P9-CNE-630

SHAKESPEARE SURVEY

# ADVISORY BOARD


Anne Barton
Jonathan Bate
Margreta de Grazia
Michael Dobson
Inga-Stina Ewbank
R. A. Foakes
Andrew Gurr
Peter Holland
John Jowett
A. D. Nuttall
Richard Proudfoot
Lena Cowen Orlin
R. L. Smallwood
Ann Thompson
Terence Hawkes

*Assistants to the Editor* Catherine Alexander *and* Paul Edmondson


1 Shakespeare and his Stage
2 Shakespearian Production
3 The Man and the Writer
4 Interpretation
5 Textual Criticism
6 The Histories
7 Style and Language
8 The Comedies
9 *Hamlet*
10 The Roman Plays
11 The Last Plays (with an index to *Surveys 1–10*)
12 The Elizabethan Theatre
13 *King Lear*
14 Shakespeare and his Contemporaries
15 The Poems and Music
16 Shakespeare in the Modern World
17 Shakespeare in his Own Age
18 Shakespeare Then Till Now
19 *Macbeth*
20 Shakespearian and Other Tragedy
21 *Othello* (with an index to *Surveys 11–20*)
22 Aspects of Shakespearian Comedy
23 Shakespeare's Language
24 Shakespeare: Theatre Poet
25 Shakespeare's Problem Plays
26 Shakespeare's Jacobean Tragedies
27 Shakespeare's Early Tragedies
28 Shakespeare and the Ideas of his Time
29 Shakespeare's Last Plays
30 *Henry IV* to *Hamlet*
31 Shakespeare and the Classical World (with an index to *Surveys 21–30*)
32 The Middle Comedies
33 *King Lear*
34 Characterization in Shakespeare
35 Shakespeare in the Nineteenth Century
36 Shakespeare in the Twentieth Century
37 Shakespeare's Earlier Comedies
38 Shakespeare and History
39 Shakespeare on Film and Television
40 Current Approaches to Shakespeare through Language, Text and Theatre
41 Shakespearian Stages and Staging (with an index to *Surveys 31–40*)
42 Shakespeare and the Elizabethans
43 *The Tempest* and After
44 Shakespeare and Politics
45 *Hamlet* and its Afterlife
46 Shakespeare and Sexuality
47 Playing Places for Shakespeare
48 Shakespeare and Cultural Exchange
49 *Romeo and Juliet* and its Afterlife
50 Shakespeare and Language
51 Shakespeare in the Eighteenth Century

Aspects of *Macbeth*
Aspects of *Othello*
Aspects of *Hamlet*
Aspects of *King Lear*
Aspects of Shakespeare's 'Problem Plays'

# SHAKESPEARE SURVEY

AN ANNUAL SURVEY OF
SHAKESPEARE STUDIES AND PRODUCTION

---

51

# Shakespeare in the Eighteenth Century

EDITED BY
STANLEY WELLS

PUBLISHED BY THE PRESS SYNDICATE OF THE UNIVERSITY OF CAMBRIDGE
The Pitt Building, Trumpington Street, Cambridge CB2 1RP, United Kingdom

CAMBRIDGE UNIVERSITY PRESS
The Edinburgh Building, Cambridge CB2 2RU, United Kingdom http://www.cup.cam.ac.uk
40 West 20th Street, New York, NY 10011–4211, USA http://www.cup.org
10 Stamford Road, Oakleigh, Melbourne 3166, Australia

© Cambridge University Press 1998

This book is in copyright. Subject to statutory exception and to the provisions of relevant collective licensing agreements, no reproduction of any part may take place without the written permission of Cambridge University Press.

First published 1998

Printed in Great Britain at the University Press, Cambridge

Typeset in Bembo 10/12pt [CE]

*A catalogue record for this book is available from the British Library*

ISBN 0 521 632250 hardback

*Shakespeare Survey* was first published in 1948. Its first eighteen volumes were edited by Allardyce Nicoll. Kenneth Muir edited volumes 19 to 33.

PR
2888
.C3
V.51

# EDITOR'S NOTE

Volume 52, on 'Shakespeare and the Globe', which will be at press by the time this volume appears, will include papers from the 1998 International Shakespeare Conference. The theme of Volume 53 will be 'Shakespeare and Narrative'.

Submissions should be addressed to the Editor at The Shakespeare Centre, Henley Street, Stratford-upon-Avon, Warwickshire CV37 6QW, to arrive at the latest by 1 September 1999 for Volume 53. Pressures on space are heavy; priority is given to articles related to the theme of a particular volume. Please either enclose postage (overseas, in International Reply Coupons) or send a copy you do not wish to be returned. All articles submitted are read by the Editor and at least one member of the Editorial Board, whose indispensable assistance the Editor gratefully acknowledges.

Unless otherwise indicated, Shakespeare quotations and references are keyed to the modern-spelling Complete Oxford Shakespeare (1986).

Review copies of books should be addressed to the Editor, as above. In attempting to survey the ever-increasing bulk of Shakespeare publications our reviewers inevitably have to exercise some selection. We are pleased to receive offprints of articles which help to draw our reviewers' attention to relevant material.

S. W. W.

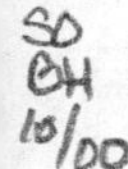

# CONTRIBUTORS

Catherine M. S. Alexander, *University of Birmingham*
Eric C. Brown, *Louisiana State University*
John Russell Brown, *University of Michigan*
Irena Cholij, *London*
Michael Cordner, *University of York*
Janette Dillon, *University of Nottingham*
William Dodd, *University of Siena*
Philip Edwards, *University of Liverpool*
Alison Findlay, *University of Lancaster*
John Jowett, *The Shakespeare Institute, University of Birmingham*
Jean I. Marsden, *University of Connecticut*
Sonia Massai, *St Mary's University College*
A. Luis Pujante, *University of Murcia, Spain*
Niky Rathbone, *Birmingham Shakespeare Library*
Katherine West Scheil, *St Joseph College, Connecticut*
Martin Scofield, *University of Kent*
Desmond Shawe-Taylor, *Dulwich Picture Gallery*
Robert Smallwood, *The Shakespeare Birthplace Trust*
B. J. Sokol, *Goldsmith's College, University of London*
Virginia Mason Vaughan, *Clark University, Massachusetts*
Marcus Walsh, *University of Birmingham*

# CONTENTS

## CONTENTS

# ILLUSTRATIONS

# SHAKESPEARE AND THE EIGHTEENTH CENTURY: CRITICISM AND RESEARCH

CATHERINE M. S. ALEXANDER

In his essay for *A Companion to Shakespeare Studies*, 'Shakespearian Criticism from Dryden to Coleridge' (Cambridge: Cambridge University Press, 1934), T. S. Eliot took much care to underpin his argument with what he described as a 'very simple' point: 'Shakespeare criticism will always change as the world changes' (p. 288). Yet while arguing for critical difference, he explored the growth of eighteenth-century criticism that was based on textual study rather than performance by singling out Maurice Morgann's essay *On the Dramatic Character of Sir John Falstaff* (1777) and applauding the piece in terms typical of 1930s character criticism. Iris Murdoch, in a 1961 *Encounter* article, 'Against Dryness', contrasted Shakespeare's unique facility 'to create at the highest level both images and people' with the empirical rationality of representations of man which she deplored in contemporary literature. She illustrated her argument with a historical parallel which considered the enduring influence of Hume and Kant and suggested

> our present situation is analogous to an 18th-century one. We retain a rationalistic optimism about the beneficent results of education, or rather technology. We combine this with a romantic conception of 'the human condition', a picture of the individual as stripped and solitary ... The 18th century was an era of rationalistic allegories and moral tales.
>
> (*Encounter* 88, 18)

Clearly these are different responses to the same period but it is not the changes which are most striking; their interest lies in the choice of examples and the approaches which reveal, through a significant similarity, another 'simple point': the recognition or imposition of the prevailingly familiar (implicit in Eliot and openly acknowledged in Murdoch) which prompts the choice and interpretation of the work of an earlier age through the critical and philosophical concerns of the present. At the end of the 1990s it is the contemporary critical and cultural issues of politicization, appropriation, production, the visual image, and nationalism which dominate the selection and critical interpretation of the body of work, from a range of disciplines, which constitutes eighteenth-century Shakespeare. This essay considers the effect of these emphases and offers an overview of the resoures which facilitate the breadth of interpretation.

The propensity to read eighteenth-century Shakespeare through the filter of late twentieth-century values (intellectually inevitable perhaps and frequently compounded by the desire to judge the cumulative cultural effect) propels eighteenth-century Shakespeare *forwards*. Material linking it/him (it is hard to determine the pronoun as 'Shakespeare' shifts from figure to construct) to its own past or connecting it to the intellectual activities of its own time is far less common. The forward propulsion is typified by Michael D. Bristol who insists, in *Big Time Shakespeare* (London and New York: Routledge, 1996), that 'Shakespeare' is a commercial product within a 'market for cultural goods and services' and contends that:

Understanding Tonson's solution to the contemporary problem of cultural technology is far more important in the long-term history of Shakespeare's reception than any quibbling over the precision of Rowe's textual scholarship. (p. 75)

Such an approach makes eighteenth-century Shakespeare teasingly familiar to an age well used to monopolies, promotion and publicity: it emphasizes the similarities rather than the differences. It is the elevation of process above aesthetic and sensibility explored by Gary Taylor in *Cultural Selection: Why Some Achievements Survive the Test of Time – And Others Don't* (New York: BasicBooks, 1996). He describes Shakespeare, for example, as a parasite 'attached to a species that eventually dominated its own niche [through 'physical, military, or economic power'] and migrated out into others, taking the parasite along and introducing it into new ecosystems that had, often, no defenses against it' (pp. 87–8). This type of reading is resisted most strongly by Harold Bloom in his insistence upon Shakespeare's survival through aesthetic superiority in his exploration of *The Western Canon: The Books and School of the Ages* (New York: Harcourt Brace, 1994).[1] Bloom praises Johnson, largely for his work on Shakespeare, as the 'canonical critic proper', contrasting his method with that of those he has identified earlier as belonging to 'The School of Resentment':

More than any other critic, Johnson demonstrates that the only method is the self, and that criticism is therefore a branch of wisdom literature. It is not a political or social science or a cult of gender and racial cheerleading, its present fate in Western universities. (p. 184)

Less aggressively, Marcus Walsh makes a similar point in the introduction to his sensitively argued exploration of *Shakespeare, Milton and Eighteenth-Century Literary Editing* (Cambridge: Cambridge University Press, 1997): 'one of my motives in writing this book has been the sense that, in some recent discussions, the eighteenth century has been judged, unsympathetically, by inappropriate and modern criteria' (p. 3).

Yet the diversity of judgement and interpretation not only reflects a clash between a reclamation of former ideologies and the overlay of the new but is a response to the magnitude of the eighteenth-century events which contributed to Shakespeare's survival and cultural dominance, and the quantity of material which records the expansion. The scale of the growth of editions and commentary, stage adaptations and the emergence of charismatic actresses, actors, and managers, the proliferation of and concomitant familiarization with references to characters and quotations in novels, verses, and art, have prompted commentators to explore and explain not just the individual progressions or developments but the conditions and the cultural nexus that may not merely provide the context but prove to be active agents in the change. Increasingly, eighteenth-century Shakespeare is read in conjunction with the promotion of nationalism, the development of a domestic aesthetic in art and literature, the expansion of and competition between publishing houses, the growth of a commercial middle class and a literate working class, and the reclamation of women's contribution to intellectual life. The reader has access to these trends through fine studies such as Linda Colley's *Britons: Forging the Nation 1707–1837* (Yale University Press, 1992) and John Brewer's *The Pleasures of the Imagination: English Culture in the Eighteenth Century* (London: HarperCollins, 1997), and to an overview of specifically Shakespearian development in Michael Dobson's 'Improving on the Original: Actresses and Adaptations' and Peter Holland's 'The Age of Garrick' in *Shakespeare: An Illustrated Stage History*, edited by Jonathan

---

[1] Jan Gorak provides an analytical critique of the role of eighteenth-century editors in determining Shakespeare's place in the Western canon, and explores the critical and theoretical issues which so incense Bloom, in *The Making of the Modern Canon: Genesis and Crisis of a Literary Idea* (London and Atlantic Highlands, NJ: Athlone, 1991). See particularly pp. 44–50.

Bate and Russell Jackson (Oxford University Press, 1996) or S. Schoenbaum's exploration of eighteenth-century constructions of Shakespeare in *Shakespeare's Lives, New Edition* (Oxford: Clarendon, 1991). But what makes the eighteenth century unique (and contributes, of course, to the breadth of interpretation) is the vast quantity of original source material which illuminates the developments from a range of perspectives.

Theatre records, letters, pictures, magazines, libraries and collections which complement text and commentary make the eighteenth century particularly tangible to the researcher, and the general reader undertaking the study of Shakespeare in the period will find the field rich in outstanding collections of facsimiles, edited assemblages of primary sources, and a growing body of commentary and criticism. The remarkable collaboration between the Birmingham Shakespeare Library and the Cornmarket Press, propelled by the Librarian Waveney Payne, celebrated the one-hundredth anniversary of the opening of the library by producing over eighty volumes of facsimiles of acting editions and adaptations of the plays, covering the period from the Restoration of the Monarchy to the death of Garrick in 1779 (London: Cornmarket, 1969). They provide easy access to material now little known but central to Shakespeare's survival. Read in conjunction with the cast lists, programme details and performance dates in Emmett L. Avery's and others' unsurpassed *The London Stage . . .* (Carbondale: Southern Illinois University Press, 1960), Charles Beecher Hogan's *Shakespeare in the Theatre 1701–1880: A Record of Performances* (Oxford: Clarendon, 1957) and the evidence of the employment of Shakespeare as an arbiter for superior English standards of wit, cuisine, sense, architecture and sex, as well as drama,[2] in the outstandingly thorough collection *The Prologues and Epilogues of the Eighteenth Century* edited by Pierre Danchin (Nancy: Presses Universitaires de Nancy, 1990– ), the facsimiles form the bedrock of theatre research and reveal more about the period than, for example, some of the tedious and uncritical anecdotal material in biographies of Garrick. The focus on the single representative of Shakespeare, however great his contribution, has led to the neglect of other actor-managers, of actors whose specialism was comedy rather than tragedy, and of the role of actresses.

Elizabeth Howe's *The First English Actresses: Women and Drama 1660–1700* (Cambridge: Cambridge University Press, 1992) is one of the few works, and certainly the finest, to redress the balance. She discusses many of the popular Shakespearian adaptations that survived well into the eighteenth century and argues that the introduction of gratuitous scenes of sex, violence and voyeurism (in Tate's versions of *Lear* and *Coriolanus*, for example, or Durfey's adaptation of *Cymbeline, The Injured Princess*), narratively unnecessary breeches parts (such as that added by John Crowne in *The Misery of Civil War*, his reworking of *Henry VI Parts II and III*) and the affecting speeches of Cibber's version of *Richard III* and Otway's of *Romeo and Juliet* (*The History and Fall of Caius Marius*) were the exploitative result of introducing actresses into roles formerly taken by men. Sandra Richards also considers eighteenth-century breeches roles, such as Charlotte Charke's early performance as Hamlet (p. 27), in *The Rise of the English Actress* (Basingstoke: Macmillan, 1993). One of the strengths of the work is the thorough bibliography, and while the anecdotal and biographical approach of the main text is sometimes a limitation, her discussion of the

[2] See, for example, Shakespeare's role as both the prophylactic antidote and approved alternative to homosexuality in Bevill Higgons's prologue to George Granville's adaptation *The Jew of Venice: A Comedy* (1701); his consumption of 'plain Beef' in the prologue to Mary Pix's *The Double Distress* (1701); his opposition to classical architecture (the proposal to build a new theatre in the Haymarket) in the anonymous epilogue to *Timon of Athens* (1703); and his 'golden Days of Wit' in the epilogue to the anonymous *The Amorous Miser* (1705). Danchin, I, 8, 15, 242.

reception of Sarah Siddons as Lady Macbeth during the Old Price Riots is valuable material missing from Shearer West's treatment of the same disturbances in *The Image of the Actor: Verbal and Visual Representations in the Age of Garrick and Kemble* (London: Pinter, 1991) and Marc Baer's exploration of their theatrical, political and cultural contexts, *Theatre and Disorder in Late Georgian London* (Oxford: Clarendon, 1992).

The 1994 reprinting of *The Memoirs of Mary Robinson*, edited by M. J. Levy (London: Peter Owen; first published posthumously in 1801) and Claire Tomalin's *Mrs Jordan's Profession* of the same year (London: Viking, 1994) reveal much about actresses whose personal appeal contributed to the revival of Shakespearian comedy in spite of (or possibly because of) their off-stage role as royal mistresses. Robinson's affair with the Prince of Wales (later George IV) which was initiated at the Royal Command Performance of *The Winter's Tale* became public after the revelation of the Prince's notes, signed 'Florizel', and generated a series of scurrilous verses and cartoons (and the stunning portraits of 'Perdita' by Gainsborough, Reynolds and Romney now in the Wallace Collection), giving the play an unexpected afterlife. The early sections of Robinson's autobiography provide incidental glimpses of an itinerant life which invite further research: she spent part of her childhood, *c.* 1763, at a boarding school run by Hannah More's sisters. She tells of a visit to William Powell's benefit performance of *King Lear* in the company of fellow pupils including Powell's two daughters, Miss Hopkins (later Mrs John Kemble), and the daughter of Hannah Pritchard (best remembered for playing Lady Macbeth opposite Garrick). This revelation of an academy for stage daughters is an unexpected one, suggesting how much is still to be discovered. Certainly the sixteen volumes of *A Biographical Dictionary of Actors, Actresses, Musicians, Dancers, Managers, and Other Stage Personnel in London, 1660–1800* edited by Philip H. Highfill, Kalman A. Burnim and Edward A. Langhans (Southern Illinois University Press, 1973–1993), and Bryan Gooch and David Thatcher's five-volume *A Shakespeare Music Catalogue* (Oxford: Clarendon, 1991) provide ample evidence of many others' involvement with Shakespeare and confirm that the definitive (and necessarily lengthy) work on Shakespeare in the Georgian playhouse is yet to be written.

A number of noteworthy facsimiles reflects the revival of interest in the eighteenth century across the arts and social sciences and provides evidence of Shakespearian proliferation. The reprinting of William Hogarth's empirical treatise of 1753, *Analysis of Beauty* (Menston, Yorkshire: Scolar Press, 1971), reveals the extent to which Shakespeare was an inspiration for his 'serpentine line', with Cleopatra's 'infinite variety' as its defining analogy. The advertisements in the endpapers, including one for the print of 'Mr Garrick in the Character of King Richard the Third', are reminders of Hogarth's importance, through his dramatic history paintings and his concern to found an English school of art, to the development of stage portraits and the visual record of Shakespeare performances. The on-going publications of the Augustan Reprint Society (from William Andrews Clark Memorial Library, University of California, Los Angeles), which has reproduced useful Shakespeare-specific texts by Lewis Theobald, Charles Macklin, Edmond Malone and Joseph Warton among many others, are a valuable source of minor contextualizing pieces such as a plan of Pope's garden and Thomas Sheridan's work on elocution.

D. Nicol Smith, in *Eighteenth Century Essays on Shakespeare* (Glasgow: James Maclehouse, 1903; 2nd edn Oxford: Oxford University Press, 1963) was the first to reprint a number of important pieces of criticism including Nicholas Rowe's 'Some Account of the Life, etc., of Mr William Shakespear' (not published since 1714), and John Dennis's 'On the Genius and Writings of Shakespear' (not published since 1721), as well as the Prefaces to the editions by Pope, Theobald, Hanmer, Warburton, and Johnson, and the essays by Richard Farmer (Shakespeare's Learning) and Maurice Morgann (Falstaff).

Although now out of print the twenty-six facsimile volumes in the 'Eighteenth Century Shakespeare' series published by Frank Cass in the early 1970s enhance Nichol Smith's valuable collection of primary sources by providing copies of the major criticism and commentary that took place outside editions of the Collected Works. Beginning with Rymer's *A Short View of Tragedy* and John Dennis's 1693 reply, the series progresses through texts by Charles Gildon, Theobald, Thomas Edwards and William Dodd, includes the three major texts by women – Charlotte Lennox, Elizabeth Montagu and Elizabeth Griffith – and concludes with papers on the Ireland forgeries by Thomas Caldecott, George Hardinge, and George Chalmers as well as the better known *Inquiry* by Malone. If one adds to this material the extensive resources of the six volumes of Brian Vickers' *Shakespeare: The Critical Heritage* (London: RKP, 1974–1981) and the growing collections of letters, many completed in the last twenty years and drawing on extensive North American holdings, then it becomes apparent how well served is the period with accessible, original sources.

Collections of correspondence are valuable records of the networks of scholarship, the connections between professional writers and amateur enthusiasts, and the collaborative nature of much Shakespearian research. They provide evidence of the reception of editions, criticism, and performance, demonstrate the importance of Shakespeare to pockets of literary aspiration and endeavour (the Warwickshire Coterie and the Blue-Stockings, for example), and reveal the widespread appropriation and application of Shakespeare's language. While *The Letters of David Garrick*, edited in three volumes by David M. Little and George M. Kahrl (London: Oxford University Press, 1963), are esssential reading, the outstanding collection remains – despite recent allegations of prudish editing by W. S. Lewis[3] – the mammoth forty-eight volumes of the *Yale Edition of Horace Walpole's Correspondence* (London: Oxford University Press; New Haven: Yale University Press, 1937–1983). The correspondence with Edmond Malone is a particularly valuable feature, and the 'notes on several characters in Shakespeare' which Walpole mentions in a letter to Malone of 11 February 1785 have been located by Lewis and reprinted in *Evidence in Literary Scholarship*, edited by René Wellek and Alvaro Ribeiro (Oxford: Oxford University Press, 1979). The notes offer a fine defence of the gravediggers' scene in *Hamlet*, cut from Garrick's 1773 adaptation, and are further evidence of the collaborative and cumulative nature of eighteenth-century engagement with Shakespeare.[4]

The five-volume collection of *The Letters of Samuel Johnson*, edited by Bruce Redford (Princeton: Princeton University Press, 1992; Oxford: Clarendon, 1994), reveals his attitude to Shakespearian criticism that post-dates his own and, when read in conjunction with the Boswell collection, the letters of Hester Piozzi, and Fanny Burney's journals and correspondence,[5] provides evidence of the ambivalent attitudes of his circle, owing more to social jealousy than concern for scholarship, to the Shakespearian work of Elizabeth Montagu.

---

[3] Timothy Mowl suggests that Lewis excluded material which alluded to Walpole's homosexuality. See *Horace Walpole: The Great Outsider* (London: John Murray, 1996), pp. 2–5, 97–8.

[4] Walpole first considered the effect of the gravediggers in the preface he wrote for the second edition of *Castle of Otranto* (1765) in an entertaining passage which leads him to question the judgement of Voltaire.

[5] Of the *Yale Editions of Private Papers of James Boswell*, the most pertinent is vol. 4, *The Correspondence of James Boswell with David Garrick, Edmund Burke and Edmond Malone*, ed. by George M. Kahrl and others (London: Heinemann, 1986). See also *The Piozzi Letters*, ed. by Edward A. Bloom and Lilian D. Bloom, 3 vols (Newark: University of Delaware Press; London and Toronto: Associated University Presses, 1989) and *The Journals and Letters of Fanny Burney*, ed. by Joyce Hemlow and others, 12 vols (Oxford: Clarendon, 1972–84).

Other revealing collections remain out of print: Elizabeth Carter's *Letters from Mrs Elizabeth Carter to Mrs Montagu* (3 vols., 1817) and Montagu's own letters, which are valuable records of women's engagement with Shakespeare, as writers, readers and leaders of fashion, deserve a new audience.[6] They may be read as a useful adjunct to the collection by Ann Thompson and Sasha Roberts, *Women Reading Shakespeare 1660–1900: An Anthology of Criticism* (Manchester: Manchester University Press, 1997), which gives short extracts, with commentary, from the work of Charlotte Lennox, Elizabeth Griffith and Elizabeth Montagu. Further evidence of an engagement with Shakespeare by those at some remove from the dominant culture may be found in *The Letters of Ignatius Sancho*, edited by Paul Edwards and Polly Rewt (Edinburgh: Edinburgh University Press, 1994), which disclose the involvement of this former slave and domestic servant with Garrick and other literary figures (see Virginia Mason Vaughan's article, pp. 57–66 below). The series of essays, *Ignatius Sancho: An African Man of Letters*, which accompanied the 1997 National Portrait Gallery exhibition of the man's life and work, reprints his published setting for 'Sweetest Bard", a section of Garrick's 1769 Jubilee Ode. It compares favourably with Thomas Arne's original music for the piece, Charles Dibdin's settings for the songs, *Shakespeare's Garland or the Warwickshire Jubilee*, and Thomas Linley's better known but similar piece *The Witches and Fairies, an Ode in Commemoration of Shakespear* (a commemorative work with words by French Lawrence performed at Drury Lane in 1776). Sancho also wrote a setting for part of *Measure for Measure* but his work is not recorded by Gooch and Thatcher and deserves to be more widely known.[7]

Selections from the *Spectator*, which provide valuable evidence of the reception of plays and players, are available in a range of modern editions but other magazine material has been less accessible. The period from 1749 onwards, when the publication of the *Monthly Review* set new trends and interests, saw an explosion in the systematic and regular reviewing of books which reveal the critical reception of text. Johnson's 1765 edition of the Collected Works, for example, was reviewed in *Monthly Review*, *Critical Review*, *Gentleman's Magazine*, and the *Annual Register*. The access to digital images of eighteenth-century material provided by the Internet Library of Early Journals project will facilitate the exploration of such resources, and enable Robert Babcock's important study of 1931 *The Genesis of Shakespeare Idolatry 1766–1799* (which uses magazine and other popular pieces to investigate the growth of bardolatry), and George Winchester Stone's 'Shakespeare in the Periodicals 1700–1740' (*Shakespeare Quarterly*, 2, 1951; 3, 1952), to be expanded. The eighteenth-century obsession with collecting, collating, categorizing and classifying – manipulating 'the available indices of reality' in George Steiner's phrase[8] – was particularly important for the preservation and proliferation of

[6] *The Letters of Mrs Elizabeth Montagu* . . ., ed. by Matthew Montagu, 3rd edn, 4 vols. (London: T. Cadell and W. Davies, 1810–13) and correspondence from the second half of her life in John Doran's *A Lady of the Last Century (Mrs Elizabeth Montagu)* . . . (London: Richard Bentley and Son, 1873). The correspondence between Carter and Montagu reveals the genesis and reception of Montagu's *Essays on the Writings and Genius of Shakespear* (London: J. Dodsley and others, 1769) and provides many examples of the application of Shakespearian quotation and allusion.

[7] Examples of the use made of Shakespeare by working women as source and inspiration can be found in Donna Landry's *The Muses of Resistance: Laboring-Class Women's Poetry in Britain, 1739–1796* (Cambridge: Cambridge University Press, 1990) and Richard Greene's *Mary Leapor: A Study in Eighteenth-Century Women's Poetry* (Oxford: Clarendon, 1993).

[8] Sensing, as a child, the 'countless systems of discourse specifically tailored to the teeming diversity of human purposes, artifacts, representations or concealment', George Steiner began to compile lists and create his own taxonomies to supplement 'the available indices of reality'. *Errata: An Examined Life* (London: Weidenfeld and Nicolson, 1997), pp. 3–4.

Shakespeare, and magazines provide useful evidence of these processes. The availability of *Samuel Johnson: A Dictionary of the English Language*, on CD ROM (Cambridge University Press, 1996) and Chadwyck-Healey's *Editions and Adaptations of Shakespeare* on CD ROM and the World Wide Web (1995) have the potential to enhance research (although the exclusion of Malone's 1790 edition from the latter is odd and, while the medium provides useful access to text, it is an unsatisfying way to explore introductory material and prefaces), and Chadwyck-Healey's *English Full Text Poetry Database* (1994), despite its under-representation of women poets, provides the opportunity to explore the extensive proliferation of Shakespearian quotation and allusion in verse.

The comprehensive accumulations and representations of original sources inform the best commentary and criticism of eighteenth-century Shakespeare. The greatest scholarly attention has been given to the editions and editors of Shakespeare. Some works offer an overview (Arthur Sherbo's 1986 *The Birth of Shakespeare Studies: Commentators from Rowe (1709) to Boswell-Malone (1821)* (East Lansing, MI: Colleagues Press, 1986) or Colin Franklin's *Shakespeare Domesticated: The Eighteenth Century Editions* (Aldershot: Scolar Press, 1991); neither making as effective use of documentary evidence as the comparable sections in Schoenbaum's *Shakespeare's Lives*) but the most revealing are those devoted to a single editor. There is a remarkable similarity in recent studies of individual editors; in their attempts to differentiate their subjects, authors have demolished the Old-Testament, inheritance model of textual transmission (Rowe the progenitor begets Pope, who begets Theobald, who spawns Hanmer and so on through Warburton, Johnson, Capell, Steevens until the ultimate issue of Malone) and make the same claim: their editor has made a unique contribution to the understanding of Shakespeare and owes little debt to his predecessors. Thus Peter Seary has argued the case for the systematic research and innovatory scholarship of Theobald in *Lewis Theobald and the Editing of Shakespeare* (Oxford: Clarendon, 1990), rescuing his reputation from the contemporary derision of Pope, Warburton and David Mallett and the posthumous disapproval of Johnson. G. F. Parker, in *Johnson's Shakespeare* (Oxford: Clarendon, 1989), insists that his editor offers a radical criticism of Shakespeare: 'radical in that it reaches to fundamental thoughts about why the plays are worth reading, and radical also in both challenging and being challenged by other, more immediately congenial, approaches to the plays' (p. 2). Edmond Malone, formerly thought to be the greatest beneficiary of the inheritance model, and widely acknowledged as the 'best' of the eighteenth-century editors (an accolade which reflects the principles of reliability and originality sought by the modern editor), has been the subject of recent studies which explore the basis of his superiority while disputing whether his achievements represent the unique accomplishment of a particular historical moment, or are part of a critical continuum or process. In the groundbreaking *Shakespeare Verbatim: The Reproduction of Authenticity and the 1790 Apparatus* (Oxford: Clarendon, 1991) Margreta de Grazia argues for the radical nature of Malone's thorough scholarship and editorial method, while Peter Martin's *Edmond Malone, Shakespeare Scholar: A Literary Biography* (Cambridge: Cambridge University Press, 1995) is particularly effective in exploring the breadth of Malone's intellectual curiosity and the complexity and influence of his social and professional connections. Martin's aim is to redress recent 'theoretical and deconstructionist' work which 'strikes at the heart of the value of historical literary research' (p. xviii). Simon Jarvis's *Scholars and Gentlemen* (Oxford: Clarendon, 1995) resists de Grazia's claims for Malone and reasserts the genealogical model of textual transmission while exploring an 'analysis of the history of textual criticism as a history of intellectual practice' (p. 188), a refreshing reclamation of scholarship over commerce and assumptions of ignorance which Walsh extends to Theobald and Capell in *Shakespeare, Milton and Eighteenth-Century Literary Editing*. Some editors remain under-represented: while their contributions may survive as Arden footnotes (albeit relegated to the bottom of the page), there is surprisingly little recent commentary on Pope or his contemporaries Sewell and Gildon; Rowe and Hanmer are discussed in terms of their illustrations as much as their editorial method; and scant attention has been paid to William Warburton or the dismissive contempt of his peers. Thomas Edwards's 1748 *The Canons of Criticism* remains almost unexplored and undisputed in its disparagement of Warburton's method.

The eighteenth century saw not only the development of character criticism (discussed, for example, by Brian Vickers in 'The Emergence of Character Criticism, 1744–1800' in *Shakespeare Survey 34*) but the acquisition by some characters – most notably Romeo, Hamlet and the supernaturals – of a metaphorical, literary or political life independent of the stage or text. This development is explored in the recent growth of cultural histories which combine performance studies, social context and reception. John Gross's *Shylock: Four Hundred Years in the Life of a Legend* (London: Chatto and Windus, 1992), Virginia Mason Vaughan and Alden T. Vaughan's *Shakespeare's Caliban: A Cultural History* (Cambridge: Cambridge University Press, 1991), Virginia Vaughan's *Othello: A Contextual History* (Cambridge: Cambridge University Press, 1994), and, to a lesser extent, Joseph A. Porter's *Shakespeare's Mercutio: His History and Drama* (Chapel Hill and London: University of North Carolina Press, 1988), use a range of eighteenth-century material, casting incidental light on the effect and influence of adaptations, and exploring a range of appropriations and influences. Shylock is central to James Shapiro's study of *Shakespeare and the Jews* (New York: Columbia University Press, 1996) but the author has a larger brief and in his exploration of the reception of *The Merchant of Venice* in eighteenth-century England he is filling 'a curious blank in accounts of appropriations of Shakespeare' (p. 213) and considering the place of Jews which is omitted from other studies of Shakespeare's role in the development of nationalism and English identity. Jonathan Bate has described the extensive political applications of Falstaff (in *Shakespearean Constitutions: Politics, Theatre, Criticism 1730–1830* (Oxford: Clarendon, 1989) and, to a lesser extent, 'Shakespeare Nationalised, Shakespeare Privatised')[9] but the widespread popularity of the figure in sequels such as William Kenrick's *Falstaff's Wedding* (1760), popular verses and novels like Smollett's *The Adventures of Humphry Clinker* (1771), and off-shoots of the 1769 Jubilee, coupled with his similarity to that other indulgent Englishman, John Bull, suggest that he too would be a fine candidate for a full length study.

The collision/collusion of commercial, national and cultural endeavours which is explored in recent character studies is particularly explicit in the biographical details on the memorial tablet in the south aisle of the Church of St Margaret, Lothbury, in the City of London, honouring the life of John Boydell and recording his death in December, 1804. It lists the following achievements:

> As an engraver he attained considerable eminence in his art; as a printseller he caused its production to become a source of commercial benefit to his country, and of such profit to himself as to enable him to afford unexampled encouragement to the English school of historic painting, and to form that splendid collection of British Art the Shakespeare Gallery.

Boydell's entrepreneurial, self-aggrandizing and chauvinistic commissioning for the Shakespeare Gallery, which opened in Pall Mall in 1789 and displayed thirty-four paintings by eighteen British artists (thirty canvases were added the

[9] 'Shakespeare Nationalised, Shakespeare Privatised', *English*, 42 (Spring 1993), 1–18.

following year and engravings of the works were sold throughout Britain and the continent) is the subject of a number of recent studies. These, and works which explore the earlier and widespread proliferation and application of images of Shakespeare and his creations, are largely responsible for our perceptions of the expansion of Shakespeare's quiddity and the shifting of attention from texts and performance.

The catalogue which accompanied the exhibition of The Boydell Shakespeare Gallery in 1996 and 1997 (first in Museum Bochum in collaboration with the German Shakespeare Society and later in Los Angeles and New York)[10] reproduces all the prints from the two volumes of *Collection of Prints from Pictures for the Purpose of Illustrating The Dramatic Works of Shakespeare by the Artists of Great Britain* (London: John and Josiah Boydell, 1803) but not the quarto engravings from *The Dramatic Works of Shakespeare* edited by George Steevens, published by the Boydells and generally known as 'The Boydell Shakespeare'. So in terms of illustration it is bettered by *The Boydell Shakespeare Prints*, edited by A. E. Santaniello (New York: Arno Press, 1979) which includes both. But the strength of the catalogue resides in its commentary on each print (an identifying quotation – shorter than the original – contextualizing information and style comment) and the series of revealing essays (first presented at a Bochum symposium in July 1995) which do much to redress W. Moelwyn Merchant's assertion that the Boydell venture was 'a massive irrelevance' (*Shakespeare and the Artist* (London: Oxford University Press, 1959), p. 66). Two of the contributors also have pieces in the 1997 *Shakespeare Jahrbuch*: Frederick Burwick's 'John Boydell's *Shakespeare Gallery* and the Stage' (pp. 54–76) reviews contemporary practice in stage design in order to demonstrate that the Shakespeare Gallery, contrary to former belief, provides evidence of stage settings, costume and acting style. In 'Shakespeare, Portraiture and National Identity' (pp. 29–53) Marcia Pointon, author of the definitive *Hanging the Head: Portraiture and Social Formation in Eighteenth-Century England* (New Haven and London: Yale University Press for the Paul Mellon Centre for Studies in British Art, 1993) considers Shakespeare's afterlife in pictorial imagery ranging from busts and portraits to banknotes and postcards.

In *Shakespearean Constitutions* Jonathan Bate explores the motivation and effect of Boydell's project but also makes extensive use of caricature to illustrate his exploration of Shakespeare and politics in Georgian England, arguing that it 'is the nearest equivalent to a study of his presence in television in our period; that is to say, it is a study in popular iconography' (p. 2). Bate's identification, through such material, of 'acts of mediation' and most particularly the cultural balancing act of 'mediation between coercion of Shakespeare and submissiveness to him' (p. 212) is one of the most sophisticated assessments of the age's relationship with Shakespeare. The 'Embodying the Author' section (pp. 134–84) of Michael Dobson's *The Making of the National Poet: Shakespeare, Adaptation and Authorship, 1660–1769* (Oxford: Clarendon Press, 1992) explores two interlinked representations of Shakespeare: the Westminster Abbey statue, erected in 1741 and immediately a contested site of meaning, and David Garrick's representation of himself as the living image. In tracing a progression from the origins of the statue through its stage appearance in *Harlequin Student*, copies, and other effigies, to Garrick's own memorial installed in the Abbey in 1797, Dobson demonstrates the processes of canonization and the effect of the elevation.[11]

The quantity of images certainly rivals printed texts and increasingly is being collated,

[10] *The Boydell Shakespeare Gallery* ed. by Walter Pape and Frederick Burwick in collaboration with the German Shakespeare Society (Boltrop: Peter Pomp, 1996).

[11] See also Ingrid Roscoe's detailed account of 'The Monument to the Memory of Shakespeare', *Church Monuments*, 9 (1994), 72–82.

exhibited and subjected to critical scrutiny. The permanent collections of many British galleries contain outstanding eighteenth-century portraits – Hogarth's 'Garrick as King Richard the Third' in the Walker Art Gallery in Liverpool; the Wallace Collection's three portraits of Perdita; and John Hoppner's 'Mrs Jordan as Viola', Reynolds' 'The Hon. Mrs Tollemache as Miranda' and his 'Kitty Fisher as Cleopatra' at Kenwood – but in the last ten years there have been a remarkable series of special exhibitions, drawing on prints, portraits, figurines, Jubilee memorabilia, cartoons, busts and medallions from private collections, reflecting a revival of interest in British art, and portrait painting in particular, which illuminate eighteenth-century Shakespeare. In 1987 the Francis Hayman exhibition, first displayed at the Yale Center for British Art, was brought to the Iveagh Bequest at Kenwood. In addition to Hayman's well-documented illustrations for Hanmer's edition of Shakespeare,[12] the exhibition (and the catalogue written by Brian Allen)[13] drew attention to his less well-known fondness for Falstaff, whom he was thought to resemble, and to the Shakespearian scenes – such as the wrestling match from *As You Like It* – which he painted to decorate the supper boxes at Vauxhall. In the same year 'Genial Company: The Theme of Genius in Eighteenth-Century Portraiture' was exhibited at Nottingham University Art Gallery and the Scottish National Portrait Gallery. Jointly organized by Joanne Wright and Desmond Shawe-Taylor (who also wrote the catalogue) it explored the visual representation of ideas particularly pertinent to Shakespeare – genius, the Worthies, the Muses, idolatry and the afterlife of fame, the audience – and provided a comprehensive, contextualized coverage of Garrick portraits. In 1994 English mezzotints from the collection of the Hon. Christopher Lennox-Boyd were exhibited at the Courtauld Institute Galleries as 'Theatre: the Age of Garrick'. In addition to displaying rare material such as the engraving by Peter van Bleeck, from his own painting, of Mrs Cibber as Cordelia, the exhibition and its catalogue provided a valuable explanation of the processes involved in the production and distribution of prints, while Lennox-Boyd's suggestion that the English enthusiasm for collecting 'heads' was because they were 'barred by faith from owning religious images' offers another perspective on the growth of Shakespearian idolatry.[14]

Norwich Castle Museum's 1996 'Art as Theatre: Shakespeare and Theatre in British Painting from Hogarth to Sargent', using holdings from the Tate Gallery, initiated a focus on Hogarth's dramatic paintings which continued throughout 1997, the tercentenary of his birth. Popular interest in theatre and painting, with a strong chauvinistic bias, followed parallel paths and Hogarth was dubbed 'Shakespeare in Painting' by Joseph Mitchell as early as 1730.[15] Elizabeth Einberg's commentary on the Tate's own commemorative exhibition 'Hogarth the Painter' is particularly fine, especially her reading of 'Mr and Mrs Garrick, 1757',[16] surely one of the most reproduced eighteenth-century portraits of recent years.

It is generally agreed that the Garrick Club holds the best collection of theatrical portraits and the Club has been generous in loaning its works to special exhibitions. The Arts Council's 'The Georgian Playhouse: Actors, Artists, Audiences and Architecture' exhibited at the Hayward Gallery in 1975 made extensive use of Garrick Club material and the catalogue

---

[12] See, for example, Marcia Allentuck's 'Sir Thomas Hanmer Instructs Francis Hayman: An Editor's Notes to his Illustrator (1744)', *Shakespeare Quarterly*, 27 (1976), 288–315.

[13] Brian Allen, *Francis Hayman* (New Haven and London: Yale University Press, 1987).

[14] Christopher Lennox-Boyd, Guy Shaw and Sarah Halliwell, *Theatre: The Age of Garrick* (London: Christopher Lennox-Boyd, 1994), p. v.

[15] Joseph Mitchell, *Three Poetical Epistles: To Mr Hogarth, Mr Dandridge, and Mr Lambert, Masters in the Art of Paintings* (London: John Watts, 1731), I, p. 75.

[16] Elizabeth Einberg, *Hogarth the Painter* (London: Tate Gallery Publishing, 1997), pp. 51–2.

1 George Romney, Banquet Scene, *Macbeth*.

remains one of the most useful source books for theatre research.[17] The Tate borrowed Grisoni's 'Colley Cibber as Lord Foppington' from the Garrick Club to enhance its own Lawrence portraits of Kemble as Hamlet and Sarah Siddons in the seminal 'Swagger Portrait' exhibition of 1993, but the most extensive display has been 'Dramatic Art: Theatrical Paintings from the Garrick Club' at Dulwich Picture Gallery in 1997. Dulwich's Director, Desmond Shawe-Taylor, discusses what the paintings reveal of eighteenth-century Shakespeare performance later in this volume. The most recent and certainly the most expensive catalogue, *Pictures in the Garrick Club*, 1997, by Geoffrey Ashton, published privately by the Club through subscription, reproduces all the well-known portraits of Garrick himself and is also a rich resource for illustrations of other eighteenth-century Shakespearian actors including Thomas King, Spranger Barry and Hannah Pritchard.

The 'Shakespeare and the Eighteenth Century' exhibition at the Fitzwilliam Museum, Cambridge, in 1997, based largely on its print collection, was particularly strong in demonstrating the popularity of the supernatural in Shakespeare (largely in the second half of the century) with depictions of Banquo's ghost by Romney (see illustration 1), Blake, Gillray and George Dance, and in its choice of caricatures. The coloured etching of Gillray's obese and ardent couple is a delight not only for

[17] Iain Mackintosh, *The Georgian Playhouse: Actors, Artists, Audiences and Architecture, 1730–1830* (London: Arts Council of Great Britain, 1975).

2 Anonymous, 1784, 'Charles the Third, King of all the Orkneys; . . . or the Effects of a Bad Conscience'.

its caption, 'Oh! that this too, too solid flesh would melt' but for its satirical legend 'Design'd for the Shakespeare Gallery'. The anonymous print 'Charles the Third, King of all the Orkneys' (see illustration 2), a parody of Hogarth's famous portrait of Garrick as Richard III, satirizes Charles James Fox's return to parliament in 1784 as a member for the Orkney boroughs, and is a fine reminder of the layering of allusion which is a characteristic of the eighteenth-century engagement with Shakespeare. The satirical use of Shakespeare was also much in evidence in the Brighton exhibition (The Royal Pavilion, Libraries and Museums, 1997) 'The Prince and his Pleasures' which revealed the extent to which the memorable images of caricature are supported by memorable texts and the value in this context of the familiarity of *Hamlet*. The constitutional implications of the Prince of Wales's relationships with women are signalled through the 'To be or not to be a Queen' legend of a print in

3 Alexander Runciman, Double Portrait of Runciman and Brown.

which Mrs Fitzherbert drags the Prince into church (anonymous, 1786), and an 1820 work by Isaac Robert Cruikshank in which the newly crowned king looks into a mirror and is startled to see his wife Caroline similarly crowned: 'To be or not to be?' Another print of the same year by William Heath shows the king leading the witnesses in his wife's trial for adultery, dressed and identified in the title as 'Falstaff and his Ragged Crew'.[18]

Setting to one side the motivations of Alderman Boydell, those of his predecessor the publisher, painter and engraver Robert Pine who held an exhibition of Shakespearian history paintings in 1782, and the overtly politicized caricatures, it is much eighteenth-century art that displays the aesthetic rather than the commercial response to Shakespeare; the attempt to recreate the admired qualities, variously expressed, of knowledge of the passions, creation of the sublime, and verisimilitude. It is

[18] The catalogue reproductions are particularly fine: Andrew Barlow, *The Prince and his Pleasures: Satirical Images of George IV and his Circle* (The Royal Pavilion, Libraries and Museum, Brighton, 1997).

art, too, that conveys not only a strong impression of performance and text but of the interconnections of the literary, dramatic and artistic worlds and the stimulation and strengths they drew from each other with Shakespeare as a shared forebear. It is pleasing to note from the acknowledgements to actors, theatres, patrons, art historians and scholars from a range of disciplines in the Dulwich 'Dramatic Art' catalogue, that such an inclusive eighteenth-century practice continues. Individual works as well as the totality of visual representations are also among the most accessible reminders of eighteenth-century Shakespeare saturation, even to the extent of becoming the subject for humour. Alexander Runciman's self-portrait with his friend John Brown (see illustration 3) was painted for David, Earl of Buchan's 'Temple of Caledonian Fame' – an attempt to rival the Temple of British Worthies at Stowe or 'The Heads of Illustrious Persons of Great Britain' engraved by Houbraken and Vertue (1743) – and as in such halls of fame, Shakespeare was a required feature. However, in Runciman's portrait, itself a pastiche of a conversation piece, the Shakespearian presence is implied in the copy of *The Tempest*, pointed to by Brown, which the two appear to be discussing. Their glazed expressions invite comparison with Trinculo and Stefano and even suggest a weariness with the prevailing pervasiveness of Shakespeare.

The study of eighteenth-century Shakespeare is far from complete. One would not expect it to be otherwise. David Nichol Smith introduced his *Shakespeare and the Eighteenth Century* (Oxford: Clarendon, 1928) with the assertion

> each age has its own point of view, its own special interests, its characteristic method of treatment; and no age can ever say the last word on anything that is a living and life-giving force. Say the last word on Shakespeare, and Shakespeare is dead. (p. 1)

The three essays in Nichol Smith's volume considered adaptations and performances, editions, and critics. The late twentieth century has contributed studies of context, culture and appropriation, and there are areas which remain under-researched or over-emphasized. I have alluded to the potentially distorting focus on Garrick and the scant attention paid to women's involvement with Shakespeare (even in the recent growth of interest in Shakespeare and art Angelica Kauffman receives little consideration) but perhaps the greatest omission is the lack of attention given to Shakespeare in Europe during this period, a significant oversight given the crucial role of Voltaire's engagement with Shakespeare to the hardening of nationalist attitudes. Michael Dobson's *The Making of the National Poet* explores adaptations of Shakespeare's plays and a number of supporting, little-known texts, demonstrating that such material was central to the development of bardolatry, but there has been little commentary on other peripheral, ephemeral, or popular material since Robert Babcock's *The Genesis of Shakespeare Idolatry 1766–1799* of 1931, and Robert Noyes's 'Shakespeare in the Eighteenth Century Novel' (*A Journal of English Literary History*, 11, 1944, 213–36) is useful for its checklists rather than criticism or contextualizing.

As I indicated at the beginning of this article, a focus on materialism rather than aesthetics leaves some lacunae: exploring the Shakespeare Effect, whether defined as Bardbiz (Terence Hawkes), Big-Time Shakespeare (Michael D. Bristol), Shakesperotics (Gary Taylor), or the length of the National Willy (Michael Dobson)[19] ignores the significance of Shakespeare to the eighteenth-century attempt to

[19] Gary Taylor coined 'Shakesperotics' to describe 'everything that a society does in the name – variously spelled – of Shakespeare': *Reinventing Shakespeare: A Cultural History from the Restoration to the Present* (London: Hogarth, 1990), p. 6. His exploration of the tactics of the Tonson publishing dynasty is particularly useful. Michael Dobson explores Shakespeare's eighteenth-century embodiment as the English sex-drive in 'Bowdler and Britannia: Shakespeare and the National Libido', *Shakespeare Survey 46* (1994), pp. 137–44.

establish a domestic literary rationale which would determine the quality of a passage and the exploration of the reader's capacity to respond to such work. Thus an important anthology like William Dodd's *The Beauties of Shakespeare: regularly Selected from each Play, with a General Index, Digesting them under Proper Heads* of 1752 is largely ignored. (As much of England seems poised to enter an age when the ability to feel – and, most particularly, to display feeling – is the approved, perhaps chiliast response, then a new, late twentieth-century emphasis in the study of the eighteenth-century Shakespeare may be imminent.) When language is considered it is often the vocabularies of commerce and promotion, the quasi-critical clichés used interchangeably for Garrick, Hogarth and Shakespeare, and the mantras of nationalism rather than the assimilation of Shakespeare's text into the national vocabulary, challenging biblical allusions in its frequency of use. Political appropriation has received much more attention than literary application.

Yet the shifts in perception and evaluation have been enormous and far reaching. The forward propulsion of eighteenth-century Shakespeare has given a new status to features of Shakespearianism which have been regarded formerly as quirky aberrations in the line of pure transmission and are now recognized as central rather than peripheral. Adaptations and sequels to plays, musical interludes, the appropriation of characters, and the proliferation of prints as well as print, are acknowledged as sustaining the playwright and part of the legitimate descent. And eighteenth-century culture, defined in the broadest social, commercial, political and historical sense, is seen as an essential agent of the process not merely its neutral context. Pope's epigrammatic observation, coined after the erection of the Westminster Abbey monument, implied that Shakespeare's popular, public re-emergence, despite being somewhat sudden and singular, was a natural act:

> After an hundred and thirty years' nap,
> Enter Shakespear, with a loud clap.[20]

Neat and appealing as the couplet may be, its sentiment is now widely regarded, as surely it must have been by many proprietorial investors in 1741, as exclusively narrow. From the perspective of the late 1990s Shakespeare's eighteenth-century entrance is seen as contrived rather than natural, and the result not of a single action nor even the sustained and cumulative outcome of editing, criticism, commentary and stage development, but of a series of cultural needs and coincidences which created particularly 'appropriate' and receptive contexts.

---

20 Alexander Pope, *Minor Poems*, ed. by Norman Ault (London: Methuen, 1964), p. 395.

# DADDY'S GIRLS: SHAKESPEARIAN DAUGHTERS AND EIGHTEENTH-CENTURY IDEOLOGY

JEAN I. MARSDEN

In eighteenth-century England, Shakespeare's works were the literary emblem of the British character, denoting liberty, courage and a specifically British genius. Shakespeare's status as the English national poet reiterated this national character; as the playwright and actor Samuel Foote explained, such is the 'Taste and Genius of the free-born luxuriant Inhabitants of this Isle' that they 'will not more bear a Yoke in Poetry than Religion'.[1] Within the context of eighteenth-century literary theory, Shakespeare represented the embodiment of English liberty, resisting the neoclassical shackles of rules and decorum. He thus stood in contrast to the French who, critics claimed, were as unwilling 'to be freed from a Sovereign Authority in the Empire of Wit and Letters as in their civil Government'.[2] With the 'Empire of Wit' standing in for 'civil Government', Shakespeare's works – if presented properly – themselves encode a national ideology of liberty and truth where literary form represents national and political character.

The symbolic value of Shakespeare's works was critical at a time when England sought to define itself in specifically national rather than religious or tribal terms. Drawing upon theories of nationalism articulated by Benedict Anderson, historians such as Gerald Newman and Linda Colley have located the mid-eighteenth century as the era when concepts of nationalism shaped British identity.[3] Anderson stresses the importance of rationalist, secular thought as a pre-condition for nationalism in eighteenth-century Europe. Such secularism allowed for a new kind of 'imagined community', one which created a 'national imagination' and supplanted the imagined religious communities of the Middle Ages and Renaissance.[4] As Newman notes, this new secular construction of identity was initially a cultural rather than a political activity, dependent on the figures such as the '*artist-intellectual*' who, Newman observes, both 'creates and organizes nationalist ideology'.[5] Thus, the evolution of nationalism can be traced vividly in the cultural artefacts of the age. As the century's great cultural icon, Shakespeare became a crucial part of the cultural activity of nationalism.[6]

---

1 Samuel Foote, *The Roman and English Comedy Consider'd and Compar'd* (1747), p. 20.

2 Peter Whalley, *An Enquiry into the Learning of Shakespeare with Remarks and Several Passages of his Plays. In a Conversation between Eugenius and Neander* (1748), pp. 16–17.

3 Gerald Newman, *The Rise of English Nationalism: A Cultural History 1740–1830* (New York: St Martin's Press, 1987); Linda Colley, *Britons: Forging the Nation 1707–1837* (New Haven: Yale University Press, 1992). John Brewer presents a fiscal–materialist interpretation of the construction of the nation state, reading English nationalism more politically than do Newman or Colley. *The Sinews of Power: War, Money, and the English State, 1688–1783* (New York: Knopf, 1989).

4 See Benedict Anderson, *Imagined Communities: Reflections on the Origin and Spread of Nationalism* (London: Verso, 1983).

5 Newman, *English Nationalism*, p. 56.

6 Even Jane Austen acknowledges Shakespeare's defining role; in *Mansfield Park*, Henry Crawford describes

Shakespeare's symbolic role in the formation of an English national identity operated on several levels. For a nation which sought to establish itself as distinct from its European neighbours, Shakespeare and his works evoked a purer national past before England was corrupted by French or classical influences. As George Lillo commented in the Prologue to *Marina* (1738), efforts to increase the number of Shakespeare plays performed in London served a useful patriotic function:

A sacred band, determin'd, wise, and good,
They jointly rose to stop th'exotic flood,
And strove to wake, by Shakespear's nervous lays,
The manly genius of Eliza's days.[7]

This general nostalgia for 'the manly genius' of an earlier England was part of the search for a national literature, a literature represented most exactly by Shakespeare.[8] More generally, Shakespeare represented a type of the ideal Briton: an adherent of liberty, scornful of rules, bold and various in his genius. Not only did his works embody these qualities, but Britons – the common reader and the critic alike – were eager to find these attributes in the man himself, an enterprise which benefitted from the little actually known about Shakespeare. Unlike Spenser, Jonson and even Milton, Shakespeare could be constructed as the true Briton par excellence; not merely the 'English Homer', he became a cultural symbol.

But, despite Shakespeare's status as national emblem and literary hero, the 'Shakespeare' performed and often read in mid eighteenth-century England was not necessarily Shakespeare verbatim. Playwrights added new scenes to the plays, or, more often, deleted scenes and even entire acts – Lillo's *Marina* was itself a retooling of *Pericles*.[9] These additions and deletions served to accommodate Shakespeare's plays to a new cultural climate; because of Shakespeare's status as national hero and representative Briton, his works *had* to be altered, however subtly, to conform to the pressures of a nationalism which sought to use Shakespeare as its cultural figurehead. Because such adaptations run counter to the canonization of Shakespeare and his works, it becomes particularly important to find those places where playwrights alter his works, recreating his plays to bring them in line with eighteenth-century theatrical and ideological demands. It is on these fault lines that I wish to focus, those places where Shakespeare's status as national hero was not enough to prevent the alteration of his works.

In the shadowy world of later eighteenth-century adaptations, Lear and Cordelia reign triumphant and Timon of Athens is provided with an adoring daughter to soften his misanthropy. The fourteen adaptations written between 1744 and 1771 constitute the last major wave of Shakespeare adaptation; they follow – and often themselves revise – the better-known adaptations written during the Restoration and later seventeenth century.[10]

Shakespeare as 'part of an Englishman's constitution'. *Mansfield Park*, ed. R. W. Chapman (London: Oxford University Press, 1970), p. 338. For more detailed descriptions of Shakespeare's role as national poet, see Michael Dobson, *The Making of the National Poet: Shakespeare, Adaptation and Authorship, 1660–1779* (Oxford: Clarendon Press, 1992) and Jonathan Bate, *Shakespearean Constitutions: Politics, Theatre, Criticism, 1730–1830* (Oxford: Clarendon Press, 1989).

7 George Lillo, 'Prologue' to *Marina* (1738). The 'sacred band' to which Lillo refers is the so-called 'Shakespeare Ladies' Club' which sponsored many productions of Shakespeare's plays during the Shakespeare revival of the late 1730s and early 1740s.

8 See Howard D. Weinbrot, *Britannia's Issue: The Rise of British Literature from Dryden to Ossian* (Cambridge: Cambridge University Press, 1993).

9 Lillo focuses his adaptation on the story of Marina and her eventual reunion with her parents. Pericles' wanderings are almost completely omitted from the plot. Lillo's prologue sums up the action:

*We've to a single tale reduc'd our play.*
*Charming* Marina*'s wrongs begin the scene;*
Pericles *finding her with his lost queen,*
*Concludes the pleasing talk.*

10 Fourteen adaptations appeared during this time: *Romeo and Juliet* (Theophilus Cibber), 1744; *Papal Tyranny in the Reign of King John* (Colley Cibber), 1745; *Pyramus*

Even though the later adaptors sought to 'restore' the Shakespeare abused by their predecessors, distinct patterns of alteration develop nonetheless, the most conspicuous 'fault line' being the plays' consistent re-creation of female character. As had the playwrights of the Restoration, the later eighteenth-century adaptors return again and again to Shakespeare's women, reshaping them to conform to a new sociopolitical context. Earlier adaptors of Shakespeare found his plays sadly lacking in female characters and supplied a host of virtuous but loving wives and mistresses whose role, by and large, was to suffer helplessly and to act as erotic objects.[11] While these adaptations were themselves fiercely political, the redefinition of female character cut across party lines; Tory propagandists such as Dryden, Tate and Ravenscroft used the same model of womanhood as the Whig playwright Thomas Shadwell. By contrast, in the mid- to later eighteenth century, playwrights sought to present Shakespeare in the guise of sentimental, rather than sensational, drama, a design reflected in their depiction of women. Where the Restoration emphasized pathos and sexual titillation, the later plays replaced these qualities with filial piety and domestic merit. Most importantly, the daughter replaces the mistress as central female figure (Lillo's *Marina* is indicative of these changes; the change in title from political figure to devoted daughter reflects the general change in emphasis). No longer the suffering victims of the Restoration adaptations, these women are benevolent angels: good daughters rather than distraught wives.

At the same time that daughters usurp wives within the adaptations, appeals to nationalism replace the Restoration's partisan politics. Unlike the Restoration adaptations, in which the political subtext was generally added in response to a specific event, such as the Exclusion Crisis of 1678–81, the eighteenth-century adaptations rarely coincide with a particular crisis. Rather, at a time when England's empire was growing far beyond the British Isles, the plays appeal to England's need to define itself as morally and politically distinct from its European neighbours. If the basis of most nationalist discourse is 'a stable and unified national self to which English men and women can remain true',[12] then the adaptations provide a body of specifically *English* literature which reiterates the British national characters at a time when what is English is changing rapidly. Within this context, the conjunction of daughterly duty and national identity is unsurprising, for it is with the female characters of the later eighteenth-century adaptations that nationalism and sentiment merge. Both gender and nationalism are cultural constructions formed in response to social and political pressures. Frequently dependent upon one another,[13] they provide recognizable and socially sanctioned identities that provoke a predictable emotional

---

*and Thisbe* (James Lampe), 1745; *Romeo and Juliet* (David Garrick), 1748; *Florizel and Perdita* (MacNamara Morgan), 1754; *The Fairies* (David Garrick), 1755; *Catherine and Petruchio* (David Garrick), 1756; *Florizel and Perdita* (David Garrick), 1756; *King Lear* (David Garrick), 1756; *Cymbeline* (William Hawkins), 1759; *A Fairy Tale* (George Colman), 1763; *The History of King Lear* (George Colman), 1768; *Timon of Athens* (Richard Cumberland), 1771; *The Sheep-Shearing: A Dramatic Pastoral* (George Colman), 1777. For a discussion of the earlier adaptations, see Dobson, *The Making of the National Poet*, and Marsden, *The Re-Imagined Text: Shakespeare, Adaptation and Eighteenth-Century Literary Theory* (Lexington: University Press of Kentucky, 1995).

11 Nahum Tate's Cordelia, for example, is defined by her love for Edgar and narrowly escapes being raped by a truly fiendish Edmund while Virgilia in Tate's version of *Coriolanus* stabs herself to prevent a similar violation. Thomas Shadwell provides Timon of Athens with two mistresses, one of whom dies pathetically with Timon in the wilderness.

12 Richard Helgerson, *Forms of Nationhood: The Elizabethan Writing of England* (Chicago: University of Chicago Press, 1992), p. 8.

13 See for example Helgerson's final chapter, 'Engendering the Nation-State', also *Nationalism and Sexualities*, ed. Andrew Parker, Mary Russo, Doris Sommer, and Patricia Yaeger (New York: Routledge, 1992), part I, '(De)Colonizing Gender' and part IV, 'Spectacular Bodies'.

response. With the Shakespeare adaptations of the mid-eighteenth century, it is the sentimentality associated with the female figure which provides nationalism with its emotional power.

As examination of the adaptations suggests, the changes to Shakespeare's daughters represent a response to this need for a clearly articulated national identity. In *Desire and Domestic Fiction: A Political History of the Novel*, Nancy Armstrong states that 'the female was the figure, above all else, on whom depended the outcome of the struggle among competing ideologies'.[14] While Armstrong refers to the growth of what she terms middle-class authority, I would like to place her comment in a more explicitly political context which considers the ideological significance of the female figure, specifically those figures created, more or less, by England's national poet. Their actions authorized at least nominally by Shakespeare's touch, the good daughters of the adaptations act as symbolic icons of Englishness. While women were not expected to participate in the political realm (facing scathing criticism if they ventured to do so), they were, nonetheless, a crucial component in the popular nationalism of the mid-to-later eighteenth century.[15] Without direct political involvement, they supported the father of their country and symbolically represented that sentimentalized domesticity which Britons must protect. (Linda Colley even attributes the growing sentimental attachment to the Royal Family to British women.[16]) In essence, women's political role was simply an extension of their domestic function.

The adaptations' not-quite-Shakespearian daughters thus represent an important shift not only in the form of drama, but in its ideological underpinnings. For the later eighteenth century, the place of daughters within the patriarchal family structure had particular moral importance. A daughter, explains James Fordyce, father and author of conduct books for young ladies, determines the well-being of a family: 'The world, I know not how, overlooks, in our sex, a thousand irregularities, which it never forgives in yours; so that the honour and peace of a family are, in this view, much more dependent on the conduct of daughters than of sons'.[17] A family's internal order and external respectability thus arise from proper daughterly behaviour. But the staging of daughterly fidelity takes on larger implications. Considered on a symbolic level in which the family acts as a type of the state, the dutiful daughter becomes the pattern of national honour: family drama becomes national drama, and the daughters of England stand responsible for the honour and peace of the nation.[18] This public interpretation of the private sphere is articulated most famously by Edmund Burke, who posited a direct relation between the structure of the family and the structure of the British government, claiming that Britain's political system 'is placed in a just correspondence and symmetry with the order of the world' and that 'we have given to our frame of polity the image of a relation in blood, binding up the constitution of our country with our dearest domestic ties'.[19] Stability within the family, the result of proper daughterly conduct, thus represents a larger stability, of social structure and of empire. Shakespeare's status as England's national poet further spotlights the

---

14 Nancy Armstrong, *Desire and Domestic Fiction: A Political History of the Novel* (Oxford: Oxford University Press, 1987), p. 5.

15 Colley, *Britons*. On the scandal attached to female political activity, see her discussion of the Duchess of Devonshire, pp. 242–50.

16 *Ibid.*, pp. 268–73.

17 James Fordyce, *Sermons for Young Ladies* (1766).

18 The political significance of the family in eighteenth-century drama has been largely ignored. One of the few books to explore family politics in drama remains Susan Staves, *Players' Scepters: Fictions of Authority in the Restoration* (Lincoln: University of Nebraska Press, 1979).

19 Edmund Burke, *Reflections on the Revolution in France* (1790), III (The True Constitutional Principles of Kingship in Britain), 2b (British liberties closely linked with an hereditary monarchy are an old inheritance and a factor of social stability).

importance of daughters within his plays; sanctified by England's poetic spokesman, their virtue constitutes a literary expression of England's national identity.

Using the dutiful daughter as an ideological marker, later eighteenth-century adaptations such as David Garrick's *King Lear* (1768) and Richard Cumberland's *Timon of Athens* (1771) emphasize domestic virtue and family ties, projecting social and political stability through the representative merit of these female figures. In this they follow the lead of countless novels and sentimental plays in which daughters love and obey their progenitors and in which the reunion of father and daughter frequently constitutes the work's emotional climax. This motif appears throughout literature of the mid-to-later eighteenth century: we see it, for example, in Kate Hardcastle's willingness to obey her father in Oliver Goldsmith's *She Stoops to Conquer*, the emotional reconciliation of Evelina and her father in Frances Burney's *Evelina* (dedicated by Burney to her own father), Matilda's devotion to her father in Elizabeth Inchbald's *A Simple Story*, and so on. Even conduct books relied upon the formula of a devoted father's letters to his presumably obedient daughter(s).[20] Shakespeare also provided a rich source of father–daughter bonds,[21] but the representation of these bonds was often not appropriate to the ideology of the patriarchal family or the well-ordered state. In Shakespeare's plays, daughters repeatedly stand opposed to authoritarian fathers, a conflict which frequently results in defiant daughters. Most famously, in *King Lear* Cordelia explicitly challenges her father's authority by responding 'Nothing' to his demand for a show of excessive filial piety. More frequently, the conflict between father and daughter is figured in the daughter's decision to marry against her father's wishes and her subsequent rejection of her father. This essential premise appears repeatedly in Shakespeare's plays and is the basis for several tragedies: Juliet defies her family in her love for Romeo, Hermia flees Athens and a marriage arranged by her father, while Cymbeline forcibly separates Imogen and her commoner husband. Even the gentle Desdemona marries against her father's will.

This conflict vanishes in the adaptations of the mid eighteenth century; these daughters are devoted, not defiant. They cherish their fathers and refuse to abandon them to old age, even rejecting love and marriage in order to minister to their needs. As represented in adaptations of *A Midsummer Night's Dream*, *The Winter's Tale*, *King Lear* and *Timon of Athens*, the bond between father and daughter becomes a necessary pillar of patriarchy. These daughters represent no threat to the power of the patriarch; they never protest their subordinate role and indeed imbue it with a sacred aura, never swerving in their reverence for their fathers, no matter how feeble or frenzied these fathers might be. Unlike a son, with whom the father must negotiate a balance of power and to whom he must inevitably relinquish power, the dutiful daughter represents no threat. In these plays the power differential between father and child is both absolute and sacred. Not only do these daughters uphold the familial power structure, they also reject or subordinate romantic love in favour of their filial piety. Their subordinate position within society is built into their position within the family. Viewed through a national lens where the King is the father of his country, these good daughters represent the ideal subject: worshipful, obedient and loyal.

---

[20] See for example George Savile, Marquis of Halifax, *Lady's New-Years Gift: Or, Advice to a Daughter* or Dr John Gregory, *A Father's Legacy to his Daughters* (1774). Published first in 1688, *The Lady's New-Years Gift* went through multiple editions in the eighteenth century, at least ten different printings between 1740 and 1800, including one edition with parallel texts in French and English (1752).

[21] According to Diane Elizabeth Dreher, 22 of major importance. *Domination and Defiance: Fathers and Daughters in Shakespeare* (Lexington, Kentucky: University of Kentucky Press, 1986), p. 1.

The adaptations present ample evidence of properly compliant daughters; bad examples are revised or quietly edited out. Thus Hermia's rebellious escape into the forest in *A Midsummer's Night Dream* appears only in Garrick's short-lived opera *The Fairies*. Garrick's version of *The Winter's Tale*, shortened to three acts and focusing upon Leontes' reunion with Perdita and, eventually, Hermione, establishes Leontes not as King, but as father, 'afloat' in tears (3.4.86) over the loss of his family circle.[22] Theophilus Cibber even recasts the Montague/ Capulet strife as a disagreement between mothers: as Old Capulet explains, the marriage of Romeo and Juliet was originally sanctioned by the two fathers, but this arrangement

> So increas'd the Anger of our Wives,
> (Whose Quarrels we are ever apt to join in)
> The Rage of civil War, broke out more fiercely.[23]

In this example of familial strife becoming political strife, the father–daughter bond remains unbroken – wives are the problem, not daughters, and Juliet actually obeys her father by loving Romeo. The daughters of this new Shakespeare are docile and affectionate; filial duty is their highest duty, and they do not intend to rebel against 'those who had a Right in the Disposal of them'.[24] Thus, altered, Shakespeare reiterates the bourgeois moral traits espoused by popular sentimental, domestic drama, and provides theatre audiences with an endorsement of the happily patriarchal family in which the father is king – and the King, father.

The national agenda underlying this rhetoric becomes most apparent in the sustained depictions of dutiful daughters in Garrick's *King Lear* and Cumberland's *Timon of Athens* (1771). In both plays, the link between nation and family is made explicit, and both explore the daughter's role as domestic and political restorative. In *King Lear*, the ancient British setting immediately suggests national overtones while Lear's role as both king and father ensures that domestic relations have national significance; the daughters who oppose him incite civil war and the daughter who demonstrates filial piety restores both the monarch and national order. *Timon of Athens*, while lacking *Lear*'s neat conflation of father and king, provides a political backdrop for Timon's travails, a backdrop which the adaptor Richard Cumberland expands into an only slightly disguised narrative of British patriotism. Although the plays begin with very different tragic trajectories, through the process of revision they end up reiterating the same story of the infirm father and his nurturing daughter. And in both cases, the national and domestic agendas coincide.

David Garrick was the eighteenth century's greatest Lear and one of its foremost adaptors of Shakespeare.[25] He created his own version of *King Lear*, basing his adaptation on Nahum Tate's controversial 1681 revision which provided Shakespeare's tragedy with both a love story and a happy ending. In Tate's version, which dominated the stage for more than 150 years, Cordelia's love for Edgar underlies her refusal to pander to Lear's vanity in 1.1. She does not marry the King of France and is reunited with Edgar after the villainous Edmund attempts to rape her on the heath. To make room for these additions to the plot, Tate eliminated segments of Lear's story, adding additional lines for Lear only in those scenes featuring Cordelia. The play's central figures thus become the young lovers rather than the aged king. In the final act, Edgar rescues Lear and Cordelia from prison, and restores Lear to the kingship, a position which Lear abdicates in favour of the happy pair. Garrick's version

22 Thomas Davies, the play's Camillo, stressed the emotional force of Garrick's Leontes; it was, he said, 'extremely affecting'. Davies, *Dramatic Miscellanies* (1784), vol. 2, p. 260.

23 Theophilus Cibber, *Romeo and Juliet* (1748), p. 2.

24 John Hughes, *Spectator* 141, 11 August 1711.

25 For Garrick's role in the Shakespeare industry of the mid-eighteenth century, see Dobson, *Making of the National Poet*, chapter 4 ('Embodying the Author') and chapter 5 ('Nationalizing the Corpus').

stands midway between Tate and Shakespeare. While Tate's adaptation emphasizes female pathos in the form of Cordelia, focusing on her lovelorn status and desperate attempts to fend off Edmund's plot to ravish her, Garrick replaces this display of female vulnerability with an appeal to sympathy, particularly through the figure of the distraught father and his devoted daughter. To accomplish this, Garrick cut Tate's play, adding virtually no new material of his own and retaining only enough of Tate's love story to make the plot understandable; at the same time, he replaced these speeches with passages from the original play.

With the Edgar/Cordelia romance abbreviated, the play's most important relationship becomes that of father and daughter. Even while removing as much Tate as possible, Garrick carefully retains Tate's references to Cordelia's filial piety, such as the scenes in which Tate – although not Shakespeare – shows Cordelia begging Gloucester for succour 'for a father and a King' (3.2). Not only does Garrick's Lear retire happily at the play's conclusion, but the inclusion of elements from Tate makes his Cordelia a more likeable daughter than her Shakespearian counterpart, explicitly devoted to her father and fetchingly in love with Edgar. She has laudable reasons for saying 'nothing' (a statement which nonetheless causes her almost constant pangs of guilt), more frequently displays her concern for her father, and does not invade England at the head of the French army. This shift in emphasis is particularly noticeable at the end of the play. In Tate's version, Edgar and Cordelia represent the restored order of the state, a point Tate stresses in the play's final speech:

EDGAR
Our drooping Country now erects her Head,
Peace spreads her balmy Wings, and Plenty
Blooms.
Divine *Cordelia*, all the Gods can witness
How much thy Love to Empire I prefer!
Thy bright Example shall convince the World
(Whatever Storms of Fortune are decreed)
That Truth and Vertue shall at last succeed.[26]

Written in support of the monarchy during the Exclusion Crisis of 1678–82, Tate's play concludes by equating 'Truth and Vertue', Cordelia, and the restored English Monarchy in the form of Charles II.[27]

By eliminating this speech, Garrick shifts the focus from Edgar to Lear, reiterating the power of the king and patriarch even as Lear plans his retirement. In Garrick's version of Tate, Cordelia becomes the means by which Lear's personal as well as political power is reestablished when a threat to her safety rouses Lear to commanding fury:

LEAR
Off, hellhounds! By the Gods, I charge you spare
her.
'Tis my Cordelia, my true pious Daughter.
No Pity? Nay, then take an old man's vengeance.
(*Snatches a sword and kills two of them; the rest quit*
Cordelia *and Exeunt.*)[28]

Originally from Tate (5.4.31–3), in Garrick's version the prison scene provides a vision of majesty restored. No longer pathetic or infirm, this Lear regains his vigour and his role as patriarch by defending his daughter. Lear's dominance alters the role of Cordelia in this reinstated order. No longer the emblem of a partisan political agenda, she becomes the good daughter and ideal subject, bestowed by her father on her bridegroom. For this dutiful daughter, familial and patriotic duties coincide; her acts of daughterly love restore a king as well

[26] Nahum Tate, *The History of King Lear* in *Five Restoration Adaptations of Shakespeare*, ed. Christopher Spencer (Urbana: University of Illinois Press, 1965), 5.6.155–61.

[27] On Tate's politics see Nancy Klein Maguire, 'Nahum Tate's King Lear: "the king's blest restoration"' in *The Appropriation of Shakespeare: Post-Renaissance Reconstructions of the Works and the Myth*, ed. Marsden (New York: St Martin's Press, 1992).

[28] David Garrick, *King Lear*, 5.4.32–4 in *The Plays of David Garrick*, ed. Harry William Pedicord and Fredrick Louis Bergmann (Carbondale, Illinois: Southern Illinois University Press, 1981), vol. 3.

as a father. Acting out of domestic impulses, she becomes a national icon.

A similar iconography emerges in Richard Cumberland's *Timon of Athens*, the only version of *Timon of Athens* staged after mid century.[29] Cumberland's play represents the culmination of the later eighteenth century's reshaping of Shakespeare in the form of sentimentalized drama. Retaining the basic contours of Shakespeare's tragedy, Cumberland simplifies and reorganizes the play, making the scope more intimate and the tone more conciliatory. His most significant innovation is the addition of a daughter much like Garrick's Cordelia around whom the play revolves. She takes control of Timon's household after his bankruptcy and accepts poverty gladly, selling everything but her plainest clothes before rushing to the wilderness to succour her father. The play's active agent, Evanthe is motivated in all circumstances by her love for her father, whether she is saving Athens or her father from ruin.

The domestic tragedy of Timon and his daughter is acted out against the backdrop of political contention, a debate described by Cumberland in nationally coded terms. While Timon entertains guests and loses a fortune, Alcibiades, a type of the ideal Briton, bold, honest and liberty loving, fights with the corrupt Athenian Senate, the same body who will ultimately turn against Timon. Cumberland presents Alcibiades' mission in terms of a generalized appeal to the values commonly associated with the British character, projecting onto ungrateful Athenians the degeneracy associated with the French:

ALCIBIADES

No, ye are Lords:
A lazy, proud, unprofitable crew,
The vermin, gender'd from the rank corruption
Of a luxurious state. – No soldiers, say you?
And wherefore are ye none? Have you not life,
Friends, honour, freedom, country to defend? . . .
Gods! that such triflers shou'd be call'd *Athenians*:
O great *Minerva*, patroness of *Athens*,
How is our fathers antient spirit fled![30]

Without ever mentioning England, in Alcibiades' speech Cumberland draws upon traits associated with Britain – honour, freedom, defence of country – and opposes them to those traits commonly associated with foreigners, particularly the French, lazy, degenerate, luxurious. His final exclamation ('How is our fathers antient spirit fled') expresses the same yearning for a purer national past as that voiced by writers such as Lillo to whom Shakespeare himself represented the 'manly genius of Eliza's days' against 'rank corruption of a luxurious state'.

Evanthe plays a central role in redeeming this unEnglish state. She pauses in her daughterly ministrations only long enough to save Athens from invasion, neatly conflating patriotism and filial piety. Explicitly linking Athens' corruption to disorder within the family, she asks the Senators:

Have you no daughters?
No sense of filial piety, no mercy?
That thus relentless you heap crime on crime.
(p. 37)

Addressing her as 'another tutelar *Minerva*', the 'repentant Senate' (p. 38) agrees to assist her father if she assists her fatherland. In a scene which evokes Volumnia's plea outside Rome in *Coriolanus*, Evanthe persuades Alcibiades not to attack Athens. ''Tis done!' she cries at the conclusion of the scene, 'my country can demand no more' (p. 50). Cumberland spells out the patriotic symbolism of the good daughter as Evanthe turns briskly from the public realm to the private, remarking: 'I've sav'd a city; grant me now, kind Gods, / To save a father' (p. 50).

Thrifty and obedient, with strong family ties and moral convictions, Evanthe embodies

[29] Shakespeare's *Timon* was not staged during the eighteenth century. All productions of *Timon* staged before 1750 were of Thomas Shadwell's *Timon of Athens: Or, the Man-Hater* (1678).

[30] Richard Cumberland, *Timon of Athens* (1771), p. 15. All further references will be taken from this text.

bourgeois values familiar to Cumberland's audience. As a dutiful daughter, her character avoids pathos (any pathos in this play derives from Timon's sufferings in the wilderness); the role is accentuated because it upholds a new ideology dependent on domestic virtue and the patriarchal family. Even the play's final scenes participate in this glorification of daughterly devotion: where Shakespeare concludes with a bitter Timon, Cumberland provides a scene of reconciliation in which the one-time misanthrope dies, claiming that his love for his daughter represents his one redeeming quality:

TIMON
Give me your pardon; I have suffer'd much,
And much I fear sorrow has shook my wits;
But in the bitterest moments of affliction,
I have remember'd still to bless my child.
(pp. 57–8)

In spite of everything, this family tie remains strong and constitutes a stability which the state of Athens will imitate, controlled by Alcibiades and counselled by Evanthe, saviour of cities and of fathers.

Cumberland's play, like Garrick's *Lear*, represents less a struggle of ideologies than an assertion of a single, dominant ideology in which nationhood is regulated by the icon of the daughter/subject. In it Evanthe is both the most prominent of the self-effacing daughters and the least Shakespearian. With the focus on the father–daughter relationship, *Timon of Athens* becomes a kind of attenuated *King Lear*; a father makes mistakes, runs mad, is found by his daughter who cares for him devotedly. But here the play's central figure is the daughter, not the father. Evanthe's father is the centre of her life, and everything else, both material wealth and romantic love, must be put aside so that she can care for her parent. These qualities are perhaps epitomized most clearly in the form which her self-sacrifice takes as Evanthe gives up her most prized possession in order to pay her father's debts:

EVANTHE
I have a picture,
*Apelles* might have own'd it: 'tis my father.
Lo, what a form he wears! A *Cretan* artist
Trac'd out the living work. There was a time,
Not all the treasure of the *Ephesian* fane,
Had brib'd me to dispose on't. Here *Faminius*,
Take it; get gold. Now I have nothing left.
(p. 25)

Evanthe's words convey the qualities appropriate in a sentimental daughter: self-sacrifice, reverence and affection. Even while remaining de-eroticized, Evanthe's admiration of her father's 'form' presents for a moment a Timon who is more than an impotent old man and recreates the image of the powerful father. Like Cordelia in the prison, she reaffirms the power of the father/king, reinventing patriarchal authority. As Evanthe demonstrates, the function of the daughter is not simply to serve but to elevate, recreate and revere the image of the father.

Perhaps the most unusual variation on the theme of fathers and dutiful daughters occurred not within the text of an adaptation but in its performance. When Theophilus Cibber's *Romeo and Juliet* first played in 1744, Cibber himself played Romeo – and his fourteen-year-old daughter Jennie played Juliet. The audience's attention was repeatedly drawn to this relationship. References to the father–daughter pairing appear first in the Prologue, spoken by Jennie, later in an epilogue which she allegedly wrote for subsequent performances, and, ultimately, in Cibber's *A Serio-Comic Apology for Part of the Life of Mr Theophilus Cibber*, published with the adaptation in 1748. In these references, the audience is invited to envision actor and actress not as star-crossed lovers, but as equally conventional characters, the needy father and the loving, supportive daughter. Cibber and his daughter recreate themselves as figures out of sentimental drama, a play for audience sympathy before the official play began. At the close of the prologue, Jennie described herself not as a lover, like Juliet, but as one: 'Who, full of modest Terror, dreads t'appear, / But, trembling, begs a Father's Fate to share.'[31] Her Epilogue, like the Prologue included in Theophilus Cibber's *Apology*, takes the role of the sentimental daughter still further:

For a kind Father fain I'd Pity move:
Pardon the Fondness of my Filial Love.
Reflect how oft' he pleas'd, oft' gain'd Renown,
And varied Shapes to entertain the Town;
While crouded Houses thunder'd his Applause:
Ye bounteous Fair, – to you I plead his Cause.
To your Protection, gen'rous *Britons*, take,
Th'unhappy Father, for the Daughter's Sake.[32]

Jennie Cibber's words evoke those of a generation of rewritten Shakespearian daughters who would make equally emotional appeals for sympathy within the confines of the Shakespeare adaptations. Her plea is virtually identical with that of Garrick's Cordelia, pleading with Gloucester and Edmund to help her father, and later still, Cumberland's Evanthe pleading with the Athenian senators. That Cibber and his daughter felt that the representation of daughterly love was a more evocative subject than romantic love underscores the emotional potency of this relationship in the eyes of the average eighteenth-century playgoer.

In the same way that eighteenth-century adaptations replace partisan politics with a more generalized invocation of British nationalism, Jennie Cibber bases her plea on a shared concept of national honour and familial love. Her appeal to the sympathy of 'gen'rous *Britons*' underlines the national context of this display of filial piety. In directing her petition to the 'Gen'rous *Britons*' of her audience, Jennie Cibber's 'Epilogue' links national pride with support of family – because her audience is (ideally) composed of true Britons, they will come to the assistance of the equally British dutiful daughter, thus helping her fulfil her national and familial duty.

The efficacy of Jennie Cibber's petition is rooted in the overlapping cultural construction of nationalism and gender which equates the good daughter with the loyal Briton. The sentimental appeal of such a figure intensifies its ideological status, engendering a profoundly nationalistic emotional response. Emblems of modest devotion, the nurturing daughters added to Shakespeare's plays fill a perceived deficiency in his works, furnishing England's national poet with appropriately British visions of female rectitude. These paragons of domestic virtue support England by supporting their fathers, their actions reinforcing the hierarchical structure of the family and by extension the bases of patriarchal society. They are thus an integral part of the British vision of properly ordered society at a time when Britain was beginning to define itself in terms not only of its military and economic prowess, but also of its moral values.[33] As prologues and epilogues such as Jennie Cibber's and the plays themselves indicate, it was difficult to separate the good daughter from the patriotic cause. The adaptations are explicit in their contention that domestic strife leads to political strife – and that peace within the family represents and even promotes national harmony. Through careful rewriting and editing, the dutiful daughter gains a place within the venerated canon of Shakespeare's works, her role sanctified by the words of England's national poet. Under the aegis of Shakespeare's divine touch, Cordelia, Evanthe and their sister heroines demonstrate that restoring the father does indeed restore the fatherland.

---

[31] In *A Serio-Comic Apology for Part of the Life of Mr. Theophilus Cibber* (1748, published with his version of *Romeo and Juliet*), p. 74.

[32] In Cibber, *A Serio-Comic Apology*, p. 87.

[33] See Newman, *English Nationalism*, especially chapter 6, 'The Moral Elevation of the English National Identity'. As Newman notes, generosity and sincerity were traits which began to be associated with the British national character in the mid-eighteenth century.

# SHAKESPEARE AND *CLARISSA*: 'GENERAL NATURE', GENRE AND SEXUALITY

MARTIN SCOFIELD

## I UNIVERSALITY AND DIFFERENCE

Most critics in the eighteenth century, unlike academic critics today, were confident of at least one assumption about great literature: that the truths it embodied were universal and that, in the words of Dr Johnson in his Preface to Shakespeare, 'Nothing can please many and please long but just representations of general nature.' It is a view which depends of course on even more basic assumptions – that there is such an entity as 'general nature' (or at least that the category is useful); and that in turn there is such an entity (or meaningful category) as 'human nature' – a certain intrinsic 'humanness' which remains in some way constant despite variations from country to country and race to race, and despite the changes in behaviour over time. But while it might be agreed that there are some constant factors in human behaviour (without which it is difficult to see how we could respond to the literature of the past at all), the notion of a 'human nature' (whether as an essence, a useful category or some kind of shadowy ideal), has become (notoriously) in recent years almost impossible to use. It is probably fair to say that some such view lay behind nearly all literary criticism from Johnson's time (and indeed before) to our own. Questioned or rejected as these ideas have been by the various forms of deconstruction, post-structuralism, new historicism and the like, literary criticism has, again notoriously, become uncertain of its foundations and has looked about for new ones. The stress has been put on relativism, on the notion that cultural values change, and on the idea that every age reads past works of literature not just differently (this was always conceded) but radically differently, not even always in 'the spirit that the author writ' (another eighteenth-century maxim, this time Pope's) but sometimes against that spirit, in readings that dissect, analyse, re-create in the image of the critic's own time. The stress has been put not on an 'unchanging human nature' but rather on the idea that human nature does change, and that literature is important above all because it both records and contributes to that process of change.

In the case of Richardson, eighteenth-century admirers were virtually united in the kind of praise they accorded him, and this praise had two main formulations: that he embodied universal truths, and that he was like Shakespeare. 'Of Nature born, by Shakespeare got' was the first line of a poem on Richardson by David Garrick; Dr Johnson for his part described Richardson as 'a writer similar in genius to Shakespeare, being acquainted with the innermost recesses of the heart' ('the heart' being a kind of constant, like 'human nature') and as having 'an absolute command of the passions, so as to be able to affect his readers as himself is affected';[1] and he also asserted that

[1] Sir John Hawkins, *Life of Samuel Johnson* (2nd edn) (London, 1787), p. 214n., quoted in *Samuel Richardson: a Biography*, T. C. Duncan Eaves and Ben D. Kimpel (Oxford, 1971), p. 388.

there were 'few sentiments [in the sense of thoughts or reflections] that may not be traced up to Homer, Shakespeare or Richardson'.[2] The trio of great names, widely separated by history, is itself a good example of the universalizing and trans-historical view of literary value. In 1813, again, *The Monthly Magazine* called Richardson 'the Shakespeare of Romance'.[3]

The tradition of comparing Richardson and Shakespeare has continued into our own day. There are a few dissenting voices like that of Walter Allen who compared Fielding with Shakespeare, and Richardson with Milton. But Mark Kinkead-Weekes put the comparison strongly when he wrote: 'The great invention of *Clarissa* can indeed be seen as the discovery of how to use comedy to probe tragedy ... What is significant is that the probing of tragedy by comedy is as centrally "Shakespeare" as the depth of characterization and the mastery of human nature that were the distinguishing features of Shakespeare for the eighteenth century.'[4] This introduces the idea of mixing the genres; and Kinkead-Weekes's whole book, entitled *Samuel Richardson: Dramatic Novelist*, puts its emphasis (as in Henry James's famous advice to the novelist, 'Dramatize, dramatize!') on Richardson's dramatic powers of immediacy of presentation, dialogue, and of writing 'to the moment' (the feature of epistolary convention where the character is writing of events immediately after they have happened or even as they happen). He also emphasized the Shakespearian quality of Richardson's exploration of character and his overall moral vision: 'Richardson was, I think, the first novelist to merit comparison with Shakespeare in both the power to explore "free" characters, and the struggle to comprehend and make the centre hold against the strongest challenge he could mount.'[5] ('Centre' here has a Jamesian sense of 'central moral view').

I shall return to these questions of moral vision in relation to the two writers; but I want also to consider the possibility of other kinds of comparisons than the ones illustrated above. What of the differences of genre between a novel of several volumes and over a million words and a play of some two to three thousand lines which lasts three hours on the stage? What of the differences between an art of immediate presentation designed to be embodied by actors, and an art of drama mediated through the epistolary convention and the convention of an 'editorial' author who arranges this correspondence and who guides the reader through it? What, above all, of the differences between a self-confessedly didactic novelist and an 'invisible' playwright who, as Johnson said, 'seems to write without any moral purpose'?

## II GENRE: TRAGEDY VERSUS COMEDY

*Clarissa* is a tragedy that might have been made a comedy. There is of course a great deal of wit and humour in the novel, and the situation and tone are not so very different, at least in its earlier stages, from Richardson's earlier novel *Pamela* where the heroine resists the seductive wiles of Mr B and the novel moves to the comic conclusion of marriage. Some contemporary readers of the earlier parts of *Clarissa* expressed to Richardson their hopes that the novel would end happily. Richardson's most energetic correspondent, Lady Bradshaig, wrote with earnest entreaties that he would not be so hard-hearted as to let Clarissa die. Richardson replied: 'I would not think of leaving my heroine short of Heaven.'[6] The reply reinforces the idea that Richardson's religious and didactic intention was a large part of the pressure that led the novel towards tragedy. He clearly developed a conception in which Clarissa would

---

2 *Ibid.*, p. 588.

3 Cited in Mark Kinkead-Weekes, *Samuel Richardson, Dramatic Novelist* (London, 1973), p. 396.

4 *Ibid.*, p. 451.

5 *Ibid.*, p. 456.

6 *The Selected Letters of Samuel Richardson*, ed. J. Carroll (Oxford, 1964), p. 104.

remain true to an absolute principle of integrity and virtue despite an emotional attraction to Lovelace, and Lovelace would remain true to a principle of Nature as opposed to morality (rather like Shakespeare's Edmund), to the principle of male sexual licence and domination, in spite of the sensitivity and intelligence which could see and admire Clarissa's own moral intelligence and virtue. 'Thou Nature art my goddess', says Edmund, and Lovelace speaks of his hopes of the Triumph of Nature over Principle. But Lovelace can feel intense remorse, and even Edmund tries to countermand the order for Cordelia's murder.

Richardson's drama of male sexuality, female virtue and parental and social prohibition suggests comparisons with Shakespeare, but not so much in the realm of tragedy as in comedy. It is not an exaggeration to say that Shakespeare characteristically treats sexuality (particularly if we confine ourselves to the subject of love before marriage) in terms of comedy rather than tragedy, and in ways which question assumptions (as in Richardson) of sexual polarity. In *As You Like It* Rosalind is banished by her wicked uncle with only Celia for an ally (as Anna Howe is to Clarissa), and teaches Orlando how to woo her by adopting a male disguise that seems to suggest a playing down of the absolute differences of male and female roles and of the absolute opposition of male and female sexuality. This mitigation of absolute sexual polarity also occurs in *Twelfth Night* where Orsino falls in love with Viola by way of being initially attracted to her as a young man; whereas his possessive and fantastical passion for Olivia evaporates into an absurd destructiveness parodic of Othello's (and close to Lovelace's) in his lines at Act 5.1.115–17:

> Why should I not, had I the heart to do it,
> Like to th' Egyptian thief, at point of death
> Kill what I love;

and Olivia comes to love Sebastian by way of her love for his disguised twin sister. (The conventions of disguise and mistaken identity are simply used as compressions or figurations of these processes). In *Much Ado About Nothing* one half of the plot turns on the question of Hero's chastity, but Don John's plot is exposed, and the brutality and arrogance of Claudio's violent spurning of his bride is also exposed and repented of (an arrogant moralism not unlike that of James Harlowe at his sister's supposed 'fall').

Shakespeare, then, tends to view the problems of pre-marital love and sexuality in a comic rather than tragic light, as amenable to the human and reconciling conventions of the genre. His 'sexual' tragedies tend to focus on marital relations: in *Othello* the jealous rage of the supposedly wronged husband; in *Antony and Cleopatra* the confusions and conflicting and self-destroying aims and ambitions of a mature man and woman both thwarted and exalted by their relationship. None of Shakespeare's tragedies centres, as Richardson's does, on the chastity, or more exclusively the virginity, of an unmarried woman. The tragedy of *Romeo and Juliet* arises from the 'fate' enjoined on them by their feuding families and an additional element of chance or accident. The question of Juliet's 'virtue' hardly arises. In this and in the ways we have already noted, it is of all Shakespeare's tragedies the one closest to comedy (although several other tragedies are intensified and made complex by their comic elements and even by the sense that they often seem to arise out of 'a comic matrix').[7] It is the lightness, the volatility, the youthfulness of *Romeo and Juliet* that gives the tragedy its unique romanticism and sadness.

But it is in *Measure for Measure*, a Shakespearian comedy which comes perhaps closest to tragedy, that we find the most suggestive parallels and contrasts with *Clarissa*. Angelo's character is of course very different to Lovelace's: the icily repressed puritan governor as opposed to the irresponsible aristocratic rake.

[7] See Susan Snyder, *The Comic Matrix of Shakespeare's Tragedies* (Princeton, 1979).

But in his sudden passion for Isabella, in particular his sexual attraction to her virtue, he shows responses akin to Lovelace's. Perhaps too, as has been suggested, Richardson half recalls some of Angelo's phrases in the language he gives to Lovelace.[8] When, for example, Lovelace is writing to Belford about the maid-servant Dorcas's fidelity to his 'bad cause', he notes: 'The vicious are as bad as they can be; and do the devil's work without looking after; while he is continually spreading snares for the others; and, like a skilful angler, suiting his baits to the fish he angles for.' (III, 247);[9] which recalls Angelo: 'O cunning enemy, that, to catch a saint, / With saints dost bait thy hook!' (*Measure for Measure* 2.2.185–6). Again, when Belford is meditating (to Lovelace) on his own and Lovelace's past follies he uses language which recalls Isabella's rebukes to Angelo:

> Lords of the creation! Who can forbear indignant laughter! When we see not one of the individuals of that creation (his perpetual eccentric self excepted) but acts within his own natural and original appointments: and all the time, proud and vain as the conceited wretch is of fancied and self-dependent excellence, he is obliged not only for the ornaments, but for the necessaries of life ... to all the other creatures; strutting with his blood and spirit in his veins, and with their plumage on his back: for what has he of his own, but his very mischievous, monkey-like, bad nature? (IV, 8)

Isabella is terser and more concentratedly metaphoric (as we would expect of Shakespeare's creation) but has the same combination of scorn for man's godlike pretensions, with the imagery of dress and animals:

> But man, proud man,
> Dressed in a little brief authority,
> Most ignorant of what he's most assured,
> His glassy essence, like an angry ape
> Plays such fantastic tricks before high heaven
> As makes the angels weep ... (2.2.120–5)

It is perhaps characteristic of Shakespeare that his most serious study of a man who is, in effect, a would-be rapist, is the study of a repressed puritan rather than of a rake. There are very few rapists in Shakespeare's plays: the only other obvious examples are Cloten in *Cymbeline*, who is a spoilt fool, and Demetrius and Chiron in *Titus Andronicus*, who are just princely thugs. There are also few or no brilliantly rakish seducer-villains in Shakespeare (perhaps surprisingly). Iachimo in *Cymbeline* comes closest to Lovelace in his wit and style and command of language, and an unscrupulous viciousness which does not even have the mitigating elements of Lovelace's genuine recognition and admiration of virtue. He also has Lovelace's witty but cynical assumption that women always have a simpering sexual awareness beneath a show of modesty: 'No need but of the most delicate hints to *them* ... Like so many musical instruments, touch but a single wire, and the dear souls are sensible all over' (III, 63) – (reminiscent of Pope in its combination of 'Every woman is at heart a rake' with 'The spider's touch, how infinitely fine! / Feels in each thread and lives along the line': Richardson has among his powers a vividly poetic feeling for language). It is also like Iachimo's sly observation (invention?) of Imogen's reading of 'the tale of Tereus': 'Here the leaf's turned down / Where Philomel gave up' (*Cymbeline*, 2.2.45–5). Mercutio might, in a story other than *Romeo and Juliet*, have fulfilled Lovelace's role – he has the wit, the passion, the crude but virile sexual language. It has of course been suggested that one reason (apart from plot) he is killed half way through the play may be that his presence would have been fatal to the atmosphere of high romantic love. But Mercutio as we know him never shows the final sexual ruthlessness of a Lovelace, and we feel he would have too much honour and honesty to stoop to Lovelace's underhand violence and deception (and perhaps too much

---

8 E.g. by Valerie Grosvenor Myer, *Samuel Richardson: Passion and Prudence* (London, 1986), chapter 7.

9 Quotations from *Clarissa* are taken from the Everyman edition (London, 1967, vol. I, 1976 vols. II–IV).

self-knowledge to be lured by a Clarissa's virtue).

A more apt and suggestive comparison with Lovelace, from Shakespeare's plays, is Lucio in *Measure for Measure*. Lucio is a gentleman (if not an aristocrat like Lovelace), and proud of his class status. He also has the sensitivity to recognize, even be awed by, Isabella's virtue ('I hold thee as a thing enskied and sainted'). At the same time he is sexually loose in his habits, frequenting prostitutes and despising them at the same time, so that his finally having to marry Kate Keepdown is to him as bad as 'pressing to death, whipping and hanging'. He has less wit and passion than Lovelace, but Lovelace shares his combination of snobbish hauteur towards and complicity with the low-life characters he exploits. In reflecting to Belford on women's love of praise he recalls a 'well-dressed, handsome girl' laughing at and enjoying the praises of a chimney sweep in the streets: 'Egad, girl, thought I, I despise thee as a Lovelace: but were I the chimney sweeper, and could only contrive to get into thy presence, my life to my virtue, I would have thee.' Lovelace has not, it appears, habitually gone with prostitutes in the past, but part of his degradation in the novel is his increasingly being drawn into the world of Mrs Sinclair and her women, a world which he has (perhaps) for a long time inhabited in a moral sense.

But for a full sense of Lovelace's 'Shakespearian' qualities we have to turn to more impressive figures than Lucio – or rather, figures at once more impressive and more disturbing. There is something of Hamlet in Lovelace's love of plotting: 'Had I been a military hero, I should have made gunpowder useless; for I should have blown up all my adversaries by dint of stratagem, turning their own devices upon them' (II, 55). Compare Hamlet's ''tis the sport to have the enginer / Hoist with his own petard'. There is something of Iago in his sophistries ('She did deceive her father, marrying you' *Othello* 3.3.209') and in his basic attitude to female sexual virtue (Iago: 'Blessed fig's end! The wine she drinks is made of grapes'); and his subtle self-justifications, almost self-deceptions (Iago: 'And what's he then that says I play the villain, / When this advice to Cassio is free, I give, and honest'; Lovelace: 'But ingenuousness was ever a signal part of my character'). This last is less of a perversion of the truth than in Iago's case, but there is something of the same sophistry or self-deception of claiming frankness or sincerity because an action *could* be construed as a good one and also because they both admit their true motives to themselves. Finally there is something of Edmund in Lovelace's sexual virility, wit and courage. The vigour of Edmund's first soliloquy in which he proclaims himself one of those

> Who in the lusty stealth of nature take
> More composition and fierce quality
> Than doth within a dull, stale, tirèd bed
> Go to th' creating a whole tribe of fops
> Got 'tween a sleep and wake.
>
> (*The Tragedy of King Lear* 1.2.11–15)

– and the sexual punning of his dialogue with Goneril ('Yours in the ranks of death') find a parallel in the vividness of Lovelace's language: 'Now fire, now ice, my soul is continually *upon the hiss*, as I may say' (II, 432) and in the sometimes fantastic inventiveness of his metaphors, which also have a touch of Hotspur in them, of Ben Jonson's characters, and of Milton's Satan 'snuffing the wide air':

> This it is to have leisure on my hands! What a matchless plotter thy friend! Stand by and let me swell! – I am already as big as an elephant, and ten times wiser! – mightier too by far! Have I not reason to snuff the moon with my proboscis? (II, 114)

That the poetic force of Lovelace's language can call up so many Shakespearian and other echoes suggests something of the extraordinary complexity of his character. But because he is a character in an eighteenth-century epistolary novel with a didactic and religious intention, he cannot become either a tragic hero like Hamlet, or a tragic villain like Iago or Edmund.[10] Rather he is degraded from his full potential and complexity rather as Milton's Satan is degraded from great heroic individualist to a shape-changer and finally a hissing serpent. Nor, because Richardson is determined to avoid a comic resolution, and determined not to 'think of leaving my heroine short of heaven', is Lovelace allowed the chance to reform of the sexual sinner of comedy, like Lucio in *Measure for Measure*, or (closer to Lovelace's own crime – and strength of character) Angelo in the same play.

> They say best men are moulded out of faults,
> And, for the most, become much more the better
> For being a little bad. So may my husband.
> (5.1.436–8)

So says Mariana, pleading for Angelo's life: but the charities possible in tragi-comedy are not possible either in tragedy (which *Clarissa* almost is) or in the religiously didactic epistolary novel. Even Caliban, who tried to rape Miranda, is pardoned at the end of *The Tempest*, and allowed to 'sue for grace'. And in *Pericles* the young lord (close in class and type to Lovelace) is allowed to be abashed and chastened by Mariana's innocence: such is the benevolent vision of Shakespeare's late romances.[11]

A dramatic and even Shakespearian inspiration, but also the constraints of genre and of history, are felt too in the creation of the character of Clarissa. Clarissa is not a pallid Victorian heroine: she has an intelligence and moral strength which put her in a class apart from either the pathos of the 'fallen woman' like George Eliot's Hetty Sorel or the wilful egoism of the nearly erring Rosamund Vincy. And her moral reasoning and prolonged effort at virtue and sincerity is allowed fuller play than that of a more substantial woman than either of the above, who dies tragically for love, Maggie Tulliver in *Mill on the Floss*. She also has a power of speech and repartee which one critic has likened to that of the Restoration female wits: her snubbing of Solmes has been compared with Millamant's snubbing of Sir Wilful (in *The Way of the World*) and she has been seen as combining the innocence of Margery Pinchwife with the trenchancy of Mrs Alithea (in *The Country Wife*).[12] Her retorts to her brother, though of course more serious and painful, are reminiscent of Ophelia's lively resistance to Laertes's possessive warnings about her honour.

---

[10] In the striking BBC Television adaptation of 1991 the tragic possibilities of Lovelace's role were interestingly and effectively increased by intensifying his remorse and by having him die in a duel with his friend Belford, rather than challenged abroad by Clarissa's cousin Col. Mordern. Given the elements of moral sensitivity in Lovelace and Belford's persistent championing of Clarissa in the novel, this was a convincing adaptation. But it moved the story away from its status as an exemplary hagiography of Clarissa and towards something more like a Shakespearian tragedy.

[11] Shakespeare nowhere, however, essays the difficult dramatic situation of having an actual seducer, still less a rapist, marry his victim. Other dramatists in the period 1594–1625 were more daring (or foolhardy). In *The Queen of Corinth* by John Fletcher, the rapist marries the victim, who has also subsequently taken the place of a second potential victim (a version of the 'bed-trick'). The two women face the rapist at the end of the play (in some ways like Mariana and Isabella) one asking for leniency and marriage and the other for his death. When the second case is revealed as a substitution, the way is free to allow the heroine to marry him. There was an indication in the first Act that the heroine/victim was originally in love with the rapist, and he with her. And the rapist is urged on by friends against his better judgement at the beginning and is bitterly repentant and (like Angelo) begs for death at the end. But the psychology of the heroine is difficult to credit, especially when she begs for marriage immediately after the rape, when the rapist is masked and therefore at that point unknown to her, and when he has also used accomplices. Nor is there any exploration of general moral issues as in *Measure for Measure*. For a discussion of this and other examples from the period, see Suzanne Gossett, '"Best men are moulded out of faults": Marrying the Rapist in Jacobean Drama', *English Language Review*, 14 (1984), 305–27.

[12] James Grantham Turner, 'Lovelace and the Paradoxes of Liberation', in *Samuel Richardson: Tercentenary Essays*, ed. M. A. Doody and P. Sabor (Cambridge, 1989), 70–88.

But we cannot imagine Clarissa talking and joking with the freedom of a Rosalind with Orlando or still less of a Helena with Parolles. Gentlemen and ladies of the early seventeenth century (if we can see Shakespeare as the ideal representative of it) found it much easier to be liberal in matters of talk about sex than Richardson and the post-puritan eighteenth century, with its tension-producing combination of aristocratic and gentlemanly licence and middle-class respectability. At the dinner at Mrs Sinclair's with Lovelace and his three friends (as Belford reports it) Clarissa shames the company by quoting Cowley against 'florid talk' and showing her displeasure by her eye, 'Not poorly, like the generality of her sex affecting ignorance of meanings too obvious to be concealed; but so resenting, as to show each impudent laugher the offence given to, and taken by, a purity, that had mistaken its way, when it fell into such a company' (II, 486). Clarissa is not prudish here but she is stern: as a figure intended to be exemplary she has to be so. The novel, as a great representative work of the mid-eighteenth century, carries the burden of new sexual and social anxieties.

On a more tragic level, Clarissa can echo Hamlet's language, as when she writes of how her doubts, perplexities and hopes 'each getting the victory by turns, harrow up my soul between them' (II, 9). On another occasion, after learning that her father has said he would 'kneel for her, if nothing else will do, to prevail upon her to oblige me', she reacts with the poignant compassion of Cordelia before the broken figure of her father in Act 4 Scene 6 of *King Lear* ('O look upon me, sir,/ And hold your hands in benediction o'er me. / You must not kneel.')

> A father to KNEEL to his child! There would not have been any bearing of that! What I should have done in such a case I know not. Death would have been much more welcome to me than such a sight, on such an occasion, in behalf of a man so very, very disgustful to me! But I had deserved annihilation had I suffered my father to kneel in vain. (II, 166)

But again the pathos is at one remove in the novel, a matter of the heroine's inward reflection. Clarissa's father never kneels, either in emotional blackmail or in Lear's pathetic contrition; and Clarissa never risks the step of fully resisting her father and of giving herself to Lovelace, which would have led either to marriage, or to a different kind of tragedy. *Clarissa*, showing a restraint characteristic of the more refined and polite eighteenth century, is about the refraining from action and the turning away from life, as opposed to the Shakespearian commitment which risks all and suffers the full sharpness of tragedy as a result. And while it might seem at first glance grudging to deny Clarissa the courage of risk-taking (since, after all, someone might say, she did run away with Lovelace), Richardson's punctilious care in pointing out that she was *tricked* into running away almost takes this particular moment of courage away from her as he endeavours to guard her against the criticisms of his most prudent and censorious (and largely female) readers.

## III THE USES OF QUOTATION

One measure both of the responsiveness of Richardson to Shakespearian suggestions and of the gap between the two authors' imaginations and between their two historical periods can be seen in Richardson's use of Shakespearian quotation. In the case of Lovelace the use is generally ironic (ironic and critical on the part of Richardson), in a way that points to the potentially tragic division in Lovelace's nature. There is the case for instance of his famous quotation of Ferdinand's speech about Miranda (*The Tempest*, 3.1.39–48):

> Full many a lady
> I've eyed with best regard; and many a time
> Th'harmony of their tongues hath into bondage
> Brought my too diligent ear. For *sev'ral* virtues
> Have I liked *sev'ral* women. Never any
> With so full a soul, but some defect in her
> Did quarrel with the noblest grace she ow'd,
> And put it to the *foil*. But SHE! – O SHE!

So perfect and so peerless is created,
Of every creature's best.

(Quotation as in Richardson, I.150). The irony arises from the way this shows Lovelace's sensitivity and genuine wonder at Clarissa, qualities that are nevertheless, as we know, not held with complete sincerity. Even the emphasis on '*sev'ral*' may suggest Lovelace's complacent self-regard for his own conquests. The idealizing love of Ferdinand is quickly seen in Lovelace's case to involve a dangerous temptation: 'All that's excellent in her sex is in this lady! Until by MATRIMONIAL or EQUAL intimacies, I have found her *less than angel*, it is impossible to think any other' (which is rather like the temptation Isabella's purity presents to Angelo). There is a different kind of irony, again, in Lovelace's quotation from *Othello* a few pages earlier: 'Thou wilt say I rave. And so I do: "Perdition catch my soul, but I *do* love her." *Else* could I bear the implacable revilings of her implacable family? *Else* could I basely creep about – not her proud father's house – but his paddock and garden walls?' There is not only irony (potentially tragic, as it is tragic in Othello's case) in the fact that perdition *does* catch his soul, but also in the contrast of his scheming and calculating desire to dominate and the half-posturing of his epistolary style, with Othello's genuine rapture.

At other times Lovelace's Shakespearian quotations simply give an added depth and subtlety to his character. In vol. IV letter X, estimating the possibility of Clarissa committing suicide he imagines that she must reason with herself in the terms of Claudio's great speech on death ('Ay but to die and go we know not where') which he quotes in full. It gives an added sense of his cultivation and poetic judgement, but it may also register the irony of his lack of reflection that Clarissa would hardly have been content with such a non-Christian objection and fear of death (though we might also recall how the pious Dr Johnson would be heard muttering the lines to himself in his later years). In vol. II letter CX (425–6) there is a subtler and more chilling use of Shakespearian quotation when Lovelace, writing to Belford about how he gloats over the idea of conquering Clarissa, adapts Hector's speech to Achilles in *Troilus and Cressida* (4.7.137–40)

Henceforth, O watchful fair one, guard thee well:
For I'll not kill thee There! nor There! nor There!
But, by the zone that circles Venus' waist,
I'll kill thee everywhere.

The arrogant brutality of Hector, already in Shakespeare a deeply ironic and sceptical treatment of Trojan heroism, is evoked to show the arrogant destructiveness, the almost self-confessed misogyny of Lovelace's obsession with Clarissa, and its self-dramatizing panache.

Clarissa alludes less to Shakespeare, but her memories of the poet's words are still significant, and what is more are less calculated, more spontaneous and, as one would expect, reflect both her taste and her virtue. We have already seen how she uses Hamlet's phrase 'harrow up my soul' (II.9), – though as if inadvertently, and without explicit self-conscious quotation in the pressure of rendering her feelings about her loss of her reputation and her 'cruel doubts and perplexities' after fleeing with Lovelace. But the most notable instance of her (again 'involuntary') quotation of Shakespeare comes in her delirious jottings when she regains consciousness after her rape. Richardson uses Clarissa's derangement to explore the hidden elements in her mind, and the episode has been described as 'the first honest attempt to deal with the unconscious since Lear and Ophelia'.[13] But while it is doubtless honest, one wonders if it succeeds artistically. The episode seems to me, indeed, to mark one of the limits of Richardson's imagination and to suggest a dimension that, unlike Shakespeare, he cannot fully achieve.

In letter XXXIII in volume III, Lovelace writes

13 Mark Kinkead-Weekes, *Samuel Richardson, Dramatic Novelist* (London, 1973), p. 231.

to Belford, transcribing some papers, some torn or scratched through, which Clarissa has written as soon as she has recovered enough physically from the rape. This itself might seem a rather awkward aspect of the epistolary technique which Richardson is forced to use: it is difficult to imagine Lovelace copying out these indictments of himself; and the only reasons he gives are that he does it for 'the novelty of the thing', and to 'show thee how her mind works now that she is in this whimsical way.' Paper VII takes a more oblique, even 'literary' form: it is a kind of poetic declamation against Lovelace, with echoes of *Twelfth Night* and the Sonnets ('Thou eating canker worm, that preyest upon the opening bud, and turnest the damask rose into livid yellowness'). In all this the device of the papers seems especially awkward, the rhetoric is formal in a limiting way, and the literary echoes only increase our sense of artificiality. In paper X Clarissa has written down (and Lovelace transcribes) a collection of quotations, including two from *Hamlet*: the Ghost's 'I could a tale unfold / Would harrow up thy soul', and Hamlet's (in adapted form)

> – Oh! you have done an act
> That blots the face and blush of modesty;
> Takes off the rose
> From the fair forehead of an innocent Love
> And makes a blister there.

It is notable that Clarissa (and Richardson) takes a speech directed against female lust to apply to Lovelace: a Freudian might doubtless say it suggests an unconscious guilt on Clarissa's part. But this would be straining the meaning: it hardly has that effect. And the main reaction I think we have to this passage, on reflection, is to feel the awkwardness of the stratagem for revealing Clarissa's inner life. And it calls up comparisons – the power of the direct Shakespearian presentation of passion and madness in Hamlet, or Ophelia or Lear – which can only make Richardson's attempt look extremely limited.

Much more telling is letter XXXV, where Lovelace describes the first meeting with Clarissa after the rape, where a genuinely novelistic drama is again possible. Clarissa's dignity and scathing contempt of Lovelace, and the latter's vain, stammered attempts at self-excuse are powerfully done, and the rhetoric seems justified by the intensity of the dramatic situation. Where Richardson can present the dramatic but formal and always 'polite' exchanges of protagonists, he can achieve considerable power. But the inner revelation of real soliloquy and the poetry of madness or derangement eludes him. And this is surely a measure of the limitation of the age: the tensions produced by a considerable permissiveness of sexual behaviour among the aristocratic classes on one hand and an anxiety about sexual licence, a middle-class propriety which inherits many of the puritan traits of repressiveness, give rise to a novel which explores just this theme, but whose technique is limited precisely by the constraints and anxieties it explores.

Richardson's concern to avoid what he called 'the horrid' also betrays this inhibition. Writing to Lady Bradshaigh, and in the course of defending himself against charges of hard-heartedness and cruelty and defending his decision not to give the novel a happy ending, he distinguishes between 'Acts of Terror and Warning' and 'Acts of Horror', and says that 'the catastrophe of Shakespeare's *Romeo and Juliet* may truly be called "horrid".[14] He quotes in particular Juliet's speech before taking the potion, with its fears of waking in the burial vault of the Capulets 'Where bloody Tybalt, yet but green in earth, / Lies festering in his shroud' etc. Richardson seems to disparage this, for he calls this 'truly horrid', and says he hopes he has avoided all Rant, Horror, indecent images and inflaming descriptions. Again it can be said that his fear of offending his genteel lady readers constitutes a limitation.

[14] *Selected Letters*, p. 104.

## IV LETTERS AND SEXUALITY

Despite its capacity for drama in Richardson's hands, the epistolary novel suffers from the limitation of presenting action at two removes: it is mediated both through the mind of the author and through the imagined mind of the letter-writer. The former mediation is that of any literature, though drama, and particularly drama seen on the stage, gives the greatest illusion of its absence. Performed drama presents, as it were, the living, suffering body; whereas the epistolary novel presents that body mediated through two levels of reflection. And what both Richardson and his protagonist Lovelace say about letters confirms this sense that the letter (at least as a means of communication rather than as a novelistic technique) denies the body. Richardson suggests that communication through letters is purer, less interrupted by accident, than ordinary conversation:

> This correspondence is, indeed, the cement of friendship; it is friendship avowed under hand and seal: friendship upon bond, as I may say; more pure, yet more ardent, and less broken in upon, than personal conversation can be even amongst the most pure, because of the deliberation it allows, from the very preparation to, and action of writing.

The phrase 'even amongst the most pure' suggests particularly an element of puritanism behind this. And he goes on a few lines later:

> Who then shall decline the converse of the pen? The pen that makes distance, presence; and brings back to sweet remembrance all the delights of presence; which makes even presence but body, while absence becomes the soul;[15]

The spiritualizing tendency of this, the sense of an escape from the physical, receives a more explicitly sexual connotation in a later remark in the same letter when the young lady to whom Richardson is writing is advised to write principally to her own sex 'since ours is hardly ever void of design, and makes correspondence dangerous'. Even at the safe physical distance implied by letter-writing the designs of men had to be closely watched.

This suggestion makes even more pointed the connection between the above letter and one of Lovelace's. He is telling Belford of a conversation with Clarissa about letter-writing, where he is trying to get Clarissa to let him read letters between her and Miss Howe:

> I proceeded therefore – That I loved letter-writing, as I had more than once told her, above all species of writing; it was writing from the heart (without the fetters prescribed by method or study), as the very word *correspondence* implied. Not the heart only; the soul was in it. Nothing of body, when friend writes to friend; the mind impelling sovereignly the vassal fingers. It was, in short, friendship recorded; friendship given under hand and seal; demonstrating that the parties were under no apprehension of changing from time or accident, when they so liberally gave testimonies, which would always be ready, on failure or infidelity, to be turned against them. (II.431)

The phrase 'The mind impelling sovereignly the vassal fingers' suggests the domination of body by the will, the (male) intellect, the exact opposite of Eliot's phrase about 'the intellect at the tips of the senses'.[16] Here the senses are at the tip of the manipulating intellect. The 'design' of men's letters, which Richardson talks about in his own letter, is of course pre-eminently the quality of many of Lovelace's *reported* letters (though not, as I shall argue below, many of his *printed* letters), particularly those at the end of volume I where he is persuading Clarissa to agree to meet him in the summer house and elope with him (an agree-

---

15 *Ibid.* p. 65; quoted in Terry Eagleton, *The Rape of Clarissa* (Oxford, 1982), pp. 43–4.

16 'Philip Massinger', *Selected Essays* (London, 1966), pp. 209–10. Laura Fasick points out that Richardson exemplifies in Clarissa a sense of the moral sensibility of the body itself as opposed to Lovelace's cold detached manipulation of the body by the mind, 'Sentiment, authority and the female body in the novels of Samuel Richardson', *Essays in Literature*, 5: 19 (Fall, 1992), 193–203.

ment she subsequently tries in a further letter to revoke, but he deliberately fails to collect the letter); or where he persuades her to go to Mrs Sinclair's.

Letters in Shakespeare's plays also (doubtless partly because of the demands of the genre, and their use generally as part of the plot where they are items on which action will turn) have more often the character of agents of design than that of free disinterested communications of friendship. Indeed, letters in Shakespeare are more often than not extremely untrustworthy or at least problematic – either because they are intended to trick or deceive, or because they are self-deceiving, or because they give bad advice or advice which the recipient is unwilling to take. (It has been said that nowhere in Shakespeare's plays is advice shown as doing any good: bad advice is followed and good advice is ignored.) In the comedies letters are used to show the affectation or pretension of the sender (Don Armado to Jaquenetta in *Love's Labour's Lost* or Orlando in *As You Like It*); or (as forged letters) to deceive and expose a recipient (Malvolio in *Twelfth Night*). The letter as a statement 'avowed under hand and seal' or 'upon hand' (to use Richardson's terms) is in Shakespeare something that is more often than not turned against the writer, either because it is intercepted by a hostile party (as the Duke intercepts Valentine's letter in *The Two Gentlemen of Verona*), or because it is read in a way that mocks the sender (as Rosalind does with Phoebe's letter in *As You Like It*).

In the history plays and tragedies letters often have a malign or negative part to play in the plot. The letter in 2.4 of *1 Henry IV* which warns Hotspur against his undertaking against the King is condemned as that of a 'frosty-spirited rogue', and the advice is (fatally) not taken. The cool reasoning of a letter is not suited to Hotspur's fiery spirit. The letters to Brutus (as if coming from Rome itself) lead Brutus to promise an action which results in failure and death. The letter of Cressida to Troilus in Act 5 comes after Troilus has seen Cressida's infidelity with Diomedes, and is condemned as 'Words, words, mere words, no matter from the heart.' Edmund's forged letter in *King Lear* brings about Edgar's alienation from his father: Goneril's to Edmund, intercepted by Edgar, reveals a further dimension of her corruption. Macbeth first tells Lady Macbeth of the witches' prophecies in a letter which does not state any criminal intention, but which might darkly seem to prompt Lady Macbeth's more ready ruthlessness ('Lay it to thy heart'). Letters are also vulnerable to delay (a turning point in the tragedy of Romeo and Juliet), crucial ambiguity (as in the order by Edmund of Edward II's death in Marlowe's play), destruction (as in Julia's tearing up of Proteus's letter in *The Two Gentlemen of Verona*) and ambiguity of author or addressee (as in Valentine's writing a letter as if from Julia, which she then gives to him, in the same play). Letters can be torn up into their constituent letters, as Julia does, and the names detached out of anger (Julia's towards her own name) or a kind of sentimental fetishism (as Julia does with the phrase 'love-wounded Proteus': 'my bosom as a bed / Shall lodge thee'.) In short, letters in Shakespeare's plays are distinctly slippery and malleable entities, more often the cause of misunderstandings and failures of communication than 'pure' or 'ardent' or displaying 'the force of friendship'.

Might one not suggest that Shakespeare's use of letters is symptomatic of an age more sceptical about writing and written correspondence than was the mid eighteenth century (when, too, writers first began to write private letters with an eye to eventual publication)? At any rate, Shakespeare's most articulate hero, Hamlet, is awkward in his letter to Ophelia; and, partly perhaps because 'presence' is such a vital matter for drama (the presence of a speaking subject), one cannot imagine any of Shakespeare's characters expressing the view of letters that Lovelace does. For in Shakespeare's plays, indeed, the general fate of letters suggests rather the pressures of 'time and accident', the vulnerability or unreliability of epistolary 'friendship given under hand and seal', and the proneness of letters 'to be turned against' their senders or recipients. They are rarely the embodiments of sincerity.[17]

Returning to Richardson we can say that a paradoxical feature of most of Lovelace's letters is that they *are* sincere. None of his 'designing' letters to Clarissa (with the exception of four letters after the rape, urging her to marry him (vol. III letters LIV, LV, LVI and LX) are given directly, but are reported to Anna Howe and others by Clarissa herself, with her comments and criticisms, and sometimes of course her innocent credulities. So Lovelace as an *epistolary* plotter is not given predominance. Rather we see him most fully in his open and undesigning letters to Belford, where paradoxically we see his sincerity, and his powers of description. And in *these* letters, physicality, the 'body' that he tells Clarissa is excluded from letters can be allowed fully through Lovelace's powers, as it were, of a novelist, so we get something like the marvellously grotesque description of Mrs Sinclair (vol. III, pp. 194–5): or the vivid Lawrentian (and Chaucerian) sense of animal life in letter XIX of vol. II (pp. 67–8) where Lovelace describes a farmyard scene as an illustration of lovers' conferring and receiving obligations:

> A strutting rascal of a cock have I beheld chuck, chuck, chuck, chucking his mistress to him, when he has found a single barley-corn, taking it up with his bill, and letting it drop five or six times, still repeating his chucking invitation; and when two or three of his feathered ladies strive who shall be the first for it [*O Jack! a cock is a grand signor of a bird*] he directs the bill of the foremost to it; and, when she has got the dirty pearl, he struts over her with an erected crest, and with an exulting chuck – a chuck-aw–aw-w, circling round her with dropped wings, sweeping the dust in humble courtship; while the obliged she, half-shy, half-willing, by her cowering tail, prepared wings, yet seemingly affrighted eyes, and contracted neck, lets one see that she knows the barley-corn was not all he called her for.

The life of the novel lies in its narrative drama and physical presentation (of which this is a small but vivid instance). But the moral message of the novel is the denial of this kind of life. Clarissa's letters only possess this dramatic power in volume I, before her elopement with Lovelace (particularly in those letters where she recounts the struggle with her family and the drama of her resistance to Solmes). In resisting her father and resisting Solmes's overtures she is resisting in the name of life, in the name of her own nature as a woman, and her letters have a corresponding passion. After her elopement with Lovelace she is forced to deny passion in the name of her sense of honour, and her letters become correspondingly a matter of moral and religious reflection, where they are not simply recounting facts. And the epistolary convention becomes in these instances a means of reflecting on moral questions rather than presenting drama. As a result, for the modern reader, the closing volume becomes the most difficult to read: the capacity of the epistolary form for moral disquisition takes over and quenches the drama.

It is difficult not to feel, in fact, that Richardson *the artist* is of Lovelace's party without knowing it; and that it is Richardson the moralist who takes over after the rape has been committed, and who has to take over then. One can go further, and say that after her elopement with Lovelace it is impossible not to feel that a certain over-delicacy and concern with mere reputation marks Clarissa's responses

[17] It should be pointed out, however, that this function of letters in Shakespeare's plays contrasts with the humanist tradition of letter-writing, as in Erasmus, where the potential authenticity of letters is stressed, together with – in terms very similar to Richardson's quoted above – their ability to make the absent present. See Lisa Jardine, 'Reading and the technology of textual affect: Erasmus's familar letters and Shakespeare's *King Lear*', in *Reading Shakespeare Historically* (London, 1996), pp. 78–97.

after her 'elopement'. In saying this I am aware that I am in the end running in the face of Richardson's whole intention – which is that Clarissa should stand for a moral principle, and stand for it in as human, self-doubting and passionate a way as possible. Lovelace is presented ultimately as tyrannical and ruthless. Had Clarissa submitted to him, the result might have been a different kind of tragedy. It might in fact have been more genuinely tragic in a Shakespearian sense – where tragedy means the following through of passionate impulse and meeting the consequences. The analogies in Shakespeare are not very close, but *Romeo and Juliet* or *Antony and Cleopatra* would I suppose be the closest. Tolstoy's *Anna Karenina* would be closer still: Anna is married, of course; and Vronsky is not a rake. But Anna's defiance of respectability is almost as great as Clarissa's might have been; and a certain destructiveness in Vronsky is brought out in the horse-racing scene. In Shakespeare, as I've suggested, *Measure for Measure* is in some ways a closer parallel of the resistance of virtuous virginity to brutal compulsion: but, with great significance for the Shakespearian vision, Shakespeare allows the problem to be explored via the genre of comedy. Angelo is allowed to avoid the worst consequences of his acts, and Isabella is allowed to learn a more human virtue.

## V RAPE, WRITING AND MORALITY

Shakespeare treats the subject of rape in any full way only in two works, and his way of doing so is significant both in relation to letters and genre and to the broader moral and historical questions I am exploring. When, in *The Rape of Lucrece*, the heroine has to communicate the news of her shame to her husband Collatine, she simply writes asking him to come to her. She dares not write down the cause of her grief in case he does not believe in her innocence, and waits until she can 'prove' it by suicide. She also feels that she can make her sincerity more apparent if she tells him what has happened to his face: 'she would not blot the letter / With words, till action might become them better.' And the poet comments:

To see sad sights moves more than hear them told,
For then the eye interprets to the ear
The heavy motion that it doth behold,
When every part a part of woe doth bear.
'Tis but a part of sorrow that we hear;
  Deep sounds make lesser noise than shallow fords,
  And sorrow ebbs, being blown with wind of
      words. (1324–30)

It is, one might say, almost a statement of the dramatist's credo, a belief in the greater emotional power of live drama as against the drama of reflective prose – or the novel. Where in any novel, one might ask, is the force of *grief* so powerfully rendered as it is, say, in the rendering of Lear's grief at the death of Cordelia, with its poignant physical touches, and the added effect, only possible on the stage, of the silent anguish and helplessness of the onlookers, Kent, Albany and Edgar?

It may be, too, that the horror of rape is especially incommunicable in written or even spoken words. At the climax of her narration to Collatine Lucrece cannot bring herself to complete her story. She manages to 'throw forth Tarquin's name', and then

'He, he,' she says –
But more than he her poor tongue could not speak,
Till after many accents and delays,
Untimely breathings, sick and short essays,
  She utters this: 'He, he, fair lords, 'tis he
  That guides this hand to give this wound to me.'
(1717–22)

And her final statement (like Othello's) is completed not by words alone but by an action: 'Even here she sheathèd in her harmless breast / A harmful knife, that thence her soul unsheathed', (where the language suggests paradoxically sexual overtones). The final revelation of her 'confession' is also the action of her suicide, and she does not have to live to face the shame of her husband's response to her words. Richardson, by contrast, is hard put to find a mode in which to render Clarissa's narration of her ordeal, and her reaction to it. The moral difference between the two heroines is of course that Lucrece kills herself and Clarissa explicitly rejects this course of action. Lovelace makes the contrast with Lucrece himself in III.220 ('no Lucretia-like vengeance upon herself in her thought'); and Clarissa herself in her rambling letter to Lovelace after the rape begins to make a vengeful comparison of Lovelace and Tarquin but suppresses it: 'A less complicated villainy cost a Tarquin – but I forget what I would say again –.' (II.212).[18]

Shakespeare's poem, though, is not one of the finest examples of his art. The harsh story is treated with a kind of brittle rhetorical distancing, with several set pieces of declamation. One feels that Shakespeare is happier artistically speaking, with the resolutions of comedy (in *Measure for Measure* or *Cymbeline* or *Pericles*) in dealing with this particular crime – resolutions which of course allow its avoidance. His only other tragic treatment of rape is in *Titus Andronicus*, that example of Senecan horror-mongering, where the violence is so extreme and the verbal response to it so coldly rhetorical, that one feels that it is an exercise in the stylization of horror, rather than a profound attempt to understand it humanely and morally.

But in terms of what one might call the iconography of rape *Titus Andronicus* has some very significant features. Like her mythological prototype Philomel, Lavinia is horribly dismembered by having her tongue cut out. The victim of rape is deprived of a voice with which to speak of her crime. But Philomel tells her story by way of art - by weaving it into a tapestry which she can show to her sister Procne. Lavinia, in a horrific variation, is deprived of hands as well as tongue: she cannot weave her story – nor can she write. She can only indicate what has happened to her by turning to the classic story of Philomel herself, in Ovid's *Metamorphoses*: she turns to the art of the past. There is a structural similarity here to the way in which Clarissa, in her first distracted writings after her violation turns partly to quotation (from *Hamlet*, among other sources) to render her deepest feelings. Beyond that Lavinia, to indicate the culprits, has to take Marcus's staff in her mouth and write in the sand 'Stuprum – Chiron – Demetrius.' This agonizing moment is perhaps too appalling for an aesthetic response: but structurally one can again see a significance which has its parallels in *Clarissa* (parallels which would of course have been far from the mind of Richardson, with his expressed distaste for the 'horrid'): the painfully hampered writing, and the recourse to Latin to make bearable the writing of the crime, are symbolically akin to Clarissa's less dreadful predicament, her fragmented and distorted writing and her inability to do more than hint at the crime that she has suffered. Despite the vast differences in degree of horror, circumstance, tone and decorum, the two writers' treatments of the crime show marked structural and symbolic similarities. But Shakespeare, perhaps ultimately without the deepest artistic conviction, chooses the mode of Senecan horror, while Richardson in a politer eighteenth century not only avoids the 'horrid' but has chosen a genre where the still horrifying facts can be – as far as possible – de-sensationalized and controlled, mediated through the triple screen of letter within letter within 'editorial' (or authorial) overview. Despite (or perhaps because of) its lack of sensationalistic power his is, in this instance, the more humane rendering.

There are two further points of comparison

[18] Ian Donaldson in *The Rapes of Lucretia: a Myth and its Transformations* (Oxford, 1982), also points out that Lovelace cites Lucretia again towards the end of the novel in conversation with Lord M and his cousins, saying that if a lady destroys herself by grief or by the dagger as Lucretia did, 'Is there more than one fault the man's and is not the other hers?' Lovelace's tone is insufferable, but Donaldson does come to the conclusion that 'it would be possible also to say that Clarissa loses the will to live' and that Richardson 'may seem too easily to accept the notion ... that rape "is a fate worse than death".'

between *Clarissa* and *The Rape of Lucrece*, which relate to social history and politics. By submitting to her rape to avoid death with dishonour – Tarquin threatens that he will kill her and then say he found her sleeping with her servant – Lucrece is able then to tell her kinsmen of the crime, and the result is that Tarquin is overthrown and with him the institution of Roman kingship. The real Lucretia therefore became a type of republican heroine, although Shakespeare only mentions the change 'from kings to consuls' in his 'Argument'. *Clarissa*, while not concerned with national politics, is also part of a profound shift of values in which a more morally sensitive and responsible middle class asserted its morality against an aristocratic code. (Beaumarchais' *The Marriage of Figaro* 1784, translated in 1785, is another manifestation of the same shift.)

But an even more significant moral difference lies in the fact that in these great representative stories of the struggle between female chastity and male will, Lucrece is protecting her chastity as a married woman and (as importantly) her husband's honour, whereas Clarissa is defending her virgin chastity and her own honour. Lucrece, in a way difficult to understand for a modern reader, laments the fact that she can no longer be regarded as a 'loyal wife': 'Of that type hath Tarquin rifled me'. She also talks of 'The stainèd taste of violated troth', which raises some complex moral questions: if she was forced to submit to Tarquin to save her own life and honour, *and* her husband's honour, how can this be seen as the violation of her troth? Shakespeare is following a Roman ethic, which was presumably felt to have some validity for his own time, where a wife's chastity was important above all because of her husband's honour rather than her own, and where any sexual violation involves some sense of guilt on the part of the woman. Lucrece can even speak of 'My life's foul deed'. Clarissa on the other hand has become a more independent moral agent, whose own honour and, more than this, whose Christian salvation, are paramount. In her case too it is virtually sexuality itself which is the great threat. She has to guard herself against her attraction to Lovelace. The preservation of the unmarried woman's virginity has become the central moral and social question of what is perhaps the greatest and most representative of eighteenth-century novels. In Shakespeare, the story of Lucrece is not one of the great achievements of his oeuvre, but he follows the Roman story and emphasis and its concern with married chastity. Elsewhere (as we have seen) his treatment of sexual morality is more various, less a matter of stark moral contrasts, and virgin chastity (while being taken very seriously in *The Tempest* and elsewhere) is never the focus of tragic conflict.

## VI CONCLUSIONS

Social and cultural historians differ markedly in their interpretations of the changes in moral attitude towards sex and marriage that took place between Shakespeare's age and Richardson's, depending partly on what kind of evidence they choose to look at. Lawrence Stone, drawing on a very wide range of social documents (though less on literary sources, apart from diaries) comes to the conclusion that sexual attitudes among the upper classes between 1500 and 1800 passed through four approximate stages: a phase of moderate toleration until the end of the sixteenth century; a phase of repressiveness that began around 1570 and lasted until about 1660; a phase of 'permissiveness, even licence' from 1660 to around 1770; and from 1770 for the next century and more a new wave of repression that coincided with the growth of evangelicalism. This would put Shakespeare at a point of transition between a phase of toleration and one of repressiveness, and Richardson, similarly, at a point towards the end of a phase of licence and before the beginnings of a new phase of repression. Both writers appear to be located at particular points of tension which provide a dynamic for their art.[19]

At the same time each writer drew, of course, on traditions which preceded their own ages: Shakespeare on a rich and complex mixture of classical literature and history, Tudor historiography, sophisticated literary predecessors, popular dramatic tradition, folk festival; Richardson more narrowly on late seventeenth- and early eighteenth-century puritan writing, Restoration drama, predecessors in the novel like Defoe, and, as I have tried to show, Shakespeare himself.

Out of these pressures and influences – in conjunction with what one has to recognize as the ultimately mysterious element of unique creativity in the writers themselves – come the distinctively different visions of sexuality. Both writers are, of course, preoccupied with the conflict of licence and law, body and spirit, as, probably, are the writers of any age. But Shakespeare puts the emphasis either on tolerant comic resolution (as in *Measure for Measure*, or *The Winter's Tale*) or tragedy in which there is no element of religious martyrdom or consolation.[20] Richardson in contrast either writes a comedy like *Pamela* in which the emphasis is didactically on Virtue Rewarded, or a type of tragedy like *Clarissa* where again the issue is presented as a stark confrontation of opposites (predatory masculine will against a religious virtue intensely concerned with propriety) and in which a clear religious didactic intention is stronger than a more Shakespearian sense of tragedy which emphasizes the essentially human intractability, waste and loss.

It is also notable how exclusively in his two major novels Richardson focuses on sexuality, and sexuality as a moral struggle; whereas for Shakespeare it is part (albeit an often dark and agonized part) of a wider vision. Rita Goldberg sees *Clarissa* as centrally representative of eighteenth-century sexual morality:

> It is almost as if the exertion of the will against an immovable identity in each individual woman provides the moral energy for a whole social world.[21]

Later she comments: 'Of the seven deadly sins the eighteenth century finds lust the deadliest.' In the light of Stone's accounts of the permissiveness of the eighteenth century up to about 1770 and indeed in the light of Boswell's diaries and even *Tom Jones* this may seem a sweeping and questionable statement. But if applied to the kind of moral and intellectual world and tradition in which Richardson moved it does not seem inapposite. Richardson's major novels, especially *Clarissa*, are posited on the central idea that sexual desire is a great threat to society and civilization, and must be tamed by rigorous social and religious laws. Shakespeare's world is less anxious, more various, with a greater sense of the varieties of sexuality and its mysterious metamorphoses and resolutions as well as its tragic intractabilities. Against Goldberg's comment on the eighteenth-century moralists' view of lust we may set Claudio's 'Sure, it is no sin; / Or of the deadly seven it is the least.' It is not that Shakespeare is more 'permissive' than Richardson: his plays are full of the darkest sense of the destructiveness of uncontrolled sexuality; and in the last plays (*The*

[19] Lawrence Stone, *The Family, Sex and Marriage in England, 1500–1800* (London, 1977). More recent research also suggests that attitudes to sexual morality (e.g. in the Church Courts) became stricter in the first decades of the seventeenth century. See Martin Ingram, *Church Courts, Sex and Marriage in England 1570–1640* (Cambridge, 1987), which throws an interesting light on *Measure for Measure*.

[20] Recent, particularly feminist, criticism and theoretical practice has, of course, questioned the degree of resolution in the comedies, particularly *Measure for Measure*: see e.g. Carol T. Neely, *Broken Nuptials in Shakespeare's Plays* (New Haven and London, 1985), pp. 101–2. The comedy of *Measure for Measure* certainly leaves a lot of problems unanswered, but a 'reconciling' reading or production still seems to me possible to make convincing, particularly in the light of the expectations of the genre.

[21] Rita Goldberg, *Sex and Enlightenment: Women in Richardson and Diderot* (Cambridge, 1984), pp. 68–9.

*Tempest* and *The Winter's Tale* in particular) there is a strong emphasis on the importance of marriage in rendering sexual relations moral and chaste. But his plays as a whole give us a complexity which is beyond Richardson's, a breadth of view far richer than the moral simplicities of *Pamela* or even the acute polarities of *Clarissa* with its 'dark and sometimes luxuriant dallyings with the beauties of death'.[22] Richardson may have rightly been seen by eighteenth-century readers as the modern writer who came closest in art and understanding to Shakespeare. Today we are more aware of the differences. But the thrill of recognition that we can get from reading writers as differently constituted, historically, as Richardson and Shakespeare, suggests that their work is more than just a record of change and difference. If we can only see where we differ from the past, and where past periods differ from each other, those differences lose their power to provoke and challenge us.

---

[22] Donaldson, *The Rapes of Lucretia*, p. 82.

# EARLY GEORGIAN POLITICS AND SHAKESPEARE: THE BLACK ACT AND CHARLES JOHNSON'S *LOVE IN A FOREST* (1723)

KATHERINE WEST SCHEIL

The prolific playwright Charles Johnson wrote seventeen plays in the first three decades of the eighteenth century. Although they have received little critical attention, his works reveal the strategies of a dramatist who diligently offered London audiences a play almost every season. He was infamous for his plagiarism, and most of his plays are derived from other sources;[1] his contemporary Christopher Bullock criticized Johnson for 'diverting the *Town* with other People's Writings, and endeavouring to acquire the Name of a *Poet* by transcribing from other *Men's Plays*'.[2] Johnson only used Shakespearian material as the basis for two plays, the 1716 afterpiece *The Cobler of Preston*, and the 1723 play *Love in a Forest*. Both adaptations were written in times of social turmoil; they are responses to specific historical conditions and events, and must be considered within that climate. This paper situates Charles Johnson's adaptations of Shakespeare in the political context of the 1720s, specifically chronicling the connections between *Love in a Forest* and the circumstances surrounding the Black Act of 1723.[3]

As a regular at Button's Coffee House, Charles Johnson circulated among the Whig literati of the early eighteenth century. In the opening lines to *Umbra* (1714), Pope identifies Johnson as one of 'Button's Wits', and the anonymous pamphlet *Characters of the Times* (1728) describes Johnson as 'Famous for many Years for writing a Play every Season, and for being at Button's every Day'.[4] Johnson's association with Button's shows that he was in touch with the political discussions of the day, as coffeehouses were central disseminators of

This article was inspired by the 1997 Aston Magna Academy, 'From Handel to Hogarth: The Culture of Early Georgian England' at Yale University. I am grateful to my fellow Academy participants and to Andrew Scheil for helpful advice and suggestions.

[1] See William J. Burling, 'Charles Johnson', *Dictionary of Literary Biography*, vol. 84, ed. Paula R. Backscheider (Detroit, 1989). Although *Love in a Chest* and *The Force of Friendship* have echoes from Shakespearian plays, neither uses Shakespeare as a direct source. See Edward Niles Hooker, 'Charles Johnson's *The Force of Friendship* and *Love in a Chest*: A Note on Tragicomedy and Licensing in 1710', *Studies in Philology*, 34 (1937), 407–11.

[2] Preface to *The Cobler of Preston* (London, 1716), p. viii.

[3] Most scholarship on *Love in a Forest* has not been kind to the play. M. Maurice Shudofsky, in an otherwise appreciative article on Johnson, calls *Love in a Forest* 'a miserable perversion' (p. 157n) and remarks that 'Pot-pourris like *Love in a Forest* do not make pleasant reading, but they go far in explaining why early eighteenth-century drama rarely rises above mediocrity.' 'Charles Johnson and Eighteenth-Century Drama', *English Literature History*, 10 (1943), 131–58; p. 134. Although Edith Holding claims to look at 'the literary, political, and theatrical context' surrounding *Love in a Forest*, she does not make any connections with the Black Act of 1723 and anti-Jacobitism. See '*As You Like It* Adapted: Charles Johnson's *Love in a Forest*', *Shakespeare Survey 32* (1979), pp. 37–48; p. 38.

[4] *Characters of the Times; or, an Impartial Account of the Writings, Characters, Education, &c. of several Noblemen and Gentlemen, libell'd in a preface to a late Miscellany Publish'd by P_PE and S__FT*, reprinted in *Popeiana* (New York and London, 1975), vol. 7, p. 19.

newspapers and periodicals; the *Freeholder's Journal* of 18 May 1723 described 'The Crowd of *Papers* that incumber the Town, and make the Tables of the *Coffee-House* look like the Counter of a *Pamphlet-shop*'.[5] Since both Drury Lane theatre and Button's Coffee House were Whig strongholds, it is not surprising that Johnson's dramas would express Whig sentiments, often vehemently anti-Jacobite in nature.[6]

Throughout his career, Johnson expressed the view that theatre should support the government. In the preface to his early play *The Force of Friendship* (London, 1710), he urges that the stage become, 'as it certainly may be, both Ornamental and Useful to the Government' and yearns for the Ancient theatre, where a poet 'taught nothing that contradicted the Constitution he liv'd under, or the Religion of his Country, and those knowing People found their Morals improv'd, their Manners polish'd, and their Judgment strengthen'd by the reasonable and noble Entertainment of the Theater'.[7] Johnson's adaptations of Shakespeare most clearly articulate this mingling of entertainment with pro-government propaganda.

Although he only uses Shakespearian material as the source for two of his plays, Johnson often expressed his reverence for Shakespeare as the standard towards which he should strive. For instance, in the Prologue to his popular comedy *The Wife's Relief: or, the Husband's Cure* (London, 1712), Johnson commends Shakespeare's 'unique genius':

> Bright Fancy, Learning, Language, Wit, and Art,
> Each in the labour'd Scene shou'd claim a Part,
> But Partial Nature lavishly bestows
> On One, what wou'd Inrich Ten Thousand Brows;
> Or 'tis with Labour she creates a Son
> Like *Shakespear*; therefore never Form'd but One:
> He sham'd the Stage of *Athens* and of *Rome*,
> And starv'd the whole *Dramatick* World to come.
> Well therefore may our Author own his Fears
> To tread, where *Avon's* Swan so oft appears . . .

In the Prologue to *The Masquerade* (London, 1719), Johnson describes Shakespeare as the measure of proper taste: 'Good Sense still triumphs on the *British* Stage: / *Shakespear* beholds with Joy his Sons inherit / His good old Plays, with good old *Bess*'s Spirit,' and in the preface to the *Tragedy of Medæa* (London, 1731) Johnson refers to Shakespeare as 'that inimitable and immortal Genius'. For Johnson, Shakespeare clearly represented a position of power and stability in a dramatic world that was fickle and uncertain towards its playwrights.[8]

As Michael Dobson has shown, the early eighteenth century was a pivotal point in the growth of Shakespeare's reputation as the National Poet.[9] Charles Johnson's treatment of Shakespeare coincides with Shakespeare's rise to prominence as a symbol of British nationalism. Johnson leveraged the cultural cachet of Shakespeare twice in his career, relying on the status of Shakespeare to sanction the political opinions expressed in his plays. Johnson's afterpiece *The Cobler of Preston* (London, 1716) is his most overtly political play, written just after the Jacobite Rebellion in 1715, and set in Preston,

---

[5] Appropriately, Johnson opened his own tavern in Covent Garden after retiring from the stage.

[6] See John Loftis, *The Politics of Drama in Augustan England* (Oxford, 1963), pp. 63–93.

[7] All references to plays are to the first edition unless otherwise noted.

[8] For example, the preface to Johnson's *Tragedy of Medæa* (London, 1731) attacks critics who 'cabal together before-hand, they meet over their Coffee, and deliberately resolve to assassinate the future Piece, without having read or seen it, if the Author does not happen to be of their Faction'. Johnson again turns to Shakespeare for guidance: 'Now I will venture to say that if half a Score only of these ingenious Criticks had attended the dramatical Performances of *Shakespeare*, when they first appeared, in the Manner, and with the same Candor and Humanity, with which they prosecuted *Medæa*, his Works must have sunk under their Prejudice; and the World would have been rob'd, by a few malevolent and ignorant half Wits, of the Labours of that inimitable and immortal Genius. And this I only mention to shew how impossible it is that any, even the best dramatick Entertainment, should live under such Treatment.'

[9] *The Making of the National Poet: Shakespeare, Adaptation and Authorship, 1660–1769* (Oxford, 1992).

the site of the first battle between the King's army and the Jacobite rebels in November 1715. The Prologue highlights Johnson's choice of the Jacobite plot as dramatic material, 'If he wants Plot, consider, Sirs, he draws / These Scenes, from the *worst Plot* that ever was.' Johnson reshapes the Sly Induction material from *The Taming of the Shrew* to make Kit Sly a Jacobite supporter. The play opens with Sly, the drunken cobbler, asserting, 'I must be a Rebel, and I will be a Rebel' (p. 1). At the end of the first act, Sly is extremely intoxicated in the house of the appropriately named Sir Charles Briton, and is unable to contain his Jacobite passions:

> Rumps and Round-Heads, Rumps and Round-Heads! I'll be a Rebel, down with the Rump, down with the Rump; and yet I do not Rebel, look'ee because I hate the Government – but because there should be no Government at all – Look'ye, I am for Passive Obedience and Non-Resistance; and so I will knock every Body down and be subject to no Body. I am likewise for Liberty and Property; that is, declare for a Spunge and no Taxes: and in order to bring this about the more expeditiously, I pronounce my self a Doxy Member of that Church which can forgive all my Sins, past, present, and to come.
>
> (p. 23)

In contrast to Sly's obvious characterization as a misguided Jacobite, Sir Charles Briton flaunts his Englishness: 'In the mean time let us not forget the Surloin of Beef I order'd to be ready by Three. That will be the chief of your Dinner, Mr *Jolly*, with a Flask of spritely *Burgundy*, to drink his Majesty's Health, and all the Royal Family' (p. 24). Johnson's audience would have recognized the references to roast beef and toasts to the King as symbols of Sir Charles's Hanoverian loyalty. At the end of the play, Sir Charles advises Sly to 'Learn to Cobble thy Shoes, and let the Commonwealth alone' (p. 45). Sly is punished for his political leanings, and forced to swear allegiance to King George I. He promises to 'mix Loyalty with my Liquor' and ends the play by vowing not to 'swallow Traytors Healths, in Bumpers down; / Nor sham Pretences of Religion forge, / But with true Protestants cry, Live King *GEORGE*' (p. 47). Barely three months after the Jacobite Rebellion of 1715, Johnson uses a Shakespearian source to condemn Jacobitism and endorse allegiance to George I.

This politically charged afterpiece held the stage for at least fourteen performances, and probably would have been more popular without the competition from Christopher Bullock's farce of the same title, put on at Lincoln's Inn Fields two weeks before Johnson's play had its first performance. Apparently, the Lincoln's Inn Fields actor Jemmy Spiller stole the draft of Johnson's play from William Penkethman, who was to play the title role.[10] Charles Akerby recounts that Bullock 'who always prided himself upon his Attachment to the Principles of *Toryism*, not only robb'd the above-mentioned ingenious Mr. *Charles Johnson* of great Part of the large Profits which he expected from the Run of a *Farce*, which was wrote, so much to the Support, and Defence of the *H—r Succession* ...'[11] Johnson's first adaptation of Shakespeare clearly was designed to make a specific political point in favour of Hanoverian Whigs. In the preface to his version of *The Cobler of Preston*, Christopher Bullock states that Johnson's play 'was penn'd for the particular Service of a *Party*', and Bullock was fully aware that Johnson was using Shakespeare for political reasons; he states that he 'did hear, there was a *Farce* in Rehearsal at *Drury-lane Theatre*, call'd the *Cobler* of *Preston*, and that it was taken from the forementioned Play of *Shakespear's*.'[12] Johnson's use of Shakespeare to stimulate anti-Jacobite sentiment was recognized as significant enough for the rival theatre Lincoln's Inn Fields to offer a

[10] The story is recounted in George Akerby, *The Life of Mr. James Spiller, the Late Famous Comedian* (London, 1729) and in Samuel Ireland, *Graphic Illustrations of Hogarth* (London, 1794).

[11] Akerby, *The Life of Mr James Spiller*, p. 24.

[12] *The Cobler of Preston* (London, 1716), Preface.

play of the same title as competition. While Johnson certainly lost profits in the theatre due to competition from Christopher Bullock's farce, Johnson's *The Cobler of Preston* was favoured by the reading public; it was reprinted in eight editions throughout the eighteenth century, including three in 1716.[13] The popularity of Johnson's play in print signals the potentially successful recipe of combining Shakespearian material with current political events.

Johnson's second reworking of Shakespeare contains a more subtle political relevance. *Love in a Forest* (London, 1723) is an adaptation of *As You Like It* with additions from *Richard II*, *Love's Labour's Lost*, *Twelfth Night*, *Much Ado About Nothing*, and *A Midsummer Night's Dream*. Johnson did not choose a well-known Shakespearian play to revive; according to surviving records, Shakespeare's *As You Like It* had not been performed at all since the re-opening of the London theatres in 1660.[14] Rather, he had other motives for his selection of source material. For his offering at Drury Lane in January of 1723, Johnson again turns to Shakespeare in a time of political crisis. The wave of Jacobite activity from the 1715 rebellion, which culminated in the 1720s, has been described as the 'most widespread and the most dangerous' period of Jacobitism.[15] The Atterbury plot revived concerns of Jacobitism, the bursting of the South Sea Bubble in 1720 encouraged hopes of a Stuart restoration, and the activities of the Blacks were a growing concern. In this environment, Johnson aligns himself with Shakespeare's reputation in order to defend his views. He accentuates the Shakespearian pedigree of *Love in a Forest* in the advertisements for the play, which only mention Shakespeare's name. In fact, Johnson's name does not appear at all in any of the notices. *The Daily Post* of 9 January advertised 'a Comedy, call'd *Love in a Forest*, Alter'd from the Comedy, call'd *As you Like it*. Written by Shakespear.' *The Daily Journal* for January 1723 similarly did not include Johnson's name in the advertisements: 'a New Comedy, call'd, *Love in a Forest*. As it is alter'd from Shakespear's Comedy, call'd, *As you like it*.' The advertisements for *Love in a Forest* deliberately focus on Shakespeare as the drawing point, not Johnson.[16]

The circumstances preceding the Black Act of 1723 figure prominently in the political context of *Love in a Forest*. Although the Black Act did not receive final royal assent until May 1723, there was much anxiety about the Blacks and the actions that would be taken against them in the early 1720s. Most accounts of the Blacks emphasize their dangerous potential, their crimes against the forest, and their status as gentry. One of the earliest descriptions of the Blacks occurs in *The London Gazette* of 22–6 March 1720, where George I issued a Proclamation referring to an earlier act against hunting in the night. The forest had long been considered the property

13 Editions were printed in Dublin in 1725 and 1767, and in London in 1775, 1817, and 1838 as part of *Cumberland's British Theatre*.

14 The other Shakespearian plays that Johnson includes were not regularly performed. From 1700, *Richard II* was performed only as Lewis Theobald's adaptation in 1719, 1720, and 1721, but Theobald does not include any of the speeches from *Richard II* that Johnson uses. *Dream* was performed only as *The Fairy-Queen* and as Richard Leveridge's *Pyramus and Thisbe* in 1716 and 1717. *Much Ado* was performed in its original version only three times in 1721. *Twelfth Night* was seen only as William Burnaby's *Love Betray'd* in 1703 and 1705. *Love's Labour's Lost* and *As You Like It* were not performed at all; Johnson's familiarity with these plays had to come from reading them. With the exception perhaps of Theobald's *Richard II*, none of these plays was a regular offering in the London theatres in this period.

15 Paul Monod, *Jacobitism and the English People, 1688–1788* (Cambridge, 1989), p. 11.

16 See Robert D. Hume, 'Before the Bard: "Shakespeare" in Early Eighteenth-Century London', *English Literary History*, 64 (1997), 41–75. For an earlier discussion of this material, see Katherine West (Scheil), '"All this we must do, to comply with the taste of the town": Shakespearian Comedy and the Early Eighteenth-Century Theatre' (Ph.D. diss., University of Toronto, 1995).

of the king, and hunting rights in the forests belonged to royalty, based on a tradition of enforcing a property qualification for hunters.[17] George rails against 'divers Persons in great Numbers, some with painted Faces, some with Visors, and otherwise disguised, to the Intent they should not be known, riotously, and in manner of War arrayed, had oftentimes then of late hunted as well by Night as by Day, in divers Forests, Parks, and Warrens in divers Places of this Realm, by Colour wherof had ensued great and heinous Rebellions, Insurrections, Riots, Robberies, Murders, and other Inconveniencies'. His complaints extend beyond simple poaching, and involve accusations of more serious activity. He warns that such actions would now be considered felonies, and cites the example of

> divers Persons, amounting to the Number of fourteen Men on Horseback, all armed with Guns, and some with Pistols, and two Footmen with a Greyhound, [who] did, in a violent and outragious Manner, on the two and twentieth Day of February last past, at Four of the Clock in the Afternoon, come into Bigshot-walk in Finchamsted Bailiwick in our Forest of Windsor, with their Faces blacked and disguised, some with Straw Hats and other deformed Habits, and did there pursue and shoot at our Red Deer, and did continue Hunting there till after Six a Clock, in which time they did kill four Deer there, three of which they carried away whole, and did cut off the Haunches of the fourth, and left the rest of the Carcase, and did terrifie and threaten the Keeper of our said Walk to shoot him, if he offered to come near them.

Emphasizing their illegality and irresponsibility, George intends that 'a speedy and effectual Stop may be put to all such outragious Practices', and offers a reward of £100 for the apprehension of any offenders. This Royal Proclamation, which preceded the Black Act, warns that the actions of the Blacks will lead to 'great and heinous Rebellions, Insurrections, Riots, Robberies, Murders, and other Inconveniencies' which must be contained. The description provides specific graphic details of the reckless treatment of the deer; similar depictions of poachers would later appear in Charles Johnson's *Love in a Forest* in 1723. Thus, as early as February of 1720, the government was taking action against what it labelled as dangerous activities by the Blacks, arguing for the need to further control the operations of this group.

Later accounts of the Blacks become more emphatic about the need for government intervention, and provide further details about this group's affairs. A description of the Blacks in Waltham-Chace printed in *The London Journal* of 10 November 1722 identifies them as gentry, and aims 'to check the Insolence of a Set of Whimsical Gentlemen who have of late started up to make their Will a Law in the Neighborhood where they live'. The forest, which is 'well stock'd with Deer' now is 'infested by a Body of artificial Negro's, (vulgarly called *The Blacks of Waltham*:) They are well arm'd and mounted, and the better to disguise themselves, black their Faces, &c. and seem to pay a sort of Obedience to one who stiles himself John, King of the Blacks.' The dangers of this organization are apparent in their leadership and their weapons. The writer underscores their menacing and malevolent intents: 'At their first Appearance 'twas believ'd they only propose to command this Chace, which they do when they please, and carry off what Deer is kill'd at Noon-Day, in Defiance of all Opposers, the keepers with their Quarter-Staves being unable to contend with Men arm'd with Carbines and Pistols. This dusky Tribe presume to punish all who dare to give an Information against any

[17] See P. B. Munsche, *Gentlemen and Poachers: The English Game Laws 1671–1831* (Cambridge, 1981), pp. 3, 5. Munsche points out that according to the Game Act of 1605, deer or rabbit hunters had to have an income of at least £40 from land, or £200 worth of goods. Munsche also defines 'game' as 'hares, partridges, pheasants and moor fowl' because 'only these animals were accorded protection under what eighteenth-century Englishmen called "the game laws"'.

Deer Stealer.' As the Proclamation by King George had earlier done, this account describes the Blacks as violent, rebellious, wanton poachers with little regard for authority.

*The London Journal* further illustrates the upper-class status of the Blacks with an anecdote. A ranger's widow received a reward for informing on a Deer Stealer,

> upon which the smutty Chief, attended by some of his Black-Guard, came up to the Lodge, and with abusive language, threatned to burn the House in case she did not refund; adding, that they were Gentlemen, and were determined to do Justice: The good Woman undauntedly reply'd, that Gentlemen would scorn to insult her after that manner, and that therefore she believ'd them to be worthless Fellows, and would not return the Money; immediately their Captain drew off his black Glove, and exposed a fine white Hand, at the same time asking, whether she thought it had been ever used to hard Labour, or belong'd to a sorry Fellow?

The noble status of this group emerges clearly here, and their wide-ranging transgressions warrant immediate retribution: 'it is hoped Means will be found to bring them to a deserved Punishment, since their Insolence is become intolerable; for with their lawless Authority, they interfere in most Disputes that happen. Most of our neighbouring Gentlemen have been insulted by them.' The writer gives several other instances of altercations between citizens and the Blacks: the group wreaked havoc on the trees of a certain gentleman after a dispute about his timber, and a similar argument with a woman over a church pew resulted in the Blacks cutting down trees in front of her house and defacing her garden. The Blacks again intervened in a quarrel between a farmer and a doctor who refused to pay for the hay he had ordered because it was damaged by rain. *The Daily Journal* of 13 January 1722 reflects the increasing legal concern over the Blacks: 'The Justices of the Peace for the County of Essex have detained most of the Inhabitants about Epping Forest, to prevent their farther Hostilities on the Game in the said Forest.'

Charles Johnson crafted *Love in a Forest* amid this climate of fear and unease. *The London Journal* of 22 December 1722, barely two weeks before Johnson's adaptation was performed, recounts that the Waltham Blacks 'still continue to go on in the lawless Manner which they have heretofore done; that they have at several Times cut down, and bark'd 600 Trees belonging to one Gentleman, and *King John* has, by Letter, threaten'd several others: So mischievous are these *masked Gentry*, that where 50 Deer used to be seen in a Herd on the Chace, there is now scarce Half a score.' As the Blacks continue their forest depredations and persist in their intimidations, the call for government intervention becomes more acute. *The London Journal* concludes, 'Their Insolence is become insupportable, and the Country Gentlemen are about to Petition the Parliament for Redress.'

Johnson's adaptation was performed and printed in January of 1723, when references to the Blacks increasingly filled the newspapers. *The Daily Journal* of 24 December 1722 contains the following story of the Blacks' violence: 'On Thursday Night last a lamentable Misfortune happen'd at Hackwood Park in Hampshire, a Seat of the Duke of Bolton's, where the Keepers apprehending that some Deer-stealers were in the Park, alarm'd the House, calling all the Servants to their Assistance; amongst the rest the Confectioner to the Family ran to their Aid, when one of the Park-keepers mistaking him for a Thief, discharged the Blunderbuss against him, loaded with sixteen Balls, which tore the unhappy Person all to pieces.' What began as poaching ended with an unexpected death, due to the unpredictable nature of the Blacks' insurgencies and the potential for their mischief to escalate.

Within a few days of the 9 January premiere of *Love in a Forest*, *The Weekly Journal: or, British Gazetteer* reported on 5 January that 'The Person who stiles himself King of the Blacks with his Company, still continues to commit fresh Disorders, and 'tis said they have murder'd some Persons who boasted that they knew and would discover some of the Company. 'Tis believ'd that their Violencies will shortly be laid before the Parliament.' Similar to the earlier anecdotes of the Blacks, this report stresses their capacity for murder, and the much-anticipated intervention of Parliament. Johnson's play coincided with these accounts; *The Daily Journal* of 22 January 1722–3 describes the activities of the Blacks: 'Complaint haveing been made to his Majesty of a Set of People who style themselves the *Blacks of Waltham*, and have a Person at their Head called *King John*, who ride about the County of Southampton in disguise, committing great Depredations on the Estates and Persons of his Majesty's Liege Subjects; a Proclamation is order'd to the Press for the discovering and seizing the said *King John* and his Accomplices, in order to their being brought to answer for their unlawful Practices.'[18] On the same page, an advertisement for Johnson's *Love in a Forest* appears; the forest setting emphasized the contemporary relevance of Johnson's play. The activities of the Blacks and the subsequent response of the Whig government are crucial in understanding the context for Charles Johnson's play.

Regardless of what actually happened in the forests, the public perceived the situation as an emergency which could escalate into heinous crimes, and thus must be contained.[19] In May of 1723 the Hanoverian government enacted the Black Act, which made it a felony to enter a forest under disguise or with a blackened face and to hunt, wound, or steal deer. It was a capital offence if the deer were taken from the King's forest,[20] and the Act made a number of other criminal offences capital crimes. However, the events of the early 1720s complicate the motives behind the Black Act and point to concerns other than simply preserving the forests from poachers.[21] In particular, the episodes related to Jacobitism in the 1720s figure prominently in the course of the government's actions concerning the forests.[22] Aftereffects of the Atterbury Plot were still resonant, since conspirator Christopher Layer was not hanged until May of 1723. The newspapers of late 1722 and early 1723 regularly discuss Bishop Atterbury's arrest and exile, as well as Layer's imprisonment and impending execution. The Black Act was instigated in the years surrounding Robert Walpole's rise to power, as the Hanoverian government demonstrated the need to maintain control of disruptive social influences. This oppressive law was an essential component in consolidating Walpole's influence, and coincided with his rise to power.[23]

As numerous historians have pointed out, Walpole's real fear was Jacobitism, not the Blacks. Several anti-Catholic measures were instigated in the early 1720s, including the suspension of Habeas Corpus and a fine for Roman Catholics. The Black Act itself has connections to Jacobitism because the Blacks were involved with the Atterbury plot.[24] The Dutch envoy L'Hermitage reported in 1723 that Sir Henry Goring, a central figure in the Atterbury Plot, 'had formed a company out of the Waltham Blacks for the Pretender's service'. According to L'Hermitage, Walpole's discovery of this connection between the Blacks and Jacobitism 'led to the bringing of the Waltham Black Act into Parliament'.[25]

A Jacobite broadside found in the state papers for the day Christopher Layer was arrested (18 September 1722) further associates the deer poachers with Jacobitism. Entitled 'The Hunting of the Newfound *Dear* with its Last

18 *The Weekly Journal: or, British Gazetteer* for 26 January carried the same anecdote.

19 E. P. Thompson, *Whigs and Hunters* (London, 1975), pp. 190–1.

20 See Pat Rogers, 'The Waltham Blacks and the Black Act', *The Historical Journal*, 18 (1974), 465–86.

21 Monod, *Jacobitism*, p. 116.

22 For instance, see *The Daily Journal* for 4 and 6 December, 1722.

23 Thompson, *Whigs and Hunters*, p. 197.

24 Eveline Cruickshanks and Howard Erskine-Hill, 'The Waltham Black Act and Jacobitism', *Journal of British Studies*, 24 (1985), 358–65.

25 *Ibid*., p. 365.

Legacy', this text casts King George I as a 'beast that's come from Dover / And some call it a Deer' who will be hunted:

And when that we do chase him,
And dress him fit for the Spit,
We will make the best of his Carcass
We will not waste a Bit.

The poem details how various parts of the King's body will be distributed, including his hide to 'make / A presbyterian Jump', and even his 'excrement will serve / To dung some — Land'. The poem ends with two triumphant stanzas, pledging to give the King's horns 'to some honest Tory' who will 'blow the tidings to the Man / That's O're the Raging Sea', concluding:

And you that will come to this feast,
Come let's goe chase the Dear,
For Hunting it is a pleasant sport
Fit for a Lord or Peer.[26]

The deer hunters in this poem are Jacobite Lords, and their prey is not a deer, but rather the King. The antagonism between the government and the Blacks, with their links to Jacobitism, became the subject for literary use in this broadside. As we will see, Charles Johnson's adaptation *Love in a Forest* involves a similar use of this conflict for dramatic material.

The Black Act had lasting ramifications for the history of English criminal law, and many historians have debated whether the act was a direct response to the forest activities, or a method of government repression. E. P. Thompson maintains that it was not the deer-stealing actions of the Blacks, but rather the challenge to authority that led to this law. John Broad argues that the Black Act 'together with the Riot Act of 1715 provided the Whigs with a machinery for law and order which could be operated in the interests of the establishment'.[27] Government control of the forests was not universally agreed upon as the best solution to the situation, and there was not unequivocal support for government intervention. Many local inhabitants saw this intrusion as disrupting the age-old methods of maintaining relationships between gentry and forest residents. In fact, the vicar of Winkfield, the Reverend Will Waterson remarked that '*Liberty* and *Forest Laws* are incompatible'.[28] Thus, Charles Johnson had a compelling reason to revive *As You Like It*, in order to justify the Hanoverian government's intervention in the forests.

In Shakespeare's *As You Like It*, Johnson found material that was relevant to this political situation. With a few changes, Johnson created a convenient framework for political commentary. Even by simply renaming the play *Love in a Forest*, Johnson calls to mind the troubling events that precipitated the Black Act.[29] Indeed, John Loftis points out that the practice of titling plays in reference to current affairs was not uncommon, even if the contents of the play did not bear out the political implications in the title.[30] Additionally, the advertisement in *The Evening Post* for the printed version of *Love in a Forest* includes the epigraph printed on the title page of the first edition, 'Nostra nec erubuit Sylvas habitare Thalia' [Our comic muse

26 As quoted in John Broad, 'Whigs and Deer-Stealers in Other Guises: A Return to the Origins of the Black Act', *Past and Present*, 119 (1988), 56–72; pp. 69–70.

27 *Ibid.*, p. 58; Thompson, *Whigs and Hunters*, p. 191.

28 Thompson, *Whigs and Hunters*, p. 49.

29 Earlier in his career, Johnson had links to prominent Whigs concerned with maintaining the forests. Johnson dedicated his play *The Country Lasses* (1715) to Thomas Pelham-Holles, Earl of Clare, who was appointed the steward of Sherwood Forest and Folewood Park in 1714 by George I. Sarah Churchill, Duchess of Marlborough, also a patron of Johnson's and to whom his play *The Victim* (1714) was dedicated, was ranger of Windsor Great and Little Parks.

30 John Loftis, *The Politics of Drama in Augustan England* (Oxford, 1963), p. 71 n1. Loftis points out that 'the trick of presenting plays with politically suggestive titles was used more than once by Lincoln's Inn Fields, whose dramatists might deplore the intrusion of party into drama but were none the less aware of their audiences' preferences', such as Benjamin Griffin's suggestively titled play *Whig and Tory* (1720), which was targeted 'to arouse the expectation of party clamour that the author had no intention of satisfying'.

(Thalia) did not blush to live in the Woods].[31] This phrase links Johnson's comic endeavour to the current events in the English woods and overtly locates his dramatic efforts in the scene of contemporary legal, social and political strife.

Many aspects of *As You Like It* reveal associations with the forest controversy. Even though Duke Senior and his followers remain poachers in both the original play and the adaptation, Duke Senior expresses reservations about their activities. For instance, in Johnson's 2.1 (as in Shakespeare's), Duke Senior remarks:

> Come, shall we go and kill us Venison?
> And yet it irks me, the poor dapple Fools,
> Being native Burghers of this Desart City,
> Shou'd, in their own Confines, with forked Heads,
> Have their round Haunches goar'd. (p. 22)

This reflection echoes the descriptions of the activities of the Blacks, such as the *London Gazette* of 22-6 March 1720 account of three deer 'which they carried away whole, and did cut off the Haunches of the fourth, and left the rest of the Carcase'. For Johnson, this remark about the slaying of deer in their own territory was ideal for strengthening sentiment against the Blacks, and reinforcing the need to protect the forest from such encroachments.

Several of the changes that Johnson makes to *As You Like It* promote government intervention in the forests. Perhaps the most significant shifts occur in the character of Jaques. Adding components of Benedick from *Much Ado About Nothing* and Berowne from *Love's Labour's Lost* to Jaques, Johnson creates a more sympathetic character. Jaques falls in love with Celia despite his admonishments about marriage – a far cry from the cynical, solitary Jaques in Shakespeare's play. In fact, the relationship between Jaques and Celia is allocated almost equal time to Rosalind and Orlando. Johnson makes several changes to Jaques in order to condemn the Blacks' depredations. In Johnson's adaptation, Jaques delivers the first Lord's speech on the wounded stag, from 2.1.:

> To Day, my Lord of *Amiens*, and myself,
> Lay in the Shade of an old Druid Oak,
> Whose antique venerable Root peeps out
> Upon the Brook that brawls along this Wood,
> To which Place, a poor sequestred Stag,
> That from the Hunter's Aim had ta'en a Hurt,
> Did come to languish; and indeed, my Lord,
> The wretched Animal heav'd forth such Groans,
> That their Discharge did stretch his leathern Coat
> Almost to bursting, while the big round Drops
> Cours'd one another down his innocent Nose
> In piteous Chace; and thus the hairy Fool
> Stood on the extreamest Verge of the swift Brook,
> Augmenting it with Tears. (pp. 22–3)

This sympathetic portrait of the wounded deer surely would have resonated with Johnson's audience when similar events were happening in the English forests.[32] By giving this speech to Jaques (a major character transformed into a sympathetic lover) instead of to the first Lord (a minor character), Johnson creates a spokesman who generates sympathy for the Whig government's actions against the Blacks.

At the end of the same scene, Jaques delivers a further moralization (which is relayed second-hand by the first Lord in Shakespeare's version): 'Are we not all Usurpers, Tyrants, worse, / To fright these Animals and kill them thus / In their assign'd and native Dwelling-Place' (p. 23). In Shakespeare's play, at the end of this speech, Duke Senior says to the Second Lord, 'Show me the place [where you left Jaques]. / I love to cope him in these sullen fits, / For then he's full of matter' (2.1.67-9). Johnson changes the Duke's lines so that he becomes a companion of Jaques in the contemplation of the wounded deer, 'Shew me this Place, / There will we sweetly moralize together, / And make

[31] Johnson's epigraph comes from Virgil's sixth eclogue, and was also used by Ben Jonson as the epigraph for the unfinished *The Sad Shepherd: or, a Tale of Robin-Hood*.

[32] Johnson's former patron Sarah, Duchess of Marlborough experienced a similar situation in Windsor Forest. See Thompson, *Whigs and Hunters*, p. 41.

our Contemplations give at once / Delight and Use' (p. 23). Instead of observing Jaques, Duke Senior here joins Jaques in his compassion, again questioning the unequivocal acceptance of poaching in which he participates. It is likely that members of Johnson's audience would have picked up on this sympathetic musing, increasing support for government intervention in the forests.

Further solidifying Johnson's political aims is the fact that the Whig actor Colley Cibber played the role of Jaques. Cibber was a prominent Hanoverian supporter: he had recently dedicated his anti-Jacobite play *The Non-Juror* to the King, netting £200 in royal favour,[33] and subsequently became Poet Laureate in 1730. At Drury Lane, Cibber's Jaques added support for the actions of the Hanoverian government. The role of Jaques was expanded not only to devise an appropriate part for Cibber, but also to provide a prominent advocate for government control of the forests.

Johnson also makes changes to Shakespeare's play to comment on the Foresters, who were responsible for patrolling the forests. In his version of Shakespeare's 4.2, Johnson clearly delineates the Foresters from the Lords. In Shakespeare's play, the Lord is referred to as 'Forrester', whereas Johnson makes the Forester a separate character. The song, 'What shall he have that killed the deer?' is sung in Shakespeare by the Lord, but Johnson specifies that the Forester, not the Lord, sings it. Johnson capitalizes on current events taking place in the forests, creating a musical comment on poaching sung by Foresters. Johnson's use of Shakespeare to sanction the repressive government actions resulting in the Black Act of 1723 marks an important point in the history of appropriating Shakespeare.

The final words of Johnson's play appear to contradict the pastoral substance of his drama, as they posit preference for the city above the country. The Epilogue questions the virtues of the country, lest the pastoral setting of *Love in a Forest* be mistaken for an approval of Tory country values over Whig support for the city. The Epilogue criticizes the '*Country* Spouse, and Rural 'Squire' who are 'Dirty and dull; —to every Pleasure lost' in favour of 'The circulating Pleasures of the Town' which are 'By regular and virtuous Laws refind'. Not only does Johnson conclude his drama by favouring the city over the country, he includes a comment on the need for 'virtuous laws' to refine the structure of civilized life, as the laws governing the forest intended. This characteristic Whig statement about the virtues of city life is a fitting conclusion to Johnson's reworking of Shakespeare.

While Johnson's play is interesting for its use of Shakespeare, it is also an important document in the history of political performances at Drury Lane. Johnson's unusual dedication of the play to the Freemasons, of which he was a member, is the earliest evidence of the Masonic influence on a specific play.[34] Harry William Pedicord had identified William Chetwood's 1730 opera *The Generous Freemason; or, The Constant Lady, with the Comic Humours of Squire Noodle and his Man Doodle* as the earliest Masonic theatre piece, but Johnson's dedication shows Masonic activity in the London theatres at least seven years earlier.[35] Although Johnson's play was performed at a Whig theatre and published by a Whig publisher, Johnson dedicates it to the Freemasons. As Paul Monod has argued, the Freemasons in England had a long history of association with the Stuart family, and thus

[33] Loftis, *Politics of Drama*, p. 72.

[34] *The Daily Post* for 15 January advertised *Love in a Forest* 'For the Benefit of the Author, a Free-Mason'. Johnson's dedication is reprinted in *Early Masonic Pamphlets*, ed. Douglas Knoop, Gwilym P. Jones, and Douglas Hamer (Manchester, 1945).

[35] See Henry William Pedicord, 'White Gloves at Five: Fraternal Patronage of London Theatres in the Eighteenth Century', *Philological Quarterly*, 45 (1966), 270–88 and 'Masonic Theatre Pieces in London 1730–1780', *Theatre Survey*, 25 (1984), 153–66.

with Jacobitism,[36] a link that Johnson would certainly want to avoid. Why would Johnson overtly choose this group for his dedication, especially in light of his earlier *The Cobler of Preston*, which vehemently denounces Jacobitism shortly after the Jacobite Rebellion of 1715?

The answer lies in the status of the Freemasons at the particular time of Johnson's adaptation. In 1717, the Grand Lodge was created, centralizing four London Lodges. Between the establishment of the Grand Lodge and 1723, five Grand Masters were elected, including the first noble Grand Master, John Duke of Montagu in 1721.[37] Philip, Duke of Wharton (1698–1731) was named the Grand Master of the Grand Lodge in 1722–3. Wharton had Jacobite sympathies, beginning with his controversial marriage to the daughter of a Tory general, and his encounter with the Pretender during his Grand Tour in 1716. The Duke of Wharton was later involved in the Atterbury Plot in 1722, and Wharton's Jacobitism is evident in his *True Briton* of 1723–4.[38] Wharton still maintained his Jacobite leanings as Grand Master, and had Jacobite songs played at his inauguration. Wharton was removed as Grand Master in 1723 and later formed the Gormogans, a new society claiming to exclude George I.[39]

Thus, the dedication of a Whig play to the Freemasons is explained by Johnson's desire to announce the legitimacy of the Freemasons as a result of the impending removal of Wharton in 1723. In addition, James Anderson's *Constitutions* of the Freemasons were also published in 1723, and Johnson appropriately coincides his dedication with the publication of the first history of the Freemasons. In fact, the *Constitutions* were advertised in *The Daily Journal* for 25 January 1722–3, in the same issue with an advertisement for Johnson's *Love in a Forest*. Johnson's inclusion of the mechanicals from *A Midsummer Night's Dream* may also be a reference to the Freemasons. In the first act of *Love in a Forest*, Charles the Duke's Fencer announces that 'the very Mechanicks, and Labourers in this Handicraft leave every Day their Occupations, and this populous City of *Liege*, and flock to visit their exil'd Sovereign, as they call him' (p. 5).[40] Johnson employs Shakespeare to show approval for the Freemasons at a crucial point in their growth as a Hanoverian court Whig institution.[41]

The success of *Love in a Forest* attests to Johnson's ability to speak to current events through Shakespeare. *Love in a Forest* was performed at least six times, including two author's benefits for Johnson. *The London Stage* lists performances for 9, 10, 11, 12, 14, and 15 January. However, according to a statement in *The British Journal* for 5 January 1723, *Love in a Forest* was to have premiered on 2 January, but was delayed because of the illness of Mrs Younger.[42] *The London Post* for 14 January 1723

36 Monod, *Jacobitism*, pp. 300, 305. Monod points out that the story of Hiram Abiff, the central Masonic mystery, can be read allegorically as endorsing the return of the Stuarts from exile.

37 T. O. Haunch, 'The Formation: 1717 to 1751', in *Grand Lodge 1717–1967*, ed. A. S. Frere (Oxford, 1967), pp. 47–91.

38 Paul Monod, 'The Politics of Matrimony: Jacobitism and Marriage in Eighteenth-Century England', in *The Jacobite Challenge*, ed. Eveline Cruickshanks and Jeremy Black (Edinburgh, 1988), p. 30; Eveline Cruickshanks, 'Lord North, Christopher Layer and the Atterbury Plot: 1720–23', in *The Jacobite Challenge*, p. 99; Monod, *Jacobitism*, p. 29.

39 Monod, *Jacobitism*, p. 301.

40 Holding, '*As You Like It* Adapted', p. 43.

41 See Margaret Jacob, *The Radical Enlightenment: Pantheists, Freemasons and Republicans* (London, 1981).

42 *The British Journal* states that 'Mr *Johnson*'s new Play, alter'd from Mr *Shakespear's*, *As you like it*, was not play'd at the Old House on *Wednesday*, as intended, by Reason of Mrs *Younger's* Indisposition, who was to bear a principal Part in that Performance.' *The Daily Journal* of 1 January carries a similar advertisement. The only cast list is printed with the first edition of *Love in a Forest*, and does not include Mrs Younger. Elizabeth Younger played such parts as Margery Pinchwife in Wycherley's *The Country Wife*, Sylvia in Farquhar's *The Recruiting Officer*, and Desdemona in *Othello*. There are only four parts for women in Johnson's play: Rosalind, Celia, Hymen, and Thisby. Mrs Younger probably was to play either Rosalind or Celia, the two main parts for women.

states that Johnson's benefit performance on 11 January had 'as numerous an Audience as has for this great while been seen; not only the Boxes, Pit and Galleries, but the Stage too being crowded with Spectators.'[43] Johnson was eager to capitalize on the timely relevance of his play, and most likely published it as its run was ending. *The Evening Post* advertises the printed edition of *Love in a Forest* for sale first in the 15–17 January issue, and continued to advertise the printed play in the 19–22 January, 22–4 January, and 24–6 January issues, as anxiety over the Blacks increased.[44]

By presenting *Love in a Forest* as a rescued play of Shakespeare's, Johnson taps into the cultural resonance of the developing 'National Poet', at a time when many of Shakespeare's plays were revived.[45] The Prologue opens, 'In Honour to his Name, and this learn'd Age, / Once more your much lov'd SHAKESPEAR treads the Stage.' Johnson immediately and deliberately attaches his play to Shakespeare's growing reputation, claiming that he has 'refin'd' 'Another Work from that great Hand'.[46] Johnson promotes *Love in a Forest* with the authority of Shakespeare, summarizing that 'New Miracles each Scene arrest the Sight, / Instruct, and please, give Knowledge and Delight.' Johnson situates his play in a lineage of immortal truth and knowledge; Shakespeare's 'sacred Truths' buttress Johnson's pro-Whig comments on the forest and sanctity of its inhabitants. By 'giv[ing] the Stage, from SHAKESPEAR one Play more', he claims only to 'tune the sacred Bard's immortal Lyre', recovering Shakespeare's views on the current politics of the Hanoverian government.

Charles Johnson maintained a position in the theatrical repertoire with a play almost every season for three decades. Because of his need to create plays which would please audiences, Johnson shows the reaction of Drury Lane theatre to contemporary social and political concerns. Drury Lane became a site of Hanoverian support, and Johnson's appropriation of Shakespearian material at two points of great political tension is an integral part of that effort. Johnson's aim is to present *Love in a Forest* as a timeless literary masterpiece retrieved from oblivion and rescued from obscurity. He both invites and shields his play from political application, offering the retitled work as a teaser to those who might be interested in such a reading. Although the intersections between Johnson's play, the Black Act, and the Freemasons are certainly not the only purposes behind his adaptation, they do lend us a better understanding of the motivations and reasons behind some of the changes made to Shakespeare's plays in the early eighteenth century.

---

[43] *The London Stage 1660–1800*, ed. Emmett L. Avery (Carbondale, 1960), 2:2; 704.

[44] *The British Journal* carried advertisements for the printed play in the 26 January, 2 February, and 9 February issues. *The Daily Post* advertised the printed edition 16, 19, 21, 22, and 23 January. *The Daily Journal* advertised the printed play 22–6 January.

[45] Paul Sawyer, 'The Popularity of Shakespeare's Plays, 1720–21 through 1732–33', *Shakespeare Quarterly*, 29 (1978), 427–30.

[46] Aaron Hill's adaptation of *Henry V* from the same year (London, 1723) also reveals a similar use of Shakespeare for political purposes. In the preface to his play, Hill encourages his audience to support his play, and by doing so to support English instead of French entertainments, just as Henry V was able to defeat the French.

# RACE MATTERED: *OTHELLO* IN LATE EIGHTEENTH-CENTURY ENGLAND[1]

VIRGINIA MASON VAUGHAN

'When Paul Robeson stepped onto the stage for the very first time', Margaret Webster recalled, 'when he spoke his very first line, he immediately, by his very presence, brought an incalculable sense of reality to the entire play.'[2] That reality emanated from Robeson's status as the first actor of African descent to impersonate Shakespeare's Othello on Broadway. Because of his biological heritage, Robeson was perceived as being more 'real' as the Moor than a white actor in blackface. Robeson's performance in the longest-running Shakespeare production ever staged on Broadway thus revolutionized the way many people felt about its hero.

As public reaction to Webster's *Othello* demonstrated, a play in performance is both a maker and a transmitter of cultural codes; it is necessarily imbricated in the broader discourses that surround it. Shakespearians concerned with the history of performance must determine the nature of those discourses and how they shaped the text's reception and transmission. For the history of *Othello*, especially, the discourses inevitably include the messy matter of racial ideology.[3]

The received view of *Othello* in the late eighteenth century seems to deny this premise, however, and to isolate the play in performance from the broad context of English culture. At a time when the justice of British enslavement of black Africans in England and the West Indies was hotly debated,[4] Othello's race and his relation to a white woman seem, in the eyes of most theatre historians, not to have mattered. Thus two contradictory discourses circulated simultaneously and, at first glance, seem to have had little or no impact on each other: (1) the pro- and anti-slavery polemics in pamphlets and magazines, and (2) criticism of *Othello* on stage in memoirs, acting treatises, and reviews.

1 My title is an allusion to Cornel West's recent analysis of race relations in the United States, *Race Matters* (New York: Vintage, 1994). Earlier versions of this essay were presented at the Shakespeare Association of America, the Higgins School of Humanities Lecture Series at Clark University, and the Shakespearian Studies Seminar at the Harvard Center for Literary and Cultural Studies; the essay has benefitted greatly from the ensuing discussions and I thank all who generously shared their ideas with me. I am also grateful to Alden T. Vaughan and R. A. Foakes for suggestions about sources and revisions.

2 Margaret Webster, *Shakespeare Without Tears* (New York: Capricorn Books, 1975; orig. pub. 1955), p. 179.

3 James C. Bulman proposes in his introduction to *Shakespeare, Theory, and Performance* that in contrast to the essentialistic approach to performance pioneered in the 1970s by John Styan, contemporary theatre historians and performance critics should examine how 'acts of representation are implicated in the dynamics of contemporary culture and in themselves acquire meaning' (London: Routledge, 1996), p. 1.

4 For historical accounts of blacks in England during this period, see Gretchen Gerzina, *Black London: Life Before Emancipation* (New Brunswick, NJ: Rutgers University Press, 1995); James Walvin, *Black and White: The Negro and English Society* (London: Allen Lane the Penguin Press, 1973), esp. chaps. 4–8; and Peter Fryer, *Staying Power: The History of Black People in Britain* (London: Pluto Press, 1984), esp. chaps. 3–8.

Perhaps because *Othello* boasts a continuous acting history from the Restoration to the present, or perhaps because of its privileged place in the canon as one of the Big Four, there is abundant perceptive commentary about its early performance history. Marvin Rosenberg began his long and fruitful career with *The Masks of Othello* in 1961. His chapter on the eighteenth century argues that 'a proper, neo-classic hero was aimed at' and demonstrates how cuts in the acting text were designed to display Othello at his best and to protect the audience from overt sexual references.[5] Rosenberg never mentions race *per se*. Carol Carlisle's thoughtful study of actor-critic responses to the Big Four, *Shakespeare from the Greenroom*, recognizes that colour had indeed created problems in the performance history of *Othello* but concludes that 'there is no interpretation of Othello advanced by an actor-critic of that period [the eighteenth century] that might not bear the stamp of nobility upon it'.[6] Julie Hankey's performance edition also offers a detailed survey of *Othello*'s acting history; she characterizes the eighteenth-century Moor as 'the hero-and-the-lover' and suggests that theatre critics such as James Boaden saw little significance in Othello as an African; rather, in Hankey's words, 'Othello was in their minds a hot and fiery southern gentleman in whom the qualities of an Englishman were not so much abandoned as exaggerated.'[7] Gino Matteo is more emphatic, insisting that the issue of race 'simply never materialised in the eighteenth-century theatre'.[8] Even so astute a critic as James Siemon is reticent on the topic of race, asserting 'the age's nearly universal insistence on Othello's nobility'.[9]

This reticence about the racial dynamics of eighteenth-century *Othello* performances, which is admittedly exhibited in my recent book,[10] reflects the traditional sources. They are either silent about Othello's race or insist that it was not an issue. William Cooke, for example, anointed Spranger Barry as the best eighteenth-century Othello in his *Memoirs of Charles Macklin* because he was the perfect hero and lover. Cooke concludes: 'those who before doubted of the poet's consistency in forming a mutual passion between such characters as the *black* Othello, and the *fair* Desdemona, were now convinced of his propriety. They saw, from Barry's predominant and fascinating manner, that mere colour could not be a barrier to affection'.[11]

In somewhat the same vein, Francis Gentleman's 1777 edition of *Othello* emphasizes that the Moor should 'be amiably elegant and above the middle stature; his expression full and sententious, for the declamatory part; flowing and harmonious, for the love-scenes; rapid and powerful for each violent climax of jealous rage'.[12] In *The Dramatic Censor*, Gentleman describes Othello as 'open, generous, free, subject to violent feelings, not, as himself expresses it, *easily jealous*, yet rouzed by that pernicious passion above all violent restraint; weak in his confidence, partial in discernment, fatal in resolution'.[13] Despite his expansive concern with character, Gentleman never men-

[5] Marvin Rosenberg, *The Masks of Othello* (Berkeley: University of California Press, 1961), pp. 29–53; quote from p. 34.

[6] Carol Jones Carlisle, *Shakespeare from the Greenroom* (Chapel Hill: University of North Carolina Press, 1969), pp. 172–263; quote from p. 200.

[7] Julie Hankey, ed. *Othello (Plays in Performance)* (Bristol: Bristol Classical Press, 1987), pp. 36–61; quotes from pp. 36 and 49.

[8] Gino M. Matteo, *Shakespeare's Othello: The Study and the Stage, 1604–1904* (Salzburg: Institut für Englische Sprache und Literatur, 1974), pp. 85–200; quote from p. 123.

[9] James R. Siemon, '"Nay, that's not next": *Othello*, v.ii. in Performance, 1700–1900', *Shakespeare Quarterly*, 37 (1986), 38–51; quote from p. 41.

[10] Virginia Mason Vaughan, *Othello: A Contextual History* (Cambridge: Cambridge University Press, 1994), pp. 113–34.

[11] William Cooke, *Memoirs of Charles Macklin* (London: James Asperne, 1804), p. 155.

[12] Francis Gentleman, ed. *Othello* (London: John Bell, 1777), p. 10.

[13] Francis Gentleman, *The Dramatic Censor*, vol. 1 (London: John Bell, 1770), p. 150.

tions colour or race. Nor is there any reference to Othello's make-up or colour in Kemble's promptbook.[14]

There are, to be sure, some hints in the standard sources that Othello's blackness was sometimes of passing interest. In a frequently cited anecdote, David Garrick is said to have answered the question, 'why Shakespeare made his hero black?' with this rejoinder:

> Shakespeare had shown us white men jealous in other pieces, but ... their jealousy had limits, and was not so terrible; ... in ... Othello, he had wished to paint that passion in all its violence, and that is why he chose an African in whose veins circulated fire instead of blood, and whose true or imaginary character could excuse all boldnesses of expression and all exaggerations of passion.[15]

Garrick drew here upon the common assumption that people living in Africa, Ethiopia, and Egypt were violent by nature, whereas people from more northern climes were steadier in temperament.[16] But what had been a cultural bias during the late sixteenth century became a fixed ideology two hundred years later when London had acquired a substantial black population.

James Boaden's memoir of John Philip Kemble echoes this received wisdom when he describes the actor-manager's Moor as 'grand and awful and pathetic. But he was a European: there seemed to be philosophy in his bearing; there was reason in his rage'.[17] Because Kemble was too northern, or English, in his self-control, Boaden implies, the actor never fully realized the role's emotional dynamics. The 29 October 1787 *Public Advertiser* echoes Boaden's assessment in its evaluation of the first act: 'in his first scenes [Kemble] was judicious, but too studiously so; and though most critically correct in his address to the Senate, evidenced he was more anxious to do justice to the text of his author than the feelings of Othello'. The reviewer praises the actor's performance in the later scenes, but, in a curious aside, comments: 'We much approve his dressing Othello in the Moorish habit ... [but] is it necessary the Moor should be as *black* as a native of Guiney?'[18]

That Kemble's Moor was too like an African from Guinea (most likely a slave to be exported to the West Indian sugar plantations) suggests that, to some viewers at least, the distinction between the white actor playing a black man and the real thing had to be maintained. This may be one explanation for David Garrick's failure in the role of Othello – not that he was too black, but that in his turban and feather, he looked too much like the black servants fashionable Londoners encountered every day. The historian Peter Fryer estimates that by the late eighteenth century approximately 10,000 black people resided in a nation whose total population was approaching nine million.[19] Despite the popular impression that there was no slavery in England during the eighteenth century, slaves were regularly bought and sold in London and the port cities of Bristol and Liverpool.[20] The majority of blacks in England had been imported by West Indian planters returning to the mother country. Slaves, many of them children, often decked in special livery,

---

[14] See the reproduction of Kemble's promptbook in *John Philip Kemble Promptbooks*, vol. 7, ed. Charles H. Shattuck (Charlottesville: University Press of Virginia for the Folger Shakespeare Library, 1974).

[15] From Frank A. Hedgcock, *David Garrick and his French Friends* (London: Stanley Paul, 1912), p. 341n.

[16] J. B. Bamborough discusses this English Renaissance conception in *The Little World of Man* (London: Longmans, Green and Co., 1952), pp. 72–3.

[17] James Boaden, *Memoirs of the Life of John Philip Kemble*, vol. 1 (London: Longman *et al.*, 1825), p. 256. Earlier in his career, Kemble produced an adaptation of *The Comedy of Errors*, called *OH! 'tis Impossible*; Boaden attributes the staging of the twin Dromios as black slaves (so that the faces of Dromio of Syracuse and Dromio of Ephesus could not be distinguished by the audience) as the reason for the production's failure (p. 33).

[18] Quoted from *The London Stage, 1660–1800, Part 5*, vol. 2, ed. Charles Beecher Hogan (Carbondale: Southern Illinois University Press, 1969), p. 1016.

[19] Fryer, *Staying Power*, p. 68.

[20] *Ibid.*, pp. 58–61.

4 Plate 2 of William Hogarth's 'The Harlot's Progress'.

accompanied wealthy white women, their blackness highlighting by contrast the mistress's fair beauty. 'Given classical names like Pompey and Caesar', contends historian Gretchen Gerzina, 'they were dressed in brightly coloured silks and satins, silver padlocked collars, and feathered turbans'.[21] William Hogarth's 'The Harlot's Progress', Plate 2, satirized this social practice with a be-turbaned black child bearing the tea kettle to his mistress's table.[22] David Dabydeen observes in his study of Hogarth's blacks that the boy's

> sartorial elegance, his silver collar and his polite domestic duties (English ladies employed black boys to wait at the tea-table, to carry their fans and smelling-salts, to comb their lap dogs, and so on) belies the sordid reality of the servitude of naked and manacled blacks in the colonies.[23]

Hogarth's engraving thus illustrates the context for actor James Quin's famous quip about Garrick's representation of Shakespeare's Moor:

[21] Gerzina, *Black London*, p. 16.

[22] See also *Hogarth: The Complete Engravings*, ed. Joseph Burke and Colin Caldwell (New York: Harry N. Abrams, 1960), plate 135.

[23] David Dabydeen, *Hogarth's Blacks: Images of Blacks in Eighteenth-Century English Art* (Athens: University of Georgia Press, 1987), p. 114.

'There was a little black boy, like Pompey attending with a tea-kettle, fretting and fumbling about the stage; but I saw no Othello.'[24] As the hero of a major tragedy crafted by the National Poet, Othello could not look like a little black slave. Garrick's diminutive stature and exotic turban thus doomed his Othello. Eighteenth-century audiences sought a Moor, as I concluded in 1994, who appeared 'as a high ranking, noble, courageous general, an English gentleman, represented by a white actor in blackface'.[25]

But does this performance preference mean that, as I once thought, race was not an issue in the late eighteenth-century interpretation of *Othello*? How could it not be an issue when cultural anxiety about Britain's black population and the future of the slave trade was at its peak, when litigation such as the highly contested Somerset case of 1772 sparked a public debate about the merits of the slave system? In the 1770s, after the Somerset ruling set a precedent that escaped slaves could not be deported to the West Indies, allowing them to claim freedom on English soil, the pro-slavery lobby countered with loud assertions of Negro inferiority and bestiality, claims that blacks had a better life on the plantations than they would in London competing for scarce employment, and predictions of an English future polluted by miscegenation. By 1783, when a new influx of blacks who had served the Loyalist cause in America arrived to claim their promised freedom, public discussion of their status accelerated. A scheme to remove the black poor from London streets and resettle them in Sierra Leone won backing even from those in favour of abolition and was actually implemented in 1786, though to little success.

London's theatres may seem far removed from this political battlefield, but the same volumes that we comb for theatre reviews – journals like *The Public Advertiser* and *The Gentleman's Magazine* – published letters, reports, and reviews from both sides. The literate gentlemen who read such magazines probably knew *Othello* well, but perhaps it was to avoid making any connections between Shakespeare's moving tragedy and the reality of most black people's lives that they insisted on the Moor's nobility and exalted status.

Outside the magazines and other standard theatrical sources, there is admittedly slender but nonetheless suggestive evidence as to how Othello was constructed within the larger culture. His blackness, of course, was a given, so it is not surprising to find Othello as the name of a slave[26] or a member of an all-black military musical regiment.[27] That Othello married a white woman was also a given. Thus the white chambermaids who flirted with the Duchess of Queensberry's black servant, Julius Soubise (notorious for womanizing and other vices), called him 'the young Othello'.[28] Othello was jealous. So, when Hester Piozzi reported the jealous quarrel between Francis Barber, Samuel Johnson's black servant, and his white wife, she called the wife 'his Desdemona'.[29]

More surprising is that literate Africans also used Othello as a self-construction when writing to a white audience. For example, when the West Indian pro-slavery lobby attacked the writings of the ex-slave Olaudah Equiano (who had gained a large and sympathetic white audience), claiming he was not African at all, he added this to the 1792 edition of his popular *Interesting Narrative*: 'An invidious falsehood having appeared ... with a view to hurt my character, and to discredit and prevent the sale of my Narrative ... it is necessary [to]

Speak of me as I am,
Nothing extenuate, nor set down aught
In malice.'[30]

---

[24] Cooke, *Memoirs*, p. 113.

[25] Vaughan, *Othello: A Contextual History*, p. 121.

[26] Gerzina, *Black London*, p. 31.

[27] Fryer, *Staying Power*, p. 87.

[28] Gerzina, *Black London*, p. 55.

[29] Hesther Lynch Piozzi, *Anecdotes of Samuel Johnson*, ed. S. C. Roberts (Cambridge: Cambridge University Press, 1932), pp. 136–7.

[30] The preface is reprinted as Appendix A in *The Life of Olaudah Equiano*, vol. 1, ed. Paul Edwards (London: Dawsons, 1969).

5 William Hogarth's 'Taste in High Life'.

If Equiano, a passionate advocate for abolition, did not otherwise identify himself with Shakespeare's Moor, he probably assumed his white readers would make the connection and respond sympathetically, as they did in the theatre, to words from Othello's suicide speech.

Ignatius Sancho is another well-known ex-slave from the period. Hogarth's engraving 'Taste in High Life' (1746) depicts him as a child. Like Pompey with the tea kettle, Sancho is dressed in fancy livery with a feathered turban, serving – as does the monkey in the engraving's foreground – as a plaything to his fashionable white mistress.[31] But Sancho was lucky. Despite his first mistress's reservations, he learned to read and, in the service of the Duke of Montagu, he found greater opportunities to exercise his musical and literary talents.

In the 1770s, after Sancho became gout-ridden and incapable of further service, the Montagus helped to set him up in London as a grocer. From his shop, Sancho associated with many of London's artists and literati, including David Garrick. His letters, published after his death in 1782, quoted frequently from eighteenth-century writers such as Pope, Sterne, and

[31] The description of plate 200 in *Hogarth: The Complete Engravings* identifies the black boy as Ignatius Sancho. Dabydeen suggests that the lady's seductive gesture implies the sexual role sometimes played by the black male slave with aristocratic white ladies; see *Hogarth's Blacks*, p. 79.

Fielding, and less frequently from Shakespeare. In one letter, he adopts Othello's words and describes himself as 'unused to the melting mood'.[32] In another, more telling, letter, he jokingly speculates as to why gentlemen should 'make elections of wide different beings than Blackamoors for their friends'. The reason is obvious, he concludes, '– from Othello to Sancho the big – we are either foolish – or mulish – all – all without a single exception'.[33] Mocking the stereotyping of black people, Sancho chooses the black best known in the dominant white culture, Shakespeare's Othello.

Equiano and Sancho were powerful spokesmen for the abolitionist cause. After gaining their freedom, both constructed identities for themselves in the white world of eighteenth-century London, yet in their writings both display the double consciousness described by W. E. B. DuBois, 'the simultaneous and sometimes conflicting awareness of being both a part of the political and social organism as a citizen, and of being a descendant of Africa'.[34] When they presented themselves to the mainstream culture, whether seriously or playfully, they chose Othello, a black hero constructed by whites, to speak for them.

Eighteenth-century publishing was, of course, controlled by white men, and it was through the efforts of white abolitionists that Equiano and Sancho's writings circulated. Would the ex-slaves have been as successful at being heard in other venues? Sancho's earliest biographer, Joseph Jekyll, reports that the grocer had a passion for the theatre and that as a young man, 'He had been even induced to consider the stage as a resource ... and his complexion suggested an offer to the manager [David Garrick] of attempting Othello and Oroonoko; but a defective and incorrigible articulation rendered it abortive.'[35] Perhaps Garrick would have arranged for Sancho's debut as the noble Moor had the plump grocer been endowed with Paul Robeson's voice and heroic figure, but it seems more likely that the performance would never have materialized.

I draw here on the distinction Dympna Callaghan makes in her recent essay, '"Othello was a white man"', between 'the display of black people themselves' (an exhibition) and 'the simulation of negritude' (an imitation or mimesis).[36] As she convincingly concludes, the actor who imitates can control the image and its signification; the person on display, in contrast, is passive, leaving the spectators in charge of determining her or his signification. White actors impersonating Othello could – and if we believe contemporary accounts, did – reinforce the stereotype of African passion. If Sancho had been able to portray Othello in the London theatres, his occupation of a speaking, subject position would have been too threatening. This may be a reason, among others, why London theatres would not accept Ira Aldridge as Othello fifty years later. Joyce Green MacDonald contends in a recent essay that by being black instead of acting black, in a 'self-authorization of blackness', Aldridge 'disrupted and complicated the economy of race in unforeseen ways'.[37] In any case, the distinction between exhibit – the thing itself – and imitation may explain why, as one historian puts it, Londoners in the eighteenth century could read about slave auctions at home and 'sensational stories of revolts on West Indian plantations quite coolly in the morning newspaper, and then shed tears that evening over similar situations presented on stage'.[38]

Although Francis Gentleman never mentions

---

32 Ignatius Sancho, *The Letters of Ignatius Sancho*, ed. Paul Edwards and Polly Rewt (Edinburgh: Edinburgh University Press, 1994), p. 40.

33 Sancho, *Letters*, p. 191.

34 Gerzina, *Black London*, p. 63.

35 Sancho, *Letters*, p. 23.

36 Dympna Callaghan, '"Othello was a white man"', in *Alternative Shakespeares 2* (London: Routledge, 1996), pp. 192–215; quotes from pp. 194–5.

37 Joyce Green MacDonald, 'Acting Black: *Othello*, *Othello* Burlesques, and the Performance of Blackness', *Theatre Journal*, 46 (1994), 231–49; quotes from p. 234.

38 Gerzina, *Black London*, p. 7.

race in his comments on *Othello*, he repeatedly frets about indecorous sexual suggestions, something Rosenberg pointed out long ago. Decorum was certainly an eighteenth-century preoccupation, and most plays were emended or cut to satisfy current tastes. For example, Gentleman describes Mercutio's reference to the 'demesnes' that lie adjacent to Rosaline's (in Garrick's version, Juliet's) thigh as 'a very indecent line of ludicrous conjuration'.[39] Though Juliet's contemplation of the loss of her maidenhead is removed from her 'Gallop apace' soliloquy in Gentleman's edition, the cuts in *Romeo and Juliet* are nevertheless minor compared to those in Gentleman's *Othello*. Moreover, Gentleman's commentary on *Othello* has a touch of hysteria about it that clearly contrasts with his sentimental acceptance of Romeo and Juliet's passion. There are, to be sure, many differences between these two tragedies, but I suggest that the impulse to clean up and cut loomed larger when it came to *Othello* because black sexuality and the prospect of miscegenation caused far more anxiety than sexual relations between two white lovers.

As Michael Neill shows in his analysis of the early illustrations of the murder scene, the figures of the white Desdemona, prone and helpless in her bed, and the black Othello who hovers over her 'foreground not merely the perverse eroticism of the scene but its aspect of forbidden disclosure'.[40] Neill shows how fear and fascination at the idea of miscegenation lurked behind audience responses to the play's final scene. William Leney's engraving of J. Graham's painting of the same scene, commissioned for the Boydell Gallery, shows a diminutive, be-turbaned figure who recalls descriptions of Garrick's performance. The engraving also suggests quasi-pornographic eroticism encoded in black and white. Like the black page whose dark skin highlights by contrast his mistress's whiteness, the black Othello hovers in the shadows of the bed curtains while Desdemona's exposed neck and breast form the picture's erotic centre. As Othello holds the light in one hand and the dagger in the other, the viewer is implicitly invited to contemplate what will happen when the black man 'tops' the helpless white female figure and kills her in an erotic embrace. Leney's engraving encodes the spectre of racial intermarriage and 'contamination' incessantly invoked by the West Indian slavery lobby, a spectre that according to Fryer, haunted England from the 1770s well into the next century.[41] Though this fear was not articulated in contemporary theatrical discourse, Cooke's denial of its existence in his description of Spranger Barry suggests its power. Moreover, the spectre's widespread circulation in larger social discourses may well explain the repeated insistence that Othello had to bear himself like an English gentleman and wear makeup that everyone recognized as artificial. Reality would be too terrifying.

However contradictory this may seem on the surface, it is less a contradiction than it is a paradox of the times and of the history of *Othello* in performance. Returning to Francis Gentleman's description of Othello –

> he is open, generous, free, subject to violent feelings, not, as himself expresses it, *easily jealous*, yet rouzed by that pernicious passion above all violent restraint; weak in his confidence, partial in discernment, *fatal in resolution*. [my italics][42]

we find striking similarities with Hector McNeill's *Observations on the Treatment of the*

[39] *Romeo and Juliet* (London: John Bell, 1774), p. 100. Gentleman used Garrick's acting edition which, among other changes, cut Rosaline from the play's beginning and added an extended dialogue between Romeo and Juliet before they expire at the end.

[40] Michael Neill, 'Unproper Beds: Race, Adultery, and the Hideous in *Othello*', *Shakespeare Quarterly*, 40 (1989), 383–412; quote from p. 385. Paul H. D. Kaplan concludes in his overview of early illustrations that the 'repeated selection of the murder scene at the end of the play reveals a taste for the melodramatic, and implies a reading of the tragedy in which Othello's violence assumes the most important position'. See 'The Earliest Images of Othello', *Shakespeare Quarterly*, 39 (1988), 171–85; quote from p. 185.

[41] Fryer, *Staying Power*, p. 161.

[42] Gentleman, *Dramatic Censor*, vol. 1, p. 150.

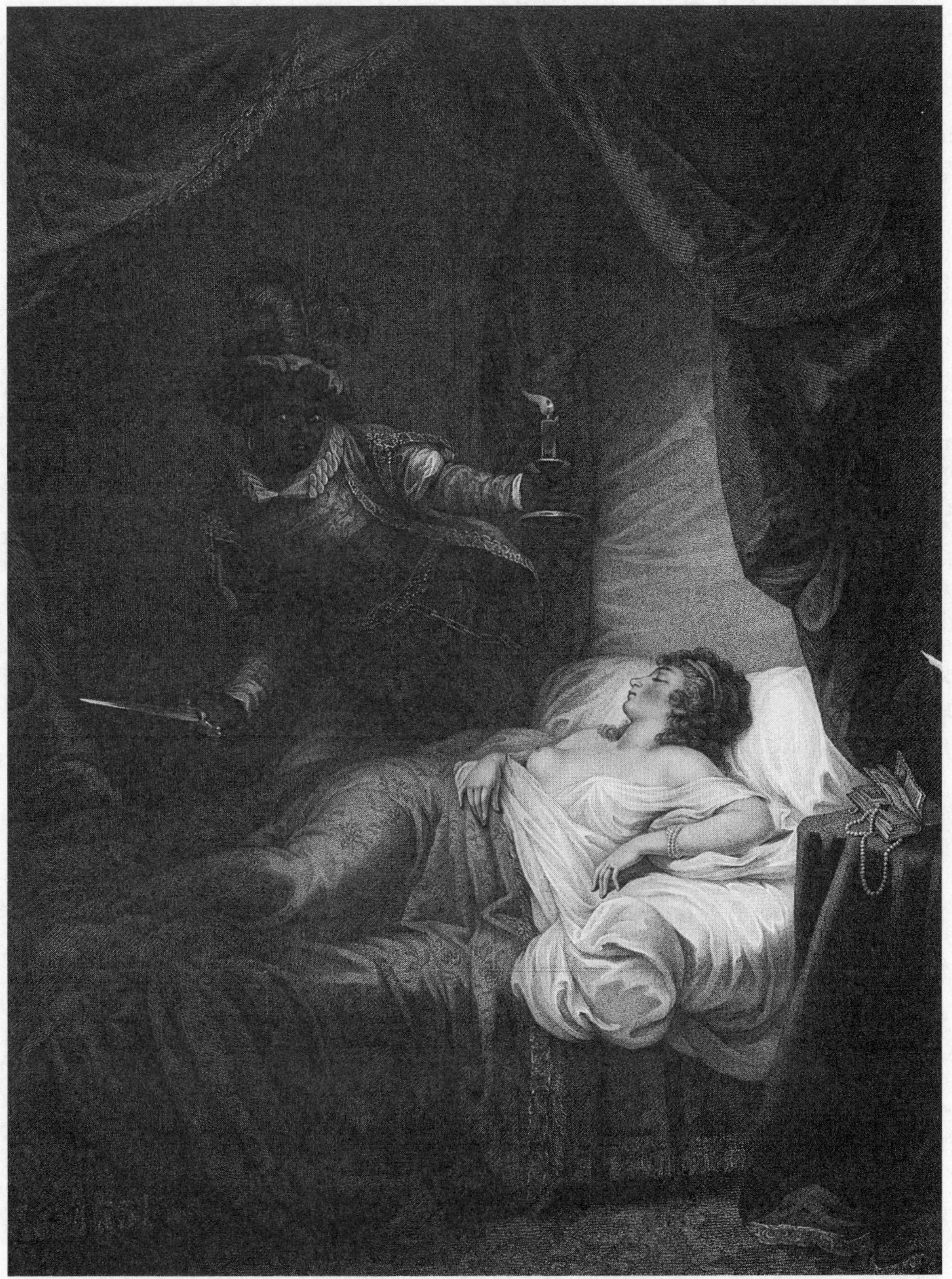

6 *Othello*: William Leney's engraving of J. Graham's painting of the murder scene, commissioned for the Boydell Shakespeare Gallery. [*By permission of the Folger Shakespeare Library*]

*Negroes in the Island of Jamaica*, a pro-slavery treatise published in 1788:

> The Negro is possessed of passions not only strong but ungovernable; a mind dauntless, warlike, and unmerciful; a temper extremely irascible; a disposition indolent, selfish, and deceitful . . . He has certain portions of kindness for his friends, generosity and friendship for his favourites, and affection for his connections . . . Furious in his love as in his hate.[43]

Perhaps Gentleman's seeming silence about race is not silence at all; perhaps it is simply the product of shared cultural assumptions – that Othello's blackness and his jealous passion are integrally connected. This linking of race with character, temperament, and values is an incipient form of the racialism that flowered in England and America during the next century.

When theatre historians look outside the standard *theatrical* resources for the late eighteenth century and examine the personal and political discourses that circulated simultaneously, the evidence is impressive that Shakespeare's *Othello* was deeply imbricated in England's growing racialism. Race mattered to performances of *Othello* but in ways that were discussed only when an inviolable line was crossed; when stage representations moved uncomfortably close to verisimilitude – when Kemble was too black, like a native of Guinea, or Garrick too like Hogarth's depiction of the slave boy Pompey with his tea kettle – only then did Othello's biological heritage merit serious comment.

As theatre historians, we should be especially careful when dealing with texts that foreground volatile issues of race, class, gender, religion, or sexual identity. Eighteenth-century reviews and memoirs were written by educated white men whose prosperous standard of living often rested on traffic in human flesh; what they did not discuss may be as important as what they did. We need to ponder their silences and, as best we can, burrow in alternative discourses to understand fully Shakespeare's role within the cultural tradition.

[43] *Gentleman's Magazine*, 1788, part 2, pp. 1093–4.

# FROM *PERICLES* TO *MARINA*: 'WHILE WOMEN ARE TO BE HAD FOR MONEY, LOVE, OR IMPORTUNITY'

SONIA MASSAI

George Lillo's *Marina* was first staged at the Theatre Royal in Covent Garden on 1 August 1738. After its lack-lustre première, *Marina* was only revived twice,[1] although the Shakespearian original was restored to the stage as late as 1854. Despite the recently renewed interest in Shakespearian adaptations and the after-life of the Shakespearian text both on stage and on the page,[2] Lillo's *Marina* remains one of the least-known early Augustan adaptations of Shakespeare.

There are several reasons for the limited critical attention devoted to Lillo's only attempt to 'improve' on Shakespeare: first, Lillo's reputation as a playwright rests exclusively on his best-known play, *The London Merchant, Or the History of George Barnwell*, an experimental domestic tragedy which secured him vast success and popularity during his life-time, and enduring credit among theatre scholars; secondly, the tendency to use Shakespeare as raw material for new plays had started to decline by the early 1730s; and, most importantly, Lillo's adaptation seems to have shared the critical and theatrical misfortunes of its Shakespearian original. Ever since Ben Jonson sarcastically described *Pericles* as a 'mouldy tale',[3] where 'we see ... many seas, countries, and kingdoms passed over with ... admirable dexterity',[4] critics have regarded this late romance as exceptionally unshakespearian,[5] as a 'curiously amorphous anomaly'.[6] Bound to the ignominy of its ancestor, *Marina* has also been doomed to critical neglect or to a biased approach, as in C. F. Burgess's tautological argument: '*Marina* is not a very interesting play, in part, no doubt, because *Pericles* is not a very interesting play'.[7]

Lillo's adaptation, however, despite its structural and dramatic shortcomings, represents a

[1] *Marina* was performed again on 4 and 8 August 1738 in Covent Garden. For further details, see Arthur H. Scouten *et al., The London Stage 1660–1800: Part 3, 1729–47* (Carbondale, Ill., 1960–8).

[2] Among the main contributions, see Jonathan Bate, *Shakespearean Constitutions: Politics, Theatre, Criticism 1730–1830* (Oxford, 1989); Gary Taylor, *Reinventing Shakespeare: A Cultural History from the Restoration to the Present* (New York, 1989); Margreta de Grazia, *Shakespeare Verbatim: The Reproduction of Authenticity and the 1790 Apparatus* (Oxford, 1991); Jean I. Marsden, *The Appropriation of Shakespeare: Post-Renaissance Reconstructions of the Works and the Myth* (Hemel Hempstead, 1991) and Michael Dobson, *The Making of the National Poet: Shakespeare, Adaptation and Authorship, 1660–1769* (Oxford, 1992).

[3] Ben Jonson, *The New Inne* (London, 1631), sig. H2r.

[4] Ben Jonson, *Every Man Out of His Humour*, in *The Complete Plays of Ben Jonson*, ed. by G. A. Wilkes, 4 vols. (Oxford, 1981–2), I, Induction, lines 269–71.

[5] It is worth noting that *Pericles*, not included in Shakespeare's First Folio, was reprinted as his in the Third Folio in 1664, Rowe included it in his edition of 1709 and it also appeared in the second edition of Pope's *Works of Shakespeare* in 1728, ten years before Lillo's adaptation. It was excluded from later editions of the complete works until Edmond Malone restored it in 1790 in *The Plays and Poems of William Shakespeare*.

[6] George C. D. Odell, *Shakespeare from Betterton to Irving*, 2 vols. (New York, 1920, repr. 1966), I, p. 257.

[7] C. F. Burgess, 'Lillo Sans Barnwell, or the Playwright Revisited', in *Modern Philology*, 66 (1968), 23.

significant stage in the history of the appropriation of Shakespeare in the second quarter of the eighteenth century. The main purpose of this article is to identify the ideological purposes that *Marina* served in 1738 and, more generally, to show how Lillo's impulse to rewrite Shakespeare stemmed not only from his wish to update the original, but also from the realization that Shakespeare's romance provided the ideal battleground within which hegemonic discourses and cultural assumptions on gender, deviant sexuality, property and propriety could be challenged.

A close, contrastive analysis of Lillo's *Marina* with its Shakespearian original will highlight what Quentin Skinner refers to as 'intentions in writing',[8] or what Umberto Eco defines as *intento operis*[9] and what I similarly regard as the text's peculiar perspective on recurrent motifs, stock characters and plot-components which source and adaptation inevitably share. I will therefore concentrate on the divergencies, rather than on the similarities, between the model and its appropriation, in order to identify *Marina*'s peculiar perspective and its ideological position in relation to the Shakespearian original, on the one hand, and the wider cultural context of the late 1730s, on the other.

The most visible alteration in Lillo's *Marina* is a stronger emphasis on the title-character. Lillo excised the first three acts in the original and expanded Acts 4 and 5 into a three-act 'single tale' (*Marina*, A4r, 25),[10] which focuses on the heroine in distress and her trial in the brothel rather than on her father's avoidance of incest and his sea-journeys, ship-wrecks and bereavements. Lillo's fascination with Marina is usually explained as the direct consequence of current taste and theatrical conventions. Trudy Drucker, for example, argues that 'Marina, an admirable figure who was strong but never masculine, ... is an example of Lillo's accommodation to the growing taste for heroic female [characters].'[11] Michael Dobson also relates *Marina* to a peculiar group of theatre-goers, by identifying the unnamed 'sacred band' praised by Lillo in the Epilogue with an influential association of London gentlewomen, commonly known as the Shakespeare Ladies' Club:

> When worse than barbarism had sunk your taste,
> When nothing pleas'd but what laid virtue waste,
> A sacred band, determin'd, wise, and good,
> They jointly rose to stop th' exotick flood,
> And strove to wake, by Shakespear's nervous lays,
> The manly genius of Eliza's days.
>
> (*Marina*, H2v, 9–14)

In the 1730s, as Dobson explains, the Shakespeare Ladies' Club came to be regarded as the champions of a 'distinctly middle-class version of domestic virtue'.[12] By opposing the current taste for Italian Opera and vulgar entertainment and reclaiming Shakespeare for the stage, the Ladies 'proved decisive', according to Pearson, 'in changing theatrical repertoires in the 1730s'.[13] By acknowledging the influence of the Ladies on his decision to 'revive' Shakespeare, Lillo therefore showed that he conformed to what Pearson defines as a 'feminine aesthetic'.[14]

One can hardly deny that his audience's expectations must have affected Lillo's choice of subject-matter. This theory, however, fails to explain why Lillo should have chosen Marina as a model of feminine virtue in distress, as opposed to other Shakespearian characters, such

8 Quentin Skinner, 'Motives, Intentions and the Interpretation of Texts', in *Meaning and Context: Quentin Skinner and his Critics*, ed. by J. Tully (Cambridge, 1988), pp. 68–79.

9 Umberto Eco, 'Between the Author and the Text', in *Interpretation and Overinterpretation*, ed. by S. Collini (Cambridge, 1992), pp. 67–88.

10 All quotations from *Marina* are followed by line-reference to George Lillo, *Marina: A Facsimile* (London, 1969).

11 Trudy Drucker, 'Marina and the Spirit of her Time', in *Restoration and Eighteenth Century Theatre Research*, 10 (1995), p. 66.

12 Dobson, *The Making of the National Poet*, p. 154.

13 J. Pearson, *The Prostituted Muse: Images of Women and Women Dramatists* (Hemel Hempstead, 1988), p. 41.

14 Pearson, *The Prostituted Muse*, p. 39.

as Perdita, Imogen or Isabella. The striking resemblance in tone and atmosphere between Millwood's London in *The London Merchant* and the underworld of pimps and bawds in Marina's Ephesus, along with the substantial additions to the original brothel scenes, suggests that Lillo was attracted not only by the resiliency of Marina's virtue but also by the very nature of her ordeal in the brothel.[15] Although some critics have lamented Lillo's bad taste in lengthening the brothel scenes, which, 'unpleasant enough in Shakespeare, ... [are] too offensive to be tolerated [in Lillo]',[16] others have more perceptively remarked on Lillo's peculiar fascination with its subject-matter. Burgess, for example, noticed the incongruity between Lillo's 'talent for low comedy' and his traditional association with sentimental and domestic drama: 'Lillo borrowed the brothel scenes from *Pericles* in their entirety and even expanded them, an unusual undertaking in view of the aversion of the average eighteenth century, middle-class audience to that which was not "genteel"'.[17] I believe that the shift of emphasis from incest in the original[18] to prostitution in Lillo's adaptation is not simply a side-effect of Lillo's decision to excise the first three acts of *Pericles* and focus on Marina, in order to please his female audience, but also a reflection of a wide-spread concern with prostitution in the 1730s.

The sudden interest early eighteenth-century writers, playwrights, philosophers and politicians took in prostitution has a parallel only in the growing concern about an apparently devastating surge of crime in general, and of theft and robbery in particular. Last regards this phenomenon as a consequence of the emergence of a new conception of patrimony and private property during the first half of the eighteenth century:

> Was there a real emergency? Could it have been that the events were exaggerated so that the authorities could assert their power and at the same time protect property which was becoming more and more valuable and more and more symbolic of status as time went on?[19]

The term 'Robinocracy', first used in contemporary political satire and pamphlets, came to embody the aristocracy and upper classes' distrust of the new philosophy of government introduced by Sir Robert Walpole, which valued money and self-interest more than tradition, and supported the emerging mercantile middle class rather than the landed interests of the gentry. John Gay's *The Beggar's Opera* (1728), for example, is based on the idea that the highly sophisticated organization of the gangs of criminals which ruled the London

---

15 Although both *Measure for Measure* and *Pericles* offer vivid accounts of the underworld and the procuring trade, it is fairly safe to assume that Lillo was never tempted to consider Isabella as a potential heroine for a new play. Isabella and Marina face a similar dilemma, i.e. the ignominious ransom of a brother and survival and self-advancement through prostitution or sexual favours, but Isabella, unlike Marina, never enters the brothel. Besides, by the time Lillo adapted *Pericles*, the popularity of *Measure for Measure* was declining, mainly because of Isabella's moral complexity. Despite Davenant and Gildon's Restoration and Early Augustan adaptations, Isabella's character had little following in post-revolutionary drama.

16 Odell, *Shakespeare from Betterton to Irving*, pp. 258–9.

17 Burgess, 'Lillo Sans Barnwell', p. 22.

18 For a wide-ranging investigation of the incest motif in *Pericles* and on the Jacobean stage, see John Pitcher, 'The Poet and Taboo: the Riddle of Shakespeare's *Pericles*', in *Essays and Studies by Members of the English Association*, 35 (1982), pp. 14–29. See also, A. J. Lewis, '"I feed on mother's flesh": Incest and Eating in *Pericles*', in *Essays in Literature*, 15 (1988), pp. 147–63; Alexander Leggatt, 'The Shadow of Antioch: Sexuality in *Pericles, Prince of Tyre*', in *Parallel Lives: Spanish and English National Drama, 1580–1680*, ed. by L. and P. Fothergill-Payne (London and Toronto, 1991); B. T. Boehrer, *Monarchy and Incest in Renaissance England: Literature, Culture, Kinship and Kingship* (Philadelphia, 1992), and Sonia Massai, '*Pericles* in Perspective: Hereditary and Elective Affinities', in *Shakespearean Revisions: 'Measure for Measure', 'King Lear' and 'Pericles', from Source to Adaptation* (Ph.D. Thesis, unpublished University of Liverpool, 1996).

19 B. W. Last, *Politics and Letters in the Age of Walpole* (Newcastle-upon-Tyne, 1987), p. 89.

underworld was surpassed and eclipsed only by the legal associations of statesmen, lawyers and politicians, who hid their criminal activities under an aura of legality and respectability. Land-owners felt that their properties were seriously threatened under the new government. For the emerging class of merchants, bankers and stock-brokers, on the other hand, the acquisition and increase of personal properties became the easiest way of gaining social respectability. At the dawn of the Industrial Revolution, when England was turning into a colonial power, private property, rather than lineage, became the fundamental principle around which society was organized, and robbery, like any other form of offence against private property, began to be regarded as a particularly serious threat to society at large.

The growing concern with prostitution can be similarly interpreted not so much as the direct consequence of an actual increase in the number of the brothels in Drury Lane and Covent Garden in the 1730s,[20] as an indirect effect of the anxiety experienced by the middle and upper classes in the face of the new values ushered in by the Walpole administration. The fact that money and financial prosperity became a priority and industry a symbol of virtue led to a significant improvement in the general attitude towards the dignity of professions. As Speck observes,

> the eighteenth century marks a crucial phase in the history of the professions ... At the outset they were all generally regarded as corrupt; ... by the end of the century they ... had acquired respectability and honesty, qualities associated with the professions ever since.[21]

Prostitution, the 'oldest profession', did not enjoy a similar revaluation, but it did start to be regarded as a 'trade', through which 'goods' were exchanged for a 'service', and which, like any other profession, created wealth, or, more commonly, a means of survival for the poorest. In Lillo's new opening to the first brothel scene, the Bawd describes her activity as a 'business' (*Marina*, B4r, 15), as a 'useful vocation' (*Marina*, B4v, 9), as a 'trade ... no worse than others' (*Marina*, C1r, 1–3), and Bolt, her pander, as 'service to the publick' (*Marina*, B4r, 21–2), their customers including 'old Batchelors, ... young Brothers, ... disconsolate Widowers, ... Husbands that have old Wives, ... and Philosophers, Lawyers, and Soldiers that have none at all' (*Marina*, B4r, 31; B4v, 1–5). This view of prostitution as a 'profession' is shared by a large number of literary and dramatic works of the period. In Theophilus Cibber's theatrical entertainment, *The Harlot's Progress* (1733), inspired by Hogarth's six famous prints, 'A Harlot's Progress' (1732), the Bawd rejoices at the thought of the 'ample Gains' to be made in the 'procuring Trade' and shows no moral qualms or remorse: 'Then mock not our Profession, / Like Courtiers we, / Secure the Fee, / And laugh at the Transgression.' The Pimp similarly extols the universal quality of his 'profession':

> Pimping is a science, Sir, ...
> The Lawyer pimps to gain a Coif,
> While Porters pimp for Hire;
> Kind Betty serves his Worship's Wife,
> The Page pimps for the Squire.
> 'Tis pimping gains a large Estate,
> Makes Varlets wear their Swords, Sir,
> For Pimps oft look as big and great,
> As any Duke or Lord, Sir.[22]

More disquietingly, as recorded by Daniel Defoe's *Moll Flanders* (1722), or John Cleland's *Memoirs of a Woman of Pleasure* (1748–9), prostitution could provide 'unfortunate women' with the means to achieve social respectability and financial comfort within wedlock. Pearson observes that in the eighteenth century women

[20] For more details and figures, see Lawrence Stone, *The Family, Sex and Marriage in England, 1500–1800* (London, 1977), p. 616.

[21] W. A. Speck, 'The Harlot's Progress in Eighteenth-Century England', in *British Journal for Eighteenth-Century Studies*, 3 (1980), p. 127.

[22] Theophilus Cibber, *The Harlot's Progress, or The Ridotto al Fresco* (Los Angeles, 1977), pp. 6–7.

had to put up with much lower standards of living than in the past:

Middle class wives and daughters were increasingly kept away from the family business and regarded as decorative adjuncts rather than working members of the family . . . The situation was still more disastrous for poor women alone, who found it increasingly difficult . . . to earn a living from the work available to them, and had to support themselves by marriage or prostitution.[23]

Marriages of interest became the target of severe censure at the beginning of the century as a form of legalized prostitution. Moreover, the progressive decline of the Puritan standards that had informed both public and private aspects of life in the seventeenth century 'encouraged', in Stone's words,

the more open admission of sexual passion into the marital relationship with a resultant reshaping of the ideal role-model of the wife to include sexual and affective functions previously performed by the mistress.[24]

The equation marriage-prostitution emerges quite clearly in Daniel Defoe's *Conjugal Lewdness, Or Marital Whoredom* (1727). The distinction between wife and kept mistress became blurred and problematic. Fictional works like Lillo's *Marina* articulate the need to re-establish it.

In order to recover this distinction, Lillo reinforced a traditional view of female sexuality, according to which women are either asexual, celestial creatures, the saint-like and God-fearing inhabitants of the temple, or rapacious witches, the presiding deities of the brothel. Marina, for example, explains to the amused Bawd that a woman should be not only honest, as in the original, but also 'modest' and 'religious' (*Marina*, C3r, 29) and have 'sense of shame', 'fear of laws' and 'rev'rence of the Gods' (*Marina*, E4r, 29–30). Lillo's Marina is emboldened by her virtue. When Bolt tries to take advantage of her, she forcefully breaks from him, and scolds him harshly: 'Hence, thou detested slave, thou shameless villain' (*Marina*, C2v, 13–14). Even under threat, Marina is proud and class-conscious. Marina is turned by Lillo into a strict, indignant chastiser of vice. She addresses the Governor as a 'Vain, rash, mistaken man' (*Marina*, E2v, 31), and when he repents, she praises him condescendingly: 'Now you're a true and worthy Gentleman, / The gracious Gods preserve you.' (*Marina*, E3r, 29–30). Chastity is a militant virtue, and, in Thaisa's case, '[a]dds whiteness to the silver robe [she] wear[s]' (*Marina*, F4r, 29). The Bawd, on the other hand, is physically repulsive, as we can infer from Valdes' merciless description of her features:

Let any one be judge, whether my chin, somewhat black and rough I must confess, or thine, that's cover'd with grey down, like a goose's rump, be the more comely. Thy face is a *memento mori* for thy own sex, and to ours an antidote against the sin you live by. (*Marina*, C1r, 11–16)

The word 'antidote' reinforces the sense of pollution, contamination and disease already present in the original. Several similar additions relate prostitution to physical decay. To the Bawd's original description of her 'creatures' as 'pitifully sodden' (*Pericles*, sc. 16, 18),[25] Lillo's Bawd adds 'stale', 'sunk' and 'diseas'd' (*Marina*, B4v, 21–2). In both the original and the adaptation the brothel is a place where 'Diseases [are] sold dearer than physic' (*Pericles*, sc. 19, 123; *Marina*, E3r, 15–16), and where 'the food is such / As hath been belched on by infected lungs' (*Pericles*, sc. 19, 193–4; *Marina*, E4r, 18–19), but Lillo drives the point home by adding a new scene at the beginning of Act 3, where Bolt addresses the Bawd as a 'retailer of stale carrion, and propagator of diseases' (*Marina*, F1v, 11–12).

The new lines added to the original exchange

23 Pearson, *The Prostituted Muse*, p. 17.

24 Stone, *The Family, Sex and Marriage*, p. 543.

25 All quotations from *Pericles* are followed by line reference to S. Wells and G. Taylor, *William Shakespeare: The Complete Works* (Oxford, 1986), unless otherwise specified.

between Marina and Lysimachus in the brothel also highlight a radical redefinition of gender roles, which reinforces the distinction not only between a prostitute and a virtuous wife, but also between an inveterate rake and an eligible husband.

The revision of Lysimachus is one of the most significant alterations in *Marina*: whereas in *Pericles* Lysimachus is a marginal figure, in *Marina* he becomes a fully rounded character. Not without irony, Lysimachus is described as a 'great man' (*Marina*, E1v, 9), a current pseudonym for Sir Robert Walpole particularly popular among his political opponents.[26] Lillo's governor, like his counterpart in *Pericles*, is a reformer and not one of the Bawd's usual customers.[27] Unlike his predecessor, however, he is tempted. Lillo's Marina is endowed with new alluring qualities, 'bewitching eyes' (*Marina*, B1r, 5) and 'luxurious charms' upon which Lysimachus cannot but feast his 'aking sense' (*Marina*, E2r, 19–20); 'when sin / Appears in such form', the governor laments, 'the firmest virtue / Dissolves to air before it'. But, unlike his predecessor, Lillo's Lysimachus is also changed by his experience in the brothel. Marina teaches him the difference between lawful love and unlawful lust: 'Shall painted clay, shall white and red, less pure / Than that which decks the lilly and the rose, / Seduce you from the bright unfading joys / Your goodness yields!' (*Marina*, E2v, 2–5). Enlightened by Marina's teachings, Lysimachus is no longer attracted only by Marina's 'form' but also by her inner qualities: 'She's all a miracle, as chaste as fair' (*Marina*, E3r, 21). At the beginning, the governor is deceived by appearances and indulges his instincts because the image of the prostitute obliterates Marina and prevents him from seeing her as his future wife: 'had I known thee before – What a thought! – But sully'd as thou art I must possess thee' (*Marina*, E2v, 9–10). Only after Marina's words have dispelled the 'detested charms of painted clay', can Lysimachus see her for what she is: 'Thou art a piece of virtue, and I doubt not. / But that thy birth and training both were noble' (*Marina*, E3v, 2–3). If Marina's beauty was the cause of his 'short liv'd error ... /, [her] goodness and [her] wisdom have corrected [it]' (*Marina*, E3r, 27–8).

Marina is also changed by her trial in the brothel. The brothel is a frighteningly new world to her, where she loses her prerogative as the potential *subject* of a lawful exchange, royal marriage, only to become the *object* of an execrable trade. When first ordered to perform her duties, she cannot understand the language used by her guardian: she first wonders whether Bolt's mind is 'sound', and then protests that he talks 'strangely' (*Marina*, C2r, 15, 19). By the time she is introduced to Lysimachus, however, she has grown familiar with the 'economic' implications of her new position. She still pleads for mercy in the name of good morals and human dignity, but she also masters a new idiom. The following speech is organized

---

26 For more details on the ironic use of the pseudonym 'great man' in contemporary satire, see J. Gay, *The Beggar's Opera*, ed. by P. E. Lewis (Edinburgh, 1973), p. 16.

27 The issue of Lysimachus' characterization in *Pericles* is still open to debate. Philip Edwards, for example, claims that Lysimachus cannot be a reformer, because he is not 'invested with the same kind of dignity and awe which we associate with those grand deceivers, the Duke in *Measure for Measure* and Prospero in *the Tempest*', see P. Edwards (ed.), *Pericles* (Harmondsworth, 1976), pp. 23–4. Wells and Taylor similarly claim that Lysimachus' lines – 'I came with no ill intent' and 'had I brought hither a corrupted mind, thy speeche had altered it' (*Pericles*, lines 1906–7; lines 1901–2, in *A Diplomatic Reprint of Pericles* (1609), S. Wells and G. Taylor (eds.), *William Shakespeare: The Complete Works, Original-Spelling Edition* (Oxford, 1986)) – must be the result of censorship. For my part, I agree with Ernest Schanzer that Lysimachus' function in the original is totally 'perfunctory' and that 'Shakespeare', unlike Lillo, 'was clearly not at all interested in the Marina–Lysimachus relationship', see E. Schanzer (ed.), *Pericles* (New York, 1972). I consequently regard Lysimachus' characterization as a reformer in the original as perfectly consistent with its overall function in the second half of the play. For more details, see S. Massai, '*Pericles* in Perspective: Hereditary and Elective Affinities', pp. 202–5.

around a double register: the first three lines belong to the moralist Marina – 'To think me, Sir, / A creature so abandon'd yet pursue me, / Is sure as mean and infamous, as wicked.' – whereas the remaining lines belong to a new Marina, who has grown aware of the different value attached to her virginity in the brothel:

> What! waste your youth in arms that each lewd
> ruffian
> Who pays the price, may fill; lavish your wealth,
> And yield your sacred honour to the hand
> Of an improvident and wastful Wanton,
> Who does not guard her own!
>
> (*Marina*, E2v, 12–19)

Should Lysimachus enjoy her as a prostitute, Marina reminds him, he would not only commit a sin but also endanger his patrimony, reputation and social position. The brothel paradoxically provides an ideal opportunity for the 'housewifization'[28] of charming Marina and for the reformation of the potentially rakish Lysimachus.

This preliminary, contrastive analysis of *Marina* in relation to its original confirms the traditional view of Lillo as a conservative moralist and opposition Whig propagandist. The additions to the brothel scenes contribute to turning the heroine into an active reformer and the hero into a reformable rake; sexual deviancy and desire are accordingly exorcised by the strength of Marina's domestic virtue. The outcome of the two main characters' trial in the brothel, the royal marriage at the end of Act 3, represents an ideal blend of elective affinities and hereditary principles, of old values, Marina's chastity, integrity and sexual restraint, and new money, Lysimachus' 'power', 'gold' and 'pomp' (*Marina*, E2r, 26–7). The succession described in *Marina*, whereby power descends from Pericles to Lysimachus through Marina, re-enacts the genesis of the first elective monarchy in England, whereby power descended from Charles II to William III through Mary. At a time when the Tories were urging the recovery of traditional values through the re-establishment of a pre-Restoration model of monarchy, and the opposition satirical playwrights were too busy exposing Walpole to ridicule, Lillo promoted an ideal of monarchy, which, although conservative when compared to the political ideals in Joseph Addison's *Cato* (1713) or John Locke's *Two Treatises on Government* (1690), has proved so enduring in England as to survive the French Revolution, the end of the British Empire, two world wars and the approach of the second millennium.

Lillo's rewriting of *Pericles* is also visibly affected by the current medical discourse on prostitution and by the reformatory zeal which characterized the predominantly middle-class, if ideologically conservative, ethical climate of the 1730s. Several factors converged to encourage a more active involvement of political and social institutions in the reformation of customs: among them, the progressive decline of the bawdy courts, religious institutions which had enforced good morals in England since the Norman Conquest,[29] and the rise of a modern notion of medicine as a social science. As Roy Porter explains, medicine 'took on more public roles . . . Doctors began to examine the relations between epidemics and environment, pressing for better public health provisions and legislations . . .'[30] Modern medical discourse and the decline of traditional institutions led to an intense programme of social reforms and the segregation of the prostitute, the polluted, gendered Other, with the opening of the first specialized clinic, the Magdalene Hospital for Penitent Prostitutes in London in 1758.

These complex social changes found their way into Lillo's *Marina*. The authorities in

[28] I have borrowed this neologism from T. Olaniyan, 'The Ethics and Poetics of a "Civilizing Mission": Some Notes on Lillo's *The London Merchant*', in *English Language Notes*, 29 (1992), 33–47.

[29] E. J. Bristow, *Vice and Vigilance: Purity Movements in Britain since 1700* (Dublin, 1977), p. 12.

[30] R. Porter, *English Society in the Eighteenth Century* (London, 1982), p. 302.

Lillo's Ephesus engage in an unprecedented trial of strength with the underworld. Whereas in the original Lysimachus did not intervene to rescue Marina from the brothel, in Lillo he sends his soldiers to close down the brothel. In the new opening of the first brothel scene, the Bawd mentions a 'new order, so much talk'd of, for suppressing publick lewdness' (*Marina*, B4r, 12–13). The Bawd's remark is likely to be a topical allusion to one of the first disciplinary measures taken by the London authorities against prostitution at the beginning of the 1730s, otherwise known as 'the 1730 drive'.[31]

The increasingly public role of medical sciences investigated by Porter is similarly documented in Lillo's *Marina*. When Bolt finally manages to gain financial independence from the Bawd, he scornfully reminds her that, as a consequence of the 'new order', she will never be able to get 'a new vamped up wench, just come out of an hospital, to accommodate a friend with' (*Marina*, F1v, 14–16). Towards the end of the same scene, Bolt's teasing provokes the Bawd to such a frenzy of rage that she swears she would rather 'die of the pip without the comfort of an hospital to hide [her] shame and misery from the world' (*Marina*, F2v, 18–20), than die unrevenged. Although the Magdalene Hospital for Penitent Prostitutes was not open until 1758, twenty years after Lillo completed *Marina*, the changed attitude towards prostitution, the new public role attributed to medicine and the collusion between the dominant medical discourse and the current literary and dramatic treatment of prostitution had already created the right conditions for the 'medicalization' of sexual deviancy. The hospital, previously an asylum, a 'place of "hospitality" for the needy', became, according to Porter, a 'centre of healing for the *sick* poor' (my italics).[32] What Porter however fails to stress is that, as the full denomination of the Magdalene Hospital suggests, the hospital was also seen as a 'reformatory', the antechamber of prison.

Despite the visible influence of current assumptions on gender and deviant sexuality in *Marina*, a closer analysis of Lillo's additions to the Shakespearian original reveals a rich subtext of dissenting voices, which questions both the traditional view of Lillo as a conservative moralist and the oppressive sense of a Foucauldian collusion between power and discourse and of a collapse of knowledge – medical, aesthetic and dramatic – into policy.

Comedy and realism undercut the black-and-white distinction between good and evil, virtue and vice. The Bawd in particular, despite her abhorrent features, is a comic and ultimately likeable character. The juxtaposition of the traditional values upheld by Marina and the new 'values' of gain, financial prosperity and sexual gratification embodied by the Bawd has devastatingly funny effects. When Marina challenges the Bawd's conception of womanhood by claiming that a woman should be honest, modest and religious, the Bawd reacts with the outraged indignation of a proud landlady: 'Honest, modest, and religious, with a pox to you! I'll make you know, before I've done with you, that I won't have any such thing mention'd in my house' (*Marina*, C3r, 31–2; C3v, 1–2). When Bolt informs her that Marina 'has been talking religion to ... Lord Lysimachus', instead of using him 'kindly', she shows the same mock outrage: 'O abominable!' (*Marina*, E3v, 20–2). Similarly, when she finds out that Marina has been rescued by the Governor's soldiers, she regards the rescue as an offence against private property: 'This is your praying Lord, plague rot him for a cheating hypocrite. And so after all my cost and pains about her to no manner of purpose, he has her for nothing' (*Marina*, F2r, 12–15). When Lysimachus' soldiers close down the brothel and suggest that the Bawd should 'do what she never thought of', that is work, her reaction is equally ironic: 'A Gentlewoman, and work! I'll see you all hang'd first' (*Marina*, F1r, 21–2).

---

[31] Bristow, *Vice and Vigilance*, p. 26.

[32] Porter, *English Society*, p. 302.

Realistic details are also added to the episode of the Bawd's purchase of Marina from the slave market: the Bawd haggles with the pirates over the price and Valdes, the Captain of the pirates, proudly remarks on the unspoilt quality of his merchandise and the egalitarian rules his men abide by – 'We have laws amongst ourselves ...; we are distinguish'd by titles and office, each man hath a right to his proportion of every prize we take; ...' (*Marina*, C1V, 4–8). Although realistic details often add to the comedy of the brothel scenes, realism is also used to criticize and expose the hypocrisy and complacency of the middle class and the reformers. Realism effectively discloses the material basis of the values embodied by the higher-rank characters and by Marina in particular. Chastity, for example, is a virtue and a precious commodity to Marina, a royal virgin and heir of kingdoms, but, as in the original, Bolt reminds her that it 'is not worth a breakfast in the cheapest country of the universe' (*Marina*, E3V, 15–16), or, to put it more plainly, that her virginity is worth nothing in the brothel unless it is sold wisely. Lillo's Marina learns faster than her predecessor and buys her way out of the brothel. Whereas Marina in the original succeeds in persuading Bolt that she could 'sing, weave, sew, and dance' (*Pericles*, sc. 19, 206) instead of prostituting herself, and Bolt is confident that when he 'will make [his master and mistress] acquainted with [her] purpose, ... [he] shall find them tractable enough' (*Pericles*, sc. 19, 220–2), Lillo's Marina bribes Bolt with gold. Bolt, on his part, is not converted by Marina's arguments, but rather pleased with the bargain: 'Nay, I don't see why a man mayn't as well do a good deed as a bad one, especially when he's paid for it' (*Marina*, E4V, 4–8).

As money becomes the supreme value, necessity becomes the strongest motivation and justification for the characters' actions. Old Wilmot in Lillo's *Fatal Curiosity*,[33] while planning the murder of a young man, whom he does not as yet recognize as his only son, reaches the conclusion that, no matter how morally objectionable, murder becomes legitimate when 'Necessity, impatience and despair, / The three wide mouths of that true Cerberus, / Grim poverty, demands' (*Fatal Curiosity*, 3.1.171–3). George Barnwell, the young apprentice in Lillo's *The London Merchant*, is similarly talked into stealing his master's money by Millwood, a young but experienced prostitute. Taken in by Millwood's lies, Barnwell is convinced that stealing is justified by a noble end: 'if my heart deceives me not, compassion and generosity were my motives' (*The London Merchant*, 2.14.4–6). Following the same logic, Barnwell betrays his master Thorougood and his friend Trueman, and kills his uncle to inherit the family patrimony. Although the names of Thorougood and Trueman, and the affirmative and peremptory confidence with which the playwright condemns Barnwell's moral short-sightedness and Millwood's wickedness might remind the reader of the black-and-white tones of an old morality, Lillo states the motives underlying his characters' actions convincingly enough for the audience to take them temporarily on board. Lillo, for example, allows Millwood to explain why she embraced and persevered in the practice of prostitution. When Trueman accuses her of abusing her 'uncommon perfections of mind and body', she replies that

> [i]f such I had, well may I curse your barbarous sex, who robb'd me of 'em, e'er I knew their worth, then left me, too late, to count their value by their loss. Another and another spoiler came; and all my gain was poverty and reproach. My soul disdain'd, and yet disdains, dependance and contempt. Riches, no matter by what means obtain'd, I saw, secur'd the worst of men from both; I found it therefore necessary to be rich; and, to that end, I summon'd all my arts. You call 'em wicked; be it so!
>
> (*The London Merchant*, 4.18.15–25)

[33] Quotations from *Fatal Curiosity* and *The London Merchant* are followed by line-reference to G. Lillo, *The London Merchant, Or the History of George Barnwell and Fatal Curiosity*, ed. by A. W. Ward (London, 1906).

Critics often offer contradictory readings of Millwood's character: according to Jones DeRitter, 'the realistic elements in Millwood's ... speech[es] are there not to make the audience sympathize with her, but rather to give Lillo the opportunity to discredit the realistic point of view by revealing ... the depths of her depravity';[34] according to Trudy Drucker, Millwood in fact 'belongs to a sisterhood of independent, assertive, self-propelled personalities moved by the wish to use their good minds to manage their lives'.[35] Despite this divergency of opinions, most critics agree that Lillo's characters are free agents and their actions prompted by reason. It is interesting to compare DeRitter and Drucker again:

> Lillo apparently believed that the ability to make moral judgements depended to a great extent on the assumption that all behavior was the consequence of rational choices; given this predisposition, any suggestion that an individual's actions could be influenced by feelings and circumstances beyond the individual's control had to be invalidated as quickly as possible.[36]

> Evidently a believer in human (including female) self-regulation in an ordered world, Lillo shared the enlightened views of a sparkling age dedicated by its most influential thinkers to reliance on reason in the quest for personal and social liberty.[37]

The most innovative aspect of Lillo's adaptation is, on the contrary, the realization that values are determined by the material basis of a character's social status and condition: to the Bawd, virtue is abominable because it is unprofitable in the brothel; to Marina virtue is precious because it is an essential asset in the temple, where the royal marriage is finally celebrated. I therefore find John Loftis' analysis of *The London Merchant* more convincing than either DeRitter or Drucker's: 'George Barnwell's (read Millwood's) crimes – fornication, theft and murder – are, to be sure, crimes by any standard ...; yet the milieu in which they are committed conditions [their] interpretation'.[38] As Loftis also points out, 'from the social dislocations accompanying the growth of the mercantile community ... came the weakening in the conviction that drama should imitate an ideal order.'[39] In one of the most significant alterations in Lillo's adaptation, Marina describes her ordeal no longer as a 'ceaseless storm / Whirring [her] from [her] friends' (*Pericles* sc. 15, 71–2), but as a 'lasting storm, That swallows, piece by piece, the merchant's wealth, / And in the end himself.' (*Marina*, B1v, 18–20). Identity is no longer the result of the mutual recognition between friends, who by definition share convictions and values, but the accumulation, piece by piece, of a merchant's wealth.

Realism discloses the material basis of values and consequently the hypocrisy of the reformers. Prostitution will continue to exist, in the Bawd's own words, while 'The necessities of Gentlemen / must be supply'd' (*Marina*, B4r, 25–6) and 'while Women are to be had for money, love, or importunity' (*Marina*, B4v, 6–7). In other words, the 'customers' are as accountable for the social evil of prostitution as those directly involved in the profession, in that they create the 'demand' that keeps the business going. As the Bawd observes in an overtly topical allusion to Walpole himself and his notorious penchant for attractive women, the 'great persecutor[s] of persons of [her] profession ... are [her] best customers and surest friends in private' (*Marina*, D4v, 25–8); hence her valedictory prophecy, according to which while such persecutors 'are entrusted with authority, as sure as thieves are honest, strumpets chaste, Or priests hate money; this same sinful nation / Is in a hopeful way of reforma-

34 Jones DeRitter, 'A Cult of Dependance: The Social Context of *The London Merchant*', in *Comparative Drama*, 21 (1987–8), p. 381.

35 Trudy Drucker, 'Lillo's Liberated Women', in *Restoration and Eighteenth Century Theatre Research*, L (1986), p. 42.

36 DeRitter, 'A Cult of Dependance', p. 381.

37 Drucker, 'Lillo's Liberated Women', p. 43.

38 John C. Loftis, *The Politics of Drama in Augustan England* (Oxford, 1963), p. 126.

39 Loftis, *The Politics of Drama*, p. 160.

tion' (*Marina*, F1r, 27–30). The Bawd shows a prophetic understanding when she objects that the authorities' attempt to 'push the lewd out of sight'[40] would not free society from the curse of prostitution: 'if they will turn iniquity out of the high-ways, they must expect to find it in their families' (*Marina*, B4r, 22–4). Not until much later on did the Victorians realize that only the institutionalization of public lewdness could guarantee a counterbalancing contrast to private virtue.[41]

To take *Marina* as an example of the bourgeois and sentimental appropriation of Shakespeare in the 1730s is only partly correct. Lillo's adaptation is not simply nostalgic, middle-class and sentimental; it is rather a dialectic confrontation between old and new models of theatre, customs and institutions. If the erection of the Shakespeare monument in Westminster Abbey took place only a few years after *Marina* was staged and the establishment of the Shakespeare myth sanctioned by Garrick's Jubilee in Stratford-upon-Avon in 1769 was well under way by the end of the 1730s, it is also true that no agreement was ever reached on the issue of what values, political ideals or social group Shakespeare stood for. As Dobson points out, by the mid eighteenth century 'Shakespeare, or a series of alternative Shakespeares, came to dramatize ... specific contemporary conflicts, rather than coming to embody a single, monolithic consensus'. In Lillo's *Marina*, as a contrastive analysis in relation to *Pericles* has shown, the bourgeois values of domestic virtue, chastity and industry were certainly imposed on the original. Shakespeare, however, was not simply enrolled by Lillo as an authoritative mouthpiece; Lillo rather adapted Shakespeare in order to undertake a dialectic critique of those very values he is traditionally believed to embody univocally and acritically. Adapting Shakespeare in the 1730s meant both looking backwards and looking forwards.

---

40 Bristow, *Vice and Vigilance*, p. 22.

41 See, for example, E. Trudgill, 'Prostitution and *Paterfamilias*', in *The Victorian City: Images and Realities*, ed. by H. Dyos and M. Wolff (London, 1973).

# 'A THOUSAND TWANGLING INSTRUMENTS': MUSIC AND *THE TEMPEST* ON THE EIGHTEENTH-CENTURY LONDON STAGE

IRENA CHOLIJ

*The Tempest* is Shakespeare's most musical play, and the one to receive the most musical attention during the eighteenth century. Yet, little has been written on its musical and theatrical history during this period. In contrast, much has been published on the Restoration adaptations of *The Tempest*, and the music associated with them; some of this information will be summarized below. The aim of this article is to chart the production history of *The Tempest* during the eighteenth century, focusing specifically on the musical requirements and amendments. Because of its fusion of human and magical worlds, and the inextricable link between music and magic, music is necessarily an integral part of the fabric of the play: 'The isle is full of noises, / Sounds, and sweet airs, that give delight and hurt not' (3.2.138–9). The underlying presence of music is more marked than in *A Midsummer Night's Dream*, whose poetry is generally perceived as more musical, and with which *The Tempest* has many parallels. Both plays were much adapted. The adaptations of *A Midsummer Night's Dream* were principally musical, and generally much abridged from the original – normally focusing on the fairy world. In contrast, although there were a few operatic versions of *The Tempest*, on the whole it was kept intact as a five-act play, but with much incidental music. It was also significantly more popular than *A Midsummer Night's Dream*.[1] The performance history of *The Tempest* is instructive in that it reflects many of the wider musical trends that affected the eighteenth-century London stage. It also demonstrates the importance of viewing productions not in isolation, but always in the context of their continually evolving history.

Early eighteenth-century theatre history has its roots in the momentous theatrical changes that took place in the late seventeenth century. Among these were the introduction of women onto the stage, the greater use of singers and musicians, the introduction of stage machinery and the birth of English dramatic opera – essentially spoken drama in which music, dancing and spectacle (machines, splendid costumes and elaborate scenery) played critical parts. In contrast to continental opera, however, in these works the principal characters did not usually sing. Three of Shakespeare's plays, *Macbeth*, *A Midsummer Night's Dream* and *The Tempest*, were altered into dramatic operas at

[1] Charles Beecher Hogan (*Shakespeare in the Theatre*, vol. 2 (Oxford, 1957), pp. 717–18) places *The Tempest* tenth and *A Midsummer Night's Dream* twenty-first in terms of relative popularity through the eighteenth century. Following Hogan I have excluded from this article discussion of *The Shipwreck*, an adaptation of *The Tempest* made for puppets (performed seventeen times at the Patagonian Theatre 1779–80) and a pantomime called *The Duke of Milan*, which was given at the Royalty Theatre in 1788. Unless otherwise stated, performance details are taken from William Van Lennep, Emmett L. Avery, Arthur H. Scouten, George Winchester Stone Jr and Charles Beecher Hogan, eds., *The London Stage 1660–1800: A Calendar of Plays, Entertainments & Afterpieces Together with Casts, Box-Receipts and Contemporary Comment*, 11 vols. (Carbondale, 1960–8).

this time. It was this operatic version of *The Tempest*, adapted by William Davenant and John Dryden and first staged in 1667, that, with one exception, was produced during the entire first half of the eighteenth century.[2]

In this adaptation the basic character names and plot remain intact, but the language is modernized, there are some different sub-plots, and several new characters are introduced, allowing for more pairings and more sexual intrigue. Miranda is given a sister, Dorinda – neither of them ever 'saw man' – whilst, unbeknown to them, also living on the island is Hippolito – 'one that never saw woman'. Caliban gains a sister, Sycorax, and even Ariel is partnered by a female spirit, Milcha. Most of Shakespeare's songs are retained, but several more are added. In particular there is a new masque of devils in the second act, and Shakespeare's fourth-act masque is replaced by a grand masque of Neptune and Amphitrite in the final act.[3] Also, whereas in the original play only characters who are, as it were, sub-human or super-human sing (the monster Caliban, the drunken Stephano and Trinculo, the spirit Ariel, and the other spirits who put on the masque), Davenant and Dryden allow one of the main characters, Ferdinand, to sing. He joins Ariel in the duet 'Go thy way', a piece that Pepys particularly enjoyed.[4]

Much of the music has survived from when the Davenant–Dryden adaptation, further altered by Shadwell, was staged at the Dorset Garden Theatre in 1674. Pelham Humfrey composed music for both of the masques and for Ariel's 'Where the bee sucks', whilst John Bannister set the songs 'Come unto these yellow sands', 'Full fathom five', 'Dry those eyes' and 'Go thy way' (the echo song). 'Arise ye subterranean winds' was supplied by Pietro Reggio, and there is act music by Matthew Locke and also possibly by Robert Smith.[5] Giovanni Battista Draghi is known to have composed music for the dances, but this is no longer extant. Nor do we have music for any of Caliban's or Trincalo's songs, which were presumably sung unaccompanied and somewhat freely. In addition, two songs for Dorinda were also published: 'Adieu to the pleasures' (1674–5) by James Hart, and 'Dear pretty youth' (1695) by Henry Purcell. The lyrics of neither of these songs is to be found in any printed texts of the play.[6]

It is difficult to know for how long the Locke/Humfrey music persisted on the London stage, for it was replaced some time early in the eighteenth century by a new setting attributed, for many years, to Henry Purcell. In an important paper given to the Royal Musical Association in 1964 Margaret Laurie demonstrated that this new music, rather than being composed by Purcell, was probably John Weldon's missing

---

[2] The exception is the 1745–6 Drury Lane season. We know from entries in Pepys's diary that the play received its première in November 1667. It was first published in 1670 (Q70) and then, in a revised form, in 1674 (Q74). For a comparison of the texts of Q70 and Q74 see *After The Tempest*, introduction by George Robert Guffey (Los Angeles, 1969). Examination of a contemporary libretto of the songs from the 1674 operatic *Tempest* can be found in J. G. McManaway's chapter '*Songs and Masques* in *The Tempest*' in *Theatre Miscellany*, Luttrell Society Reprint no. 14 (Oxford, 1953), pp. 69–96.

[3] The fifth-act masque was added in 1674.

[4] Writing in his diary for 6–7 November 1667 Pepys describes the Davenant–Dryden *Tempest* as 'the most innocent play that ever I saw, and a curious piece of Musique in an Echo of half-sentences, the Echo repeating the former half while the man goes on to the latter, which is mighty pretty' (*The Diary of Samuel Pepys* edited by Robert Latham and William Matthews (London, 1974), vol. 8, p. 522). Pepys later asked Bannister to write down for him the tune of this Echo piece 'which pleases me mightily' (*Diary*, vol. 9, p. 189 – 7 May 1668).

[5] Peter Holman (*Four and Twenty Fiddlers: The Violin at the English Court 1540–1690* (Oxford, 1993), pp. 336–8) argues that three of the act tunes normally ascribed to Matthew Locke were probably composed by Robert Smith, to whom they are attributed in US–NH: filmer MS 7 ff. 23′–4.

[6] For a discussion of the music see Peter Dennison, *Pelham Humfrey* (Oxford and New York, 1986), pp. 94–109. All the music has been transcribed and edited by Michael Tilmouth in *Matthew Locke: Dramatic Music*, Musica Britannica vol. 51 (London, 1986).

setting.[7] The *Daily Courant* advertisement for the Drury Lane performance of *The Tempest* on 31 July 1716 announced: 'All the musick compos'd by Mr Weldon and perform'd compleat, as at the Revival of the play'.[8] This particular production had opened at Drury Lane on 7 January 1712, when it was advertised 'With new Scenes, Machines, and all the Original Decorations proper to the Play', though with no specific reference to the music. There is no absolute proof that the so-called Purcell setting was indeed composed by Weldon, and for this 1712 revival, but Laurie's evidence points overwhelmingly in that direction. Unfortunately, we lack prompt-books or contemporary acting editions of the play from this period, which could help date the introduction of this setting; the Purcell/Weldon version has some significant differences in its text from the earlier setting – mostly cuts affecting the longer musical numbers.

It is, however, misleading to think of the Purcell/Weldon music as having been composed by one person and all introduced at the same production. Although there was no doubt a critical point when a substantial amount of the new music was introduced (possibly 7 January 1712), a slower evolution had also been occurring – just as had occurred, indeed, with the earlier operatic *Tempest*, where some of the music for the 1674 opera had already been used in performances since 1667. The one piece that can certainly be associated with both the earlier operatic *Tempest* and the Purcell/Weldon setting is Henry Purcell's 'Dear pretty youth'.[9] However, the dances in the Purcell/Weldon setting also had earlier origins. The dance following 'Arise ye subterranean winds' is taken from Lully's *Cadmus and Hermione* (produced in London in 1686), whereas Laurie thinks that the remaining two dances are, because they appear 'archaic in comparison with the rest of the score', possibly remnants of Draghi's music from the 1674 production.[10] I also wonder about the authorship and timing of those two exquisite Ariel songs 'Come unto these yellow sands' and 'Full fathom five'. The tune of 'Come unto these yellow sands' was adopted by D'Urfey for his celebratory song 'Now comes joyful peace', written after the signing of the Treaty of Utrecht on 31 March 1713, and published in the undated *Musa et Musica*, vol. 2 and then in *Wit and Mirth*, vol. 5 (1714).[11]

As already noted, the text used in the Purcell/Weldon setting is shorter than in the Locke/Humfrey setting, with the fifth-act masque completely rewritten. This is to allow for much more expansive musical treatment, which is immediately evident in the choruses. The longest of these is 'The Nereids and Tritons' in the fifth-act masque, where two lines of text occupy 47 bars of music, followed by an instrumental postlude of 24 bars. Of course, it is not just the choruses that have been expanded. The Purcell/Weldon setting also

[7] Margaret Laurie, 'Did Purcell set "The Tempest"?', *Proceedings of the Royal Musical Association*, 90 (1963–4), pp. 43–57.

[8] As quoted in Laurie, 'Did Purcell set "The Tempest"?', p. 52. The advertisement actually appeared on 30 July. *The London Stage* fails to record these words for this performance, first noting them only for the following performance on 7 August.

[9] References to the music in the Purcell/Weldon setting are to the edition by Edward J. Dent, originally published by the Purcell Society in 1912 and subsequently reprinted separately by Novello (not dated). A full list of sources for this setting of *The Tempest* is given in Franklin B. Zimmermann, *Henry Purcell, 1659–1695: An Analytical Catalogue of his Music* (London, 1963), pp. 336–7. Whereas the various manuscript scores may have had their origins in theatrical sources, the publication by Harrison *c.* 1786 *The Musick in the Comedy of the Tempest*, is quite clearly a 'scholarly' edition of the music, not representing actual theatrical practice. The only manuscript which shows evidence of theatrical use is BL: Add MS 37027, which is also the only manuscript dating from the early decades of the eighteenth century.

[10] Laurie, 'Did Purcell set "The Tempest"?', p. 44. One of these dances, the 'Salors Dance', is found only in BL Add MS 37027 (f. 18). It is not present in the Dent edition.

[11] Laurie, pp. 45–6. Also Bryan S. Gooch and David Thatcher, *A Shakespeare Music Catalogue*, 5 vols. (Oxford, 1991), vol. 3, pp. 1507–8 (no. 14702).

makes more virtuosic demands on its solo singers, as is evident when comparing, for example, the treatment of the opening words in Reggio's 'Arise ye subterranean winds' with that of the setting attributed to Weldon. Similar demands are made in the masque of Neptune and Amphitrite, where the difficulties of Neptune's part, in particular, no doubt reflect the agile vocal abilities of the bass Purbeck Turner.[12] Other roles, too, require good singers. Ariel's song 'Dry those eyes', although not as fiery and extrovert as some other numbers, nevertheless calls for controlled, sustained, lyrical singing of a kind quite different from that needed in the more straightforward 'Come unto these yellow sands' and 'Full fathom five'.

Both the Locke/Humfrey and Purcell/Weldon settings are substantial musical compositions totalling, in performance, some forty minutes and one hour respectively.[13] Much of the music, however, though enhancing the entertainment, is not essential to the plot. And even when it does seem dramatically desirable it is often the function of the music, rather than any specific lyrics, which is of importance. Thus, although Davenant and Dryden's operatic *Tempest* was acted throughout the first half of the eighteenth century, it seems that the music attached to different productions often varied. For example, it appears that Humfrey's masque of Neptune and Amphitrite was replaced in the early years of the century by Purcell's masque from *Timon of Athens*.[14] Also, the *Daily Courant* advertisement on 30 July 1716, in alerting us to Weldon's music, suggests that this may be a revival of music that had been dropped in the interim. It seems likely that the masque was later sometimes omitted, or replaced by something else, or much shortened.[15] The theatrical manuscript BL: Add MS 37027, for example, has a somewhat curtailed final masque. This manuscript also completely omits Ariel's rather lengthy 'Dry those eyes'.

As well as cuts, however, there were also additions. It is clear from advertisements that dances, for which unfortunately we lack most of the music, were an important feature of the Davenant–Dryden operatic *Tempest*. They seem to have become especially prominent from the 1720s onwards. For example, for the performance at Drury Lane on 6 June 1723 we learn that the dancing was 'After the Turkish Manner, as it was perform'd by the Kister Aga and the Eunuchs of the Seraglio, for the Diversion of the Grand Signior at the last Bairam Feast'. At Drury Lane on 22 May 1727 there was a 'Dance of the Winds', a 'Grand Devils Dance' and 'The Dance of Waterman', whereas on 11 April 1737 the play included a 'Comic Dance of Fantastical Spirits (in Grotesque Characters)', the 'Waterman's Dance' and 'a Grand Ballet of Sailors'.

As well as dances new songs were added. The advertisements for the Drury Lane performance on 28 November 1740 state: 'in which will be sung two additional new songs, composed by Mr Arne'. Unfortunately, we have no further information concerning these songs. Since Mrs Cecilia Arne took the parts of Milcha and Amphitrite in this performance, it is possible

[12] Philip H. Highfill Jr, Kalmin A. Burnim and Edward A. Langhans, *A Biographical Dictionary of Actors, Actresses, Musicians, Dancers, Managers and Other Stage Personnel in London, 1660–1800*, 16 vols. (Carbondale and Edwardsville, 1973–93), vol. 15, pp. 58–9. He is listed as singing Neptune in the *Daily Courant* advertisement for the performance on 31 July 1716. It cannot be certain that the part was written for him but, since earlier advertisements fail to mention the masque and its singers, he is the first singer advertised in this part.

[13] Timings based on the recordings made by Christopher Hogwood and the Academy of Ancient Music (Locke/Humfrey) and John Eliot Gardiner with the Monteverdi Choir and orchestra (Purcell/Weldon). The Locke/Humfrey setting is significantly shorter, however, if the act tunes are omitted.

[14] See, for example, the advertisements for performances at Drury Lane on 5 March 1705, and 1 and 21 January 1707.

[15] When Kemble reintroduced some Davenant–Dryden elements into his 1789 production of *The Tempest* he used only sections of the two masques, as will be discussed later in this article.

that Arne's songs were written for either of these characters, and more probably Milcha. In the 1674 printed text, however, Milcha is only assigned the solo song 'Full fathom five', though joining Ariel for 'Dry those eyes'. No setting of either song by Arne survives, though Milcha may have sung other texts.

During the 1740s there was a move to restore Shakespeare's plays to their original versions. And so, for the 1745-6 season at Drury Lane, the Davenant–Dryden adaptation was replaced by Shakespeare's own play. Nevertheless, the legacy of the more musical adaptation is evident in this new production, not least in its retention of the fifth-act masque. *The General Advertiser* for 30 January 1746, announcing the following day's performance of *The Tempest* 'As written by Shakespeare', informs us that this revival contained a 'GRAND MASQUE, new set to Musick by Mr Arne', and concluded 'wi[t]h a Musical Entertainment (compos'd by Mr Arne) of NEPTUNE *and* AMPHITRITE'. With the Grand Masque was also advertised 'proper Chorus's and Dances', while the Musical Entertainment was to include Mrs Young, Mrs Sibella and others as 'Sea Nymphs'. The whole play was to be 'interspersed with Dances by Mr Muilment, Mr Desse, Miss Scot and others'.

Music for the various dances does not survive, nor does Arne's setting of the Musical Entertainment of Neptune and Amphitrite. Much of the Grand Masque, however, is extant. Evidently copied from an imperfect source, this masque can be found in BL: Add MS 29370. In the First Folio the instruction 'They sing' is given only for the twelve lines beginning 'Honor, riches, marriage, blessing' (4.2.106–17), which are also the only lines set in italics. Arne, however, used the entire text (4.1.60–117 and 128–38) excluding, as far as we can tell, just lines 64–9, 117 and 138. These were set as a series of recitatives followed by arias for each of the goddesses (Ceres, Iris and Juno), ending in a grand chorus with all three of them. Unfortunately, because of the imperfect state of the source copy, we lack virtually all of Iris's aria, as well as the last part of Ceres's aria.

Judging from Arne's music Mrs Sibella, who sang Ceres, was the least accomplished of the three sopranos in this production.[16] Her aria, accompanied (as are the others) by two violins and basso continuo, is really quite simple, with all the words set syllabically. In contrast, the short section we have of Miss Esther Young's aria, as Iris, shows her superior vocal talents. Both these singers, however, serve merely to warm the audience up for the exuberant flourishes of Juno, sung by Cecilia Arne. Juno maintains her position of superiority in the final trio, where she has the most prominent part. This last number builds to a splendid climax as the three sopranos are joined by alto, tenor and bass singers, and the orchestra of flute, violins, viola and basso continuo is augmented by trumpets, timpani, horns and oboes.

Also included in BL: Add MS 29370 are three songs for Ariel. The first of these, 'Come unto these yellow sands', is a simple, lyrical enough, but not terribly inspired composition, which lacks a chorus. This is followed not, as we might expect, by a setting of 'Full fathom five', but by an accompanied recitative of a non-Shakespearian text. The words are as follows:

> Behold your faithful Ariel fly
> To the farthest India's sky
> And then again at your command
> I'll traverse o'er the silver sand
> Doing thy hest what e'er it be
> Not with ill will but merrily.

This recitative is followed by a setting of Ariel's rather sing-song words 'E'er you can say come and go' (4.1.44–7), which suggests that the recitative replaced Ariel's line 'What would my potent master? Here I am' (4.1.34). Like 'Come

16 Mrs Sibilla (or Sybilla) was the stage name of the German soprano Sibilla Gronaman, who had sung in Arne's *The Temple of Dullness*, *Rosamond* and *Alfred* in 1745 (*Biographical Dictionary*, vol. 14, p. 357).

unto these yellow sands' this is a straightforward, and not very notable, setting.

A fourth Ariel song which needs to be mentioned here is Arne's charming and still well-known setting of 'Where the bee sucks'. This is not contained in the manuscript, presumably because it was so frequently issued as a single song-sheet in the second half of the eighteenth century. All four of these songs for Ariel were probably written for the 1746 Drury Lane production. However, they were not sung then. Instead they were replaced with compositions by Wilhem Defesch. This was due to an unfortunate incident concerning Mrs Clive. We learn of this from the *Memoirs* of Dr Charles Burney:

> Arne & she had probab[l]y had a quarrel before he went to Ireland; for she refused to sing his Music. And when he new set the Tempest, and she undertook the part of Ariel, he sent her the beautiful and characteristic air: 'Where the bee sucks there suck I' – she sent it back untried, and employed Defesch, a good contrapuntist, but a dull composer to set all the songs in her part.[17]

Burney described the same incident more colourfully in his article in Rees's *Cyclopædia*:

> Mrs Clive, after a quarrel and battle with Dr Arne, behind the scenes of Drury-Lane theatre, would perform none of the doctor's music, and when he had new set the Tempest, and prepared for her his charming air in the part of Ariel, 'Where the bee sucks', she refused to sing it, and employed Defesch to set the same words, and whatever else she had to perform in all her parts, which was a greater loss to the public, than disgrace to Dr Arne, who was as superior to Defesch in genius, as Mingotti was to Clive in the art of singing.[18]

The quarrel referred to, between Kitty Clive and Thomas Arne, would appear to be the one related also by Burney in his *Memoirs*:

> When one night M^rs^ Clive having undertaken a song in w^ch^ she was imperfect: as she was given to be out of time as well as tune; at a hitch, she calls out loud to the band, "why dont the fellows mind what they are ab^t^?" At the end of the Act Arne went up stairs to remonstrate against her insolence, when the only satisfaction he obtained, was a slap on the face. In return, he literally turned her over his knee and gave her such a manual flagellation as she probably had not received since she quitted the nursery; but as a proof that she had made a good defence, he came back without his wig, all over blood from her scratches, & his long point ruffles torn & dangling over his nails.[19]

This explains why Arne's 'Where the bee sucks' was first published in a collection of songs associated not with the theatres but with the Pleasure Gardens, where it was sung by Arne's wife. The song appears in *The Second Volume of Lyric Harmony Consisting of Eighteen entire new Songs and Ballads . . . as perform'd at Vaux-Hall Gardens By M^rs^ Arne, M^r^ Lowe & M^r^ Rheinhold. Compos'd by Thomas Augustine Arne* (London, 1746).

A unique copy of Defesch's songs for *The Tempest*, long thought lost, was discovered at the Marylebone Public Library in 1986.[20]

[17] Slava Klima, Garry Bowers and Kerry S. Grant, eds., *Memoirs of Dr Charles Burney 1726–1769* (Lincoln and London, 1988), fragment 40, p. 63.

[18] Abraham Rees, *The Cyclopædia; or, Universal Dictionary of Arts, Sciences, and Literature*, 39 vols. (London, 1819), vol. 11.

[19] *Memoirs*, fragment 40, p. 63.

[20] *The Songs in* The Tempest *or the Enchanted Island As they were perform'd at the Theatre Royal in Drury Lane by M^rs^ Clive and M^rs^ Mozeen. Set to Musick by W^m^ Defesch* (London, [1746]). I am grateful to Evan Owens and Elizabeth Gibson for drawing my attention to these songs, after which I wrote my article 'Defesch's "Tempest" Songs' in the *Musical Times*, 127 (1986), 325–7. At the time I was unaware of the Burney anecdotes, and I should like to thank John Parkinson for informing me about these. However, I disagree with Parkinson's interpretation of the events, as expressed in a letter to the *Musical Times* in August 1986 (p. 427). He suggests that Defesch's songs were written not for the 1746 production but 'for a later revival'. The later revivals in which Mrs Clive played Ariel were of the Davenant–Dryden alteration, whereas Defesch's songs were clearly written for Shakespeare's play. One of these songs, 'While you here do snoring lie', belongs to a scene cut in the alteration, and the text Defesch set of 'Where the bee sucks' is the Shakespearian version (with Lewis Theobald's emendations) rather than the

Contrary to Burney's dismissal of Defesch's works as 'in general dry and boring'[21] these *Tempest* pieces are quite delightful as was evident from a BBC broadcast on 24 August 1986. There are five songs in total: four for Mrs Clive as Ariel, and one for Mrs Mozeen (formerly Miss Edwards) as Miranda. The songs appear to be printed in the order in which they belong in the play.

The first song is a setting of the non-Shakespearian text also set by Arne – 'Oh bid your faithfull Ariel fly'. Its words, however, are slightly different from those used by Arne:

> Oh bid your faithfull Ariel fly
> To the farthest Indies sky,
> And then at thy afresh command
> I'll travers o'er the silver sand.
> I'll climb the mountains, plunge the deep
> For I like mortals never sleep.
> I'll do your task, what e're it be,
> Not with ill will, but merrily.

The setting is fairly simple, though there are expressive melismas on 'travers' and 'merrily'. Its position as the first song in the collection suggests that it was sung during Ariel's initial appearance during the second scene of the first act.[22]

Miranda's song which follows is also of a non-Shakespearian text:

> All fancy sick I am from love
> Made up with hopes and fears.
> Say why should joy my heart thus move,
> Yet fill mine eye with tears.
> So great the bliss which I receive,
> My life my dear from thee,
> That fear alas does make me grieve,
> Thou ne'er canst love like me.

It is a da capo song, accompanied throughout by flute and basso continuo. There is more harmonic interest in this piece than in the first, reflecting Miranda's confused emotional state, and there are some telling examples of word-painting on 'joy' and on 'fear alas', which rises chromatically. Otherwise, though, this piece is somewhat uninspired. It was presumably sung after Miranda's first encounter with Ferdinand, at the end of the first act.

In the next piece, 'While you here do snoring lie', an oboe joins the accompanying violins and basso continuo. A slow introduction, with heavy dotted figures and languid oboe line, depicts the sleeping Gonzalo and his companions. Defesch uses accompanied recitative for Ariel's opening three lines (2.1.295–7), moving from G minor to a brighter B♭ major for a lively triple-metre setting of the final three lines. The vocal part, though not complicated, is effective, and there are judicious touches of word painting throughout.

Ariel's third song, an agreeable setting of 'A're you can say' (4.1.44–7), has a number of similarities to Arne's setting of the same text, though Defesch's piece is more delightful than Arne's. However, Defesch did not surpass Arne in his setting of Ariel's final song, 'Where the bee sucks'. Nevertheless, Defesch's is a perfectly competent composition, despite its triple metre making the word-setting a little awkward in places. It is also unusual for being in da capo form. In this final piece Defesch took the opportunity of introducing his longest expressive melismas, with eight bars on 'fly' and eleven on 'hangs'.

It is a little surprising that Defesch did not set Ariel's songs 'Come unto these yellow sands' and 'Full fathom five'. Perhaps the music from the Purcell/Weldon version continued to be used, or perhaps the songs were omitted. Unfortunately, we lack a prompt-book or acting edition of this production. All we can surmise is that John Lacy, the manager of Drury Lane,

altered lyrics in Davenant and Dryden's play. Parkinson also suggests that Arne's 'Where the bee sucks', although first published in 1746, may have been written for the 1740 production. However, Burney's anecdotes imply that Arne's song was composed for Mrs Clive, and she only first took on the role of Ariel in 1746; in 1740 Ariel was played by Miss Cole.

21 Charles Burney, *A General History of Music*, vol. 4 (London, 1789), p. 670.

22 This is the position it occupies in later *Tempest* productions.

used the Theobald edition of the play (published in 1733) as his basic text. Theobald made two distinctive emendations to the lyrics of 'Where the bee sucks', which were not adopted by any other editors. In the first line he changed the second 'sucks' to 'lurk', and in the fifth line he altered 'Summer' to 'sunset'. Both changes are to be found in Arne's and Defesch's songs.

Why the 1746 production of Shakespeare's play received only six performances is hard to determine, since we lack any contemporary comment on the production. Burney suggests that Mrs Clive managed to sing Defesch's songs 'into public favour',[23] but this was clearly not enough. During the 1745–6 season the more popular Davenant–Dryden alteration had continued to play at Goodman's Fields, where it remained for the following season. And when Mrs Clive and Mrs Mozeen next played Ariel and Miranda at Drury Lane (on 26 December 1747) it was in Davenant and Dryden's adaptation. The last appearance of the Davenant–Dryden play during the eighteenth century was at Drury Lane on 27 April 1750.

For six years there were no *Tempest* performances on the London stage. Then, on 11 February 1756, a new operatic adaptation was produced at Drury Lane. Tate Wilkinson recalls its reception:

> The Tempest as an opera in three acts, with recitatives etc. was introduced that season, with a paltry dialogue ... Signora Curioni, an Italian singer, performed in it, but it was dreadfully heavy. – It went through with great labour eight nights, but not without the aid of the garland dance, well performed by sixty children, at the end of the second act, and the pantomime of Fortunas, or the Genii, after that.[24]

The identity of the librettist is disputed, but the music was composed by J. C. Smith.[25] The previous year his operatic adaptation of *A Midsummer Night's Dream*, entitled *The Fairies*, had been produced at Drury Lane, with slightly better fortune. William Coxe speculates on the failure of Smith's *Tempest* opera which, incidentally, only received six performances:

> The great success of the Fairies, encouraged Smith to make another attempt in the same species of composition, by setting to music the songs in the Tempest – But although the airs were by no means inferior to those in the Fairies, yet the piece did not meet with the success it deserved; a principal cause of this failure, was probably owing to the negligent manner in which it was brought on the stage. The season was too far advanced, and the decorations were indifferent.[26]

In fact the opera was, according to the prompter Richard Cross, received with 'Great Applause' on its opening night, bringing in receipts of £180. But, as Stone puts it, 'its novelty waned and few seemed to care for it after that'.[27] Some, like Theophilus Cibber, were even quite damning:

> and *The Tempest*, castrated into an opera. – Oh! what an agreeable Lullaby might it have prov'd to our Beaus and Belles, to have heard *Caliban*, *Sycorax*, and one of the Devils trilling of Trios.[28]

The libretto was published by J. and R. Tonson in 1756. The story is taken not just from Shakespeare but also from Davenant and Dryden, as can be seen, for example, in its use of the echo song between Ferdinand and Ariel, and the sailors' sub-plot. Thus, the characters Ventoso and Mustacho are borrowed from the earlier adaptation, but there is no Dorinda,

---

23 Entry on Defesch in Rees's *Cyclopædia*.

24 Tate Wilkinson, *Memoirs of his own Life*, 4 vols. (York, 1790), vol. 4, p. 213. The garland dance (not part of the opera) is only noted in the advertisements from the second performance onwards, and the opera was only followed by *Fortunatus* at its last performance, on 16 March 1756.

25 There is debate about Garrick's involvement in the libretto, which he himself denied (in a letter to James Murphy French, 7 December 1756).

26 William Coxe, *Anecdotes of George Frederick Handel, and John Christopher Smith* (London, 1799), p. 47.

27 George Winchester Stone Jr, 'Shakespeare's *Tempest* at Drury Lane during Garrick's management', *Shakespeare Quarterly*, 7 (1956), p. 3.

28 Theophilus Cibber, *Two Dissertations on the Theatres* (London, 1756), p. 36. Although the opera has one trio, there are no devils and no Sycorax.

Hippolito, Milcha or Sycorax in the opera. Nor is there any need for a masque. The title page of the libretto states: 'The songs from Shakespear, Dryden, etc'. Of the thirty-two songs introduced, the lyrics of four are taken from Shakespeare's *The Tempest* and another four from Davenant and Dryden's 1674 alteration. Ariel's 'Where the bee sucks' is not included, as these words had already been used in Smith's opera *The Fairies* the previous year. Other texts were appropriated from Ben Jonson, Edmund Waller, George Granville, Abraham Cowley, John Dryden and John Hughes.

Not printed in the libretto is an introductory dialogue, by way of prologue, which is present in the manuscript submitted to the Lord Chamberlain for licensing.[29] In this dialogue Heartly persuades Wormwood of the merits of English opera, and of the need to encourage English musical talents. It was spoken at the opening night, when it was 'much hiss'd & dislik'd'. However, when it was omitted from the following performance, it was 'call'd for, & had some Applause'. Although not printed in the libretto of Smith's opera, the dialogue was printed, in revised form, in the *St James's Magazine* for October 1762.[30]

Smith's music for *The Tempest* was published in full score by John Walsh in 1756. As with *The Fairies*, issued by Walsh the previous year, the score lacks most of the recitatives. However, it does include two very fiery accompanied recitatives. The first, with the eleven lines beginning 'Myself will fly on board', is an extension of Ariel's opening number 'Arise ye subterranean winds'. Full of rushing semiquaver and demi-semiquaver scales and arpeggios, it sets the appropriate stormy atmosphere for this tempestuous opening scene. The second is Prospero's twenty-one line speech beginning 'Now does my project gather to a head'. Here, there are local bursts of activity in the strings in response to such lines as: 'chase the ebbing Neptune' (ascending scales), 'fly him, when he comes back' (descending scales), 'set roaring war', 'bolt' and 'shake'.

Smith's opera contains three duets, one trio, and twenty-eight solo numbers. The overture is taken from his Italian opera *Il Ciro riconosciuto* (1745)[31] and there is an instrumental hornpipe to herald the sailors' entry in the first act. The libretto suggests that the final love duet between Ferdinand and Miranda should give way to a grand concluding chorus. The printed musical score, however, contains no chorus.

It is difficult to judge the effectiveness of Smith's opera looking just at the printed score. Smith's writing seems competent. Inevitably, one or two numbers, such as 'Dry those eyes', seem a little dull, yet others appear worth revival. Prospero's 'In tender sighs he silence breaks', for example, is potentially quite a humorous piece, with the scotch snaps and several pauses suggesting Prospero is gently mocking the young lovers – a sentiment quite different from Shakespeare's intention. Although Smith's opera received only six performances, several pieces had an independent afterlife. For example, Ferdinand's 'To what my eyes admir'd before' was printed in the second volume of *Clio and Euterpe*,[32] 'Full fathom five' sometimes replaced the so-called Purcell setting in concert performances of the Purcell/Weldon music,[33] and the duet, 'Whilst blood does flow within these veins' appears in BL: Add MS 31669 (ff. 30–2), a collection of vocal duets

29 Larpent MS 123.

30 Dougald MacMillan, *Catalogue of the Larpent Plays in the Huntington Library* (San Marino, 1939), p. 22.

31 Andrew D. McCredie, 'John Christopher Smith as a dramatic composer', *Music and Letters*, 45 (1964), 23–38; p. 26.

32 *Clio and Euterpe*, vol. 2 (London, 1759), p. 110.

33 William Coxe (*Anecdotes*, p. 48) comments: 'It must not be omitted, that when the Tempest, set to music by Purcell, was represented at the Concert of Ancient Music, the celebrated air, "Full fathom five", by Smith, was substituted for that of the original composer. It was universally admired, and has ever since been retained.' LCM: MS 990, which has music from the Purcell/Weldon setting, contains this substitution of 'Full fathom five', transposed down a semitone to D major, but with the chorus of the earlier setting added on.

compiled by R. J. S. Stevens in 1797. However, it was Caliban's two songs, 'No more dams' and 'The owl is abroad', which proved particularly popular. As we shall see, several of Smith's songs were used in later stage productions of *The Tempest*.

Two seasons later, on 20 October 1757, Garrick re-introduced Shakespeare's original *Tempest* at Drury Lane. Unlike the abortive attempt to restore Shakespeare's text in 1746, this production was a successful one, remaining at Drury Lane for twenty years. The principal musical innovation on this occasion was William Boyce's music for the fourth-act masque.[34] Boyce's setting is a far cry from Arne's of eleven years earlier. The text is drastically shorter, employing or adapting only fifteen lines of Shakespeare's play (4.1.106–13, 116–17 and 134–8). To these are added an introductory eight lines:

> Hither Hymen, speed your way,
> Celebrate this happy day.
> Hither, Ceres, haste away,
> Celebrate this happy day.
> With blithsome look and jocund mein
> Come and tread this short grass green.
> Leave behind you grief and care,
> Come and bless this happy pair.

Just two soloists are required, a soprano and a tenor, and neither part is vocally demanding.[35] The masque is divided into three sections, each linked by a short recitative, of which the first is accompanied. The key structure is simple, with the central piece in G major and the outer two in C major. Metre and orchestration is varied between the numbers.

It is difficult to ascertain exactly what other music was used in this 1757 production. A book of the songs and choruses was apparently issued gratis at the theatre, but there are now no extant copies.[36] The nearest we have to a prompt-copy is the Bell edition of 1774. This claims to present the text 'As performed at the Theatre-Royal, Drury-Lane'.[37] While in broad terms this description may be accurate enough, in some of the musical details this is not the case. As may be expected in an acting edition, the Bell publication shows a number of omissions from Shakespeare's text. It also has the altered words of the fourth-act masque as set by Boyce, although the layout is not entirely accurate.[38] However, it is with Ariel's songs that the Bell edition is least helpful. Some care is taken with the final two. 'Where the bee sucks' contains Theobald's emendations, which suggests that Arne's setting was used. And 'Before you can say, come and go', not identified as a song in the First Folio, is here clearly marked 'AIR'. It was probably Smith's composition that was used, since Isabella Young, the Ariel on this occasion, had also taken the role of Ariel in Smith's opera two seasons earlier.[39] Smith's additional second stanza, however, is not included.

The remaining three Ariel songs are problematic, since they are all printed as they are in the First Folio, and not as set by any composer.[40] Smith's settings of 'Come unto these yellow sands' and 'Full fathom five' may well have been used initially, but I suspect that they were later replaced by the Purcell/Weldon settings. The remaining Ariel song, 'While you here do snoring lie', however, was not set by

---

[34] The autograph manuscript of this masque is at Ob: MS Mus d 14. There is a copy at LCM: MS 92.

[35] Newspaper cast lists name only Hymen and Ceres in the Masque, whereas the 1774 Bell edition of *The Tempest* assigns the opening eight lines to Juno. The autograph score, however, reveals that the introductory recitative was in fact by Ariel.

[36] These books were available from the opening night onwards and were still being advertised in playbills as late as 2 December 1771 (playbill at the Birmingham Central Library).

[37] According to its title page.

[38] The repeat of the words beginning 'Honour, riches, marriage, blessing' occurs four lines too late in the Bell edition, and the first designation 'Recitative' is eight lines too early.

[39] Smith set the five lines as given in the Bell edition. Arne and Defesch used a different opening word, and set only four of the lines.

[40] This is particularly true of 'Come unto these yellow sands' and 'Full fathom five'.

Smith, and I doubt that Defesch's composition was used. That the song was indeed sung is implied in a review of a later Covent Garden adaptation of the play in 1776:

> The omission of *Sebastian* and *Antonio's* plot to murder *Alonzo* must be missed, if, abstracted from the merit of the scene, we consider only the loss of Purcell's divine air, which he set for *Ariel*, who wakes the King and *Gonzalo* with, *While you here do snoring lie, etc!*[41]

Unfortunately, the reviewer does not help us to identify the composer, as Purcell did not set these lyrics. Nor did Weldon, since this was one of the scenes omitted in the Davenant–Dryden adaptation. However, there is extant an anonymous setting of these words, once thought to be by Arne. It was first published by John Caulfield *c.* 1825,[42] and the attribution to Arne suggested by Alfred Roffe in 1878.[43] This attribution has since been rejected by John Parkinson, though solely on the grounds that Arne is not named 'in any other source'.[44] The setting is fairly short and simple, and I see no reason to doubt that it could be of eighteenth-century origin.

During the twenty years that this particular production ran at Drury Lane a number of other songs were added. For example, Vernon as Ferdinand, Champness as Caliban, and both Mrs Baddeley and later Mrs Smith as Miranda all introduced songs into their roles.[45] I suspect that most of these were taken from Smith's opera. Champness had played Caliban in Smith's opera, and no doubt introduced his 'No more dams' and 'The owl is abroad' into the play. Judging by which Smith pieces we know were used in later stage productions, I believe that one of Ferdinand's songs was almost certainly 'To what my eyes admir'd before', and Miranda's song was probably 'Sweetness, truth, and ev'ry grace'. In addition, it seems that some extra Arne songs were also introduced by Mrs Arne as Ariel on 4 April 1767. Whether these were some of Arne's earlier settings, or new compositions, is unclear.

As well as all these songs, dancing naturally played an important part in this production. The première on 20 October 1757 promised 'a Grand Dance of Fantastic Spirits (occurring after 'Come unto these yellow sands'); and a Pastoral Dance proper to the Masque by Delater, Giorgi, Sga Lucchi etc'. Similar comments are made in most subsequent advertisements.

Garrick's version of *The Tempest* was superseded at Drury Lane by Sheridan's new production in January 1777. However, several days before it opened, an operatic adaptation of *The Tempest* was offered at Covent Garden. Since no prompt-book or acting edition of this adaptation survives, almost all we know about this production comes from newspaper advertisements and reviews. The première was on 27 December 1776, and the following day's *Morning Post, and Daily Advertiser* describes its chief characteristics:

> An Operatical mutilation of Shakespeare's comedy of the *Tempest*, was performed here last night; *Miranda* and *Ferdinand* have now each of them two airs, notwithstanding which the whole is here reduced into three acts. The alterations consist of cuttings and transpositions; the *masque* is judiciously brought from the fourth act into the last scene, by which means the piece is wound up much more dramatically than it was wont to be.

41 *The Morning Post, and Daily Advertiser*, 28 December 1776.

42 *A Collection of the Vocal Music in Shakespear's Plays* (London, 1864), vol. 1, believed to have been issued separately *c.* 1825 (Charles Humphries and William C. Smith, *Music Publishing in the British Isles From the Beginning until the Middle of the Nineteenth Century*, 2nd edn (Oxford, 1970), p. 100).

43 Alfred Roffe, *The Handbook of Shakespeare Music* (London, 1878), p. 77.

44 John A. Parkinson, *An Index to the Vocal Works of Thomas Augustine Arne and Michael Arne* (Detroit, 1972), p. 10.

45 Vernon is first listed as Ferdinand 'with proper song' (later 'songs') on 30 October 1762; Champness as Caliban 'with songs' on 5 May 1767; Mrs Baddeley as Miranda 'with a song' on 16 March 1769 and Mrs Smith as Miranda 'with a new song' on 12 May 1773.

Attention is drawn also to the omission of the assassination attempt on Alonzo, as quoted earlier. The reviewer was clearly not impressed by the singing:

Mrs *Farrell* [Ariel] has certainly a fine tenor kind of voice, but she is very far from possessing that delicate kind of pipe, which the invisible agent certainly requires[,] not to say any thing of her figure upon the occasion, which instead of '*being able to lye in a cowslips bell!*' – is a full head and shoulders taller, and some few inches wider across the girt than the present *Prospero.*

This contrasts with the opinion of the reviewer in the *London Chronicle* for 26–8 December 1776:

we are in justice obliged to confess that the alterations of the Tempest are extremely well concerted. The music is excellent, and its merit is considerably heightened by the masterly manner in which it is executed by the orchestre. As to the vocal parts, Miss Brown [Miranda] deserved the highest applause; Mrs. Farrell did likewise great justice to her musical task. The rest of the performers paid the strictest attention to their parts.

Similar sentiments are expressed in *The Gazetteer and New Daily Advertiser* for 28 December 1776, where we also learn that the work was 'received with great and universal applause', but that 'Mr Mattocks [Ferdinand] did not exceed his usual line of mediocrity'.

More information about the music is given in the review in the *Morning Chronicle, and London Advertiser* for 28 December 1776:

The Music, which is partly the composition of Purcel, of Smith, Arne, and Fisher, has considerable merit, though the Airs are very unequally set. The performers in general did justice to their characters. Mrs. Farrell (who possesses one of the finest voices we ever heard, and sings with a degree of distinctness and power of execution, which reminded us of the old method before the ear was sported with by the modern custom of introducing a variety of unnatural shakes, which are not only difficult to execute, but which distract the attention, and deprive the hearer of knowing the words of the Airs sung) deservedly met with the warmest applause. Miss Brown looked prettily in Miranda . . . and spoke the words with more feeling and propriety than she is accustomed to exhibit.

The review ends, as does that in the *London Chronicle* quoted above, with the three airs that 'were most applauded'. These are Mrs Farrell's 'Arise ye subterraneous [*sic*] winds' and 'Where the bee sucks', and Miss Brown's 'Sweetness, truth and every grace'. The setting used for the first song is undoubtedly the Purcell/Weldon one, despite the omission of one line. Theobald's emendations make it clear that Arne's 'Where the bee sucks' was sung, and Miranda's song is taken from the Smith *Tempest* opera of 1756. Apart from these, we also know of a fourth song used in this production, a setting of 'Bid your faithful Ariel fly' composed by Arne. This was published in his collection *The Syren* (London, 1777), where it is headed 'The New Air in the Tempest Sung by Mrs Farrell In the Character of Ariel'. Unfortunately, none of Fisher's music has survived. Nor do we know anything about the dances, except that they were performed by 'Mr Aldridge, Miss Valois, and others'.[46]

The Covent Garden operatic adaptation received only seven performances between its première on 27 December 1776 and its final night on 13 May 1779. Its demise was no doubt due, at least in part, to the unexpected popularity of Richard Brinsley Sheridan's production of *The Tempest*, which opened at Drury Lane on 4 January 1777.[47] This ran for ten years,

[46] *The Gazetteer and New Advertiser* for 27 December 1776.

[47] Sheridan and Thomas Linley Senior were joint managers of Drury Lane at the time, though Sheridan has traditionally been associated with making the alterations to the play. The only 'proof' we have of Sheridan's direct involvement concerns catalogue entries seen by W. A. Harrison, referring to printed *Tempest* song texts 'altered by R. B. Sheridan' (J. Greenhill, W. A. Harrison and Frederick J. Furnivall, eds., *A List of all the Songs and Passages in Shakespeare which have been set to Music* (London, 1884), p. xx). Harrison did not see an actual copy of the song booklet. If the entries refer to the copies of the 8-page *Songs and Chorusses in the Tempest* (London, 1777) the attribution to Sheridan must have been made independently; there is no mention of Sheridan in the 1777 publication.

with a notable eighteen performances in its opening season.

The 1777 Drury Lane *Tempest* was a revision of the previous Drury Lane production. No acting text was published, but a carefully marked-up prompt-copy survives at the New York Public Library.[48] This shows quite a few cuts to the Bell 1774 edition, including the omission of the initial storm scene (which was replaced by a chorus and special effects). The play, however, remained in five acts and, in line with other productions, this latest Drury Lane *Tempest* alteration featured 'New Music, Scenes, Dresses and Decorations'. The new music was composed by Thomas Linley Junior, and the scenery was designed by de Loutherbourg. The dancing included a 'Dance of Spirits' in the first act, with the 'Grand Ballet' *The Double Festival* at the end of the fourth act, both by Gallet, as well as a 'Fantastic dance' in the third act. The prompt-book (p. 258) also calls for a 'Pigmy Dance' in the third act, which replaced the 'dance of fantastic spirits' in later performances.[49]

Linley's contribution to this production is preserved in a manuscript copied by the theatre scribe Joseph Gaudry in 1780, two years after Linley's tragically premature death.[50] It comprises an opening storm chorus, replacing the text of the initial scene, four songs for Ariel – one including a chorus – and a concluding chorus to 'Where the bee sucks'. This last chorus is, in fact, an arrangement of William Jackson's choral extension of Arne's song.[51] To the four-part chorus Linley has added horns, oboes, bassoons and strings. The same accompaniment, but with the addition of trumpets and timpani, is also used in the storm chorus. The words of the chorus are:

> Arise, ye spirits of the storm,
> Appal the guilty eye;
> Tear the wild waves, ye mighty winds,
> Ye fated lightnings fly,
> Dart thro' the tempest of the deep,
> And rocks and seas confound,
> Hark how the vengeful thunders roll,
> Amazement flames around.
> Behold the fate-devoted bark
> Dash'd on the trembling shore;
> Mercy the sinking wretches cry!
> Mercy! – they're heard no more.

This piece became one of the 'smash hits' of the eighteenth century, and was used in *Tempest* productions well into the nineteenth century.

Linley's Ariel songs were written for his star pupil, the young Ann Field.[52] The first two, 'O bid your faithful Ariel fly' and 'Come unto these yellow sands' were clearly written to show off Miss Field's vocal prowess. Unlike Arne and Smith, Linley also composed a four-part chorus to conclude 'Come unto these yellow sands'. The remaining Ariel songs, 'While you here do sleeping lie' and 'Eer you can say', are significantly less virtuosic, and seem more to resemble the earlier settings, particularly those by Defesch. Of these four songs 'O bid your faithful Ariel fly' is the only one which gained any lasting popularity.

It is clear from both the prompt-book and copies of word books of the songs[53] that Linley's was not the only music used. 'Full fathom five' was apparently sung not by Ariel but 'by a Spirit'.[54] Since the final two lines are marked as sung by a chorus of spirits this

---

48 Acc. no. 709081. The prompt-book was prepared by William Hopkins (Edward A. Langhans, *Eighteenth Century British and Irish Promptbooks* (New York, 1987), p. 190).

49 The prompt-book was prepared after the initial season.

50 BL MS Egerton 2493 ff. 2–57.

51 Jackson's Quartetto was first published in *Six Quartets Op 11* (no. 6) (London, n.d.). The *British Library Catalogue of Printed Music* and the *British Union-Catalogue of Early Music* both give a publication date of *c.* 1780, but the piece was certainly known several years earlier.

52 The *Biographical Dictionary* entry on Ann Field (vol. 5, pp. 240–2) assigns her no date of birth, but notes that this was her first theatrical role.

53 *Songs and Chorusses in the Tempest, as it is Performed at the Theatre Royal in Drury-Lane* (London, 1777). There are two extant copies, one at the Folger Library and the other at the Huntington Library.

54 *Songs and Chorusses*, p. 5.

suggests it was the Purcell/Weldon setting of the words, rather than Smith's, that was used. However, three songs from Smith's opera were used: Caliban's 'The owl is abroad' and 'No more dams', and Ferdinand's 'To what my eyes admir'd before'. As already implied, Arne's setting of 'Where the bee sucks' was also used. Such was the popularity of this song that it appears to have been sung at least twice during the play. It was first sung in its correct position, without choral addition. It was then given, in place of the Epilogue, as the closing number: '*Finalle* / Where the Bee Sucks & repeated / *As Quarteto & Chorus*'.[55]

One other song is given in the word-book, and this is Stephano's 'The Master, the Swabber, the Boatswain and I'. The only apparently eighteenth-century tune for these words that has come down to us is that published by Caulfield.[56] Labelled 'Stephano's songs, as sung by Mr [John] Bannister', there are settings of 'I shall no more' and 'The Master, the Swabber', with the two preceded by a three-part setting of the catch 'Flout em and scout em', here attributed to Henry Purcell. According to the prompt-book, all three of these songs were sung in the 1777 production. John Bannister, however, first played the part of Stephano at Drury Lane only on 22 February 1797. Nevertheless, it is possible that John Moody, who preceded Bannister in this role, may also have used these tunes presented by Caulfield. There are two interesting things to note about the settings. First, the tune used for 'I shall no more' is also the one, according to Caulfield, which was used for the Gravedigger's song in *Hamlet*.[57] It is, in fact, a ballad tune known as 'The Children in the Wood'.[58] Secondly, 'The Master, the Swabber' has only the first five lines (up to 'tang') and the final line set, with a pause on the word 'tang'. The intervening lines, which were presumably at least said if not sung, may have been considered, by Caulfield, too obscene to print.[59] As for the catch, 'Flout em and Scout em'. I do not know if there is any theatrical tradition behind the music printed by Caulfield.

Two final musical observations need to be made concerning the 1777 Drury Lane *Tempest* production. First, the prompt-book makes clear that the fourth-act masque was omitted and replaced by a dance. Secondly, there are numerous cues in the prompt-book for 'music', such as the 'marvellous sweet music' heard by Alonzo and Gonzalo in the third act. Unfortunately, we lack music both for these effects and also for the dances. However, we do know that some of the background music was 'played behind the scenes' by a musical instrument – 'the Invention of Mr Merlin'.[60] John Joseph Merlin specialized in creating combinations of pianos and harpsichords.[61] Exactly which instrument was used on this occasion is not clear; once again, the music has not survived.

A long and detailed review of the 1777 Drury Lane production appeared in *The Morning Chronicle, and London Advertiser* for 6 January 1777. Among other comments is a description of Ann Field's contribution: 'The child who performed the part of Ariel, acquitted herself very creditably; her manner of acting was extremely pleasing, and her singing delicate and pretty, but as may naturally be expected from a child, rather too weak'. We also read that the 'shower of flammable matter', presumably accompanying the storm chorus, filled the stage with smoke, and left the audience coughing

---

55 As written at the foot of p. 278 in the prompt-book.

56 *A Collection of the Vocal Music in Shakespear's Plays* (London, 1864), vol. 1, pp. 15–16.

57 Compare *A Collection of the Vocal Music in Shakespear's Plays*, vol. 1, p. 16 with vol. 2, p. 90.

58 William Chappell, *Popular Music of the Olden Time* (London, 1855–7), vol. 1, pp. 200–1.

59 The words given in *Songs and Chorusses*, p. 6 differ slightly from those in the First Folio. However, the differences lie in those lines which Caulfield has omitted.

60 *The Public Advertiser* for 6 January 1777.

61 Edwin M. Ripin and others, *The New Grove Early Keyboard Instruments* (London, 1989), p. 185. See also *Biographical Dictionary*, vol. 10, pp. 201–2.

violently for two acts. From advertisements at the beginning of the following season we learn that the storm chorus was moved to the beginning of the second act, a position it retained into the nineteenth century.[62]

The final performance of the Sheridan production of *The Tempest* was on 4 June 1787. Just over two years later, on 13 October 1789, London witnessed its final major *Tempest* adaptation of the century. This was an alteration by John Philip Kemble published by J. Debrett in 1789,[63] which 'restores' some of the Davenant–Dryden material long since abandoned by other managers. Dorinda and Hippolito are resurrected, as is the masque of devils and the masque of Neptune and Amphitrite.

Musically, Kemble seems to have chosen the most popular *Tempest* numbers from the previous seventy-five years. From the Purcell/Weldon *Tempest* we have Ariel's songs 'Come unto these yellow sands' and 'Full fathom five', as well as the masques just mentioned. However, the masques are drastically shortened. The devils' masque, sung by furies and placed in the third act, comprises only the opening duet and first chorus. From the masque of Neptune and Amphitrite just the solo number 'Halcyon days' is used. However, the four lines of text are marked 'Duet' and the last two lines are repeated, with the heading 'Chorus of Tritons, Nereids, etc', so this is clearly a rearrangement of the original. Not surprisingly, Arne's 'Where the bee sucks', with Jackson's extension, is also included. However, it is unclear whether or not Linley's version of Jackson was used.[64] At least two of Linley's other pieces were, however, used. These are the storm chorus, which opens the second act, and the solo 'O bid your faithful Ariel fly'. It is unclear whether Linley's music was also used for Ariel's remaining song, 'Before you can say'. Although Linley's opening word is 'Eer', in the 1777 word-book of the songs it is given as 'Before', which is how it stands in the prompt-book. If not Linley's, then I suppose Smith's setting may have been used.

We know that four other songs were also sung in this production. Two of these are Stephano's songs 'I shall no more' and 'The Master, the Swabber', which have been discussed above. The remaining two songs, however, were specially written for this production, and were composed by Michael Kelly. Kelly took the part of Ferdinand, and Miranda was played by his on- and off-stage lover Mrs Anna Maria Crouch. Kelly's songs comprise a solo for Miranda, and a duet for the pair of them. The words of Miranda's solo are:

To see thee so gentle a creature distrest,
With tears fills mine eyes, and with sorrow my
    breast;
O wou'd I possess'd of my father the art,
Or that I had his power, or he had my heart.
With tears I'll entreat him, with sighs I'll assail,
Can the sigh of my soul with my father e'er fail.[65]

The setting is undistinguished but is fully orchestrated for horns, oboe, bassoon, strings and basso continuo. A similar orchestra, but with two oboes, accompanies the duet. The words are:

---

[62] The prompt-book at the New York Public Library, as already noted, was clearly prepared after the initial season, since it shows the storm chorus in its revised position.

[63] J. Debrett also published a fifteen-page booklet: *The Airs, Chorusses, etc. in The Tempest, or, The Enchanted Island, As it is now Performed at the Theatre-Royal, Drury Lane* (London, 1789). There is a unique copy of this booklet at the Birmingham Central Library (S 347.31789).

[64] Linley omits Jackson's section which has additional words and is set in G minor. Although neither the 1789 nor 1807 printed texts of the play supply these extra words, nineteenth-century musical sources make it clear that Jackson's full setting was used for the 1807 production. However, since quite a few changes were made musically for the later production, that does not preclude Linley's version from possibly having been used in 1789.

[65] Words taken from the musical score (published by Longman and Broderip, London n.d.). There are minor textual differences in the 1789 printed play and word-book of the songs.

What new delights invade my bosom,
In every vein what rapture plays;
Whilst on thee I fondly gaze.
O thou art source of all my pleasure,
Treasure of my soul art thou.
Without measure, am'rous pleasure
Crowns my nights and wings my days.

Again, the setting is not particularly notable.

Finally, there were four performances of *The Tempest* at the Haymarket Theatre between 15 November 1793 and 4 January 1794. The cast lists suggest that it was Kemble's adaptation that was used at the theatre. There is no evidence of any new music being used in this production.

What emerges from this brief survey of the eighteenth-century production history of *The Tempest* is a rather flexible, audience-sensitive attitude towards Shakespeare's play. There were experiments, but devices which were known to work were repeated. Music and spectacle are expensive yet, done effectively, attract audiences. So, visiting dancers were exploited, and the presence of good singers in the company encouraged new, and additional, songs, some of which demanded virtuosic abilities. Large amounts of new music periodically superseded earlier settings, yet old favourites were constantly resurrected. And thus the century ended rather curiously, with the last productions of *The Tempest* in the eighteenth century (and indeed the first of the nineteenth) using a text containing alterations stemming back to 1667 and a medley of popular musical settings spanning the entire eighteenth century.

# *DOUBLE FALSEHOOD* AND THE VERBAL PARALLELS WITH SHELTON'S *DON QUIXOTE*[1]

A. LUIS PUJANTE

## I

The first English translation of *Don Quixote* (Part I), by Thomas Shelton, was entered in the Stationers' Register on 19 January 1610/11,[2] and published in 1612. In the winter of 1612/13 a play called *Cardenno* or *Cardenna* was presented by the King's Men at court, and again on 8 June 1613.[3] Then in 1653 Humphrey Moseley entered a manuscript in the Stationers' Register as '*The History of Cardenio*, by Mr Fletcher & Shakespeare'.[4] So far as is known, no manuscript of the play has survived. On the face of it, the play was a work of collaboration between the two playwrights, in the line of *The Two Noble Kinsmen*. Moreover, Cardenio is the name of a character in the first part of *Don Quixote*, and represents a well-known episode which could have been the source of the lost play.

Then in 1727 a play called *Double Falsehood* was produced at Drury Lane by Lewis Theobald as an adaptation from Shakespeare, and published the following year. The title-page stated: 'Written originally by W. Shakespeare; And now Revised and Adapted to the Stage By Mr Theobald.' In his preface the adapter stated, among other things, that he was in possession of three manuscripts of the original play, and took for granted that 'the Tale of this Play' was 'built upon a Novel in *Don Quixot*'.[5] Indeed, even a plot summary shows a very close narrative parallel with the story of Cardenio as told by Cervantes, despite the fact that the names of the main characters are different (Julio for Cardenio, Leonora for Lucinda, Henriquez for Don Fernando and Violante for Dorothea).[6] This suggests that the adaptation may have been based on the lost *Cardenio*. However, it is unlikely that Theobald had known of the Moseley registration, since it was not found until long after his death. Hence his rejection of Fletcher's authorship, which he denies in his preface to *Double Falsehood* against the opinion of some contemporaries (though in the preface to the second edition, published in the same year, Theobald seemed to accept the possibility of Fletcher's part-authorship).[7] Other than that, *Double Falsehood* develops like a tragicomedy comparable to Shakespeare's last plays, and fits tantalizingly into the pattern of betrayal or

1 This article is a revised version of a paper given at the International Shakespeare Conference, Stratford-upon-Avon, 1996, within the Intertextuality Seminar.

2 Edward Arber, *A Transcript of the Registers of the Company of Stationers*, vol. 3 (London, 1875–94), p. 204.

3 E. K. Chambers, *William Shakespeare. An Account of Facts and Problems*, vol. 2 (Oxford, 1930), p. 343.

4 Chambers, *William Shakespeare*, vol. 1, p. 538.

5 *Double Falsehood*, ed. Walter Graham (Cleveland, 1920), p. 29.

6 For a detailed comparison of the narrative parallels see Eduard Castle, 'Theobalds "*Double Falsehood*" und "*The history of Cardenio*" von Fletcher und Shakespeare', *Archiv für das Studium der neueren Sprachen*, 169, 3n.4 (Juni 1936), 182–99.

7 See John Freehafer, '*Cardenio*, by Shakespeare and Fletcher', *PMLA*, 84, 3 (1969), p. 509.

disloyalty, spousal contracts, marriage and final reconciliation that can be found in these works.

The complex problems deriving from these facts have stimulated studies in various directions. Leaving aside eccentricities,[8] we can see that some writers who have dealt with the *Cardenio/Double Falsehood* problem have tended to disregard Theobald's claims and to think that Theobald's adaptation was a fabrication or a forgery, the most extreme advocate of this theory being Harriet Frazer.[9] However, most scholars who have examined the issue seem to agree that there are more reasons to believe the information and the claims as they have come down to us than to disbelieve them.[10] Thus, in his well-documented article, John Freehafer concluded, among other things, that: (1) the original authors of *Cardenio* were Fletcher and Shakespeare; (2) the main source of the original *Cardenio* was the Cardenio episode in the 1612 Shelton translation of *Don Quixote*; (3) the original *Cardenio* was very probably cut and perhaps altered during the Restoration period, and further altered by Theobald; and (4) the lost *Cardenio* survives in *Double Falsehood*.

Recent research has made the forgery theory even more improbable. A note in a London newspaper of 1770, brought to notice in 1984, advertised a revival of *Double Falsehood* and a 'new edition' of the text, adding: 'The original Manuscript of this play is now treasured up in the Museum of Covent-Garden Playhouse'.[11] Even though the theatre building burned down in 1808, this newspaper information confirms Theobald's claim that there were original manuscripts of his adaptation. More recently, Stephan Kukowski has shown that there are many distinctive traces of Fletcher in *Double Falsehood*, whereas what seems to be Shakespeare's contribution is comparatively small, and that, therefore, the play cannot be a forgery, 'unless, that is, Theobald had inadvertently forged the wrong writer'.[12] Then, in a thorough study of linguistic markers in *Double Falsehood*, Jonathan Hope has concluded that the forgery theory looks 'very unlikely indeed', that the evidence gathered suggests the collaboration of Shakespeare and Fletcher, and that most scenes in *Double Falsehood* would seem 'to mix material from different scenes of any original text'.[13] Finally, the forgery thesis is implicitly disregarded by recent editors of English adaptations of Shakespeare: the Cornmarket series in the sixties, and the CD-Rom Chadwick-Healy in 1995 have included *Double Falsehood* in their collections, without committing themselves as to how much genuine Shakespeare has survived in the play. Further conclusions do not seem to be possible. As Stanley Wells has put it: 'For the present, and perhaps for ever, *Double Falsehood* is the nearest we can come to *Cardenio*.'[14]

If a basic consensus has been reached that *Double Falsehood* is not a forgery, but a real adaptation by Theobald of the lost *Cardenio*, then we must agree, particularly with Graham and Freehafer, that the use of the Cervantian source in the Shelton translation is one of the fundamental aspects of the issue. It is not only that most situations in *Double Falsehood* can be

[8] Such as Charles Hamilton's *William Shakespeare and John Fletcher. Cardenio or The Second Maiden's Tragedy* (Lakewood, 1994). Hamilton claims to have discovered a manuscript play which is in Shakespeare's own hand and which, according to him, is the lost *Cardenio*.

[9] See her *A Babble of Ancestral Voices: Shakespeare, Cervantes and Theobald* (The Hague, 1974).

[10] See, among others, Gamaliel Bradford, 'The History of Cardenio', *Modern Language Notes*, 25, 2 (1910), 51–6; Walter Graham, ed., *Double Falsehood*, Introduction; E. H. C. Oliphant, *The Plays of Beaumont and Fletcher* (New Haven, 1927), pp. 282–302; Alfred Harbage, 'Elizabethan-Restoration Palimpsest', *Modern Language Review*, 35, 3 (1940), 287–319; Clifford Leech, *The John Fletcher Plays* (Cambridge, Mass., 1962), pp. 144–68; John Freehafer, '*Cardenio*'.

[11] Brean S. Hammond, 'Theobald's *Double Falsehood*: An "Agreeable Cheat"?', *Notes and Queries*, 229 (March, 1984), 2–3.

[12] Stephan Kukowski, 'The Hand of John Fletcher in *Double Falsehood*', *Shakespeare Survey 43* (1990), p. 27.

[13] *The Authorship of Shakespeare's Plays* (Cambridge, 1994), pp. 91–100.

[14] *Shakespeare. A Dramatic Life* (London, 1994), p. 373.

traced back, *mutatis mutandis*, to a similar passage or situation in the Cardenio episode of *Don Quixote*, but that, as Graham and then Freehafer pointed out, in *Double Falsehood* there are significant verbal parallels clearly demonstrating the use of Shelton's *Don Quixote*. In this respect, Freehafer went through the Cardenio story both in the reissues of Shelton and in the various English translations of *Don Quixote* published between Shelton's 1612 version and *Double Falsehood*, and concluded that nothing in Theobald's adaptation points to the use of any translation or edition of *Don Quixote* later than that of 1612.[15]

However, as this paper will attempt to show, the Shelton translation has a stronger presence in *Double Falsehood* than has been established so far. In what follows I will first go over the verbal parallels found by Graham and Freehafer as presented by them, and then over a number that to my knowledge have not been noticed before. For the sake of clarity, and with a few exceptions, I will set out the parallels in separately numbered items, usually followed by a comment, except when they are obvious or self-explanatory. At the end I will also attempt to show the way in which certain textual features in these parallels support some conclusions in recent research which make the forgery theory improbable.

## II

Of the seven cases observed by Graham, four belong to the passage dealing with Dorothea/Violante disguised in the mountains, and two others to the stages preceding the enforced wedding between Lucinda/Leonora and Don Fernando/Henriquez. The seventh case, while being perfectly valid, is rather of the discursive/contextual type and will not be discussed here.

(1) Shelton, bk. iv, ch. i, pp. 253–4[16]

How much more grateful companions will these crags and thickets prove to my designs, by affording me leisure to communicate my mishaps to Heaven with plaints, than that of any mortal man living, since there is none upon earth from whom may be expected counsel in doubts, ease in complaints, or in harms remedy?

*Double Falsehood*, 4.2.39–47[17]

How much more grateful are these craggy Mountains,
And these wild Trees, than things of nobler Natures;
For These receive my Plaints, and mourn again
In many Echoes to Me. All good People
Are faln asleep for ever. None are left,
That have the Sense, and Touch of Tenderness
For Virtue's sake: No, scarce their Memory:
From whom I may expect Counsel in Fears,
Ease to Complainings, or Redress of Wrongs.

Graham's first case, belonging to the Dorothea/Violante passage, is conclusive. Though not exact verbal parallels, the two passages are highly coincidental, not only as regards the textual structure and the basic order of the elements, but also in the way particular words, ideas or phrases are used literally, replaced by close equivalents, or slightly expanded. These traits will also be found in many of the passages to be discussed afterwards. However, the other verbal parallels pointed out by Graham need to be supplemented, qualified or further commented on.

---

[15] Freehafer, '*Cardenio*', pp. 501–2. Before *Double Falsehood* was published in 1728, Shelton's version was reissued in 1620 (now with the second part of *Don Quixote*), 1652, 1672–5, 1706 and 1725, and the following translations appeared: John Phillips (1687), John Stevens (1700; a revision of Shelton's), Peter Motteux (1700–3), Edward Ward (1711–12; a verse paraphrase of Motteux's), and John Ozell (1719; a revision of Motteux's), as well as Edmund Gayton's translation of the Cardenio episode (published in his *Pleasant Notes upon Don Quixote*, 1654). See Carmelo Cunchillos, *Traducciones y ediciones inglesas del 'Quijote' (1612–1800). Estudio crítico y bibliográfico* (Universidad de Zaragoza, 1984. Unpublished Ph.D.).

[16] References are to Miguel de Cervantes Saavedra, *The History of the Valorous & Witty Knight-Errant Don Quixote de la Mancha*, trans. Thomas Shelton (London and New York, 1900).

[17] References are to Lewis Theobald, *Double Falsehood*, ed. Walter Graham (Cleveland, 1920).

(2) Shelton, bk. iv, ch. i, p. 254

This body, since it is not Lucinda, can be no human creature, but a divine.

*Double Falsehood*, 4.2.57

Since she is not *Leonora*, she is heav'nly.

Thus Cardenio/Julio's words on seeing Dorothea/Violante in that same narrative passage. However, the specific parallel between 'divine' and 'heav'nly' begins even before Julio *sees* Violante in that scene of *Double Falsehood*, since he says 'from Heaven' (4.2.9) and 'heav'nly' (4.2.32 and 34) from the moment he *hears* her play and sing her song. Incidentally, in what is his sixth parallel (the song of Cardenio), Graham seems to be right when he thinks that Violante's song may derive from Cardenio's lament (Shelton, bk. iii, ch. xiii, pp. 236–7), as Dorothea sings no song in the original passage in *Don Quixote*.

(3) Shelton, bk. iv, ch. i, pp. 255 and 262

Lady, whatsoever you be, stay and fear nothing
***
*** is it possible that you art named Dorothea?

*Double Falsehood*, 4.2.87–8

Stay, Lady, stay: can it be possible,
That you are Violante?

As quoted by Graham, the Shelton sentences are in fact made up of two from different stages of the narrative, thus suggesting that the writer of the original passage of *Double Falsehood* used 'Stay, lady, stay' because he remembered having read it seven pages before. While not denying this possibility, we might wonder whether the parallel with 'stay', apart from being perhaps a little strained, is really necessary. In Shelton, the complete sentence uttered by Cardenio when he interrupts Dorothea reads: 'Lady, is it possible that thou are named Dorothea?' In other words, inattentively or otherwise, in the second Shelton quotation Graham left out the word 'lady' at the beginning of the sentence, which, when seen complete, makes the verbal parallel more evident and the first Shelton quotation unnecessary, or at least not wholly relevant.

(4) Shelton, bk. iii, ch. xiii, p. 243

For, Sir, I know you very well.

*Double Falsehood*, 2.4.23–4

LEON. Know you Julio, Sir?
MESS. Yes, very well; and love him, too, as well.

This parallel refers to the message Lucinda/Leonora sends to Cardenio/Julio to warn him of her enforced wedding. The Shelton sentence quoted by Graham is what the messenger says to Cardenio; in *Double Falsehood* the messenger's words are an answer to Leonora. However, the parallel is actually longer. In Cervantes the messenger is telling Cardenio how he was asked by Lucinda to deliver a letter to him:

a very beautiful lady did call [me] from a certain window ... 'Brother, if thou beest a Christian, as thou appearest to be one, I pray thee, for God's sake, that thou do forthwith address this letter to the place and person that the superscription assigneth (for they be well known), and therein thou shalt do our Lord great service; and because thou mayst not want means to do it, take what thou shalt find wrapped in that handkerchief.' And saying so, she threw out of the window a handkerchief, wherein were lapped a hundred reals, this ring of gold which I carry here, and that letter which I delivered unto you ... And after, perceiving the pains I might take in bringing you it ... and seeing that you were the man to whom it was addressed, – for, sir, I know you very well. (Shelton, bk. iii, ch. xiii, p. 243)

In the equivalent passage of *Double Falsehood*, Leonora, from her window, calls a passer-by:

LEON.
How tediously I've waited at the Window ...
(...)
Sir, –
[*Enters* Citizen.]

CITIZ.
To me?

LEON.
As You were of a virtuous Matron born,
(There is no Doubt, you are:) I do conjure you
Grant me one Boon. Say, do you know me, Sir?

CITIZ.
Ay, *Leonora*, and your worthy Father.

LEON.
I have not Time to press the Suit I've to you

With many Words; nay, I should want the Words,
Tho' I had Leisure: but for Love of Justice,
And as you pity Misery – But I wander
Wide from my Subject. Know you *Julio*, Sir?

CITIZ.
Yes, very well; and love him too, as well.

LEON.
Oh, there an angel spake! Then I conjure you,
Convey this Paper to him: and believe me,
You do Heav'n service in't, and shall have Cause
Not to repent your Pains. – I know not what
Your Fortune is; – Pardon me, gentle Sir,
That I am bold to offer This.
[*Throws down a Purse with Money.*]
(2.4.1–30)

In a similar way to the first verbal parallel commented on earlier, the two passages are coincidental in the textual structure and the order of the elements, as well as in the way particular words, ideas or phrases are used literally, replaced or expanded. Also, the longer Shelton passage shows how the fact that the messenger knows Cardenio very well (as Graham pointed out) is anticipated by Lucinda towards the middle, when she tells the messenger that both the address and the addressee are 'well known'.

(5) Shelton, bk. iii, ch. xiii, p. 245
I carry about me a poniard secretly, which may hinder more resolute forces by giving an end to my life.
*Double Falsehood*, 3.2
Stage direction, '[Leonora] *Shows a dagger.*'

This last Graham parallel refers to a later stage in that part of the action, when Lucinda/Leonora is about to be married to Don Fernando/Henriquez against her will. Graham comments: 'Leonora then threatens to kill herself if Julio does not hide while the wedding takes place.'[18] However, the Shelton quotation should have begun in the previous sentence, which reads:

procure to be present at this sacrifice, the which if I cannot hinder by my persuasions and reasons

Then the stage direction in *Double Falsehood* should have been quoted with the sentence that precedes and follows it:

– see, I'm arm'd, and vow.
[*Shows a dagger.*]
To fall a bleeding sacrifice before Thee. (3.2.73–4)

In other words, Theobald's Leonora shows a weapon that Cervantes's Lucinda says she has and wants to carry 'hidden', but in fact Leonora also *speaks* about carrying a weapon, and what she says ('I'm armed') is clearly a textual reduction of Shelton's 'I carry about me a poniard.' Next, the presence of the word 'sacrifice' in both parallel passages does not seem to be an accidental coincidence, despite the fact that in Shelton 'sacrifice' is used figuratively for the enforced wedding. It is true that, as Graham says, in *Double Falsehood* Leonora threatens to kill herself if Julio does not hide during the wedding, but later in the scene, after Leonora swoons and 'a Paper drops from her', it becomes clear that she intended to 'do the Violence to herself' with the dagger, thus coinciding with Lucinda's intention in Shelton of 'giving end to [her] life'.

## III

In his important article on the *Cardenio* problem, John Freehafer devotes space to the intertextual relationship between *Double Falsehood* and Shelton's *Don Quixote*, refers to 'the six impressive instances' pointed out by Graham and cites some brief new ones which are quoted and discussed next.[19]

(6) Shelton, bk. iii, ch. x, p. 200
... with a thousand oaths and promises.
*Double Falsehood*, 1.2.141–2
the Interchange
Of thousand precious Vows.

Freehafer finds that Julio's words in *Double Falsehood* derive from the equivalent passage in *Don Quixote*, in which Lucinda confirms her

[18] Graham, *Double Falsehood*, Introduction, p. 6.
[19] Freehafer, '*Cardenio*', pp. 501–2.

faith to Cardenio as quoted above. While not denying this possibility, it also seems that Lucinda's words in Shelton have been transferred to a different situation in *Double Falsehood* concerning Violante, the other female character. After seducing her, Henriquez recalls what he did to her in the following way:

> A Promise first of Marriage – Not a Promise only, for 'twas bound with Surety of a thousand Oaths; – and those not light ones neither. (2.1.19–21)

In Shelton it is the seduced Dorothea who comments on the incident in the following ways (bk. iv, ch. i, pp. 262–3 and 264):

> [Don Fernando] took an image that was in my chamber for witness of our contract, and added withal most forcible words and unusual oaths, promising unto me to become my husband

> And then Don Fernando turned again to reiterate and confirms his oaths, and added to his former other new saints as witnesses. [. . .] And at his departure from me he said . . . that I might be secure of his faith, and that his oaths were firm and most true

In other words, in *Double Falsehood* the seducer's recollection of the incident derives from these three comments by Dorothea in Shelton, but it also seems that one of his expressions ('a thousand oaths') originates in Lucinda's words to Cardenio as quoted by Freehafer – in none of the three here can we see an exact parallel.

However, Freehafer's contribution to the verbal parallels can best be seen in brief significant points. Thus he observes that the chief characters in the original *Cardenio* must have retained their Cervantian names, since the names of some minor characters in *Double Falsehood* appear to derive from the Shelton translation. Freehafer mentions two. One is the 'Master of the Flocks', who is called 'Master' by Shelton (bk. iv, ch. i, p. 269), but 'Countreyman' or '*Rustick*' by later translators. The other is 'Roderick', which seems to derive from a marginal note in Shelton, and, though the Stevens translation of 1700 also mentions that name, it differs from Shelton and *Double Falsehood* in the other parallel passages.[20] However, among the minor characters in *Double Falsehood* deriving from Shelton two more names could be added to the ones pointed out by Freehafer: Lopez and Camillo. To be sure, Lopez was and is one of the commonest of Spanish surnames, but an Alonso Lopez appears in *Don Quixote* four chapters before the Cardenio episode begins. As to 'Camillo', it may derive from Camilla, one of the female characters in the tale of the 'Curious-Impertinent', inset in the Cardenio episode.

Freehafer also noticed that minor characters like Fabian, Gerald and Lopez appear briefly in the play but not in the dramatis personae, and concluded that their brief presence in *Double Falsehood* represents 'a remnant of a comic underplot that has been largely expunged'.[21] But as regards the dramatis personae, yet another small detail could confirm Freehafer's observation. In *Double Falsehood* place names are conspicuous by their absence. In the original story of Cardenio Cervantes is not too specific, either: Cardenio comes from one of the best cities in Andalusia, but which one? And there is the Duke Ricardo, but Duke of what? However, Cervantes does mention the Andalusia region a number of times, and tells how both Cardenio and Dorothea fly away to Sierra Morena, where Don Quixote and Sancho are wandering at that stage of the novel. But in *Double Falsehood* Sierra Morena becomes 'the Mountains', and Andalusia is expanded to 'Spain' ('France' is the only other place name used in the play).

Interestingly, 'Andalusia' appears in *Double Falsehood* at the end of the dramatis personae: 'SCENE, the *Province of* Andalusia *in* Spain.' This may be a remnant from the original *Cardenio*. Admittedly, the indication of place is not frequent in manuscripts or early editions of Elizabethan/Jacobean plays. But there are

20 See note 15, above.

21 Freehafer, '*Cardenio*', p. 505.

exceptions: 'Messina and its neighbourhood', in Beaumont and Fletcher's *Philaster*' 'Sparta', in John Ford's *The Broken Heart*: 'Florence', in Middleton's *Women Beware Women*; or 'an uninhabited island', in Shakespeare's *The Tempest*, to name just a few. Therefore, the lost *Cardenio* would not be alone in specifying the scene. Alternatively, it may have been added by Theobald himself, thus compensating for possible omissions of the place name in the adaptation, and perhaps even in the dramatis personae – here no character, not even the duke, is mentioned with relation to a place name, unlike the dramatis personae of so many Elizabethan/Jacobean plays.

## IV

So far, I have tried to show that most of the verbal parallels between *Double Falsehood* and the Shelton translation pointed out by Graham and Freehafer could be amplified either in textual extension or in number. Now I propose to bring in a number of new verbal parallels that, to my knowledge, have not been noticed up to now. As a rule, I will concentrate on intertextual and even literal coincidences that have a narrative support. Minor verbal echoes or coincidences that are not linked to the story line will not be considered. Unless stated otherwise, the parallels involve the same narrative situations with the respective characters, even though, as in the following one, the speaking characters are different.

(7) Shelton, bk. iii, ch. x, p. 201, and ch. xiii, p. 241

> he [Don Fernando] would . . . come to my father's house, under pretence . . . that he went to see and cheapen certain great horses that were in the city were I was born.
>
> Don Fernando . . . resolved to send me to his eldest brother, under pretext to get some money of him for to buy six great horses, that he had of purpose.

*Double Falsehood*, 1.1.34–8

> by *Julio*, good *Camillo's* son,
> [. . .]
> He [Henriquez] doth sollicit the Return of Gold
> To purchase certain Horse, that like him well.

(8) Shelton, bk. iii, ch. xiii, p. 244

> and the success of this affair shall let you to perceive whether I love you well or no. I beseech Almighty God that this may arrive unto your hands before mine shall be in danger to join itself with his [Don Fernando's].

*Double Falsehood*, 3.1.6–13

> She bids me fill my Memory with her danger;
> [. . .]
> Lower, she tells me here, that this affair
> Shall yield a Testimony of her Love:
> And prays, her Letter may come safely and sudden.
> This pray's the Heavens have heard, and I beseech 'em,
> To hear all Pray'rs she makes.

This case, which has to do with the letter Lucinda/Leonora sends to Cardenio/Julio telling him of her enforced wedding with Don Fernando/Henriquez, can be added to the Graham parallel dealing with the way Lucinda was going to send the message (item 4). Here the parallel is typical of the way in which the Shelton text tends to be transformed in *Double Falsehood*. The last lines reproduce two very specific words within the Shelton passage ('affair' and 'danger'), and although the verbs or verbal expressions in Shelton are not used literally, the idea is the same: 'shall let you to perceive whether I love you well' is rewritten 'Shall yield a Testimony of her Love', and 'I beseech Almighty God' becomes 'And [she] prays.' Obviously, the speaking character having changed (Lucinda in *Don Quixote*, Julio in *Double Falsehood*), the verbal expressions are affected, while the nouns can be literally transcribed. Moreover, the change from prose to verse does not prevent single words from being easily incorporated, whereas verbs, periphrases, etc., are adapted to verse with more difficulty.

(9) Shelton, bk. iii, ch. xiii, p. 245

> for if thou carriest a poniard to defend thy credit, I do here likewise bear a sword.

*Double Falsehood*, 3.2.59–60

What! stay, and see thee ravish'd from my Arms?
I'll force thy Passage. Wear I not a Sword?

This parallel belongs to the interview between Cardenio/Julio and Lucinda/Leonora just before the latter's enforced wedding to Don Fernando/Henriquez. As it involves Cardenio/Julio's reaction on hearing that she carries a poniard, it can be added to the Graham parallel discussed above (item 5). Besides, it is also possible that Lucinda's reference to Cardenio's bearing a sword had been used more literally at the beginning of the scene, when Leonora says to herself before the enforced wedding: 'thus provoke a Man, / that bears a Sword ...' (3.2.18–19).

Later in the same passage and scene, respectively, there is a highly specific verbal parallel when Lucinda/Leonora faints at her wedding:

(10) Shelton, bk. iii, ch. xiii, p. 248
All the house was in a tumult for this sudden amazement of Lucinda.
*Double Falsehood*, 3.2.170
*Don Bernard*, this wild Tumult soon will cease.

The next eight parallels deal with incidents in the lives of Cardenio/Julio and Dorothea/Violante when they are in the mountains. In the following one the information has been clearly compressed and some details omitted, though some textual parallels are evident.

(11) Shelton, bk. iii, ch. ix, pp. 192–3 and 194
we did not see him [Cardenio] a good many of days, until by chance one of our shepherds came by with our provision of victuals; to whom he drew near, without speaking a word, and spurned and beat him, well-favouredly, and after went to the ass which carried our victuals, and taking away all the bread and cheese that was there, he fled into the mountain with great wonderful speed ... We requested him likewise, that whensoever he had any need of meat ... he should tell us where we might find him, and we would bring it to him with great love and diligence.

although the shepherds do offer him meat willingly, yet will not he receive, unless he take it with buffets.
*Double Falsehood*, 4.1.10–12
Why, now and then he [Julio] takes our Victuals from us, tho' we desire him to eat; and instead of a short Grace, beats us well and soundly, and then falls to.

(12) Shelton, bk. iii, ch. ix, p. 193
And, touching his dwelling or place of abode, he said that he had none other than that where the night overtook him.
*Double Falsehood*, 4.1.13–14
MAST. Where lies He?
I SHEP. Ev'n where the Night o'ertakes him.

(13) Shelton, bk. iii, ch. ix, p. 194
for when he is taken with this fit of madness
*Double Falsehood*, 4.1.24–5 and 97–8
He seems much disturb'd: I believe the mad Fit is upon him.

I fear, his Fit is returning. Take heed of all hands.

(14) Shelton, bk. iii, ch. ix, pp. 192–3
almost two days in the most solitary places of this mountain
*Double Falsehood*, 4.2.5–6
These wild and solitary places, Sir,
But feed your Pain.

(15) Shelton, bk. iv, ch. ii, p. 270
the state in which I am, and thou mayst behold – ragged, naked, abandoned by all human comfort.
*Double Falsehood*, 4.2.92–3
And I, as far from any earthly Comfort
That I know yet, the much-wronged *Julio!*

(16) Shelton, bk. iv, ch. i, p. 254 and 255
they beheld a young youth behind a rock ... attired like a country swain

and thereby they knew the supposed swain to be a delicate woman
*Double Falsehood*, 4.1.134–7
Savours of soft and female Delicacy.
He but puts on this Seeming
[...]
He plays the Swain, rather to cloak some purpose

This parallel and the next two concern the life of Dorothea/Violante in the mountains disguised as a boy. In *Double Falsehood* the comments on her feminine delicacy have been transferred to the Master of the Flocks. This transference helps to support the presence of this character in this part of the play, and particularly the motivation for his sexual harassment of Violante afterwards (both the character and his sexual intentions are mentioned very briefly by Cervantes when narrating the original incident between Dorothea and her master).

(17) Shelton, bk. iv, ch. ii, p. 270

The audients of her sad story felt great motions both of pity and admiration for her misfortunes

*Double Falsehood*, 4.1.173–8

I will be a Woman; and begin
So sad a Story, that if there be aught
Of humane in you, or a Soul that's gentle,
You cannot chuse but pity my lost Youth.

In the *Double Falsehood* quotation a similar case of transference can be observed with the same purpose as in the previous parallel. Here it is Violante herself who is asking the Master not to take sexual advantage of her. Incidentally, the Master of the Flocks is also given a rudeness that finds no antecedent in Cervantes's brief reference to him. This aspect may have been transferred from young Andrew's master, who beat his boy because he demanded his wages from him, and had to face Don Quixote's sense of justice. Now Andrew reappears in the course of the Cardenio episode, and the previous incident is recalled by Don Quixote, who calls Andrew's master a 'rude fellow' (Shelton, bk. iv, ch. iv, p. 301). I offer this only as a possibility, but this description might well be the textual source for 'brute fellow' with which Roderick characterizes the Master of the Flocks after thwarting his sexual harassment of Violante (4.1.99).

(18) Shelton, bk. iv, ch. i, p. 261

and the traitor caused tears to give credit to his words, and sighs to give countenance to his intention.

*Double Falsehood*, 4.2.62–6

Yon Maids . . .
[. . .]
Be wise; and to an Oath no more give credit,
To Tears, to Vows, (false Both!) or any Thing
A Man shall promise

In the Shelton text Dorothea is telling her hearers about her seducer. In the *Double Falsehood* quotation the lonely Violante, under the influence of her seduction, rhetorically warns all maids in a like situation. Seeing the use of 'Oath' and 'promise' here, this rhetorical address might also derive partially from Lucinda's words to Cardenio and from Dorothea's story as quoted above (item 6).

The last two parallels belong to the end of the story and the play. As a comparison shows, the reunion and final reconciliation of the chief characters is not worked out in *Double Falsehood* in exactly the same way as in Cervantes.[22] One of the differences is expressed in the parallel that follows, which involves a transference:

(19) Shelton, bk. iv, ch. ix, p. 369

The curate presently repaired to take off the veil of her face and cast water thereon.

*Double Falsehood*, 5.1.1, 4.2.47 and 50–1

Stage direction, '*Enter* . . . Leonora *veil'd* . . .'
Stage direction, '*Enter* Leonora *veil'd* . . .'
*Don Bernard* finds beneath
This Veil his Daughter.

In Cervantes Dorothea, who wears a veil, faints on seeing her spouse Don Fernando. In *Double Falsehood* the veil is worn by Leonora, Lucinda's counterpart.

(20) Shelton, bk. iv, ch. ix, p. 371

Witness shall also be thine own handwriting

*Double Falsehood*, 5.2.171–3

Here is a letter, Brother,
[. . .]
The Writing, yours.

This last parallel, one of the shortest, is also one of the most interesting. The situation is the same in both works: Don Fernando/Henriquez is called to account for breaking his promise of marriage to Dorothea/Violante after seducing her. In the Shelton sentence Dorothea is reminding Don Fernando of his promise. In the

[22] The dénouement of *Double Falsehood*, which contains the theme of the restoration of lost children to their parents, is more in line with the ending of Shakespeare's romances than with that of the Cardenio story in Cervantes. See Bradford, 'The History of Cardenio', p. 56.

*Double Falsehood* lines Roderick addresses his brother Henriquez and shows him the letter he wrote to Violante (in 2.2.27–31) after having enjoyed her. However, in Cervantes, despite the fact that Dorothea told her story in great detail, she did not say that Don Fernando had written her a letter. If Cervantes had thought of this then, he might have mentioned it as an aggravating circumstance of the deception. Be that as it may, it turns out that the letter written by Henriquez to Violante in *Double Falsehood*, read earlier in the play and shown now as evidence against Henriquez, is not based on a letter, note or document mentioned by Dorothea in *Don Quixote*, but only on this brief reference at the end of the Cardenio episode which involves a contradiction in Cervantes.[23]

## V

The study of sources does not consist only in parallel-hunting, but it benefits from the establishment of real verbal parallels (i.e., not vague echoes).[24] By the same token, the study of literary relationships that aspires to go beyond verbal parallels needs a firm ground. Supplementing the parallels found by Graham and Freehafer has shown how much more the Shelton translation was at the basis of the play than has been thought before. Therefore, although echoes of Shelton and others can also be found outside the narrative development, the number of significant close parallels in equivalent passages now establishes conclusively Shelton's translation of *Don Quixote* as a proximate source: so proximate that it appears to have been at the writer's elbow in the course of the writing.

Moreover, if *Double Falsehood* is not a fabrication or a forgery, but a real adaptation of the lost *Cardenio*; if one of the methods of adaptation consisted in reducing the original work (*Double Falsehood* is a very short play), then either Theobald, or perhaps his Restoration predecessors in possession of the manuscripts, or both, did away with much Jacobean material in adapting the original *Cardenio*, and part of it could well have derived from Shelton. As Freehafer observed,[25] *Cardenio* was probably much more heavily indebted than *Double Falsehood* to the Shelton translation. It is also probable that the reduction affected the scenes attributed to Shakespeare (at least, up to and including 2.2) much more than those set down to Fletcher: a comparison between *The Two Noble Kinsmen* and Davenant's revision of this play shows that the latter 'left not a line of the passages most confidently ascribed to Shakespeare intact, although several of Fletcher's passages survive with only minor alterations'.[26] And Theobald had no qualms, either, about changing and excising a Shakespearian text at will, as we can see in his adaptation of *Richard II*.[27]

If we now turn to the verbal parallels quoted above, we can observe that only two belong to the Shakespearian scenes of *Double Falsehood* (items 6 and 7), and the remaining eighteen to the Fletcherian ones, six of them being present in 4.2, perhaps the most Fletcherian-sounding scene. Here we could be reminded of Kukowski's argument: having shown a fair number of Fletcherisms in *Double Falsehood*, several of them occurring together, he concluded that, if Theobald were creating a deliberate forgery, 'he would be attempting to produce more lines that sound like Shakespeare, and fewer that

[23] The original Spanish that Shelton translated as 'Witness shall also be thine own handwriting' reads: 'Testigo será la firma que hiciste' (literally: 'Witness shall be the signature thou didst'; more idiomatically: 'Let your own signature testify', according to J. M. Cohen's translation, Harmondsworth, 1950, p.328). But Don Fernando had not signed any letter or document, either. Some commentators of *Don Quixote* have noticed the inconsistency in Cervantes, as well the linguistic unusualness in Spanish of 'hacer una firma' (to 'do' a signature).

[24] See René Wellek and Austin Warren, *Theory of Literature* (Harmondsworth, 1973), pp. 257–8.

[25] Freehafer, '*Cardenio*', p. 502.

[26] See Kukowski, 'The Hand of John Fletcher', p. 81.

[27] See Freehafer, '*Cardenio*', p. 506.

sound like Fletcher'.[28] Though the evidence may not be too ample or conclusive, it is worth pointing out that some of these Fletcherisms are also present in the *Double Falsehood* quotations of the parallels, and that most of them are not literal borrowings from the Shelton text, but verbal alternatives to, or departures from, it. Among the various Fletcherian features identified by Kukowski, we can here observe the expression 'all good people' (item 1), one instance of ''em' (item 8), and fourteen cases of feminine endings (items 1, 2, 4, 5, 8, 16, 17 and 20), one of them occurring together with ''em' (in 'beseech 'em', item 8).[29]

The establishment of all these verbal parallels could well yield more results. Here we would need detailed stylistic analyses of the similarities and differences in the parallels, perhaps with the help of computers.[30] This way we might even find scraps or tricks of style not only of Fletcher, but of Shakespeare and Theobald. It is to be hoped that this would not provide new ammunition for those few who believe that the whole thing was a forgery.

---

28 Kukowski, 'The Hand of John Fletcher', p. 88.

29 Here I leave out, therefore, the lines ending in 'danger', 'comfort', and 'credit' (items 8, 15 and 18, respectively, which are words borrowed literally from Shelton).

30 What is called 'neural computation' has been applied to stylistic analysis, and specifically to the works of Shakespeare and Fletcher. See Robert A. J. Matthews and Thomas Merriam, 'Neural Computation in Stylometry, I: An Application to the Works of Shakespeare and Fletcher', *Literary and Linguistic Computing*, 8 (1993), 203–9.

# EIGHTEENTH-CENTURY PERFORMANCES OF SHAKESPEARE RECORDED IN THE THEATRICAL PORTRAITS AT THE GARRICK CLUB

DESMOND SHAWE-TAYLOR

> But he who struts his hour upon the stage
> Can scarce extend his fame for half an age;
> Nor pen nor pencil can the actor save,
> The art and artist share one common grave.
>
> (David Garrick, Prologue to *The Clandestine Marriage*, 1766)

'The theatrical profession, unfortunately, is one made up of perishable properties.'[1] So wrote the actress Anne Mathews in 1838, despairing of ever describing her husband Charles's performances. The same thought lies behind David Garrick's affecting couplets printed above, with their deliberate echo of Macbeth's 'poor player, / That struts and frets his hour upon the stage / And then is heard no more'. But Garrick's verses are not strictly honest: the pen might not be much use, but the pencil (as a paint-brush was then called) could save an actor and his art. Garrick invented theatrical painting: his artists – William Hogarth, Francis Hayman, Johann Zoffany and many others – clearly had an input, but the idea was his. It is also a distinctly British branch of painting, a peculiar hybrid – part history, part *genre* and part portraiture. The world's best collection of this unique art form belongs to the Garrick Club, London.

This article examines how Shakespeare was interpreted, acted and produced in the theatre of the eighteenth century through the evidence of these paintings. They must however be consulted with care, for theatrical painting is more than mummified performance. It operates on three levels: as an invaluable (though somewhat unreliable) record of an actor's style; as an insight into the society which produced it; and as a work of art in its own right.

## THE ACTOR'S ART

The first thing everybody comments upon when discussing actors in the eighteenth century is their *person*: not just their looks, but their deportment and presence. In 1765 a talent spotter reported to David Garrick on the actor James Dodd: 'his *person*', he writes, 'is good enough, but his motion ... [has] ... more the stalk and *menage* of a dancing-master than the ease of a gentleman'.[2] Dodd fails in something which cannot be *acted* and which it is probably too late for him to learn; he fails to be a gentleman. This is an age in which the children of nobility were sent at a very early age to dancing masters in order that they should learn not only to stand and gesture properly, but to look as if doing so cost them no effort or thought. Actors, especially tragedians, must do

[1] *Memoirs of Charles Mathews*, 4 vols. (London, 1838), II, pp. 283–4.

[2] Letter from Dr Hoadly to Garrick, 23/5/1765, quoted in David Thomas and Arnold Hare, *Restoration and Georgian England 1660–1788* (Cambridge, 1989), p. 255.

this too, without the '*menage* of the dancing-master'. When John Philip Kemble engaged a French tutor for his younger brother Charles, so that he could play princely parts, he estimated that it would take twenty years to acquire the necessary grace of action.[3]

Though he had little else to recommend him, David Ross was in point of fact a gentleman and made a minor stage career out of his aristocratic bearing.[4] Johann Zoffany's painting of 1757–67 (illustration 7) depicts him as Hamlet, in the act of reading, as indicated in Act 2, Scene 2. This is how an eighteenth-century gentleman dresses and stands. The rules of deportment can be checked against the useful illustrations in François Nivelon's *The Rudiments of Genteel Behaviour* of 1737 (illustration 8). Ross holds his shoulders back, gestures with elegant asymmetry and places his feet at the recommended (90 degree) angle to each other.

Of course he is a soul in torment: this can be deduced from his frown, the slight discomposure of his wig and the turning down of his left stocking. These are stock conventions: the turned stocking is visible in Spranger Barry's performance (see illustration 18) and was probably invented around the turn of the century by Betterton.[5] The idea comes from Ophelia's description of Lord Hamlet:

> with his doublet all unbraced,
> No hat upon his head; his stockings fouled,
> Ungartered, and down-gyvèd to his ankle,
> (2.1.79–81)

As down-gyving goes this looks rather token, but then, following the rest of Ophelia's account would have seemed hopelessly indecorous at the time. To them, Hamlet was firstly a philosophical Prince and secondly a tortured soul. Later in the century Charles Kemble was commended for those 'fine instincts' in his interpretation of the same art which 'taught him the unseemliness of launching bitter sarcasms at Claudius before his courtiers'.[6] We no longer think of such courtly 'seemliness' as an important part of Hamlet's character.

7 Johan Zoffany, *David Ross as Hamlet* 1757–67. Oil on canvas, 77 × 64 cm.

[3] Jane Williamson, *Charles Kemble, Man of the Theatre* (University of Nebraska, 1970), p. 20.

[4] *Catalogues of Pictures at The Garrick Club*, 1909, p. 55, no. 120, and *Garrick Club Catalogue*, 1997, no. 726.

[5] See the 1709 Rowe edition of Shakespeare (Trussler, *British Theatre*, p. 132).

[6] Jane Williamson, *Charles Kemble, Man of the Theatre*, p. 3 quotes Westland Marston *Our Recent Actors* (Boston, 1888), pp. 113–14.

Though it may have been painted as late as 1760, Zoffany's image of David Ross provides an insight into the theatrical style of the first half of the eighteenth century. The complete absence of setting, for example, draws attention to the design of the stage at this date. From 1674 until 1774 more than half of the acting area at Drury Lane theatre was found in the 'apron stage' – the part in front of the proscenium arch – which was flanked by doors for the actors and boxes for the audience.[7] The architecture of this apron stage was the unchanging architecture of the theatre, not of the scenery. Hence such absurd stage directions as this from the 1773 Bell edition of *Coriolanus* (Act I, Scene I): 'a wood ... Enter at one door Cominius'.[8]

8 Plate from François Nivelon, *The Rudiments of Genteel Behaviour*, 1737.

There is nothing in Ross's style of acting to show an awareness of his great contemporary, David Garrick. He looks like a left-over from the days when acting had more to do with impressive declamation than psychological impersonation. A performance in the 1720s or 1730s would probably have looked to us much more like an opera than a play. A treatise on acting written in 1755 recalled the forced gestures of the previous generation and their recitation which was 'a kind of singing'.[9] James Quin, the star of these early years, apparently spoke 'with very little variation of cadence, and in a deep full tone, accompanied by a sawing kind of action'.[10] These writers had learned to expect more, for they were living in the age of Garrick.

## GARRICK AND THE NATURAL REVOLUTION

'Inimitable Shakespeare! but more matchless Garrick! always as deep in Nature as the Poet' (William Pitt).[11]

It was in 1741 that the British stage underwent its revolution, for in this same year Charles Macklin played Shylock at Drury Lane and David Garrick played Richard III at Goodman's Fields. David Garrick's person and deportment were up to the dignity of any tragic part: contemporary reviews especially commend the 'peculiar happiness in his address and action'.[12] But he used them in a novel way. As he himself put it, when he encountered the obsolete style still in vogue amongst provincial strollers: 'we in Town are Endeavouring to bring the Sock & Buskin down to Nature, but

[7] Burnim, *David Garrick Director*, p. 62.

[8] *Ibid.*, p. 97.

[9] John Hill, *The Actor*, 1755, p. 239, quoted in *Restoration and Georgian England*, p. 345.

[10] Trussler, *British Theatre*, pp. 174–5.

[11] Burnim, *David Garrick Director*, p. 107.

[12] *The Gentleman's Magazine*, of 1742, quoted in *The Georgian Playhouse*, 1975; see also Price, *Theatre in the Age of Garrick*, p. 25.

9 Johan Zoffany, *David Garrick as Macbeth and Hannah Pritchard as Lady Macbeth in 'Macbeth'*. Oil on canvas, 102 × 127.5 cm.

they still keep their Strutting, Bouncing, and Mouthing, that with Whiskers on they put me in mind of ye late Czar of Russia who was both an Ideot & a Madman'.[13]

What does 'bringing down to Nature' involve? Zoffany's depiction of Garrick in *Macbeth* (illustration 9) may give some idea. He is playing opposite Hannah Pritchard's Lady Macbeth, a famous pairing which lasted from 1748 to 1768. Macbeth has just murdered Duncan; his wife urges him to return the daggers to the scene of the crime so as clumsily to frame the grooms.

MACBETH
I'll go no more.
I am afraid to think what I have done,
Look on't again I dare not.
LADY MACBETH
Infirm of purpose!
Give me the daggers. (2.2.48–51)

They are both still in the dress of the eighteenth century. In the first performance Garrick daringly played the scene with unbuttoned waistcoat and other 'discomposures in his dress', but his friends advised him against repeating the

[13] Burnim, *David Garrick Director*, p. 59.

experiment.[14] The revolution in acting style was more durable. Zoffany shows a posture convulsed with horror: the body recoiling from the death-chamber, arms seeming to fend it off, and a jerky awkwardness to the whole figure. A contemporary description conveys the effect of this scene: 'You heard what they spoke, but you learned more from the agitation of mind displayed in their action and deportment ... The wonderful expression of heartfelt horror, which Garrick felt when he shewed his bloody hands, can only be conceived and described by those who saw him'.[15] What Garrick brings to the part is an immediacy of passion: this moment's start of horror may soon give way to some other contrasting reaction. All accounts of his acting draw attention to this thoroughbred nervousness and alacrity of response. He was famous for his transitions from one aspect of a character to another.[16] As a demonstration piece he would in the course of five to six seconds alter his expression 'successively from wild delight to temperate pleasure, from this to tranquillity, from tranquillity to surprise, from surprise to blank astonishment, from that to sorrow'.[17] When he seemed to have aged prematurely, Dr Johnson had a ready explanation: 'his face has had double the business of any other man's'.[18] How did this appear to the old guard? Theophilus Cibber, son of the prime ranter Colley Cibber, saw in Garrick only 'his over-fondness for extravagant Attitudes, frequent affected Starts, convulsive Twitchings, Jerkings of the Body, sprawling of the Fingers, flapping the Breast and Pockets ... the Caricatures of Gesture'.[19]

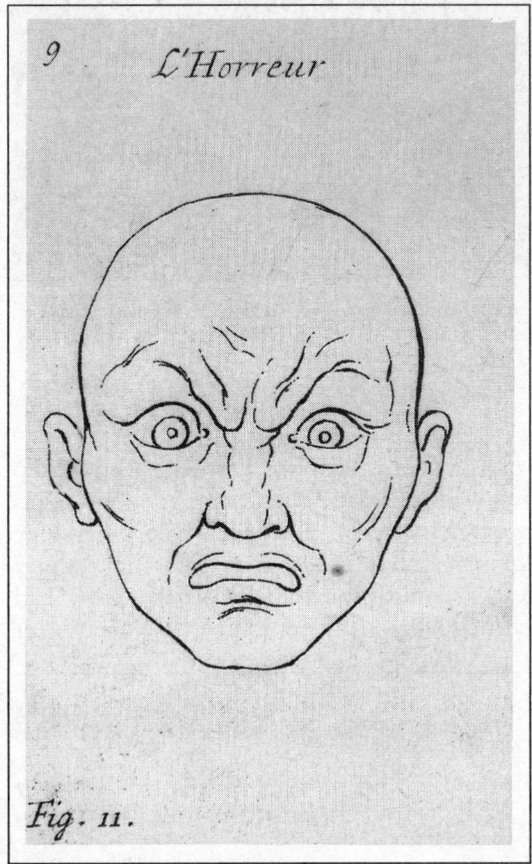


10 Plate 10 from Le Brun, *Méthode pour apprendre à dessiner les passions*, 1702.

Garrick's style did not just rely on instinct: he was well aware of the systematic studies of expression which were fashionable at the time. As a party piece, he used to wear the various expressions described in Le Brun's *Conférence sur l'Expression* of 1698, a treatise constantly referred to by artists and actors in the eighteenth century (see illustrations 10 and 17).[20] His 'heartfelt horror' in Zoffany's depiction – the face staring directly out of the picture, with knit brows, open mouth and wide eyes – comes straight from Le Brun's plate illustrating exactly that emotion (illustration 10). The most striking similarity lies in the conventions of the illustra-

14 *Restoration and Georgian England*, p. 327. John Hill, *The Actor*, 1755.

15 Price, *Theatre in the Age of Garrick*, p. 20; *Dramatic Miscellanies*, Dublin 1784.

16 *Ibid.*, p. 3.

17 Burnim, *David Garrick Director*, p. 1.

18 Price, *Theatre in the Age of Garrick*, p. 18.

19 Theophilus Cibber, quoted in Price, *Theatre in the Age of Garrick*, p. 15.

20 See Jennifer Montagu, *The Expression of the Passions* (New Haven and London, 1994), p. 85 and Adolphus, *Memoirs of John Bannister*, 1839, I, pp. 30–1.

tion itself, which Zoffany has deliberately mirrored. The straight view, with incised expressive lines within the schematic rugger-ball, gives to Le Brun's treatise an air of diagrammatic precision, of scientific inquiry. This was how the treatise was viewed – as a kind of descriptive inventory of the soul.

Le Brun is important for the period because he represents a way of generalizing the emotions. Charles Macklin felt that an actor should have a 'philosophical knowledge of the passions', knowing their '*genus*, *species* and characteristics' as a botanist might those of plants.[21] To us this over-rational pedantry of the passions is comical: Aaron Hill's treatise on acting written in 1746 asserted that there 'are only ten dramatic passions', which he lists and describes so that actors may practise them in their mirrors.[22] Those lacking Garrick's natural talent might look up *terror* in Roger Pickering's *Reflections upon Theatrical Expression in Tragedy*, of 1755, where they would learn that 'in astonishment and surprise, arising from terror, the left leg is drawn back to some distance from the other' and so on.[23] The important thing for the eighteenth century was that generalizing meant dignifying. A frightened man is contemptible; an artist revealing the secret principles of Terror is instructive and uplifting. In Zoffany's painting Garrick's features are generalized and dignified: they are expanded, regularized and given a sweeping pattern; they seem to be worn by the face like a noble mask. Even in the extreme of terror there is no contortion or grimace: Macbeth may be bad, but he's still a gentleman.

Johann Zoffany (1733–1818) came to London from his native Frankfurt in 1754; he was discovered by Garrick, while working as a drapery painter, who set him to produce a series of records of stage performances. Out of these commissions Zoffany became the leading exponent of theatrical painting. There is no other example in the century of such an extraordinary fruitful collaboration between patron and painter.

11 Sir Thomas Lawrence (studio), *John Philip Kemble as Hamlet 1801*. Oil on canvas, 82.6 × 54.6 cm.

## THE SUBLIME KEMBLES

Sarah Siddons and her brother, John Philip Kemble both made sensational London debuts in 1782 and 1783 respectively. Together they dominated tragic acting for the next thirty years. Comparison with Garrick, who had recently retired in 1776, is inevitable. Sir Walter

[21] Macklin, *The Art and Duty of an Actor*, quoted by G. Taylor, in *The Eighteenth-Century English Stage*, p. 57.

[22] Aaron Hill, *Essay on the Art of Acting*, 1746, quoted by G. Taylor, in *The Eighteenth-Century English Stage*, pp. 64–5.

[23] *Restoration and Georgian England*, p. 45, Roger Pickering, *Reflections upon Theatrical Expression in Tragedy*, 1755, p. 31.

Scott sums up the account: Garrick was equally at home in comedy and tragedy; Kemble was humourless; Garrick was short though well-formed, 'Kemble, on the contrary, was tall and stately, his person on a scale suited for the stage and almost too large for a private apartment, with a countenance like the finest models of the antique and motions and manners corresponding to the splendid cast of his form and features.'[24] Kemble's more imposing stage presence made Garrick seem positively homely in retrospect. Zoffany's image of Garrick and Mrs Pritchard (illustration 9) reminded Kemble of a cook and a butler quarrelling over a kitchen knife.[25] Kemble's more measured style of acting made Garrick seem a fidget.[26]

This may suggest a return to the pre-Garrick years, when larger-than-life actors moved stiffly and declaimed impressively. Various things distinguished the Kembles from the ranting era of James Quin and Colley Cibber. His declamation was more dignified and his acting was more intellectually 'paced'. He built up the dramatic tension slowly and, according to Hazlitt, was capable of 'working up a character from a single "line" of thought or characterization "and never letting it go."'.[27] It is no accident that Kemble excelled in reflective and introverted parts like Hamlet and Cato. Two Lawrence portraits in the Garrick Club depict Kemble as Hamlet (illustration 11) and as Cato in Joseph Addison's play (illustration 12). Sir Thomas Lawrence (1769–1830) was primarily a fashionable portrait painter on the scale of life, as can be deduced from these two examples, though they are in fact scaled-down replicas of life-size images. These are 'portraits-in-role', frozen abstracts of the essence of a part, conceived in the grandest and most universal fashion, rather than simple records of a specific moment in performance. Both depict the drama of thought, not feeling. Hamlet's macabre banter with a grave-digger has been turned into a celebration of the power of the intellect, which, even from the edge of the grave, can contemplate the stars. We are reminded of Hamlet's celebration of man – 'In apprehension how like a god!' – rather than his gloomy conclusion, which would have been more appropriate for this setting: 'And yet, to me, what is this quintessence of dust?'

Above all Kemble made an ideal Roman: heroic, noble and self-controlled. He was sometimes referred to as the 'last of the Romans'.[28] According to Sir Walter Scott, 'other perfor-

12 Sir Thomas Lawrence, *John Philip Kemble as Cato in 'Cato' by Joseph Addison* 1812. Oil on mahogany panel, 109.9 × 73.7 cm.

[24] Kelly, Linda, *The Kemble Era* (London, 1980), pp. 34–5.

[25] *Ibid.*, p. 47.

[26] George III's opinion, quoted in Kelly, Linda, *The Kemble Era* (London, 1980), p. 22, see also Burnim, *David Garrick Director*, pp. 55 and 60.

[27] Trussler, *British Theatre*, p. 207.

[28] Kelly, *The Kemble Era*, p. 202.

mers might excel Kemble in the full burst of instant and agitating passion ... but we cannot conceive of anyone delineating, with anything approaching the same felicity, those lofty Romans, feeling and partly exhibiting, yet on the whole conquering the passions of nature by the mental discipline to which they had trained themselves'.[29] Addison's Cato is the part Scott must have had in mind (see illustration 12). This scene (Act 5, Scene 1) depicts the stiff upper lip of an Augustan Hamlet. As Cato prepares for his suicide, the stage directions read, '*Cato, solus, sitting in a thoughtful posture; in his hand, Plato's book on the Immortality of the Soul. A drawn sword on the table by him.*' Cato is literally being philosophical about his own death. As in Lawrence's depiction of Hamlet, the anguish of a doubting mortal is replaced by the exultation of an expanded intellect, contemplating the immortality of the soul, as taught by Plato. Again the effect is achieved by a transfiguring light, inspired by the lines:

> And yet, methinks, a beam of light breaks in
> On my departing soul. (Act 5, Scene 1)

If Kemble is less shifting in his moods than Garrick, this does not mean that his face is vacant. It is rather expressive at rest, by the very nature of its form, rather than in motion, by the nature of its stimulus. The science which analysed the character of the face was called *physiognomy*, and it enjoyed a revival at this time following the publication of the first volume of Johan Caspar Lavater's *Physiognomische Fragmente*, in 1775. An age-old principle, invented by Aristotle and systematized by Le Brun, says that men have the characters of the species they most resemble. Kemble as Cato is aquiline: he has the narrow face, frowning brows, shaded eyes and long hooked nose of an eagle. This means of course that he has an eagle's piercing gaze and regal character. In case we miss the reference there is an eagle carved on the arm of his chair. During a row with Sheridan, Kemble is supposed to have bellowed, 'I am an EAGLE, whose wings have been bound down by frosts and snows.'[30] The physiognomic characterization belongs as much with the part as with the actor: the eagle is the symbol of the Roman Republic, and Cato is the personification of all its virtues. It is Rome itself which is facing death with dignity; as Cato declares (Act 2, Scene 1), 'My life is grafted on the fate of Rome.'

13 George Henry Harlow, *Sarah Siddons as Lady Macbeth*, 1814. Oil on canvas, 61 × 38 cm.

According to Aristotle, tragedy should inspire Pity and Terror; if Garrick excelled in the former, Kemble and his sister excelled in the latter. In the precise language of the time,

[29] *Ibid.*, p. 181.
[30] *Ibid.*, p. 87.

they were sublime. Sarah Siddons's performance of the sleep-walking scene in Lady Macbeth (her *tour de force*) would regularly cause members of the audience to faint away.[31] Luckily this moment is recorded in a small image (illustration 13) by Lawrence's pupil, George Henry Harlow (1787–1819). Sarah Siddons introduced a daring innovation: instead of holding a candle, as Mrs Pritchard had, she made as her trade-mark the wringing of her unencumbered hands.[32] The effect was electrifying: 'It seemed', wrote Hazlitt, 'almost as if a being of a superior order had dropped from a higher sphere to awe the world with the majesty of her appearance … her gestures were involuntary and mechanical. She glided on and off the stage like an apparition.'[33] This last sentence describes a peculiar characteristic of both the Kembles – their imposing rigidity. Harlow's image of Sarah Siddons, like Lawrence's image of her brother as Hamlet (illustration 11), has a frontality and a vertical rigidity which is a far cry from conventional deportment, as seen in the acting of Ross (illustration 7). The Kembles were statuesque: the two factors which, according to James Boaden in 1827, caused Sarah Siddons to change her style were the larger theatres and 'her delight in statuary, which directed her attention to the antique and made a remarkable impression upon her as to simplicity of attire and severity of attitude'.[34] But the examples here have more the sublimity of a primitive standing stone, than the grace of a Greek Venus or Apollo. Not everyone was so struck by these unbending postures: Hazlitt thought Kemble was 'the very still life and statuary of the stage … an icicle upon the bust of tragedy'.[35] Such frigidity was especially absurd off stage: a contemporary remembered Kemble at breakfast looking as if he had eaten a 'poached curtain rod'.[36]

## COSTUME

Writing in 1791, Tate Wilkinson provides a summary of the standard attained in Regency stage costume: 'strict propriety of habiliment not any manager has yet arrived at, even in London … though it is so highly improved these last twenty years'.[37] It is easy to see this improvement by comparing the Hamlet of David Ross with the Richard III of G. F. Cooke (illustrations 7 and 14). Unfortunately such comparisons can be misleading as so much depends not upon the actor but the part. Richard III was historically dressed in Garrick's time. This is because the audience knew the history: as Lichtenberg pointed out, they were familiar with the costumes of 'England's Henries and Richards' from 'school and from engravings, medals and firebacks; they even wore them at *masquerades*.[38] They are less concerned with Scottish history: figure 3 shows Garrick as Macbeth in modern dress (though not the guard's uniform which was the norm). It was not until 1773 that Garrick's rival, Macklin, mounted Macbeth in a version of ancient Scots costume.[39] Suddenly Garrick's coat and waistcoat looked ridiculous: the *St James Chronicle* of 30 October 1773 described him amongst the witches as a '*modern fine gentleman*, … a Beau, who had unfortunately slipped his Foot and tumbled into a Night Cellar, where a Parcel of Old Women were boiling Tripe for their Supper'.[40] Hamlet was the part which came last to historical costume – Garrick was still acting the part in modern dress in the 1770s – evidently British interest in

---

31 *Ibid.*, p. 22.

32 *Restoration and Georgian England*, p. 364; Trussler, *British Theatre*, p. 208.

33 Kelly, *The Kemble Era*, p. 49.

34 James Boaden, *Memoirs of Mrs Siddons*, II, 1827, pp. 288–92, quoted in *Restoration and Georgian England*, p. 49.

35 Kelly, *The Kemble Era*, p. 69.

36 *Ibid.*, p. 104.

37 Tate Wilkinson's memoirs of 1791, quoted in *Restoration and Georgian England*, pp. 321–2.

38 *Restoration and Georgian England*, pp. 330–1.

39 *Ibid.*, p. 329.

40 *St James Chronicle* of 30/10/1773, quoted in Price, *Theatre in the Age of Garrick*, p. 59.

history did not extend to medieval Danish fencing accidents. Lichtenberg sums up the stage's relationship with history: 'where the public is not yet awake to a certain point of antiquarian interest, the player should not be the first to disturb their slumbers'.[41]

The first actor–manager to make a conscious policy of disturbing these slumbers was Kemble, who shared with Sir Walter Scott a love of 'dramatic antiquities'.[42] For Kemble historically accurate sets and costumes contributed to the whole spectacle of a play, along with orchestrated crowd scenes and minor characters learning to act. His Hamlet (illustration 11) looks vaguely Elizabethan, while his Cato (illustration 12) is a remarkable advance on previous classical costume on the eighteenth-century stage. Until his time the Roman 'shape' – a tutu-like version of Roman armour – was worn by all ancient men, whether or not they were soldiers, often playing opposite women in contemporary ball-gowns.[43] Cato wears an authentic Roman smock, of the type worn underneath a toga in public and on its own in private.

But an interest in history doesn't necessarily mean knowledge. Kemble's 'historical costumes', like those of his predecessors, were probably more remarkable for their strangeness than their accuracy. According to the playwright and antiquarian James Robinson Planché, 'the alterations made in the costume of the plays founded upon English history in particular, while they rendered them more picturesque, added but little to their propriety; the whole series, *King Lear* included, being dressed in the habits of the Elizabethan era, . . . and, strictly speaking, very inaccurately representing the costume even of that period'.[44] With this in mind Planché set about educating his audience from scratch with a series of illustrated guides to the dress of Shakespeare's plays, the first of which, *Dramatic Costume: Costume of Shakespeare's Historical Tragedy of King John*, came out in 1823.[45] Planché collaborated with Kemble's younger brother Charles on a simultaneous production of *King John*, with historically accurate costumes, which 'initiated a new departure in theatrical art'.[46] Some idea of the innovation can be gained from the exotic costumes worn by George Frederick Cooke as Richard III and Shylock (illustrations 14 and 15), which have clearly been specially researched and designed.

14 Charles Robert Leslie, *George Frederick Cooke as Richard III*, 1813. Oil on canvas, 44.5 × 29.2 cm

[41] *Restoration and Georgian England*, pp. 330–1.

[42] Kelly, Linda, *The Kemble Era*, p. 102, see also p. 74.

[43] *Restoration and Georgian England*, p. 321

[44] James Robinson Planché, *Recollections and Reflections*, p. 36.

[45] See Williamson, *Charles Kemble*, p. 167.

[46] *Ibid.*, p. 7.

## THE ROMANTIC STAGE: GEORGE FREDERICK COOKE AND EDMUND KEAN

G. F. Cooke (1756–1812) was an exact contemporary of J. P. Kemble. But having spent most of his career touring the provinces, his sensational debut as Richard III and subsequent brief London career (1800–10) seemed to offer the capital a new acting style. It is for this reason that he can be bracketed with the much younger Edmund Kean (1789–1833), who made his London debut as Shylock in 1814 and whose meteoric career was effectively burnt out in 1825. It was as Richard and Shylock that Garrick and Macklin launched themselves; it was in the same parts that Cooke and Kean defined their identity in contrast to the Kembles. Both their repertoires were made up of such outcasts and tortured villains: Cooke also specialized in Richard II, Iago, Kitely, Macbeth and Sir Giles Overreach; Kean in Othello, Hamlet and Iago.

15 Thomas Phillips, *George Frederick Cooke as Shylock in 'The Merchant of Venice'*, 1803. Oil on canvas, 76 × 63 cm.

Neither Shylock nor Richard III was ever John Philip Kemble's strongest role (Walter Scott recalls how he 'could never *look* the part of Richard'); he was evidently content to leave them to Cooke.[47] John Genest, writing in 1832, compared the two actors: 'Cooke did not possess that elegant figure of Kemble, but his countenance beamed with great intelligence – his eyes were fiery, dark, and at times terribly expressive, particularly in the worst passions of our nature ... his attitudes [were] less picturesque than Kemble's ... but they were just, appropriate and natural'; Kemble excelled as Coriolanus and Hamlet; Cooke as Richard III, where his figure was good, 'his face better, his voice better, his habitual manner better, as being more quick, abrupt and impetuous'.[48] Another contemporary critic felt that Cooke's Richard was 'somewhat deficient in the kingly and heroic part', but shone in 'all the subtle, ludicrous, sarcastic turns of the character ... We have seen Richard rendered more awful and terrific, but never more thoroughly detestable ... His delivery of the passage ... "Why I can smile and murder while I smile", ... conveyed the idea of a man, sensible of his personal deformities and the barriers which separated him from the rest of his brethren, hugging himself up and enjoying a horrible satisfaction in the possession of a faculty by which he hoped to overreach the rest of mankind and secure the grand object of his eye.'[49]

The small portrait of Cooke as Richard III by Charles Robert Leslie (1794–1859) (illustration 14) brings these descriptions to life. Richard is clearly delivering a soliloquy (perhaps even the one mentioned above);

47 Kelly, *The Kemble Era*, pp. 159–60.

48 John Genest, *Some Account of the English Stage* (Bath, 1832), VIII, p. 194, quoted by A. Hare, in *The Eighteenth-Century English Stage*, pp. 131–2.

49 *Restoration and Georgian England*, p. 374; *Monthly Mirror*, 1800, pp. 318–21.

unlike Kemble's Hamlet, Cooke actually addresses the audience, with an insinuating directness which was usually reserved for comedy. He bows to us in a reasonably graceful posture, though his deformity is hinted at in the unusual twist of his right arm. This might seem at least a courtly, if not kingly, act of courtesy, except that the bow is so sarcastic, so exaggerated in its mock obsequiousness. It is as if he cannot conceal his contempt for the objects of his dissimulation. He is indeed 'hugging himself up and enjoying a horrible satisfaction' in the possession of his satanic cunning.

His Shylock portrayed by Thomas Phillips (1770–1845) (illustration 15) is a snap-shot of scorn, with flashing eyes, swivelled head, turned down mouth and bared teeth. His wispy beard, receding yet long dark hair and exotic costume, turn Cooke's Shylock into a terrifying outcast. Depictions of Garrick in villainous roles show a handsome man *playing* a monster. Cooke wasn't so handsome: according to a contemporary, 'his features are thoughtful, bold and marked, and calculated to give the expression of scorn, envy, hatred, brutal ferocity and overbearing pride with unrivalled force and effect'.[50] He isn't here playing a monster; he has become one.

Edmund Kean is probably the most vividly described actor in history. For Coleridge his acting was 'like reading Shakespeare by flashes of lightning'.[51] For Hazlitt it was 'like an anarchy of the passions, in which each upstart humour, or frenzy of the moment, is struggling to get violent possession of some bit or corner of his fiery soul and pygmy body – to jostle out and lord it over the rest of the rabble of short-lived and furious passions'.[52]

The Garrick Club owns a small oil sketch of Kean as Richard III, executed with a characteristic liveliness of touch by a neglected master of theatrical scenes, George Clint (1770–1854) (illustration 16). It perfectly conveys the 'fiery soul' twisting the 'pygmy body' into a contortion of passion. Kean was clearly less dignified and more natural than Kemble: Hazlitt recalls, 'we used to admire Mr Kemble's figure and manner, and had no idea that there was any want of art or nature. We feel the force and nature of Mr Kean's acting, but then we feel the want of Mr Kemble's person'.[53] Another reviewer felt that he was so 'matter of fact' that he was like a 'poet who disdains metaphor'.[54] Kean's Richard here is not just matter of fact, he is mean, insinuating, even cringing. At first sight one might assume Richard is drawing his sword to perpetrate some crime, which would at least have some heroism to it. In fact he is playing his most abject role in the play – the

16 George Clint, *Edmund Kean as Richard III*. Oil on canvas, 52.5 × 41.3 cm.

50 Quoted in A. Hare, in *The Eighteenth-Century English Stage*, p. 130.

51 Donohue, *Theatre in the Age of Kean*, p. 59.

52 Dobbs, *Drury Lane*, 1972.

53 Kelly, *The Kemble Era*, p. 198.

54 Donohue, *Theatre in the Age of Kean*, p. 59.

improbable lover. He kneels to Lady Anne, whose husband he has murdered, and offers his sword and naked breast:

> Lo! here I lend thee this sharp-pointed sword;
> Which if thou please to hide in this true breast,
> And let the soul forth that adoreth thee.
> (Act I, Scene 2)

For all his 'anarchy of passions' Kean's acting and Clint's painting are still subject to expressive systems: Kean here clearly wears the expression of 'Desire', as recommended by Le Brun (illustration 17). This is the appropriate expression for his situation, though an extra tilt of the head takes away the dignity of the Le Brun and conveys the fawning of an otherwise vicious dog.

## ACTING AND PAINTING

Garrick's contemporaries were very aware of a tradition of acting extending back even to Shakespeare's time. What about theatrical painting? What are the antecedents of this special branch of painting? The short answer is that it is a cross-breed of two forms and yet is distinct from both.

Its nearest ancestor, especially in comedy, is *genre*, or the depiction of everyday life. The Dutch masters of the seventeenth century excelled in this department and taught English followers, like Hogarth, the importance of a faithful, atmospheric and expressive depiction of interiors. Charles Lamb said of Hogarth that he could tell a story in furniture. This is all the more important for theatrical painting as, unlike even Hogarth's brand of genre, it illustrates a specific text.

Its other line of descent comes from the noblest form of painting – called *History Painting* – which is the depiction of subjects from pagan or Christian literature. This was more something to boast about than the genre connection: Lawrence referred to one of his theatrical portraits (like illustrations 11 and 12) as 'a sort of half-history picture'.[55] There are treatments of Shakespearian subjects entirely within this tradition: this requires that Shakespeare is conceived as a poet rather than a writer and that a scene is imagined without actors. For James Barry, and many other history painters, the Death of Cordelia is not fundamentally different from the Sacrifice of Iphigenia or any other of a thousand 'standard' subjects for artists. However this approach to Shakespeare is surprisingly rare and doesn't really belong in the category under discussion. True theatrical painting is distinct from conventional history painting in that it depicts a particular individual *playing* a timeless hero. The full drama of the situation is there and yet we are almost always allowed to see the actor behind the role, to imagine that he could step out of character if he so wished. This requires a kind of distance, a self-conscious exaggeration, which allows the

17 Plate 11 from Bowles's *Passions of the Soul, from the Designs of the late Celebrated Monsieur Le Brun*, 1780s.

[55] D. E. Williams, *The Life and Correspondence of Sir Thomas Lawrence*, 1831, I, p. 197.

18 Francis Hayman, *Spranger Barry as Hamlet, Mary Elmy as Gertrude and Lacy Ryan as the Ghost in Shakespeare's 'Hamlet'*, 1755–60. Oil on canvas, 127 × 108 cm.

19 Johan Zoffany, *Sophia Baddeley as Fanny Sterling, Robert Baddeley as Canton and Thomas King as Lord Ogleby in 'The Clandestine Marriage' by David Garrick and George Colman*, c. 1770. Oil on canvas, 102 × 128 cm.

gesture to draw attention to itself, perhaps even (though this is a risky adventure in tragedy) to point up some contrast between the actor and the part.

The art of theatrical painting depends upon juggling these different traditions and levels of reality in order to create a pictorial equivalent (rather than mere record) of the stage spectacle. Francis Hayman (1708–76) was a friend and contemporary of Hogarth with an impressive range of skills: history, genre, portraiture, conversation pieces, book-illustration and even scene-painting. Today he is known best for a purely imaginary depiction of the wrestling scene from *As You Like It* (Tate Gallery). The Garrick Club's treatment of Spranger Barry as Hamlet in the scene in Gertrude's bedchamber (illustration 18) inclines towards history, yet he is clearly seeking to reconcile his ideal image of this moment of the play with a specific performance. The scenery is imaginary; the candlelight dramatic and impossible in a theatre of this date.[56] The strange ring of blue light surrounding the flame is a paranormal phenomenon, derived from Shakespearian belief that

[56] *Garrick Club Catalogue*, no. 49.

lights burn blue in the presence of ghosts.[57] The lighting on the figures is manipulated so that the living receive a much stronger glare than the pallid moonlight which bleaches out the colour from the face and armour of the ghost. The background here also plays tricks on the eye: partly suggestive of a mirror, partly of an aperture, we seem to be looking at a material through which only a ghost might pass. It is perhaps even deliberate that Gertrude starts up from her chair to help Hamlet (she doesn't see the ghost), and in this way leaves an empty throne to her right hand which her husband should be occupying.

All these are stage directions and 'special effects' supplied by the artist; the performances on the other hand are supplied by the actor. 'Silver-tongued' Barry, as he was called, was a typical product of the 'Pre-Garrick' era: stately rather than electric, he was apparently 'full of grace and dignity', but 'deficient in representing the violent emotions of the soul; nor could a countenance so placid as his ever wear the strong impressions of despair or horror'.[58]

Though ambiguously poised, Hayman's depiction of Hamlet is intended to speak more of Elsinore than of Drury Lane. More self-consciously *theatrical* images tend to depict comedies rather than tragedies. The most brilliant comic painting in the Garrick's collection – Zoffany's depiction of Thomas King and others in David Garrick's *Clandestine Marriage* (illustration 19) – takes us away from Shakespeare himself, but the situation is clearly Shakespearian: a kind of modern dress Olivia and Malvolio.

Lord Ogleby (the central character here) is a testy, burnt-out gallant with a heart of gold. He is kept alive by a daily administering of nostrums and potions and yet is 'full of attentions to the ladies, and smiles, and grins, and leers, and ogles, and fills every wrinkle in his old wizen face with comical expressions of tenderness' (I, 1). The moment depicted here is the one of maximum comic entanglement. Ogleby is staying with Sterling, a rich merchant, to negotiate an advantageous marriage between his impoverished nephew and Sterling's daughter, Fanny. Unfortunately Fanny is already secretly married and chooses this moment to come clean. However her manner of presenting the case is so modestly roundabout, so full of unspecified references to secret passion, that Ogleby thinks she is declaring her love for *him*. Of course the old ogler can't resist.

OGLEBY

There's no standing this: I have caught the infection – her tenderness dissolves me. (*sighs*)

FANNY

And should you too severely judge of a rash action which passion prompted, and modesty has long concealed –

OGLEBY (*taking her hand*)

Thou amiable creature – command my heart, for it is vanquished. – Speak but thy virtuous wishes and enjoy them.

FANNY

I cannot, my lord . . . (*exit in tears*)

(Act 4, Scene 1)

The comedy of Zoffany's image depends upon the ludicrously unheroic manner of Ogleby's declaration of love. He shrugs his shoulders and smiles a wan, hesitant and apologetic smile. It is as if an instinct of gallantry has talked him into the declaration against his better judgement, as if he is in the grip of a Pavlovian habit of courtship – 'There's no standing this.' The nearest precedent for his expression occurs in Reynolds's *Garrick Between Comedy and Tragedy*, where Garrick is shown shrugging his apologies to Tragedy for yielding to his baser comic instincts. Ogleby is also poised in the centre of the painting making a choice – between Fanny or nothing. And still it is with visible reluctance that he has decided to put himself under starter's orders for one last time.

---

[57] See *Richard III*, Act 5, scene 3, line 181.

[58] See Brian Dobbs, *Drury Lane, Three Centuries of the Theatre Royal, 1663–1971* (London, 1972), p. 103 and *Restoration and Georgian England*, p. 368.

This is the comedy of the *situation*. The comedy of the *painting* derives from Zoffany's ability effortlessly to sail a course between depicting a real and a stage event. The trees are just bland enough to be stage-flats and just leafy enough to be trees; the brightly picked-out figures have just a hint of stiffness and isolation from the simple background to suggest the hyper-glitter of costume in the footlights. The gestures and expressions have just enough of exaggeration to freeze a moment of comic posturing, and celebrate a great actor's ability to be larger than life.

Zoffany's great gift is this same tactical artificiality of the comic actor. In part this is a faithful record of the special reality of the stage: of wobbly sets, over-acting, grease-paint and foot-lights. In part it is a deliberately invented pictorial equivalent of this stage-reality: a kind of tongue-in-cheek hamming it up in paint.

## CONCLUSION

Why should the Georgian period be such a golden age for theatrical painting, a new genre which has been in steady decline ever since? The coincidence of the careers of David Garrick and William Hogarth is one powerful explanation. Both artists reached an immeasurably larger audience than their predecessors; both excelled in an exciting new combination of comedy and tragedy. This fortunate meeting of minds, which to a lesser or greater extent affected most of the Georgian artists represented in the Garrick Club's collections, may not have been entirely coincidental. In the culture of Georgian England there is a species of self-awareness which seeks to divide artistic experience into constituent parts. In the novels of the period author, reader and character are separately addressed and identified; in a mock-heroic passage even such a nebulous entity as *style* is pulled out of the amorphous experience of reading and formally introduced. In the same way theatrical painting illuminates the separate layers of theatrical experience. It makes the viewer aware of divisions between actor and part, between scenery and landscape, between painting and 'reality'. This self-consciousness means that theatrical painting is naturally comic. It is no surprise that the vast majority of theatrical paintings in the collection of the Garrick Club depict comedies. Even Zoffany's renderings of tragedy tend to make us smile. It is not that they fail to convey the emotions of tragedy, simply that they do so through an essentially comic medium, rather as Charles Rosen wrote of the operas of Mozart, 'Mozart was, indeed, capable of tragedy in his dramatic works, but in comic opera.'[59]

The Romantic idea that Shakespeare could only really be understood in the imagination of the reader dented the prestige of the actor and reduced the opportunities for comedy. It also introduced a kind of *unity* of imaginative experience which weakened the divisions upon which theatrical painting thrived.

---

59 Charles Rosen, *The Classical Style; Haydn, Mozart, Beethoven* (London, 1971), p. 164.

# EIGHTEENTH-CENTURY EDITING, 'APPROPRIATION', AND INTERPRETATION

MARCUS WALSH

Eighteenth-century literary editing, of Shakespeare as well as Milton and other authors, has sometimes been characterized as tending to alter and construe the text in the light of distinctively eighteenth-century, and often distinctively personal, tastes and knowledges. That view has been subject to especially serious and repeated challenge in the last few years,[1] but survives at some points in the writings of distinguished Shakespearian commentators, including Margreta de Grazia and Gary Taylor.[2] In my own study of the subject, *Shakespeare, Milton, and Eighteenth-Century Literary Editing* (Cambridge University Press), to some of the materials and arguments of which this essay will recur, I have attempted to demonstrate that a number of the significant works of eighteenth-century scholarship and scholarly editing are based on coherent and often well-formulated theoretical understandings of interpretation, which profess to establish authorial readings, and to understand an original, authorially intended, meaning.[3]

In presenting this argument I have been very conscious of resisting a powerful explanatory metaphor, which has operated particularly dominantly in recent work on the theatrical and cultural history of Shakespeare, in the eighteenth century as in other periods: that is, the metaphor of 'appropriation', of readers and other 'users' challenging an original or 'authorial' meaning of the text, understanding the text in their own way and turning it to their own uses. A number of significant recent studies have explored the operations of 'appropriation' in Shakespearian performance and cultural construction in the eighteenth century: notably, Michael Dobson's *The Making of the National Poet* (Oxford, 1992), Jonathan Bate's *Shakespearean Constitutions* (Oxford, 1989), several essays in Jean I. Marsden's collection *The Appropriation of Shakespeare* (Hemel Hempstead, 1991), and Marsden's monograph *The Re-Imagined Text: Shakespeare, Adaptation, and Eighteenth-Century Literary Theory* (Lexington, 1995). Of course, the authors of these books are for the most part concerned not with textual explication, but with the uses of texts. My argument will be precisely that in this important body of recent discourse a sufficiently clear distinction has not always been made between eighteenth-century appropriative uses of the Shakespearian text in the theatre and elsewhere, and in broader critical commentary, on the one hand, and the more narrowly focused interpretative processes of textual editing and editorial annotation on the other.

'Appropriation' as a concept and as an inter-

---

1 Notably by Peter Seary, *Lewis Theobald and the Editing of Shakespeare* (Oxford, 1990); Simon Jarvis, *Scholars and Gentlemen: Shakespearian Textual Criticism and Representations of Scholarly Labour, 1725–1765* (Oxford, 1995).

2 Margreta de Grazia, *Shakespeare Verbatim: the Reproduction of Authenticity and the 1790 Apparatus* (Oxford, 1991); Gary Taylor, *Re-inventing Shakespeare: a Cultural History from the Restoration to the Present* (New York, 1991).

3 *Shakespeare, Milton, and Eighteenth-Century Literary Editing: the Beginnings of Interpretative Scholarship* (Cambridge: Cambridge University Press, 1997).

pretative practice has a long history in relation to both sacred and secular classics.[4] In recent Shakespearian criticism it has become an *idée reçue*, and its users do not therefore always elaborate its provenance. It is apparent, however, most explicitly perhaps in the rather carefully theorized work of Jonathan Bate, that it derives from two main sources. One of these is materialist literary theory, and especially that of Walter Benjamin and the contemporary German writer Robert Weimann.[5] The second, perhaps more significant for Anglo-American Shakespearian criticism, is a line of hermeneutic theorizing taking its rise from the work of Hans-Georg Gadamer, and pursued by many thinkers including Paul Ricoeur and Hans Robert Jauss, whose essay 'Literary History as a Challenge to Literary Theory' has been especially influential.[6] Gadamer, though warning against an 'overhasty assimilation of the past to our own expectation of meaning', nevertheless insists that as interpreters we must recognize, and indeed cannot escape, the prejudices of our own historical mode of being, and must accept that we stand always within tradition. Interpretation is a matter of reciprocal relationships, and understanding can only be attained by the fusion of our own horizon with that of the work itself. For Jauss, rejecting 'the prejudices of historical objectivism' in favour of an 'aesthetics of reception and influence', the literary work is 'not a monument that monologically reveals its timeless essence', but 'an orchestration that strikes ever new resonances among its readers and that frees the text from the material of the words and brings it to a contemporary existence' (pp. 20, 21).

'Appropriation' has clearly been a valuable as well as an influential idea. Theoretical positions avowedly derived from Gadamer have played a major role in some recent discussions of the question of how we deal and historically have dealt with the 'classic', of why certain literary works written in past centuries continue to live for and to be at some level available to succeeding generations. I think especially of the work of Gerald Bruns and Joel Weinsheimer.[7]

Yet 'appropriation' in this sense involves difficulties in its practical application to interpretation. In this paper I should like to note some reservations which have been entered against these hermeneutical accounts of 'appropriation' in general, to develop rather more particularly my own reservations about its application to the study of the editing of secular literary texts in the eighteenth century, and briefly to evidence respects in which eighteenth-century scholarly editorial practice seems to me not 'appropriative'.

An important rebuttal is a review article by E. D. Hirsch on Gadamer's *Truth and Method* (*Wahrheit und Methode* (1960)).[8] Gadamer's denial that true interpretation can reside in 'the

---

[4] Gerald L. Bruns provides a richly informative and suggestive account in his *Hermeneutics Ancient and Modern* (New Haven and London, 1992).

[5] Benjamin, 'Eduard Fuchs, Collector and Historian', in *One-Way Street and Other Writings*, tr. Edmund Jephcott and Kingsley Shorter (London, 1979), pp. 349–86; Weimann, *Shakespeare and the Popular Tradition in the Theater* (Baltimore, Maryland, 1978); '"Appropriation" and Modern History in Renaissance Prose Narrative', *New Literary History*, 14 (1982–3), 459–95.

[6] Jauss, 'Literary History as a Challenge to Literary Theory', chapter 1 of his *Toward an Aesthetic of Reception*, tr. from the German by Timothy Bahti (Brighton, 1982), pp. 3–45; Paul Ricoeur, 'Appropriation', in *A Ricoeur Reader: Reflection and Imagination*, ed. Mario J. Valdés (Hemel Hempstead, 1991), pp. 86–98.

[7] See especially Bruns, *Hermeneutics Ancient and Modern*; Weinsheimer, *Eighteenth-Century Hermeneutics: Philosophy of Interpretation in England from Locke to Burke* (New Haven and London, 1993).

[8] 'Gadamer's Theory of Interpretation', *The Review of Metaphysics*, March 1965; reprinted in *Validity in Interpretation* (New Haven, 1967), pp. 245–64. Hirsch's reading of Gadamer in this review and elsewhere has been questioned: for example by Paul Ricoeur in his 'Construing and Constructing: A Review of *The Aims of Interpretation* by E. D. Hirsch, Jr', *Times Literary Supplement*, 197 (25 February 1977), p. 216 (re-printed in *A Ricoeur Reader*, pp. 195–9 (p. 197)); and by Joel Weinsheimer in his *Philosophical Hermeneutics and Literary Theory* (New Haven and London, 1991), pp. 24–5.

genuine re-cognition of an author's meaning', Hirsch insists, leads towards the doctrine of textual autonomy, and thence to the doctrine of the indeterminacy of textual meaning. If the meaning of a text is 'a never-exhausted array of possible meanings lying in wait for a never-ending array of interpreters ... no actual interpretation could ever correspond to the meaning of the text'. Gadamerian hermeneutics replace the author as the main authority for meaning by a principle of tradition which is consensual, and this leaves open the question of what basis there might be for discriminating between different, opposed, interpretations. For Hirsch, Gadamer's central concept of the fusion of horizons, as a process by which textual meanings are '*codetermined* by the historical situation of the interpreter', does not solve the essential problem; in the fusion of horizons the text is not understood, but appropriated. 'How can an interpreter', he asks,

> fuse two perspectives – his own and that of the text – unless he has somehow appropriated the original perspective and amalgamated it with his own? ... how can it be affirmed that the original sense of a text is beyond our reach and, at the same time, that valid interpretation is possible?

In his answer to Gadamer, and indeed throughout his two major works, *Validity in Interpretation* and *Aims of Interpretation*, Hirsch has been concerned to disprove what he calls 'the fallacy of the inscrutable past', the belief that the minds of our predecessors are necessarily alien, and the texts they produced necessarily opaque. Such a historicist scepticism is unjustified:

> It is one thing to say blankly that we can never 'truly' understand the texts of a past age; it is quite another thing to venture the less absolute and no doubt true conception that we sometimes cannot possibly acquire all the cultural givens necessary for understanding an old text.

The hermeneutics of appropriation have of course been concerned with avoiding a deadening 'historicism', particularly associated with the old philology, in our reading of literary texts. To undertake a merely pedantic reconstruction of the past is to risk 'narcosis'. Nonetheless, Hirsch insists, there are equal though opposite dangers in the 'antidote' offered by Gadamer and others, 'that we vitalize the inscrutable texts of the past by distorting them to our own perspective'.[9]

Hirsch has no intention of denying the fact of difference between the present horizon of a reader, and the horizon of a work written in the past, but he nonetheless argues for the possibility of sameness in the construing of textual meaning. Hirsch's well-known and important (though much questioned) solution to this problem is his distinction between the determinate *meaning* of a work, and the (potentially infinitely variable) significance of that meaning to its readers. The logic of Gadamer's argument, Hirsch alleges, leads him into the contradiction of saying at the same time 'that a written text has a self-identical and repeatable meaning' and that 'the meaning of a text changes'. Hirsch insists however that:

> There is a difference between the meaning of a text (which does not change) and the meaning of a text to us today (which changes). The meaning of a text is that which the author meant by his use of particular linguistic symbols. Being linguistic, this meaning is communal, that is, self-identical and reproducible in more than one consciousness.
>
> (*Validity*, p. 255)

Hirsch revised his understanding of meaning and significance, qualified his disagreement with Gadamer, and further addressed the question of the ways in which we can use past literature, in an essay published in 1984.[10] Acknowledging that 'literature is typically an instrument designed for broad and continuing future application', and that the meaning of a work of literature must hence embrace many exemplifications brought to it by future readers,

[9] Hirsch, *Validity in Interpretation*, pp. 245–6, 249, 250, 253–4, 40; *Aims of Interpretation* (Chicago, 1976), p. 39.

[10] 'Meaning and Significance Reinterpreted', *Critical Inquiry*, 11 (1984), 202–25.

Hirsch rejected his earlier claim that 'future applications of meaning, each being different, must belong to the domain of significance', and accepted Gadamer's argument that application can be part of meaning (pp. 209, 210). Hirsch nevertheless continues here to resist a free remaking of meaning according to the interpreter's wishes. He explicitly rejects what he takes to be the 'Gadamerian mode of interpretation', in which 'meaning is *made* to conform to the critic's view about what is true', as not acceptable 'as a learned activity which pretends to historical and scholarly accuracy' (p. 218). Identity of meaning in different applications by different subsequent readers 'is preserved only when the application is an instance subsumed by the original intention-concept', and application remains for Hirsch 'mainly concerned with the changing realm of significance' (pp. 214, 215, 218). Indeed it is clear that Hirsch allows the notion of 'application' chiefly in the critical rather than the interpretative domain:

> in most applications of texts, and thus in most of our commentary about texts, meaning is not interpreted; meaning is assumed. In most commentaries ... we deal with judgment, value, and cultural connection – in short, with significance. (p. 215)

This seems to me experientially true, and it is crucial for my argument. Text-editorial decisions, and explicatory annotation, being characteristically engaged with detailed issues of wording and meaning, are precisely the place where meaning is *not* assumed. For this reason, text-editing and annotation are to be distinguished from other, more evidently appropriative, critical activities. Notions of, or arguments for, 'appropriation', however credible in themselves, do not in my view adequately describe the activities of verbal discrimination, interpretation, and explanation which scholarly editors in the eighteenth century, and since, have practised.[11]

Hirsch's hermeneutics, especially in their distinction between meaning and significance, in their repudiation of historicist scepticism, and in their preference for a restricted notion of 'application', clearly are at odds with some common assumptions, as I have described them, of some recent works on the history of the appropriation of Shakespeare. 'Of course', writes Jonathan Bate, 'we do all impose our own predilections on Shakespeare and make the plays mean what we want them to mean' (p. 209). Rather, by Hirsch's account, unless our applications are amongst possible instantiations of the original intended meaning, we make the plays *signify* what we want them to signify. 'The history of appropriation may suggest', Bate remarks, 'that "Shakespeare" is not a man who lived from 1564 to 1616 but a body of work that is refashioned by each subsequent age in the image of itself' (p. 3). But this statement reveals, I think, in the light of Hirsch's arguments, two kinds of apparent ontological and hermeneutic confusion: between meaning and significance, between what a thing is, and how it is used; and between Shakespeare as an individual historical subject (whom we cannot know), and the verbal meaning of Shakespeare's text (which, being linguistic, is in principle sharable).

Now certainly 'appropriation' is both a practical and a proper heuristic model in analyses of the history of the many kinds of cultural uses of Shakespeare, from thoroughgoing adaptations of his plays for the stage (as discussed by Jean Marsden and Michael Dobson), through the uses of Shakespeare in late eighteenth and early nineteenth-century political caricature (as discussed by Jonathan Bate), and even in the appearance of the Bard as a figure on a £20 note, as a hologram on a credit card, or as an image in an advertisement for Flower's Best Bitter (as discussed by Bryan Loughrey and

[11] My position is analogous to that of Josephine Guy and Ian Small, who argue more broadly in their *Politics and Value in English Studies* (Cambridge, 1993) that there is 'a radical disjunction between concepts commonly used by text-editors and those used by literary theorists'; see especially pp. 141–3, 151–2.

Graham Holderness).[12] 'Appropriation' is similarly no doubt a useful concept in considering the work of 'aesthetically orientated' editors such as Bentley and Warburton, whose explanatory comments on *Paradise Lost* (in Bentley's edition of 1732) and on the plays of Shakespeare (in Warburton's edition of 1747) very often might be thought to be concerned with 'significance', even where they claim to be dealing with matters of 'meaning'. One important and familiar element of 'appropriation' in such editorial work is the free exercise of conjectural emendation unsupported or inadequately supported by textual or interpretative evidence. As Thomas Edwards alleged, in his attack on Warburton in *The Canons of Criticism* (1748), the conjecturing 'Professed Critic' claims the 'right to declare, that his Author *wrote* whatever He thinks he *ought* to have written', 'to alter any passage which He does not understand', and to correct his author 'into all possible perfection, and of that perfection the Professed Critic is the sole judge' (Canons, 1, 2, 6).

Nonetheless, however useful the idea of 'appropriation' may be from these points of view, it seems to me to work very much less well in our analysis and historiography of the work of such scholars and editors as Lewis Theobald or John Upton or Edward Capell. No form of editing or explication can entirely avoid some degree of appropriation, but, as Simon Jarvis has recently insisted, 'any inquiry into the history of Shakespearian textual criticism needs first of all to grasp its relative autonomy from the other miscellaneous kinds of "appropriation" with which it is often lumped' (p. 8). Unlike the adaptations of Tate or Cibber or Garrick, and unlike the 'theatre texts' which purported to reproduce the text of individual plays as actually performed at Covent Garden or at Drury Lane, scholarly editions after Pope neither made nor suggested substantial overall changes to the surviving early texts of Shakespeare. Certainly Theobald and others conflated early texts – Quarto and Folio *Hamlet*, notably – but they did so with a view to preserving all of the words of the Scripture, not in a wilful attempt to create something new. Further, conjectural emendation, often considered a characterizing procedure of eighteenth-century editors, not only became less common as the century wore on, but also was increasingly used (I shall argue) as an interpretative rather than an appropriative activity.

I might begin my own statement of resistance to the extension of the idea of appropriation to eighteenth-century scholarly editing by looking at two distinguished and important contributions, by Jonathan Bate and Jean Marsden, to the recent discussion.

I have suggested that there is a distinction to be made between theatrical adaptation as appropriative, and textual editing as at least potentially non-appropriative. Jonathan Bate, in his *Shakespearean Constitutions*, refuses such a distinction, specifically arguing against the denial of 'traditional textual scholarship . . . that an edition is an appropriation'. Bate ascribes to 'traditional textual scholarship' the belief – at least as characteristic, in my view, of the eighteenth-century scholar editors as of the Greg/Bowers text-editorial tradition – that 'printing-house errors can be detected and a text that is true to the author's intentions reconstructed'. Bate rejects this belief on the grounds, very familiar and persuasive of course in recent Shakespearian scholarship, firstly that Shakespeare did not authorize publication of his plays, and that therefore none of the printed texts can properly be said to embody authorial intention; and secondly that the Shakespearian text is not stable, but 'raw material that is designed to be worked upon in the theatre – which is to say, material that is designed to be appropriated' (*Shakespearean Constitutions*, p. 208). Both of these grounds might be questioned. Does the absence of a personal

[12] 'Shakespearean Features', in Jean I. Marsden, ed., *The Appropriation of Shakespeare: Post-Renaissance Reconstructions of the Works and the Myth* (Hemel Hempstead, 1991), 183–201.

Shakespearian *imprimatur* necessarily evacuate the printed texts of Shakespearian authority? Is intention to print identical with, or an indispensable pre-condition for, intention to mean? Is plurality and diversity in the surviving textual witnesses equivalent to indeterminacy? Stagings are evidently variable, and have been from the beginning, but does their variability prove the infinite variability of the textual material on which they are based, or does it rather show (what would be trivially and inconsequentially true) that any text may be altered *ad infinitum* in the course of its application history, and that many texts have been? It is a historical fact that 'no two editions of Shakespeare are identical' (as Jonathan Goldberg, here quoted by Bate, points out); this certainly demonstrates that the (plural though in principle determinate) surviving textual evidence may (as in the case of the writings of other authors) be interpreted by editors in a variety of ways. Does it also prove the radical instability of the Shakespearian text?

For present purposes, however, I would like to follow Bate's assertion where it leads, to a conflation of editorial decision-making with dramatic adaptation. Bate goes on to say that many readers:

> set great store by the idea of authorial 'consent'. A 'true' revision or interpretation, it might be said, is one to which Shakespeare would 'consent', which is true to the 'spirit' of the 'original' – one could imagine Shakespeare giving his posthumous assent to the Kean-Hazlitt revision of Shylock or, more locally, Theobald's alteration of F's 'and a Table of greene fields' to 'and a' babbled of green fields'.
>
> (p. 209)

Such a notion of authorial 'consent' is, we can agree, untenable. As Bate himself points out, 'opinions about what Shakespeare would or would not consent to are circumscribed by the opiner's preconceptions about Shakespeare'. To appeal to 'authorial consent' is implausibly to locate intention in an extra-textual biographical subject. To appeal to 'posthumous assent', still worse, runs against an essential distinction which E. D. Hirsch has made, most clearly in his response to Steven Knapp and Walter Benn Michaels's celebrated essay 'Against Theory', between the author's original intention – what she or he *intended* at the time of writing – and the intention which might later be speculatively attributed to 'an author'.[13] There is however a more credible appeal to the author's verbal intention, which allows a distinction between Kean-Hazlitt and Theobald, between theatrical adaptation and production on the one hand and textual editing on the other. The Kean-Hazlitt revision of Shylock may be represented as a matter of *use*, an appropriation to the horizon of Kean and Hazlitt's time, properly a matter of significance. Theobald's famous conjectural emendation, however, may be represented as a matter of meaning, not merely a text-editorial recovery of original wording lost at some stage of transmission, but also an interpretative attempt to establish original intended meaning. We know that the surviving text of Shakespeare is (to use Gary Taylor's metaphor) at least at some points 'diseased'. In cases of textual disease, where no surviving witness provides an adequate reading, conjecture is essential; to avoid it is merely, as A. E. Housman pointed out, to practise 'the art of explaining corrupt passages instead of correcting them'.[14] That Theobald's emendation is conjectural, founded on no authority of copies, does not necessarily make his decision 'appropriative'. Conjecture, or interpretative choice, is an inevitable part of editing as an interpretative act, and a conjecture *ex ingenio* is not essentially different in nature from, or necessarily less persuasive than, a choice between two witnessed readings. The point is famously made in Richard Bentley's assertion, in his edition of Horace (1711), that 'nobis et ratio et res ipsa centum codicibus

[13] 'Against Theory?', in *Against Theory: Literary Studies and the New Pragmatism*, ed. W. J. T. Mitchell (Chicago and London, 1985), pp. 48–52 (p. 50).

[14] In his edition of Manilius's *Astronomicon*, book I (London, 1903), pp. xxxii, xli.

potiores sunt'.[15] It has been repeated with some variations many times since, for example in Housman's insistence that the presence of a reading in a codex merely confirms a choice made on prior interpretative grounds, or in G. Thomas Tanselle's argument that an editorial conjecture 'may be more certainly what the author wrote than any of the alternative readings at a point of variation'.[16] The essential distinction is not between a witnessed and an unwitnessed reading, but between the unsubstantiated 'improvement' of a work by an editor's own standard – which we may call 'aesthetic' or 'appropriative' – and an editor's employment of apposite and rational interpretative criteria in an attempt to reconstruct an author's intended reading – which I would wish to call 'interpretative'. Theobald claims explicitly to be undertaking just such an exercise. The editor is a 'Critick', that is, in Theobaldian usage, an interpreter, and wherever he finds a reading 'manifestly corrupted, deficient in sense', he must correct it by what Theobald calls a 'reasonable emendation'. Where originals are lacking, we must conjecture, or 'guess' at a new reading; 'but these Guesses change into Something of a more substantial nature, when they are tolerably supported by Reason or Authorities' (*Shakespeare Restored*, pp. iv–v, 133). Theobald's point is in fact well illustrated by the arguments and information he deployed in making his famous emendation to *Henry V* 2.3.16, to which Bate's comment refers. For Theobald, emendation must be based on appropriate knowledge, in this case 'a *competent Knowledge* of the *Stage* and its *Customs*'. He refutes Pope's surmise that 'a table of green fields' must have been a marginal instruction to a property man of that name, with an account distinguishing the roles of prompter, property man, and scene-keeper in the Jacobean theatre. Theobald supports his own conjectural emendation, 'a' babl'd of green fields', on the basis of the coherent sense it makes in its context, its closeness to the 'Traces of the Letters', and its truth to human experience: 'To *bable* ... is to mutter, or speak indiscriminately, like ... dying Persons when they are losing the Use of Speech' (*Shakespeare Restored*, 1726, pp. 137–8). Theobald's emendation can of course never be established as, nor does he claim it to be, a certainly accurate reconstruction of a now lost original. Whether or not a given reading is 'manifestly corrupted, deficient in sense', and how the reading is to be corrected, are of course interpretative judgements. Such judgements may be made, Theobald insists, by a process of rational argument based on relevant historical data. It is not self-evident where subjective appropriation is to be attributed to that process.

My second representative modern commentator is Jean Marsden. Acknowledging at several points in her Introduction to the collection of essays entitled *The Appropriation of Shakespeare* her indebtedness to Jauss, Marsden asserts and assumes that appropriation is both inevitable, and an exercise of power by the reader or consumer over the text:

> appropriation ... comprehends both the commandeering of the desired object and the process of making this object one's own, controlling it by possessing it ... In the world of literary studies, the process is both necessary and unavoidable ... Scrutinised dispassionately, every act of interpretation can be seen as an act of appropriation – making sense of a literary artefact by fitting it into our own parameters ... we possess it by reinventing it as surely as if we had secured its physical presence by force.
>
> (p. 1)

This orthodox statement begs a number of the questions that have been debated by hermeneutic theorists: might interpretation consciously choose parameters which belong to the work and its author, rather than those of the interpreter? might it choose to locate authority

[15] Bentley's note on Odes 3.27.15.

[16] See especially Housman, *Astronomicon*, I.lx; Tanselle, 'Classical, Biblical, and Medieval Textual Criticism and Modern Editing', *Studies in Bibliography*, 36 (1983), 21–68 (p. 55; see also pp. 26, 62–3).

in the work and its author, rather than in the interpreter? Is such an exercise of power as Marsden describes inevitable?

Marsden's *Re-Imagined Text* is an extended study of Shakespearian adaptation and literary theory in the eighteenth century. In these pages Professor Marsden regularly asserts, very credibly, that during the course of this period, and particularly because of the success of the eighteenth-century editorial project, the locus of interest turned from the theatrical performance to the printed book: 'Shakespeare becomes an author to be read' (p. 9). Perhaps less credibly she assumes that, as a necessary consequence of this move from the public space of the theatre to the private space of the closet, 'the emphasis shifted to subjective interpretation', and indeed to personal and emotional response (pp. 6, 127). Such an argument about the tendency of the printed book is neither unimportant nor unfamiliar. Gerald Bruns writes of a complicated post-Reformation story that is yet to be told,

> about how the printing press produced a culture of reading radically different from anything that had existed before: a culture in which the individual reader can appropriate the act of reading, where reading can now mean (or seem to mean) reading for oneself, say, independently of the sort of institutionalized setting in which one would be read to ceremoniously by a figure of forbidding authority: read to moreover from a text that one was not allowed to touch and rarely even to see . . .
>
> (*Hermeneutics Ancient and Modern*, pp. 162–3)

The Bible, once a shared and public text, becomes available to the private reader, more or less free, or apparently free, from the prescribed meanings of Church authority. Like Marsden, Bruns associates print with private reading, with appropriation, with reading for oneself. The question nonetheless remains: do the principles and practice of textual editing and commentary, and more especially those of the eighteenth-century editors of literary texts, necessarily invite or enable such subjective reading?

Marsden is concerned chiefly in this book with Shakespeare adaptation and criticism rather than with editing, with activities which we have learnt to think of as naturally appropriative, as inevitably tending from meaning to significance. Nonetheless it is striking that Marsden can take as a given that individual reading must be a subjective act, an appropriation, 'making sense of a literary artefact by fitting it into our own parameters'. This is a model of reading, certainly a model of *interpretation*, which the eighteenth-century scholar editors would have recognized, but would not, I believe, have endorsed. While Marsden speaks of the text as cut off from Shakespeare, as 'textualized', Theobald and a number of other eighteenth-century editors and readers thought of Shakespeare's original text (though not its faulty surviving witnesses) as a scripture bearing its author's intended meaning. Marsden's assumptions about the nature of reading are founded on the work especially of Jauss, but they bear a striking resemblance to some much older theorizations, and in particular – by no means surprisingly, given the large historical context of which Bruns reminds us – to certain Protestant arguments for private readings, and private meanings. Those arguments gave to Romanist apologists the opportunity for gleeful accusations that, were a Protestant pastor to enquire how the different members of his congregation read the Scripture, he would find a mere confusion of individual understanding: as the Catholic apologist John Gother puts it, 'This Man's Bible, and That Man's Bible; Such an one's Bible and Such an one's Bible; infinite Number of Bibles'. There was however a rather different Anglican biblical hermeneutics available to the eighteenth century; a hermeneutics which assumed that the Scriptures had a determinate and unchanging meaning of which the author's intention, rather than the tradition of the Church or the individual light, was the essential criterion. John Wilson asserts in 1678 that the Scriptures have an immutable sense '*Originally* and *Essentially* in themselves, given them by their Author when they were first indited'. In 1741 Isaac Watts warns the student against '*warping* the Sense of the Writer to *our own Opinion*', for we must come to the work of any author with 'an honest Design to find out his true Meaning'. It is possible to argue (as I have attempted in my recent study) that the assumptions and indeed many of the methods of the eighteenth-century scholar editors have an affinity with this rather different tradition in biblical hermeneutics.[17]

For Jean Marsden the mid century was a time 'when neoclassical formalism and attempted objectivity were being replaced by more individualized *readings* of the plays', when critics found in the irregular beauties of Shakespeare's work 'proof that literature must be approached intuitively', 'evidence of the superiority of "feeling" over the now outmoded and incomplete notion of reason' (pp. 9, 128). 'Neoclassical formalism', however, is scarcely a homogeneous and uniformly applicable category, and Marsden's account of the rejection of 'reason' in favour of 'feeling' is perhaps a simpler version of the trajectory of the culture and epistemology of the period than many observers would accept. It is more than possible to argue the reverse of Marsden's position: that the neo-classical assumptions of Pope or Bentley operate in the direction of subjective appropriation of Shakespeare and Milton to their own values, and that the editorial project of interpretation begins at precisely the point where editors question neo-classical assumptions about the proper forms and languages of literature. Intuition, arguably, is characteristic of the neo-classical moment in editing and textual commentary. The appeal to historical evidence and rational interpretative argument, on the contrary, is a distinguishing claim of the scholar critics such as Theobald and Capell who turned against the methods of Pope and Warburton.

These trends in eighteenth-century editing need to be differentiated. Marsden asserts that each and every new edition published in the years 1730 through 1765 gave rise to complaints that:

> ... rather than studying the text at hand, the editor has followed his own whims, egotistically foisting 'chimeral conjectures and gross mistakes' upon an ignorant and unwary public ... Angry critics portray editors as eager to strike out every word they cannot comprehend, and in their lack of knowledge of Shakespeare's language and customs, 'there is danger lest peculiarities should be mistaken for corruptions, and passages rejected as unintelligible which a narrow mind happens not to understand'. (p. 116)

This suggests that every new editor was engaged in, or was perceived to be engaging in, an act of appropriation, submitting Shakespeare's text to the Procrustean bed of his own understanding. In fact, however, all of Marsden's substantiating instances here belong to the years 1748 to 1756, and most are explicitly or implicitly attacks upon the free and often highly personal practice of conjectural emendation in William Warburton's edition of 1747. It is certainly possible to argue for a line of scholarly editing, represented particularly in the work of Theobald and Capell, which defined itself partly in opposition to Warburton's methods, and aspired to, and substantially achieved, an understanding of Shakespeare in the terms of his own language and culture, rather than an accommodation of Shakespeare to eighteenth-century standards of thought and expression.

The characteristic metaphor of such editors was 'restoration', that is, the restoration (however naive it must seem to modern eyes) of a true authorial original. For Theobald, the object is 'the True Text', and the purpose of every editorial amendment 'a real Restoration of the genuine reading'.[18] A Virgilian quotation became a resonant motto of his concern. Wishing to draw attention to what he thought to have been the damage inflicted on the text of the great poet by his first player editors, Alexander Pope used as an epigraph for his edition

---

[17] Gother, *The Catholic Representer. Or the Papist Misrepresented & Represented* (Second Part, 1687), p. 55; Wilson, *The Scriptures Genuine Interpreter Asserted* (1678), p. 5; Watts, *The Improvement of the Mind* (1741), p. 123.

[18] *Works of Shakespeare* (1733), I.xxxvi, xl.

of 1725 the account of Aeneas's meeting with the spirit of Deiphobus:

> – Laniatum corpore toto
> Deiphobum vidi, & lacerum crudeliter ora,
> Ora, manusque ambas, populataque tempora raptis
> Auribus, & truncas inhonesto vulnere nares!
> Quis tam crudeles optavit sumere poenas?
> Cui tantum de te licuit?[19]

In a nicely Scriblerian revenge, Theobald used the first three lines ('Laniatum ... / ... / ... ambas') as his own epigraph on the title-page of *Shakespeare Restored* (1726). Theobald's epigraph is preceded by a sub-title: 'Designed Not only to correct the said Edition, but to restore the True READING of *SHAKESPEARE* in all the *Editions* ever yet publish'd.' So the epigraph follows a double assertion of the purpose of restoration. For all their differences, part of what is at issue for Pope and Theobald is the exercise of power over the text. *Cui tantum de te licuit?* The text of Shakespeare is seen as having been indecently wounded; not merely diseased or damaged, but subjected to illicit and dishonest violence. For Theobald, and for such subsequent scholars as Capell and Upton, editing begins with allowing what they take to be the author's text its own life and authority. The exercise of a peremptory or personal power over the text is precisely what is disavowed at the outset.

Our modern sense of the inevitability of 'appropriation', and our insistence on its functioning in a print environment, may make us less than hospitable to such eighteenth-century positions. Marsden recognizes and describes but is not wholly sympathetic to the characterizing concern of eighteenth-century editors, and some eighteenth-century critics, with detailed explication of the text, and the restoration of authorial wordings and meanings. She quotes George Steevens's comment, in a review of Benjamin Heath's *A Revisal of Shakespeare's Text*, that Heath 'has taken more pains to understand Shakespeare's meaning than his words, two studies which have so mutual a relation that they ought to be inseparable', and goes on to remark that:

> On the most basic level, Steevens asserts that an author's meaning is dependent on the specific words that he or she wrote ... This assumption lies behind the mid-century paranoia of losing Shakespeare, both the cultural construct and his works, and reveals a major shift away from the critics and adapters of the Restoration who used Shakespeare's language as an excuse to re-write his plays. For critics and editors such as Steevens, such rewriting would be impossible, for by substituting new words, the early adapters were tampering with Shakespeare's 'meaning' and thus diluting his genius. (pp. 117–18)

In fact Steevens's dictum does not bear on mid eighteenth-century attitudes to Shakespeare's language as such, nor specifically on adaptation, but (as is clear from its context) on the relation between the establishment of the words of the text and the explication of those words, a relation central to eighteenth-century scholarly editing, and indeed, it might be argued, to editing in general as an interpretative activity. Steevens's insistence that an author's meaning is dependent on his words might seem unsurprising, but Marsden appears to imply that 'meaning' is not a more or less determinate quality to be found in an original text but must stand in quotation marks. Hence the eighteenth-century project of textual restoration and explanation, thought rational and coherent enough by its practitioners, is associated with what is labelled 'the almost hysterical fear', 'the mid-century paranoia' of 'losing Shakespeare'.

As scholarly editing of secular literary texts began and established itself in England in the eighteenth century, editors and commentators adopted more and more firmly the assumption that it was their responsibility to select authorial

[19] *Aeneid*, 6.494–7, 501–2: 'And here [I] saw Deiphobus ... his whole frame mangled, his face cruelly torn – his face and either hand – his ears wrenched from despoiled brows, and his nostrils lopped by a shameful wound ... Who chose to wreak a penalty so cruel? Who had power so to deal with thee?' (Loeb translation).

words and to explain authorial meanings. These are professions almost too regular to require illustration. Lewis Theobald sets out to restore the author's sense and the author's 'genuine Words'.[20] Edward Capell insists, in the Advertisement to his *Notes and Various Readings* to Shakespeare published in 1774, that 'the sole intent of the "*Notes*," is – to *establish* the Author's text, and to *explain* it'. The assumption is that the editor must carry out both the *ars intelligendi* and the *ars explicandi*, not only understanding the text but also making available its meaning to the reader.

Interpretation as the recognitive understanding of a past text depends on a reconstruction of its author's horizon. The turn of the eighteenth-century editors from appropriation to interpretation involved a movement toward the belief that earlier literature must be understood within relevant contexts of its own moment of production. Historical knowledge is for scholar-editors such as Theobald and Capell not a self-sufficient antiquarianism but an enabling interpretative tool. Theobald, in the Preface to his 1733 edition of Shakespeare, insists that an editor should be 'well vers'd in the History and Manners of his Author's Age' (I.xlv–xlvi), and describes his policy and practice in his editorial annotations:

> Some Remarks are spent in explaining Passages, where the Wit or Satire depends on an obscure Point of History; Others, where Allusions are to Divinity, Philosophy, or other Branches of Science. Some are added to shew, where there is a Suspicion of our Author having borrow'd from the Antients ... And some . . to explain an obscure and obsolete *Term*, *Phrase*, or *Idea*. (I.xliv)

To prepare himself for his editorial task Theobald read, according to the claim made in his Preface, the Italian novels, Hall and Holinshed, Plutarch, Chaucer and Spenser, the plays of Ben Jonson and of Beaumont and Fletcher, and 'above 800 old *English* Plays', the last specifically in order 'to ascertain the obsolete and uncommon Phrases in him'. His reading certainly extended beyond that, to Hakluyt, to Stowe and Camden, to Wyatt, Surrey, Lodge, and Daniel, and much else. This extensive reading – 'all such reading as was never read' – is regularly put to text-editorial and interpretative use. Pope and Rowe, unable to make sense of Hamlet's fancy of playing at *loggats* with my Lady Worm's skull (5.1.88), had amended to *loggers*; Theobald, recalling equivalent uses in Ben Jonson's *Tale of a Tub* and in a Statute of Henry VIII, is able to explain that *loggats* was a game, and thence to restore the Folio reading (*Works of Shakespeare*, 1733, VII.347). Samuel Johnson's clearest statement of a similar kind of contextualizing and explanatory intent is perhaps that of the 1756 *Proposals* for his edition:

> The editor will endeavour to read the books which the authour read, to trace his knowledge to its source ... by comparing the works of Shakespeare with those of writers who lived at the same time, immediately preceded, or immediately followed him, he shall be able to ascertain his ambiguities, disentangle his intricacies, and recover the meaning of words now lost in the darkness of antiquity.[21]

John Upton, in his *Critical Observations on Shakespeare* (1746; second edition, with expanded Preface, 1748), speaks of 'knowledge in ancient custom and manners, in grammar and construction' as being essential for the editor. Typical of Upton's interpretative uses of literary historical knowledge, though more extended than most, is his discussion of Shakespeare's uses of the vice figure. References to the vice in Jonson's *The Devil is an Ass*, *Staple of News*, and *Alchemist* substantiate his understanding that 'THE INIQUITY was often the VICE in our old Moralities', and allow him to reject emendations by previous editors of the phrase 'the formal Vice, Iniquity' (*Richard III*, 3.1.82), to 'the formal wise Antiquity'. Here, as in Theobald, contextualizing knowledge enables both a text-editorial judgement, and the interpretation

20 *Shakespeare Restored* (1726), p. 7.

21 *Johnson on Shakespeare*, ed. Arthur Sherbo (New Haven, 1968), VII, p. 56.

on which it is based (*Critical Observations*, pp. 137–8, 393–7).

The most thoroughgoing scholarly exercise in contextualizing interpretation of Shakespeare before Malone is offered in three volumes of Edward Capell's *Notes and Various Readings*, which appeared in 1779–81, long after the publication of his edition of the plays as a virtually bare text in 1768. Of these three volumes perhaps the most remarkable is that entitled *The School of Shakespeare: or, authentic Extracts from divers English Books, that were in Print in that Author's Time.* The *School* is based substantially on Capell's own extensive collection, which included works by, amongst others John Scogins and Erasmus, Ulpian Fulwell and Milton, Chaucer and Sidney, Florio's Montaigne and Lyly's *Euphues*, and much else besides. But the *School* is not mere undifferentiated background. It was based, Capell claimed, on consultation of every book 'that seem'd likely to contribute anything towards [Shakespeare's] illustration'. Every single representative extract in the *School*, so far as I can see without exception, is chosen to cast *interpretative* light on particular Shakespearian usages or allusions. So the phrase 'take eggs for money' is illuminated by a passage from Stowe's *Annals*, and the 'pin and web' is explained by a careful description from Sir Henry Wotton's *Remains.* It is clearly Capell's purpose, through these instances, to help his reader understand such Shakespearian uses of these phrases as in Mamillius' boldly childish assertion that he would rather fight than be fooled, or in Leontes' jealous suspicion that Polixenes and Hermione would think the world blind to their wickedness (*Winter's Tale*, 1.2.163, 293).

Passages which allow recognition of lost aspects of Shakespeare's horizon, matters of custom, or theatre practice, or law, for instance, are prominent in Capell's *School*, but its chief purpose, as Capell made clear in the Preface to his edition of 1768, was to provide examples of words and usages which had been thought to be peculiar to Shakespeare, in order to establish what in Shakespeare's own time was their 'true force and meaning'. This quest for the 'true force and meaning' of the words as used by Shakespeare, as of other authors, including Milton, can be traced back to editors working very much earlier in the century. Indeed I think it might be traced beyond that to a hermeneutic principle regularly articulated by English writers in relation to the Bible, in John Locke's insistence for example that he that would interpret Paul correctly 'must understand his Terms in the Sense he uses them, and not as they are appropriated by each Man's particular Philosophy',[22] or in John Wilson's or Samuel Clarke's arguments that the linguistic context within which we interpret Scripture cannot be our own, but 'the Scripture use of Speaking', understanding any Scripture word 'as it really signifies in the original texts'.[23] We find editors doing what they can to explain the words of Shakespeare long before adequate English lexicographical resources were available to them. Lewis Theobald could appeal to Skinner's *Etymologicon Linguae Anglicanae* in explaining Hamlet's word 'unaneled' as meaning '*Not being anointed*, or, *not having the extream Unction*', and to Spelman's *Glossary* in explaining 'even Christian' as 'fellow Christian' (*Hamlet*, 1.5.77, 5.1.28); no dictionary however could help him to account for the reading of the early editions at *Macbeth* 3.2.15, 'We have *scorch'd* the snake, not killed it', and he could only make sense of the passage by his own knowledge of the most immediately relevant contemporary linguistic context, Shakespeare's other plays, which offered him the alternative possibility *scotch'd*, meaning 'slash'd' or 'cut'.[24] As the century progressed, editors benefited from, and contributed to, a substantial development of lexicographical resources which facilitated the verbal

22 *Paraphrase and Notes on the Epistles of St Paul* (1707), pp. xxii–xxiii.

23 *Scriptures Genuine Interpreter Asserted*, pp. 160, 163; *Scripture-Doctrine of the Trinity* (1712), pp. xix, xxiii.

24 *Shakespeare Restored*, pp. 53, 185–6.

explanation of earlier writings. In the Preface to his edition Theobald promised 'a complete and copious glossary', which was never published, though it may have been begun. Johnson's *Dictionary* is the most important glossary to any edition of Shakespeare published in the eighteenth century, of course; it is evidently related to his work on his edition, and Shakespeare is the most represented author amongst Johnson's illustrations. Later glossaries include Richard Warner's voluminous manuscript draft, and brief published sample, of a *Glossary to the Plays of Shakespeare, on a more extensive Plan than has hitherto been attempted* (1768); and the Glossary which Capell included in his edition, a word list for which Capell's *School of Shakespeare* provided, in effect, the illustrative quotations.

These exercises in what was essentially historical lexicography are one important indication of a fundamental shift from the aesthetic to the authorial, from the appropriative to the interpretative, in eighteenth-century editing. Another is an increasing tendency for choices between textual variants, and decisions whether to resort to conjecture, to be made in the light of Shakespeare's own *usus scribendi*, his figurative habits, his tendency to anachronism, his idiolect, his metrics, rather than on the basis of the editor's own taste. Rejecting Pope's emendation of a Shakespearian quibble in *The Merchant of Venice*, – 'Not on thy Sole, but on thy soul, harsh Jew' (4.1.122) – Theobald recognizes such an expression as 'the very Antithesis of our Author', and reaffirms the editor's duty to interpret rather than to improve: 'if I restore his Meaning, and his Words, he himself is accountable to the Judges for writing them' (*Shakespeare Restored*, pp. 168–9). Samuel Johnson similarly refrains from reducing Shakespeare's language to his own or general contemporary standards of correctness. In Claudius's line on Polonius's burial, for example, Johnson prefers 'In *hugger-mugger* to inter him' (*Hamlet* 4.5.82), the F and Q reading, to 'In *private* to inter him', the emendation made by Warburton and other editors: 'That the words now replac'd are better', affirms Johnson, 'I do not undertake to prove; it is sufficient that they are Shakespeare's'.[25]

Also relevant to the argument about 'appropriation' are the uses and effects of two other prevalent interpretative procedures in eighteenth-century scholarly editing: 'conference of places' and paraphrase. The explanation of obscurities by reference to equivalent but clearer parallels had of course been a fundamental validating principle in classical editing and scholarship and in biblical hermeneutics, and it was persistently used in eighteenth-century editing and commentary on the vernacular classics. Lewis Theobald more than once announces his willingness 'to expound the Author by himself; which is the surest Means of coming at the Truth of his Text'.[26] It is a characteristic and persistent method both in *Shakespeare Restored* and in his edition. Amongst the numerous possible examples are his use of a parallel from *Antony and Cleopatra* to defend the Player Queen's expression 'as my love is *sized*' (against Pope's emendation to 'fixed'), and of parallels from *Macbeth*, *Love's Labour's Lost* and *The Merchant of Venice* to demonstrate Shakespeare's familiarity with the physiological understanding that lies behind Gertrude's description of Hamlet's hair standing 'like life in excrements' (*Hamlet* 3.2.160–1, 3.4.112).[27] Theobald's text-editorial and interpretative uses of parallels are typical though early. Many of his contemporaries and successors, especially perhaps Zachary Pearce in his *Review of the Text of Milton's Paradise Lost* (1732–3) and Edward Capell in his editorial apparatus on Shakespeare, regularly employed the method and stated the principle. Samuel Johnson, in the *Proposals* for his edition, promises to supply the meaning 'by the autho-

[25] *Johnson on Shakespeare*, VIII, pp. 981, 996.

[26] *Shakespeare Restored*, p. 128.

[27] For an especially developed example, see Theobald's use of parallels to defend his emendation of *Hamlet* 1.3.130 to 'sanctified and pious *bawds*' (*Shakespeare Restored*, pp. 26–8).

rities of other writers, or by parallel passages of Shakespeare himself'.[28] John Upton is to be found insisting that the 'careful and critical reader' – that is, the understanding reader – 'would compare one passage with another; for such authors are the best interpreters of their own meaning' (*Critical Observations*, pp. 137–8).

Of especial significance in eighteenth-century editing is the explanatory paraphrase. Here we might go back to Hirsch's quarrel with Gadamer. Gadamer asserts that, as readers are rooted in their own history, 'one understands differently when one understands at all'. For Hirsch this is 'literally nonsense'; one cannot be said to understand 'only when one does not understand' (*Validity*, pp. 252–3). Hirsch resolves what he sees as a contradiction by insisting on the difference between understanding and explanation. What is to be understood is a meaning not an expression, and mere repetition of an expression is no guarantee that understanding has been achieved. It follows, concludes Hirsch, 'that one tends to *express* a meaning differently when one understands at all'. It is in fact precisely this possibility, of rendering a determinate meaning in alternative terms, that makes it possible to use paraphrase as an essential method of explanatory commentary.[29] The running paraphrase was a main component of seventeenth and eighteenth-century biblical commentaries, which typically presented themselves in the form of 'Paraphrase and Annotation'. A striking formal parallel with these is provided by George Smith Green's full-length prose version of *Paradise Lost*, published in 1745, with the notes of Nicolas de St Maur;[30] Green's prose paraphrase is avowedly designed to explain Milton's poem, 'to make it more intelligible'. A more occasional though nonetheless persistent use of paraphrase was characteristic of the discourse of eighteenth-century interpretative editing, of Shakespeare as well as of Milton. For instance, where Pope had 'degraded' the word *mining* in Hamlet's lament about 'rank corruption, mining all within' (*Hamlet*, 3.4.139), Theobald uses paraphrase to defend the reading given in both F1 and Q2: 'The poet describes Corruption as having a corrosive Quality, eating its secret way, and undermining the Parts that are skin'd over.' Samuel Johnson's edition fulfils the promise made in his *Proposals*, that 'when the diction is entangled, it will be cleared by a paraphrase or interpretation'.[31] So he is able to explain Hamlet's expression, 'Ere I could make a prologue to my brains' (4.2.31), and avoid a Warburtonian emendation: 'Before he could summon his faculties, and propose to himself what should be done, a complete scheme of action presented itself to him . . . This appears to me to be the meaning.'[32] Such explanatory rewordings are everywhere.

Such evidence as I have been able to offer here for the interpretative tendencies and methods of eighteenth-century editing is inevitably selective. I have been re-presenting for the most part one side of a debate which of course had opponents in its own time, and did not, even on the most partial view, yield a clear victory for re-cognition over appropriation before the late 1740s. In some respects questions of 'appropriation' must arise, in relation to the nature of the annotator's authority, the processes by which annotators select the materials they use (and the implications of that selection), and the annotator's intended audience. In its institutional, economic, social, and political connections editing is bound to be a product of, and to play its part in producing, the public literary culture of its own time. These are issues which Simon Jarvis and Joseph Levine in particular have recently addressed.[33] And a crucial

28 *Johnson on Shakespeare*, VII, pp. 56–7.

29 Compare Hirsch, *Validity in Interpretation*, p. 136.

30 *The State of Innocence: and Fall of Man. Described in Milton's Paradise Lost. Render'd into Prose . . . By a Gentleman of Oxford* (1745).

31 *Johnson on Shakespeare*, VII, pp. 56–7.

32 *Johnson on Shakespeare*, VIII, p. 1004. Warburton had proposed 'Mark the prologue to my bane'.

33 Jarvis, *Scholars and Gentlemen*; Joseph M. Levine, *The Battle of the Books: History and Literature in the Augustan Age* (Ithaca and London, 1991).

question is the *use* made of the scholarly printed edition; not only what editors thought they were doing in establishing and explaining texts, but how the form and content of the new editions enabled or shaped new kinds of reading. This question is raised by Jean Marsden's assumption that all private reading is inevitably subjective, and is stated rather more explicitly in Roger Chartier's suggestive remark that 'a transformation in the forms and the mechanisms through which a text is proposed authorized new appropriations, thus it created new publics and new uses'.[34] Certainly the eighteenth-century scholarly edition represents an example of such transformations in form, and at least enabled new appropriations.

Yet eighteenth-century scholarly editions are not wholly appropriative, and not appropriative in some of the ways that have been claimed. Theobald, Capell, Johnson, and others were engaged in a project at least partly re-cognitive, devoting scholarly effort to recover the horizon of the past, in order to understand its writings. John Upton insists both on the difference of past writings, and our duty to understand that difference rather than to appropriate it to modern conceptions, in particularly energetic and indignant but not unrepresentative terms:

> it is to be remember'd, that things are not as we judge of them, but as they exist in their own natures, independent of whim and caprice. So that I except against all such judges, as talk only from common vogue and fashion; 'why, really 'tis just as people like – we have different tastes now, and things must be accommodated to them.'
>
> (*Critical Observations*, p. 385)

In making this claim Upton did not suffer, any more than most of his contemporaries, from the naive delusion that the determinate sense of a past writing 'is at all times immediately accessible to the interpreter' (I take these words from Jauss's rejection of what he calls the 'platonizing dogma of philological metaphysics').[35] That accusation might apply to Pope, who could claim, in his *Homer*, that 'Men of a right Understanding generally see at once all that an Author can reasonably mean.'[36] It does not apply to Upton or Theobald or Johnson or Capell, the chief end of whose scholarship was interpretation, the understanding of the messages of the past. E. D. Hirsch, in the course of his rejection of sceptical historicisms, insists that 'all understanding of cultural entities past or present is "constructed". The various languages of a culture (taking "language" in the broadest possible sense) are acquired through learning, and not inborn' (*Validity*, p. 43). What I have found myself describing in the work of the eighteenth-century editors is, I think, just such a process of acquisition and application of the learning that enables understanding.

---

34 *The Order of Books: Readers, Authors, and Libraries in Europe between the Fourteenth and Eighteenth Centuries*, tr. Lydia G. Cochrane (Cambridge, 1994), p. 15.

35 'Literary History as a Challenge to Literary Theory', p. 28.

36 *The Twickenham Edition of the Poems of Alexander Pope*, vol. VII: *The Iliad of Homer*, bks I–IX, Maynard Mack *et al.*, eds. (London and New Haven, 1967), p. 82.

# *SHAKESPEARE SURVEY*: BEGINNINGS AND CONTINUITIES

PHILIP EDWARDS

'We are approaching the mid-year of our century, and it is time for us to take stock, to inquire what in fact we have accomplished in study and on stage, and, by considering what yet remains to be done, to direct our path for the future.' This rather Baconian sentence comes from Allardyce Nicoll's Preface to the first number of *Shakespeare Survey* in 1948. One of the main features of the early numbers was a 'Retrospect' on what the first fifty years of the century had contributed to some one branch of Shakespeare studies. Now, at the end of the twentieth century, after fifty years of publication, here is a brief, personal retrospect on *Shakespeare Survey* itself.

In the autumn of 1945 Allardyce Nicoll returned to England from his years in the United States as Professor of Drama at Yale and, during the war, working for the British Embassy in Washington. He took up his post as Professor of English Language and Literature in the University of Birmingham with very clear plans, and he carried them all out within three years. He wanted to found a Shakespeare study-centre at Stratford-upon-Avon, just over twenty miles from Birmingham, and hold there an annual international Shakespeare conference, and he wanted to found a new Shakespeare yearbook, something like but not too like the *Shakespeare Jahrbuch*.

Nicoll was no stranger to the Midlands and its theatrical activities. He had a house at Malvern, on the slopes of the Herefordshire Beacon, where one of his neighbours was Sir Barry Jackson, founder of the Birmingham Repertory Theatre, and also, from 1929, of the Malvern Festival, which had made a special feature of Shaw's plays. Sir Barry had just been appointed Director at the Shakespeare Memorial Theatre in Stratford. A close link between the Stratford theatre and the proposed new study-centre there was fundamental in Nicoll's planning. Fundamental also was internationalism. It was to be the purpose of the new study centre, or institute, with its annual conference, and a new yearbook, to bring together an international community of Shakespeare scholars and theatre-directors, split up and kept apart during the long years of World War II. Nicoll had great faith in the power of Shakespeare's writings to break down nationalist antagonisms, and in the common bond of the appeal of the plays in theatres throughout the world.

During the winter and spring of 1945–6 Nicoll was gathering support for his projects. It would be of the greatest interest to know how and when Cambridge University Press came into the picture as publisher for the new yearbook. Nothing is on record. Cambridge were the publishers of Nicoll's monumental histories of English drama. They had also published the successful and influential *Companion to Shakespeare Studies*, edited by Harley Granville-Barker and G. B. Harrison, in 1934. George Rylands (who, at the age of ninety-four as I write this, is the only surviving member of the original Advisory Board) regards the *Companion* as a forerunner of *Shakespeare Survey*. It certainly demonstrated the Press's interest in theatre-study as an integral element in Shakespeare scholarship. R. J. L. Kingsford was then Secretary and Richard David Assistant Secretary of Cambridge University Press. They both worked with the greatest commitment to the launching of the new yearbook, and took a close personal interest in every aspect of the publication. David had been a pupil of George Rylands and had acted as Lear in one of his productions. His edition of *Love's Labour's Lost* was one of the first to appear in the new Arden series (in 1951). He became a frequent reviewer of current theatrical productions for *Survey*. With these interests in theatre and in scholarship, it seems possible that David was influential in the Press's adoption of the new venture. But there was H. S. Bennett as well. He was associated with Nicoll's proposals from the first and he was a Syndic of the Press. He also greatly admired Rylands' work with the Marlowe Society.

In August Nicoll assembled his supporters at Mason Croft in Stratford, the former home of Marie Corelli, at that time the Midlands headquarters of the British Council, whose officers, Ernest Burbridge and Phyllis Mann, were untiring in their support. This gathering, with Peter Alexander, H. S. Bennett, George Rylands, C. J. Sisson, F. P. Wilson and John Dover Wilson, was recorded as the first Shakespeare Conference, though it was a small and private affair. Rylands was the youngest of the group, and thought it an honour to be among these senior scholars. There was real excitement in the air, and a sense of new beginnings. Rylands recollects with particular pleasure the heated debates about the productions which took place over tea at Mason Croft after the theatre. These, and the closing sessions chaired by David which became a feature at later Conferences, when directors and actors came to discuss the week's productions and answer questions, seemed to him a practical demonstration of how worthwhile it was to bring together the theatre and the academic world.[1]

Decisions made at the Conference about the proposed yearbook were firm enough for Nicoll to make an announcement in the press, and to draft a press notice for Cambridge University Press to issue to 'the trade', soliciting review copies of books on Shakespeare. This last was not in fact released until November – partly because there was as yet no title for the yearbook. The press release spoke of 'a new series of yearbooks ... which will provide a critical survey [*crossed out and* review *inserted*] of notable current activities in Shakespeare studies and in the staging of Shakespeare's plays'. 'It is hoped that this yearbook will become the recognized forum for the discussion in English of Shakespeare and his work.'

The sponsors of the proposed journal were given as the University of Birmingham, the Shakespeare Memorial Theatre, and the Shakespeare Birthplace Trust. (The latter, then and for many years later under the direction of Levi Fox, was giving Nicoll's developments at Stratford enthusiastic support.) The names of these sponsors were printed on the title-page of the first number, and the University of Manchester was added in 1950. This list of sponsors remained for the entire eighteen years of Nicoll's editorship (with 'Shakespeare Memorial Theatre' becoming 'The Royal Shakespeare Theatre' in 1963). Then the list was silently dropped, no doubt in recognition that financial subsidies had long since ceased. (A grant from the Rockefeller Foundation was also acknowledged in the first number.) The Advisory Board was given as the six names cited above, but by the time the press notice was issued in November 1946, Nicoll had written to Cambridge University Press adding the names of H. B. Charlton and Una Ellis-Fermor.

Nicoll had appointed me as Assistant Lecturer in English at Birmingham in the summer

---

[1] I am most grateful to Dr Rylands for seeing me at King's in June 1997 and talking to me about the early days of *Survey*.

of 1946, and he now asked me to act as the Secretary of the new publication, with an 'honorarium' (untaxed) of £50 per annum. My initial recollection is of argument about the title. '*Shakespeare Survey*', an early choice, was felt to be dull, and in any case (some of the Board felt) had been pre-empted by E. K. Chambers with his book *Shakespeare: A Survey*. But *Shakespeare Survey* it became.

Nicoll promised to let the Press have copy for the first number by 1 September 1947, even though at the time (November 1946) the contents of the volume had not been decided, and he kept his word. The general lines of the volume were clear in his mind from the beginning, and it is astonishing how firmly Nicoll's original conception of the make-up of the first number has been maintained through fifty years and three different editors. Some features of the policy were: a special theme for each volume (this much encouraged by the Press); a 'retrospect' on this theme; the use of papers delivered at the previous Stratford Conference; extended criticism of a selection of United Kingdom productions; a review of the past year's studies divided into three sections (Critical Studies, Life and Times, Textual Studies); a report on a major archive; fresh documentary material or a reconsideration of known documentary material; news of international events and developments; new articles embodying original research or interpretation.

It was perhaps greedy of the first volume to contain reproductions of the two most important visual representations of the Elizabethan theatre, the de Witt drawing of the Swan, and the Peacham drawing of *Titus Andronicus*, but it is only the latter which received a reconsideration, and Nicoll was very keen to have the de Witt drawing in a number whose special theme was the Elizabethan theatre. The photograph of the Peacham drawing was taken by Nicoll himself. In July 1947 he drove I. A. Shapiro and me from Birmingham to Longleat at high speed in an American style car whose floating movement was so different from that of the bone-shakers I was accustomed to that I was afraid I might be sick. Longleat had been housing a girls' school and the estate was very neglected. We made our way up the magnificent front steps past ruminating cows and piles of cattle dung. The eighteenth-century book-case housing the Peacham manuscript was in an outbuilding, along with bales of stationery for the school. Nicoll had his own portable apparatus for photographing manuscripts (which he used to carry round Italy with him in those days before the photocopier was invented) and he photographed the *Titus Andronicus* drawing, plus a letter by Donne for Shapiro.

*Shakespeare Survey I* came out on time on 23 April 1948. The superb quality of the lavish photographic plates contrasted strongly with the inferior paper – still of wartime standard. Typographically, the book was outstanding, a credit to the designers, craftsmen and readers of a printer and a publisher who were both working in the same establishment at Cambridge. Particularly attractive was the large font and the wide page, abandoned in 1970 for double columns and smaller type, which (I think) narrowed and restricted the flow of the discourse itself.

With its theme of the Elizabethan theatre and 'the theatrical influence on Shakespeare's writing', *Shakespeare Survey I* became Nicoll's manifesto. His masterly opening Retrospect on 'Studies in the Elizabethan Stage since 1900' was informed by his belief in the power of time to dissolve error and uncover the truth about Shakespeare, and his belief that this truth (not too far from its ultimate delivery) would be found in the matrix of his writings, the theatre. The plays had to be recognized as plays and not as poems, and their nature was to be understood by relating them to the physical, social and economic conditions and circumstances of the theatres which saw their birth. Nicoll noted with approval (p. 3) the tendency to discuss groups of plays 'not in terms of Shakespeare's supposed psychological development, but in those of changing tastes in the audience or of the shifting personnel of his company'. There seems to be a fairly direct reference here to a major article in this first number by a former graduate student of Nicoll's, G. E. Bentley, on 'Shakespeare and the Blackfriars Theatre', which argued that Shakespeare's striking redirection of his plays towards romance in his last years was a response to the acquisition of the Blackfriars theatre by the King's men in 1608.

Understanding Shakespeare's plays in terms of their theatrical origin demanded for Nicoll a scrupulous attention to the diversity of Elizabethan playing places, and the practices of presentation within them. He had been giving great encouragement to the research of his senior lecturer, I. A. Shapiro, on the available visual evidence, and was able to print in this first number Shapiro's stern and exacting scrutiny of early depictions of Bankside and their value in determining the site and the shape of the Globe and neighbouring playhouses.

At one end of the scale, then, there was the historical evidence, which, painfully unearthed, might lead us towards the essence of Shakespeare. But almost as important for Nicoll was the living testimony of contemporary theatre. This was a testimony that had to be truly delivered, and the cause of true delivery underlay Nicoll's collaboration with Barry Jackson (who had shown his great interest in earlier drama at Malvern). Living theatre could be a laboratory to recreate the simple strength of the Elizabethan theatre, and in the vitality of its own performance discover qualities inherent in the plays inaccessible either to readers or to audiences at conventional commercial productions. But in this respect the path of progress after the pioneer work of Poel and Granville-Barker was uncertain. Both George Rylands and Una Ellis-Fermor, reviewing productions in London and Stratford in this first number, found cause to lament the throwing away of hard-won gains in a failure to concentrate on speaking the verse, and in impeding the flow of the play by cumbersome settings and awkward scene-changes.

Nevertheless, the importance to Nicoll of the living theatre as interpreter of the plays is clear from the space given in this first volume to a dialogue between Micheál Macliammóir and Hilton Edwards on their own Shakespeare productions and Charles Landstone's review of 'Four Lears', in London, Bristol, Huddersfield and Liverpool. *Survey 4* printed an excellent reflective essay by John Gielgud on the quality of acting in 1950, and this respect for the actor as interpreter has followed right through the life of the publication, with (for example) interviews with Judi Dench (Gareth Lloyd Evans, *27*) and Peggy Ashcroft (Inga-Stina Ewbank, *40*).

*Survey I* gave an impressive list of international correspondents, twenty-eight from twenty-seven countries, and there were five pages of 'International News' about productions and publications and translations. The small print allotted to this feature corresponded to its lack of excitement, but the panel continued, with changes and additions to the correspondents, and the 'International News' (or 'Notes' as it became) throughout Nicoll's editorship. Both the panel and the feature disappeared in the first of Kenneth Muir's volumes. The fortunes of Shakespeare abroad were also the subject of special articles, such as Henri Fluchère's Retrospect on Shakespeare in France, 1900–48, in *Survey 2*.

I ought to qualify my statement that Nicoll made *Shakespeare Survey I* his manifesto. It provided space for his belief in theatrical determinism; it did not impose it. Una Ellis-Fermor's assertion in the review of the year's criticism that 'the critic's primary concern is with the artist and the poet' (p. 118), and her welcome for George Wilson Knight's *The Crown of Life* may seem defiant, but her remarks were well within the range of editorial tolerance. *Shakespeare Survey* was intellectually cautious and conservative to begin with, and it remained so, but it was not narrow. The balance it maintained between textual and documentary research, criticism of different allegiances, theatrical history and contemporary productions was admirable. Its hospitality was not spineless or indecisive. It was an aspect of Nicoll's Baconian optimism in the 'exantlation' of the truth about Shakespeare. He had his own conviction about the best approach, but all (or most) approaches might be legitimate in the cooperative and cumulative endeavour towards the final unveiling. One of the strongest features of the early numbers was the succession of Retrospects, the critical marking out of progress made and of work needing to be done. On biography, on chronology, on *Hamlet*, on the Roman plays, on the comedies: above all perhaps on criticism itself – a mammoth 15,000 word Retrospect in *Survey 4* (1951) by Kenneth Muir (who was invited on to the Advisory Board in 1954). The cumulative effect of these *comptes-rendus* is expectation and hope: the past leading to the future. The Retrospect became less important in later years – not because of editorial policy, but perhaps because belief in the value of the past has been ebbing away.

In 1959, Allardyce Nicoll retired as Professor of English at Birmingham, though he stayed on at the Shakespeare Institute until 1961. His successor was T. J. B. Spencer, who, with Frank Kermode, joined the Advisory Board in 1960. Nicoll organized and edited the bumper volume entitled *Shakespeare in his own Age*, a compendium on life and thought in Shakespeare's day, which appeared as *Shakespeare Survey 17* in 1964, the quatercentenary of Shakespeare's birth. The next volume, *Survey 18*, published in 1965, was Nicoll's last, and at the age of seventy he handed over the editorship to Kenneth Muir. It has to be faced that this succession raised a problem. Terence Spencer had been appointed to succeed Nicoll as director of the Shakespeare Institute as well as Professor of English at Birmingham. He did not himself wish to take on *Shakespeare Survey* because of his onerous responsibilities as editor of *The Modern Language Review*, but he felt that *Survey* had been founded as part of a whole which included the Institute and the Conference, and should be recognized as an integral part of that whole. He believed that *Survey* could be directed by an editorial board at the Institute under the continued sponsorship of the University of Birmingham. This proposal was not accepted by the Advisory Board and the Press, and so the editorship passed to Liverpool, where Muir was King Alfred Professor of English Literature.

Muir made few radical changes in editorial policy. In his preface to his final volume fourteen years later (1980) he quoted the aims announced by Nicoll in *Shakespeare Survey I*, and said that he had pursued the same aims. New names appearing among the Advisory Board were as much an indication of the toll of time as of changes in approach to the study of Shakespeare. Allardyce Nicoll died in 1976, and the seventies also saw the untimely deaths of Advisory Board members Peter Ure, J. C. Maxwell and Terence Spencer himself. Reviewers of current theatrical reproductions included Gareth Lloyd Evans, John Russell Brown and Peter Thomson as well as Richard David. Many outstanding essays were published during these years – by (for example) C. L. Barber, Anne Barton, Philip Brockbank, Inga-Stina Ewbank, Helen Gardner, R. B. Heilman, G. K. Hunter, R. A. Foakes, Northrop Frye, Harry Levin, Molly Mahood, A. D. Nuttall, Robert Weimann.

I succeeded Kenneth Muir as King Alfred Professor of English Literature in 1974. I think it was in the year 1977 that I was puzzled by a letter from Cambridge University Press asking me for my views on the future direction of *Shakespeare Survey*. I had been a member of the Advisory Board for a year or two and assumed that soundings were being taken among its members now that Muir was reaching the age of seventy. I soon discovered, to my great embarrassment, that Muir had been assuming that I would follow him as editor, but had neglected to mention the matter to me. Once this was cleared up the far more appropriate appointment of Stanley Wells was made.

Stanley Wells was at this time (1980) still working on the Oxford Shakespeare with his headquarters in Oxford. He had formerly been for many years a Fellow of the Shakespeare Institute, and in his first Preface as editor (1981) he saluted Allardyce Nicoll as 'my mentor and friend'. He succeeded Philip Brockbank as Director of the Institute in 1988, and so *Shakespeare Survey* came home.

With just three editors in fifty years, and with such close links between those three editors, it is not surprising that there should be so strong an impression of continuity in the conduct and ethos of *Shakespeare Survey*. It was a virtue rather than a vice of the original *Survey* that in spite of the obvious predilections of its founder, it never committed itself tacitly or openly for or against any of the prevailing schools of criticism represented shall we say by Leavis, Wilson Knight and Northrop Frye. That cautious tolerance has continued in the years of Wells's editorship, which have seen fundamental and unparalleled changes in the objectives and procedures of criticism and in the language of critical discourse. Recognition of the revolutionary atmosphere was slow. I am surprised to find that I made the first reference in the journal to Greenblatt's *Renaissance Self-Fashioning* – in 1983. By now there have of course been a great many contributions with strong feminist, neo-historicist, or neo-freudian allegiance with as many from those who continue to challenge the aims and principles of some of the newer schools. But, generally speaking, it has mainly been in the pages of those who have toiled in the salt-mines of reading through and reporting on 'The Year's Contributions to Shakespeare Studies' that the impact of the new criticism has been recognized and assessed. However, in 1988 *Shakespeare Survey 40* devoted itself to 'Current Approaches to Shakespeare through Language, Text, and the Theatre', and that volume is full of angst and questioning about the procedures of critical discussion, with Terence Hawkes's 'Take me to your Leda' as a good example of bringing fundamental issues of the purpose and direction of criticism to the fore.

One might reflect on what the themes of three successive recent numbers of *Survey* have to say about its 'ideology'. *Survey 46* (1994) was 'Shakespeare and Sexuality', *Survey 47* was 'Playing Places for Shakespeare', and *Survey 48* was 'Shakespeare and Cultural Exchange'. Though indeed the vocabulary is very different, these last two numbers carry on directly from the early insistence of Nicoll that the theatre, historically and immediately, is the interpretative centre of Shakespeare study, and his belief in internationalism: that is to say, that Shakespeare binds nations together, but that each national culture transmutes what it receives and enhances the totality in which it shares. The first volume however is an insistence of a different kind: that time marches on. By and large, *Shakespeare Survey* has been a stabilizing force in the choppy seas of critical debate in recent years. Its caution is inherited, stemming partly from its mission to survey the past and reconnoitre the future rather than to invade and occupy the future. If its early faith that the time was not far off when all would be known, and all would be agreed, has subsided, its wariness has saved it from the disappointment of false apocalypse.

# DESTINED LIVERY? CHARACTER AND PERSON IN SHAKESPEARE[1]

WILLIAM DODD

Over the last twenty years or so, post-structuralist attacks on the 'subject' have led to the questioning of many traditional assumptions about the nature of character in literature and drama. The very concept of character has been held to carry politically reactionary implications. More recently, however, theoretically sophisticated critics have felt a need to salvage this concept while continuing to reject what is often called the bourgeois, liberal humanist view of the subject. In this article I would like to explore two related aspects of character in Shakespearian drama that seem to me to be particularly relevant to the current debate. The first is that of character as an 'effect' of verbal interaction. The second concerns the problem of a character's agency. I will then test the claims made by discussing part of *Measure for Measure* 2.2.

Recent studies by Jean-Christophe Agnew, Douglas Bruster, and Lars Engle have shown that the rapid expansion of the market into a pervasive, 'placeless' phenomenon in later sixteenth century England was beginning to affect the entire tissue of social existence, above all in the fast-growing capital.[2] As dramatists were well aware, the mushrooming London theatres were both an expression of this accelerating market economy and a site in which to reflect upon it in their explorations of human behaviour.[3] The sea-change that took place has been aptly summed up by Agnew:

> As the ritual and ceremonial ground of drama dissolved beneath their feet, actors stretched a safety net of story and spectacle across the widening chasm of disbelief. Innovations in character and plotting, novel arrangements of theatrical space, and new rhetorical and authenticating devices – these were the players' answers to the material problems growing out of a declining civic patronage, to the political tensions produced by a deepening religious conflict, and, not least of all, to the performative exigencies imposed by the changing expectations and responses of occasional audiences.[4]

As the boundaries between the world of the play and the world of the spectators became sharper, the need for compensating mimesis became greater. The shift from the depiction of biblical figures or moral abstractions to the

[1] An earlier version of this article was given as a paper in a Forum on *Theories of Shakespearean Character* chaired by Terence Hawkes at the Sixth World Shakespeare Congress, Los Angeles, 7–14 April 1996. Research for it was made possible by funding from the University of Siena. I am grateful to Sonia Massai for her helpful criticisms.

[2] Jean-Christophe Agnew, *Worlds Apart: The Market and the Theater in Anglo-American Thought, 1550–1750* (Cambridge, 1986); Douglas Bruster, *Drama and the Market in the Age of Shakespeare* (Cambridge, 1992); Lars Engle, *Shakespearean Pragmatism: Market of His Time* (Chicago, 1993).

[3] Dekker in *The Gulls Horn-Book* describes the theatre as 'your poets' Royal Exchange'; Jonson in the Induction to *Bartholomew Fair* ironically presents dramatic conventions in terms of a commercial contract. On this and other evidence for contemporary awareness of the theatre as a kind of exchange or market, see Agnew, *Worlds Apart*, pp. 118ff.

[4] *Ibid.*, pp. 104–5.

portrayal of historical or fictional individuals meant that playwrights and players had to work to make them lifelike. *Dramatis personae* were no longer 'givens' or ready-made texts of a collective religious culture: their existence had to earn some degree of 'conditional credibility' for the duration of the performance, and possibly beyond.[5] And they needed to appear capable of interacting with each other.

Some years ago I proposed that one significant way in which dramatic speech can be 'authenticated' is by allowing characters to perceive and exploit the metadiscursive and metacommunicative dimension of verbal intercourse much as we do in real conversation.[6] They can be represented as *aware* not only of what is being said but also of how it is being said. They may, for instance, distinguish between signifier and signified ('When I said "a mother", / Methought you saw a serpent', *All's Well*, 1.3.136–7), or name the illocutionary force of a sentence ('Now, by Apollo, King, thou swear'st thy gods in vain', *Lear* F, 1.1.159), or interpret meaning according to the context of speech ('I do beseech your Majesty impute his words / To wayward sickliness and age in him', *Richard II*, 2.1.142–3). Characters thus appear to recognize themselves and others as speakers and hearers, thereby objectifying the communication situation *while* they are participating in it. They give the impression that they are involved in an ongoing *dynamic*, in which they respond to responses ('Well, well, I see / I talk but idly, and you mock at me', *Richard II*, 3.3.169–70) or to other interactional phenomena emerging *here and now*, in the theatrical present. Marks of this kind of awareness are sufficient by themselves to implicate the rest of the communication situation, since in social reality such marks presuppose an overall communicative competence. It follows that characters endowed with metadiscursive awareness implicitly ascribe *intentionality* to themselves and others, thereby creating the prerequisites for the representation of *decision*, which Peter Szondi sees as the core of intersubjective drama. What we sometimes think of in semantic or substantial terms as a character's inner being is, then, in cases like this, a sense effect produced by the semiotic phenomenon of metadiscourse, though various other factors may sustain this effect.[7] That this inner being can never be made fully present, is if anything an advantage.[8] All the spectators need is room for inference and a few cues from the explicit text as to what can plausibly be inferred. The physical presence of an actor speaking the lines will usually be enough to convince them that inference is appropriate.[9]

If on the one hand the commercial theatre audience is encouraged to ascribe personhood to fictional or fictionally recreated characters, on the other it is invited to play a fictional role itself in this new game of make-believe[10] – a game very different from the ritual involvement in a single transcendent reality of earlier religious drama. The audience's moment-by-moment knowledge of the dramatic action and its anticipated responses are increasingly built into the strategy of the play. Because spectators now occupy a dynamic reception position

---

[5] See Agnew, *Worlds Apart*: 'Whereas the theater of the Middle Ages had formed part of an ongoing communal ritual, the theater of the Renaissance more closely resembled an occasional discretionary compact struck between performers and audience ... A conditional credibility, not faith, was the playwright's aim ...' (pp. 110–11).

[6] See my 'Metalanguage and Character in Drama', *Lingua e Stile*, 14 (1979) 1, 135–50.

[7] In *Faultlines* (Berkeley, 1992), Alan Sinfield suggests: 'Further indicators of subjectivity might be self-reference and self-questioning (including soliloquy), indecision, lying' (p. 59).

[8] Cf. Mikhail Bakhtin: 'A person has no internal sovereign territory, he is wholly and always on the boundary; looking inside himself he looks *into the eyes of another* or *with the eyes of another*' (quoted in Engle, *Shakespearean Pragmatism*, p. 62).

[9] In a performance involving 'boy actresses' and/or disguised or cross-dressed characters, such confidence may easily be shaken of course.

[10] See Kendall L. Walton, *Mimesis as Make-Believe* (Cambridge, Mass., 1990).

within a story normally assumed to be happening for the first time and once only, they have to be *persuaded* to accommodate the play's new individuals in their own make-believe world, and, god-like, to confer personhood on them as well as to judge them.[11] Hence the increasing use of the kind of authenticating marks I have just described.

The growing tendency to represent character as an effect of interaction clearly responds to changes taking place in early modern English society. At this time individual identity was coming to be seen as at least partly open to negotiation – as fashioned, earned, confirmed or demolished in a person's encounters with others. Shakespeare's awareness of this development is made explicit in a well-known speech of Ulysses in *Troilus and Cressida*:

> [man] Cannot make boast to have that which he
> hath,
> Nor feels not what he owes, but by reflection –
> ...
> no man is the lord of anything,
> Though in him and of him there be much
> consisting,
> Till he communicate his parts to others.
> Nor doth he of himself know them for aught
> Till he behold them formèd in th'applause
> Where they're extended –
> (3.3.93–4, 110–15)[12]

That Ulysses' account, for all its classical and biblical origins, should be couched in theatrical terms is revealing. The theatre clearly offers Shakespeare a privileged vantage point as well as an effective vocabulary for exploring the effect of contemporary social and economic trends on the individual. Lars Engle notes that Ulysses provides here

> a theory of human value which contradicts his 'degree' speech by making individual worth entirely dependent on continual cultivation of fickle public demand. A man, says Ulysses, 'cannot make boast to have that which he hath / Nor feels not what he owes but by reflection' [3.3.93–4]; that is, we know and measure ourselves in others' responses.[13]

Ulysses' thinking is informed by the playwright's awareness of how the expanding market economy is unsettling traditional structures of thought and identity – by accelerating upward and downward social mobility; by increasing the geographical mobility of persons, who are now drawn or driven in great numbers to London; by opening a struggle for the control of what Linda Charnes calls 'the textual production of cultural authority'; by penetrating the language and perhaps the very modalities of human relations.[14] The public theatre was uniquely equipped to represent this emerging mode of identity construction in its fictional interactions, holding up a mirror in which spectators could contemplate and evaluate the very processes of their own social and individual becoming. This must have been an extraordinarily hypnotic novelty at the time. The appearance in Shakespeare's plays of phrases like 'Richard loves Richard; that is, I am I', 'I am not what I am', 'I am not that I play', with their semi-blasphemous allusion to Jehovah's 'I am that I am', is symptomatic both of the public's fascination with the new fluidity of identity and of the theatre's capacity to cater to it – among other things by setting identity adrift in the multiple frictions of actor and role, character and disguise.

Let me now turn to a complementary aspect of

[11] On the judgemental role of the audience, see Edward Burns, *Character: Acting and Being on the Pre-Modern Stage* (Basingstoke, 1990), p. 128.

[12] For some illuminating recent discussions of this speech, see Robert Weimann, 'Society and the Individual in Shakespeare's Conception of Character', *Shakespeare Survey 34* (1981), 23–31; Linda Charnes, *Notorious Identity* (Cambridge, Mass., 1993), pp. 97ff.; Engle, *Shakespearean Pragmatism*, pp. 156ff.

[13] Engle, *Shakespearean Pragmatism*, p. 156.

[14] Charnes, *Notorious Identity*, p. 164, note 6. Earlier in this note, Charnes points out that 'early modern England was starting to register in every aspect of life what Agnew calls "the antagonism of market relations." These shifts were viewed as threatening not just the social privileges of the aristocracy but the ideological underpinnings of gender, class, and power' (p. 163).

character, one which has been a bone of contention for some time among Shakespearians, namely the problem of 'agency' in drama. How far does it make sense to talk about characters as if they were self-willed individuals capable of rational action? Post-structuralist theory has done much to demystify the traditional idea of the subject as 'the complex but nonetheless unified locus of the constitution of the phenomenal world . . ., the bearer of a consciousness that will interact with whatever the world is taken to consist in'.[15] The assumption that the subject is 'the free, unconstrained author of meaning and action, the origin of history' has been seriously questioned.[16]Accusing this 'liberal-humanist' conception of the subject of perpetuating suspect social and political structures, its post-structuralist critics have replaced it with the notion of a 'decentered, heterogeneous, constructed, contradictory subjectivity'.[17] The subject is thus no longer seen as determining history but as determined *by* history, constructed and conditioned by oppressive institutions and ideologies. However, various Shakespearian commentators not unsympathetic to such theory – Linda Charnes, Walter Cohen, Christy Desmet, Lars Engle and Alan Sinfield, among others – have recently begun to argue 'for a qualified re-emergence of agency as a valorized category'.[18] Charnes, for instance, though taking it as axiomatic that identity is socially constituted and that psychological structures are forged by social structures, recognizes that this is not a one-way process: 'subjective structures also reconstitute and inflect social structures'.[19]

What shape might this new, more conditional agency take in drama? A number of critics who reject the post-romantic view of a character as an autonomous agent endowed with a unique inner essence, tend to treat a character's 'subjectivity' not as a location or content or property but as an *effect* – typically (though not uniquely) an effect of *friction* between *discourses* in Foucault's sense of the word.[20] To give just one example, Alan Sinfield writes: 'Macbeth's subjectivity is not his unique, ineluctable possession, but constituted from rival stories that are current, though not equally authorized, in his society . . . Macbeth entertains more than one discourse at a time, and interiority is projected by an audience or reader as the place where discourses intersect.'[21] This has proved to be a rewarding approach in many respects, but it is one which has been felt to give an incomplete picture of the way many characters function in drama and especially Shakespearian drama. Thus some writers, most notably Engle and James Siemon, have turned to the writings of the Bakhtin Circle for a less oppressive model of human agency in language. Engle notes that 'Bakhtin denies the autonomy of individuals with less emphasis on the ubiquity of constraint and more on the omnipresence of dialogic encounters.'[22] Thus, though individuals are no longer held to be the discrete, independent subjects of humanist tradition, they are nevertheless seen as actively engaged in the dialogical construction of society. Siemon proposes using the Bakhtinian

---

15 Paul Smith, *Discerning the Subject* (Minneapolis, 1988), p. xxvii; quoted in Walter Cohen, 'The Subject of Shakespeare and the Subject of History', *Shakespeare Jahrbuch* (East) 126 (1990), 60–4, p. 60.

16 Catherine Belsey, *The Subject of Tragedy* (London, Methuen, 1985), p. 8.

17 Smith, *Discerning*, quoted in Cohen, 'Subject of Shakespeare', p. 60.

18 Engle, *Shakespearean Pragmatism*, pp. 61, 63. Brian Vickers, in a head-on attack on neo-structuralist views of the subject, sees no reason for qualifying this re-emergence: 'Agency belongs to the characters, who are presented as self-moving, self-willed, and thus coming into relationship with other characters having complementary, or conflicting values, desires and goals. Out of their interplay the dramatist builds a determinate literary work' (*Appropriating Shakespeare*, New Haven, 1993, p. 75).

19 *Notorious Identity*, p. 14.

20 Engle, *Shakespearean Pragmatism*, p. 60, has a variant on this in which rival discourses are counterposed to the composite entity 'actor-agent' and not simply to each other.

21 *Faultlines*, p. 64.

22 *Shakespearean Pragmatism*, p. 62.

concepts of utterance and voice to combat the post-structuralist tendency to treat 'textuality' or 'discourse' as superpersonal forces. In an analysis of *Richard II*, he shows that a character is neither a stable, autonomous entity nor a mere mouthpiece of all-powerful discourses. Rather, it is a dynamic phenomenon involved in and produced by a complex network of utterances, each of which is itself an arena of different voices, 'a meeting ground for the struggles and agreements of social forces, accents, intonations . . .'[23] The interactive mode of character creation I outlined earlier is compatible with these recent approaches, I believe.

Nevertheless, it seems to me that there is still a missing link between character in its aspect of agency and character as an arena of discourses, utterances, or voices. When competing discourses or voices converge in a single character, they do not give off sparks by themselves. In order actually to *be* competitive in drama they need to be *perceived* as competitive – otherwise they will not influence the course of the action and their incompatibility may well pass unnoticed. Generally this means that they need to be *experienced* as conflicting by the character who voices or embodies them in his or her actions. Discourses of aristocratic oligarchy and discourses of absolute monarchy may, in early modern England, be conflictual in general political terms, but for them to become theatrically conflictual they have to be *lived* by their bearer as incompatible. We need in other words to posit that characters may be, and in Shakespeare often are, represented as *selves* (unitary if not unified selves) capable of taking these discourses in charge and assuming responsibility for their ideological conflictuality by living them as their *individual* dilemma. Characters thus conceived (and only these) will voice their discourses from the *first-person standpoint*. In other words, they will not simply vehicle these discourses but they will relate to them or entertain them as *values*. Values, according to Charles Taylor, are one of the cornerstones of selfhood, given that 'it belongs to human agency to exist in a space of questions about strongly valued goods, prior to all choice or adventitious cultural change'.[24] The Bakhtinian notion of human selfhood as 'a form of answering and as thus taking responsibility for one's responses to surrounding discourse' similarly admits the essential role of values.[25] But since characters are fictional creations, how can we know whether the competing discourses have become values, are experienced 'first-personally' by them? The answer, presumably, is that they will show emotional stress. The greater their commitment to rival discourses, the greater the anxiety they will display. Negative affect of this kind will, I suggest, be interpreted by an audience as a symptom that a character is a self struggling to take moral responsibility for competing discourses and registering what it costs him or her. I follow Taylor in taking 'self' as having an essential moral component:

> To know who I am is a species of knowing where I stand. My identity is defined by the commitments and identifications which provide the frame or horizon within which I can try to determine from case to case what is good, or valuable, or what ought to be done, or what I endorse or oppose. In other words, it is the horizon in which I am capable of taking a stand.[26]

---

23 James R. Siemon, '"Subjected thus": Utterance, Character and *Richard II*', *Shakespeare Jahrbuch* (East) 126 (1990), 65–80, p. 65. Further theoretical support for the rejection of what Siemon calls the 'totalizing claims' of textuality or discursive formations can be found in Pierre Bourdieu's critique of the realism of the structure in his *Outline of a Theory of Practice* (Cambridge, 1986), p. 72.

24 *Sources of the Self* (Cambridge, Mass., 1989), p. 31.

25 See Engle, *Shakespearean Pragmatism*, p. 62.

26 *Sources of the Self*, p. 27. David Aers has recently argued that various aspects of the 'modern' self date back at least to the middle ages: 'There is no reason to think that languages and experiences of inwardness, of interiority, of divided selves, of splits between outer realities and inner forms of being, were unknown before the seventeenth century, before capitalism, before the "bourgeoisie", before Descartes, before the disciplinary regimes addressed in Foucault's *Discipline and Punish*' ('A Whisper in the Ear of Early Modernists', in *Culture and History 1350–1600*, Detroit, 1992, ed. D. Aers, p. 186).

Siemon, in his illuminating discussion of the way 'speech and speaker are shaped in dialogical interrelation with their multiple interlocutors' in *Richard II*, comments as follows on the passage in 1.3. in which Gaunt disowns his earlier advice to Richard about the banishment of Bolingbroke:

> Gaunt takes back what he said because, in effect, he did not say it: approached in a particular discourse (bid to argue juridically 'as a judge' instead of paternally 'like a father'); confronted with a relationship constructed according to certain values (the aristocratic honor culture's higher standards for 'my child' than for a 'stranger'); fearing a critical response from his interlocutors on the basis of these values if lenient rather than 'strict' (seeking to avoid 'slander' as 'partial'); and anticipating amelioration of an overly harsh judgment by his interlocutors on the basis of lineage values he assumes they share (hoping some will restore his 'own' and his 'life' which an heir would represent in those values). Despite the potential self-contradictoriness in this account, its burden is tellingly summed up in Gaunt's protest that far from being interpretable as simple expressions of his will, his express judgments upon his son as just previously upon himself are not his own: 'You gave leave to my unwilling tongue / Against my will to do myself this wrong.' The personal pronouns here eloquently testify against the notion of a solitary ego as the origin or proprietor even of the words of its 'own' mouth. Gaunt's 'yes' to the sentence was not 'yes' at all, but appears here represented as a dialogized utterance, pre-formed and mediated among a complex of struggling social evaluations and differentiations.[27]

Siemon elegantly proves that the origin of Gaunt's words cannot be identified in a 'solitary ego'. But this does not prevent them from being taken in charge by the simulacrum of a self. As is implied by his 'alas' (a standardized signal of anxiety), Gaunt is conceived as a self who exists 'in a space of questions about strongly valued goods'. Tension between these goods provokes dismay. His utterances are certainly mediated through other utterances, but his anxious response to them reveals that 'Gaunt', in the last analysis, is *that which takes these in charge*. When he says:

> You urged me as a judge, but I had rather
> You would have bid me argue like a father.
> Alas, I looked when some of you should say
> I was too strict to make mine own away,
> (1.3.230–3)

his self emerges in the form of an affective preference. Gaunt's 'self' is that which wishes he had been understood as a father when he was forced by circumstances to speak as a judge. It is that which, showing symptoms of distress, seeks to reinstate and take responsibility for a meaning that he had failed to communicate earlier.

What puts a premium on the bonding of affect with values in the creation of character is the public theatre's involvement in the dynamic market economy of contemporary London. Its capacity to portray fictional selves electrified by conflicts between values makes it an ideal site for exploring the moral and emotional turmoil unleashed when the contingent, pragmatic modes of evaluation fostered by a market economy come into collision with traditional essentialist values. The measuring of such values against their practical consequences, their cost in human terms, is a central feature of Shakespearian drama. Throughout the plays and Sonnets, as Engle has shown, we find

> both a view of social interaction as an economy, a diffuse network of discursive transactions which hang together according to humanly established (and thus mutable) patterns of exchange, and a tendency to treat truth, knowledge, and certainty as relatively stable goods in such an economy rather than gateways out of it.[28]

In addition to this general affect, the *specific* emotions characters show will define the particular moral and ideological stance they take towards the discourses in question. It has been

[27] '"Subjected thus"', p. 60. The unspecified edition from which Siemon quotes follows the (longer) quarto version for Gaunt's speech.

[28] Engle, *Shakespearean Pragmatism*, p. 3.

suggested by Theodore Sarbin that what we today call emotions is really a variegated collection of situated actions which serve to establish moral identity roles (as distinct from social roles):

On this formulation, grief, anger, jealousy, and exultation, for example, are the names of roles played out in the service of maintaining or enhancing one's moral identity. They are patterned actions in the same sense that greetings and farewells are patterned actions. But the patterns of conduct of identity roles are intimately connected to values. It is in support of one's values that the actor makes judgments about the conduct of self and other. The judgment about the effect of an action on one's identity determines whether the actor will enact an identity role, making use of dramatistic rhetoric to convince self and/or other of the legitimacy of his or her moral claims.[29]

Emotions are thus like miniature dramas which we learn to perform from childhood onward and which define our moral self-image. If this is true, then a character's emotional response to given discourses or events will not only suggest the value she or he attaches to them but it will also provide an important clue to the character's own moral identity or ethos. It is Kent's *indignation* at Lear's brutal rejection of Cordelia, or at Oswald's insolence, that reveals the quality of his commitment to feudal values – far more than his explicit declarations of fealty. The overall pattern of a character's emotional responses thus helps to define its ideological orientation towards the world. As Robert C. Solomon has pointed out,

Our emotions are not only projections; they are our *projects*. They are not only directed towards intentional objects; they are laden with *intentions to act*. Emotions are concerned not only with 'the way the world is' but with the way the world *ought* to be. Every emotion, in other words, is also a personal ideology, a projection into the future, and a system of hopes and desires, expectations and commitments, intentions and strategies for changing our world.[30]

Seen from this angle, then, a character is the resultant of the emotional stances it assumes towards the persons, events, discourses and utterances which form its environment.[31] Sometimes these stances will merge into a logically coherent whole, sometimes they will remain incompatible. In the latter case, as Alan Sinfield has pointed out, characters will either appear as selves capable of entertaining this incompatibility, or as radically *fissured*. Sinfield suggests, for instance, that although Macbeth's subjectivity is 'one swaying between divergent possible selves' and is 'radically insecure' it nevertheless appears 'adequately continuous'. Lady Macbeth, on the other hand, is 'sacrificed to keep Macbeth's story going': she 'cannot articulate complexity' and her character 'breaks down when it has to change'.[32]

We need of course to allow for the fact that in many cases a character's set of emotional stances may not be a unique individual combination but a manifestation, rather, of what Pierre Bourdieu calls a *habitus*. This term is used by Bourdieu to refer to 'systems of durable, transposable *dispositions*' produced in a group or community by a particular environment – for instance, 'the material conditions of existence characteristic of a class condition'. These dispositions generate regular patterns of behaviour that are neither the 'product of obedience to rules' nor, though 'objectively adapted to their goals', do they involve 'a conscious aiming at ends or an express mastery of the operations necessary to attain them'.[33] *Habitus* is a concept which has more explanatory power than, say, social type, since it embraces a wider range of features that might otherwise be mistaken for

[29] Theodore R. Sarbin, 'Emotions as Situated Actions', in *Emotions in Ideal Human Development*, eds. L. Cirillo and S. Wapner (Hillsdale, N.J., 1989), p. 87.

[30] Robert C. Solomon, *The Passions* (Notre Dame, 1983), p. 212 (his emphases).

[31] This, of course, is not the whole picture. Another central feature of character construction that I have no space to deal with here is the way characters are constituted by the kinds of speech acts they use.

[32] Sinfield, *Faultlines*, pp. 64–5.

[33] Pierre Bourdieu, *Outline*, p. 72 (his emphases).

an individual conformation. Laertes' turbulent response to his father's and sister's death is a pure expression of the *habitus* that fashions the behaviour of sons and brothers in a late-feudal, patriarchal court environment. It is precisely this which enables Claudius to exploit him so easily for his own purposes. Claudius's failure to manipulate Hamlet, on the other hand, is a symptom of the extent to which the son of his murdered brother turns out to be 'more than kin and less than kind': Hamlet is deeply estranged from his *habitus*, contemplating the actions and emotions it prescribes at times with radical scepticism, at times with genuine nostalgia for its lost simplicities. This dissonance is one of the factors that helps to create such a strong impression of Hamlet's autonomous agency.

To recognize that many – though, it is important to stress, by no means all – Shakespearian characters are constructed so as to represent persons with complex but unitary selves in no way implies that we should refrain from exploring their relationship to 'discursive formations' and the like. These can and should be unpacked, but I believe that it is insofar as they are taken in charge by a character-as-self that they enter most effectively into the multivocal arena of utterances and thus contribute most powerfully to the ongoing dynamic of the play.

Let me now try to flesh out some of the preceding remarks by examining part of Isabella's first interview with Angelo in *Measure for Measure* 2.2.

At the beginning of the encounter Isabella's abhorrence for Claudio's fault deprives her arguments of conviction and rhetorical force. But when she begins to ground her reasoning on the principle that man is sinful by nature and thus must both seek mercy and be merciful, she is able to assume a firmer and less conflictual discursive position. Her rising vehemence signals the personal value to her of the arguments she is deploying, while Lucio's approving comments on her performance serve to objectify what we might call her emotional self production.[34] Why, then, is Angelo so slow to be moved, responding coolly and with a logic as good as or better than Isabella's? It helps create suspense of course, but more to the point here is the implication that it takes time for a speaker to produce significant psychological effects on another self – which of course is a way of suggesting that this other *is* a self. In addition, the audience is given time to feel the full impact of Isabella's passionate appeal and thus to desire its success. Spectators are manoeuvred into a position where they want Angelo to be persuaded. This is tantamount to acknowledging him as a person susceptible to emotions like their own.

Isabella's argument that

> man, proud man,
> Dressed in a little brief authority,
> Most ignorant of what he's most assured,
> His glassy essence, like an angry ape
> Plays such fantastic tricks before high heaven
> As makes the angels weep (2.2.120–5)

makes the first visible breach in Angelo's defences. Lucio's charting of the emotional temperature ('He's coming; I perceive't', line 128) focuses the audience's attention on the fact that Angelo has an inner self susceptible of interpretation as well as of persuasion. Even before it is manifested in words, Angelo's transformation-through-interaction is shown as being the

34 Various critics have thrown light on this episode by reading Isabella's argumentation against a background of Renaissance rhetorical theory and practice. For a recent example, see Christy Desmet, *Reading Shakespeare's Characters* (Amherst, 1992). My reason for underplaying the rhetorical dimension here is (apart from one of space) that I believe the unfolding of dramatic dialogue here cannot be fully comprehended in terms of the way speaker and responder deploy strategies according to their predicted effects. While Shakespeare's (and his characters') rhetorical skills contribute essential elements to the interaction, they are, I believe, frequently subordinated to the dramatist's simulation of the *contingency* of reciprocal negotiations of personhood.

outcome not of an impersonal discursive or narrative logic but as a response, parallel to that of the audience, to the ongoing *performance* of another self. This is confirmed when Isabella makes a move ('That in the captain's but a choleric word, / Which in the soldier is flat blasphemy', lines 134–5) which surprises and impresses Lucio ('Art advised o' that? More on't', line 136) and puzzles Angelo ('Why do you put these sayings upon me?', line 137). We see Angelo, like Lucio, objectifying Isabella's use of proverbial (male) wisdom, and by seeking to discern her intention in using it, acknowledging her as the subject of her speech. Personhood is thus won on the field by Isabella through the negotiations of verbal interaction.[35] But Angelo's metadiscursive framing is itself caught up in the ongoing contest. His identification of Isabella's previous move as one of citation of pre-constituted discourse is now exploited by Isabella to make it impossible for him not to *acknowledge* her next point: 'Because authority, though it err like others, / Hath yet a kind of medicine in itself / That skins the vice o'th'top' (lines 138–40). In other words, Angelo has not only recognized Isabella as an intellectually autonomous source of her speech, thereby defining himself as a self capable of ascribing intentionality to another self, but he has also placed his own capacity to do so on record, admitted it as evidence. Consequently he cannot now elude Isabella's interpellation of him as a *person*, when she says 'Go to *your* bosom; / Knock there,' etc. (lines 140ff.). The 'you' Isabella invokes is one that he has placed in the arena, exposed to negotiation, accepted as fashioned moment by moment in social exchanges.

It is instructive to compare this episode with George Whetstone's three renderings of the encounter. The prose version in his *Heptameron of Civil Discourses* was printed in 1582, four years after his play of *Promos and Cassandra*, in which the interview is both narrated in the 'Argument' and dramatized in 2.3. As T. J. B. Spencer has suggested, Shakespeare probably read the novella as well as the play (the name Isabella appears in the former but not in the latter). There, Cassandra's plea and Promos's reply are both presented in direct speech, the latter being prefaced by the narrator's remark that 'Promos's ears were not so attentive to hear Cassandra's ruthful tale as his eyes were settled to regard her excellent beauty.'[36] The narrative thus *forecloses* any possibility that the interaction might take an unpredictable turn. It leaves no space for Promos to recognize Cassandra as a *person*. The 'Argument' of the play reports in advance how: '*Promos* regarding her good behaviours, and fantasyng her great beawtie, was much delighted with the sweete order of her talke ...'[37] Like her beauty, Cassandra's talk is an *aesthetic* attraction, not a sign of personhood. In the dramatized version Promos responds as follows to Cassandra's second and last speech pleading for leniency: 'Faire Dame, I see the naturall zeale thou bearest to *Andrugio*, / And for thy sake, (not his desart) this favour wyll I show ...' (2.3.38–9). He then expands on this in a brief soliloquy:

I do protest, hir modest wordes hath wrought in me
 a maze.
Though she be faire, she is not deckt with garish
 shewes for gaze;
Her bewtie lures, hir lookes cut off fond sutes with
 chast disdain.
O God, I feele a sodaine change that doth my
 freedome chayne. (2.3.49–52)

As he develops this episode in dramatic

[35] Cf. Daniel Dennett, 'Conditions of Personhood', in *The Identities of Persons*, ed. A. O. Rorty (Berkeley, 1976): 'whether something counts as a person depends in some way on an *attitude taken* toward it, a *stance adopted* with respect to it ... our treating him or her or it in this certain way is somehow and to some extent constitutive of its being a person' (p. 177, Dennett's emphases).

[36] 'The Story of Promos and Cassandra', in *Elizabethan Love Stories*, ed. T. J. B. Spencer (Harmondsworth, 1968), p. 120.

[37] In Geoffrey Bullough, *Narrative and Dramatic Sources of Shakespeare*, vol. 2 (London, 1958), p. 445.

dialogue Whetstone thus assigns Cassandra's words a more important role. But it is still their aesthetic rather than interactive quality that affects Promos; and they continue to be overshadowed by her looks. What is signally absent in Whetstone is anything resembling Isabella's *interpellation* of Angelo's person, and his *acknowledgement* of hers.

At this stage of the encounter in Shakespeare's version we see two dimensions of personhood interacting: what we might call the semantic self as a given of human nature – the sinful, postlapsarian self evoked in the thematic content of Isabella's speeches – and the interactional identity that is forged moment by moment in the theatrical here-and-now. It is both fitting and ironical that the theatrically-produced identity translates the universal fallen condition of man into the contingent *falling* condition of a particular man, as Angelo not only discovers a natural guiltiness within himself but enacts it in a theatrically very specific way.[38] His response, 'she speaks, and 'tis such sense / That my sense breeds with it' (lines 145–6), is more than a rational recognition that he is, after all, part of fallen humanity: it is a recognition of this recognition, a further move in a complex game of framing which gives the impression that Angelo and Isabella are endowed with what Charles Taylor calls 'radical reflexivity'.[39] What shakes Angelo is not simply Isabella's discourses as rhetorical arguments, or her prone and speechless dialect, but the combining and subsuming of these in the 'sense' produced by a speaking subject. This 'resultant' is what finally provokes Angelo's individual recognition of the other as a person before his *given* fallen nature sets his senses breeding. He acknowledges as much in this aside, since he presents his transformation as a *consequence* ('such ... that') of Isabella's challenge. At the same time, his reduction of Isabella to an object of his speech (to a 'she' instead of a 'you') and his pun on 'sense' show him endeavouring to escape from her presence-as-person. The jump from 'sense' as rational meaning produced by a self, to 'sense' as sensual appetite is quite arbitrary: the identity of the word is used as an alibi for a transition which has no logical or cultural coherence. Behind this slippage we glimpse a deeper tension – that between Shakespeare's sense of the existential openness of personal interaction and the closure of a preordained narrative. Angelo, regardless of the possible worlds opened by dialogue, must succumb to lust. Nevertheless, he cannot simply write off the effects of this dialogic emergence: the personhood Isabella has earned here continues to affect the form of his verbal behaviour even in their second encounter. At the opening of 2.4, Angelo is shown as still unable to give free reign to his lust as the narrative logic requires. He resorts again to punning in order to force Isabella's opening words ('I am come to know your pleasure', line 31) into a new mould of meaning: 'That you might know it would much better please me, / Than to demand what 'tis' (lines 32–3). Angelo is made incapable of a frontal attack precisely by his inescapable awareness of the personhood of Isabella that emerged during their previous interview. What we have observed in 2.2, then, is how interactional dialogue can become a site for the production of the self as *agency* – self as aware of and responding to transpersonal 'discourses', as opposed to being simply voiced or subjugated by them; self as capable of *choosing* whether or not to put on the destined livery.

In depicting personhood here as the product of negotiation, Shakespeare is clearly responding, among other things, to the way the increasingly 'placeless' market was affecting social relations in early modern England. His

[38] Anne Ferry, in *The 'Inward' Language* (Chicago, 1983, p. 41), notes that when sixteenth-century writers look into themselves, what they usually find is general humanity rather than a unique individual identity.

[39] Taylor, *Sources of the Self*: 'we can ... become aware of our awareness, try to experience our experiencing, focus on the way the world is *for* us. This is what I call taking a stance of radical reflexivity or adopting the first-person standpoint' (pp. 130–1).

presentation of this encounter embodies an emerging awareness that 'the self was a contingent, arbitrary, and instrumental affair, not a natural or supernatural calling', as Agnew puts it.[40] But such dramatic interactions do more than manifest or objectify a social process: they help to provide the new, negotiated personal identity with a moral legitimation. Stage dialogue, by its very nature, exposes acts of verbal manipulation and violence to a kind of scrutiny not normally possible in real life and in so doing sets up implicit norms of 'correct' interpersonal discourse. Characters who respect these norms show respect for others, and thus in their turn earn the respect of the judging audience. Agnew has argued that 'Elizabethan society operated in a state of diminished and diminishing transparency' as an expanding market economy challenged traditional structures and values, provoking a crisis of representation.[41] If this is so, the theatrical transparency of imagined interactions hints that a new road to authenticity may be available. By sharing in the construction of the implicit norms celebrated in dramatic dialogue, spectators may develop a sharper awareness of what it takes to see through the less transparent verbal manifestations of the bewildering contemporary world.

At this point in the interview between Isabella and Angelo, plot logic and interactive logic come apart. What has taken place on the dialogic level is an act of *hearing*, an act constituting persons, as two individuals starting out from a 'differentially consequential interaction'[42] for an instant achieve a commonality of viewpoints ('She speaks, and 'tis such sense ...').[43] What presumably ought to have ensued on this level is that Angelo should have accepted Isabella's request for mercy and eventually, perhaps, made her a proposal of marriage. But there is a narrative logic that cannot be eluded – that of the fictional story adapted from the source, and that of the vaster Christian narrative of fallen human nature: Angelo's moral rectitude must be overwhelmed by his passions. Does this mean that Angelo, like Lady Macbeth, must fall apart as a character? As Sinfield has noted, some characters seem constructed so as to express a sense of being selves capable of *entertaining* a conflict, others seem to split into two different, irreconcilable functions or discourses. There can be little doubt from Angelo's soliloquies that he comes under the former category. Compared with Promos, in whom no trace of an interactive self emerges through *hearing* the other, Angelo is a more tragic character. He is faced with incompatible options, each of which carries strong affect. On the one hand he genuinely desires to engage morally with other persons, on the other he 'hotly lusts' to use his power for sexual ends.

It seems to me that what we observe at this point is a clash between two principles or systems. One has its roots in essentialist values, to which the semantic structures of the adopted narrative are bound. This system is what Leeds Barroll takes as the framework for his investiga-

---

40 Agnew, *Worlds Apart*, p. 113.

41 *Ibid.*, p. 110.

42 The term is Barbara Herrnstein Smith's. In *Contingencies of Value* (Cambridge, Mass., 1988) she argues against the assumption that what takes place in verbal transactions is really *communication*. 'What there is, rather, is a *differentially consequential interaction*: that is, an interaction in which each party acts in relation to the other differently – in different and asymmetric ways and in accord with different specific motives – and also with different consequences for each' (p. 109). Although I do not share her conviction that verbal interaction is at rock bottom a linguistic market, there can be little doubt that it is often, even typically, engaged in by speakers to 'gain certain goods'.

43 Charles Taylor, observing that we can only attain personhood 'by being initiated into a language', claims that a crucial feature of conversation is that 'in talking about something, you and I make it an object for us together, that is, not just an object for me which happens also to be one for you, even if we add that I know that it's an object for you, and you know, etc. The object is for us in a strong sense, which I have tried to describe elsewhere with the notion of "public" or "common space"' (*Sources of the Self*, p. 35).

tion of character in early modern drama in his book *Artificial Persons*. He suggests that

> in a transcendentalist climate of opinion, it is assumed that all men essentially wish to be united or gain identity with some superhuman hypothetical 'personality'. Because of 'original sin', human fallibility, or other conditions taken to be inherent in mortals, men were also understood as being unable to comprehend the existence of this desire for unity in themselves.
>
> ... in the transcendentalistically oriented society, individual crises or tragic causations function within a concept of man's fallen condition. And in such a cultural context, the translation of psychological assumption into the mimesis of dramatic causation and process will espouse the redundancies of an appeal to the root concept of original sin or its ideological synonyms ...[44]

This system, however, comes into collision here with a competing principle – an emerging economy of contingent evaluation that both shapes and measures the consequences of discursive interaction, in a significant manifestation of Shakespearian pragmatism. As Engle has shown, this pragmatism is manifested in 'Shakespeare's capacity to bring abstraction up against an event or situation which tests it', and to evaluate discourse 'by the uses agents make of it, or the consequences in which discursive situations enmesh agents'.[45] The way these two principles interact in the dialogic production of personhood is an issue that remains to be explored in depth in Shakespearian criticism. The penetration of modes of evaluation characteristic of post-Reformation mercantile society into the very tissue of interpersonal discourse exposes traditional conceptions of the human individual to constant reappraisal. Some of the clearest traces of this confrontation are, I believe, to be found at those junctures where Shakespeare allows his 'given' characters to place their selves at risk by embracing (or wilfully shying away from) the openness of dialogue as they *negotiate* rights and obligations that were formerly part and parcel of their social standing. Our sense of their personhood, our impression that at such moments they are 'unified subjects meaningfully acting in the world',[46] surely owes much to the way that transactional dialogue offers characters a *point d'appui* from which they can objectify, at one and the same time, their old, static, 'given' selves and their new, dynamic, negotiated selves.

---

44 Columbia, S. Carolina, 1974, pp. 103, 254.

45 Engle, *Shakespearean Pragmatism*, p. 57. See also Charnes, *Notorious Identity*, p. 81. Thomas McAlindon's recent reaffirmation of Shakespeare's essentialism ('Cultural Materialism and the Ethics of Reading: or, the Radicalizing of Jacobean Tragedy', *Modern Language Review*, 90 (1995), 4, 830–46) while a useful reminder that essentialist conceptions play a vital role in the dramatist's thinking (as well as that of his contemporaries), fails in my opinion to allow for the pragmatic implications of the dramatic and theatrical dynamic so persuasively depicted by Engle and Charnes.

46 Cohen, 'The Subject of Shakespeare', p. 64.

# PREJUDICE AND LAW IN *THE MERCHANT OF VENICE*

B. J. SOKOL

## I

The legally institutionalized prejudice seen in *The Merchant of Venice* is repulsive from a modern perspective. I will argue that this play portrays deeply ironic images of social prejudice that offended Elizabethan standards of decency and fairness as well as ours. Paradoxically, these contemporary Elizabethan standards come into focus when the play is viewed from a perspective involving legal history, for they in fact trumped the prejudicial laws of Shakespeare's time.

In the updated approach to Shakespeare of his provocative book *Kill All the Lawyers?*, a practising American lawyer Daniel J. Kornstein advises Shylock to appeal against Portia's judgement.[1] And he makes frequent reference to modern legal doctrines, often specifically American, to show how these have evolved or advanced since Shakespeare's time. Yet Kornstein sometimes discusses issues and principles which have persisted in the Anglo-American legal tradition since Shakespeare's time, which may guide us to the shared social and moral vocabulary of Shakespeare and his age.

I share Kornstein's view that Shylock is presented by Shakespeare as distinctly ill-intentioned, yet still a man wronged and unjustly treated. I also agree that this 'minority view' in literary criticism negates certain *prima facie* appearances of the play, but it is a valid and necessary one because in the play's fictionally constructed world, as in the real world, 'appearances deceive'.[2] But I will base my position more historically than Kornstein's; to launch my own discussion I will note what is illuminating in his advice to Shylock, and how inaccuracies and anachronisms detract from it.

A first error is that this advice ignores Elizabethan jurisdictional and legal peculiarities relevant to *The Merchant of Venice*. The question of what jurisdiction, if any, Shakespeare had in mind for the play's fictional lawcase has been much debated. I have argued for the special appropriateness of a jurisdiction which was originally derived from Italy, but well known to Elizabethans. This was the jurisdiction of the pan-European traditional International Law Merchant. Uniquely in England, some Law Merchant tribunals allowed a combination of summary civil and criminal judgement (as is seen in the 'pie-Powders' court of Ben Jonson's *Bartholomew Fair*).[3] This very

---

[1] Daniel J. Kornstein, *Kill All the Lawyers?: Shakespeare's Legal Appeal* (Princeton University Press, 1994), 'Fie upon Your Law: *The Merchant of Venice*', pp. 63–89; the 'imaginary appeal' is outlined pp. 83–5.

[2] Kornstein, *Kill All the Lawyers*, pp. 77–9. A similar theme is given a very sophisticated basis in René Girard, '"To Entrap the Wisest"', in *Shylock*, ed. Harold Bloom (New York: Chelsea House, 1991), pp. 291–304, esp. pp. 297–300.

[3] My '*The Merchant of Venice* and the Law Merchant', *Renaissance Studies*, 6 (1992), 60–7, hereafter referred to as 'Law Merchant', argues that English *pie poudre* courts of the Law Merchant provided a model uniquely appropriate to the play, partly because they were able to

combination of judgements in the trial scene of *the Merchant of Venice* therefore need not have provided, *pace* Kornstein,[4] any grounds for an appeal.

Others of Kornstein's law points are less a-historical. He discusses at length a social need for appropriate limitations on the freedom to make contracts,[5] and there were parallel (if subtly different) sixteenth-century discussions of enforcement or relief from the provisions of 'sealed bonds' like Shylock's.[6]

Even more interesting, in spite of partial anachronism, is Kornstein's citation of a modern principle of 'equal protection of the laws', under which he condemns the 'vile Alien Statute' invoked by Portia against Shylock.[7] Despite his revulsion at the *un*equally protective 'Alien Statute' of Venice cited by Portia, at first glance such a statute would seem hardly remarkable from an Elizabethan perspective. In 1601 Elizabeth arranged to expel from England all 'Negars and blackamoors'.[8] In 1594 she seemed hesitant to punish the unfortunate Doctor Lopez,[9] but Jews were so *un*equally protected in her realm as to be officially outlawed.[10] Although they were not enacted, other Elizabethan anti-Alien laws were repeatedly proposed, and economic surveys were undertaken to investigate their applicability. Roman Catholics also suffered legal disabilities in Shakespeare's time, and possibly Shakespeare's family suffered under these.[11] Yet, despite these circumstances, I will argue that legal and social inequality based on prejudice *is* intended to be seen as unjust within the context of *The Merchant of Venice*.

## II

To bring this into focus, I will first trace allusions in the play to legalistic biblical materials. In the course of his dramatic handling of a litigious and mercantile Jew, Shakespeare drew so heavily upon biblical stories concerning especially property relations and legal vindication that *The Merchant of Venice* contains the most extensive biblical references in all his work. Current legal topics were also apparently meditated upon by Shakespeare for *The Merchant of Venice*. I believe that the play reflects a contemporary crisis about justice. Historically, this resulted from no simple matter of 'law before equity' or any converse formula, but rather from the philosophic casualties of a battleground between conflicting and combative jurisdictions.[12]

---

combine civil and criminal judgements. Fascinatingly, Jewish Law tribunals in pre-expulsion England also attended to both criminal and civil matters – see Sir Frederick Pollock and F. W. Maitland, *The History of English Law Before the Reign of Edward I*, 2 vols. (Cambridge University Press, 1898, 2nd edn repr. 1968), vol. 1, p. 474.

4 Kornstein, *Kill All the Lawyers*, p. 84.

5 *Ibid.*, pp. 68–79.

6 See 'Law Merchant', pp. 64–5.

7 Kornstein, *Kill All the Lawyers*, pp. 79–81.

8 Eldred Jones, *Othello's Countrymen: the African in English Renaissance Drama* (London: Oxford University Press, 1965), pp. 12–13.

9 See David S. Katz, *The Jews in the History of England 1485–1850* (Oxford: Clarendon Press, 1994), pp. 49–101. The execution for treason of Lopez in 1594 occasioned a wave of Elizabethan anti-Semitism which was engineered 'in Essex's interest' according to J. R. Brown, ed. the Arden Edition *The Merchant of Venice* (1955; London: Methuen, 1977), p. xxiii. (Except where otherwise noted, all references to the play will be from this edition.) But *Merchant* was unlikely to have been occasioned or influenced by the Earl of Essex's manipulation of the Lopez affair, since Shakespeare was allied with an anti-Essex faction; see my 'Holofernes in Rabelais and Shakespeare and some manuscript verses of Thomas Harriot', *Etudes Rabelaisiennes* 25 (1992), pp. 131–5.

10 In 1148 an English court upheld the first prosecution based on the infamous Jewish 'blood libel' (the case of William of Norwich) – see R. Po-chia Hsia, *The Myth of Ritual Murder* (New Haven: Yale University Press, 1988), p. 2, and Frank Felsenstein, 'Jews and Devils: Semitic Stereotypes of Late Medieval and Renaissance England', *Journal of Literature and Theology*, 4 (1990), p. 17. Following this, increasing restrictions and agitation led to the first European expulsion of Jews, from England in 1290.

11 E. A. J. Honigmann, *Shakespeare: the 'Lost Years'*, (Manchester University Press, 1985), pp. 115–25.

12 I argue in 'Law Merchant' that *The Merchant of Venice* is

Certainly the riddle of where true justice lies was made more complex both in *The Merchant of Venice* and in Shakespeare's London by the presence of economically important alien sub-communities. Those were generally tolerated, although their rights, for instance to trade and to employ English men and women, suffered periodic verbal attack and occasional outbursts of unofficial anti-foreigner rioting. So Shakespeare's allusions to social and ethical questions concerning aliens, as in Gobbo's ruminations on employment by Shylock, touched live issues. Yet not entirely live, for it is most likely that Elizabethan London did not provide Shakespeare or his audience with visible prototypes for the legal treatment and actual behaviour of Jews.[13] There were, however, many refugee households, and foreign merchants or visitors whom Shakespeare could have asked about continental Jews; with certainty, by early Jacobean times, Shakespeare had contacts with artisans who numbered among London's alien communities.[14]

The balance of evidence indicates that Shakespeare's personal associations were unlikely to have produced close observation of any Jews.[15] One of the surprises of *The Merchant of Venice*, therefore, is that he imagined a Shylock exhibiting a propensity often seen in tolerated Jewish minorities, which is his enthusiastic voluntary turning to Christian courts and lawyers.[16] Shylock's doomed pursuit of a Venetian legal underpinning for his revenge against Venice embodies some of the most complex human motives portrayed in the play.

## III

In his pursuit of revenge Shylock repeatedly makes references to Old Testament stories of the legal vindication of the oppressed and of the restoration of their denied freedom or rights. One such reference is made in a moment of anticipated triumph, when all seems to be going Shylock's way in his lawcase against the Christian merchant Antonio. Highly gratified by the apparent progress of the case, Shylock exclaims

---

set in the context of profound jurisprudential problems arising from the competition for profitable business of King's Bench with Common Pleas, the intellectual jostling of common law with equity, and the common lawyers' attack on the powers of the special jurisdictions of Borough Courts, Merchant Law, Admiralty, Staple Courts, etc. (not officially over until 1977!).

13 A community of Sephardi Jews was present in Shakespeare's London: see Lucien Wolf, 'Jews in Elizabethan England', *Transactions of the Jewish Historical Society*, 11 (1928), 1–91, which states, pp. 21–2, that the Marranos were tolerated 'so long as they did not break the law or outrage public sentiment', although once, in 1592, they departed from secrecy to 'assemble for Divine worship in London' under diplomatic protection. According to Katz, *The Jews*, p. 108, these Marranos were generally so secretive that 'The only Jews of most people's acquaintance were biblical figures, literary characters, and entirely imaginary.' On contrary speculations see below.

14 As seen from the 1612 lawsuit *Bellot vs. Mountjoy*, discussed in S. Schoenbaum, *William Shakespeare: A Compact Documentary Life* (New York: New American Library, 1986), pp. 260–4 and E. K. Chambers, *William Shakespeare: A Study of Facts and Problems*, 2 vols. (Oxford: Clarendon Press, 1930), vol. 2, pp. 90–5. On Shakespeare and the mainly foreign Southwark sculptors see my 'Painted Statues, Ben Jonson and Shakespeare', *Journal of the Warburg and Courtauld Institutes*, 52 (1989), 250–3.

15 On whether Shakespeare knew any of the 'hundred or more' Jews in his London see James Shapiro, *Shakespeare and the Jews* (The Parkes Lecture: University of Southampton, 1992), pp. 1–7. This is generally sceptical, but notes, p. 17, that Thomas Coryate 'expresses no surprise [. . .] that Amis [a Jew Coryate met in Constantinople] had spent thirty years in a London that many scholars assume was free of Jews'.

Shakespeare's acquaintance with converted Italian Jews could be argued if he knew of John Florio's partial Jewishness, or else through the highly unlikely actuality that: (1) Emilia Bassano Lanier was intimate with Shakespeare, as alleged by A. L. Rowse, ed., Emilia Lanier, *The Poems of Shakespeare's Dark Lady* (London, 1978), pp. 6–37; (2) all of the musical Bassano family in England were Jews, as is well argued by Roger Prior, 'Jewish Musicians in the Tudor Court', *Musical Quarterly*, 49 (1983), 253–95, p. 253; (3) the staunchly Christian Emilia Bassano even knew of her ancestral faith; (5) she confided about this to Shakespeare. Only if these concur is it possible that Emilia's Jewishness might have influenced *The Merchant of Venice*, as alleged in A. L. Rowse, *What Shakespeare Read – and Thought* (New York: Coward, McCann and Geoghegan, 1981), p. 172.

16 As detailed by Robert Kirsner in 'Rabbi Sem Tob the

of the seemingly unbiased Christian justicer Portia/Balthazar: 'A Daniel come to judgment: yea, a Daniel!' (4.1.219). Significantly, the name 'Daniel' means in Hebrew 'God has judged'.

Shylock does not refer directly to the biblical book of Daniel in which the exiled Jewish hero is first valued for skill in interpreting dreams and visions, but then, for his piety, is thrown into a lions' den. Yet there is a parallel between various demands for the rigid application of Venetian laws in Shakespeare's play and the legalistic basis for Daniel's ordeal; Daniel is punished through the application of an inflexible law of the Medes and Persians obtained by his enemies solely in order to catch Daniel out.[17]

Let us delay discussion of such stories of jurisprudential chicanery to note first that Shylock explicitly refers to Daniel as a shrewd lawyer, rather than as an unfairly treated Jewish alien. Shylock's reference must then be to the story in the book of Susanna in which Daniel appears as a resourceful detective/advocate. In this apocryphal book of Shakespeare's frequently employed Geneva Bible, Daniel wins a court case for the innocent but vulnerable Susanna, and thereby defends justice itself. He astutely represents her, saving her person and her reputation despite the apparent hopelessness of confronting the perjured testimony of two salacious Elders. These lying old men are not only establishment figures, but also possess the crushing moral authority of actually being judges. What is crucial in Shylock's allusion is that Daniel's advocacy for Susanna before the court of the people defends the friendless weak against the socially powerful. It is also important that Daniel's defence of Susanna relies on a cunning legal stratagem; he separates the two false witnesses and traps them into contradictory statements. The risky legal adventures of Susanna lead to a biblical conclusion that God 'saves those who hope in him', even if they are in desperate straits.

As his own hopes rise, Shylock begins to identify himself with a socially weaker party avenged and vindicated by law, and so remembers Susanna's legal rescue by Daniel. His joy in seeming to win his law case with Portia's aid shows Shylock's complex motives, which include not only revenge against powerful Antonio, but also a desire for public acknowledgement of his rights, and thus for social recognition.

Shylock's intended foul revenge is only ambiguously legal, and is necessarily incapable of rendering the good he desires. Nevertheless, in the complexity of his motivation Shylock is unique among fictional Jews of the age. These were typically stereotyped as monsters of furtive, gloating, mass-murdering perfidy. Correspondingly, Shylock's broken-hearted ending is unlike the merely physical dismemberment through torture that demolishes other Elizabethan literary Jew-monsters.

## IV

Shylock's excitement when he lauds Portia's Daniel-like astuteness is not only villainous gloating. The peculiarly urgent significance he attaches to his anticipated legal victory is clarified by a consideration of Shylock's lengthier allusions early in the play to the legal manoeuvres recorded in the Book of Genesis of the patriarch Jacob. These are manoeuvres that Shylock finds wholly good. Shylock first men-

Poetic "Melamed" of Fourteenth Century Spain', the *Sepharad 1492–1992* conference (7–10 May 1992) at San Francisco State University. To illustrate typicality Professor Kirsner told me a parallel anecdote from his own life: the congregation of the Feinberg synagogue of Cincinnati Ohio, divided in the 1950s over whether to seat women with men during religious services or to preserve traditional segregation, asked an eminent Christian judge to decide the issue (he chose integration).

17 Daniel 6:4. The conspiratorial legal moves of the envious rivals against Daniel are emphasized in the twelfth-century text of *The Play of Daniel* (Egerton Ms. 2615) and in W. H. Auden's poem 'Daniel [...] a sermon' written to accompany the play's 1958 performance: these texts are printed in the album booklet of the performance, Decca DL 9402.

tions Jacob's wrested inheritance, 'wrought' by his 'wise mother' (1.3.68), thus making the only approving comment on mothers in *The Merchant of Venice* (all others are bawdy, cynical or both).[18] This allusion introduces an explicitly approving account by Shylock of the trickery Jacob used to gain an advantage over the revenge upon Laban. Both biblical stories, purportedly told to justify lending money for interest, are oblique to this purpose, but both have other compelling resonances in *The Merchant of Venice*.

An important factor common to both of these stories is that they involve peculiar dealings with animals. This fact, if not its significance, is obvious in Shylock's account from Genesis 30–1 of how 'Jacob graz'd his uncle Laban's sheep' (1.3.66), but it arises also in connection with his allusion to how Jacob became holy Abraham's 'third possessor' (1.3.68–9), that is, the third Hebrew patriarch. Genesis 27 tells how Jacob's 'wise mother' Rebekah helped him to trick the second patriarch, Isaac, into giving to him a deathbed blessing intended for the first-born son Esau. To this end Rebekah covered Jacob with the 'skins of the kids' so that he appeared to blind Isaac's touch to be a 'hairy man' like Esau, and she dressed him in animal skins smelling of the hunter Esau. This looks like a direct application of a technique of benevolent deception still practised by shepherds today; to save an orphaned lamb they place the skin of a stillborn lamb over it to trick the stillborn's mother into accepting it as her own. Shakespeare, raised near the Cotswolds, knew of such techniques of husbandry, as many in his audiences may have done. For them Shylock's allusion to the biblical pastoralist's ruse was a first hint in *The Merchant of Venice* of an inspired use of trickery.

The story of Jacob and blind Isaac re-echoes in the play in the ludicrous episode of the 'confusions', or practical jokes, perpetrated by Launcelot Gobbo on his 'more than sand-blind' father, who refuses him blessings, finding him *too* hairy (2.2.30–95). This burlesque emphasizes how in the Bible divinely controlled fate, acting through means that may even seem unjust, selects a destined heir through deception.

After alluding to Jacob's inheritance, Shylock gives Antonio a rendition of the story of Jacob's revenge on Laban which, in the context of their ongoing financial negotiations, has sinister implications.[19] Involving a crafty contract, in effect a 'merry bond', which yields redress for a legitimate grievance, this story again describes Jacob's trickery. After Laban has repeatedly cheated Jacob of the rewards due for decades of labour, Jacob negotiates for a final wage all the (normally rare) black or parti-coloured offspring of his flocks. Jacob then employs specialized animal breeding techniques, to his great advantage.[20] By inducing all the best animals of Laban's flocks to conceive 'streak'd and pied' offspring, he gains all the profits of the herds.[21]

This biblical story, like the tale of Jacob

[18] Aside from Shylock's perceptions of Rebekah and Leah, the play excludes images of powerful women and of women valued as other than possessions. So, all of Portia's shrewd actions require denial of gender while her rival Antonio loses all his vigour when offering a breast in false-feminine nurturance. My 'Constitutive Signifiers or Fetishes in *The Merchant of Venice*?', *The International Journal of Psycho-Analysis*, 76 (1995), 373–87, finds these issues central.

[19] These implications are not analysed in John Scott Colley, 'Launcelot, Jacob, and Esau: Old and New Law in *The Merchant of Venice*', *Yearbook of English Studies*, 10 (1980), 181–9, which sees Shylock's reference to the biblical story of Jacob and Laban only in relation to the story of Jacob and Esau. Colley references only the Bishops' Bible.

[20] Vexed questions of just what Jacob's special methods of cattle breeding were, and particularly whether they were natural or miraculous in operation, are discussed in an essay on the tradition that maternal imagination may affect embryos: M. D. Reeve, 'Conceptions', *Proceedings of the Cambridge Philological Society*, 215 (1989), 81–112. Reeve's discussion of exegetical and textual problems relevant to Jacob and Laban, pp. 85–92, does not consider Shakespeare or the Bible translations that he used.

[21] That Laban's coloured animals have especially high value is richly ironic in the racial contexts of *The Merchant of Venice*, as we shall see.

acquiring Esau's blessing and birthright, might seem to us only an account of crafty cheating. But the Renaissance responded differently to Jacob's tactics.[22] The episode of the coloured sheep is followed in Genesis by Jacob's explanation to his two wives (Laban's daughters) that God Himself ordained his success (31:4–10). In the Geneva or 'Breeches' translation of the Bible often used by Shakespeare the passage is glossed marginally: 'This declareth that the thing which Iacob did before, was by Gods commandement, and not through deceite.'[23] Next Jacob tells his wives that in a dream God's angel showed him the way to his safe vindication, and the Geneva Bible glosses: 'This Angell was Christ.' Thus Shakespeare's audience may well have held Jacob's cunning legal moves to be an unorthodox but no less justified means of attaining an outcome ordained divinely, an outcome vindicating the oppressed.

Just like Jacob, whom he describes making a seemingly foolish but wily contract with oppressive Laban, Shylock obtains a silly-seeming 'merry bond' from Antonio. His aim is also to obtain compensation. Analogously with Jacob wearing animal skins, Shylock later mimics animality in his insistence on taking Antonio's flesh (justifying accusations he is a 'cut-throat dog' or 'wolf'). Antonio, for his part, notices merely that Shylock's story of Jacob's practice against Laban does not excuse the taking of monetary interest (nor does Shylock take any from Antonio on this occasion). There is deep irony in how the Christian merchant impatiently understands Shylock's stories in a mercantile light only, and cannot hear how much the Jew admires the third biblical patriarch's skill in obtaining a 'merry' legal redress for injustices.[24]

The picture unseen by Antonio in Shylock's story, of the powerless foreigner Jacob besting the established local patriarch Laban, explains why Shylock does not retire in defeat after the egregious theft of his wealth and his daughter. He seeks rather for vindication *on the terms of Venetian justice*, and yearns to present such an excellent legal case against Antonio that it is sure to succeed.[25] Just as Othello must show himself the most superb of Venetian soldiers to overcome the racial prejudices that he has internalized, so Shylock must show himself to be the most adroit Venetian litigant and businessman.

There are things in Shakespeare that cannot be appreciated without imagining that some of his characters have mental interiors. Why did Antonio fail to comprehend the point of Shylock's story about Jacob's divinely inspired revenge, and also why isn't he made suspicious by Shylock's willingness to lend him money without taking interest? Is he distracted even more than his unworldly 'want-wit' sadness described at the play's start might account for, or deaf to the ominous drift of Shylock's question: 'Hath a dog money? Is it possible / A cur can lend thee three thousand ducats?' (1.3.116–17)? In twenty lines Shylock five times repeats that Antonio has abused him as a 'dog' or 'cur'. Antonio's response is, 'I am as like to call thee so again, / To spet on thee again' (1.3.126). Thus Antonio flaunts his hatred of the Jew while he puts his life in hands that must be clenched at hearing his hate.

This may seem suicidal. Indeed by the time of his law trial Antonio's melancholy has deep-

[22] On divine validation of the trickery of Esau see Colley, 'Launcelot, Jacob and Esau', p. 186. Condoned trickery constitutes a huge theme reflected in Solomonic justice, Jesuit teachings on equivocation, the trick statue in Tirso de Molina's *Don Juan*, Duke Vincentio's 'craft' in *Measure for Measure*, etc.

[23] *The Bible*, trans. L. Tomson (London: Christopher Barker, 1597).

[24] Barbara K. Lewalski, 'Biblical Allusion and Allegory in *The Merchant of Venice*', in *Shylock*, ed. Harold Bloom (New York: Chelsea House, 1991), pp. 236–51, suggests in a note, p. 250, that Antonio may allude to the biblical justification of Jacob's action. But Antonio's impatient remark that Jacob's 'venture [. . .] sway'd and fashion'd by the hand of heaven' cannot 'make interest good? / Or is our gold and silver ewes and rams?' (1.3.86–90) shows that he has not understood how, for Shylock, trickery of the unjust may provide a divinely ordained recompense.

[25] See 'Law Merchant', pp. 64–5.

ened to the point where he craves only death. Using animal imagery in ways new to the play, he speaks of himself as a sacrificial lamb. Correspondingly, he and Gratiano relabel the former 'dog' Shylock as a 'wolf', perhaps recalling the name of the infamous Doctor Lopez. But unlike the historical Lopez,[26] Shylock makes an excellent legal case for himself, which despite prejudice seems to give him ascendancy.

At this point Shylock gleefully seizes the dramatic and linguistic initiative, transforming the Christians' animal images by saying that he intends to use Antonio in no other way than they use 'many a purchas'd slave, / Which (like your asses, and your dogs and mules) / You use in abject and in slavish parts, / Because you bought them' (4.1.90–3). In other words, Shylock spitefully reviles the Christians by claiming to imitate their low moral stature. Despite sentimentalists' readings, Shylock similarly concludes the famous 'Hath not a Jew eyes?' speech not with a noble plea for equality, but by spitefully justifying a Jew's desire for Bacon's 'wild justice' of illegal revenge on the basis of ferocious 'Christian example' (3.1.60–6). However, in his argument about asses and slaves Shylock may extend his sarcasm into an even more bitter and unexpected area than such levelling ethical nihilism. In the First Folio punctuation (more clearly than in the Arden), his ambiguous retort may even propose that the Christians might support bestiality:

> You haue among you many a purchast slaue,
> Which like your Asses, and your Dogs and Mules,
> You vse in abiect and in slauish parts,
> Because you bought them. Shall I say to you,
> Let them be free, marrie them to your heires?
>
> (TLN 1996–2000)

We will find the legal and ideological aspects of such a suggestion crucial. Before addressing them, we may note that Shylock, in taxing the Christians on keeping slaves, may recall with bitterness the Scholastic doctrine that 'all Jews collectively inherited servile status to Christians'.[27] It may also reflect the legal status of Jews as the king's property in England between the Conquest and their expulsion.[28]

But usually (or in practice) such semi-feudal ownership was more constrained by decency than Shylock's mercantile 'asses/slaves' equation,[29] which obliterates distinctions of human life, animal life and material goods. Indeed the very making of such an equation might seem to condemn Shylock's morality, compared with the Christians'. But the play quite promptly upsets this distinction, by showing two Venetian men blithely regarding their wives as their absolute property, as disposable as so much livestock:

> BASSANIO
> Antonio I am married to a wife
> Which is as dear to me as life itself,
> But life itself, my wife, and all the world,
> Are not with me esteem'd above thy life.
> I would lose all, ay sacrifice them all
> Here to this devil, to deliver you.
> [...]
>
> GRATIANO
> I have a wife who I protest I love, –
> I would she were in heaven, so she could
> Entreat some power to change this currish Jew.
>
> (4.1.278–88)

On hearing these edifying offers, Shylock remarks with wholly justified sarcasm, and also in dismay for his apostate daughter, 'These be the Christian husbands!'

## V

Often without explicit censure, *The Merchant of*

---

[26] See Katz, *The Jews*, pp. 49–101.

[27] Hsia, *The Myth of Ritual Murder*, p. 114, discusses Aquinas' and Duns Scotus' views.

[28] See Pollock and Maitland, *The History of English Law*, vol. 1, 468–75, and William Holdsworth, *A History of English Law*, 16 vols. (London: Methuen, 1903–), vol. 1, pp. 45–6.

[29] Pollock and Maitland, *The History of English Law*, vol. 1, 471, explains: 'the Jew, though he is the king's serf, is a freeman in relation to all other persons'. See R. A. Routledge, 'The Legal Status of the Jews in England, 1190–1790', *The Journal of Legal History*, 3 (1982), 91–124.

*Venice* repeatedly presents characters confusing human with animal life, thereby suggesting ethical equations of life with property. Thus Shylock dismisses his lazy servant Gobbo with comparisons to unprofitable livestock (2.5.45–50).

Later Shylock seems to equate his paternal relationship with cash when he polishes Marlowe's Barabas's 'O girl! O gold! O beauty! O my bliss!' to: 'My daughter, O my ducats! O my daughter!' (2.8.15). But Shakespeare, as opposed to Marlowe, tempers his Jew's mercenariness in relation to his daughter when the human/animal *distinction* becomes crucial in Shylock's shocked response to learning of Jessica's bartering of Leah's love-token turquoise ring for a monkey.

Shylock's hatred of Antonio is also not limited by a cash nexus; no amount of 'moneys' can buy off his revenge on his reviler and tormentor. Yet he explains this with bitter animal/human sarcasm, pretending that his hatred is as inexplicable as an animal phobia: 'men there are love not a gaping pig! / Some that are mad if they behold a cat!'

There are many other strange concatenations of hatred with animal imagery in the play, as when Shylock sarcastically mocks his own supposed mercenariness by asserting that a financial option on Antonio's human flesh is 'not so estimable, profitable neither / As flesh of muttons, beefs, or goats' (1.3.162–3). These concatenations are focused and elucidated by an oddity of legal history. To find the appropriate connection we must take a close look into some little regarded elements of the play.

## VI

Seemingly minor excrescences of Shakespearian texts may hold clues to deep themes and meanings. One such excrescence produces a conundrum and tonal crux of *The Merchant of Venice* when, in supposedly idyllic Belmont, the newly married Lorenzo accuses Launcelot Gobbo of the 'getting up of the negro's belly' (3.5.35). This accusation is framed in a scene containing much quibbling, and might seem to disclose no more than the insignificant tastelessness of a bawdy mini-subplot. But the complex wording of Gobbo's reply to Lorenzo's accusation serves rather as a key, or the second half of a key, to unlock the cupboard of prevalent social attitudes as portrayed in Belmont. Evaluation of these attitudes is crucial for a proper understanding of the play.

The first half of the key provided by Gobbo's overtly crude excuse for his fornication is found in the concept behind a repulsive legality noted by Sir Edward Coke. Coke discusses a law symptomatic of fear and hatred which made a marriage between a Christian and Jew equivalent to the *clamantia peccata* of sodomy and bestiality. According to his *Institutes*, 'the party so offending should be burnt alive'.[30] Indeed an unusual case of such a burning in 1222 is discussed in Pollock and Maitland's monumental *History of English Law*,[31] which also ponders an alternative view that burial alive was more appropriate than burning for Christians married to Jews.[32]

---

[30] Sir Edward Coke, *Third Part of the Institutes of the Laws of England* (London, 1644), p. 89. A note in a contemporary hand in the British Library copy 508.g.5(2.) adds, 'But if converted he shall not be burnt'.

[31] Pollock and Maitland, *The History of English Law*, vol. 2, p. 584: 'Stephen Langton [...] degraded and handed over to lay power a deacon who had turned Jew for the love of a Jewess. The apostate was delivered to the sheriff of Oxfordshire, who forthwith burnt him [... This] prompt action seems to have surprised his contemporaries, but was approved by Bracton'. Archbishop Langton's proceedings became quite famous for legal and political reasons discussed in F. W. Maitland, 'The Deacon and the Jewess; or, Apostacy at Common Law', *Collected Papers*, ed. H. A. L. Fisher, 3 vols. (Cambridge University Press, 1911), vol. 1, pp. 385–406. Pollock and Maitland, vol. 2, p. 394 cites a converse case where one partner in a Jewish marriage converts to Christianity, a rare instance where a full divorce allowing remarriage was allowed, and another case in which 'a Jewish widow was refused her dower on the ground that her husband had been converted'.

[32] *Ibid.*, vol. 2, p. 549.

However, for our discussion, not rare punishments but the legal equivalencing of Jewish miscegenation with bestiality is most significant. For, even beyond biblical injunctions, Shakespeare's age viewed the *clamantia peccata* of bestiality with an anxiety fuelled by ideological terror.[33] Although actual indictments in Elizabethan England for bestiality were rare, and convictions still rarer,[34] the offence was violently condemned. According to the analysis of Keith Thomas, this was because it violated an insecure yet crucial division of humans from animals.[35] So nudity, long hair, night work, nocturnal burglary (for, said Coke's *Institutes*, night was 'the time [...] wherein beasts run about seeking their prey'), the play-acting of animal roles and even swimming caused great anxiety.[36] No wonder then, wrote Thomas:

> Bestiality, accordingly, was the worst of sexual crimes because, as one Stuart moralist put it, 'it turns man into a very beast, makes a man a member of a brute creature.' The sin was the sin of confusion; it was immoral to mix the categories. Injunctions against 'buggery with beasts' were standard in seventeenth-century moral literature, though occasionally the topic was passed over, 'the fact being more filthy than to be spoken of.' Bestiality became a capital offence in 1543 and, with one brief interval [1553–62], remained so until 1861. Incest, by contrast, was not a secular crime at all until the twentieth century.

In accord with what Keith Thomas identifies as persistent early-modern 'discourses on the animal nature of negroes',[37] the doctrine equating Jewish–Christian miscegenation with bestiality is extended to Moorish–European miscegenation also when envious Iago repeatedly describes newly married Othello and Desdemona as beasts coupling.[38] In the light of such equivalencing, suggesting ideological damnation beyond any aesthetic repugnance, we may understand why Portia so strongly abhors the prospect of marriage with a Prince having 'the complexion of a devil', even if 'he have the condition of a saint' (1.2.123–4).

The legal equivalencing of miscegenated human marriages with the terrible *clamantia peccata* of bestiality may also help explain why *The Merchant of Venice* contains nearly eighty references to animals, and why the most striking of these are to animals breeding.[39] In fact, Jewish Law prescribes a more humane standard of care for animals than Christian interpreters of Shakespeare's time recognized when they overlooked or anthropocentrically allegorized Old Testament demands for kind treatment.[40] Nonetheless, of all the characters in the play Shylock uses negative animal imagery most often (thirty-three times), and most vehemently. In Shakespeare's creation of Shylock it seems Jewish dietary restrictions were taken as characteristic of revulsion for all beasts, despite the many Old Testament laws protecting them.[41]

---

33 For a lawyer's view of this *clamantia peccata* see Coke, *Institutes of the Laws of England*, pp. 58–9.

34 See statistics in 'Bestiality and Law in Renaissance England' pp. 147–50, an appendix to Bruce Thomas Boehrer, 'Bestial Buggery in *A Midsummer Night's Dream*', *The Production of English Renaissance Culture*, ed. David Lee Miller, Sharon O'Dair, and Harold Weber (Ithaca: Cornell University Press, 1994), 123–50.

35 Keith Thomas, *Man and the Natural World: Changing Attitudes in England 1500–1800* (Allen Lane: London, 1983), pp. 38–9, 94–117, 118–19, 134–5.

36 *Ibid.*, pp. 38–9. Slightly later human transfusion of animal blood, and still later vaccination, were opposed on the same basis.

37 *Ibid.*, p. 42; on later-emerging racialist theories of human polygenism see *ibid.*, p. 136.

38 Caroline Spurgeon, *Shakespeare's Imagery and What It Tells Us* (Cambridge: Cambridge University Press, 1935), p. 335, reveals that 'contemptuous or repellent' animal images dominate *Othello*. Othello at last compares himself to a 'base Indian' or in the Folio text a 'base Judean' (TLN 3658), and then stabs himself imaged as a 'circumcised dog'.

39 This search was done using the University of Toronto's *TACT* text analysis program applied to William Shakespeare, *The Complete Works*, ed. Stanley Wells and Gary Taylor, Electronic Ed. (Oxford: Oxford University Press, 1989).

40 Thomas, *Man and the Natural World*, pp. 22–4 and 151; but p. 137 claims that some common people ignored this and regarded animals 'in the way that Jews had before them, as essentially within the covenant'.

41 Exodus 23:5 and 12; Deuteronomy 22:4; Proverbs 12:10; Hosea 2:18 even speaks of a holy covenant with beasts.

So, as mentioned earlier, Shylock describes an irrational detestation of animals or of certain music when asked to explain his hatred of Antonio:

> What if my house be troubled with a rat [. . .]
> Some men there are love not a gaping pig!
> Some that are mad if they behold a cat!
> And others when the bagpipe sings i' th' nose
> Cannot contain their urine. (4.1.44–50)

But Shylock's allusions to animal or music-phobia are a disingenuous opposite of what they claim to be: rather than describing an unfounded aversion, they recall how Antonio persistently called him a dog, and how the music of a Venetian festival covered the theft of his wealth and daughter.[42] Again, he images unpleasant animal/human interactions to represent more ugly human/human ill-will.

A mock denial of ill motives where these are crucial, a sly or spiteful self-denigration, and deliberate confusion of the animal with the human, characterize also the covert message of Lancelot Gobbo's dismissal of responsibility for his fornication. Like Shylock's jest about hating Antonio for 'no reason', Gobbo's self-exoneration for having illicitly impregnated an unseen and nameless female 'negro' or 'Moor' is ostensibly humorous. It caps a scene of quibbling, perhaps not really merry, in Belmont. This begins with Jessica cornered by her erstwhile servant/ally Gobbo, now elevated in rank, who over-familiarly, uncomfortably and blasphemously (by denying grace) wrangles that she must be 'damn'd' either with Jewish ancestry or else (if she is not Jewish) with bastardy. Next, in a parody recalling Shylock's commercial grievance against Antonio's interest-free lending which 'brings down / The rate of usance here with us in Venice' (1.3.39–40), Gobbo laments Jessica's religious conversion because:

> this making of Christians will raise the price of hogs, – if we grow all to be pork-eaters, we shall not shortly have a rasher on the coals for money. (3.5.21–3)

Although he is now a licensed clown, Gobbo's use of commercial/animal imagery in connection with Christian conversion may make the auditor begin to wonder if there is something untoward in his raillery.

At this moment Jessica's new husband Lorenzo enters, and she reports to him how Launcelot:

> tells me flatly there's no mercy for me in heaven because I am a Jew's daughter: and he says you are no good member of the commonwealth, for in converting Jews to Christians, you raise the price of pork. (3.5.29–33)

To this gibe against his wife and his marriage, Lorenzo retorts with a counter-accusation of miscegenation against Gobbo: 'I shall answer better to the commonwealth than you can the getting up of the negro's belly: the Moor is with child by you Launcelot!' To this Gobbo makes his riddling reply:

> It is much that the Moor should be more than reason: but if she be less than an honest woman, she is indeed more than I took her for. (3.5.37–9)

Lorenzo comments on this, 'How every fool can play upon the word!', presumably pointing towards quibbles including the multiple puns: 'more'/'Moor'; 'more' = greater vs. more = pregnant; and take = understand vs. take = sexually use.

Yet there is more going on in Gobbo's complexly phrased rationalization than simply his skill with what Lorenzo later calls the 'tricksy word'. Gobbo says that if the pregnant Moor is 'less than an honest woman' (and therefore *is* a woman) she is 'indeed more' than he took her for. This amounts to a confession or boast that Launcelot took her for less than a woman of any kind, for he 'took' her as an animal. With the greatest effrontery he frankly

[42] Jessica says at 3.2.6 that Shylock's murderous intention predated her elopement, but Ruth Nevo, *Comic Transformation in Shakespeare* (London: Methuen, 1980), argues persuasively, pp. 130–1, that by emotional logic it must develop afterwards.

admits that racial miscegenation was, for him, just bestiality.

## VII

Gobbo's 'humorous' crudeness about the pregnant Moor creates a unique and valuable episode of the play, yielding a context in which racial prejudice is stripped of its more usual disguise of politeness and social grace. The Clown's indecent racialism is not wholly different from the casual bigotry of the higher-born Belmontese visitors and natives, and it serves to point up what may tend to be confused or overridden by their charm.

Due appreciation of our distance from Shakespeare's age does not obscure his depiction of the 'better' classes of Belmont as comfortable and indeed satisfied with their offhanded disdain for aliens and minorities. Possibly the reason that their collective attitudes of scorn and unthinking bias have rarely been explicitly commented upon is that the racialist attitudes of the socially 'superior' characters of *The Merchant of Venice* need not affront us unless we choose to be painfully responsive to them. If we choose to enjoy a comedy with clear winners and losers, or to identify with a 'winning side', we may easily accept the self-estimation of the play's blithely overweening characters and evade whatever may taint their charismatic gloss, fashionable charm and eventual triumph.

Moreover Shakespeare makes the taking of an ethical stance which can question the dominant group's position very difficult for both Elizabethan and modern audiences. *The Merchant of Venice* is deliberately designed to evoke a specific anxiety inhibiting any disapproval of its luxury-loving Belmontese. Those who attack their leisured 'good life' may appear boorishly Malvolio-like or untutored in pleasure. Some of the finest poetry of the play specifically warns off resistance to Belmont's softer charms, disparaging that dangerous curmudgeon 'The man that hath no music in himself' (5.1.83). Many critics even go farther, identifying in wealthy Belmont a kind of utopia, a place of giving without stint and a community of unlimited selfless love. I would argue, rather, that a lesson is dearly bought in the play's last Act: that adult love distinctly requires both a clear sense of the self and an understanding of the need for limitations in giving.[43]

Despite the warnings and temptations of Belmont's elite, I believe that their mixture of bigotry and cruelty with social privilege and charm is a product of Shakespeare's deeply intentional irony. Such irony adds a clanging impact to the unruffled expression, at a moment of joy, of a racialist metaphor for mistaken or misled perception:

> Thus ornament is but the guiled shore
> To a most dangerous sea: the beauteous scarf
> Veiling an Indian beauty; in a word,
> The seeming truth which times put on
> To entrap the wisest. (3.2.97–101)

Bassanio's aberrant association of an in-reality ugly 'Indian beauty' with a trap and a sea of danger passes without any comment in the scene, as it does in most explicit criticism.[44] Yet corresponding unnoted particulars problematizing value are unquestionably manifest elsewhere in the play.

For example, the word 'good' is used in a particularly cynical way by Shylock when he carefully explains that by calling Antonio a

---

[43] I argue in 'Constitutive Signifiers' that Antonio's selfless code is necessarily defeated by Portia and the marriage contract.

[44] What Bassanio has in mind is made explicit in Montaigne's sceptical 'An Apology', *Essays* (New York: Modern Library, 1933), p. 429: 'The Indians describe [beauty as] blacke and swarthy, with blabbered-thick lips, with a broad and flat nose, the inward gristle whereof they loade with great gold-rings, hanging downe to their mouth'. The Oxford text places Bassanio's lines in an aside, exonerating the others present from sharing his vision. Other editors emend, not seeing the implied contrast of Indian with the beauteous. Yet, as the Arden editor tersely notes, p. 82, 'the Elizabethan aversion to dark skins gives sufficient meaning to the passage'.

'good man' he means merely good for the ducats owed (1.3.11–15). The same word appears sixty-three times in the play, mainly used by the Venetian men to mean profitably effective or in conventional epithets (as in 'good signors' or 'good Leonardo'). But ethical 'good' is also discussed by Nerissa and Portia (1.2.10–28, 3.4.10, 4.1.257, 5.1.91); on varied uses of a single word hinge differences between material concerns, empty social conventions, and moral concerns.

If varied uses of a single word in *The Merchant of Venice* require irony-detecting discrimination, harder problems of interpretation arise in regard to the chauvinism of its Belmont. Veiled distinctions must be sifted without the aid of Shylock's very helpful key to his own comment on Antonio being only financially 'good':

> Ho, no, no, no, no: my meaning in saying he is a good man, is to have you understand me that he is sufficient. (1.3.13–15)

The only sure external test for literary irony requires a certainty about assumed values unavailable in *The Merchant of Venice*, where virtually all values presented are problematized. There may be clues, however, to an intended literary irony in the stylistic or structural quirks of over-emphatic expression or repetition (as there are in the hyper-altruistic zeal of the cannibalistic letter-writer of Swift's *A Modest Proposal*). Accordingly, in basically monocultural Belmont one hears excessively many casual slurs against foreigners, some like Bassanio's aspersion quite violent, which may imply an habitual trend of prejudice there.

Discrimination on this point is perplexing. Are we being tested when we are invited to join the clear lead of Nerissa in approving Portia's repetitively jeering characterizations of her foreign suitors? Are Portia's remarks really witty, or are they desperate antidotes to her initially depressed weariness with 'this great world' (1.2.1–9)? Arguably, Portia's anti-foreigner invective may be an extra-dramatic 'stand-up comic' bid for the pit's vulgar laughter.[45] But in most instances her comments are not mere banter, for they purport to represent her offstage experiences of the Neapolitan, Palatine, French, English, Scottish, and German suitors' odd behaviours. Yet the culminating instance of Portia's anti-suitor gibes cannot be excused as wry reportage. In this she gratuitously dismisses the courtship of the Prince of Morocco *before she has seen or met him*; she denigrates his 'complexion of a devil' after seeing only his (presumably black) 'forerunner [...] who brings word the prince his master will be here to-night' (1.2.118–25). So Shakespeare presents us with the image of absolute racial *pre*judice.

We are placed at risk of being seduced by elements in the play asking for our tacit allowance of Portia's stark prejudice against Morocco. For one thing, the Belmontese world of genteel privilege, luxury and wit discourages all punctilious distinctions or unsuave scruples. In such a world, the harshness of racial discrimination may seem attenuated, as are the later cruelties of the sexual ring tricks, by being attuned to near-musical conventions of teasing and charm. A great majority of modern critics greatly favour what they hear as the social harmonies of Belmont,[46] which drown out for

---

45 René Girard, *A Theatre of Envy* (Oxford University Press, 1991), p. 249 suggests *The Merchant of Venice* speaks to two simultaneous audiences, a 'refined' one on an ironic plane and a 'vulgar' one in accord with their bigotry. I propose that Shakespeare had a more complexly constituted audience in mind in my *Art and Illusion in 'The Winter's Tale'* (Manchester University Press, 1994), pp. 65–6.

46 Many seem influenced by the lauding of idyllic Belmont in C. L. Barber, *Shakespeare's Festive Comedy* (1959; rpt. Cleveland, OH: Meridian, 1963), pp. 163–91. Barber's chapter title, 'The Merchants and the Jew of Venice: Love's Communion and an Intruder', epitomizes a view that 'Shylock and the accounting mechanism which he embodies are crudely baffled in Venice and rhapsodically transcended in Belmont' (p. 173). This classic pro-Belmont argument is more temperate than many of its descendants: for instance, Colley, 'Launcelot, Jacob and Esau'; J. S. Coolidge, 'Law and Love in *The Merchant of Venice*', *Shakespeare*

them Portia's prejudgement of the not-yet-seen, soon stunningly seen, '*tawnie Moore all in white*' (Folio stage direction, TLN 514).

But by making this one clear instance of Portia's wholly unsupported prejudice resemble her former wryly 'observant' nationality quips, the play tempts us to lose our own ethical bearings. Here, as often, *The Merchant of Venice* seems deliberately to make difficult its demands on audiences; here these are demands of the sort Peter Davison believes implicitly made with regard to racism: 'often in Elizabethan and Jacobean drama, and especially in [*Othello*] the audience is called upon to exercise judgement, to distinguish facts from its prejudices'.[47] But the misleading parallel of Portia's remarks on Morocco with her earlier ones on other suitors, rather than confusing us, may challenge us to identify a tonal difference. Such a difference does arise, because Portia cannot describe Morocco or his behaviour. Her barb must therefore be purely verbal. Although in Shakespeare's age punning could present true wit or even profundity, it could also portray moral shallowness.[48] Portia's equivocation between Morocco's 'complexion' meaning skin colour and his 'complexion' in the sense of humoural make-up or character does mark an unamiable decline in the quality of her repartee. It displays none of the fashionable skill in Theophrastian character sketching she has shown before – we may even feel vicarious embarrassment on account of her descent from high-spirited wryness into desperately brittle hilarity.[49]

But Shakespeare makes it impossible for audiences to dwell long on Portia's racial prejudice, although for some its acrid taste may linger. For when the Prince of Morocco arrives he indeed at first displays an unbalanced personality, or unfortunate 'complexion'. In a seeming anticipation of racial prejudice he shows himself vainglorious and magniloquent, over-vaunting his heroic valour and sexual 'blood'. So he begins, 'Mislike me not for my complexion', boasts of virility, and claims that he can 'Pluck the young suckling cubs from the she-bear / Yea mock the lion when a roars for prey' (2.1.1–38). Again, as with Shylock, animality is actually asserted by an individual who is subject to social prejudice. This is of course in accord with the prejudicial English marriage law.

Morocco's embattled vanity leads him to mis-choose the golden casket, which occasions Portia's gruesomely dismissive couplet:

> A gentle riddance, – draw the curtains, go, –
> Let all of his complexion choose me so.
> (2.7.78–9)

Her racialist relief is expressed with perhaps a telling displacement of idiom, wherein 'gentle riddance' substitutes for a more usual locution such as 'fair' or 'good riddance' (*OED*, 'riddance', 4). This may suggest that for Portia 'gentle' behaviour, good breeding, prevails over any other good.

On another plane, Portia's elation with being safe from marriage with Morocco may imply more than racial aversion. The defeat of any unwanted suitor may give her some relief from the feelings of oppression and powerlessness under the mortmain of her father's will: 'I may neither choose who I would, nor refuse who I dislike, so is the will of a living daughter curb'd

---

*Quarterly*, 27 (1976), 243–63; M. J. Hamill, 'Poetry, Law and the Pursuit of Perfection: Portia's role in *The Merchant of Venice*', *SEL*, 18 (1978), 229–43. Stephen J. Greenblatt, 'Marlowe, Marx, and Anti-Semitism', *Critical Inquiry*, 5 (1978), 291–307 (rpt. in Greenblatt, *Learning to Curse: Essays in Early Modern Culture*, NY: Routledge, 1990, pp. 40–58), contrasts Shylock's Venetian 'economic nexus' with Portia's world, 'not a field in which she operates for profit but a living web of noble values and moral orderliness' (p. 295), and seemingly excuses Marx's notion of the loathsome 'Jewishness' of capitalism.

47 Peter Davison, *Othello* (Basingstoke: Macmillan, 1988), p. 65.

48 On wordplay central to a Shakespeare play see my 'A Spenserian Idea in *The Taming of the Shrew*', *English Studies*, 66 (1985), 310–16; for an ignoble pun see *King Lear*, 1.1.11–12.

49 Production may highlight Portia's decline from witty discernment, may elide this, or may make it ambiguous and confusing. The last may be best, as it leaves uneasy responses unguided.

by the will of a dead father' (1.2.23–5). Anti-patriarchal motives may well inspire Portia's anti-foreigner gibes, all of which are made against sexually acquisitive men.[50] Yet, if Portia's sense of oppression is lightened by Morocco's defeat, she lacks compassion for a fellow-sufferer under the will that oppresses her. Shakespeare pointedly shows Portia administering to Morocco (and only to him) the oath required under the will, 'if you choose wrong / Never to speak to lady afterward / In way of marriage' (2.1.40–2). In accepting this stipulation, hazarding his sexual and dynastic future, Morocco is fully as brave as he claims to be. Because he risks a heavy loss for her, it is difficult to hear the pat, sententious couplet above, in which Portia welcomes his destruction.

Characteristically, the play complicates the issue. The Prince of Arragon soon after finds a mocking fool's head in his chosen silver casket, which seemingly releases him from his vow of permanent celibacy: 'take what wife you will to bed, / I will always be your head: / So be gone, you are sped' (2.9.70–2). Arragon's only punishment for his mistaken choice is humiliation. His choice of silver, although showing insincerity, may also reflect that he is white, not 'tawnie' or golden like Morocco. I would not insist on this contrast of Arragon's and Morocco's fate, but will note that it aligns with the variation in Portia's remarks about these suitors. Her sneers about Morocco's 'complexion of a devil' far exceed her brief gibe on Arragon's folly, suggesting that racial prejudice in Belmont is so virulent as to make miscegenation with bold Morocco more unacceptable than marriage with vain and foolish Arragon.

## VIII

If all laws are enacted only to support the interests of powerful élites, or if law typically only strait-jackets human desires (these are the alternatives often proposed by recent commentaries on Literature and Law), then law can have little to do with literature's longstanding fascination with justice. But, conversely, part of the strong theatrical appeal of *The Merchant of Venice* may derive from what it shares with many other literary and folkloric portrayals of justice enacted. This is the satisfaction of a desire that may even be a human instinct, the desire to see redress of grievances and the orderly advancement of social good. Even a troubling critique of society, exposing the deficiencies of law, may hinge on a hope for such 'good'.

To carry a bit farther our prior discussion of the varied uses of the epithet 'good' in *The Merchant of Venice*, let us note that its application in an often-repeated and insincerely conventional form of address is once applied even to 'good Shylock' (3.3.3). This is Antonio's phrase when he is about to be arrested for debt, when his vital interests are at stake. The hollowness of this form of address could not be more poignantly indicated than by its use in imploring a reviled enemy.[51] But its typical hollowness in use is once made even more explicit, by means of an inversion. This occurs in another highly charged context, when Solanio, regretting his former cynical banter about Antonio's depression (1.1.47–56), brings the news of Antonio's merchant losses. Solanio here eschews what he calls his former 'slips of prolixity', and consciously if brokenly tries to rehabilitate the worn-out phrase 'good Antonio', and recover its meaning:

> it is true [. . .] that the good Antonio, the honest Antonio; – O that I had a title good enough to keep his name company! – (3.1.10–14)

[50] Lynda E. Boose, 'The Comic Contract and Portia's Golden Ring', *Shakespeare Studies*, 20 (1988), 241–54, p. 247, finds Portia's 'covertly manipulative subversions of passive aggression' used against 'the male system of female suppression'.

[51] The locution 'good sir[s]', listed only four times by Bartlett, is actually very commonly used in Shakespeare's plays (62 times). In *Hamlet*, 2.1.47, Polonius explains its insincerity to his spy Reynoldo.

That the very word 'good' can be used so feelingly in *The Merchant of Venice*, as well as in self-interested, sarcastic, and unthinkingly conventional ways, surely indicates that we must confront this play with very alert attention.

With such attention we have noted that the play's pervasive animal imagery, bearing both legal and ideological ramifications, rears up in a 'witty' exchange between a Clown and a newly married Jew and Christian to disgrace its often critically vaunted world of Belmont. Although Jessica identifies Portia as a near-goddess in the same short scene, Launcelot's guilt-dismissing 'confession' still exposes the submerged racialist values of Portia's realm. Well in advance of Gratiano's frighteningly obscene (not bawdy, nor erotic) castration jests, which cap Belmont's gender struggles while ending the play, Gobbo's ugly sexual gloating demonstrates how all the resolving finalities of the comedy are undercut by chronic confusions. These are confusions between seeking wealth or pleasure, fitting societal moulds, and possessing full humanity.

# 'MANY A CIVIL MONSTER': SHAKESPEARE'S IDEA OF THE CENTAUR

ERIC C. BROWN

## I

Critics have long noted Shakespeare's debt to Sidney's *Arcadia*, particularly for *King Lear*.[1] One passage in the *Arcadia* that critics have overlooked not only bears marked similarity to several of Shakespeare's plays but also encapsulates an idea that fascinated Shakespeare throughout his entire career: the centaur. During a jousting exercise, the character of Musidorus, a prince of Thessalia in the guise of a shepherd, is urged by Pamela to 'do something upon his horse'. While on his steed, prancing upon the ground in a rhythmic dance, 'he (as if Centaurlike he had bene one peece with the horse) was no more moved, then one is with the going of his own legges: and in effect so did he command him, as his down limmes ... that it seemed as he borrowed the horse's body, so he lent the horse his minde'.[2] This union of horse and man resembles, for example, that in *Hamlet*: Claudius describes 'a gentleman of Normandy' whose horsemanship seemed like 'witchcraft'; such was the man's skill that '[h]e grew into his seat, / And to such wondrous doing brought his horse / As had he been incorpsed and demi-natured / With the brave beast' (4.7.68–74). This idea of horse and rider as 'demi-natured', incorporated as one centaur-like composite, pervades Shakespeare's work. In sonnets 50 and 51, he elevates the bond between horse and rider to one of emotional interchange. In 50, the speaker relates that 'The beast that bears me, tired with my woe, / Plods dully on to bear that weight in me, / As if by some instinct the wretch did know / His rider loved not speed, being made from thee' (lines 5–8). The idea is echoed in *A Lover's Complaint*, when the maid says of her suitor, '"Well could he ride, and often men would say, / 'That horse his mettle from his rider takes'; / ... And controversy hence a question takes, / Whether the horse by him became his deed, / Or he his manège by th' well-doing steed"' (lines 106–12). Similarly, in *Julius Caesar*, Antony remarks that his horse 'is a creature that I teach to fight, / To wind, to stop, to run directly on, / His corporal motion governed by my spirit' (4.1.31–3). The very words of Sir Philip Sidney – 'he borrowed the horse's body, so he gave the horse his mind' – resound in Shakespeare's portrayal of Antony. This idea of the centaur has hitherto been given insufficient critical attention, both as a cultural mode of thought current in Shakespeare's day and as a particularly Shakespearian *idée fixe*. The

[1] Geoffrey Bullough, *Narrative and Dramatic Sources of Shakespeare*, vol. 7 (London: Routledge and Kegan Paul, 1966), p. 48, concludes that 'Shakespeare knew *Arcadia* well', and that especially in *Hamlet*, 'the adventures of Musidorus and Pyrocles gradually revealed by Sidney seem to have influenced Shakespeare'. As to *King Lear*, see for instance Kenneth Muir, *The Sources of Shakespeare's Plays* (New Haven: Yale University Press, 1978), p. 196.

[2] Sir Philip Sidney, *The Countesse of Pembrokes Arcadia*, intro. Carl Dennis (orig. 1590; rpt. Kent, Ohio: Kent State University Press, 1970), p. 122.

abundance of centaurian images and mythology in his writing needs also to be explored, most notably in *Othello*, in which the pattern of human–bestial hybrids reaches something of a fever pitch.

Perhaps since Horace's *Ars Poetica*, the fantastic hybridization of the human and bestial has played an ambivalent role in art. In the first line of that treatise, Horace asks, 'If a painter chose to join a human head to the neck of a horse ... could you, my friends, if favoured with a private view, refrain from laughing?'[3] While he affirms that 'painters and poets have always had an equal right in hazarding anything', Horace nevertheless decries such liberty if 'savage should mate with tame, or serpents couple with birds, lambs with tigers'. However, as one critic recently puts it, the 'Horatian catalogue of "inventive" hybrids should be considered a commonplace in Renaissance thought'.[4] Shakespeare writes relatively little of most classical hybrids. Harpies occur a handful of times; a dance of twelve satyrs in *The Winter's Tale*; a single reference to the minotaur in *1 Henry VI* and the sphinx in *Love's Labour's Lost*; the infamous analogy 'Hyperion to a satyr' and Ophelia's 'mermaid-like' floating in *Hamlet*; and a variety of other 'mermaid' references throughout the canon.[5] Yet allusions to the specific components of the half-horse, half-man hybridization – their nature and mythology – appear with surprising regularity. Certainly, the classical centaurs differ from most of their hybrid brethren in their active commerce with human society. They were often upstanding symbols of reason governing the passions, and some commentators have suggested that they were indeed 'dignified and noble', and 'not associated with most other monstrous forms', representing instead 'good actions'.[6] But there is a volatility in the horse-human mix that makes them a 'monstrous form' of a very particular sort.[7] For Shakespeare, there is no simple dichotomy of bestial and human, but rather a fluid interchange between the two that both strengthens and dissolves their apparent difference. (Jonathan Bate observes this paradox of centaurs when he calls them 'arrested in a perpetual state of semi-metamorphosis'.)[8] This notion of hybridizing foregrounds a further complexity of centaurs that Shakespeare would dramatically exploit: two apparently disparate traditions that, together, constitute most centaur iconography.

---

[3] Horace, 'The Art of Poetry', in *Horace: Satires, Epistles, and Ars Poetica*, trans. H. Rushton Fairclough (Cambridge, Mass.: Harvard University Press, 1970), p. 451.

[4] John F. Moffitt, 'An Exemplary Humanist Hybrid: Vasari's "Fraude" with Reference to Bronzino's "Sphinx"', *Renaissance Quarterly*, 49 (2), (1996), 315.

[5] See for harpies *The Tempest* (3.3.53–84), *Much Ado* (2.1.253), and *Pericles* (17.47); 'Here a dance of twelve satyrs' in *The Winter's Tale* (4.4.340 s.d.); 'Thou mayest not wander in the labyrinth. / There Minotaurs and ugly treasons lurk' in *1 Henry VI* (5.5.144–5); *Love's Labour's Lost* (4.3.318); *Hamlet* (1.2.140 and 4.7.148); and mermaids in *Errors* (3.2.45, 170), *Antony* (2.2.214–16), *Dream* (2.1.150), *Duke of York* (3.2.186), *Lucrece* (line 1411), and *Venus* (line 777).

[6] Richard Barber and Anne Riches, *A Dictionary of Fabulous Beasts* (Woodbridge: Boydell, 1996), p. 37. As testimony to this view, a compendium by Conrad Lycosthenes, *Prodigorum ac Ostentorum Chronicon* (Basilae, 1557), p. 668, depicts a peculiar breed of centaur, two of whose four arms resemble a toad's, and whose ears are those of a dog. Despite the seemingly monstrous nature of this conglomerate, the author pleasantly reports 'amici sunt hominum et mulierum, quia illis nullam inferunt molestiam': friends to all, because they mean no harm. On hybrids in general, see also Joyce E. Salisbury, 'Human Beasts and Bestial Humans in the Middle Ages', in *Animal Acts: Configuring the Human in Western History*, ed. by Jennifer Ham and Matthew Senior (New York and London: Routledge, 1997), pp. 9–21; and Beryl Rowland, *Animals with Human Faces* (Knoxville: University of Tennessee Press, 1973).

[7] In a treatise partly devoted to human-beast hybrids, Ambroise Paré sees the combination of horse and human in a more malignant light. He reports that during the year 1254, in Verona, 'a Mare foaled a Colt with the perfect face of a man, but all the rest of the body like a Horse: a little after the Wars between the Florentines and Pisans began, by which all Italy was in a combustion.' See *The Workes of that Famous Chirurgion* (London, 1649), p. 586.

[8] Bate, *Shakespeare and Ovid* (Oxford: Oxford University Press, 1993), p. 194.

In *The Prince*, first published in 1532, Machiavelli composed one of the more notorious passages on centaurs. He writes that 'Achilles and many other ancient princes were brought up by the centaur Chiron, who was to nurture and instruct them. Having a teacher who is half animal and half man can only mean that a prince must know how to use both natures; he who has the one without the other is not likely to survive'.[9] Machiavelli may have been the first to personify Chiron in this fashion. But as George C. Taylor remarks, 'great humanists from Plato to Lewis Mumford have given serious consideration to the idea that on one side man is constitutionally a beast, at times worse than other beasts, on the other side a god in intellect and ethics. Shakespeare stands out among Renaissance thinkers particularly attracted by this idea'.[10] Interpreted *in malo*, centaurs are rapacious and libidinous revellers: there is Nessus, slayer of Hercules, and there are the famously truculent centaurs who took part in the battle with the Lapiths. Interpreted *in bono*, these same centaurs are renowned for skill in prophecy, medicine, and hunting: there is Chiron, the wise and careful instructor of the great Greek heroes. (Achilles, Hercules, Jason, and Theseus all reportedly learned through his instruction.) For Shakespeare, these mythological indeterminacies are especially crucial. They allow for a plasticity in metaphor that mimics the paradoxical state of centaurs themselves. Hercules, an especially prominent hero in their mythology, can banefully slaughter the horse-men, even as he is instructed by them, and even as he is himself slain by them. The horse and human components continually intermingle, just as the centaurs both menace and cultivate archetypal humanity.[11] Thus 'Chiron' is for Shakespeare both the mentor of mankind and a murderous rapist in *Titus Andronicus*.[12]

An additional importance of the centaur is that, in general, the early history of the creature corresponds in remarkable ways to the politics of expansion in the sixteenth century. Kollman writes that

> it took ... centuries before the horse became common in the Near East, and there is every possibility that the people who distributed the horse were, in fact, the Kassites. As barbarian nomads, they might have ridden their horses, and, to the Near Eastern cultures that were accustomed to chariots and asses, such a sight might have been sensational enough to have caused the confusion that ... horse and man were one animal.[13]

In fact, Shakespeare read of just such an account in Pliny's *Natural History*, translated by Holland in 1601. (Critics have long noted that Pliny's *History* was a source for portions of *Othello*.)[14] In a chapter on 'The first inventers of diverse things', and amidst a detailing of various military innovations, Pliny writes that 'Bellerophon

---

[9] Niccolo Machiavelli, *The Prince*, ed. and trans. James B. Atkinson (Indianapolis: Bobbs-Merrill, 1976), p. 281.

[10] George Coffin Taylor, 'Shakespeare's Use of the Beast in Man', *Studies in Philology*, 42 (1945), 530. Beryl Rowland has made a study of Chaucer's use of human and horse, without mentioning centaurs, in 'The Horse and Rider figure in Chaucer's Works', *University of Toronto Quarterly*, 35(3) (1966), 246–59. Cf. Joan Hartwig, 'Donne's Horse and Rider as Body and Soul', in *John Donne's Religious Imagination: Essays in Honor of John T. Shawcross*, ed. by Jean R. Frontain and Frances M. Malpezzi (Conway, Ariz.: UCA Press, 1995), pp. 262–83.

[11] In an informative essay on the centaur in literature, Judith Kollman proposes that 'to Shakespeare the centaur meant something fairly similar to what it had represented in Classical Greece: namely, a threat to established social order. The centaur remains a creature of two worlds, yet belonging to neither'. See 'Centaur', *Mythical and Fabulous Creatures: A Source Book and Research Guide*, ed. Malcolm South (New York: Greenwood, 1987), p. 235.

[12] Douglas Stewart, 'Falstaff the Centaur', *Shakespeare Quarterly*, 28 (1977), 5–21, makes one of the most penetrating investigations of the mythical Chiron as an 'anti-centaur'.

[13] Kollman, *Mythical and Fabulous Creatures*, p. 226.

[14] See Bullough, *Sources*, vol. 7, p. 211, and Muir, *Sources of Shakespeare's Plays*, pp. 188–9, who cite extensive borrowings. For other evidence, see also Muir, 'Holland's Pliny and *Othello*', *Notes and Queries*, 198 (1953), 513–14; J. L. Simmons, 'Holland's Pliny and *Troilus and Cressida*', *Shakespeare Quarterly*, 7 (1976), 329–32.

shewed first how to ride on horsebacke ... [and] the Thessalians, called Centaures, inhabiting neere to the mountain Pelius, were the first that fought on horsebacke.'[15] Thus he speculates that the first riders of horses became transformed, through the peculiar magic of myth, into the centaurs. (Sidney may have been cleverly suggesting this in giving his Prince Musidorus, whose homeland was Thessaly, centaur-like attributes.) The novel appearance of horses was emphatically resurrected during the conquest of the New World, and the resurgence of a 'real' sixteenth-century centaur became embodied in the figure of the Spanish conquistador. As Stephen Greenblatt puts it, the 'peoples of the New World could not bring the strangers into focus; conceptual inadequacy severely impeded, indeed virtually precluded, an accurate perception of the other'.[16] Such 'conceptual inadequacy' found one of its most unusual avatars in the misperception of horse and man as one entity.

The New World centaurs can be traced through the 1603 publication of Montaigne's *Essays*, translated by John Florio, in which an interesting chapter appears some one-hundred pages after the famous 'Of the Cannibals', generally regarded as a source for Shakespeare's construction of Caliban in *The Tempest*.[17] The essay, 'Of Steeds, Called in French Destriers', is of course connected with horses, one of Shakespeare's favourite topics.[18] Montaigne begins with an etymological discussion, but soon meanders his way into discussion of horses and riders glorious enough to challenge even the Duke of Bourbon's in *Henry V*, who proclaims his mount 'is indeed a horse, and all other jades you may call beasts' (3.7.23–4). If Shakespeare was combing the *Essays* for accounts of the New World, he likely would have noticed Montaigne's account of the conquering Spanish horsemen:

> These new discovered people of the Indies, when the Spaniards came first among them, esteemed that as well men as horses, were either gods, or creatures far beyond, and excelling their nature in nobilitie. Some of which, after they were vanquished by them, comming to sue for peace and beg pardon at their hands, to whom they brought presents of gold, and such viands as their countrie yeelded; omitted not to bring the same, and as much onto their horses, and with as solemn Oration as they had made unto men, taking their neighings, as a language of truce and composition.[19]

The report bears some semblance to *The Tempest*, when Stefano drunkenly believes Caliban and Trinculo to be one supernatural quadruped, of which he remarks 'Have we devils here? Do you put tricks upon's with savages and men of Ind, ha? ... Four legs and two voices – a most delicate monster!' (2.2.57–90). Both the conflation of horses and men in the conquest of the Indies, and the hybridization of Caliban and Trinculo in *The Tempest*, embody the idea of the mythological centaur. Shakespeare's familiarity with travel accounts of

---

[15] *The Historie of the World. Commonly Called, The Naturall Historie of C. Plinius Secundus*, trans. Philemon Holland (London, 1601), vol. 1, p. 189.

[16] Greenblatt, *Marvelous Possessions: The Wonder of the New World* (Chicago: University of Chicago Press, 1991), p. 11.

[17] Recent considerations include William M. Hamlin, *The Image of America in Montaigne, Spenser, and Shakespeare* (New York: St Martin's, 1995); M. R. Woodhead, 'Montaigne and *The Tempest*: An Addendum', *Notes and Queries*, 29 (1982), 126; and Gail K. Paster, 'Montaigne, Dido, and *The Tempest*: "How Came that Widow in?"', *Shakespeare Quarterly*, 35 (1984), 91–4. T. Sipahigil sees *Othello* as influenced, as well, in 'Montaigne's *Essays* and *Othello*', *Notes and Queries*, 21 (1974), 130.

[18] In *Shakespeare's Debt to Montaigne* (Cambridge, Mass.: Harvard University Press, 1925), p. 24, George Coffin Taylor contends that *Antony and Cleopatra* may have been partly influenced by this essay. Caesar recalls Antony's action during famine, 'Thou didst drink / The stale of horses' (1.4.61–2), and the lines bear some resemblance to Montaigne's discussion of horsemen who, lacking 'other beverage', 'were forced to drinke the stale or urine of their horses'. The quote appears on the same page as that of the men and horses treated as one entity.

[19] Montaigne, *The Essayes*, trans. John Florio (orig. 1603; rpt. New York: The Modern Library, 1933), p. 253.

the New World often pertained to expressly centaurian incidents.[20]

Shakespeare's knowledge of New World accounts need not, of course, be limited to Montaigne, nor was it confined to later accounts of the Virginia Colony. Rather, his perusal of travel-books went back some time, and among various other accounts, he knew Richard Eden's translation of the first three Decades of Pietro Martire.[21] The text of Eden's translation was first published in 1555, and includes the following description of a battle between Indians and Spanish: 'the governour had unbarked [sixteen] horses which were also at the battayle, and so fiercely assayled the Barbarians on the backehalfe, that they brake theyr array and scattered them as it had byn flockes of sheepe, overthrowing, woundynge, and kyllynge them on every side. Which thynge the seely wretches so imputed to a miracle ... For wheras before they had never seene any horses, they thought that the man on horsebacke and the horse, had byn all one beaste, as the antiquitie dyd fable of the monster *Centaurus.*'[22] Here again, the connection is made between ancient myth and modern perception; the 'monster Centaurus' is realized in the cultural novelty of horse and rider juxtaposed. Shakespeare may well have also drawn on this account for his caricature of the hybrid Caliban and Trinculo in *The Tempest*, but the account may also have spurred on the dramatizing of beast and man in *Othello*, the possibility of which I discuss below. Perhaps more importantly, Eden's translation provides yet another instance of man and horse interwoven, and offered Shakespeare greater metaphorical depth for an idea with which he was already preoccupied. Somewhat unexpectedly, the only overt mention of 'America' in all of the Shakespeare canon, and one of the few of the New World, appears in *The Comedy of Errors*. Dromio of Syracuse, in his geographical study of Nell the kitchen maid, declares that 'America, the Indies' might be found 'upon her nose, all o'er embellish'd with rubies, carbuncles, sapphires, declining their rich aspect to the hot breath of Spain, who sent whole armadas of carracks to be ballast at her nose' (3.2.136–40). One might expect that amidst the confluence of hot-breathed Spanish invaders and the Indies, hints of Shakespeare's initial attraction to centaurs might be found, as well. And indeed, *The Comedy of Errors* exhibits the idea of the centaur as a prominent force.

R. A. Foakes mentions of *The Comedy of Errors*, 'the idea of being made a beast operates ... generally in the play, reflecting the process of passion overcoming reason, as an animal rage, fear, or spite seizes on each of the main characters'.[23] The centaurs are evoked almost immediately by the name of the inn, the 'Centaur'. This play was possibly adapted by Shakespeare through Warner's version of the *Menaechmi* of Plautus (not published until 1595), but it is more probable that Shakespeare had at least consulted the Latin original.[24] Plautus had no such inn in his play, nor did Warner include one in his translation; the innovation is Shake-

[20] Much has been written on the possibility of New World accounts as sources, or at least contextualizations, for Caliban in *The Tempest*. See William M. Hamlin, 'Men of Inde: Renaissance Ethnography and *The Tempest*', *Shakespeare Studies*, 22 (1994), 15–44; and cf. Ben Ross Schneider, Jr., '"Are We Being Historical Yet?": Colonialist Interpretations of Shakespeare's *Tempest*', *Shakespeare Studies*, 23 (1995), 120–45.

[21] See Bullough, *Sources*, vol 8, p. 240.

[22] *The First Three English Books on America*, ed. E. Arber (Birmingham, 1885), p. 194. Arber, too, writes that 'William Shakespeare read this third Text' (p. vi).

[23] Foakes, p. xlv. See also Harold Brooks, 'Themes and Structure in *The Comedy of Errors*', in *Shakespeare: The Comedies*, ed. Kenneth Muir (Englewood Cliffs, N.J.: Prentice-Hall, 1965), p. 22, who writes that 'The dominant imagery, of man as beast, reflects the ideas of illusory appearance and malign metamorphosis; above all, it mirrors the threats to identity and to status in the cosmic order.'

[24] See Bullough, *Sources*, vol. 1, pp. 12–39 for Warner's version. For Shakespeare's knowledge of the Latin, see also the Arden *Errors*, ed. R. A. Foakes (London: Methuen, 1962), pp. xxiv–vi; and the New Cambridge *Errors*, ed. T. S. Dorsch (Cambridge: Cambridge University Press, 1988), pp. 8–9.

speare's. The inn serves as a kind of signpost for centaur icons, and Charles Garton persuasively argues that the twin Antipholuses derive their name from the centaur, Pholus, whom Shakespeare probably knew from Ovid's *Metamorphoses*. Pholus was one of the more prominent of classical centaurs, present at the Battle of the Lapiths, as well as the major figure in the myth recounted by Garton.[25] The myth constitutes part of the twelve labours of Hercules; the hero encounters this centaur in his pursuit of the Erymathian Boar, the fourth labour. Apollodorus relates the meeting as follows: 'When he crossed Pholoe Heracles stayed with the centaur Pholus ... He offered meat to Heracles while he himself ate raw flesh. When Hercules asked for wine Pholus said that he was afraid to open the wine jar because it belonged to all the centaurs jointly. Heracles told him to take courage and opened it himself. Drawn by the smell of the wine, the centaurs appeared soon afterwards at the cave of Pholus, armed with rocks and fir trees.'[26] Passion overcoming reason was frequently the failure of the classical centaurs, whose thirst for wine often spelled their doom. Of just such a lapse the Duke accuses Antipholus of Ephesus and others, saying 'I think you all have drunk of Circe's cup' (5.1.271). This off-handed phrase neatly fuses the seduction of reason, the confusion of intoxication, and the chaos of beastliness into one sweeping metaphor. Garton points out that in both the myth and the play, 'Hospitality, meat, and wine are prominent ... and in both lead on to uproar and violence.'[27] The tale of Pholus concludes with Hercules wreaking havoc among the creatures with bow and arrows, eradicating nearly the entire race (including, unintentionally, Chiron); Pholus himself is slain upon accidentally dropping an arrow into his own foot. Shakespeare was well acquainted with the Hercules lore, especially his twelve labours.[28] Further, in the ninth book of the *Metamorphoses*, the dying Hercules catalogues his labours and recounts among them that 'Ageinst the force of mee, defence the Centaures could not make.'[29] The lure of Hercules for Shakespeare may even be due in part to the fact that the hero is a centaurian figure, being half-man and half-god; and like the centaurs by whom he is taught and whom he destroys (and who destroy him), he is also traditionally a figure of paradox. He is at once Seneca's *Hercules Furens* and the gluttonous libertine of Aristophanes' *Birds*.

In comically refashioning elements of the Pholus myth, Shakespeare turns the tragic demise of the centaur race from a tale of chaos reigning to one of chaos reined-in. The 'gossips' feast' (5.1.408) that suggestively concludes the play creates a full inversion of the

---

25 Garton, 'Centaurs, the Sea, and *The Comedy of Errors*', *Arethusa*, 12 (1979), 233–54. See also Elizabeth Truax, *Metamorphosis in Shakespeare's Plays* (Lampeter: Edward Mellen, 1992), pp. 32–6. In canto 12 of Dante's *Inferno*, when Dante and Virgil come upon the centaurs at the river of blood, in the Circle of the Violent, three are named: Chiron (the leader), Nessus (the pilgrim's transport across the ford), and Pholus. Kollman, *Mythical and Fabulous Beasts*, p. 233, calls this 'the most significant literary use of the centaur during medieval times.'

26 Apollodorus, *The Library*, trans. Michael Simpson (Amherst, Mass.: University of Massachusetts Press, 1976), p. 94. Shakespeare could have gleaned the myth from Natale Conti's *Mythologiae* (Venice, 1567). Garton, 'Centaurs', p. 238, suggests Virgil's *Aeneid* as a possible source: in Book 5, a ship-race involves a vessel called the *Centaur*, and its captain receives as prize a slave woman and her two twins.

27 Garton, 'Centaurs', p. 236. A pun on 'Pholus' and 'phallus' in *The Comedy of Errors* may also be apparent. In transforming the play of Plautus, Shakespeare replaced with the name 'Dromio' the original name of the parasite character, 'Peniculus'. Perhaps to maintain the effect of the previous comical epithet, Shakespeare omits the bawdy 'Peniculus', but replaces it with the equally wanton 'Antipholus', effectively linking the name even further to the rest of *The Comedy of Errors* because of the enhanced double play on the name of the centaur 'Pholus'.

28 A good recent treatment of Hercules in Shakespeare, especially in the sense of paradox, is Jeff Shulman's 'At the Crossroads of Myth: the Hermeneutics of Hercules from Ovid to Shakespeare', *ELH*, 50 (1983), 83–105.

29 Ovid, *Metamorphosis*, trans. Arthur Golding (London, 1567; rpt. New York: Centaur Press, 1961), 9.235.

Pholus myth, celebrating the harmonious effects of a concluding banquet.[30] Another of Shakespeare's earliest plays contains one of the most comic instances of his idea of the centaur. In *The Taming of the Shrew*, as Petruchio arrives at his wedding in a lampoon of convention, Biondello relates that 'his horse comes with him on his back'. When Baptista declares, 'Why, that's all one', Biondello corrects him: 'Nay, by Saint Jamy ... / A horse and a man / Is more than one, / And yet not many' (3.2.77–84). In an essay mostly focusing on other horseplay in the comedy, Jeanne Roberts aptly remarks that Petruchio comes to his wedding 'like a parody of the centaur at the wedding feast', and that 'there have been some overtones of the monster in Petruchio right from the start'.[31] Beatrice concocts a similar image of the centaur in *Much Ado about Nothing* when she says of Benedick, 'if he have wit enough to keep himself warm, let him bear it for a difference between himself and his horse, for it is all the wealth that he hath left to be known a reasonable creature' (1.1.64–8). The collapse of difference between Benedick and his steed evokes the same comical conflation as between Petruchio and his own: horse and rider are nearly one entity, and occasionally less than one.

While the parodic qualities are important here, equally important is the manner in which these centaur tableaux become inverted. In *The Taming of the Shrew*, a short while after Petruchio's odd appearance, Grumio describes the tribulations of the post-wedding journey. In a significant counterpoint to Petruchio's equestrian buffoonery, Kate finds herself fallen 'under her horse', her husband leaving her in this state, 'with the horse upon her', to berate his servants (4.1.66–8). The inversion here marks 'how he is more shrew than she' (4.1.76), but also how he is more centaur, too. Petruchio tops his horse, a horse tops Katherina; and yet, despite the shifting of the power structure that this latter 'topping' heralds, a bond emerges. Centaur and anti-centaur overlap, linking the newly betrothed even as Grumio's tale appears to demonstrate their difference. Nor are their positions of power unqualified. Petruchio's earlier centaurian apparition does belie a bit of the monster, and Kate's later fall, while mired in muck, nevertheless signals a kind of emotional highground. He becomes violent, she mollifying. This bucking of horse into rider appears elsewhere, as well. The speech of Pirithous near the close of *The Two Noble Kinsmen* details a more tragic union and inversion of horse and man. Recalling Sidney's Musidorus, cavorting ably on a dancing horse, the knight Arcite approaches his demise atop a black steed, 'dancing, as 'twere, to th' music / His own hooves made' (5.6.59–60). Unlike that Prince of Thessaly, Arcite finds himself quite toppled when his horse becomes irate, reacting to a spark set by his own horseshoe. At first, Arcite maintains his seat; indeed, despite the horse's best efforts, 'neither curb would crack, girth break, nor diff'ring plunges / Disroot his rider whence he grew' (5.6.74–5). The animal finally resorts to an unusual method, creating a distinctly inverted centaur image:

> On end he stands –
> That Arcite's legs, being higher than his head,
> Seemed with strange art to hang.
> [A]nd presently

---

[30] See also David Bevington, *Action is Eloquence: Shakespeare's Language of Gesture* (Cambridge, Mass.: Harvard University Press, 1984), pp. 159–60, on the use of banquets in several plays, and Maggie Kilgour's *From Communion to Cannibalism: An Anatomy of Metaphors of Incorporation* (Princeton: Princeton University Press, 1990) for the manifold implications of dining and consumption in Renaissance England.

[31] Jeanne A. Roberts, 'Horses and Hermaphrodites: Metamorphoses in *The Taming of the Shrew*', *Shakespeare Quarterly*, 33 (1983), 165. See also Joan Hartwig, 'Horses and Women in *The Taming of the Shrew*', *Huntington Library Quarterly*, 45 (1982), 285–94. For a similar treatment of horses, see Deborah B. Wyrick, 'The Ass Motif in *The Comedy of Errors* and *A Midsummer Night's Dream*', *Shakespeare Quarterly*, 33 (1982), 432–3.

Backward the jade comes o'er, and his full poise
Becomes the rider's load. (5.6.77–82)

In this incident, the 'strange art' is not unlike the 'wondrous doing' of *Hamlet*'s 'gentleman of Normandy' (who also 'grew unto his seat'). An interchange occurs, but this time at the urging of the horse. The consequences resemble those of *The Taming of the Shrew*: the centaur image disrupts the wedding of Arcite and Emilia, yet in its inversion seems to allow for the wedding instead of Emilia and Palamon. That the simultaneous point of union and separation of this trio should be presaged in such an image is consistent with a creature in a 'perpetual state of semi-metamorphosis'.

Such inversions continue in perhaps the most blatant use of the centaur image in another early comedy, *A Midsummer Night's Dream*, in the figure of Bottom. His cephalic metamorphosis turns topsy-turvy the picture of a centaur with the upper body of a man and lower body of a horse. Deborah Wyrick rightly argues that 'if Shakespeare had merely wanted to display a hybrid monster, he could have followed the Theseus legend by creating a Minotaurian Bottom complete with bull's head'.[32] As Wyrick implies, there are obvious comic reasons for 'Bottom' *not* being strictly bull-headed, and instead becoming an inverted 'ass-centaur'.[33] The ribald humour, of course, necessitates his having an ass for a head. But as an inverted centaur Bottom also blends well with Theseus' dismissal of the 'battle with the Centaurs, to be sung / By an Athenian eunuch' (5.1.44–5) as an appropriate subject for the royal entertainment. Just as Bottom inverts and displaces the figure of a proper centaur, so too his own play of Pyramus and Thisbe replaces the centaurs in performance. Louis Montrose notices the appropriate alliance between centaur mythology and pervasive cultural modes of thought in Elizabethan England in *A Midsummer Night's Dream*. As a play that participates in the same inversion of mythological models as *The Comedy of Errors*, *A Midsummer Night's Dream* 'actually calls attention to the mechanism of mythological suppression by an ironically meta-dramatic gesture', as when Theseus rejects the centaurs 'because they are already too familiar ... The first performance narrates a wedding that degenerates into rape and warfare; the singer and his subject – Athenian eunuch and phallic centaur – are two antithetical kinds of male-monster.'[34] Most critics and editors have taken Theseus' reference to the battle with the centaurs to signify the Battle of the Lapiths, in which Theseus ironically took part. As he informs Philostrate, however, 'We'll none of that. That have I told my love / In glory of my kinsman Hercules' (5.1.46–7). The reference could equally be to the battle with Pholus and his cohorts, in which Hercules nearly eradicated the centaur race

---

32 Wyrick, 'The Ass Motif', pp. 444–5. M. E. Lamb, '*A Midsummer Night's Dream*: The Myth of Theseus and the Minotaur', *Texas Studies in Language and Literature*, 21 (1979), 478–91, and David Omerod, '*A Midsummer Night's Dream*: The Monster in the Labyrinth', *Shakespeare Studies*, 11 (1978), 39–52, both ingeniously bring attention to Bottom as a Minotaur in the maze of the woods outside Athens. (Either essay might be augmented by recalling Bottom's potentially double-edged sobriquet, 'Bully'.)

33 The *Physiologus*, one of the most widely read books during the Middle Ages, catalogues some fifty or so beasts, each of which was given a particular allegorical significance. Among the creatures detailed was the onocentaur, or 'ass-centaur': 'Formerly, Isaiah the Prophet pointed out that the sirens and ass-centaurs and hedgehogs will come into Babylon and dance [cf. Is. 13:21 and 34:14]. Physiologus treated the nature of each one, saying ... the ass-centaurs from their breasts up to the figure of a man and that of an ass from there down. "Thus the man of deceitful heart is confused in all his ways" [Jas. 1:18] ... Such beasts, sirens or ass-centaurs, represent the figures of devils'. See the *Physiologus*, trans. Michael J. Curley (Austin: University of Texas Press, 1979), pp. 23–4. If Bottom falls into this tradition, it is clearly with a sense of ironic inversion mimicked by his inverted appearance. The buffoonish figure hardly seems ready to signal the apocalypse.

34 Louis A. Montrose, 'Shaping Fantasies: Configurations of Gender and Power in Elizabethan Culture', *Representations*, 1 (1983), 45.

from existence with his arrows. The depiction of Hercules battling the lascivious centaurs would only emphasize Montrose's point. The castrated singer reciting the exploits of Hercules loosing his arrows, much like 'Cupid, all armed', who 'loosed his love-shaft smartly from his bow / As it should pierce a hundred thousand hearts' (2.1.157–60), is an even more poignant exposition of the singer's and subject's antithetical nature.

Even in *Titus Andronicus*, another play written not so far off in time from *The Comedy of Errors*, a reference made to centaurs is no more clearly to the Battle of the Lapiths. As Titus slits the throats of Demetrius and Chiron, he utters his wish 'To make this banquet ... / More stern and bloody than the Centaurs' feast' (5.2.201–2). First, the name Chiron certainly resonates with centaur lore, although Shakespeare inverts Chiron's beneficent qualities in this play, as noted earlier. However, if Shakespeare intended the name Chiron as a reference to the famous centaur, it is all the more appropriate that the allusion to the 'Centaurs' feast' is not to the Lapiths, but rather to the Pholus myth and Hercules' battle. For in the conclusion to this battle, Hercules' instructor Chiron dies from an arrow accidentally loosed by the hero. Such tragic possibilities of the centaur find expression in various ways, gory violence often vying with base lust for the premier role. Perhaps Shakespeare's most infamous allusion to centaurs occurs in *King Lear*, during Lear's raging speech on the moor. Implicating primarily his own 'pelican daughters' (*Lear* F 3.4.71) Goneril and Regan, Lear rails 'Let copulation thrive ...':

The fitchew nor the soiled horse goes to't
With a more riotous appetite. Down from the waist
They're centaurs, though women all above.
But to the girdle do the gods inherit;
Beneath is all the fiend's. (4.5.112–24)

Here, the King evokes the lustful nature of the centaur, and projects that nature onto the lower half of women.[35] His denigration of female sexuality, aligning it not only with centaurs but devils, carries out a trend toward misogyny that centaurs themselves so often pursued. Ironically, one of the few references available to Shakespeare concerning female centaurs cast them in a quite different light. In the *Metamorphoses*, Ovid relates the story of a famous female centaur, Hylonome, and her beautiful beloved, one Cyllarus, during the Battle of the Lapiths: 'Full many Females of his race did wish him too theyr make, / But only dame Hylonome for lover he did take. Of all the halfbrutes in the woodes there did not any dwell / More comly than Hylonome.'[36] The vision of a 'comly half-brute' fairly well sums the paradoxical nature of many centaurs. What is most striking, though, is the stress on fidelity. Lear's accusations of 'riotous appetite' seem all the more embittered in contrast. Additionally, Michael Andrews points out the resonance of Lear's speech with his ensuing words to Cordelia: 'I am bound / Upon a wheel of fire, that mine own tears / Do scald like molten lead' (4.6.39–41). The image of punishment derives from the Ixion myth, and the Tartarean wheel he spins upon; Andrews correctly observes that Ixion was the

[35] Jeanne Roberts (quoted in Kollman, *Mythical and Fabulous Beasts*, p. 235) argues that 'Lear's image sequencing is doubly disturbing because it evokes not only the collapsing of human and bestial but also the reversal of male and female roles. In the course of his speech the woman has moved from the position of horse to that of rider, although the final metaphor is blurred – in fact from the waist most centaurs are horses.' I find the final metaphor, rather than intending the image to be that of a female centaur, from the waist down a libidinous horse, to mean 'centaur-like' from the waist down, evoking only the licentiousness of the conventional centaur instead of its physical form.

[36] Ovid, *Metamorphoses*, 12.443–6. Claudette Hoover expresses a problematic view in 'Women, Centaurs, and Devils in *King Lear*', *Women Studies*, 16 (1989), 353, when she claims that the 'centaur was, after all, half man and half stallion ... and they were always male'. In addition to Ovid's reference to Hylonome, Stephen Bateman, *The Doome Warning All Men to the Judgement* (London, 1581), p. 10, reports on the curious race of 'Apotharni', a tribe of human-horse hybrids in which the females were bald and 'long bearded'.

'progenitor of the centaur', and that the 'Centaur image is conspicuously appropriate.'[37] This sequence of images and allusions demonstrates well Shakespeare's familiarity with centaur mythology, and his occasionally slippery treatment of it. Lear damns his daughters as centaurian, only to accept his role as their progenitor, himself consigned to the glooms of a mythical underworld.

In 'The Improvisation of Power', Stephen Greenblatt recalls Machiavelli's discussion of Chiron and notes that it serves as 'an early instance of the celebration of psychic mobility that has continued to characterize discussions of Western consciousness to the present time'.[38] Indeed, as Greenblatt rightly intimates, this emblem of the centaur is at the heart of Shakespeare's *Othello*. As in *Troilus and Cressida*, Shakespeare introduces in *Othello* the figure of the 'Sagittary'. This mythological concoction was said to have fought as an archer against the Greeks during the Trojan war, in some versions slaying more than twelve thousand warriors in a single day. In Shakespeare's play, Agamemnon exclaims that 'the dreadful sagittary / Appals our numbers' (5.5.14–15), focusing on the fear and panic produced by the creature rather than its proficiency with artillery. Such fear and panic, as evident in Eden's translation of Pietro Martire, were emphasized in other accounts of the New World that especially parallel the idea of the centaur in *Othello*. This play exemplifies Shakespeare's consideration of the creature as a means of exploring the interchange and hybridization of beast and man generally. I deal with the play here as one of metamorphosis, highlighted by centaur mythology, lore and imagery.

## II

In 1552, Françisco Lòpez de Gomara finished *The Pleasant History of the Conquest of the West India, now called new Spain*. Gomara served as chaplain to Cortes upon the latter's return from the Indies, and while never travelling across the Atlantic himself, Gomara composed through second and third-hand accounts a somewhat glorified history of Cortes' conquest. Before the conquest of Mexico, Cortes took special care with the sixteen horses he was to bring to the New World. They had been brought to the Indies on Columbus's third voyage, but were still extremely scarce and valuable. According to Jon White, 'those sixteen horses were to be "their fortress", "their one hope for survival" – in fact, "they owed it all to the horses"'; the conquistadors would additionally subjugate the New World 'riding ... Moorish fashion', adopting the methods of their enemies.[39] In 1578, the enormous popularity of Gomara's book in Europe led Thomas Nicholas to translate 101 of the original 252 chapters into English, and the work was published in London that year and again in 1596. Nicholas relates an episode concerning 25 March 1519, and the miraculous Battle of Cintla. Waiting for Cortes and his cavalry to reinforce the embattled Spaniard, the soldiers witness the sudden appearance of a 'horseman with a speckled horse', who begins to turn the tide of the battle against the Indians:

> In thys meane tyme the horsemanne faded away, and was not seene, and wyth hys absence the Indians beganne afreshe, and enclosed the Chrystians in the same daunger that they were in before: then the horsemanne appeared again neere oure menne, and made marvellous may among the enimies, whereupon our menne seeying this succoure, gave the onset agayne with great courage, and slewe and hurt many Indians, but at the best season, the horseman vanished awaye cleane out of sighte, and when the

[37] Andrews, 'Lear's Wheel of Fire and Centaur Daughters', *Renaissance Papers* (1965), 21–4.

[38] Stephen Greenblatt, *Renaissance Self-Fashioning: From More to Shakespeare* (Chicago: University of Chicago Press, 1980), p. 224. On the 'zoomorphic images' in *The Prince*, see Ezio Raimondi, 'The Politician and the Centaur', trans. Michael Moore, in *Machiavelli and the Discourse of Literature*, ed. by Albert Russell Ascoli and Victoria Kahn (Ithaca: Cornell University Press, 1993), p. 145–60.

[39] Jon White, *Cortes and the Downfall of the Aztec Empire* (New York: St. Martin's, 1971), pp. 60–4.

> Indians sawe not the horseman, with fear of whom they fledde, thinkyng that he hadde bin a Centaure, and that the horse and man was all one incorporate, they returned agayne with lively courage, and used our Christians worse than they hadde done before. Then the horseman returned the third time, and put the Indians to flight with great hurte, whom our footmen pursued with great slaughter.[40]

White makes an interesting critique of this battle, writing that 'it seems as if the horsemen did not do the damage directly, but that the sudden appearance of these "centaurs" ... caused so much demoralization that the Indians faltered ... The Indians had no idea how to deal with this supernatural beast, half animal and half man, and simply stood paralyzed while the pounding hoofs and flashing swords cut them down.'[41] One is reminded again of the Sagittary in *Troilus and Cressida*, whose mere appearance 'appals' the Greeks into retreat. Just as ancient cultures figuratively transformed barbarian invaders into hybrid forms of beast and man, so too the Indians purportedly transform the invading conquerors from civilized Europe into centaurs. Rumours of these episodes would surely have had import for Elizabethan England, which repeatedly confronted the prospect at the close of the sixteenth century of these same Spanish 'centaurs' conquering more than just the distant Indies. The latter part of the 1500s saw several attempts at a Spanish invasion of England, the Spanish Armada of 1588 being only the most famous. As R. B. Wernham recounts, 'Three times armadas gathered in Ferrol and Coruna for direct attacks upon England', the first two thwarted by fierce storms, and John Loftis relates that throughout her reign, 'Elizabeth was confronted ... by the threat of a Spanish invasion supported by a rebellion of English Catholics.' Harrison offers many instances similar to the one in which Queen Elizabeth in 1597 'spoke several times of the King of Spain, his wishing to kill her'.[42] The parallels, then, between the Spanish subjugation of the Indies and their threatened invasion of England reside partly in the notion of Catholic Spain as ideologically uncivilized, heathenish barbarians. Further, the violating sexual aggression of the Spaniard King into the sanctified realm of the Virgin Queen Elizabeth reverberates with the same violence as the drunken centaurs raping the Lapith women – again a breaking of an understood bond or treaty. As in *Love's Labour's Lost*, in which Shakespeare ridiculed the Spanish Armada in the figure of Don Armado, these anxieties play themselves out noticeably in *Othello*, particularly in the figure of Iago, for that villain has Spanish connotations as well.

The work of Gomara disturbed one of the men who had actually accompanied Cortes, Bernal Diaz del Castillo, who completed *The True History of the Conquest of Mexico* in 1572 largely as a response to his literary predecessor. Diaz revised Gomara's purported revelation during the Battle of Cintla, perhaps with a tinge of sarcasm. Apparently, 'previous to the arrival of the main body of the cavalry under Cortes, Francisco de Morla appeared in the field upon a grey dappled horse' – Gomara claimed that Morla served only as an avatar at best, insisting that 'it was [really] one of the holy apostles, St Peter or St Jago, disguised under his person'.[43] That the patron saint of Spain, James or 'Iago', should offer salvation to the conquering Spanish in the guise of a pagan beast elicits a note of sarcasm from Diaz. But his sudden appearance as the champion of Good was not, at least, unprecedented. Rea points out that 'the most important aspect of St James in Spain ... is

40 Gomara, *The Conquest of the West India*, trans. Thomas Nicholas (Ann Arbor: University Microfilms, 1966), p. 44.

41 White, *Cortes*, p. 169.

42 Wernham, *The Return of the Armadas* (New York: Oxford University Press, 1994), p. 4; Loftis, *Renaissance Drama in England and Spain* (Princeton: Princeton University Press, 1987), p. 71; G. B. Harrison, *A Second Elizabethan Journal* (Boston: Routledge and Kegan Paul, 1931), p. 242.

43 Bernal Diaz, *The Conquest of Mexico*, trans. Maurice Keating (La Jolla, CA: Renaissance Press, 1979), p. 47.

his association with the Reconquista (the military expulsion of the Moslems from the Iberian peninsula, and the re-Christianization thereof)'. For St James was not only a symbol in the Spanish mind of the superiority of Christianity, but 'was reputed to have *participated* in battle to destroy the infidel occupiers'. Thus 'Santiago' became 'the Moorslayer'.[44] The name Iago, then, embodies both the inherently contradictory conflation at the Battle of Cintla of Christian man and pagan beast, and the representation of Spanish freedom. (The name itself is something of a centaur.) But even more directly relevant to Shakespeare and his contemporaries, the name too was a 'war cry of those Spanish arch-enemies. (A name, indeed, of one of the ships of the Armada)'.[45] All of England was confronted with Iago, a decidedly sagittarian aggressor.

The performance of *Othello* in 1604 before the court of James I draws particular attention to Iago; Shakespeare partly mirrors the image of the English James with an exposition of Iago as the Spanish other. However, Iago's connotations with such 'otherness' go deeper, and one might also compare Iago with his etymological ancestor, Jacob in Genesis. Othello could well have paraphrased in his final speech the words of Esau to Isaac concerning his duplicitous brother: 'Was he not iustely called Iaakob? for he hathe deceived me these two times: he toke my birthright, and lo, now hathe he taken my blessing.'[46] The displacement of Esau by Jacob parallels that of Othello by Iago in a variety of ways.[47] Most relevant to Jacob's supplanting of Esau may be the 'beastliness' of Esau, whose hairy arms Jacob mimics with the skins of goats, for as he laments to his mother, he is not 'rough' like his brother, but 'smothe' (Genesis 27:11). Jacob must become part beast. The maelstrom of Machiavellian and biblical forces of reputation, power and beastliness at play in *Othello* nevertheless derives from Shakespeare's particular idea of the centaur. In the eye of this maelstrom lurks Iago.

As in *The Comedy of Errors*, centaur allusions in *Othello* appear almost immediately. After rousing Brazantio and alerting him to Desdemona's disappearance, Iago urges Roderigo to 'Lead to the Sagittary the raisèd search, / And there will I be with him' (1.1.160–1). In effect, he promises to join with the Moor under the sign of the Sagittary.[48] Thus *Othello* discloses the 'Sagittary', and the fearsome, warlike centaur is appropriate for the malicious metamorphosing that Shakespeare explores in the play. The initial meeting of Othello and Iago at the Sagittary, their convening in a place where bestial and human might well be expected to

---

44 John A. Rea, 'Iago', *Names*, 34(1) (1986), 97–8. See Barbara Everett's '"Spanish" Othello: the Making of Shakespeare's Moor', *Shakespeare Survey 35* (1982), 101–12, for an overview of correspondences between *Othello* and Spain. She argues that Iago 'was of all names the most recognizable both as Spanish and as James', and that St James was commonly known in Spain as Santiago Matamoros, St James the Moor-killer (p. 103). Cf. H. Thomas, *Shakespeare and Spain* (Oxford: Clarendon, 1922).

45 Rea, 'Iago', p. 97.

46 See Genesis 27:36 in *The Geneva Bible. A Facsimile of the 1560 Edition*, intro. Lloyd E. Berry (Madison: University of Wisconsin Press, 1969). Subsequent biblical citations are taken from this text.

47 Norman Nathan, 'Iago, Iachimo, Jaques, Jaques de Boys, Jaquenetta, St Jaques, and Jacob', *Names*, 35 (3–4) (1983), 325–7, finds many echoes of the biblical Jacob and Esau in the relationship of the Antipholus twins, as well.

48 See also Lena Cowen Orlin, *Private Matters and Public Culture in Post Reformation England* (Ithaca and London: Cornell University Press, 1994), pp. 196–201, who perceives the Sagittary's mythical influence in the play as oriented around the celestial sign of the archer. T. Sipahigil, '"Sagittary/Sagittar" in *Othello*', *Shakespeare Quarterly*, 27 (1976), 200, reads 'Sagitary' not as a zodiacal centaur sign on an inn, but rather as a 'sagittaria', a 'class of light and fast ships used in the Mediterranean from the twelfth through the seventeenth centuries'. Jean Roberts, *The Shakespearean Wild: Geography, Genus, and Gender* (Lincoln: University of Nebraska Press, 1991), p. 101, remarks, 'the name of the Sagittary . . . evokes both the heavenly constellation and the hybrid human bestial archer of the legend, thus potentially betokening either blessed sensuality or forbidden lust'.

come together, prefigures the bonding of the two characters in 3.3, and serves as a vanguard for the broader pattern of joining and separation within the play. More importantly, Iago and Othello combine over the course of the play in the same hybridization of beast and man that creates the centaur, or sagittary: equine imagery will frequently serve Shakespeare in describing their relationship. Emphatically, the pattern begins beneath the sign of one of the deadliest and, to Shakespeare, most 'appalling' centaurs. But a few lines earlier in the scene, another exchange occurs that adroitly anticipates the Sagittary image that follows.

Othello and Desdemona apparently honeymoon at the Sagittary. Page duBois points out that 'in many of the episodes in the Centaur myth, the horse/men sustained ... hostility to legal marriage and to the forms of exchange typical of Greek civilization', and this is clearly illustrated in the Battle of the Lapiths, a melee that fairly ruins the wedding-day of Pirithous and Hippodame.[49] Indeed, the most likely reason for the Sagittary allying with the Trojans, both traditionally and in *Troilus and Cressida*, is the shared hostility towards the laws of marriage between centaurs and the Helen-stealing Paris. That Othello and Desdemona would stay as newlyweds under the sign of the Sagittary immediately foreshadows, and threatens, the imminent destruction of the couple. Iago will assume the role of sagittary/centaur, and truly, as Othello later relates, Iago 'best know[s] the place' (1.3.121).[50] (And one recalls here, too, Biondello's centaurian song in *The Taming of the Shrew*, and the invocation there to 'Saint Jamy'.) In taunting Brabanzio, Iago cries that 'Because we come to do you service and you think we are ruffians, you'll have your daughter covered with a Barbary horse, you'll have your nephews neigh to you, you'll have coursers for cousins and jennets for germans' (1.1.111–15). Iago details the conjugal bliss to Brabanzio by transforming the image of Othello into a horse, mating with the human figure of Desdemona. (The covering of Desdemona with a Barbary horse also echoes those coverings of Katherina and perhaps Arcite, as well.) Here too a pattern begins that continues throughout: the centaurian configuration of Desdemona and Othello that gradually mutates into, and is consequently displaced by, Iago and Othello. Desdemona, in effect, occupies the position of 'Hippodame', both susceptible to centaur-destruction, and yet incorporating and sustaining the horse-hybrid, as Hippo-dame does within her very name. Thus, when Iago further tortures Brabanzio by informing him that his 'daughter and the Moor are now making the beast with two backs' (1.1.117–19), he is not only mimicking Rabelais, but also evoking the licentious image of the centaur: a single beast possessing, of course, two backs.[51]

Shakespeare uses the centaur in *Othello* to develop the triptych of characters that form the overriding triangle of jealousy in the play: Othello, Iago, and Desdemona. As already mentioned, Iago forecasts in Act 1 his eventual displacement of Desdemona and virtual betrothal to Othello by means of his language regarding the Sagittary. Iago seems at first to be the most adoptive of the Machiavellian centaur type: one willing to use both fraud and force, the wisdom of man and the brutishness of a beast. Supposedly unlike Cassio, whose 'soldiership' is 'Mere prattle without practice' (1.1.25–6), Iago knows both the machinations of deceit and the turmoil of the battlefield. Nevertheless, he sees himself to Othello as 'much like his matter's ass', with the qualification that he 'follow[s] him to serve [his] turn

49 DuBois, *Centaurs and Amazons* (Ann Arbor: University of Michigan Press, 1982), p. 28.

50 To further illustrate the link with Spain, Orlin, *Private Matters*, p. 207, argues that in astrological spheres, 'James the Greater/Santiago rules the sign of Sagittarius'. Her subsequent observations on the animal imagery in *Othello* form a useful supplement to this discussion.

51 For a slightly different take, cf. William C. Watterson, '"O Monstrous World": Shakespeare's Beast with Two Backs', *The Upstart Crow*, 13 (1993), 79–93.

upon him' (1.1.42–7). Iago is the complete Machiavellian centaur, and yet he already is metaphorically cleaving in two, ready to transfer his parts onto another, and finally to divorce Desdemona from, and thus meld with, the Moor. As he asserts, 'Were I the Moor I would not be Iago' (1.1.57); but as the play progresses, this becomes less and less true. Othello's beginnings seem also to be those of the complete centaur. He is the paragon of beast and man: a composite centaur, already marginalized by his ethnicity, his 'sooty bosom' (1.2.71), but also a valiant and valuable insider in the Venetian power structure. To Brabanzio, he is the black, savage half – the 'foul thief' (1.2.63) – while Desdemona, the innocent, nevertheless forms half of the 'beast with two backs'.[52] Desdemona is textually bestialized as well, both as 'white ewe' (1.1.89), and more tellingly as the possessor of a 'greedy ear' who, much like 'the cannibals that each other eat', 'Devour[s] up [the] discourse' of Othello (1.3.142–9). As Iago's treachery unfolds, and displaces Desdemona more and more, she herself will maintain attachments to centaurs, even as she is distanced from Othello.

Iago's reasons for his subterfuge are never completely elucidated. One possibility he alleges is that Othello has slept with Emilia. Or more accurately, he asserts, 'the lusty Moor / Hath leapt into my seat' (2.1.294–5). Thus Iago wants vengeance, an eye for an eye, a 'wife for wife' (2.1.298). The language Iago here chooses is revealing. Othello has assumed a 'riding' position with Emilia, displacing Iago. If Iago is to get even with him, he too must displace Othello and 'leap into his seat', creating a centaur tableau of his own. In Iago's plan, however, it is Othello who 'will as tenderly be led by th' nose / As asses are' (1.3.393–4). The moor must become fully the beast. Iago does not begin his assault proper, the 'monstrous birth' is not truly 'ingendered' (1.3.395–6), until the second act, at which point the source of anxiety up to that point disappears: the Turkish fleet on its way to attack the island of Cyprus sinks in a storm. Like the Spanish aramadas of the mid-1590s, that never quite reached England over the uncooperative seas, the Turkish fleet never reaches the Venetian territory. The ship 'Iago' of the 1588 Armada never did, either; Shakespeare concocts, however, a quite different ending. For while the Turkish fleet is drowned in the first scene of Act 2, Iago appears on Cyprus shortly thereafter.

The plot to disgrace Cassio that evolves on the island is particularly emblematic of centaur myth. Kollman notes that 'the average centaur is a potentially uncontrollable creature, although the violence does not always manifest itself specifically as sexual violence'. Furthermore, she notes that 'it was wine . . . that drove the centaur, famous Eurytion, distracted in the palace of great-hearted Peirithoos . . . His brain went wild with drinking, and in his fury he did much harm in the house of Peirithoos . . . Since his time there has been a feud between men and Centaurs, and he was the first who found his own evil in heavy drinking.'[53] Cassio's drunken belligerence on the night of his swordfight with Montano similarly exhibits the exacerbation of rage by the potency of drink. Oddly in this scene, Cassio (who owns 'very poor and unhappy brains for drinking' [2.3.30–1]) is tempted and spurred on by Iago and the latter's English drinking songs. The suddenly Anglophilic Iago, who cheers at one point 'O sweet England' (2.3.81), adopts and contorts the English songs in much the same way that he ensnares Cassio. He absorbs, as the Spanish attempted to do, the sovereignty of that which

[52] The Victorian artist Edmund Dulac may well have had Othello in mind when he created the picture immortalized by Yeats in his poem 'On a Picture of a Black Centaur by Edmund Dulac'. Therein, a black centaur bears a human, while green parrots chatter in the background. Dulac, of course, was also a popular artist for *The Tempest* and *Macbeth*. See Colin White, *Edmund Dulac* (New York: Charles Scribner's Sons, 1976), pp. 93–7.

[53] Kollman, 'Centaur', pp. 227–8.

is 'most potent' about England. And by its retranslation into his own mouth, Iago transforms the songs into instruments of more heinous seduction. He transmutes that which is James's into Iago's. Adding to the similarity with the centaurs (for drinking as vice alone certainly is not relegated only to these creatures of myth), Iago tells Montano that Cassio's vice ''Tis to his virtue a just equinox' (2.3.116). Cassio's personality is split evenly between vice and virtue, monster and man. Or as Cassio himself says, 'I ha' lost my reputation, I ha' lost the immortal part of myself, and what remains is bestial!' (2.3.257–8).

Iago's melding with Othello becomes complete in the pivotal third act. Othello unnervingly suggests to Iago, 'Exchange me for a goat / When I shall turn the business of my soul' (3.3.184–5) to believing the latter's suggestions of infidelity. His words here quite closely mirror the tale of Jacob in Genesis, in which Jacob does indeed exchange Esau for a goat. From this point on, until the final revelations of treachery, Othello willingly complies with Iago's behests. Othello's alteration into a beast couples Iago's own resituation as reasoning plotter, but the two become intermingled. They are, like the centaur, 'arrested in a perpetual state of semi-metamorphosis.' Iago assumes the imaginary place of Desdemona when he relates to Othello his supposed encounter with Cassio:

I lay with Cassio lately,<br>
...<br>
In sleep I heard him say, 'Sweet Desdemona,<br>
Let us be wary, let us hide our loves',<br>
And then, sir, would he grip and wring my hand,<br>
Cry 'O, sweet creature!', then kiss me hard,<br>
As if he plucked up kisses by the roots,<br>
That grew upon my lips, lay his leg o'er my thigh<br>
And sigh, and kiss, and then cry 'Cursed fate,<br>
That gave thee to the Moor!' (3.3.418–30)

Othello's reply, 'O, monstrous, monstrous!' (3.3.431), anticipates the betrothal into a centaur form of Iago and Othello shortly thereafter, as they kneel and pledge union with one another.[54] Othello says 'I greet thy love, / ... with acceptance bounteous', and Iago utters the fateful words 'I am your own for ever' (3.3.472–82). Iago's 'bloody thoughts' become Othello's. They surge over the 'Pontic sea, / ... Till that a capable and wide revenge / Swallow them up' (3.3.456–63), like the Turkish fleet swallowed up by the waves of the Mediterranean, or the Spanish turned back by the Atlantic. The jealous abomination that the Othello–Iago hybrid creates is depicted in the fourth act.

'A horned man's a monster and a beast', says Othello. The paradox Shakespeare is exploring is pinpointed more by Iago's response, however: 'There's many a beast then in a populous city, / And many a civil monster' (4.1.60–2). Such paradoxical interchange mirrors their own relationship, and recalls the tradition of centaurs as themselves 'civil monsters'. Their union purposefully excludes Desdemona. But while Othello and Iago begin to operate together, she too becomes associated with centaurs. Bianca refers to her unwittingly as a 'hobby-horse' (4.1.151). The epithet in its immediate context connotes a harlot, as a derogatory term for one's fixation, but in the broader expanse of the play, the centaur-like image of a mummer wearing the attached figure of a horse, as in a morris dance, also must come to mind. In *Love's Labour's Lost*, the 'hobby horse' also reflects the same lasciviousness as centaurs, as when Don Armado asks, 'Call'st thou my love hobby-horse?' Moth responds, 'No, master, the hobby-horse is but a colt, and your love perhaps a hackney' (3.1.29–31). Finally, it is as a result of Desdemona's handkerchief that the 'hobby-horse' appellation occurs to Bianca at all, and this handkerchief – a device borrowed

[54] Cf. James R. Aubrey, 'Race and the Spectacle of the Monstrous in *Othello*', *CLIO*, 22 (1993), 221–38; and Karen Newman, *Fashioning Femininity and English Renaissance Drama* (Chicago: University of Chicago Press, 1991), pp. 71–94.

by Shakespeare from Cinthio's *Gli Hecatommithi* – parallels centaur mythology once again.

As already mentioned, it is the centaur Nessus who eventually slays Hercules. As Ovid relates the myth, Nessus is pierced by an arrow for attempting the rape of Hercules' beloved. The arrow, 'with poyson foule of Lerna Snake embrewed', killed him, but not before he doused a shirt with his own blood 'and gave it to Dyanayre, / Assuring hir it had the powre too kindle Cupids fyre'. Some time later, 'tatling fame / ... Told Dyanyre that Hercules did cast a liking too / A Ladie called Iolee. And Dyanayra (whoo / Was jealous over Hercules) gave credit to the same.' She then sends the sanguinary shirt to Hercules, who 'receyving it without mistrust therein, / Did weare the poyson of the Snake of Lerna next his skin'.[55] Hercules is verily eaten alive by the acidic poison, and dies in slow agony. Shakespeare uses the metaphor in *Antony and Cleopatra*, when Hercules-like Antony proclaims in torment, 'The shirt of Nessus is upon me' (4.13.43).[56] In *Othello*, the allusions are not as overt but are potentially more suggestive. First, Othello describes the handkerchief's origins as given to his mother by an Egyptian clairvoyant. This seer informed her that 'while she kept it, / 'Twould make her amiable, and subdue my father / Entirely to her love; ... / She, dying, gave it me, / And bid me, when my fate would have me wived, / To give it her' (3.4.58–65). The ostensible power of the handkerchief is as an aphrodisiac, a love-potion in cloth form. But as with the shirt of Nessus, the power to 'kindle Cupid's fire' belies the ultimate effect: to poison mortally the bearer. Both Hercules and Othello succumb to the insidious potency of the charms. For by means of this handkerchief, this 'ocular proof' (3.3.365) given by Iago, Othello falls headlong into the pit of jealousy. Similarly, Deianira's jealousy provides the impetus to bid her lover to wear the shirt; Othello's jealousy makes him demand Desdemona produce the handkerchief. The theme of poisoning runs through *Othello*. Iago remarks that the thought of Othello leaping into his seat 'doth, like a poisonous mineral, gnaw my inwards' (2.1.296), and Othello first proposes the use of poison to kill his wife. Lodovico calls the finale an 'object' that 'poisons sight' (5.2.374). But if the figure of Cassio is seen as the manifestation of the poison fed Othello by Iago (he 'pour[s] this pestilence into his ear', (2.3.347)), it is also a significant parallel that Cassio says of himself, 'Had I as many mouths as Hydra, such an answer would stop them all. To be now a sensible man, by and by a fool, and presently a beast!' (2.3.297–9). For it was the many-headed Lernean Hydra that provided the poison that killed both Nessus and Hercules. And were Cassio indeed such a venomous creature, the exact pattern he describes would befall those who came in contact with him. Through Iago's transmutation of Cassio into just that poison, it is Othello who goes from sensible man, to fool, to beast – a quite degenerative centaur.

After Iago taunts Brabanzio that he will 'have [his] daughter covered with a Barbary horse', Desdemona echoes this curiously. She tells Emilia that 'My mother had a maid called Barbary' (4.3.25), from whom Desdemona learned the song of 'willow'. The very inclusion of the word 'Barbary' links Desdemona, through the willow song, with the centaur allusions at the onset of *Othello*. John Draper notes that 'Shakespeare's two commonest references

[55] See Ovid, 9.119–333, for a complete retelling of the myth.

[56] Several critics have noted the resemblance between the shirt of Nessus and the handkerchief of Othello: Bate, *Shakespeare and Ovid*, p. 181, calls Iago's deceitful language the 'verbal equivalent to the poisonous shirt of Nessus with which Deianira is deceived into destroying another great martial hero, Hercules', while Robert Miola, *Shakespeare and Classical Tragedy: The Influence of Seneca* (Oxford: Clarendon, 1992), p. 135, writes that 'the parallels defy accident'. He goes on to cite, as the probable source for Shakespeare's knowledge of the 'centaur's magic cloak', Seneca's *Hercules Oetaeus*, although Golding's Ovid seems to me more probable. See Bate, *Shakespeare and Ovid*, pp. 206–7, for a treatment of this myth in *Antony and Cleopatra*.

to Barbary are not only incidental but indirect: the plays have four allusions to Barbary horses and at least two to Barbary pigeons, both of which were a usual sight in England.'[57] In *Othello*, as elsewhere, Barbary often conjures up the image of the horse. That a maid named Barbary should impart to Desdemona the tragic song that prefigures her demise is more than ironic. Though as loyal as Ovid's Hylonome, she suffers under aspersions more akin to those hurled at Lear's centaur daughters. Her death is not so much a division from Othello, with whom she has already parted ways, but from her self – a splitting into body and song. (Not unlike Richard II, who bids his soul 'Mount, mount . . . / Whilst my gross flesh sinks downward' (5.5.111–12), only a few lines after asserting, 'I was not made a horse' (5.5.92).) The body perishes at the hands of Othello; the song lingers on, as it did through Barbary, through the singing of Emilia (5.2.255), until Iago smites her. Iago remains, but with his contrivances discovered, separates from himself as well – Othello, his other half since the third act, kills himself. The mortal blow comes from a weapon weighty with implication: 'a sword of Spain' (5.2.260). Iago thereafter becomes simply an abstract beast: a 'Spartan dog, / More fell than anguish, hunger, or the sea' (5.2.371–2). His own poisoning instruction finally proves too virulent for the mollifying verses of Barbary, the Chiron-like maid.

What progresses as a play of interchange among Iago, Othello, and Desdemona ends with nearly total dissolution. Few single images could embody as vividly the same potential for these contrary forces as the centaur. Not all of the bonding or severing of bonds in *Othello*, of course, derive from conceptions of the creature. But the steeping of the play in so many aspects of this idea – the Nessus and Hydra myth, the method of conspiracy against Cassio, the foreboding 'Sagittary', and the possibility of accounts Shakespeare had read concerning the Spanish centaur-like creations – makes those metaphors of bonding that do include equine imagery all the more resonant. But a last and eerily poignant example of the centaur's significance in Shakespeare's day may best summarize the plight of Othello. The widely read mythographer Natalis Conti comments that 'the ancients told of the misfortunes the Centaurs suffered' in order to 'suppress the temerity of impure and criminal men'. He concludes, 'For he who abuses wine, gives in to impure desires, steals the goods of others, [and] does not know that temperance and equity must be exercised in all things is forced . . . to spend the last days of life among strangers.'[58] Shakespeare's centaurs are at times explorations of beast and man, horse and rider, at other times models for the possibilities of myth. In *Othello*, finally, one has the sense that the play's primary characters are living their lives, like Conti's centaurs, sadly among strangers. No single relationship survives unscathed, and as the play unfolds, it becomes more and more clear how little the characters know or, in the case of Iago, care for the inner workings of the others. Othello himself, straddling racial and personal lines, never manages the delicate fusion embodied by these 'civil monsters'. But then, the centaur may have preoccupied Shakespeare most for that very reason: its apparently seamless union of difference is really arrested in a perpetual state of struggle. To be a 'stranger / Of here and every where' (1.1.138–9) may be Othello's first and final lot – the boundaries between horse and man, after all, underscore those perplexing borders between one human and another. And in *Othello*, the negotiation of those borders begins and ends with utter estrangement.[59]

---

57 Draper, 'Shakespeare and Barbary', *Etudes Anglaises*, 16 (1961), 308. Possibly the most famous instance is Claudius' wager in *Hamlet* – 'six Barbary horses' (5.2.112) that Laertes will lose the match against the Prince of Denmark.

58 From *Natale Conti's Mythologies: A Select Translation*, trans. Anthony DiMatteo (New York and London: Garland, 1994), pp. 372–3.

59 I would like to thank Mark Thornton Burnett and Gale H. Carrithers, Jr, for their extremely helpful suggestions and comments on this essay.

# SHAKESPEARE'S INTERNATIONAL CURRENCY

JOHN RUSSELL BROWN

Answering a comparatively simple question, may sometimes help clarify a more difficult one. So by considering why Shakespeare, who wrote four hundred years ago, is more frequently performed than any other dramatist and staged in theatres all around the world, it may be possible to ask how present-day scholarship and criticism, a huge new industry, might best be employed.

Shakespeare's almost universal currency today makes theatre seem a backward-looking art: it has produced no other voice in our own time that is so widely acceptable. The most respected theatre directors turn repeatedly to Shakespeare's scripts as if nothing modern has so fired their imaginations. Giorgio Strehler, Ariane Mnouchkine, Peter Brook, Peter Stein, Suzuki Tadashi, Robert Lepage: all of these, each from a different country, have mined Shakespeare repeatedly for productions that are startling in effect, contentiously modern, and, often, sensuously beautiful as well.

Why should theatre be so fixated on Shakespeare, and variously so, all around the world? The easiest answer is to say that Shakespeare was a very wise man and a genius, but other geniuses of the theatre have not so transcended boundaries of language, race, social customs, politics, religious belief; and few writers of any kind have proved so immune to the changes brought about by time.

Sometimes we are told that Shakespeare's great merit lies in his poetry: in the subtlety with which he wrote, the endless fascination that even his simple-seeming words possess for those who study them; in the compassion, good sense, fine distinctions, alert sentiments that are implicit in his words; in the music of his speeches as they are spoken, and imprint themselves in our memories. But if Shakespeare's use of the English language were the only or the chief cause of his popularity today, that would not explain why the plays have proved able to cross all boundaries of time and place, and of cultures. They survive without the advantage of his verbal brilliance when translated into many other languages, whether comparatively simple and limited in vocabulary or rich in sound and associations, whether idiomatic and unliterary or gravely archaic and esoteric. Around the whole world, Shakespeare holds attention today without his poetry giving great pleasure and gaining close attention. What is the secret, then, that accounts for his value in foreign exchange, his international currency?

To start with the most obvious: the variety of the plays points to part of the explanation, for Shakespeare seems never to have been content to repeat himself without introducing significant changes. For over twenty years, one or, more usually, two plays followed each other, year after year; and in every one, Shakespeare modified how he wrote, tackled further and more difficult themes, invented amazingly original characters, filled the stage with surprising images, minted new words and used old ones in new ways. To read through the whole volume of the *Complete Works* is to travel far in the mind and in many directions. Some kind of discontent must have driven him from which we benefit today, a perpetual desire to move forward into new territory. Harold Pinter, near the start of his own career, imagined Shakespeare confronting all possible difficulties on the road ahead only to assert that 'He survived them all.'[1] In much the same vein, Peter Brook, the director, has written that Shakespeare today is still a 'model' for actors and directors, no matter what new experiment they have in hand.[2]

To persistence and unflagging invention must surely be added the good fortune to have been born in the right place and at the right time. Theatre is a collaborative art which no one person can practise on his or her own, and also an art that is fully alive only with an audience to enjoy it and contribute to its making. In both respects, Shakespeare arrived at the right time. As a writer, he was not alone. Before his early death, Christopher Marlowe vied with him in popularity and productivity. Providing theatres with plays was a task that attracted many ambitious young authors at that time – poets, politicians, moralists, and future priests among them. They answered a steady demand for new plays: whenever one was performed for the first time by the Admiral's Men (the only company of that time for which we have records), no matter what it was about or whether its author was well known or neophyte, the takings at the theatre went up – either it was crowded or prices of admission had been increased for the special attraction.[3] The contrast with our theatre is striking: today original texts are always considered a risk by the management, no matter how strong the writer's reputation. Most new plays are tried out in readings and then in one or more workshops, to all of which admission will probably be offered free of charge.

It was Shakespeare's good fortune to write for a theatre that was up-to-date, widely popular in appeal, and fashionable. It was patronized by the leaders and rulers of the nation, by the witty and the youthfully ambitious, by long-established families and by the newly prosperous professional class. Lawyers commissioned special performances for their own pleasure and actors from the theatres performed in celebratory shows and pageants paid for by the Merchants' Guilds of the City of London. To newly built and very splendid theatres came the equivalents of both blue- and white-collared workers, taking time-off in the middle of the working day. On public holidays, audiences might overflow the available accommodation.[4] At the universities, theatre was patronized by both faculty and students, college halls being made available for performances despite the unavoidable inconvenience this caused. Touring outside London was a regular business for the professional theatre companies and hardly a town of any size was without a building or open-air site in which plays could be staged; people must have thronged to see these provincial performances since a number of the surviving records tell of injuries in clashes around the place of performance.[5]

Such widespread popularity, in his own time, meant that the theatre for which Shakespeare wrote was neither a literary nor an 'Art' theatre, as we understand those terms. Infected as they very obviously were with a delight in poetry and rhetoric, and with the wise sayings and mythical figures of classical literature, its dramatists also drew upon less sophisticated sources:

1 *Show* (New York, February, 1964), p. 102.

2 'So it is that in the second half of the twentieth century in England where I am writing these words, we are faced with the infuriating fact that Shakespeare is still our model' *The Empty Space* (London: MacGibbon and Kee, 1968), p. 95.

3 See Peter Thomson, *Shakespeare's Theatre* (London: Routledge, 1983), pp. 56–7.

4 See, for example, Andrew Gurr, *The Shakespearean Stage, 1574–1642* (Cambridge: Cambridge University Press, 1980), p. 196.

5 See Alan Somerset, '"How chances it they travel?": Provincial Touring, Playing Places, and the King's Men', *Shakespeare Survey 47* (1994), pp. 45–60, 54–5.

old-fashioned rituals and ceremonies surviving from pagan times, popular ballads, fairy stories, sports, games and competitions. The most serious of plays would be likely to include scenes of broad and topical comedy and, often, various chases and fights, disguises and dances. Numerous minor figures would fill out processions and a great deal of music was played upon drums, trumpets, and some stringed and woodwind instruments. Unlike many ambitious dramatists in later ages – in the twentieth century especially – Shakespeare's contemporaries, and he among them, were interested in more than argument, analysis, interesting characters, or the representation of every day life on the stage. These they did provide, and in plenty; but their audiences loved what were called 'shows', 'alarums and excursions', 'activity', 'antics', and displays of many kinds, as well as 'high astounding' words and 'ravishing' poetry of which they may have had only limited understanding.[6] The new dramatists became adept at pleasing all these appetites with the result that plays were the most sought-after entertainments of the age.

Lucky in time and place, Shakespeare thrived on the opportunities offered by an active and pleasure-giving theatre. Seeing his plays performed in other languages than English is to realize how much of their vitality and viability is due to popular showmanship and an imaginative use of the physical elements of the actors' performances that he understood very well as a member of the leading Elizabethan acting company. Much in the performance of one of his plays will work on the audience's imaginations without the help of the words of the text; the mere succession of events on stage can hold an audience's attention.

Moreover, in the theatre, Shakespeare's plays are visually and physically alive in the very being of the actors, capable, even in mute performance, of many fine, surprising, and meaningful effects. This becomes obvious when they are seen in countries which are more ceremonious in daily life than present-day United States or Europe – for example, in Japan. At the start of a production of *King Lear* at the Panasonic Globe Theatre in Tokyo in 1991, the entire court entered in due order and silently took up appropriate positions. Later, when the king made his entry, they prostrated themselves full-length on the floor of the stage. Lear's absolute power, not mentioned in the text at this point, was everywhere apparent and impossible to ignore because the director had used ceremony with a seriousness that was Asian and Elizabethan, and had nothing to do with Western urban or rural living. Later the unmoving, self-contained, and outwardly respectful figures of Lear's daughters drew absolute attention when they did break out of that fixed ordering, both when speaking to their father and when hearing what their sisters have to say to him. With each movement calculated according to the rules and limits of an expected ceremonial in which each person faced the king, glances or small signs of inner tensions were so clearly marked that they gave an impression of suppressed rivalries and fears. With everyone alert and almost entirely still, physical performance and movements on stage had a power beyond the meanings transmitted by the words which were spoken, so that the scene became ominous as it riveted the audience's attention.

In trying to explain the worldwide currency of Shakespeare's plays, we should *see* its action, in our mind's eye, staged with that respect for ceremony that was instinctive in his own times. In the same scene of *King Lear*, the Dukes of Cornwall and Albany have almost nothing to say but are brought into focus several times, notably when Cordelia turns to speak of her sisters' 'husbands' (1.1.95–9) or when the king, without preparation, calls the two dukes by

[6] Thomas Dekker's Prologue to his *If It Be Not a Good Play, the Devil is in it* (1612) contains one of the best known descriptions of the audience's reception of a play; quoted, with numerous others, in Andrew Gurr, *Playgoing in Shakespeare's London* (Cambridge: Cambridge University Press, 1987), p. 225.

name, treats them equally as his two 'beloved sons', and invests them, and not their wives, with his power (1.1.126–38). Why do they not reply, or why are they not allowed opportunity to do so? Perhaps they should come forward, with or without their wives, and almost certainly they should kneel. What are their wives thinking as they also say nothing, and how do they relate to their husbands at this moment? Ceremony can set the stage and ensure that the audience senses powerful undercurrents of thought and feeling. By use of this physical language the play has a silent life which in some countries around the world may be more eloquent than when it is performed nearer to its original home.

In the comedies, ceremonies express sentiments that would otherwise be hidden and also accentuate the necessities or absurdities of what happens. In *As You Like It*, for example, Adam, the loyal but frail and aged servant, behaves with reverence towards his two very different masters; Rosalind tries to honour an unknown wrestler and he stumbles in silent response; the Banished Duke maintains the propriety of a court when he is in a forest with none of the outward trappings of pomp to help him; the huntsman who killed the deer (4.2.) is honoured boisterously, dressed up in the still bloody hide of the slain animal; Touchstone approaches the old shepherd, Corin, and the youthful and easily nonplussed William (3.2. and 5.1.) with an air of courtesy at odds with what he is saying. A little later, this fool assumes a knightly dignity to hold forth about honour in front of the entire court, in the middle of which, his chosen mate has to be ordered to 'bear your body more seeming, Audrey' (5.4.42–101); presumably she does so and, probably, absurdly so, because she makes no verbal reply. Shortly before the end of this comedy, the god Hymen enters and commands a solemn ordering of events (5.4.105).

Ceremony is only one part of the physical language of theatre that renders Shakespeare's plays viable around the world and gives to foreign-language productions some advantages over those in English. In Asian countries where the practice of martial arts is a thriving part of contemporary life, fights and martial display will draw close attention. A production of *Romeo and Juliet* in Seoul, South Korea, in 1995, staged the street brawls of the early acts using the staves and drums of the folk dances that could be seen regularly in city and village squares. Energy and mastery of detail established both individuality and shared commitment to opposition: the young people of Verona in this performance had a seemingly effortless and sustained readiness for action – vigorous, aggressive, proud, instinctive – and this spectacle turned the opening events of the tragedy into dangerous and compelling drama. In this setting, the other violence of the lovers' passion seemed more necessary and also strangely gentle in contrast.

In countries where warfare is a present reality, the marching and counter marching, the frequent stand-offs, the build-up and breakdown of military power, the physical difference in the soldiers' appearance before and after battle, are some of Shakespeare's visual effects that make the history plays compelling narratives and vivid demonstrations of intransigence, violence, suffering, fear, the will to power, and much else besides that reflects and magnifies a daily reality – all present on stage and breathing with immediate life which is besides and even beyond the force of any words that are spoken. Viewed with the eyes of this audience, the rapid alterations of fortune in the Henry the Sixth plays are nicely judged hammerblows that propel the action forward and ensure the rapt attention of audiences.

In many parts of Asia, technically difficult and accomplished physical performance, accompanied with music, is an established tradition in theatre – as, for example in the Kathakali and Kutiyattam of India, the Kabuki of Japan, and Beijing Opera and it derivatives in China. When influenced by such performances, an Asian actor is more externally expressive than a

European or North American, and able to respond, boldly and clearly, to the changing demands of Shakespeare's text with seemingly fresh and boundless invention. Such acting can make a strong visual impression that matches and, occasionally, outreaches what the words themselves communicate. In 1995, *Much Ado About Nothing* was played in the public garden on the waterfront of Shanghai where the stage was a broad flight of shallow steps in front of an impressive memorial of the city's liberation and also much of the area around: entrances and exits were hugely extended and the characters would sometimes talk to each other when ten or fifteen metres apart. The narrative and comedy both survived, partly because the actors had gestures and presence to sustain them on such a scale and partly because the play is written in a demonstrative style which supplies the actors with much to do, as well as to speak. Speeches have a directness and quick alteration of mood that invite active performances: as Benedick says, appropriately, 'I stood like a man at a mark, with a whole army shooting at me' (2.1.231–1). *Much Ado* is a subtle and witty play that performs well in intimate spaces, but it is also an energetic play with opportunity for strongly physical performances and sensational stage effects including extrovert dancing and disguising, a church scene that is violently disrupted, a crazily disorganized trial scene, an attempted duel followed by a mourning vigil, much arriving, partying, processing, and departing, much watching, conspiring, and mistaking, and a good deal of weeping and swooning.

Shakespeare's plays have survived with comparatively few stage directions of any authorial authority, but their texts give many other cues as to what should be done as well as said:[7] how people should walk, amble, or run; bend down, kneel, or kiss; touch each other, turn away, or hide from sight. They call for specific gestures, for the closeness of one character to another so that sometimes the eyes can be seen and sometimes not, for entrances and exits, several persons together or one at a time. They require letters to be delivered, clothes to be changed, weapons to be drawn. They require actors to change direction of address, to speak to one particular person or to many, or to the audience. Shakespeare, as he wrote, imagined the persons of a play in activity as well as speech. Once the text is in rehearsal, actors are fully engaged with all their faculties in what the text implies that they should do, as well as in what they should say. In contrast, some contemporary dramatists will write as if the supply of speeches were the full extent of their business. As Peter Nichols put it:

> it's about all we've got, because really plays are people on stage talking to each other. They're not much else. Or singing to each other or dancing with each other. Mostly talking to each other.[8]

Shakespeare's texts give instruction for physical performance in a more detailed and more constantly present way than their explicit cues for action indicate: varying syntax, sound, and silence also dictate how the actors appear to the audience. For example, even without the control of metre which must be lost in any translation, specific words repeated in a series or over a short passage of time, or the varying length and form of sentences (sometimes with many subordinate clauses or with whole catalogues of instances or epithets), or the pauses suggested by incomplete sentences, will all insist that the speaker varies breath and expends energy in very specific ways: and this activity in order to speak will, inevitably, alter physical presence and posture. Confidence or a lack of it becomes physically very evident as some speeches run on heedlessly, or as others build in effect or change force rapidly and frequently. When speech is slow and weighted down with

---

7 Rudolf Stamm's *Shakespeare's Theatrical Notation: The Early Tragedies* (Berne: Francke Verlag, 1989) systematically considers the use of such cues.

8 William Demastes, 'Peter Nichols On His Art, Politics, and Peers: An Interview', *Journal of Dramatic Theory and Criticism*, 3, 1 (1988), 107.

ponderous ideas, or broken up hesitantly, or stops suddenly, the actor's physical performance changes in accord with the different modes of thought and sensation.

All these small changes in speech patterns and syntax, together with the changes in physical performance that they require, are largely independent of the sounds of the particular words of the original texts and are effective in whichever language is spoken. In a silent reading they are details that may not be much noticed, if at all, but, in performance, they provide a continuous element in what the play becomes for an audience, part of what every actor does on stage, visible and audible in a non-linguistic but musical or percussive way. In very active performances the combined effect can be huge and it will seldom be small, because the dialogue was not written to represent 'talk' as it might register in everyday conversation: these speeches were designed to be delivered so that they can be heard by a thousand people or more and, when so spoken, the extra effort required of the actor will accentuate the visual signs of a changing involvement in the drama. Speech involves physical action and that action displays the speaker's changing involvement in the drama for all to see.

When sensitively and boldly enacted in response to the promptings of speech, Shakespeare's plays are like a dance, and one with the ability to catch attention and express the ongoing drama. For example, consider Henry the Fifth's address to his soldiers at the siege of Harfleur:

> Once more unto the breach, dear friends, once
>     more,
> Or close the wall up with our English dead.
> In peace there's nothing so becomes a man
> As modest stillness and humility,
> But when the blast of war blows in our ears,
> Then imitate the action of the tiger.
> Stiffen the sinews, conjure up the blood,
> Disguise fair nature with hard-favoured rage.
> Then lend the eye a terrible aspect,
> Let it pry through the portage of the head
> Like the brass cannon, let the brow o'erwhelm it
> As fearfully as doth a gallèd rock
> O'erhang and jutty his confounded base,
> Swill'd with the wild and wasteful ocean.
>
> (3.1.1–14)

The sequence of long and short phrases will vary the need to pause for breath and gather inner momentum for the following words. A number of separate phrases, linked and yet distinct in syntax, must be spoken so that they hang together but change frequently in tone, reference, and length of phrase. The speech starts with three phrases in one line and the repetition of 'Once more'; it addresses 'dear friends' as actual people standing in front of the speaker and then, in a moment, switches to 'our English dead' as if some of those friends were now envisaged as just so many stones with which to patch up a damaged wall. Speaking of 'the action of the tiger', a number of ideas follow each other, each instinct with action but lengthening in phrase. The subject matter changes, however, so that speech makes particular points about parts of the human body – the eye and the forehead – and also has to take in more solid and larger ideas, from the compact 'brass cannon' sweeping out to encompass a huge expanse of an ocean, both 'wild and wasteful'. Implicit in Shakespeare's dialogue is a physical dynamic, that involves varying control and expenditure of breath. These work together with a varying emotional and imaginative committal that changes the force, speed, weight, phrasing, pointing, and application of speech. In the actor's person, an audience can *see* and *feel* what is happening: the drama is verbal, but also palpable and unmissable.

Remembering also the stage shows and ceremonies together with various instructions to the actors implicit in the text, it becomes clear that Shakespeare was as keenly aware of what a person is, does, and becomes, as he was of what he or she says; that is how he imagined the plays as he wrote and one of the main reasons why they have been found to be viable on stages all around the world and in our present, far distant, times.

As extraordinary as Shakespeare's success in performance all around the world is the variety of meanings that his plays have been given in those performances. They seem to respond to local interests and different audiences, ready to be all things to all peoples and speak to whatever issues may dominate the minds of their audiences. *Othello* in China may be about the power of individuality, not about jealousy, passion, miscegenation, double standards in sexual morality, deception, evil, holiness, or damnation. In Germany, *The Merchant of Venice* is likely to be about anti-semitism, but recently it has been performed there as an exposure of man's inhumanity to women and especially of the cruelty of young men to the most defenceless women. In parts of India, *King Lear* may be about what is unchanging and indestructible in life; in Italy about how one's man's mind may withstand the world and everyone in it, in charge of his own destiny in the face of appalling loss and pain. In Czechoslovakia, *Hamlet* has been about political power, surveillance and trust; or about madness and stupidity; in Moscow, it has been about the necessity of being independent at all costs. Elsewhere *Hamlet* will be a play about inheritance, death, intelligence, sexual revulsion, fate. That Shakespeare's plays can bear so many interpretations is another reason why they are done so frequently and in so many countries, responding to whatever is the local political, moral and theatrical context. It is also a reason why they continue to be performed long after the society from which they sprung has lost many of its chief characteristics.

Ingmar Bergman's account of his own production of *Hamlet* for the Royal Theatre in Stockholm explains how one of many interpretations came about. At first it seemed an entirely personal matter, as Bergman told an interviewer:

> You have found something that is very interesting for you, just in *Hamlet* . . . You feel you can make it the way that nobody else can make it. You have suddenly found a personal view of the play. It's very simple. Then you feel – it's very lustful and very nice – because it's as if you have it as a secret a very long time.[9]

By the time he started rehearsals, he was 'furious', he said, at the frustrations encountered in setting up the production; and shocked and alarmed by the assassination of the politician Olaf Palme, who was a friend, that had happened only weeks earlier in Stockholm. Bergman's mind-set was able to light up the playtext with unusual brilliance. The critic from the London *Times* (12 June 1987) commented:

> Passionately sensual, tightly knit and persuasively motivated, the production thrillingly creates a close group of individuals, all intent on accumulating knowledge of one another, and frequently remaining on stage after their scenes, watching from beyond the perimeter of a downstage circle where the action is concentrated.

The lights are suddenly taken up as Horatio greets Hamlet: the prince laughs a lot and then suddenly turns serious; wearing dark glasses, over-acting to the Players. He gropes and violates Ophelia, jabs Rosencrantz (or perhaps Guildenstern) in the crutch. Gertrude puts lipstick and red high-heeled shoes on Ophelia as she prepares to encounter Hamlet. Watching the performance of *The Mousetrap*, Claudius is drunk and has a bottle in his hand; in the next scene he enters with a dishevelled whore whose wig comes off as he manhandles her; he is covered with sweat and strips off his clothes before attempting to pray, by which time the whore is asleep on the floor. And so on: a violent world in which the characters seem to hack their way towards what they despairingly want. At the end of the play, the full size of the stage is revealed for the first time: it is the inside of a theatre and through its scene-dock crashes

[9] G. William Jones, ed., *Talking with Ingmar Bergman* (Dallas: SMU Press, 1983), p. 37.

Fortinbras with storm troopers; they are accompanied by a television crew and an interviewer, to record the incident.

Little of the re-thinking in this angry, tough, and sensual production could be called Shakespearian in the strictest sense; the play in a Swedish translation had been wrenched into another world, to suit the stage and audience of that world. Many familiar readings were lost, but further suggestions of motive, passion, and achievement had been discovered and accentuated, picking up small clues as they caught the imagination of this director from within the words of the text. But a great deal of the text did remain, not least the so-called simple words, such as *yes* and *no*, or *mother, father, son*, and many demanding words like *love*, and *think* and *do* – words that are unmistakable in any language and carry the core of this tragedy's action.

Shakespeare's plays respond uncommonly well to major re-interpretation and survive all kinds of additions, subtractions, and wilful changes to what was originally set down on paper. Two demonstrations of this pliancy could be seen in Tokyo within a week of each other in October 1992. One, at the Panasonic Globe, was called *A Broken Macbeth* and took many liberties with the text: Lady Macbeth survived, for example, and at the end of the play read her husband's letter once more; the three Witches were silk-robed and resplendent spirits, and three ghosts of Macbeth's victims were added who were acrobatic and often played comic tricks – both trios made appearances throughout the play, like a chorus in a musical. The play started with the entire cast gyrating to cries of 'Fair is foul, and foul is fair' and these words, in English, recurred again and again during the performance. Macbeth was galvanic in action, literally running around the stage in amazement and fear, or trembling hugely and then controlling his fear with oversized responses that were both frightening and funny. In the banquet scene, he was suspicious of everyone, not taking his eyes off his guests until sometime after he has actually sat on the Ghost of Banquo. The *Hamlet* that was playing concurrently, produced by the Bluebird Theatre Company, was cast with women in all the male roles, and men in the two female ones. The acting style was childish and, occasionally, crudely operatic; the production seemed to be saying that all men are idiots – frantic, irredeemable idiots – except, possibly, an androgynous Hamlet struggling to be sensible; and his stronger intelligence destroyed him. Gertrude was a slow-witted hulk, presumably to imply that she was condemned to be so in order to survive in this male world. Although this production might well be judged boring and unskilful, it was in fact extremely popular: the young audience sat crowded together, apparently intent on every word and action.

Many experiences like these mark both the openness and attractiveness of Shakespeare's plays. They are not confined by the obvious meanings of any specific statement of intent and so they can live from one generation to another and travel from one country to another. This versatility is not a sign of weakness or lack of serious thought in their composition. Rather it proves the strength of their characters, stories, and structures: these seem indestructible, whatever themes are chosen or whatever textual changes are made. Indeed, a main reason for Shakespeare's international currency seems to be that he grounded action firmly and then invited, very positively and openly, a diversity of interpretation.

Two qualities of the writing are largely responsible for allowing this freedom in interpretation. First, the characters and the stories are developed and presented in a way that suggests that all is not explained or resolved. It is noticeable that in all the plays there is at least one character who does not fit entirely, but goes beyond the thoughts and feelings of the majority of persons presented on stage. These strangers tend to unsettle ordinary reactions and disrupt ordinary expectations. Othello is an obvious example: an 'extravagant and wheeling stranger', as Roderigo calls him (1.1.138). He raises fears and alarms in the minds of other characters because he is a Moor; because he is a general who is devoted to a young and inexperienced girl – though one of great strength of mind; a practical and successful soldier who believes in magic spells and 'prophetic fury' (3.4.55–75) and yet quotes Christian scriptures with approval; a passionate man involved in events that 'would not be believed in Venice' (4.1.242); a man capable of great feats of arms who becomes a helpless victim of a violent fit and lays down on a bed to 'roar' (5.2.205). An audience will find itself wondering at the underlying compulsions that drive this man and had encouraged Desdemona to love him; questioning, too, the reception he had encountered in the state of Venice and its Turkish wars.

In all Shakespeare's tragedies, at least one stranger is used in this unsettling way: in *Titus Andronicus*, it is Aaron; in *Romeo and Juliet*, the Nurse, Mercutio, Peter, Friar Lawrence are all of a different mould from that of the noble families they serve. In *Hamlet*, perhaps, Pyrrhus in the Player's speech, 'horridly tricked / With blood of fathers, mothers, daughters, sons' (2.2.460–1), is the most obvious stranger, speaking of the inhumanity of self-justified vengeance. The First Player is a stranger too, a professional artist for whom such pretence has all the effects of reality and none of its substance. In this play Shakespeare has introduced many discordant figures: Fortinbras, the pirates' Messenger, the Gravediggers, Yorick as represented by his mirthless skull, the 'churlish' Priest: all of them standing outside the main bonds joining together the other persons in this play, and all capable of suggesting different perspectives on those persons.

In *Macbeth*, the witches are the obvious strangers, strong when they meet together for secret and midnight rites. So too are the Porter, the 'Old Man' whom Ross encounters without any reason in the narrative, and the Doctor who describes the off-stage English King and the 'strangely visited people' whom he can miraculously cure (4.3.140–59). As 'Bellona's bridegroom' (1.2.54), the hero himself is, in some sense, a stranger too, and the audience becomes increasingly aware that he has no place in civilized life, complete with 'honour, love, obedience, troops of friends' (5.3.27).

In the comedies, the most obvious stranger is Shylock, in many ways looking forward to Othello. But in *The Merchant of Venice*, this disruptive function is also performed by Jessica and Tubal, by Launcelot and his father who as clowns have an inherited strangeness, and by Antonio who in his isolation sees himself as the 'tainted wether of the flock' (4.1.113). Briefly the audience is told of 'the moor [who] is with child by you, Launcelot', someone who would further threaten the peace of Belmont and the ease of comedy if she were to come on stage (3.5.35–7). Characters who are not easily accommodated or assimilated in accepted ways of thought and feeling are found in all the comedies, the various clowns, chiefly, but also those who follow very limited and highly individual tracks through the action. For example, in *As You Like It*, as well as Touchstone the play's clown, Charles the Wrestler, Audrey, William, Corin, Sir Oliver Martext, the two pages, Hymen, and, most notably, Jacques are all characters with their own individual 'measures' (5.4.191) or ways of thinking and being; and, off-stage, there is the 'old religious man' who converts Duke Frederick so that the comedy may happily conclude (5.4.158). Perhaps the 'poor sequestered stag' whom Jaques encounters off-stage (2.1.33) and the deer whose death is celebrated on-stage in Act 4, Scene 2, should both be in this reckoning, since they too have power to disturb established attitudes of mind.

Shakespeare used strangers in all the plays to 'disable' conventional 'judgements'[10] and sometimes to reveal an untamable world of thought, passion, and action. By their means he took human experience to unfamiliar limits

[10] The phrase is taken from *As You Like It*, 4.1.32, 5.4.74.

without losing contact with familiar responses – and with a world that is all too easily and thoughtlessly recognizable. Recognizing this structural device, we should not be surprised at the varieties of interpretation the plays have received, both from critics and from theatre directors. To sit at home and let familiar images and closed arguments possess our minds is no way to respond to these texts. Nor should we be surprised that the plays prove attractive and amendable to many different societies or that in theatres of various traditions they are constantly being rediscovered and re-interpreted.

The second quality in Shakespeare's writing that encourages varying interpretations and helps to account for his currency around the world is its suggestiveness: his speeches do not say everything. Shakespeare left space, as it were, for the actors to invent or improvise the motives for their words, their actions, and their hesitations. The text says only so much: it lays down what a hearer will hear but only indicates the thoughts and images which accompany the spoken words in the minds of either speakers or hearers. Actors are invited to explore, to look for ways in which they can take upon themselves the words and actions of their characters. In doing this, the text is constantly bending, taking on new colours, being spoken with new point, in new tempo, volume, pitch, tone or texture. The language seems to fit all wearers and show off each individual actor's sense of character; it does not dictate all that should be effected. Translations will usually be less flexible, but each translator will have responded to the freedom offered by bending the new version so that a particular sequence of choices has been made. The plays will never be translated once and for all time, but reissued again and again with each new translator and according to changes in their intended audiences and in the wishes of directors and actors who reinterpret them according to their own instincts and visions.

Such fluctuations of meaning and effect are common to all theatre texts which must await their performers, but Shakespeare seems to have written with exceptional openness so that a great variety of actors, in a great variety of times and places, can enter in and make the words their own. It is this which accounts for the freshness of good Shakespearian performances when it seems as if the entire play has just been discovered and brought to unexampled life. This also accounts for a freedom, good humour, and adventure that characterizes good rehearsals of the plays: actors will often surprise themselves as they test what they can do with the text, laughing out loud with pleasure as a new discovery brings new life to a character or to a scene. This is why actors want to return to the same roles, time and again, finding them different as they join each new cast or as they encounter them in a different time and place. Only a writer who had a strong imaginative confidence could give such wide scope for reinterpretation.

A strange paradox comes to mind in considering Shakespeare's plays in present-day performances around the world. Theatre, the art which cannot be engaged in alone, provided the means for Shakespeare to become known for his own highly distinctive work – we can recognize that writing anywhere – and yet at the same time he was able to set his collaborators and critics free to create on their own accounts, to emphasize whatever themes and establish whatever meanings they wish. Moreover, his plays call upon the full physical and mental participation of actors, so that the most inward and personal qualities of the performers are made evident in each re-enactment of their roles. These unique and highly individual texts positively invite reinterpretation, discovery, and imaginative and instinctive collaboration and, because of this, they have been staged, in many different styles and in many languages, to a growing and diverse audience all around the world.

In view of Shakespeare's international currency, the time has come to take his plays out of the closeted world of literary studies where signs inscribed in the text and verbal description of meanings are the primary objects of research. In that environment, even the writing of stage-histories yields little more than anecdotal accounts of what has been done with specific details of the text. Such studies do not account for the international currency of Shakespeare's plays which depends on their performative qualities, their instigation of physical, living-and-breathing realizations on a stage before an audience – qualities which those working in the theatre instinctively respect and enjoy. By giving close attention to the physical aspects of performance, linking a study of text with a study of acting and staging, scholars and critics will deal with those aspects of the plays that ensure their worldwide viability today. As he wrote the plays, Shakespeare imagined individual persons in action as well as speech and it is with such a subject that critics and scholars must be engaged. By making this the object of their study, they can teach others how to respond more fully and might be able to indicate how new plays for our own times could be given a comparable viability.

# REPEOPLING THE GLOBE: THE OPENING SEASON AT SHAKESPEARE'S GLOBE, LONDON 1997

MICHAEL CORDNER

Rebuilding the Globe Playhouse on London's Bankside cost Sam Wanamaker, the scheme's only begetter, more than forty years of zealous and tenacious labour. That extended history of delay and disappointment had one fortunate consequence. The resplendent building which now adorns the Southwark waterfront is a decisively different phenomenon from the one which would have been erected, say, in 1960 or in 1975 if, by some miracle, the necessary money had then become available. Only in 1989, for instance, did new scientific discoveries make available a way of using chemicals to impede the spread of fire in thatch. Before that date, safety regulations would have imposed an inauthentic tiled roof on the reconstruction. Similarly, numerous details of the final design were strongly influenced by the researches of John Orrell, whose key book on the subject, *The Quest for Shakespeare's Globe*, was only published in 1983. Orrell's conclusions have in turn been modified by archaeological discoveries made during the recent excavations on the Rose and Globe Playhouse sites, and the results of that rethinking have also been incorporated in the new building. And, finally, the construction of the new Globe has been intimately shaped by the 'vast knowledge of historic timber framing' painstakingly acquired by Peter McCurdy, who only became associated with the project in 1991.[1] In a host of both large and small ways, therefore, the new building results from a distinctively 1990s confluence of up-to-date scholarship, newly reclaimed craft skills and technical innovation.

Compared with this lavish investment of energy in determining and reconstructing the Globe's physical features, recent academic work on the kind of acting it was designed to host and foster has been much more tentative. An actor, preparing to tackle demanding roles there, might reasonably enquire about up-to-date writing on, for example, the distinctive technical challenges which different kinds of Shakespearian soliloquy pose for their performers. It would be difficult to know what books or articles to recommend in reply to such a query. The study of Shakespeare in performance has become a major industry in the last few decades; but the overwhelming focus of attention has been on the notation and analysis of specific past performances – the study of what has historically been done with and to the texts, not the exploration of the texts' own possibilities and demands and the traps they may pose for the unwary or ill-prepared interpreter.

This scholarly inertia meant that the adventurous actors who took part in the first full season at the reconstructed Globe in the summer of 1997 were very much on their own. Their programme was ambitious – two Shake-

[1] Jon Greenfield, 'Design as Reconstruction: Reconstruction as Design', in J. R. Mulryne and Margaret Shewring (eds.), *Shakespeare's Globe Rebuilt* (Cambridge, 1997), p. 81.

speare plays, *Henry V* and *The Winter's Tale*, and two non-Shakespearian, Middleton's *A Chaste Maid in Cheapside* and Beaumont and Fletcher's *The Maid's Tragedy*. It was also generically diverse – a history play, a romance, a city comedy, and a court tragedy. All the plays demanded large casts and spread the acting weight widely among them. None of them was of the kind where a few starry performances could compensate for meagre casting in other roles. What was immediately apparent was that the players could rely on the active enthusiasm and trust of the spectators, buoyed up by delight and pride in the building and the project. At the performance of *Henry V* I attended, the opening Chorus's modest query – 'Can this cock-pit hold / The vasty fields of France?' (lines 11–12) – immediately inspired from the pit jubilant assertions of confidence in its capacity to do just that.

Entering the Globe is an exhilarating experience. The building worked its magic on all four of the audiences with whom I saw shows there over three days in late August 1997. All shared a sense of heightened expectation mingled with confident partisanship. The Globe is a paradoxical mixture of a proven success – a famous playhouse which carries the cachet of having premiered some of the greatest English plays ever written – and a radical move into uncharted territory, since an open-air amphitheatre on this scale and to this design is wholly without parallel in modern Britain. The heady interest and enthusiasm aroused by this opening season make clear how well those running the Globe have communicated to the public the excitement of performing in such a building in the late 1990s. As a result, the Globe is now confidently established as a successful *modern* playing-space which also happens to be a recreation of a late Elizabethan building. Thus a crucial first victory for the actors has been won. But a massive voyage of discovery still lies ahead. Inevitably some of this year's work was hesitant and insecure, while at other points actors resorted to familiar tricks and stock routines. If a preoccupation with some of the things which went wrong seems sometimes to predominate in the remainder of this article, that is because, with an eye to the future, negative examples may have even more to teach us than positive ones. But such caveats are in no way intended to undermine the scale of the artistic directorate's achievement this summer.

The Globe is not a performance-space where actors can hoard their privacy and insist on the supremacy of inter-character relationships. It is an auditorium where the audience is empowered in a wholly unfamiliar, exhilarating, unpredictable, and sometimes perilous way. Before this summer, for example, I had never attended a performance of *Henry V* where the opening line of 'Once more unto the breach, dear friends, once more' (3.1.1) was greeted by applause in the manner of an audience at a pop concert welcoming the opening melody of a hit song. Fully visible to the players, but also to itself, this audience is enfranchised to be more interventionist than spectators clustered, for instance, in the dark recesses of the main theatre at Stratford-upon-Avon will ever feel inspired to be. Audience members, especially those standing in the pit, are themselves an intrinsic part of the spectacle and potentially influential performers in it. No actor can thrive at the Globe who seeks to deny or evade this central reality. One key challenge it poses to its performers is that, while accommodating themselves to this fact and learning to relish it and exploit it to the full, they must also devise techniques for simultaneously sustaining the credibility and intensity of their characters' involvement in the unfolding narrative. In what follows I will not attempt to offer a full description and analysis of the four productions in this inaugural season, but will instead focus principally on the ways in which directors and players measured up to the unnerving, but potentially liberating, nature of these new performer/spectator dynamics.

By general consent, the least successful of the season's productions was *The Winter's Tale*. I see no reason to dissent from that judgement. There were indeed moments when it seemed as if its director, David Freeman, was intent on providing us with a practical encyclopaedia of errors which his successors must at all costs avoid. His positioning of his actors, for instance, was constantly puzzling. For the first third of 5.1, Leontes sat with his back to the right-hand stage-pillar, facing across stage towards the other pillar. He was thus totally masked from a third of the audience, many of whom rapidly became disengaged and restless. The entirety of 2.2 – Paulina's rescuing of the newly born Perdita from prison – was played upstage, close to the right-hand tiring-house door, which served as prison entrance. The logic seemed to be that the jailer would perforce stay close to the gateway it was his function to protect, and that this therefore decreed that Paulina must also stay tethered to that part of the stage. But this naive literalism need not apply on the unlocalized stage of the Globe. Fidelity to it here meant that an important scene was played far from the majority of the audience and obscured for some of the time from many of them by one or other of the pillars. These misjudgements were then compounded by an early, tactlessly obtrusive entrance for Leontes, in anticipation of 2.3, from the left-hand stage-door, which rendered Paulina's two concluding speeches inaudible from where I sat. Many more such mishaps could be catalogued. The season's other directors did not make such elementary mistakes. So why did this one? Sheer technical incompetence would be one unkind answer; but Freeman is a highly experienced director. It seemed almost as if he had resented the challenges set by this stage and perversely refused to submit to the disciplines it imposes.

His handling of soliloquy was similarly fallible. At one extreme, Camillo (Ade Sapara) was allowed to cling to old-style proscenium arch technique, his soliloquies and extended asides numbly addressed to some unpeopled spot in the middle distance. This fearful refusal to acknowledge our presence disabled his entire performance. Leontes (Mark Lewis Jones), on the other hand, seemed on occasion to relish playing directly to the audience. But the manner in which he did so was itself problematic. A victim in the pit was selected to exemplify the claim that 'many a man there is, even at this present, / Now, while I speak this, holds his wife by th'arm, / That little thinks she has been sluiced in's absence', and then another was singled out to qualify as the adulterous betrayer, 'Sir Smile, his neighbour' (1.2.193–7). But the actor's delight in the effect he was having was far too transparent. A swaggering, but nervous, player, only too grateful for the response he was provoking, stood before us, not a Sicilian king, made wretched by his suspicions, and anxious to bequeath some part of his diseases to us. This is a playing-space which can only too swiftly separate an incautious actor from his role in ways which damage the forward impetus of the performance.

Other kinds of direct address also proved troublesome. Hermione (Belinda Davison) played parts of her self-defence in 2.1 straight to the audience, treating us as an extension of the courtiers assembled on stage. But as a consequence she frequently ignored the latter for extended periods of time, reducing them to the status of mere stage decoration. Thus abandoned, they became limply disengaged – mere observers of a spectacle in which they seemed to have no personal involvement. It was almost as if Freeman thought that in this theatre an actor could either speak directly to the audience or to the other players on stage, but not perform both actions simultaneously. As a result, energy drained away from the scene.

Directors and actors seemed similarly foxed by, or indifferent to, the demands of the play's language. This frequently witty text produced in this performance only a tiny number of laughs generated by verbal cues. Melodramatic extremes of delivery were indulged – top-of-the-voice anger for Leontes, whining pathos for Hermione, and so on – but few subtler nuancings of tone or tempo of delivery were attempted. When not in one of these extreme fits, the players mainly favoured a drably matter-of-fact delivery. In one variant on this, Leontes spoke the 'spider steeped' speech (2.1.41–7) with his feet firmly placed, hands on ceremonial chain, in a lucid, almost expository way, then glossed it retrospectively with a sudden spurt of non-verbal aggrievedness. Such acting off the line was a recurrent mannerism and confessed an inability to make the language itself a convincing agent of emotional communication. Nothing here suggested that Freeman took seriously the often expressed hope that the reconstructed Globe will prove to be a theatre where the verbal energy of the language of pre-civil war drama can be liberated into fresh theatrical potency.

In his programme note Freeman remarked that 'Mahler said something somewhere along the lines that you can conduct the notes of a score, the text, or you can conduct the score's shadow.' His own preference was clearly for the latter approach. But were the shadows he pursued really ones cast by Shakespeare's text? In 4.4, the sheep-shearing festival, the actors who played Leontes, Hermione and Paulina (Joy Richardson) reappeared in fresh costumes among the throng. This was not simply convenient doubling to swell the crowd, since our attention was recurrently drawn to them. Thus, 'Hermione' embraced and comforted the sobbing Perdita (Anna-Livia Ryan) after Polixenes (Michael Gould) had harangued her. So the absent mother was yet present. Similarly, 'Leontes' was positioned closely, and admiringly, beside Perdita during the early part of the flower debate with Polixenes. More emphatically still, 'Leontes', with his forehead now adorned with horns, later danced with Perdita in her queen-of-the-revels finery, raising her from the ground, and swaying with her mounted around his waist. The dance was at that point suddenly aborted, with Perdita miming consternation and distress. Some interpretations of 5.1 discern an adumbration of incestuous feeling in the warmth of Leontes's greeting to Perdita. But what is gained by anticipating that possibility in this flamboyant way in the preceding scene? And what kind of anticipation is it, since this is not Leontes we are watching, but the actor of Leontes moonlighting as an anonymous shepherd, whose intimate contact with Perdita's body is yet in some way presumably meant to inform our understanding of the king's sexuality?

All this while many a 'necessary question' (*Hamlet*, 3.2.42–3) of Shakespeare's play was being neglected. The humdrum work of preparation, by which climaxes are steadily built and rendered comprehensible to an audience, seemed not to interest Freeman. In 4.4, the disguised Polixenes and Camillo wore scarfs which masked all the lower part of their faces. Their watchful presence during the earlier part of the scene can crucially enrich the texture of the action and elucidate Polixenes's later eruption into vitriolic denunciation of Perdita; but here their muffling disguise effectively rendered them totally uncommunicative to us during this crucial period. In the same way, the Old Shepherd (Patrick Godfrey) was placed far upstage right, and masked from many spectators by a pillar, during the love duets of Florizel (Jonathan Slinger) and Perdita, while the more central areas of the stage were purposelessly occupied by countryfolk bearing on numerous sheep-fleeces and milling desultorily around. But Polixenes's denunciation of his son and Perdita will transform the Old Shepherd's existence, and the concluding segment of the scene will partly focus on how he copes with that. Exiling him to the margins of the stage at this point gives the actor no chance to prepare the ground for his re-emergence into prominence. Similar carelessnesses multiplied throughout the scene.

All the imaginative energy in the staging had been poured into incidents like Leontes's horn-dance with Perdita, moments of Freeman's devising, not Shakespeare's. This is not playing the text's shadow; it is more a matter of inventing a kind of counter-text and playing that. But once again Freeman was not radical enough, and it was the actors who paid the penalty of his failure of nerve. 4.4 of *The Winter's Tale* is an enormously long scene, complexly articulated, and brilliantly inventive, but fiendishly difficult to make evolve in performance with the necessary fluency and variety. Freeman's actors were condemned to play most of its 843 lines, hamstrung by a director who, preoccupied with his own counter-text, was putting little thought into how to grade and shape the diverse beats of Shakespeare's own scene. Dutifully delivering the lines their author had assigned them, they often seemed to be in some other performance than the one which really interested Freeman. A truly radical director would have followed the logic of his own obsessions and drastically cut and redesigned the scene, so that his pre-occupations could claim the space they needed to become dramatically lucid. Lacking the courage to take that step, he was condemned to spend his time doodling in Shakespeare's margins. In quite fundamental ways, this *Winter's Tale* broadcast its director's unwillingness to think seriously about the demands imposed both by the text he had agreed to direct and the playhouse in which he was staging it.

Richard Olivier's production of *Henry V* confronted the challenge of working in the Globe in a totally different way. The programme for the show, for instance, insisted on the authenticity of its costuming. Calvin Klein underwear, we were assured, had been banned, and the actors would be 'entirely dressed in recreated clothing of the period', by which was meant the period of the play's composition, not of the historical events it dramatizes. The gentlemen, therefore, sported Elizabethan ruffs, incorporating, according to the companionable programme, 'as many as 20 yards of fine linen hand sewn and gathered into a neckband of 15 inches'. Authenticity was also cultivated in the casting. This was the only one of the season's shows to have an all-male company.

The linch-pin of the production was the performance of Mark Rylance, the Globe's Artistic Director, as Henry. He brought to the role wide experience in Shakespeare, including much admired performances of Ariel, Benedick and Hamlet. The warrior king was not, by conventional expectation, the most natural casting for him. His voice lacks the trumpet notes the role is usually thought to demand, and his most characteristic acting personality mingles gentleness, shyness, solitariness, sly, inventive wit, and an undertow of melancholy. Rylance's characters typically view their world from a slightly divergent or detached position. The ability to take stage-centre and demand from others their unquestioning obedience, fundamental to the victor of Agincourt, was not obviously native to him.

Rylance soon demonstrated that he could use the Globe with a relaxed intimacy nowhere apparent in the *Winter's Tale* company. As he addressed the Archbishop of Canterbury (John McEnery) early in 1.2, his tone was edgy and concerned, laying especially pregnant emphasis on the 'blood' that might soon be shed 'in approbation / Of what your reverence shall incite us to' (lines 19–20). Canterbury had swiftly been put on his mettle, his suave preparation of his tactics in 1.1 now looking a shade theoretical in the face of this challenging questioning from Henry. But Rylance combined his pressure on his fellow player with fluent involvement of the entire playhouse in the encounter. As he spoke, his eyes played lightly across the pit and the galleries. This, he signalled to us, was a fully public event, with potentially massive reverberations. Also hinted at was Henry's political skill, which called for as many witnesses as possible to the church's expected, indeed demanded, sanctification of a French invasion.

Throughout the play's long course, Rylance's ability to sustain in this way a simultaneous dialogue with his fellow actors and with the audience never slackened. He could, for instance, risk not looking at the traitors in 2.2, as they read the commissions which indicted them. Thus, 'What see you in those papers, that you lose / So much complexion?' (lines 69–70) was spoken without his having seen the change he confidently asserted. The staging of their exposure had been so carefully structured by Henry that their responses were, in effect, predetermined. What principally mattered now was the way their self-disclosure could be rhetorically managed by Henry for the benefit of a larger national audience, for which the playhouse audience deputized. This self-conscious shaping of the incident was pursued into the briskly business-like and upbeat way in which, as the traitors departed under guard, Rylance proceeded to voice 'Now lords for France' (line 179). One chapter was swiftly and confidently closed, and a new one opened with similar authority. He then compounded the effect by briefly kneeling on 'Let us deliver / Our puissance into the hand of God' (lines 186–7), before rebounding to his feet and off towards the exit on the scene's concluding couplet. His attendant lords, following his cue to kneel, found themselves left momentarily earth-bound as their king darted from the stage. Such witty deftness was a recurrent motif in the performance. This was a Henry who, in the midst of berating the Dauphin for his gift of tennis balls, could find time to juggle three of the offending balls in the air with calm aplomb. By the play's middle stages the suppleness with which he commanded the spectators' attention was such that he could even earn a laugh from the final word in the following couplet from Henry's reply to Montjoy in 4.3: 'There's not a piece of feather in our host – / Good argument, I hope, we will not fly' (lines 113–14). Turning wordplay of that kind into gold means that an actor has taught an audience to listen with particular care and an alert expectation of pleasures to come.

In the eve-of-Agincourt scenes this Henry who commanded the audience so confidently began to hide from us, as doubt and worry crowded in on him. He completed his disguise by smutching his face with grime. He then spoke a substantial segment of the 'Upon the King' soliloquy (4.1.227) kneeling, indeed almost prostrated on the stage, with his face concealed from the audience, though he remained perfectly audible throughout. Similarly, during the 'O God of battles' prayer (4.1.286), though he was now turned once again towards the pit, one hand, with his battle-glove clutched in it, hovered maskingly in front of his face. Only with the reappearance before his men on 'What's he that wishes so?' (4.3.18) was his former confidence in directly addressing characters and audience alike fully restored. And, with it, came the ability to spread laughter – by, for example, the affectionately ironic pause with which he separated out 'with advantages' in the prediction that the old warrior 'will remember, with advantages, / What feats he did that day' (4.3.50–1). So Rylance's performance combined clarity of outline and adroit humour with a sustained ability to address fellow characters and spectators simultaneously without for a moment slackening his hold on the continuity of his conception of the role.

The play's design did not allow any of the other actors the luxury of concentrating on a single character. If doubling had been problematic in *The Winter's Tale*, here it was often enriching. Thus, Vincent Brimble, who, as Gower, recalled Falstaff's name when Fluellen (David Fielder) could not (4.7.43–9), had earlier, as Mistress Quickly, narrated the fat knight's death. The actors cast as the three English traitors, seduced by French gold, enjoyed an immediate resurrection as the principal nobles in the French court. William Russell played both the French King, with his anguished memories of previous English depredations in France, and Sir Thomas Erpingham, the oldest veteran on the English side. John McEnery added to his portraits of the Archbishop of Canterbury whose approval sends others to die in battle and the braggart soldier

Pistol, unwilling to follow Henry 'into the breach', a third incarnation as the Governor of Harfleur, who saves his town by surrendering it. Christian Camargo doubled the war-hungry Dauphin and his peace-favouring mother. And Toby Cockerell was both the Cheapside boy, whose French proves adequate to translate for the terrified Le Fer, and the French Princess, with her eagerness to learn English in implicit anticipation of a French defeat.

The roll-call of characters in *Henry V* is so massive that doublings and treblings of this kind must have been fundamental to Shakespeare's planning of it. Some of the multiple assignments in the present production may correspond to Elizabethan ones; others may not. Some, into which I was tempted to read significance, may have been the inadvertent product of sheer casting necessity. But the piquancy of juxtaposition and cross-reference resulting from tackling a play on this scale with a relatively small body of players was constantly striking.

It also, however, invited more versatile playing than it mostly received here. Rory Edwards, for instance, doubled Orléans, the aristocratic warlord of the Agincourt scenes, and Burgundy, the conciliating peacemaker of the court negotiations in 5.2, but found no way of making each a distinct presence. Well-intentioned and energetic as the company undoubtedly was, only John McEnery in his Archbishop persona and, especially, Toby Cockerell as the French Princess were capable of consistently playing in the same league as Rylance. Otherwise, this was at best a second-eleven company. Were crucially wrong decisions taken by the casting director, or had there been a problem in persuading first-ranking actors to play at the Globe in its first full season? I suspect the latter is the true explanation. In a BBC2 documentary broadcast on 25 August 1997, Fiona Shaw, asked if she would like to act there, agreed that she would, but only after she had watched a number of performances there. The subtext seemed to be that she expected numerous mishaps in the early years and would like the chance to learn from others' disasters. A performer's carefully built-up reputation is his or her most precious possession, and one unwise professional choice can damage it massively. Chariness about committing one's fortunes to an untried venture, especially one which, like the Globe, demands a radical rethinking of one's craft, is therefore perfectly comprehensible. But the Globe is now a proven hit with audiences, and the best work done there in 1997 demonstrates that responsive and thoughtful actors have no reason to fear it. We may therefore anticipate a richer line-up of talent in future seasons. This year's company, however, was too often industrious, but o'erparted.

One consequence of this was a facile reliance on stereotyping. One example was a Dauphin who thought it apt to climax his exhortation to his countrymen – 'let us do it with no show of fear' (2.4.23) – with a falsetto giggle. This was rewarded with the kind of anti-French laugh the audience was only too willing to provide and the production to encourage. Similar jingoism greeted the mention of other foreign threats. Thus, in 1.2, the reference to 'the weasel Scot' (line 170), for example, provoked energetic hissing. Its eruption did not, I take it, mean that the audience included a contingent of National Front supporters. The hissers were themselves, in effect, playing a role. They had the impression that this would have been the 'Elizabethan response' at such a moment, and they were obligingly supplying it. All the dangers of National Heritage theatre beckon here. A 1997 audience in the Globe was not responding directly, and from the context of their own lives and histories, to the experience of watching a modern company perform a 1599 play in a late twentieth-century reconstruction of the most famous Elizabethan playhouse, but was instead enfolding the event in a bizarre time-warp of its own devising. This is a trend which must be resisted.

In one other crucial way this production was content to be pageant theatre. Henry might confess that 'Our gayness and our gilt are all besmirched / With rainy marching in the painful field' (4.3.111–12), and the Chorus speak of the English soldiers' 'lank lean cheeks and war-worn coats' (4.0.26); but what we saw on stage paid little heed to this. A certain weariness of limb was occasionally mimed; but the nobles' armour remained as unblemished and immaculate on the field of Agincourt as when we had first seen it. This was not a version of the play which made the struggle and endurance of a prolonged military campaign dramatically palpable to us; but Shakespeare's text does do exactly that. There was a persistent failure of imagination here, which produced an extraordinary reading of the conclusion to Henry's speech to the Governor of Harfleur. The brutality of the king's threats has much preoccupied modern commentary. Henry, with an exhausted army behind him, warns the town that, if it does not surrender immediately, then its inhabitants must

look to see
The blind and bloody soldier with foul hand
Defile the locks of your shrill-shrieking daughters;
Your fathers taken by the silver beards,
And their most reverend heads dashed to the walls;
Your naked infants spitted upon pikes,
Whiles the mad mothers with their howls confused
Do break the clouds, as did the wives of Jewry
At Herod's bloody-hunting slaughtermen.
(3.3.116–24)

This savage echo of Marlowe's Tamburlaine before the gates of Damascus is a potentially defining moment for the actor. Henry never otherwise sounds remotely like this; so this speech marks one expressive limit in charting the interpretative demands of the role. The minimum narrative requirement is that it should be voiced with a conviction sufficient to render the town's immediate surrender plausible. But kings who make such threats must be willing to carry them out. Otherwise, they risk discrediting any future threats of force necessity may lead them to make. So the speech can be a moment of discovery for Henry about what military command may demand of the men who undertake it and/or a moment of revelation for the audience about the conduct of which 'the warlike Harry' (Prologue, 5) may prove capable. Rylance inched his way through the speech improvisatorily, with recurrent glances at his supporting commanders, as if for inspiration for further horrors with which to intimidate the French. Then, on its last words, he looked once again at his comrades and smirked jovially at them. We were to understand that the whole thing was a ruse, a jape, a fantasy which was sure to dupe the credulous French, but which there was no actual risk of the good-hearted English carrying out. It was a serious misjudgement, since it reduced the entire encounter to the status of a hollowly theatrical comic routine. In the face of such directorial 'imperfections', there was nothing which our 'imaginary forces' (Prologue, 23 and 18) could for the moment do to reconnect us with the harsh imperatives of actual warfare, to which Shakespeare's text is so tellingly attuned. For all its incidental pleasures, Olivier's production was finally too timid, as if constrained by a sense of decorous limits beyond which it must not press. First-season nerves may have generated uncertainty about how much of the play's full range it was prudent to risk exploring at this early stage of work in a radically novel performance-space. However that may be, such caution will need to be eschewed in future seasons if the Globe is to live up to its full potential.

The *Henry V* cast, amplified by four actresses, also provided the company for the Middleton comedy. *A Chaste Maid in Cheapside* is an extraordinary, but rarely performed, work, which received its last major London revival as long ago as 1966. That neglect is partly explained by its sheer technical demands. The speed with which it articulates a complex action, interweaving the fates of an ornate array of characters, demands a matching athleticism and ingenuity from its players. It is also a tough-minded text, evoking a ruthlessly competitive and predatory world, which it never sentimentalizes. Its ideal actors must have the nerve, when Middleton requires it, to shock and chill their audiences.

In Malcolm McKay's production the action constantly spilled off the stage into the pit and beyond. A posse of drunken Puritan women cavorted through the audience, singing 'Shall we gather at the river?' The 4.4 duel between Sir Walter Whorehound (Rory Edwards) and Touchwood Junior (Christian Camargo) began on the stage, was continued through the pit, and returned to the stage again for its climax. Moll Yellowhammer (Katie MacNichol), attempting to elude pursuit, ran through the pit, climbed a rope ladder to the level of the upper gallery, clambered over the balcony, and vanished out of sight past admiring, but startled, spectators. In a theatre where traditional barriers between actors and audience were already eroded, this production seemed to want to collapse them entirely and generate, whenever possible, a kind of street theatre.

McKay's direction of the dialogue similarly worked to consolidate the links between player and spectator. Middleton is notoriously addicted to the use of asides, but McKay actually increased their number. As the turbulent Kixes (John McEnery and Eve Matheson) flashed once again from domestic harmony to no-holds-barred warfare and back again in 3.3, Touchwood Senior (Steven Skybell) bemusedly asked us, in a line Middleton had forgotten to script, 'How do they do that?' Soliloquies too were reshaped to the same end. The great set-piece solo for the willing cuckold Allwit (Mark Rylance) – 'The founder's come to town' (1.2, 11ff.)[2] – contained numerous rephrasings and additions. When some of the audience giggled at his description of his wife as 'even upon the point of grunting' (line 30), i.e. about to give birth, he rebuked them, in the manner of a stand-up comic, with an unMiddletonian 'Do you mind?' In Allwit's question, 'what affliction nature more constrains / Than feed the wife plump for another's veins?' (lines 46–7), the last two words were altered to 'another man's prick'; and when this earned the expected guffaws, Allwit/Rylance, adopting the tone and rhythms of the great English comic Max Miller, pointed to one laugher and confided, 'He knows what I'm talking about'.

This soliloquy of Allwit's poses stern technical challenges. We have first met this major character only ten lines earlier, with no information about him having been previously provided. He now launches into a paradoxical, pithily phrased celebration of his cuckold's life. Rylance coped lucidly with it, adopting a rapid, clipped, intensely excited delivery for its first part, and then beckoning us into his confidence with 'He gets me all my children' (line 18). But the use of the elbow-nudging Max Miller ad lib later – 'He knows what I'm talking about' – was less certainly appropriate. Miller's whole comic persona was notoriously based on making his audience feel that he and they shared the same, implied but not quite spoken, dirty thoughts. In contrast, Allwit's characteristic gesture is to proclaim a blithe indifference to conventional masculine pride and a delight in having all sexual demands lifted from him by Sir Walter's supplanting of him in bed. 'These torments', he smugly boasts, 'stand I freed of' (line 48). He therefore flaunts his immunity from precisely those erotic obsessions which bonded Miller to his audience. Looking for cues to assist their own work in the practice of modern comics is clearly a good move; but here the wrong model had been selected. Eve Matheson as Lady Kix was guided by a surer instinct when she borrowed, with intelligent variation, some of the mannerisms and rhythms patented by Jennifer Saunders for her role in the TV series *Absolutely Fabulous*, since both characters are built on rapid-fire discontinuities of mood and abrupt switches between ultra politeness and bitchy put-downs. As a result, Matheson's was the performance

[2] Quotations from, and act, scene and line references to, *A Chaste Maid in Cheapside* are to the Revels Plays edition, ed. R. B. Parker (London, 1969).

which most effortlessly succeeded in being true to the toughness of Middleton's writing and engagingly accessible to a 1990s audience. The production as a whole would have offered a richer experience if McKay had encouraged other players to profit from her example.

His programme note professed admiration for Middleton as the author of 'a broadside against a grubby, cheating world' and a portrait 'of what we might now call dysfunctional families', but also professed to believe that the play's text is a medley of Middleton's work and 'songs, slang and satire stirred into the theatre pot by the comics who wanted to add their own spice and tuppence worth'. I know of no textual evidence to support the latter surmise; but McKay's affecting to believe it functioned as an implicit rationalization of his own directorial practice. It also inadvertently aligned his own interventions with those of the overweening comics who, in his account, interpolated their inferior gags into Middleton's script.

The disadvantages of his approach showed up most grossly in the playing of Matthew Scurfield as the goldsmith Yellowhammer, the chaste maid's father. His soliloquy in 4.1 epitomized all that went wrong with his performance. A disguised Allwit has revealed Sir Walter's licentious past to Yellowhammer in order to block the intended marriage between Moll and the knight. Yellowhammer responds at first with the desired outrage; but, when left alone, he begins to think more pragmatically. He recollects his own sowing of wild oats when a teenager and concludes:

> The knight is rich, he shall be my son-in-law;
> No matter, so the whore he keeps be wholesome,
> My daughter takes no hurt then; so let them wed:
> I'll have him sweat well ere they go to bed.
>
> (lines 247–50)

The last line refers, of course, to the treatment of venereal disease by sweating the victim in a steam tub. The chill complacency of Yellowhammer's final resolve is characteristically Middletonian. As long as they do all they can for him medically, Sir Walter's libertine excesses will be no bar to his marrying Moll. It is a moment to test any actor. Scurfield had neither the stomach nor the nerve for it. He threw the final line away – anyone who did not know the text would have had no chance of catching what it meant – and capped it with his own '*Why* not let them marry?', played direct to the audience in crude pantomime style. Middleton's line, if allowed to register, is likely to command silence in an audience, or perhaps provoke a sharp intake of breath. But Scurfield substituted instead hearty melodrama and actorish excess. He looked very pleased with himself. He fell into this trap again and again. At Moll's apparent death in 5.2, the only question that concerns Middleton's Yellowhammer is what the neighbours will think: 'All the whole street will hate us, and the world / Point me out cruel' (lines 92–3). At this point Scurfield interpolated, again straight to the audience, 'It's all right for you lot' – another fatal dilution of the bleak clarity of the original text. Where Scurfield was so elated by his ability to prompt come-back from the audience that he had to reassure himself once again that he could still do it, the play itself requires of the actor an ice-cold self-restraint to match the character's amoral solipsism. Beside the poised and challenging clarity of Middleton's writing, Scurfield's antics seemed adolescent and narcissistic. His misjudgements, however, went hand in glove with the production's general approach. McKay might praise Middleton's 'angry, brilliant verse', but nothing in his production conveyed that anger. Instead, we were offered stock comic routines and a facile playing of the audience. An early Gala Shakespeare concert for the Globe project was greeted by a *Guardian* reviewer with the hope that the rebuilt theatre would not 'be giving us Carry On, Merrie England'.[3] There would be a real danger of that unwelcome possibility being realized if the

[3] Barry Day, *This Wooden 'O': Shakespeare's Globe Reborn* (London, 1996), p. 151.

worst aspects of McKay's adulteration of Middleton's steely masterpiece became a model for future Globe stagings of Jacobean comedies.

Lucy Bailey's production of *The Maid's Tragedy* obeyed very different imperatives. She had been invited by Rylance to direct a Beaumont and Fletcher play of her own choice and selected this one, according to her programme note, because it was 'a brilliant piece of storytelling'. That respect for the playwrights' mastery of their craft produced a more austere, less self-opinionated production than McKay had inflicted on *A Chaste Maid*. For Acts 2 to 5 a blue cloth covered the entire stage-floor area between the two stage-pillars and back to the tiring-house facade. In the extended duets which compose a large part of the action Bailey made no attempt to supply unnecessary visual decoration but plotted the relevant figures' movements on the blue cloth with geometric precision. In 2.1, Amintor (Jonathan Slinger), prostrated by learning the true reason why Evadne (Geraldine Alexander) had married him, knelt before her supplicatingly on his 'Thou hast ta'en an oath' speech (lines 252ff.).[4] Then, suddenly revolted by his humiliation, but without the self-control to rise, he edged away from her on his knees. But his need to wring concessions from her soon again overwhelmed him, and he moved back towards her, still kneeling, to embrace her pleadingly around the waist. Her poised, sardonic composure contrasted eloquently with the servility of his posture. The undermining of a prime courtier's self-esteem by his ruler's absolutist whim could not have been more graphically rendered. Glacial stillness was again Evadne's weapon when dealing in 3.1 with the sudden eruption of her royal lover's jealousy. The King (Nicholas Le Prevost) paced uneasily to and fro as he interrogated her, while she mirrored the adamantine confidence of her responses by literally refusing to give ground to him. In the early stages of her transformative encounter with her brother Melantius (Mark Lewis Jones) in 4.1, she behaved with the same suave immobility of body; but, as his verbal onslaughts became more violent and more telling, her growing emotional disarray was matched by an accelerating agitation of movement, until their positions were decisively reversed, as he remained commandingly still while she moved in inchoate patterns away from and back towards him. The visual language of the production in such scenes was spare and unfussy, but delicately attuned to the ebb and flow of advantage and power in the tense struggles for mastery to which the play is addicted and from which it derives so much of its power to tease and astonish an audience.

Bailey was also alert to the persistent wit of the writing. Indeed on occasion she was inclined to amplify it. In 1.1 the explanation by Lysippus (Andrew Bridgmont) of the causes of Aspatia's 'infectious grief' (line 97) prompted shocked concern from Melantius but suppressed giggles among the attendant courtiers. There is no hint of the latter in the text; but, in retrospect, that double vision came to seem like a model for the complex and unstable amalgam of empathetic concern and ironic laughter which subsequent scenes often called forth from the audience. Early in 2.1, the crass gaucheness of Amintor's 'Much happiness unto you all!' (line 126) to a group which included Aspatia (Anna-Livia Ryan) earned the derisory response it deserved. But, after Evadne's revelation, his bitter 'Are these the joys of marriage?' (line 215) earned a different kind of laughter – one which acknowledged that the wretched speaker was forging black humour out of the pain of his enduring humiliation. The next segment of the speech (lines 215–28) was spoken boldly to the audience, and on 'If we do lust, we'll take the next we meet' (line 225) his stare challenged the audience to acknowledge that, if burdened with his fate, they too might embrace such

[4] Quotations from, and act, scene and line references to, *The Maid's Tragedy* are to the Revels Plays edition, ed. T. W. Craik (London, 1988).

cynicism. It was brave and confident playing and provided a revealing contrast with the miscalculated handling of Leontes's 'Sir Smile' speech which I discussed earlier. The director/actor collaboration had here clearly left the player sure of his ground and willing to take risks. This was the more striking, since *The Maid's Tragedy* was performed by the *Winter's Tale* company, their mood totally transformed from the demoralized group I had seen perform the Shakespeare play two days earlier.

One of the most piquant moments in the Evadne/Amintor confrontation in 2.1 comes towards its end, when Amintor exclaims, 'What a strange thing am I!', and Evadne replies, 'A miserable one, one that myself / Am sorry for' (lines 319–21). Her next speech reprises that thought, but framed in a decisively different way. She is explaining why she cannot grant his self-abasing request that she kill him: 'I must have one / To fill thy room again if thou wert dead, / Else, by this night, I would: I pity thee' (lines 327–9). The extreme paradox of claiming to pity someone who is also your victim provided one trigger for laughter here. The stunned inability of Amintor to know how to cope with the systematic undermining of every shred of dignity he once possessed offered a similar cue to the audience. But so firmly grounded was the playing that laughter never became the sole or predominant reaction. If we did not quite pity Amintor, yet his agony and wretchedness were made so palpable to us that our attitude, like Evadne's, was fluctuating and equivocal. Even the loudest laugh did not dissipate the scene's tension or the momentous sense that a man was being taken apart piece by piece. The same remained true even during the multiple deaths with which the play concludes. Here some of the laughter certainly reflected resistance to what some spectators presumably regarded as an arcane Jacobean preference for a bloodbath to round off the show. Yet even they, after their moments of noisy self-assertion, fell silent again. The production's inner tension and steadiness of grasp reasserted itself each time, and the enthusiasm which greeted the cast as they took their bows was rapt and emphatic. The actors even looked a little surprised at its intensity.

I should at this point say that the performance I attended was an evening one. Friends who saw *The Maid's Tragedy* at a matinée reported a less favourable impression of the production. For them, the Globe's audience's penchant for unrestrained laughter simply won out. The play was originally staged by the King's Men at the Blackfriars Playhouse, and no record survives of a Globe performance. Editors tend to surmise that successful plays, including this one, would have been switched back and forwards between the two venues. This may be correct; but it is equally possible that some plays were so tailored for the Blackfriars that performing them at the larger open-air amphitheatre might have been judged inadvisable. Certainly the focus on the stage provided by the dying natural light and the generalized stage-lighting from the upper galleries was an invaluable support to the performance of *The Maid's Tragedy* I witnessed. But I would also add that Bailey's preparation of the production was such that her players were able to take full advantage of those circumstances.

Learning to perform ambitious and demanding scripts from four centuries ago in a radically unfamiliar playing-space is bound to entail an extended process of trial and error. The long-term vitality and health of the enterprise will depend on the open-mindedness and flexibility with which subsequent directors and casts learn from the successes and miscalculations of this season's pioneers. For anyone fascinated by the riches of the pre-1642 dramatic repertoire the project holds the promise of great revelations to come. But reefs also lie ahead. The excitement of playing to and with such an active and interventionist audience can transform the actor into a kind of addict, constantly needing the fix of another audible response from the spectators to buoy him up. This is the malady to which

Matthew Scurfield so comprehensively succumbed in *A Chaste Maid in Cheapside*. Similarly, the double function of the space – as heritage site and living playhouse – contains the risk that its directors may feel drawn to producing a kind of museum theatre. As we have seen, there were hints of that in Richard Olivier's *Henry V*. But in Mark Rylance the Globe has an artistic director who is a generous encourager of others' work, an experimenter eager to find new ways of staging the early modern repertoire, and a player whose witty ease in handing the auditorium demonstrates what can be done there. The next few years on the Bankside promise many excitements.

# SHAKESPEARE PERFORMANCES IN ENGLAND

ROBERT SMALLWOOD

I was unwise enough to remark, at the start of last year's essay, on the comparative quietness of the preceding year in terms of Shakespearian theatre. The balance has been more than redressed by no less than sixteen productions that seemed worth considering in 1997. I treat them, not precisely in Folio order, but still in a 'Comedies, Histories, Tragedies' progression.

Jonathan Miller's production of *A Midsummer Night's Dream*, which opened at the Almeida Theatre late in 1996, offered a new – if not quite wholesomely refreshing – vision of the play by casting virtually every role at least a decade older than one had ever imagined it, thus putting on display some reprehensibly silly behaviour by a whole lot of people who were clearly of an age to know better. Played on a set (designed by the Quay Brothers) that looked like a dilapidated hall of mirrors, and in costumes of 1930s elegance (the work of Clare Mitchell), the production began with a more-than-middle-aged, dinner-jacketed, cigar-smoking Theseus (Robert Swann) and an Hippolyta (Angela Down) in splendid ball gown, both of them, one felt, much more likely to take an interest in the quality of the claret at the next court dinner than in nuptials four days, or four years, hence. She seemed utterly disdainful that such an event should even be contemplated, mouthing the word 'revelling' after him in contemptuous disbelief. The tiresome interruption of their languor by an ancient, irascible Egeus (John Franklyn-Robbins) and his preferred son-in-law, Jonathan Coy's plump, moustached, balding Demetrius, left poor old Theseus wholly perplexed about what to do. Sylvestra Le Touzel's plummy-voiced Hermia, well on the wrong side of thirty, was applauded (politely, of course) by Hippolyta as she rejected her father's choice of husband. She seemed liable to a charge of cradle-snatching in directing her favours at Angus Wright's gangling, fearfully posh, and (in this context) surprisingly young Lysander, all goofish inarticulacy, who would later be transformed by Puck's magic (administered in the form of eye-drops from a little bottle) into a smooth-talking cad of a seducer.

There was much in the production from which one could take pleasure, but as a serious exploration of the play's poetry, or of its concern with the transforming power of the imagination and the destabilizing force of love, it offered little. Alongside the strange, irrational world of Shakespeare's love comedy one encountered a firmly rational world of social comedy – Coward with a touch of Wodehouse – clever and engaging, certainly, but also strangely irrelevant. This was most apparent in the fairy world. Oberon and Titania – the perhaps overdue experiment of *not* doubling them with Theseus and Hippolyta symptomatic of the rationalist approach – became, in Norman Rodway's and Angela Thorne's performances, a couple of ageing aristocrats, he a clubbable old buffer, ostentatiously at ease with himself, his smoker's cough getting in the way of the verse even as he contemplated, with a certain wry distaste, the flora of Titania's bank; she, in gold lamé dress, cloche hat, and feather stole, lamenting the terrible weather in accents of cut-glass precision such as one might expect from a society hostess reporting on the fête in her castle grounds. Their servants, very below stairs, were led by a Cockney Puck in butler's white gloves, smouldering with resentment at his proletarian dependency: '*look* how I go', he said with a rebellious whinge; 'up and down, up and down', he grumbled at the endlessness of his chores.

Such concern with social realism worked best for the *Dad's Army* version of the mechanicals' scenes, with George Formby songs – it had been 'Smoke gets in your eyes' for Theseus and Hippolyta and would be 'I'll be with you again' for the Oberon and Titania reconciliation – and a wonderfully fussy, Betjemanesque Quince from Frank Williams, who snorted 'rubbish' at all the phoney sentimentality of the laments at Bottom's losing his 'sixpence a day' and took the prompt corner in the final scene to read quietly along with his fellows' performance in proprietorial pride. 'Pyramus and Thisbe' had its moments of amusement, particularly in Toby Jones's failure as Snug to find the right moment for Thisbe's demise, her death throes continuing well beyond the rendition of 'Underneath the Arches' that the bergomasque became. The performance over, the lovers were left to face what was clearly the profoundly uninteresting prospect of bed, Hippolyta, appalled at the mention of 'new jollity', stalking off alone, Hermia, who had glared at Lysander on the remark 'lovers to bed', leaving with Helena ahead of the young(ish) men, and Theseus sauntering off on his own, clearly much impressed by the notion of solitary dreaming proposed in 'Underneath the Arches'. The slow, melancholy return of the fairies and Puck's instruction to the audience, at the end of his epilogue, to 'hop it' completed the sense of joylessness wherein lay the proffered joke of it all – and up to a point, indeed, it was amusing. But somehow it seemed to patronize the play, to invite a detached smile at the youthful eagerness and commitment of its characters, and perhaps also of its author. Pleasure in the production demanded knowledge of the play in other versions, for its purpose was to amuse by exploiting the gap between what it offered and normal expectations. And it did this with a certain elegance.

Equally determined to adjust one's focus on its play was Bill Alexander's version of *The Merchant of Venice* that opened at Birmingham Repertory Theatre in February. If Miller's *A Midsummer Night's Dream* had left us with few of the play's characters to find sympathetic, Alexander, taking further his work at Stratford in 1988, was determined to make sure that everyone in Venice and Belmont was at least unlikeable, and if possible contemptible. Ruari Murchison's set presented walls and pillars of decaying and sooty brick, a dark and stagnant-looking canal in the background, and a general sense of murk and shadow. A screen, and a suggestion of a distant glimpse of the sea, cheered things up only a little for Belmont. Fotini Domou's costumes, dark and vaguely Victorian, offered little to brighten the mood. In this gloomy environment Don Warrington's world-weary Antonio seemed perfectly at home and the cheap and tasteless attempts of his friends to cheer him up futile and insensitive – and incomprehensible, for there seemed no great reason to care about such a miserable toad. He learned with grim misery that Charles Edwards's blond, elegant, transparently self-seeking Bassanio intended to woo Portia, though there was no particular suggestion that his own sexual jealousy lay behind this. David Schofield offered a hard, upright little Shylock, precise and deliberate in his skullcap and sleek black overcoat. He had a heavy accent, a bitter hatred, a resilient pride, and a sardonic sense of humour. He never sought our sympathy, though he achieved it at times willy-nilly, at least in a negative sort of way, as the loathsome, yapping Salerio and Solanio (future recruits to the brownshirts without doubt), baited him or

20 *The Merchant of Venice*, directed by Bill Alexander for Birmingham Repertory Theatre. Charles Edwards as Bassanio, David Schofield as Shylock, Don Warrington as Antonio.

kicked insanely at his front door. His daughter Jessica, making gauche attempts at the sign of the cross before her elopement, was the focus of everyone's attention when she arrived at Belmont and they forced her to read Antonio's letter about her father's cruelty. She burst into bitter tears at Lancelot's jokes about the price of pork and had firmly occupied her father's place as society's victim by the end: she was left on stage after the lovers' final exits to suffer the withering, baleful glare of Antonio in the evening's final image.

Not that being with the lovers would have offered her anything better: Lorenzo (William Mannering) had shown himself feeble and inept in his attempts to offer comfort to his wife's grief; Gratiano (John McAndrew) had revealed a streak of savage violence in the trial scene that made one think that Nerissa was in for some nasty surprises; while Bassanio and Portia were clearly made for each other, he shallow and self-congratulatory (as well as sartorially tasteless: the purple suit in which he went a-wooing would have looked vulgar on the commissionaire of a pretentious hotel); she, in Cathy Tyson's triumphantly unattractive portrayal, obsessive in her desire for him, callous and giggly in her response to her other suitors, and merciless in her humiliation of Shylock in the trial scene. Even Lancelot Gobbo managed to become disturbing in Jah-Man Aggrey's bitterly unfunny performance, rastafarian locks on end as he played both himself and his father ('one speak for both', as Bassanio says) in a bewilderingly schizophrenic presentation of misplaced energy.

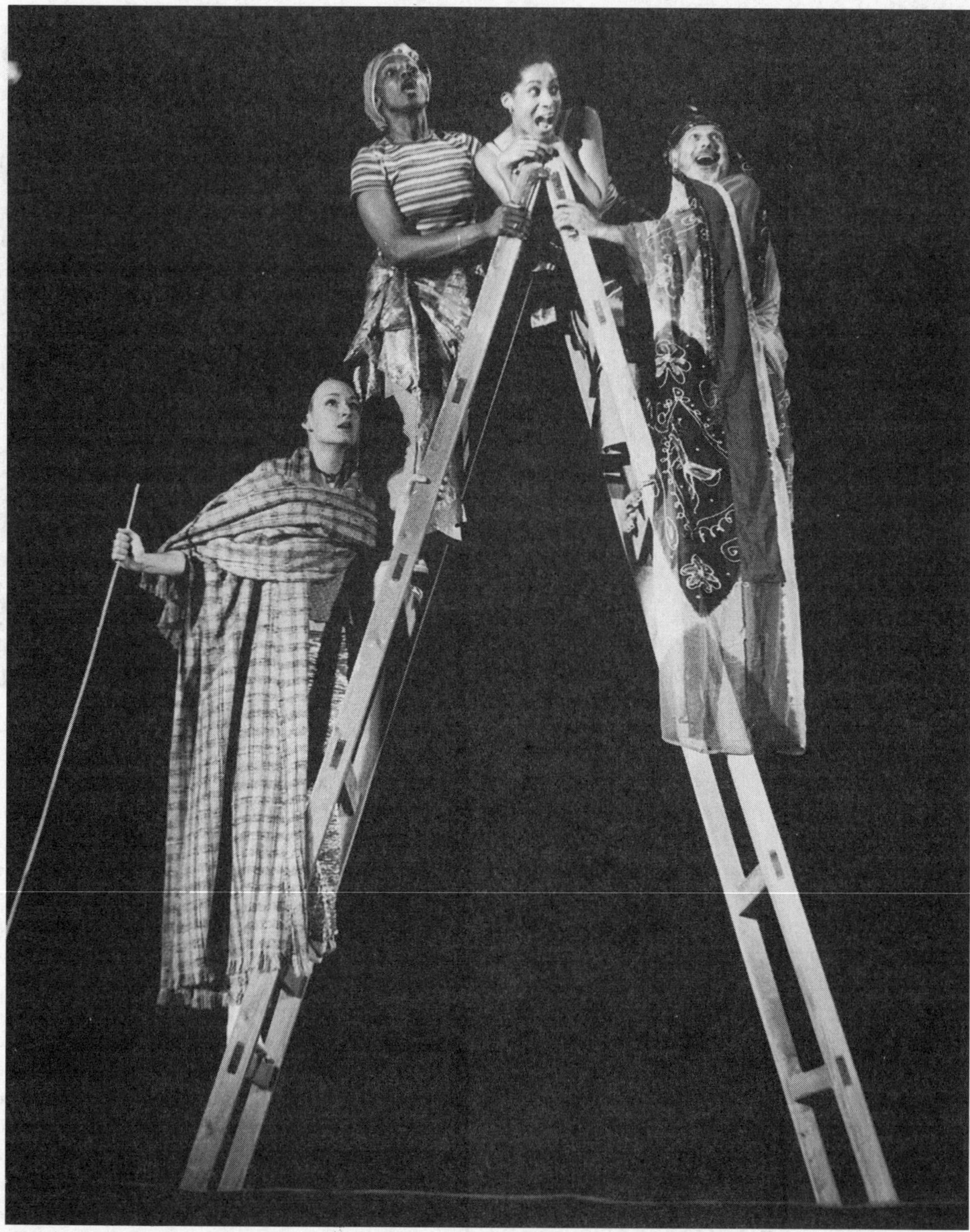

21 *All's Well That Ends Well*, directed by Irina Brook for the Oxford Stage Company. Rachel Pickup as Helena, Anni Domingo as the Widow, Clara Onyemere as Diana, Kaleem Janjua as 'Mariana' (the Neighbour). Act 3, Scene 5 (watching the march-past).

'What an odious play this is', wrote Jeremy Kingston, reviewing the production for *The Times*, and the long journey towards odiousness that it has clearly been making through a series of recent productions certainly passed another milestone here. Pity for Jessica seemed the only decent emotion left to us.

From a new 'problem comedy' to one for which the epithet is of more venerable vintage – but once again to a director bent on a novel and unexpected reading. Irina Brook's production of *All's Well That Ends Well* at the Oxford Playhouse in the late summer attempted to create a world in which the folk-story origins of the play might operate more freely by presenting it in a pastiche African world. The attempt, though energetic and forceful, was doomed to failure. Rachel Pickup's Helena, however, was so full of energy, so gracefully and intelligently spoken, and so committed in her love for Emil Marwa's boyishly naive Bertram, that much of this wonderful play's essence seemed to survive the mistaken directorial concept.

From a theatrical property basket the cast of white and black actors were presented, as the play began, with shawls and robes that suggested an African world, and when not actually performing they sat round the stage, punctuating the dialogue by playing on drums and bells. Not once did the concept help the play and at times it was violently at odds with it, not least when Bertram refused Helena with all the weight of sixteenth-century social hierarchy behind him ('A poor physician's daughter my wife!') and Jeff Diamond's King of France responded in terms that assume the absolute power of a Renaissance monarch, with every syllable he uttered made absurd by the fact that the crown he wore was a tambourine without a skin found in the property basket; or when Helena cured the king, not in secret through the medical legacy of her father ('prescriptions of rare and proved effects'), but through a sort of cod witch-doctor's dance projected onto a screen with the entire cast watching. When a Shakespeare play is genuinely absorbed into a different ethnic culture, and re-presented in the light of it, the results are frequently illuminating; the external imposition of pseudo-versions of ethnicity (as with the Globe production of *The Winter's Tale* reviewed elsewhere in this volume), is patronizing and phoney.

But for all its self-imposed problems, the production at many points demonstrated the theatrical power of this strangely neglected play, scenes such as Helena's confession to the Countess (a fine performance by Madlena Nedeva of this most sympathetic of roles, though robbed of some of its scope by the excision of Lavatch, with whom she has such a patient and generous relationship), or Bertram's rejection of Helena after the fun of the choosing dance (here very competitive and overtly sexual, in a way that seemed perfectly legitimate), or Bertram's wooing of Diana (with its valuable opening lesson in how to fail in a chatting-up routine by getting the girl's name wrong), or the comic cruelties of the interrogation of Parolles, all coming off with fine theatrical energy. There was an interesting unscripted glimpse of the opening moments of the 'bed trick', with Helena, in Diana's very identifiable veil, leading Bertram lovingly by the hand to the consummation she has so long yearned for. The ending took the sentimental choice of a penitent Bertram kneeling to Helena and kissing her on 'more welcome is the sweet', a kiss that might have come two acts earlier as Helena begged it ('strangers and foes do sunder and not kiss') if Bertram had not been diverted by Parolles's loud (and calculated) drumming at the crucial moment. The production ended, perfectly in character, with a directorial misjudgement, the Epilogue being spoken, not by the King, but by the mysterious witch-doctor figure who had doubled Reynaldo and the 'Gentle Stranger'. But for all its oddities, it had still revealed that the play's theatrical energy is more or less indestructible if the role that drives it has been adequately cast; and in Rachel Pickup's performance of Helena it undoubtedly had. The

22 *Measure for Measure*, directed by Michael Gordon for English Touring Theatre. Michael Hadley as the Duke, Catherine Cusack as Isabella. Act 3, Scene 1.

buoyancy and emotional commitment of her appeal to the 'leaden messengers' not to harm the arrogant young man who is, so unworthily, the object of her love, were not easily to be forgotten.

Another so-called 'problem comedy' with another director determined to 'bend it to his awe', was *Measure for Measure*, directed by Stéphane Braunschweig (his first production in Britain) for Nottingham Playhouse, but also shown at the Edinburgh Festival and at the Barbican. Braunschweig was his own designer, creating a cylindrical set in dark brown wood on a stage that revolved to cacophonous electronic noise, part of the drum cut away to reveal a cavernous void with a great staircase seen from several different angles through the evening, the outside, where many scenes were played, leaving a narrow track with secret little doors into that uninviting interior. On that narrow track a furtive, balding figure, in a modern three-piece suit in dark grey, began the evening by whispering 'Escalus' through one of the little doors. Another balding figure in dark grey three-piece appeared (Roger Watkins's Escalus), to be followed soon by a third, of virtually identical appearance (Paul Brennen's Angelo). Here, clearly, was the Establishment, the men in grey suits and in their fifties who run the show – even to the extent of pushing round the revolve from time to time to advance the story. That duty fell most often, unsurprisingly, to Jim Hooper's rather detached, unattractive Duke, apt to smirk to himself as he put his plans together, for whom Lucio's adjectives 'unweighing' and 'shallow' seemed apt enough.

Such simple symbolism as having the Duke move the scenes along was frequently more heavy-handed. Escalus had not arrived unencumbered at the start, but was carrying a sword and balance which were later handed over to Angelo. When we first met Lucio (suavely if undemonstratively played by Danny Sapani), he was wearing red horns on his head and reading the *Financial Times*. (The horns later proved to be a little jokey hat, but the director's devilish point had been made.) On one occasion, as the set swung round, we caught a glimpse of Angelo descending the staircase; and he had wings, in far from angelic black. Immediately before Angelo's first meeting with Isabella that winged vision appeared again, but now seen through Masaccio's painting of Adam and Eve being expelled from Paradise – which, as the sole decoration of that austere interior space, also made its bluntly self-evident point. Less self-evident was why, in a basically modern-dress production, Mistress Overdone and her clients all wore Elizabethan costumes, though the explanation may well be no more elusive than the fact that this allowed the display of excessively prominent cod-pieces (and that it looked incongruous in contrast with the modern policeman's uniform of Harry Gostelow's Constable Elbow). It can presumably only have been his character's name that condemned Tony Cownie, as Pompey, to trying to be funny in a toga.

But if the production often seemed to be trying too hard to lay the play open for our measured examination, it captured some moments with extraordinary vividness. Across the front of the stage, from little upright chairs, Brennen's thin-lipped Angelo and Lisé Stevenson's passionately committed Isabella (in St Teresa cream and brown habit), faced each other; and we waited to see who would move to bridge the space between them. He was first from his chair, standing above her, his finger raised in insistence on the legal argument he had to make; but it was Isabella who first made physical contact, falling on her knees before him, her hand on his breast, as she demanded that he go to his bosom, then lying in his lap as she reached her finger to his lips and begged that his heart might not 'sound a thought upon your tongue / Against my brother's life', he twitching the while with fear and longing. Their second interview took place on the staircase, the ebbs and flows of the argument marked in their movements up and down, the sound of their footsteps echoing its urgencies, their cheekbones prominent and their eyes dark hollows in the uncompromising side light. At the moment when Angelo put his proposition to her in its lewdest simplicity they were at the top of the steps, she just below him, her back to him, his hands twitching above her shoulders; she turned to face him in horror, then backed slowly, precariously, down the long staircase, he following, pathetic yet frightening, his sexual yearnings and threats now spilling out in shameless viciousness: a fine, self-consciously deliberate, piece of theatre.

Also boldly demonstrative in its presentation of the idea 'is't not a kind of incest?' was the interview between Isabella and Claudio, clearly her *younger* brother in Oscar Pearce's fresh-faced, curly-haired performance. Through bars, we watched an encounter of growing physicality: he lay with his head in her lap as she told him of Angelo's bargain; that position had been reversed by the time he began to wonder about being ready to die and soon he was all over her, kneeling across her to beg 'Sweet sister let me live'; and again came the reversal, she forcing him to the ground in her anger, and finally astride him as she threatened 'no word to save' him. By the end of that scene she was sitting on the front edge of the stage beside the Duke, their legs swinging in cheerful unison, her head on his breast, his arm around her and his eyes rolling in anticipation, as they planned what they both clearly thought was the brilliant scheme of sending Mariana to Angelo's bed in her place.

That upbeat image immediately before the interval was quickly overwhelmed in the second half. The Duke's astonished disbelief when the messenger from Angelo failed to bring the pardon produced a silence daring in its length. Then the Duke and Stephen Ventura's Provost (another man in a grey suit) moved to Plan B. They smirked delightedly at the news of Ragozine's death, though the Duke would soon be retching with disgust at the arrival on stage of the pirate's head in a bag as blood-stained as Abhorson's apron had been as he sat polishing and sharpening his huge sword. (Pompey, as novice executioner, wore an apron of startling whiteness.) The production ended with the same trio of bald, middle-aged men who had begun it, listening to the appeals for justice of two beautiful young women with long blonde hair. Isabella had torn off her veil in anguish when the Duke told her that her brother was dead and the long black dress that Jayne McKenna wore as Mariana was almost as nun-like as Isabella's. And there they stood, the victims, legal, social, and sexual, of the male Establishment, with Lucio presiding over the proceedings from high on the staircase. As the reversals and revelations of the final scene unfolded, the pace slowed. The unmasking of the Duke caused Isabella to sink into a chair and provoked a groan of shame from Escalus, who then sat hunched and still for the rest of the play. Mariana reappeared from marriage in bridal white to stand beside Angelo, a white carnation in his buttonhole; and thus they stayed, motionless until the end. Isabella came to her knees with prompt obedience and spoke her appeal for Angelo's life with cold logic, as though repressing the anger she felt now that the nature of the Duke's game had become clear to her. She then sat with her head in her hands until the extraordinary reappearance of Claudio. Before that Barnadine had responded to the prospect of being handed over to the Friar's 'advice' by throwing his cloak over his head and remaining an unmoving heap for the rest of the scene. Claudio was revealed when a panel in the wooden boarding opened high above the stage. From off his head he pulled a bloody bag, then stood there, naked, like Michelangelo's David, holding a severed head – presumably Ragozine's, though perhaps it was Goliath's, or Medusa's. (Or were we somehow being invited to connect him with Adam in the Masaccio painting?) Isabella stood frozen to the spot, staring up at him – as well she might – oblivious of the Duke's proposal; Claudio stared back at her; neither moved again. With Lucio pinned to the wall in horror at the prospect of marrying a punk, the Duke came slowly down stage to sit in the chair where Angelo had sat when first tempted by Isabella and, seemingly exhausted, spoke the final lines with his hand on his brow, his commitment to what he was saying dwindling with his voice, his subjects turned to statues behind him. 'What's yet behind, that's meet you all should know', he said wearily, then he too passed into oblivion, and what had always been a deliberately slow production ground to a halt as darkness came.

Rather less concerned to impose his own particular gloss on *Measure for Measure* was Michael Gordon, who directed, for the English Touring Company, a production that played at various venues during the autumn and that I caught up with at Cambridge Arts Theatre. This was an infinitely more straightforward version than Braunschweig's, played in vaguely nineteenth-century costume on a simple set (designed by Conor Murphy) backed by a geometric pattern that suggested the bars of a prison, and with a raised playing area that offered no escape from emotional exposure. It was taken throughout at a crisp pace, uncluttered by 'business' or elaboration, and delivered a virtually full text in two and a half hours, including an interval. At times one felt that it was so determined not to slow down that some of the complexities went unexplored: in Michael Higgs's presentation of Angelo's soliloquy following the first interview with Isabella, for example, or Michael Hadley's of the

Duke's 'Be absolute for death' to Claudio, where haste seemed in danger of blurring the progress of emotional and intellectual discovery. For the most part, however, the sense of drive and energy served the narrative well, the urgency of the need to save Claudio, the immediacy of Angelo's desire for Isabella and the speed of his response to it which so nearly defeats the Duke, all appropriately emphasized by it.

The production was notable chiefly for the professional Shakespearian debut of Catherine Cusack as Isabella. She brought to the role a quality of stillness and self-containment, and a sense of ardent honesty and directness, that made her declaration 'More than our brother is our chastity' entirely unsurprising. When the Duke put to her the proposal that Mariana should take her place for the appointment with Angelo she paused and took time to consider (pauses were rare enough to be conspicuous in this production), trying the idea before her conscience and then giving her consent with a certain solemnity. No wonder that her reaction to her brother's desire to live by her pollution had been so contemptuously uncompromising, and her appeal to Angelo so straightforwardly intense, oblivious of the effect that her ardour (and her touch on his breast on 'Go to your bosom'), were having on him. When Mariana agreed to the exchange plan she and Isabella changed their outer robes, Mariana thus taking on the appearance of a nun and Isabella looking like a schoolgirl in a navy blue gymslip, the respective special interests of Angelo and the Duke, the director seemed to be suggesting, thus provided for. At the end, the various expressions of thanks from the Duke were treated as dismissals from the stage, each character withdrawing with a respectful bow until only the Duke and Isabella remained. He then knelt to her for the final proposal: 'What's mine is yours.' She waited a long time before raising him to his feet, but then let go his hand, stepped back, and stared at him, intensely but without commitment, until the lights went out.

Another production where the interpretative hand of the director seemed comparatively light was Mike Alfreds's of *The Winter's Tale* for his Method and Madness Company, with costumes, set, and lighting all the responsibility of Paul Dart, which was on tour from January before a month at the Lyric Hammersmith around midsummer. I saw it at Warwick Arts Centre and found it engaging in a not particularly memorable way. And here, is the dilemma of a reviewer of Shakespeare productions for such a journal as this: is one's task to highlight the eccentric, to give prominence to the production that is determined to show its play in a new light, however ill-judged; or should the worthy, the mainstream, the sensibly unsurprising occupy one's attention? There was nothing eccentric, or ill-judged, about this version of *The Winter's Tale*, but nor was there (and here one feels ungrateful) much about it to write – well, if not home, then to *Shakespeare Survey*, about, unless it be the interesting doublings that occur when eight actors perform the two dozen or so roles that the text demands: Raad Rawi as contrastive studies in fatherhood, Leontes and the Old Shepherd; Terence Wilton, hen-pecked figure of fun as Antigonus in Sicilia, reappearing as that figure of theatrical fun in Bohemia, Autolycus; and Fergus O'Donnell dying in the first half as Leontes's son Mamillius (played on his knees, the tone of the production permitting such *faux-naïf* ways of suggesting infancy) and returning in the second half as his son-in-law Florizel. The play's exploration of the pattern of loss and restoration was strengthened by these necessity-derived inventions. Odd, then, it might seem, that the more flamboyant double of Hermione and Perdita was eschewed, but the tricksiness that this involves for the final scene would have been alien to the tone of simplicity and directness that the production sought.

It began with actors costuming each other in robes of the Arabian-nights-with-fur-fringes style and there was a lot of changing of carica-

23 *Cymbeline*, directed by Adrian Noble for the Royal Shakespeare Company. Front row: Patrice Naiambana as Caius Lucius, Edward Petherbridge as Cymbeline, John Kane as the Soothsayer, Joanne Pearce as Imogen, Damian Lewis as Posthumus. Act 5, Scene 6.

ture theatrical beards as actors switched from role to role. There were problems, inevitably, in producing much of a sense of a court in shock at Leontes's tyranny, or in elation at his daughter's and his wife's return, or of the high jinks of a sheep-shearing festival, with a stage so sparsely peopled; but there were incidental bonuses too, such as the interesting handling of Time's medial intervention, spoken with great intensity and concentration by all eight actors as a Chorus. This was not a production to change the course of the play's theatrical history, but it was well paced, unfussily staged, and directly and intelligently spoken. What more should one ask for? – well, more memorable individual performances, of course.

One got them in the other of the 'late plays' on offer this year, Adrian Noble's RSC production of *Cymbeline* that opened on Stratford's main stage in February. The problems of *Cymbeline* are notorious, yet within this remarkable monster are some of the most wonderful things in Shakespeare, if only a director can find a way to unlock them. Adrian Noble's key was of Japanese origin, though the production rather alluded to the world of kabuki than imported its conventions coherently. Indeed, when the reference got too precise – tiptoeing servants, a long-handled parasol carried over the Queen, warriors of vaguely samurai appearance – the detail got in the way of what was genuinely useful about this suggestion of another theatrical world, its provision of a theatrical equivalent to the storyteller's 'Once upon a time'. Not surprisingly, it proved most effective at the start. However early one arrived, a hooded figure in long white robes was to be seen sitting by a fire. Gradually he was joined by others, in ones, twos, small groups, until there were a couple of dozen of them, all identically clad in white, gathered to hear a story told by a figure in red, who would later turn out to be the Soothsayer and who, at 7.30, stood up to say 'There was a king called Cymbeline.' It was distinctly easier to understand than the opening speech in the Folio and though we quickly returned to the authentic text, the presentation of the opening scene as a kind of chorus, each character standing to identify themselves as they were mentioned, was undoubtedly helpful in getting this difficult beginning across to audiences unfamiliar with the play.

Equally effective was the great white cloth, suspended, sail-like, within the blue cube of Anthony Ward's set, swooping forward or back across the stage to provide changes of location – like the lever at the side of the child's drawing board wiping the slate clean for a fresh start – as the play shifts back and forth, from Cymbeline's abode, to Wales, to Rome, so potentially confusingly but here so easily followed. Down the left-hand aisle of the auditorium the stage continued outwards on a ramped track, a road to 'beyond beyond', as Imogen calls it, perfectly suited to the journeying motif of the play that the great sail reflected: 'Safe mayst thou wander, safe return again', as Pisanio says. The ramp took characters out, and round the back, and on again, enwrapping us in the story's wanderings and coincidences and wonders.

Any production of *Cymbeline* stands or falls by, and probably only exists for, its Imogen. Joanne Pearce's great quality in the part was the buoyancy of hope and optimism, the rapt energy of love and commitment, that she radiated and that seemed to put her in touch with the forward momentum that drives the play, apparently magically, towards its happy ending. 'When shall we hear from him', she asked impatiently, turning the moment of lament at her husband's departure to hope for the future; 'O, for a horse with wings', she said, and the absolute commitment of her yearning created a grim contrast with our awareness of what is planned for her on the journey she is so eager to start. To perhaps the most taxing challenge that Shakespeare provides for a woman actor – to make us share her grief at her husband's death when we *know* it's only a dummy, and a dummy of the wrong man to boot – she rose impressively, taking head-on the whole gamut of emotion, from the forlorn pretence at the start that it's a nightmare ('I hope I dream') to the terrible step-by-step recognition of what seems the brutal, bloody truth of bereavement and of the mutilation of the man she loves. It was an impressive achievement.

There were good performances elsewhere too: from Edward Petherbridge as Cymbeline, long white robe, long white hair, long white face, a sort of priest-king, never seeming quite focused on the affair in hand, carried on his golden chair into battle like a sacred talisman, growing slowly in awareness and power in the final scene, from wide-eyed bewilderment to confident control – '*My* peace we will begin'. Of Guy Henry's Cloten (or 'Cloaten', as he kept insisting – a splendid directorial idea, this, for turning the hesitancy of an editor's footnote into a running theatrical joke), I was less certain. It was a genuinely funny performance, attempting that frightening combination of stupidity and violence that the role requires, but somehow it was impossible to believe that this willowy and melancholic figure could carry out the plan he enunciates for raping Imogen and then kicking her back to court. There was an ironic detachment about the performance, as though somehow, deep down, Cloten knew that he was a no-hoper. Paul Freeman's Iachimo, on the other hand, managed to find the role's opportunities for laughter while remaining profoundly threatening. 'No tragically potent scoundrel ever came out of a trunk', wrote Granville Barker long ago, but as the lid opened, slowly, and first one hand, then the other, gripped the trunk's side before the face appeared, sniffing the air for the scent of the woman whose ruin he seeks, the sense of danger was potent. This was an older Iachimo than I remember, not the usual macho figure, confident of his sexual prowess, but a dissolute, embittered man who does what he does, not out of desire for the beauty and purity of Posthumus's wife, but through contempt and envy of the idealism of Posthumus's love for her. And Damian Lewis's Posthumus certainly offered that sense of naive unworldliness, the green-jerkined country boy out of place in the urbanity of red-cloaked Rome. His directness and simplicity, in the soliloquy of deranged sexual jealousy, kept it painful, and pitiable, when it can so easily topple into the absurd. The Welsh boys (Jo Stone-Fewings as Guiderius, Richard Cant as Arviragus) managed to be amusing, and likeable, but never silly, in their earnest quaintness, and Joanna McCallum's Queen, with her gold gong ear-rings and slit-eyed make-up, adroitly trod the narrow line between genuinely evil step-mother and the transparent wickedness of pantomime.

All in all, then, an impressive team offering an enjoyable production of the play, though not without some uneasinesses and disappointments, some trivial, some more serious. Audiences unfamiliar with the play are always going to struggle to identify the ghosts of Posthumus's parents in the penultimate scene; it seemed a pity, therefore, to dress them – I think the headgear was responsible – as if they were surgeons come to perform an operation on their offspring. The gold-masked Jupiter, on the other hand, playing peep-o over the white sail, seemed to me to achieve a nice balance between amusement and grandeur in response to the impossible theatrical challenge that Shakespeare has thrown at the director. More significant was the tendency of some actors occasionally to stand back from their parts and point up the absurdity of the situation; there is no point in performing this play if one is going to condescend to it as if it were a silly piece of melodrama. Why, then (to take one example), did Paul Freeman's Iachimo deny himself the slightest hope of convincing us of his penitence in the final scene by treating the phrase 'I faint' to mean, not 'my guilt is making me feel unwell', but 'I am now going to collapse completely unconscious and one second later bob back up again'? The tightropes of the amazing final scene were for the most part walked with great dexterity: the safety-valve laughs that the text provides – 'More matter yet', 'When shall I hear all through?', 'I left out one thing' – taken splendidly, the moments of powerful emotion movingly presented at face value. It seemed a pity thus to spoil the delicate balance between wonder and awareness by laughing at the play. I was puzzled also by some of the music: by the decision to provide a setting that drained the exquisite funeral dirge of all its grace and beauty and by the idea of having Cloten (rather than one of the musicians he has hired) sing 'Hark, hark the lark', this time to a setting of great elegance, thus further hindering our ability to see him as the brutal threat to Imogen's chastity that he is. More fundamentally, the never-never-land far-eastern setting lost much of the play's political dimension, and of its relevance to the continuing issue of Britain's relations with the rest of Europe, of the fact that Cymbeline's final treaty with Rome is not unconnected with our Treaty *of* Rome. Still, no production of a play, least of all of *Cymbeline*, can get all of it, and this one, with its fine mixture of clarity in telling the story and sense of wonder at its progress, got a lot – even solving, with the wafting of silk flags, the thump of drums, and the clash of gongs, and some eerily impressive shadow play, the age-old problem of staging a battle.

*Cymbeline* had been preceded on Stratford's main stage by two other comedies that opened, in accordance with the pattern of the new-style season, in the closing weeks of 1996, Michael Boyd's production of *Much Ado About Nothing* and Ian Judge's of *The Merry Wives of Windsor*. A more energetically hostile set of reviews than

24 *Much Ado About Nothing*, directed by Michael Boyd for the Royal Shakespeare Company. Siobhan Redmond as Beatrice, Alex Jennings as Benedick (and remains of tree). Act 4, Scene 1: 'Tarry sweet Beatrice'.

those that greeted Boyd's production it would be hard to find. And yet, if it's true that the main directorial duty is to cast the play well, then Michael Boyd did a splendid job, for it's hard not to suppose that Shakespeare was thinking of Alex Jennings when he penned the role of Benedick, and had he foreseen the future of women's roles on the English stage after 1660 his thoughts might easily have drifted north of the Border to find the appropriate Beatrice to put opposite him, precisely the contrastive sharpness to set against the Jennings bonhomie. Siobhan Redmond gave an incisive, astute, intelligent Beatrice, with a cautious, almost prickly, defensiveness that ill concealed the sense of hurt she carried from that occasion – some while ago, one felt in this production – when she was foolish enough to allow Benedick to win her heart of her with false dice. That the Jennings Benedick escaped our censure for what we might otherwise have thought such caddish behaviour was largely due to his charm, of course, but also to his ability to convince us that in fact he never even noticed the emotional damage he was doing. 'What, my dear Lady Disdain', he said (apparently surprised and delighted to see her), in response to what ought to be the clean ace service of her first remark to him, and then tucked her arm chummily under his: 'Are *you* yet living?' But his early wide-eyed, rather boyish, *insouciance* in no way impeded his movement to absolute seriousness and dignity as he delivered his challenge to the seemingly incurably boyish Claudio of Rhashan Stone, any more than Siobhan Redmond's early defensive sharpness prevented her immediate, and touchingly vulnerable, susceptibility to the overhearing scene. There was no real problem with the central relationship in this production.

But if there was much right with this, the main motor of the play, there was much far from right with the theatrical world in which it was presented. This was one of those productions so brimming with directorial ideas (a malady most incident to directors working on the Stratford main stage for the first time) that one struggled at times to see the wood for the trees. Some of these ideas were pared away as the season progressed: the Messenger at the beginning ceased to be Don Pedro in exaggerated disguise; we were spared the inevitability of turning against Beatrice before a line had been spoken when she gave up petulantly snapping the bow of a cellist doing her (not very adequate) best; the mirror behind which Beatrice learned so much about herself ceased to turn, twice, with her and those she is overhearing having to follow it through ninety degrees each time. But for all that the production became simpler, it remained too complicated and fussy, and one was aware of this the moment it began as a host of figures from Leonato's household (bakers' assistants, artists in residence, the musical staff), bustled about the stage. One might have supposed that they were there to people a believable social world, but that seemed to be the last of the production's aims. It was not even possible to say whether Tom Piper's set depicted indoors or outdoors. A receding white ceiling and upstage door, brick walls, a colonnade, all seemed to propose indoors, but a large tree suggested otherwise, while its trunk's thrusting through the floorboards made one wonder if one was supposed to think of sexual violation. (If one was, and one followed the idea through, the fact that its erectness had been chopped down in its prime for the second half seemed a brave punishment for its thrustfulness.) If one were trying to offer a literal-minded explanation for the set I suppose one might have said 'orangery', but I'm not sure that that would have taken one any further forward. More important was the fact that the set looked much later than seventeenth century, whereas the characters were all in firmly seventeenth-century costume. Such unsettling dislocation is, of course, good for one, but one would have liked to *feel* the benefit more distinctly.

The failure of the figures to match the background was presumably an aspect of the production's constant exploration of the picture motif. One arrived in the theatre to see an enormous picture frame around the proscenium arch and within the picture thus delineated watched Beatrice posing while her portrait was painted. Upstage was a little collection of picture frames, while a cartoon sketch towards a full-length wedding portrait of Hero and Claudio was obscenely ripped and penetrated by Borachio to demonstrate his plot against Hero to Don John (whose spirits, it has to be admitted, 'toil in *frame* of villainies'). The conveniently-to-hand picture frames were then used by George Seacoal, and his fellow guardians of the law, as hiding places, *Ruddigore*-fashion, to steal up on Conrade and Borachio, who were finally captured in them – 'framed', indeed. All this was, in some sense, a response to an aspect of the text, as was the large mirror which appeared on several occasions through the play, the mirror in which the reflection of Don John distorted alarmingly as he snarled his independence of social norms – I must 'eat when *I* have stomach, and wait for no man's leisure' – the mirror in which Beatrice saw herself as a little boy, the mirror through which Claudio saw the ghost (or I suppose it was the ghost) of Hero in the tomb scene. The most significant event of the story takes place (off stage) at a bedroom window, and windows have frames. The play is constantly concerned with how people perceive themselves, with shifting perspectives, with the interpretation of visual evidence, and there's a part of us that's ready to be grateful for having these things thus 'brought to light'; but there's an equal impulse to resent excessive directorial intervention. Was all this helpful illumination or were we being led by the nose? One didn't quite know which to think – and then one found a director illustrating Borachio's remark to Conrade that 'it drizzles rain' by having him urinate against what remains of the tree-trunk, and perhaps one did know what to think after all.

From the same area of directorial invention (or intervention) came the little boy who dominated many playgoers' responses to this production. He appeared first to Benedick before his gulling scene (where the text – here cut – in fact requires a boy to fetch a book from a chamber window), looking at Benedick silently as the latter darned his sock, a little figure dressed in a miniature version of Benedick's suit, whose existence Benedick seemed uncertain of as he stared at him with a kind of puzzled wistfulness. He reappeared behind the mirror which had hidden Beatrice during her gulling scene, imitating her actions as she gazed yearningly at him. And at the end of the play, as that disturbing upstage door swung open, we saw him again, and again through glass, in the position where, at the end of the preceding scene, Claudio had seen Hero's ghost; and now he was holding a sapling. Why Beatrice saw herself reflected as a seven-year-old boy was clearly the sort of literal-minded question to be kept at bay, and to try to turn this juvenile apparition into some relative of Cupid was equally to kill the idea with excessive precision. Perhaps he was proposed as a vision of what Beatrice and Benedick had lost by their earlier failure, or might never have if they didn't manage this time to overcome their trepidation about self-commitment. Whether one found this silent infant a suggestive directorial gloss on the play's relationships, creatively puzzling, or a tiresome irrelevance, seemed almost to be a touchstone of one's attitude to interpretational direction of Shakespeare.

Within all this 'direction' there were some interesting individual performances supporting those of the principals: a Hero and a Claudio from Emily Bruni and Rhashan Stone who explored much more fully than usual the uncertainties, the pain, and the final hesitation of one of Shakespeare's more troubling love relationships, Hero frequently pulled around the stage like a human parcel by her father or by Don Pedro, Claudio kneeling in tears of shame as he was reunited with Hero at the end; a brave stab at that most difficult of propositions, the villain in the comedy, by Damian Lewis, who turned Don John into a sexually ambivalent psychopath – something of a handful as a house guest; and a Dogberry from Christopher Luscombe who brought petty officialdom to new heights as he fussed and twitched and knowingly winked his pernickety way to revelation of the villainy. His Verges (Toby Longworth) was too young, but Luscombe made an amusing virtue of necessity by asserting his view that 'when the age is in the wit is out' straight to Leonato, the oldest man on the stage. Dogberry's East End vowels marked him off sharply from the posh people around Leonato with whom he sought pathetically to hob-nob, and his entry and exit down the theatre aisle, from outside the proscenium frame that encloses their world, again marked him as the outsider – though ironically the outsider who saves that world from self-destruction: 'What your wisdoms could not discover, these shallow fools have brought to light'.

But in spite of some fine individual performances, it is the abundance of directorial ideas that stays in the memory from this production. One example must suffice for many: the oddest final dance I've ever seen in a production of this play. It went on for several minutes, beginning in stately manner with the couples properly

25 *The Merry Wives of Windsor,* directed by Ian Judge for the Royal Shakespeare Company. Susannah York as Mistress Ford, Edward Petherbridge as Ford being 'as extreme in submission as in offence'. Act 4, Scene 4.

paired, but gradually became chaotic as more and more people joined in, the couples separated, the music got louder, the rhythm of the thudding drum-beat more ominous, drowning out the melody carried on the strings. And as dancing time and music time became completely dislocated, the huge veils that disguised the women on their arrival swirled in the air and slowly the white ceiling, which had, all the evening, made the playing space seem so claustrophobic, eased open like some gigantic car sunshine roof and we saw a dark blue sky and what might have been a moon, and the music, and the dancing, subsided, and the couples re-formed and made their exits (a little tentatively, it seemed to me) and our attention was rivetted on that upstage door. Would Don John, brought with armed men back to Messina, be behind it, one wondered; and there instead was that enigmatic, angelic little boy, with his enigmatic, but surely promising, little tree. Was it all a manifestation of Beatrice's description of the dance of marriage and repentance, beginning in state and ancientry but then falling into the cinquepace faster and faster before sinking into the grave? Certainly there was no difficulty in allowing one's imagination to turn the wild discordancy of the middle part of the event into a dance of death, the wafting veils into shrouds, and the oblong, tapering roof of the stage into a giant coffin lid, lifted to allow a macabre peep at the goings-on below, with only the boy, and his sapling, left to create a future. For all the critical fusillade this *Much Ado About Nothing* received for over-earnest directorial interference, it would be a duller world if sound judgement and good taste were to deprive us of productions as thought-provoking, intriguing, and eccentric as this.

Excessive thoughtfulness was not an accusation likely to have been brought against Ian Judge's cosy image of Elizabethan Windsor, with its fairy-tale castle, its picture-book schoolchildren, and its little box hedges. *The Merry Wives of Windsor* is a fine example of Shakespeare's *craft*, a bourgeois comedy with farcical elements and some anticipation of the world of pantomime, and it received in the RSC version a bourgeois production with farcical elements and rather more than anticipation of the world of pantomime. The one potentially disturbing area of the play, its exploration of class division – for in both its plots impecunious outsiders from a higher social sphere have come to Windsor in search of rich women – was simply ignored. Fenton (Jo Stone-Fewings) was hardly distinguishable in social status from the natives of Windsor, while Leslie Phillips's Falstaff, florid and bumbling in his cheap ginger toupée, had clearly forgotten that he finds Ford's wife 'well favoured' only because 'the jealous wittolly knave', her husband, has 'masses of money', and was apparently genuinely committed, with no ulterior financial motive, to the seduction of Susannah York's self-contented, alluring Mistress Ford, forlornly hopeful though that was at his time of life. This was an amusing marshmallow of a Falstaff, not really *big* enough, in any sense, to pose a threat to Windsor's prim self-satisfaction. There was something almost pathetic about his presenting a red rose to Mistress Ford, in his Mr Toad check suit, one of the many costumes that lurched amusingly between the sixteenth and twentieth centuries, modern patterns in Elizabethan styles, farthingales with Salisbury's handbags, city banker's pinstripes with fully starched ruffs, all impinging simultaneously on our awareness of the small-town world of the play. Ian Judge is very good at keeping a production bustling along – 'hurry music' must be one of his most regular commissions – and this was no exception, with the brisk scene changes to Tim Goodchild's set often entertaining in themselves: the little suburban hedges whisked on for the outdoor scenes; the staired and banistered interior, very affluent, for Ford's house, so perfect for those group searches and chases; the cosy interior of the Garter where we encountered Falstaff in his bathtub, complete with plastic duck, following his less voluntary ducking in the Thames.

There were good supporting performances in the vividly differentiated series of caricature parts that the text provides, though the production had no more success than its predecessors in making Nym and Pistol spring to life. There was a shameless (very shameless) stereotype of peppery gallic absurdity from Guy Henry as Dr Caius, constantly pretending he'd understood more than he had; a very funny Slender from Christopher Luscombe, fastidiously adjusting the disobedient forepiece of his straw-coloured hair and obediently trying to do as his uncle tells him in a heterosexual wooing that was clearly a mistake for him; a good contrast between the wives, Joanna McCallum's Mistress Page uncomplicated, confident, bustling, Susannah York's Mistress Ford winsome, a little nervous, just possibly susceptible to Falstaff's blandishments; an unflappable, dogged Page from Paul Greenwood, fierce in his distrust of Fenton for the unanswerable reason that, as a prospective son-in-law, 'he knows too much'; an eager busybody Mistress Quickly from Cherry Morris, blithely without a qualm of conscience as she took money from all Anne Page's suitors; and, the most interesting performance of the evening, a pathetically insecure, repressed, hesitant, peaky Ford from Edward

Petherbridge, frenetic in his search of every scrap of linen in the buckbasket, but embarrassing, too, in the humiliation to which his suspicions, and his grovelling later apology for them, condemn him, the connections with Posthumus and Claudio (those other jealous lovers elsewhere in the Stratford season) interestingly there, below the surface. If it hadn't been for the final scene, in which the not uninteresting idea of alluding to Hallowe'en in the children's costumes for Parson Evans's troupe of fairies at Herne's Oak suddenly drifted five days later and we were invited to perceive Falstaff as the guy on top of the bonfire while firework noises filled the auditorium, one would have left the theatre more or less contented that a reasonably professional, if rather shallow, job had been done. The razzmatazz of a danced curtain call was pure Ian Judge, and the final image of Falstaff, defying the text and absenting himself from the country fire to which he'd just been invited (no doubt he'd had enough of fires for one evening), in order to sit under the oak tree sharing his page's sandwiches, had precisely the right sentimental ring to provide the *envoi* to this production.

Both the year's major history plays came from the RSC: Ron Daniels's version of *Henry V* was a touring production, with a separate company, seen at Stratford in September before a national tour; Gregory Doran's production of *Henry VIII* was part of the 1996–7 Swan season. Daniels's *Henry V* offered the play in twentieth-century costume, in a simple box set designed by Ashley Martin-Davies, its walls inscribed with names, like the Vietnam memorial in Washington, a high door at the back for major entrances and exits, and a huge ramp that rose to deliver Henry and his men to the breach in Harfleur's walls. Shakespeare's first scene having been cut (as well as all the second scene's discussion of the threat from Scotland), it opened with Henry studying a flickering old film of a First World War battle, his own shadow cast ominously across the screen as he did so. He and his court were in ceremonial, perhaps naval, uniform, the gold braid piled thickly on Henry's chest and shoulder. Norman Rodway, doubling the Chorus, in high-buttoned military tunic, and Canterbury, in the same high-buttoned tunic made clerical by the simple addition of a cross, offered a comic version of the Salic law speech, relishing the names (Childeric, Ermengare, and so on) as quaint and unbelievable curiosities – as indeed they seemed in the context of the military world with which we had been presented, on stage and on film. War decided on, the braided finery became workaday army uniform, perhaps First War perhaps later, and so this sixteenth-century play about a fifteenth-century battle began to unfold in its twentieth-century guise.

On the whole it worked rather better than might have been expected. Rodway's Chorus, wafting in and out of the play (besides Canterbury he played the Governor of Harfleur, Erpingham, and Burgundy), spoke with an energy and intelligence that clearly derived from an enthusiastic commitment to the images he was creating. I'm not sure that the doublings helped: the distinctive nature of the audience's relationship with the Chorus is a symptom of the play's theatrical self-consciousness and to require responses to the same actor at other levels of imaginative commitment may be to risk its dilution. There was much directorial interference with the connections between the Chorus and adjacent scenes: not only did the cutting of the first scene destroy the bathetic contrast between the ostentatious appeal for a 'muse of fire' and the spectacle of two princes of the church trying to get out of paying their taxes, but the reversal of the first and second scenes of Act 2 removed that other ironic juxtaposition, the quarrel of Nym and Pistol after we have just heard about the youth of England being 'on fire'; the last scene of Act 3 (the French commanders impatient for dawn) was moved to follow the fourth Chorus, thus postponing the fulfilment of the Chorus's promise of Henry visiting 'all his host', while

26 *Henry V*, directed by Ron Daniels for the Royal Shakespeare Company. Henry V (Michael Sheen) threatens Harfleur through microphone and loudspeakers. Act 3, Scene 3.

the fifth Chorus was omitted altogether, depriving Henry of that most elaborate of compliments, the comparison with 'conquering Caesar'. The losses from all this seemed greatly to outweigh the modest gains of time, though the move directly from the Chorus's description of the 'nest of hollow bosoms' to the exposure of the traitors perhaps offered a bonus in theatrical urgency. In modern dress, the fact that Scroop had been Henry's 'bedfellow' took on a particular resonance, the King's accusation against him becoming a passionate lament for lost trust and departed love, full of bitter recriminations. The disarming of the three traitors by Nicholas Day's Exeter, looking curiously like King George V, and the ripping off of the epaulettes that proclaimed the honour they had abused, was a sharply effective sequence before the departure from Southampton, with signalling lamps, kitbags, ammunition boxes, the roar of helicopter engines, all the accoutrements of a twentieth-century army on the move, presented to us.

The comic scenes of *Henry V* are not Shakespeare's most unequivocally distinguished writing and their particular version of the late sixteenth-century vernacular survived the journey to modern-dress presentation less successfully than other parts of the play. Campbell Morrison's bumptious bruiser of a Pistol appeared, with his fellow bikers, in black leathers before the forbidding fence of a demolition site, Nym with his flick-knife making an odd combination with Bardolph and his sword. In the second of their scenes there was, for me anyway, a theatrical first: Falstaff's coffin (of fairly standard width, as it turned out) was carried on by the four mourners; they stood around it, even sat on it, for their obsequies and then, departing for the wars, left Dona Croll's West Indian Cockney Mistress Quickly (who had given a touching, unsentimental account of Falstaff's death) to drag it off on her own. The little gang at war proved more full of song than the text really suggests, operating as a little glee club during parts of the siege of Harfleur, their songs a forlorn attempt to keep at bay the terror which at one point had Nym vomiting into an ammunition box. Their annihilation provided some of the production's more poignant images: the corpse of Bardolph dangling from the gallows against a threatening sky, the King holding his head in despair as he caught sight of him, scarcely able to articulate his exit line 'And on tomorrow bid them march away'; the humiliated, leek-spitting Pistol hobbling forlornly from the stage as the formalities of the final peace negotiations were being set up; and the Boy (posthumously identified in this production as 'Davy Gam, Esquire') – a chirpy, poignant performance this from Nina Sosanya – caught by the French cavalry, running this way and that in frantic search of an escape, and finally knocked to the ground and trampled to death.

As befitted figures who seemed to come from an altogether different military epoch from the one inhabited by the English forces, that same French cavalry actually rode unwieldy silver hobby-horses. Hobby-horses with their means of motive power decently veiled from sight by heraldic caparisons, their riders anonymous beneath their helmets, can have a certain iconic theatrical threat (as John Barton was wont to show in history-play productions two or three decades ago); two-legged hobby-horses parading solemnly about the stage like ostriches, their riders' faces clearly visible, though not without a strange, other-worldly elegance, inevitably provide a poor match for the heavy artillery that the English had brought to the battle. The French court scenes had already established this contrast: the operatic formality of the King and courtiers in their pale blue frock-coats, their hair in pig-tails, was shattered by the arrival of Exeter, in khaki and gaiters, with his battle threats; or, later, as the exquisitely titled earls knelt in elegant obeisance to their liege, an azure silk curtain wafting as backdrop to their lavender costumes, the vision was blasted away by the sound and smoke of gunfire as English tommies swarmed across the stage from the siege of Harfleur. At the end, too, for the peace negotiations, the contrast was maintained: in autumnal light, and before a giant wreath of poppies, the French paced slowly on in high top hats and tail coats to hand over their country, and their princess, to their conquerors, who were waiting for them, in military uniform, though now in the ceremonial gold-braided version of it seen in the opening scene.

With the odds so weighted against him, it was something of a triumph that Michael Sheen still managed to maintain some audience sympathy for Henry. A sense of potential vulnerability and of boyish charm and quickness were present alongside the astute political instinct and the uncompromising determination – a touch of the Tony Blairs, indeed. He constantly ruffled his mop of curly hair in eagerness and anxiety, and the smile that so often flashed across his face illuminated it instantaneously. He threatened the destruction of Harfleur through microphone and crude loudspeakers, the reproduction seeming to flatten out the sound into a merciless coldness. His brother Gloucester became appalled at the savagery of his threats and tried to switch off the microphone; Henry smashed him to the ground and went on, clearly believing that the very credibility of the expedition, and of his own kingship, depended on overcoming this first real obstacle. He thus committed himself fully, at least for the moment, to the threats he was making, only to radiate the immensity of his relief when the need to carry them out was removed. For 'Once more unto the breach' he addressed his auditors individually, performing the actions he described as though to wind himself up as well as them, while 'Crispin, Crispianus' was subdued, low-key, profoundly committed to the idea of the brotherhood being 'remembered'. His soliloquy 'Upon the King' was interestingly taken as the utterance of a man much disorientated and angered by the conversation he had just had with Michael Williams and John Bates, less self-pitying than it is sometimes apt to seem, and after the battle he broke down in tears of relief at his victory and of remorse at the roll-call of the English dead, reading their names from the labels of the body-bags in which their corpses were laid out in terrible symmetry across the stage. There was genuine emotion, too, in Henry's conversation on their shared Welshness with Alan David's excellent Fluellen, as there was also in the relief of the kiss that ended his wooing scene with Katherine, for all the energetic charm of the boy king had seemed to be getting nowhere with Karine Androver's wanly beautiful princess, wearing the black of mourning for her lost countrymen, defeated France personified, who stood awkwardly two inches taller than he (and on purpose too, for she wore high heels) and maintained supremacy by her silence. From first to last, indeed, Sheen's performance was one of admirable variety and immediacy, and if the production overall seemed no more than a worthwhile experiment, in its title role one was surely watching an actor with an exciting Shakespearian future.

Gregory Doran's RSC production of *Henry VIII* at the Swan Theatre made splendid use of that exciting space. Robert Jones's simple and effective set had large double doors upstage, beneath a gallery where the musicians sat, with the words 'All is True' engraved across them in large roman capitals. The doors opened at intervals through the play (thus obscuring their ominous legend) for its great public shows to spill onto the stage: a version of the Field of the Cloth of Gold at the beginning, bass drum thudding, the entire company singing 'Deo Gratias', and a resplendent Henry trucked down stage astride a golden horse; the elaborate coronation procession for Anne Boleyn in her golden robe; and the christening at the end, Henry again trucked in, enthroned, more of 'Deo Gratias' in chorus, lots more gold, drumbeats and pomp, and a little bundle (palpably not a baby) to prophesy over. It was all 'sufficient', as Sir Henry Wotton wrote about that fateful early performance, 'to make greatness very familiar, if not ridiculous' – and that was clearly the intention, for as each of these glamorous, carefully orchestrated, public manifestations of power concluded, it was ironically undercut. In the earlier instances this was achieved by having the pieces withdrawn again upstage behind the doors, like so many toys being put back in the cupboard, as the real power play of sordid political manoeuvring took over the space again and the label 'All is True' (for truth is a malleable political commodity) returned; and at the finale, as Paul Jesson's Henry stood there for what seemed an interminable time, trying desperately to keep the paternal beam on his cheeks (and we were surely meant to be aware of the actorly effort), and gold confetti fell from the roof, we were suddenly aware that Anne Boleyn (Claire Marchionne) had appeared at his left, her fingers tremblingly touching the neck that was soon to be severed by the executioner's axe – a victim, like so many others we had met, of the monarchy whose continuance we had just been invited to celebrate.

The production's juxtaposition of these gaudy power shows with the everyday world of intrigue and jostling for position around the King was extremely effective. In contrast to the golden shows, the costumes in other scenes were mostly in subdued colours, greys, blacks, dark greens, a world in which the crimson robe and biretta of Ian Hogg's Wolsey, his podgy

27 *Henry VIII*, directed by Gregory Doran for the Royal Shakespeare Company. Opening tableau (Field of the Cloth of Gold); on the truck: Gardiner (Paul Benthall), Queen Katherine (Jane Lapotaire), Henry (Paul Jesson), Wolsey (Ian Hogg).

features and peering little eyes interrupting the silken sleekness, shone out like a beacon. This was a cardinal who took his power for granted and carried it without affectation, who spoke his native Suffolk accent plain and bluntly, who seemed strangely plausible when he came to plead with Queen Katherine to give her cause over to the King, and who accepted the collapse of his power (an event that is a lesson to us all in the perils of misfiling) with gently amused detachment.

His principal adversary, Queen Katherine, pulled, in Jane Lapotaire's excellent performance, and exactly as the authors must have intended, most of the audience's sympathy in her direction. She spoke with a slight Spanish accent, which marked her off as the 'stranger' which she so often feels herself to be, and moved through the play with the sort of commanding dignity which made her frequent references to herself as a 'poor weak woman' seem more than usually ironic. The trial scene was played as if the entire auditorium were the clergy and lawyers assembled at the Blackfriars and she commanded the space superbly in her impassioned self-defence, quite rightly upstaging Henry who sat on his stool centre stage staring glumly in front of him. The scene with her women – 'you find me here part of a housewife' – surrounded by the linen they are engaged in mending, took the singing of 'Orpheus with his Lute' from sedate madrigal style gently into Spanish rhythms and finally into flamenco dance, each of the women and, last of all, hesitantly, Katherine herself, joining in. It seemed to me a legitimate, and poignant, reminder of her native country which she now feels is her sole hope of comfort, before the arrival of Wolsey reasserts the English, and the male, hegemony. For much of this scene the director had Anne Boleyn on stage as one of Katherine's women, playing the lute for the song, sitting there through much of the interview with the cardinals, the youthful beauty of her silent presence creating further pain for the ageing Queen. For her final scene Katherine was stooped and pale, appearing (it was a drab, loose gown that did it, replacing the court dress of earlier scenes) emaciated and frail, as if she had lost half her body-weight since we last saw her. The problem of staging her vision was avoided by reducing it to a simple beam of ethereal light, a cop-out that, in an intimate space like the Swan, has much theatrical discretion in its favour. A final, pathetic moment of bitterness came, after she had been carried out to die, when Caputius (Rex Obano) ripped up the letter whose contents she had just been at such pains to recount, as if aware of the futility of expecting Henry to take the slightest notice of it.

Paul Jesson's Henry, round-faced, crew-cut, ebullient, was an admirably enigmatic creation – and a triumph for the costume department, which managed to make him seem half as wide again across the shoulders as anyone else on stage (or in Tudor England). His unquestioning trust in Wolsey in the early stages might have been mental laziness, or a sort of boyish naivety; it did not seem at all incompatible with an obvious affection for Queen Katherine, whose hand he took, tenderly and comfortingly, as they sat together to hear the Surveyor speak of the possibility of his dying 'without issue'. 'Go thy ways, Kate', he shouted with Petruccio-like enthusiasm at the end of her speech in the trial scene, and if we hadn't already heard Suffolk speak of his conscience having 'crept too near another lady', his protestations of love for her, and of tenderness of conscience in himself, would have been perfectly believable, for Jesson presented them straightforwardly and at their face value – for (rightly I'm sure in this play) this was a performance that played every scene for what it was worth, without worrying too much about consistency. 'Creeping' was not, in any case, the word that would have come to mind to describe Henry's first approach to Anne Boleyn in this production, for the masquers who arrived at Wolsey's party were hardly 'shepherds', as the Folio proposes. They were satyrs whose masculinity stood jauntily erect before them, sweeping the women into a dance that threatened rape, asserting the ruthless male dominance of this world of Henry's court, a dominance to which Anne Boleyn had to succumb with as good a grace as she could muster as Henry directed her to the 'next chamber' (down through the trapdoor) that Wolsey had so thoughtfully provided for the fulfilment of the King's desires. And yet, for all the role's casual self-esteem and bullying self-assertion, for all the unthinking, unquestioning acceptance of absolute power, Jesson never allowed us the easy route to outright dislike of the man, for he, like the rest, was seen to be driven by the dictates of the power game, by the inexorable requirement that he beget an heir to continue the dynasty of which he is but the temporary representative. The expression of anguish on his face at the news that Anne's child was, after all, a girl, presented him, too, as the victim of history, so that all the carefully orchestrated enthusiasm at the christening came to seem like just another public performance. 'As I have made ye one, lords, one remain', he said fiercely at the end of the council scene, and added, thoughtfully, 'So I grow *stronger*, you more honour gain'. It was as if he recognized, grimly and bitterly, that now, at this stage in the reign, after the deaths and executions of so many who had served him in the past, it was only the *strength* of his grip on power that mattered; the 'honour' was a superfluity that others might squabble over if they liked. This was an excellent performance at the centre of a thoughtful and impressive production.

Among productions of the tragedies, Matthew Warchus's of *Hamlet* for the RSC on Stratford's main stage was certainly the most controversial. The divisive issue was the cutting. Warchus took out a thousand lines, but it was not that evenly distributed, internal snipping that we are used to and that allowed Adrian Noble to take the same number of lines from *Cymbeline* without anyone complaining. The Warchus method involved the blatant removal of conspicuous sections of the play, most obviously all of the political plot involving Norway and Fortinbras, and including the entire first scene, with important rearrangements in what remained, so that what we watched was a goodish way along the road that leads from 'version' to 'adaptation', concentrating exclusively on that area of the play that presents Hamlet in relation to his family and to his conscience. The production had something of the quality of a photograph taken through a telephoto lens: part of the view was lost, but what remained came closer to you.

And 'closer' was undoubtedly the point. Alex Jennings's Hamlet was among the most immediate, the most emotionally engaging and affecting, in a long time. His relationship with the audience was inevitably vivid, for the production did everything it could to intensify it, starting as it meant to go on with us alone with Hamlet, his face spotlit in the darkness, a solitary, intimate presence. He was scattering his father's ashes from an urn as images of his loving boyhood relationship with him flickered on a home movie behind him, the sentimentalized memories of the little boy in the snow with daddy in his Dr Zhivago hat taking us straight into Hamlet's state of mind. The play was to end with the same grainy, flickering, silent film, so that the action was framed in this manifestation of the Ghost's sternest command: 'Remember me'. The victim of such a beginning was Horatio, whose sensitivity and trustworthiness is the first thing we meet with in the text, but who seemed here, despite Colin Hurley's sincerest efforts, a less significant and a vaguer figure than usual, bewildered by the thought-processes of his quicker-minded friend, only slowly (and perhaps only just) earning that place beside him at the end to speak what were (in this Fortinbras-less finale) the play's last words, cradling the dying young man in his arms while the home movie returned to show the small boy, similarly clasped in his father's embrace, in a final image that evoked one's pity in proportion to one's ability to overcome resentment at its blatant touch on the trigger of the sentimental.

And 'trigger' is an apt enough term in a production with a gun-toting central character – though, insofar as I understand the term 'gun-*toting*', I imagine it implies confidence and dexterity with the weapon, qualities which Alex Jennings's Hamlet scarcely evinced. We saw him first with his revolver in the little attic lumber room to which he'd retired with some of his books and private possessions, gingerly pulling it from the brown paper carrier bag in which he'd apparently carried it home from the Elsinore gunshop. It provided a splendid theatrical image, this nutshell of a room in the middle of the stage's comparatively infinite space, a boyhood secret place at the top of the house, cluttered and confined, a physicalization of the isolation and claustrophobic disarray of his own mind. Clutching the gun mistrustfully he pointed it at the audience, almost as if threatening us not to object to the repositioning of 'To be or not to be', brought in here, roughly in line with its position in the bad quarto, to precede the arrival of Rosencrantz and Guildenstern. Since we'd missed that earlier wish that his flesh (whether sullied or solid) would melt – the first soliloquy began with 'That it should come to this' delivered with lashing bitterness at his mother's departing back after her suavely self-satisfied attempts to coax him out of grieving – to see him here contemplating death, and more particularly self-slaughter, as he turned the gun from the audience to his own temple, was not without its aptness. The gun stayed with him through

28 *Hamlet*, directed by Matthew Warchus for the Royal Shakespeare Company. Alex Jennings as Hamlet, Paul Jesson (with Yorick's skull) as the Gravedigger. Act 5, Scene 1.

much of the rest of the play, decently hidden for the most part in its carrier bag, but, after fumbling attempts to load it, bullets spilling onto the floor, it was pointed for a long time at Claudius in the prayer scene. Claudius knelt with his back (presumably meaningfully) to the great 'Christ of the Andes' statue that stood upstage left in Mark Thompson's vast and threatening set, its arms outstretched, over against the huge square pillar whose brutal immovability seemed to symbolize the forces against which Hamlet was fighting. Hovering there in the shadows by the pillar, Hamlet took trembling aim at his uncle's back, the occasion to 'do it, pat' presenting itself so obviously that the need to find a reason for putting it off became frighteningly urgent. Moments later a shot was indeed fired, an immediate, thoughtless, lightning reaction that despatched Polonius, and the remaining bullets were saved for Claudius – saved too long, for they went into him only after the envenomed rapier and the poison had done their work. Thus Hamlet's splendidly simple plan – just buy a gun and shoot the bastard – came to its futile conclusion, though the fact that Claudius twitched convulsively as the first bullet found its mark perhaps allowed one the grim satisfaction of supposing that there was just enough life left in him for a fraction of the plan to be fulfilled. And after the last shot had assaulted our ear-drums and the barrel was empty, and Hamlet, slumped in his uncle's chair, had surveyed the carnage, the rest was, ironically indeed, silence.

If one could stop worrying about what was missing and commit to the telephoto lens quality of the production, there was no denying its absorbing and exciting theatricality. Alex

Jennings spoke with all that intelligent, graceful command of the verse that one has to come to expect of him, and made one feel the isolation and pain of Hamlet with unrelenting intensity. This was an enormously sympathetic Hamlet, a centre of intense energy, impatient to get on with his plan, impatient with the players in the rehearsal, a thwarted man of action whose presence, wandering, armed, around the house, clearly posed a real threat to Claudius. The opening sequence was a fine piece of theatre with its violent lurch from Hamlet alone with his memories over his father's ashes to the brash and noisy vulgarity of Claudius's wedding party, champagne corks popping, pop music blaring, coloured lights flashing, and Hamlet, in his black suit, dumped into the middle of it all by the flying out of the screen on which his memories had been projected, his shield from the horror of the present. That deft control of the stage was apparent throughout. Two examples must suffice: the bleak graveyard, with its authentic municipal-cemetery plastic grass to act as receptacle for the delving discoveries of Paul Jesson's ebulliently self-assured grave-digger, in his local-authority-issue orange overall trousers, peering through bottle-glass spectacles as he crooned 'September Song' with its wickedly apposite refrain 'I haven't got time for the waiting game', while a dank, greyish snow drifted down; and the eerie, jerky presentation of 'The Murder of Gonzago' as a shadow play on a screen in front of which Hamlet pranced in brilliant crimson jacket, white face and painted-on smile – circus master, clown, MC – and the shadow of Lucianus, bending to administer the poison, loomed huge and distorted in front of Paul Freeman's suave, expensively suited Claudius, while Hamlet joined in with sing-song recitation of the incriminating lines, until even the hard-headed self-control of the usurper could take no more.

There were other fine performances around Alex Jennings, besides Freeman's and Jesson's: a rosy-cheeked Polonius from David Ryall, seeming very much the amiable old buffer, comfortably sure of his rightness in asserting his affection for his daughter by denying her access to the man she loves, apparently completely harmless and bumbling until one saw him at his filing cabinet checking his records of others around Claudius – and one had a horrible inkling that the bumbledom might be a front for something distinctly nastier. Susannah York's Gertrude, bland and sweetly pretty, frustrating and infuriating for Hamlet to deal with, nevertheless *had* moved, by the play's final stages, into an awareness of the true situation that allowed the possibility of an alliance with Horatio to be emerging. There was a brave attempt at the fragmented story of Ophelia from Derbhle Crotty, transparently in love with Hamlet as he with her, terrified by his anguished night visit (one of the production's dumbshow interpolations), heartbroken and baffled by the nunnery scene, and tottering on in red high heels and skimpy minidress in her madness, spilling the pills she is taking and wildly mistaking them for flowers, collapsing, vomiting – was it the drugs, or what did that song say about being tumbled? – a brave performance that risked treading the terrible theatrical boundary where one doesn't know whether it's the character that's embarrassing or the acting. And from Edward Petherbridge we had the telling double of Player King and Ghost, the Ghost suddenly there at the party, looking like anybody else (only just a little paler you know); clutching Hamlet's hand as he described his torments, locking on with a convulsive grip so that one wondered at the severity of the frostbite that must ensue for his son; sitting down on the corner of his widow's bed in his silk dressing gown, elegant and silver-haired, watching his wife in her petticoat, precisely, surely, 'as he lived'. There was no shortage of interesting performances around the engrossing account of the title role that Alex Jennings gave us. As telephoto shots go, this one seemed to me to achieve a remarkable sharpness of focus.

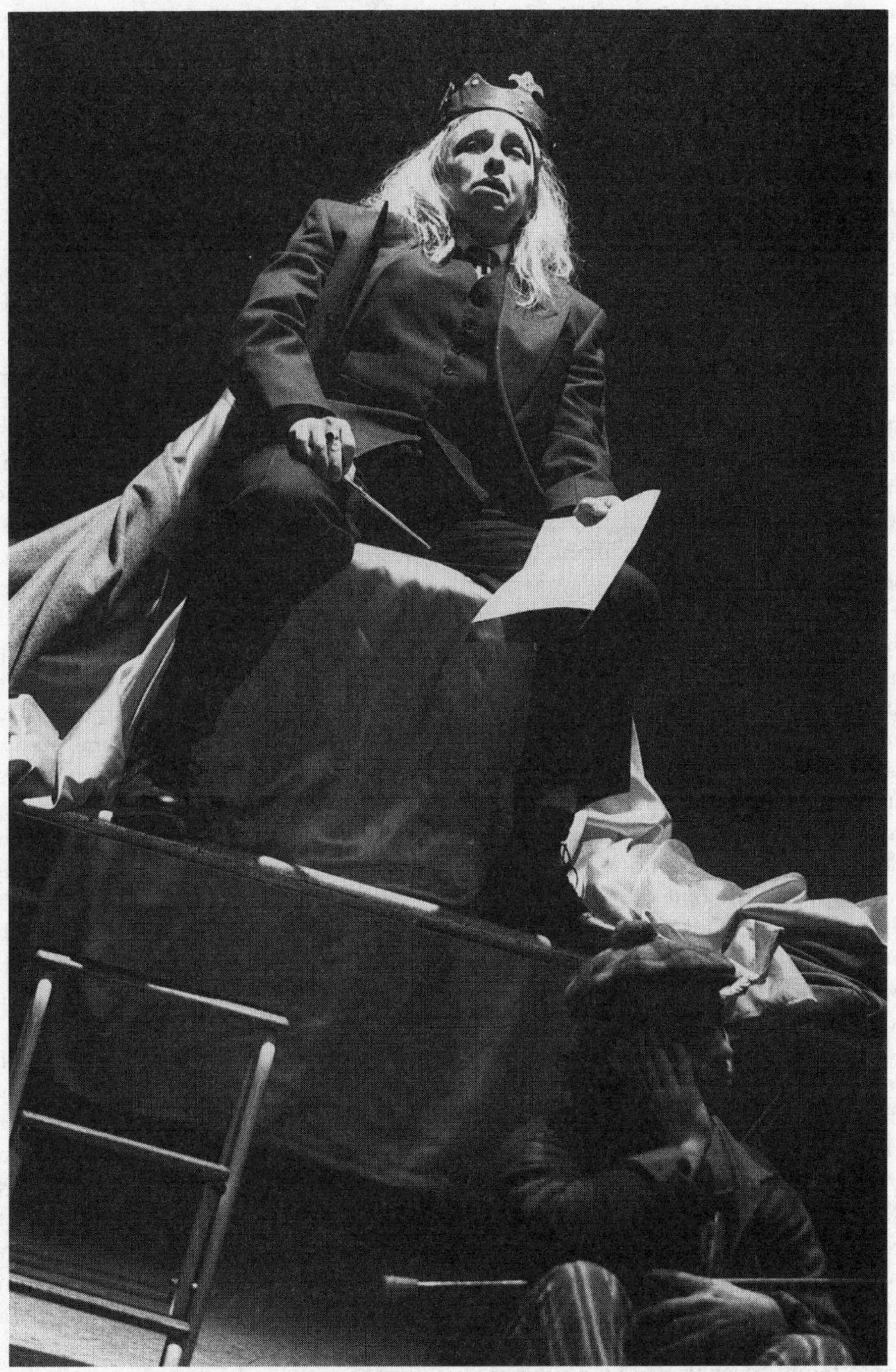

29 *King Lear*, directed by Helena Kaut-Howson for the Haymarket Theatre, Leicester. Kathryn Hunter as Lear, Marcello Magni as the Fool. Act 1, Scene 1.

No less than three productions of *King Lear* were to be seen within a few hundred yards of each other in London during the summer and autumn: Helena Kaut-Howson's, with Kathryn Hunter as Lear, was at the Young Vic in July having been seen originally at the Leicester Haymarket in February; Sir Peter Hall's version, with Alan Howard in the title role, opened at the Old Vic in August; and Richard Eyre's production, with Ian Holm as the King, was in repertoire at the Royal National Theatre's Cottesloe auditorium from the spring.

The Kaut-Howson production, designed by Pawel Dobrzycki, was notable most obviously for presenting a woman as King Lear, though in its Leicester version (much of this was pared away at the Young Vic where I also saw it, though enough remained for the point to be discernible) its presentation of the play as the dream, or hallucination, of a dying patient in a geriatric hospital was also surprising. At Leicester the play began with an ancient, crotchety woman sitting in a wheel-chair in a seedy-looking nursing home, watching *East Enders* on the television. Some of her family, bored and indifferent during the visiting hour, sat near her and a hospital orderly, in tam o' shanter hat, was desultorily sweeping the floor. Suddenly the old woman suffered some sort of seizure, alarm bells rang, doctors and nurses brought in life-support apparatus and hurried her behind screens. Moments later the screens parted and there was a little white-haired old man in a black suit three sizes too big for him sitting up on the end of his bed, his fool beside him in tam o' shanter and holding a candy-striped broomstick; and the first scene of *King Lear* was ready to start. At the end of the evening we faded back into this framing fiction, the screens were drawn back round the bed, the heart-beat monitor stopped, and a junior house doctor in white coat stepped forward to deliver Edgar's closing lines to the waiting family. Presumably it was all an attempt to explain why a woman should be performing King Lear, an attempt always heavy-handed and hardly necessary, for with it only vestigially remaining at the Young Vic, the central performance remained no more nor less convincing than it had been and there was still no great difficulty in accepting the idea of wheelchairs becoming chariots, a bathtub Tom's hovel, and the hospital bed the one in which Lear awakened to Cordelia.

Responses to this central performance were remarkably varied among reviewers (and, indeed, among one's own students) for the degree of persuasiveness seemed to be partly subjective: some found an eccentric midget in a freak show, others a moving performance of the sufferings of androgynous old age. The performance was indisputably a curiosity, but not, I think, a freak. It was highly effective in its presentation of Lear's journey towards increased awareness; it was intelligent and often incisive in its handling of the language; and it was unfailingly interesting as a technical tour de force. What it lacked, for me, was any vestige of emotional engagement, and that derived, I think, from a constant awareness of the visual, and vocal, unexpectedness and oddity of what one was experiencing. In that oversize black suit, long, wispy Dr Who hair, tiny white goatee beard like some ancient Confucian philosopher, Lear 'tottered about the stage with a walking stick' (in Charles Lamb's phrase) looking disconcertingly like some dotty Victorian parson. One watched fascinated, but never (for me, anyway) in serious danger of suspending disbelief.

In contrast with this oddly distancing central performance the production was elsewhere offering us a series of very immediate images: Goneril and Regan (Kate Seaward and Gabrielle Reidy), crop-haired, slit-skirted, fur-coated, towering over their father as he cursed them; Edmund (Jeremy Brudenell), cool, handsome, blue-eyed, going into battle in his SS hat; Albany (David Acton) with his pipe and suede shoes, probably ex-RAF and clearly a decent sort of cove; and Edgar (Simon Roberts) naked as Poor Tom and escaping, in a memorable image, down a man-hole cover from a frightening version of the search; Cordelia (Hayley Carmichael) in faded jeans for the first scene but reappearing with her French army in a General de Gaulle hat; a Fool from Marcello Magni full of little theatrical juggling tricks to amuse the audience (though perhaps these were largely to compensate for a certain incomprehensibility in his delivery of the lines and quite why his corpse was propped up in deathly witness of the blinding of Gloucester it was hard to say); the blinding itself, carried out hideously realistically with a corkscrew; and battle scenes that brought stark memories of images from the recent conflict in Bosnia. All these were so vivid and immediate in their effects that Lear by contrast seemed a curious escape from a world of fairy tale: Tom Thumb or Rumpelstiltskin kept coming disconcertingly to mind. And the voice, though always crisp and clear in its articulation, so patently lacked, in its rasping preciseness, any range or depth that much of the emotional colour was inevitably lost. Bewilderment was there, and resentment; pain, too, at times, and a certain touching wistfulness, but on anger, majesty, rage, pathos, grief, we were seriously short-changed. Nor was there any real sense of the great curve of Lear's journey, for this figure began distinctly off his rocker and remained a strutting, peevish, rather nasty little person until he got out of that absurd ill-fitting suit and into a white hospital robe for the reconciliation with Cordelia, though his appearance for the Dover Beach scene in his Fool's tam o' shanter was touching. The final entry was also effective, with Cordelia's corpse flung across his wheel-chair which had clearly become her childhood pram in his bewildered imagination and which he rocked in the forlorn effort to awaken her. There were, indeed, many things to admire in Kathryn Hunter's performance, and it was indisputably a courageous attempt, but in the end that meanly nagging little question 'Why bother?' kept edging its way back into one's mind. And from the internal evidence of the production an answer did not present itself with complete conviction.

From one *King Lear* more interesting technically than emotionally one moves to another. Peter Hall's rather old-fashioned production offered an uncut Folio text in basically Elizabethan costume, all white ruffs, black dresses and black doublets-and-hose, with crimson velvet capes, for the opening scene, though with departures later, here and there, from the Elizabethan theme: Goneril wore black trousers under a black gown for much of the evening; Edmund often seemed temporally indeterminate in military greatcoat and black leather; and Lear himself, for the awakening to Cordelia, was in oversize buff pyjamas. John Gunter's set began as a plain greyish box with precisely symmetrical doors at the sides and rear and windows above, all of them closing to near invisibility. Successively achieving that invisibility (for me anyway) was the jagged fissure right down the back wall which breathtakingly split open for the storm scene, fork lightning running down either side of it as Alan Howard's Lear appeared in the space between, hanging on to the electrified edges for 'Blow winds and crack your cheeks' – as comprehensive an image as could be of his world split apart. After that initial surprise, later openings of the fissure were inevitably more tame, but it still produced some fine stage pictures: a cave, a rock, a blasted sapling and Greg Hicks's near-naked Edgar framed in the space for 'Yet better thus ...'; bright, optimistic light and Cordelia in blue and white and a silver breast-plate, looking like the statue of Joan of Arc in every French village church, her little army behind her; howls and smoke and, back-projected onto a screen (had someone been to see the RSC's *Cymbeline*?), swirling flags and crashing bodies for the battle; at the third blast of the trumpet Edgar, encased head to foot in black armour, helmet closed, huge silver sword gleaming – and Edmund's chances suddenly seeming, as Cassius Clay used to say of those of his opponents, 'slim or none'; and, last of all, the fissure split wide for the story's final revelation: Lear with Cordelia's corpse in his arms.

Alan Howard's first Shakespearian role for some years found him undiminished in thoughtfulness, in verbal inquisitiveness and experimentation, and in vocal (particularly *vibrato*) athleticism. I found him consistently interesting, often intriguing, rarely moving. Not a syllable was inaudible in this immense role, but that was partly because each syllable was treated as a separate entity, weighed and examined on the tongue, as it were, before being released to the waiting world – and about the length of the wait there was often a certain unpredictability, as though he was trying to catch us on the hop. 'Attend the lords of France and Burgundy ...', he said, very slowly, followed by a long pause; then, all of a sudden, he snapped 'Glosta', picking his messenger at the last moment, wrong-footing them all. But when, a little later, he switched his attention from Burgundy to France, there was no vestige of a pause and we were all caught out again, momentarily failing to realize that he'd changed his direction of address. 'No I will weep', he said all in one go, and paused, apparently at a full stop; then he went on with a new thought: 'No more in such a night', as if all one phrase, followed by another pause after which came the third sentence: 'To shut me out'. The performance was full of such syntactical conjuring tricks. Peter Quince's Prologue seemed predictable by comparison.

This was a Lear apparently much in need of physical contact. He frequently touched Poor Tom's bare arms and shoulders, as if puzzled and worried by their nakedness. He kissed the elder daughters (Anna Carteret as Goneril, Jenny Quayle as Regan) on each cheek then, lengthily, on the mouth, after their love speeches, and even as he cursed Goneril as a 'disease in my corrupted blood' he was embracing her. Cordelia (Victoria Hamilton) held his hand throughout her failure to express her love and, having placed back on his head the 'crownet' which he had just instructed his sons-in-law to part between them (for only he could have failed to realize that he would need it to meet the rulers of France and Burgundy), she again held his hand for much of the interview with her prospective husbands. Combined with the loving persuasiveness in the explanation of her inability to heave her heart into her mouth, all this physical affection made the wild and whirling rage of his rejection seem unbelievable, a performance merely.

Which is what it so self-consciously was. His lank, straggly wig and oddly sidling walk at his first entrance immediately set one thinking about the techniques that an actor might employ to play Lear; throughout one found oneself thus observing him at one remove, always aware that this was a younger man pretending to be four score and upward. In the first scene he sat with his head on one side and a mirthless grin on his face, as if he had, indeed, ever but slenderly known himself. Inevitably, therefore, it was the daughters who had diagnosed this who could cope with it, for no one in this production was expecting the love test, though the division of the kingdom had clearly been leaked in advance. On Dover Beach his words were a monologue (or perhaps an aria) spoken without reference to Gloucester's presence – though it has to be said that the delayed acknowledgement gave the ultimate recognition an extra charge. But here, as elsewhere, it was of the technical means that one was most aware: the meticulously orchestrated stages of the ascent to full volume in the storm scene; the carefully timed movement through the syllables in the awakening to Cordelia; the laboured crawl across the stage to sniff at (and gloat over) the corpses of his elder daughters before crawling back to straighten and tidy that of Cordelia – a little moment of tenderness that achieved the truthful simplicity so elusive elsewhere. Emotional engagement was thwarted by one's constant awareness of how exactly the performance had been scored.

Emotional engagement there was, here and there, elsewhere: in the ferocious contempt of David Yelland's fine, aristocratic Kent for Stephen Noonan's insolent, shaven-headed Oswald, and in the quiet resignation with which he accepted his consequent spell in the stocks; in the sudden dawning revelation of love and understanding as Dennis Quilley's Gloucester, honest and not over-intelligent, and appalled at the behaviour of Cornwall and Regan particularly because they were guests in *his* house, realized that 'Edgar was abused'; and in the utter devotion to Lear of Alan Dobie's buff-suited, sad-eyed little Fool, his precarious juggling act not quite what it was, his northern vowels giving an appealing directness to all those 'thou's', his attempts to hide his growing exhaustion pitiful. There was a vigorous, and interestingly arrogant, Edmund from Andrew Woodall and Greg Hicks managed to keep us aware of the emotional sufferings of Edgar as he presented the physical sufferings of Poor Tom. The production, though sometimes a little slow, was always clear, intelligent, and unpretentious. Yet somehow it never quite caught fire.

It was Richard Eyre, offering the play in the simple oblong of the Cottesloe's rectangular configuration, who seemed most nearly to release its power. Around a covered table the family met, Lear, crop-haired and grey-bearded, strutting truculently in at the beginning to take his seat at the head, facing Cordelia, his elder daughters with their husbands, and Kent and Gloucester, on either side: eight people round a table, that was all it took to decide the fate of the kingdom. Peremptorily Lear barked the order to an astonished Gloucester (clearly not at all used to being the errand boy) to attend France and Burgundy then snapped at him for being so foolish as to take the map with him. So much had been set up in these opening moments: the testy old man, supremely confident of his own authority, his hands drumming his impatience on the table, the awe in which he is held, the absolute clarity of his mind which even allowed him a little snarl of laughter at the idea of crawling towards death – though a nervous attempt to join in by other members of the family was quickly glowered into silence. His satisfaction at his elder daughters' declarations was perfunctory, impatient, his anxiety to hear Cordelia – he had walked round the table to give her a little kiss on the head as he wondered who 'doth love us most' – pathetic, his childish rage when she disappointed him violent. It was eclipsed, however, by his fury when Kent defied him. He clambered up onto the table to pronounce the banishment in a towering passion that filled the theatre and struck terror into more than his subjects.

Ian Holm's performance was one of power and authority throughout, spoken with crisp and searching intelligence, vocally craggy (none of the Howard search for melodies here), and ducking nothing. Standing against the rain-lashed blackness of the end wall and defying the sound effects of wind and thunder, he made every syllable of 'Blow wind and crack your cheeks' clear and direct; casting off his 'lendings' in a surge of fellow feeling, he embraced Poor Tom's filthy body in a gesture that created an astonishing image of human tenderness and compassion, then pottered about the stage hand in hand with him, their shared nakedness pathetic, faintly absurd, two bare forked animals pretending to talk philosophy; and at the end, after all he had given, there was still energy left to hobble on carrying the corpse of Cordelia unaided and to place it, with a snarl that turned into a terrible sob, beside the bodies of her sisters which had just been wheeled in on something akin to a railway porter's four-wheeled truck. Moments later, after collapsing in Edgar's arms and kissing his godson for the final service of loosening his button, he too found his place on that brutal little truck and Kent pulled the whole wretched family away.

It was a production of simplicity, directness, and pace, the one obvious extravagance of Bob Crowley's admirable design (apart from the rain), being the astonishing moment when the two end walls, large and solid enough to contain the doors through which all entrances and exits had hitherto been made, crashed inwards to the floor of the stage as the storm began, the whiff and wind they created in the

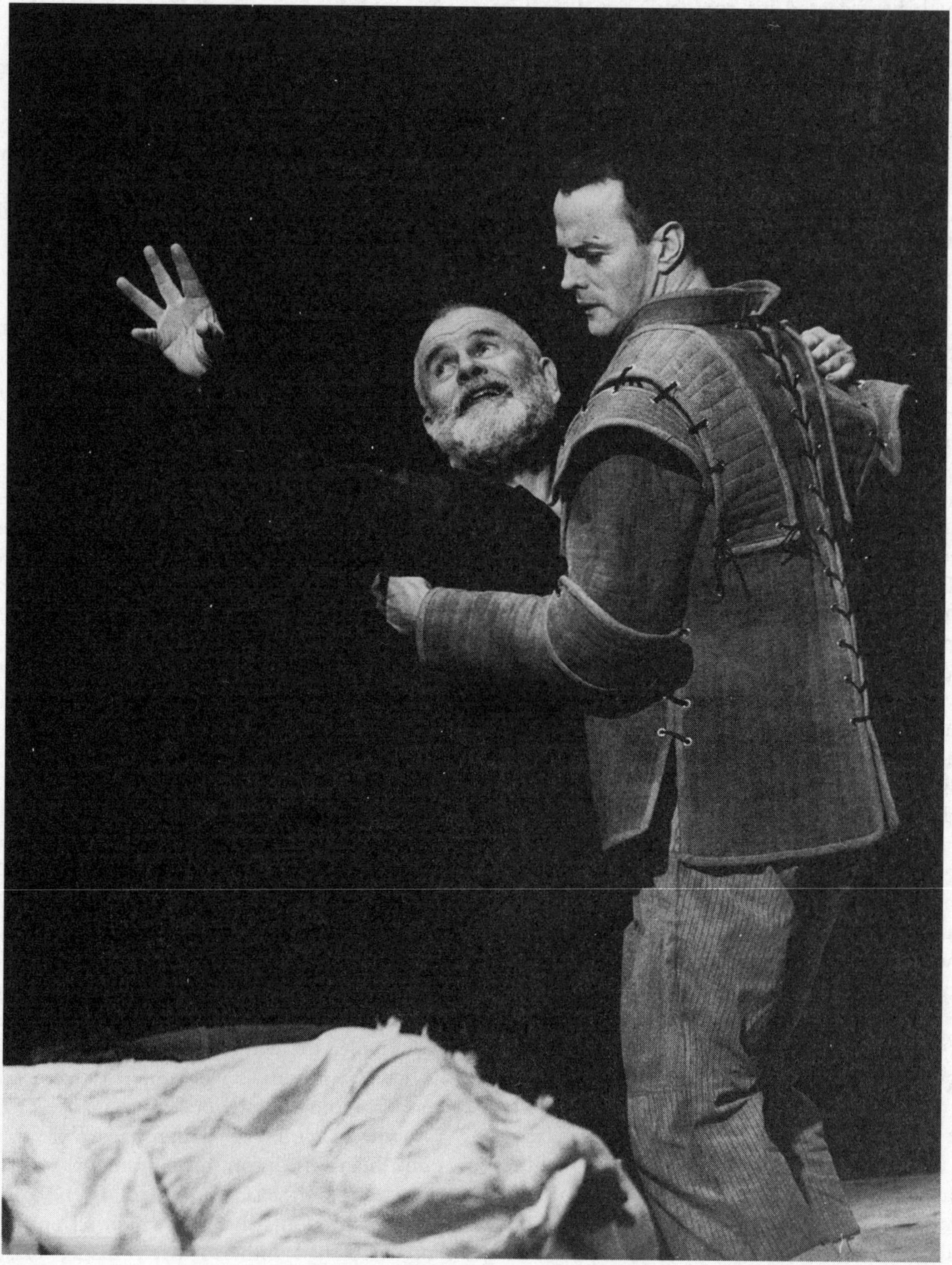

30 *King Lear*, directed by Richard Eyre for the Royal National Theatre. Ian Holm as Lear, Paul Rhys as Edgar. Act 3, Scene 6.

auditorium producing an answering gasp. The timelessness of the costumes, hints of Renaissance here, of the First World War there, and the tennis-court-like intimacy of the traverse playing space, presented the play's seething emotional relationships unrelentingly before the audience's examination.

There were many fine performances around Ian Holm's. Michael Bryant, white-bearded and clad, even to the pom-pom on his old felt hat, in what looked remarkably like a Father Christmas outfit in the wrong colour – a threadbare buffish grey – presented a Fool whose jokes had long since ceased to be funny but who couldn't help continuing to go through the routines, with his little soft-shoe shuffle to point the punch line and Lear the only audience old enough to remember that anybody ever thought these rhymes and tags amusing. In the hovel, near his end, he stumbled and stuttered over the last of them, too exhausted to remember his lines but still driven by that professional's compulsion to keep the show on the road. Bewildered and uncomprehending he just managed to find the strength to help Lear onto the litter and disappeared from the play – or almost so, for in the Dover Beach scene Lear appeared wearing that old hat with the pom-pom, and cracked up as he looked at it and spoke of our coming to 'this great stage of fools'. (The hat then became the inspiration for the idea of shoeing a troop of horses with felt.)

Timothy West's Gloucester had a rather Edwardian decency about him, a certain smugness as he admitted to fathering Edmund, an injured self-esteem when Lear sent him on errands, and a believable gullibility in his dealings with his sons. Paul Rhys gave to Edgar a wide-eyed innocence sufficient to provoke an 'aah', shared with the audience, from Edmund as he found his 'practices' so 'easy'. We had watched Edgar before the play began making observations through smoked glass of an eclipse of the moon (projected onto the end wall), and carefully making notes in his earnest, scholarly way. He ended the first half of the play holding the stage on the line 'Lurk, lurk'; and he concluded it too, a clear-eyed figure alone capable of contemplating a future. We never wholly lost sight of him as Poor Tom, his sense of pity, often manifested in a little smile that expressed shared pain and compassion for Lear and for Gloucester, movingly clear through all his pretences. He was an impressive figure by the end, the only person who could possibly have concluded the play (just as he had marked its beginning and centre), for David Lyon made Albany's journey from initial timidity to supreme command a comparatively short one, looking rather like an eighteenth-century clergyman and behaving with all the moral seriousness, and military hesitancy, one would expect from such a figure. David Burke's Kent was a finely energetic performance, the Geordie accent he adopted as Caius giving a splendid buoyancy to his long tirade of insults to Oswald, every one of them savoured, as though he was thinking 'just one more, and it'll be even more perfectly appropriate than the last, and after it I'll *hit* you'.

Finbar Lynch's Edmund really ought not to have taken in his father – or anyone else for that matter. The charm, and the twinkle, were elegant enough, but the brutal, ruthless drive were evident beneath the surface, the villainy transparent to all but the naive and myopic persons who share the family genes. Lynch had decided (not uninterestingly) to make clear his Edmund's definite preference for Goneril over Regan, his farewell kiss with her ('yours in the ranks of death') sizzling with sexual passion and commitment; even in his death throes he was struggling to clamber onto her body. His preference for Goneril was hardly surprising, given the pathological sexuality of Amanda Redman's platinum-blond Regan, whose refusal to offer a helping hand to her dying husband was one of the production's most chilling moments, her eyes burning for the power and sexual freedom that his death would give her. Barbara Flynn's Goneril, more intelligent in her destructiveness and more restrained in her sexuality (though still making her point obviously enough in a figure-revealing dress laced to below the waist), seemed the safer bet. To the role of Cordelia Anne-Marie Duff brought an impressive stillness of commitment in her love for her father but also a fine sense of determination and power as she returned to fight his cause. Her speech 'O dear father, / It is thy business that I go about', given with an echo effect as an oration to an invisible army, sounded like a 'mission statement'.

But for all that one admired the supporting performances, it is to Ian Holm's Lear that one's thoughts return and to the sense of latent, pent-up power that the performance suggested: the rage seething below the surface as he stood confronting Goneril, articulation strangled into little animal growls, the whip with which he had returned from hunting twitching in his hand, she (and we) terrified he would use it; the fury explosive, but just held in, as he was asked to regard his contemptible son-in-law as 'the fiery duke'; the tiny, balding little man cutting with ease through the sound effects on 'Blow wind'; and the huge energy and pride with which he made every centimetre count on 'Ay, every inch a king'. There was nothing sentimental about the awakening to Cordelia: a proud caution kept him apart from her until late in the interview, when, very tottery on his feet, he gave her a quick, nervous little hug on 'old and foolish' and there was a faint answering smile from her that evinced the profoundest understanding and forgiveness. That hug was repeated in their next scene as they were brought in from the battle with wrists bound and he threw his arms, thus tied together, over her head on 'he that parts us'. Such small illuminating details were there throughout: in the final moments, struggling to deal with Kent's revelations, he pulled aside the cloth that covered Regan's face on that trolley of corpses and said, with a little dismissive wave of the hand, 'this is a dull sight'. Of such small matters major performances are constructed and in a production of great intensity and directness this was undoubtedly a major performance.

31 *Othello*, directed by Sam Mendes for the Royal National Theatre and the Strasburg Festival. Simon Russell Beale as Iago. Act 2, Scene 1: 'That Cassio loves her, I do well believe it.'

I stay at the Royal National Theatre and end this essay as I began it, with a Shakespearian love story transposed by its director to the 1930s. Sam Mendes's production of *Othello* at the Cottesloe (must all the National Theatre's Shakespeare be in the studio space that makes tickets so difficult to come by?) was an admirably unpretentious piece of work, put together with profound intelligence and a fine sensitivity to the rhythms of the play. Anthony Ward's simple set (using the Cottesloe in its square configuration) presented a tiled central square with a walkway round it and, supported on wooden stilts, a slatted upper level. This verandah space seemed to me to owe much to the last studio *Othello*, Trevor Nunn's for the RSC in 1989, not just in the general suggestion of a colonial world, but also in many of its details: the sound of cicadas, the cane furniture, the jug of 'real' lemonade on Desdemona's table, the sense of a gentleman's club about the Venetian senate – cigars, brandy, old oak desks, and Desdemona sending something of an electric shock through them all when she arrived in a close-fitting crimson satin evening dress. But the most telling similarity was in the point of taking the break: in the middle of 3.3, on 'I am very sorry that you are not well', the handkerchief having just fallen to the floor, where it would remain, ominously, through the interval.

For the opening episode in Venice military uniforms were navy blue, but for the Senate scene Othello, like his wife, was in evening dress (the event at the Sagittary had clearly been an elegant one), but with his black tie unlaced. His failure to retie it before meeting Clifford Rose's dignified and politically astute Duke suggested either immense familiarity with his employers or a foolish assumption of it. In a production so precise and sensitive in its details it seemed to me a mistake; there weren't many. In Cyprus the men all wore pale khaki-drill uniforms, with Claire Skinner's slender and delicate Desdemona in a long soft turquoise dress, barefooted for the scenes on her verandah, her fair hair worn bobbed. Maureen Beattie's Emilia was distinctly more frumpish, her hair rolled at the back, her buttoned cotton-print dress of chain-store origins, and her Scottish vowels expressing pithy common sense in every syllable.

The production created a vivid sense of an occupying garrison for whom internal disturbances such as Cassio's drunken brawl represent a desperate danger. The proclamation (2.2) was presented as a military parade, junior officers lined up to hear the CO's orders and saluting before marching off to put them into operation. The drinking party (played to the sound of a rainstorm outside that increased the sense of claustrophobia) beautifully captured a mess-room world, crates of drink rattling in, a sentimental mood for 'King Stephen' (exquisitely sung by Simon Russell Beale) and, moved to follow it, a rowdy chorus for 'Let the canakin clink', the 'canakin' turning out to be the card in a card-game that means you have to drink off a glassful of liquor if you are dealt it – and Iago made sure that Cassio nearly always was. The fight that followed was fast and savage and the entry of David Harewood's physically impressive Othello a stunning moment as, with enormous authority, he plucked Cassio and Montano apart. Left alone after it, Iago picked up the playing cards as he was ruminating his next move and took out a Queen of Hearts for Desdemona, a Jack of Hearts for Cassio, and (wittily apt racist choice) an Ace of Spades for Othello. His plans thus progressed, he put the three cards mockingly, possessively, into his breast pocket.

This was a production dominated, more so than usual, by its Iago. Simon Russell Beale was on impressive form, his weight seeming to increase his threat, the ugly roll of fat on the back of his neck, accentuated by the tight-collared uniform from which it bulged, the near-shaven head, and the podgy face, all adding to the sense of repellent menace. His diction had a searching clarity about it, the words tightly measured, every phrase distinctly presented, but never in a way that drew attention to itself or slowed down the proceedings. In the scene of the arrival in Cyprus he read the little rhyming saws from a book fished out of his suitcase until he came to the last – 'She that was ever fair' – which he invented on the spot while gazing at Desdemona as she sat in her travelling slacks, her feet up on his knee, having to stop himself deliberately with the ending in 'small beer'; it gave his remark a few minutes later in his soliloquy ('Now I do love her too') an interesting resonance. There was an extraordinary tenderness about the comforting embrace he gave her later, after she had been 'bewhored', and from which he recovered his equilibrium only after retiring upstage for a little convulsion of sexual frustration.

Not that Russell Beale used this relationship to 'explain' Iago. His hatred for Othello stood out with stinging energy in the opening conversation with Roderigo and at the end of the Senate scene the ferocity of his loathing caused him to fling a file across the room on 'I hate the Moor.' But he straightened his tunic, picked the file up again, and sat down to plan, for planning was something he clearly enjoyed a lot – 'How, how?'; then, the idea 'engendered', he settled back to read the newspaper and listen to the Savoy Orpheans on the wireless. As he brought Othello to the fit from which he would soon kick him (reasonably gently) back into consciousness, he reproduced his every movement, repeating the crucial words into his ear. Then, with Othello unconscious on the floor, the shadows from the ceiling fan passing rhythmically across his twitching body, he laughed – a brilliant, chilling, contemptuous laugh of satisfaction, which turned into an extraordinary retch, as though the boundaries of destruction and pain that he was treading had made him sick with excitement and fear. And some of that pain was certainly his own, for behind all the loathing, all the bile, all the ruthlessly calculated destructiveness, there was the pain of utter emptiness, of a man emotionally crippled. At the end his defiant gaze across the bed and into the audience was calm, unhistrionic, remorseless. This was a very fine performance, its intensity and concentration unremitting.

David Harewood's Othello was slightly less assured. Apart from a hair-cut so obviously *not* of the 1930s that one could not understand how it had slipped by the director's precise eye for detail, he looked splendid – tall, powerful, athletic, graceful – and spoke with an impetuous energy that was never unjust to the meaning or, indeed, the nuances, of Shakespeare's lines: there was a nice sense, for example, of affectionate amusement in his recollections of Desdemona's response to his military narratives. To the sinuousness and grace of Othello's language, however, to its hypnotic patterns of sound, he was less fully responsive; some of his pauses seemed misplaced and some of his rhythms a little too staccato; and in the two great scenes of disintegration he seemed to me to start shouting too soon, which inevitably trapped him with nowhere to go except louder still. He was also, it has to be said, too young for the part, a figure in the prime of manhood with absolutely no need to worry yet about the 'vale of years'. (This had a curious knock-on effect in making Roderigo seem more unbelievably stupid than usual in crediting the blatant untruth of Iago's 'she must change for youth'.) There was about Harewood's Othello, however, a fine directness and simplicity that made him pitifully vulnerable to Iago. In the murder of his wife he was very fine, savouring each word of 'Put out the light' with terrible deliberation, and stifling her in a scene of frantic violence, she lashing out, kicking, screaming, he grunting rhythmically as he forced the pillow down, both of them arriving at stillness together: a terrible violation of the wedding sheets upon which the event occurred.

Beyond the central pair of Beale and Harewood there was a mass of excellent work in the supporting roles. Claire Skinner's pale and slender beauty brought a great vulnerability to the role of Desdemona, but with it also a kind of self-assured wilfulness as she pressed Cassio's suit in her convent-schoolgirl's voice and took care to present herself, 1930s-style, as 'modern woman': wearing clothes that were impeccably fashionable but just a touch assertively so, ostentatiously making barefoot appearances in the governor's residence, playing the willow song in a sophisticated blues version on her little gramophone. Maureen Beattie's Emilia provided a vivid foil for Desdemona. Astute and sad, and getting a little dowdy, she was pitifully in love with her husband, whom she kissed eagerly when giving him the handkerchief and received a cold-blooded push of rejection for her trouble – it was clear throughout how much he hated being touched. Her sudden understanding of the truth in the final scene made her give a passionate anger to the word *lie* so that it burned with meaning: 'You told a lie, an odious damnèd *lie*' welled up from the depths of her own straightforward honesty, and also, indeed, from the depths of the play, for upon that simple syllable its whole destructive engine is built. Colin Tierney gave us an elegant, handsome public-schoolboy of a Cassio, a little patronizing in agreeing to have a drink with members of the infra-dig Cyprus regiment, gazing at Desdemona in a way that made Iago's task easier, overwhelmed by the discoveries of the final scene and frightened by the authority he is to inherit. Crispin Letts's Roderigo was rather older and distinctly more disreputable than usual, reaching Cyprus as a stowaway in a trunk, a man eaten up by lust for Desdemona, gazing yearningly at the couch where Iago makes him imagine he will be spending the next night with her. So put out of mental focus was he by his obsession that he seemed genuinely capable of the self-delusion of ''Tis but a man gone' in agreeing to kill Cassio, and as Iago stabbed him – with an amazing 'tut, tut' on 'kill men i'th' dark?' – the sudden dawning realization on his face was absurd as well as pitiful. From Clifford Rose there was a nice authoritative double of the Duke and Lodovico, keeping his eye, in both roles, on the political goal of what is good for Venice; and from Trevor Peacock a touchingly sympathetic fuddy-duddy Brabantio, embarrassed (and embarrassing for everyone else in that war-room Senate) in exposing his emotions to his government colleagues, pushing his daughter away as she tried to embrace him before his exit, their last moment together.

Sam Mendes had brought together a fine company, adroitly cast, and created for them a world in which the play could be explored in a clear, relevant, unfussy, and genuinely illuminating way. The production was never self-indulgent (though often fresh and surprising), never clever for the sake of being so (though always incisively intelligent), and it never put the play at the service of a directorial concept (though it was throughout full of originality). It seems a good enough place to end an account of a year that has offered a remarkable range (in extent and in quality) of productions of Shakespeare.

# PROFESSIONAL SHAKESPEARE PRODUCTIONS IN THE BRITISH ISLES, JANUARY–DECEMBER 1996

*compiled by*

NIKY RATHBONE

Most of the productions listed here are by professional or semi-professional companies. Information is mainly taken from newspaper reviews held in the Birmingham Shakespeare Library.

## ALL'S WELL THAT ENDS WELL

Manchester Royal Exchange: September 1996
Director: Matthew Lloyd
Designer: Ashley Martin-Davies
Performed in the round, in the company's touring theatre tent, and set in the Second World War.

The Prince Theatre, the Prince of Orange pub, Greenwich, London: October 1996.
Director: Paul James

## ANTONY AND CLEOPATRA

Northern Broadsides, tour continues. See *Shakespeare Survey 50*

1157 Theatre Company at the Tabard, London: June 1996
Director: Alasdair Middleton
Warm baths taken on stage were used as a symbol of Egyptian degeneracy.

## AS YOU LIKE IT

The RSC at the Royal Shakespeare Theatre, Stratford: April 1996–
Director: Steven Pimlott
Designer: Ashley Martin-Davis
Music: Jason Carr
Rosalind: Niamh Cusack

The BAC, Lavender Hill, Battersea, London: June 1996
Director/Music: Peter Brewis
Designer: Caroline Grebbell

Open Hand Productions, the Oxford Shakespeare Festival: July 1996

The Northcott Theatre, Exeter, in Rougemont Gardens: July 1996
Director: John Durnin
Rosalind: Tanya Ronder
A semi-musical production, set in the 1920s.

Bold and Saucy Theatre Company with Open Hand Productions, played in Oxford college gardens: July 1996

Contraband Theatre Company, in Queen's Park, London: August 1996
An all-female cast, with the exception of Touchstone, played by a man in drag.

R. J. Williamson Productions, tour of northern England, with *Much Ado About Nothing*: August 1996–

Theatre Unbound, tour of open-air sites, with *Much Ado About Nothing*: July 1996–

## THE COMEDY OF ERRORS

The New Shakespeare Company at the Open Air Theatre, Regent's Park: May 1996–
Director: Ian Talbot
Designer: Claire Lyth

The RSC at The Other Place, Stratford and tour: June 1996–
Director: Tim Supple
Designer: Robert Innes Hopkins
The RSC/Natwest regional tour production for 1996/7.

Open Hand Productions at the Cambridge Shakespeare Festival: June 1996

## CORIOLANUS

West Yorkshire Playhouse, at the Mermaid Theatre, London: June 1996
Director Steven Berkoff. A revival of the 1995 production. See *Shakespeare Survey 50*.

Brave New World Theatre Company at Moray House Studio Theatre, Edinburgh Festival: August 1996
Director: Spencer Hinton
Performed by a cast of seven.

## HAMLET

Mappa Mundi, tour continued. See *Shakespeare Survey 50*

Traffic of the Stage, tour continued. See *Shakespeare Survey 50*

Lincoln Shakespeare Company: March 1996
Director: Karen Crow
Set in a collapsing east-European state.

The Factory, Sligo, Ireland: March 1996
Director: Niall Henry
Designer: Rebecca Jobson

The Soho Group, London: tour: May 1996
The play within a play was performed by oriental shadow puppets.

The Oxford Stage Company, tour: July 1996
Director: John Retallack
Designer: Matthew Wright
Music: Karl James
Hamlet: Ian Pepperall
The Ghost and Claudius were played by the same actor.

Open Hand Productions, Cambridge college gardens: July 1996

The Greenwich Theatre, London and limited tour: October 1996
Director: Philip Frank
Designer: Julian McGowan
Hamlet: Michael Maloney
Modern dress.

Glasgow Citizens: September 1996–
Director/Designer: Philip Prowse
Hamlet: Cal MacAninich

Theatre Babel, Glasgow, tour, with *Julius Caesar*. October 1996–
Revival of their 1995 production. See *Shakespeare Survey 50*.

Fecund Theatre, Bradford, tour: November 1996
Intended to appeal to a young audience. The production used imagery drawn from Christianity and video footage to signal major plot developments.

The Library Theatre, Manchester: November 1996
Director: Chris Honer
Designer: Nick Beadle
Hamlet: Stephen Mapes

Two-Way Mirror, the Springfield Theatre, London: November 1996

Director/Hamlet: Ricardo Pinto
Music: Michael Dresser

Kaboodle Productions, Liverpool at the Liverpool Everyman: November 1996
Director: Lee Beagley
Hamlet: Dominic McHale
The production opened in a modern classroom, the teacher assigning roles, to emphasize the play-acting theme of the play. Projected images of war formed the background.

Norwich Playhouse: November 1996
Director/Ghost: Julian Glover
Hamlet: Jamie Glover
Gertrude: Isla Blair

*Film version*

*Hamlet*
Castle Rock Entertainment USA release December 1996, UK release February 1997
Director/Hamlet: Kenneth Branagh
Claudius: Derek Jacobi
Gertrude: Julie Christie

*Adaptations*

*Hamlet*
Nathan Evans, performing solo, with puppets, at the Demarco Foundation, Edinburgh Festival, September 1996
An unhappy, lonely child of divorced parents acts the story of *Hamlet* to himself.

*I Hamlet*
The Rose Theatre Company, tour: October 1996
Three actors, male and female, performed the role using masks and puppets, and exploring issues of identity, gender, madness and death.

*Elsinore* by Robert Lepage
Nottingham Playhouse and the Royal National Theatre, London: November 1996
An almost solo performance by Lepage, transforming himself into all the major characters, and performing within a revolving orb. The intended opening at the Edinburgh Festival was cancelled due to technical problems.

*Ophelia* by Bryony Lavery
Stantonbury Campus and Clollae Theatre Companies, Milton Keynes: December 1996
Director: Rosemary Hill
The play was set in Elsinore, but incorporated female characters from other Shakespeare plays in an exploration of feminine emotions. An amateur production, included for its subject-matter.

*Hamlet*
A new ballet by the Royal Danish Ballet, Copenhagen. Extracts performed at the Harrogate Festival: September 1996
Choreographer: Peter Schaufuss
Designer: Steven Scott
Music: Traditional classical music by Riued Langgaard (1893–1952) was used, together with new rock music by the Black Sun rock group for Hamlet's soliloquies. First staged at Elsinore.

*Qui Est Là?*
Centre International de Créations Théâtricales, Bouffes du Nord, Paris: December 1995–March 1996
Director: Peter Brook
Fragments of *Hamlet* constantly modified by the voices of great directors of the past: Meyerhold, Artaud, Craig, the Noh master Zeami. Although this production has not yet been seen in the British Isles it is included for its interest as a production by one of the most innovative directors of Shakespeare.

## HENRY IV PART 1

Albion Touring Theatre Company, tour, with *A Midsummer Night's Dream*: August 1996–

## HENRY IV PARTS 1 AND 2

The English Touring Theatre Company, tour: October 1996–
King Henry: Timothy West
Prince Hal: Samuel West

## HENRY VIII

The Royal Shakespeare Company at the Swan Theatre, Stratford: November 1996–
Director: Gregory Doran
Designer: Robert Jones
King Henry: Paul Jesson
Queen Katherine: Jane Lapotaire

## JULIUS CAESAR

Off the Shelf Theatre, Coram's Fields, London: July 1996
An open-air production.

Theatre Babel, Glasgow, tour of Scotland, with *Hamlet*: September: 1996–

## KING JOHN

Tabard Theatre, Chiswick: March 1996
Director: Kate Bone
Designer: Rachel Jarvis
King John: Sandra Evans (*sic*)

## KING LEAR

The Stratford Theatre Company at the Waterside Theatre, Stratford: April 1996
Director: Brian Larcher
Lear: Emmanuel Toutougi
A mixed amateur and professional cast. The production was played in the round.

Ludlow Castle: June 1996
Director: Val May
Lear: Barrie Ingham
A modern setting.

Traffic of the Stage, tour, with *Twelfth Night*: September 1996
Director: Harry Meacher
A Lear driven to dotage by shame and defeat at the hands of his two beautiful daughters.

Southward Playhouse, London Fringe: September 1996
Director: Jack Shepherd
Lear: Oliver Cotton
A small-scale production in a modern setting with a minimal set.

The Naked Pony, tour of south-east England, France, Poland and Macedonia: September 1996–
Director: Hadrian Garrard
Lear: David Arbus

*Adaptations*

*Edmund son of Gloucester*, written and directed by Christ Lambert
Exiled Theatre Company at the Brewery Arts Centre, Cirencester: May 1996
The cast included Edmund, Gloucester and Lear and the action covered the first eighteen years of Edmund's life, immediately preceding the action of *King Lear*.

*Cordelia* by Marc van der Velden
Theatre La Blance, Denmark, at the Young Vic, London as part of the LIFT Festival: June 1996
A play for children about caring for old people. The old Fool has died and Cordelia, disguised, takes on his role.

*King Lear*
Mardjanishvili State Academic Drama Theatre of Tbilisi, Georgia at the Edinburgh Festival: August 1996
Director: David Doiashvili
A free adaptation in which Regan and Goneril both have a child by Edmund.

*(King) Lear*
Parthenos Productions, the Actors Centre, Tristan Bates Theatre, Covent Garden, London: August 1996–
Director: J. E. Damassa
Lear: Sue Rheam
A female Lear, cross-dressing in a black leotard, frock coat and drop earrings.

*King Lear, the Panto*
Oddsocks Theatre Company as the Pembroke Players, supposedly a group of strolling Elizabethan players, tour: November 1996–

## MACBETH

The English Touring Company. Continuation of their 1995 tour. See *Shakespeare Survey 50*.

The Abbey Theatre, Dublin: February 1996
Director: Patrick Mason
Designer: Joe Vanek
Macbeth: Des McAleer

The New Victoria Theatre, Stoke on Trent: February 1996–
Director: Rob Swain
Macbeth: Edward York
A fast, high-tech, modern-dress production,

Actions and Words, tour of Kent: March 1996
Director: David Beston
Set in the eleventh century, and particularly directed at school students.

Theatr Iolo, Cardiff, tour of Welsh castles and schools: March 1996–
Performed in Welsh.

Fenland Theatre Company, Wisbech: March 1996
Director: Michael Burrell
A mixed amateur and professional production.

Illyria Theatre Company, tour: May 1996–
Director: Oliver Gray
Macbeth: Marc Danbury

The Brewery Arts Centre, Kendal: May 1996
Director: Anne Pierson
Macbeth: Hugo Chandor

The Royal Shakespeare Company at the Royal Shakespeare Theatre, Stratford: May 1996–
Director: Tim Albery
Designer: Stewart Laing
Macbeth: Roger Allam

Box Hedge Theatre Company, tour of open-air sites: June 1996–

Stray Theatre Company, tour: July 1996–
Director: David Lightbody
Music: Liam Clancy
A new West Highland professional theatre company. The young and sexy witches were transformed into the three murderers.

The Gatehouse Theatre Company at Stafford Castle: July 1996
Director: Julia Stafford Northcote
Macbeth: Robert Beck
Lady Macbeth: Ruala Lenska
The witches were played by men in simple black costumes.

Free Stage Theatre Company, Minsk, Belorussia at Ravenscraig Castle, Kirkcaldy, Scotland: August 1996
Producer: Richard Demarco
Director: Valery Arnisenko
Macbeth: Oleg Garbouz
The witches appeared as a chorus on the battlements, the part of Duncan was cut. The second August production by Demarco at Ravenscraig, which he sees as an extension of the Edinburgh Festival.

Teatr Ludowy-Krakow, Poland, at the Edinburgh Festival: August 1996
Director: Jerzy Stuhr

Motivated by the close, loving relationship between Macbeth and his wife.

Roar Material at the Yard, Hulme, Manchester: October 1996
Directors: Camden McDonald, who also played Macbeth; Phil Dennison, who also played Duncan.
Set in urban wasteland, with the witches as punkettes, Hecate in drag, and the cast costumed in combat fatigues. The Yard is a new functional performance space of bare concrete surfaces.

Chester Gateway: October 1996
Director: Jeremy Raison
Designer: Kit Surrey
Macbeth: Sam Graham
A black box set with enormous doors and a large circle on the floor as a focal point. The actors were Scottish and Scots accents were used throughout.

Mappa Mundi and the Sherman Theatre, Cardiff, tour: October 1996–
Director: Lloyd Llewellyn-Jones
Set in 1930s Nazi Germany.

York Theatre Royal, October 1996
Director: John Doyle
Designer: Mark Bailey
All the actors acted as a chorus of witches, seductive and attractive. Duncan was played by a woman to indicate his/her gentle character. The set was a plain black box.

The Duke of Cambridge, London fringe: December 1996
Director: Alistair Barrie
Macbeth: Catherine Bready
An all-female cast.

*Television version*

*Macbeth*
Director: Michael Bogdanov
Acted by residents of the Ladywood council estate, Birmingham, and filmed for transmission as part of the BBC2 Performance season, autumn 1996.

*Adaptations*

*Lady Macbeth* by Jean Binnie
Millstream Theatre Company, tour: February 1996–
A new play in which Lady Macbeth seduces Macduff.

*The Dark: A Macbeth* by Nicholas Jonne
Theaterstorm at Ealing Green Arts Centre, London Fringe: May 1996
A multi-lingual chorus torment a caged Macbeth by recalling the events of the play.

*The Porter's Daughter* by Peter Lily
Northumberland Touring Theatre Company: June 1996

*Lady Macbeth* and *Visions of Ophelia*
Aki Isoda, one woman show at Shakespeare's Globe, London: July 1996
First performed in Japan, 1990.

*Macbeth*
Gilded Balloon, played in the open around the Royal Mile, Edinburgh Festival: August 1996
A modernized text played in a gangland, drug wars setting by a mixed amateur and professional cast.

*Macbeth*
The Smallest Theatre in the World, Edinburgh Festival and tour: August 1996
A cast of one playing to an audience of one in his sidecar theatre. Marcel Steiner has been touring festivals worldwide for twenty-five years.

## MEASURE FOR MEASURE

Bold and Saucy Theatre Company and Open

Hand Theatre Company, performing in Oxford college gardens for the Oxford Shakespeare Festival: July 1996

## THE MERCHANT OF VENICE

The Lyric Theatre, Belfast: January 1996
Director: David Grant
Designer: Stuart Marshall
Shylock: Richard Croxford
Set in America, reflecting anti-semitism in the 1920s, with a rather young Shylock.

The Arches Theatre, Glasgow: February 1996
Director: Andy Arnold
Designer: Graham Hunter
Shylock: Michael Derrington
Set in the nineteen-thirties.

The Worcester Theatre Company at the Swan Theatre, Worcester: February 1996
Director: Jenny Stephens
Designer: James Merrifield
A modern dress production, set in a marble hall reminiscent of Ruskin's *Stones of Venice*.

Lafayette Workshop, New York at the St Bride's Centre, Glasgow: August 1996
Set in Italy between the wars.

Salisbury Playhouse: October 1996
Director: Jonathan Church
Designer: Ruari Murchison
Set in the nineteenth century, with Belmont seen as the traditional enchanted place.

The Royal Lyceum, Edinburgh: November 1996
Director: Kenny Ireland
Designer: Sarah Williamson
Shylock: Tom McGovern
A young, barely middle-aged Shylock. The set was composed of Impressionistic gauzes, reminiscent of Turner watercolours.

The Crucible, Sheffield: November 1996
Director: Deborah Paige
Shylock: David de Keys
A bleak production with Shylock shown as an old man, always alone in his scenes with the Christians, and Portia portrayed as a worldly woman.

*Television production*

Channel Four Schools Service: February 1996
Director: Alan Horrox
Shylock: Bob Peck
Portia: Hayden Gwen

## THE MERRY WIVES OF WINDSOR

Spotlight Theatre Company: Free Shakespeare in the Park, Temple Newsam, Leeds: June 1996
Producer: Pam Jones

Advena, Wimbledon Studio Theatre and tour: October 1996
Director: Justin Rhodes
The production used a multi-media presentation with a large screen backdrop onto which video images were projected.

## A MIDSUMMER NIGHT'S DREAM

The Royal Shakespeare Company, UK and international tour continues.
See *Shakespeare Survey 49*.

Leicester Haymarket: February 1996
Director: Matthew Lloyd
Designer: Ashley Martin-Davis
Music: Jim Sutherland

Open Hand Productions at the Cambridge Shakespeare Festival, open-air production in the college gardens: June 1996

Albion Theatre Company (Norwich), tour of National Trust open-air sites in south-east England with *Henry IV Part I*: July 1996
Set in the Victorian period.

The Duke's Theatre, Lancaster, promenade production in Williamson Park: July–August 1996
Director: Ian Forrest
Designer: Liz Ascroft
Set in Edwardian England.

Hopeful Monsters at the Chelsea Centre Theatre: August 1996
Director: Lucy Gordon-Clark
Music: James Munro
A modern-dress production using madrigals adapted to electronic sound.

Shakespeare in the Park, The Grassy Knoll, Battersea: August 1996
Director: Alan Paterson
Designer: Bruce French
A knockabout production with the lovers and Puck doubling as fairies and mechanicals.

The Ninagawa Company at the Mermaid Theatre, London: September 1996
Director: Yukio Ninagawa
Designer: Tsukasa Nakagoshi
Music: Ryudo Uzaki
First UK production 1995. See *Shakespeare Survey 50*.

Griffin Theatre Company. Drayton Court Theatre, London Fringe: October 1996
Director: Fraser Grant

Liverpool Playhouse: October 1996
Director: Richard Williams
Designer: David Collis
Music: Joanna MacGregor
A modern-dress production with the wood created by ladders descending from the flies.

Advena at Wimbledon Studio Theatre: November 1996

The Almeida Theatre, London: November 1996–
Director: Jonathan Miller
Designers: The Quay Brothers
Oberon: Norman Rodway
Titania: Angela Thorne
Set in a decayed stately home in the 1930s where the down-at-heel upper-class fairy aristocracy were waited on by Puck, a butler out of *Remains of the Day*.

*Adaptations*

*Bottom's Dream*
An adaptation for children by Edward Bond.
Classworks Theatre, Cambridge, tour: March 1996
Director: Claudette Bryanston
Designer: Lisa Lillywhite
Music: Ned Bennett

*A Midsummer Night's Dream*
Maison Bertaux, tour: April 1996
Director: Metin Marlow
Designer: Zerling Hughes
An adaptation which fragmented the play. Staccato monologues were delivered against a background of changing projected colours.

## MUCH ADO ABOUT NOTHING

Bristol Old Vic: February 1996
Director: Andy Hay
Designer: Mick Bearwish
Beatrice: Amanda Harris
Benedick: Duncan Bell
Set in 1940s Italy.

Forest Forge, Ringwood, tour: March 1996
Director: Kevin Shaw
Designer: David Haworth
Set in the twenties, on a private cruise yacht.

Heartbreak Productions, open-air production, touring English heritage properties: June 1996–
Director: James Bolam

The Anglo-Irish Company at Drayton Court Theatre, Ealing: June 1996
Director: Mark Fitzgerald
A traditional late sixteenth-century setting.

Robert J. Williamson's company, second Leeds Shakespeare Festival and tour of northern England with *As You Like It*: July 1996–
Director/Benedict: Robert Williamson
Set in the nineteen-twenties.

Bold and Saucy Theatre Company with Open Hand Productions, the Oxford Shakespeare Festival, Oxford college gardens: July 1996

Illyria Theatre Company, tour: July 1996–

Open Hand Productions, Cambridge college gardens: July 1996

Theatre Unbound, tour of open-air sites, with *As You Like It*. July 1996

The RSC at the Royal Shakespeare Theatre, Stratford: November 1996
Director: Michael Boyd
Designer: Tom Piper
Beatrice: Siobhan Redmond
Benedick: Alex Jennings

## OTHELLO

Factotum Theatre Company, Haywards Heath, Sussex, tour: March 1996–
Director: Wilia Gilbert
Set in the nineteenth century. The final scene of the play was played as a prelude to the action.

*Film version*

*Othello*
Castle Rock Entertainment, UK release 1996
Producer: Oliver Parker
Othello: Laurence Fishburne
Iago: Kenneth Branagh
Desdemona: Irene Jacob
The text was severely cut, and additional scenes such as Desdemona's wedding night added.

## PERICLES

*Adaptation*

*The Legend of Pericles*
Greenbelt Theatre Productions tour: September 1996
Director: James Roose-Evans
Designer: Bruno Santini
The production stressed the redemptive ending of the play.

## RICHARD II

The Royal Shakespeare Company, European tour
See *Shakespeare Survey 50*.

## RICHARD III

Open Hand Productions in Cambridge college gardens, Cambridge Shakespeare Festival: July 1996

*Adaptation*

*Richard III*
Oddsocks as the Pembroke Players, tour: July 1996
A humorous adaptation.

*Film versions*

*Looking for Richard*. USA release 1996, UK release: January 1997
Director/Richard: Al Pacino
A freewheeling analysis of the play intercutting footage of selected scenes with commentary from Al Pacino and other actors, scholars and critics.

*Richard III*
Bayly/Pare Productions, Mayfair Entertainment and United Artists: 1996
Producer: Richard Loncraine
Director: Richard Eyre
Richard: Ian McKellen
Based on the 1990 Royal National Theatre production, set in the 1930s.

*Richard III*
Director: James Keane
Richard: Frederick Warde
This item is included for interest. A very rare print of this 1913 film was discovered in Los Angeles and screened there in October 1996, with other screenings planned.
This is advertised as the oldest complete US feature film, pre-dating *Birth of a Nation*. It is 55 minutes long and lavishly filmed with a large cast of extras. Frederick Warde, a British actor, born 1872, also starred in the film *King Lear*, 1916.

## ROMEO AND JULIET

Means and Ends Company at the New End Theatre, London: January 1996
Director: Simon Parry
Designer: Matt Edwards
Video footage was used in an attempt to link this traditional production with contemporary events in Europe.

West 28th Street Theatre Company at the Ashcroft Theatre, Croydon: March 1996
Director: Mark Helyar
Played in modern dress, with schools workshops.

Norwich Playhouse: March 1996–
Directors: Henry Burke and Zoe Seaton
Designer: Spencer Chapman

The Tabard Theatre, London: April 1996
Director: Kate Bone
Designer: Steve Dennis

Theatre Set Up, tour of open-air sites: July 1996
Director: Wendy McPhee

Creation Theatre Company, Magdalen College, Oxford: August 1996
Director: Sebastian Doggart
Juliet: Nina Bowden
In an otherwise professional production, the actress playing Juliet was a thirteen-year-old, the age of Juliet in the play.

Northern Broadsides, tour with *Antony and Cleopatra*: autumn 1996
Director: Barrie Rutter
Nurse: Ishia Bennison
A modern-dress production. The actors all remained on stage acting as Chorus, and as observers of the action.

The New Victoria Theatre, Stoke on Trent: October 1996
Director: Rob Swain
A modern-dress production.

*Adaptations*

*Romeo and Juliet*
Shakespeare in Education schools tour: February 1996–
Director: Andrew Jarvis
The production stressed the materialism of the society in which the play is set.

*Romeo and Juliet*
The Custard Factory, Birmingham, tour: February 1996–

*Romeo and Juliet*
Grupo Gulpan, Brazil, in Battersea Park, London: July 1996
A circus theatre group mainly performing on stilts.

*Romeo and Juliet*
Oddsocks tour: September 1996
The Bard's best bits.

*Romeo and Juliet*

*Film version*

*Tromeo and Juliet*
The Troma Company, USA 1996
The text was totally re-written for the present day, and set among punks in downtown Manhattan

## THE TAMING OF THE SHREW

The Eye Theatre, Eye, and tour of open-air sites: July 1996
Director: Tom Scott
Set in the 1930s, and including the Christopher Sly prologue and epilogue.

Bold and Saucy Theatre Company, the Oxford Shakespeare Festival, Oxford college gardens: July 1996

Open Hand Theatre Company, Cambridge Shakespeare Festival, Cambridge college gardens: July 1996

Cannizaro Park, Wimbledon, open-air production: August 1996
Director: Jenny Lee
A professional director with a mixed amateur and professional cast.

## THE TEMPEST

Strathclyde Theatre Group: February 1996
Director: Kate Robinson
Slides projected onto a white linen curtain provided the island scenery. When Caliban appeared he was symbolically represented on slide as a toad.

The Seagull Theatre, Lowestoft: May 1996
Director: Rory Kesey
Music: Paul Hobbs
The parts of Ariel, Gonzalo, Sebastian and Trinculo were played by women.

Hatrick Theatre Company, the Richardson Studio, the Everyman Theatre, Cheltenham: June 1996

Regent's Park Open Air Theatre, London: June 1996
Director: Patrick Garland
Prospero: Denis Quilley
Set in the 1820s.

The Soho Group, London, tour: July 1996
Director: Luke Dixon

Trinity Arts Theatre Company, Kent tour of open-air venues: July 1996

Contact Theatre Company, Manchester, Oldham Coliseum and tour: September 1996
Director: Benjamin Twist
Designer: Neil Warmington
Music: Richard Taylor

Shared Experience at the Wolsey Theatre, Ipswich and tour: October 1996–
Director: Nancy Meckler
Prospero: Michael Cashman

*Adaptations*

Cherub Company, London at the Casson Studio Theatre, Leatherhead and tour: September 1996
An adaptation using masks, mime, puppetry and music.

## TROILUS AND CRESSIDA

The RSC at the Royal Shakespeare Theatre, Stratford: July 1996–
Director: Ian Judge
Designer: John Gunter
Music: Ian Kellan
Troilus: Joseph Fiennes
Cressida: Victoria Hamilton
Pandarus: Clive Francis

## TWELFTH NIGHT

Oxford Stage Company, tour continues. See *Shakespeare Survey 50*.

KDC Productions, London Fringe: January 1996
Director: David Cheetham
Set in the 1970s, with Orsino played as a rock and roll millionaire.

The RSC at the Royal Shakespeare Theatre, Stratford, UK tour and Vienna: March 1996–
The 1994 production revived with a new cast.
Director: Ian Judge
Designer: John Gunter
Malvolio: Edward Petherbridge
See *Shakespeare Survey 49*.

Imaginary Forces and Clear Day, tour: April 1996–
Designer: Michael Thomas
Illyria was located in the Balkans, and the production used Georgian choral music. The production was first staged at the Bridewell Theatre, London in 1995, and has been re-staged for a fourteen-week UK tour.

Wales Actors Company, tour of Welsh open-air sites: May 1996–
Director/Orsino: Paul Garnault

Bold and Saucy Theatre Company with Open Hand Productions in Oxford college gardens for the Oxford Shakespeare Festival: July 1996
Director: Sarah Davey

Pentacle Theatre Company, Shakespeare in the Park, The Grassy Knoll, Battersea: August 1996
Director: Philip Ayckbourn

Traffic of the Stage, tour with *King Lear*: September 1996–
Set in the Regency period.
Director: James Reynard

Action and Words Theatre Company, London, tour with schools workshops: November 1996
Director: David Beaton
Set in the 1970s.

*Film version*

*Twelfth Night*
Renaissance Films 1996
Director: Trevor Nunn
Music: Shaun Davey
Viola: Imogen Stubbs
Olivia: Helena Bonham-Carter

*Adaptations*

*Twelfth Night Fever*
The Key Theatre, Peterborough: September 1996
Adapted and directed as a rock musical by Derek Killeen and Michael Cross
Music: Carlton Edwards
An amateur cast with professional theatre back-up in the third rock musical Shakespeare adaptation by this team.

*Twelfth Night*
Adapted and abridged for schools by Andy Rashleigh
Unicorn Arts Theatre Company, London: September 1996
Music: Neil Brand
A rock musical for children. Feste as the DJ of Radio Illyria used songs to explain the plot.

## THE TWO GENTLEMEN OF VERONA

Trestle Theatre Company, The Globe Theatre, London: August 1996
Director: Jack Shepherd
Music: Claire van Kampen

Designer: Susan Coates
Proteus: Mark Rylance
Valentine: Lennie James
Performed in modern dress, on a temporary stage. The official opening of the Globe was in 1997.

*Adaptation*

*Two Gentlemen of Soho* by Josh Lacey
The Warehouse Theatre, Croydon: April 1996
In 1599 Julia, disguised as a boy, sets off for London.

## THE WINTER'S TALE

Third Party Productions, British and foreign tour: January 1996–
Director: Anthony Matheson
Patrick Knox, as Time, acted as controller of the action.

Riding Lights Theatre Company, York; UK tour: May 1996–
Director: Paul Burbridge
Designer: Sean Cavanagh
A professional cast of six in a modern-dress production which developed the play's themes of forgiveness, reconciliation and resurrection.

The Lincoln Shakespeare Company: November 1996
Director: Simon Clark
Music: Laurie Bennett and Damien Waters
Artists and sculptors were invited to contribute artworks to create a post-apocalyptic setting for this production.

*Adaptation*

*The Winter's Tale*
The Orange Tree Theatre, Richmond, schools production, tour: June 1996

## ATTRIBUTED PLAYS

*The Birth of Merlin*
Theatre Babel at the Tramway, Glasgow: December 1996
A single rehearsed reading of the play.

## POEMS AND SONNETS

*The Rape of Lucrece*
Shakespeare's Globe, Southwark: November 1996
Stage readings of five versions of the story.

*Venus and Adonis*, adapted by Michael Craven
Theatreworks at the Players Theatre, Dublin: October 1996
Venus: Liz Schwartz
Mythic creatures acted as a chorus carrying the narrative forward.

## MISCELLANEOUS

*Contested Will* by Olly Figg
Etcetera Theatre, Camden, London: January 1996
A play about William Ireland's Shakespeare forgeries.

*Dead White Males* by David Williamson
The Nuffield Theatre, Southampton: February 1996
A critical approach to post-structuralist, feminist and multicultural approaches to teaching Shakespeare in universities, seen through the eyes of a male lecturer and his relationships with the female students. The latest work by the Australian playwright.
With John Woodvine.

*The Herbal Bed* by Peter Whelan
The Royal Shakespeare Company at The Other Place, Stratford: May 1996
Director: Michael Attenborough
Designer: Robert Jones

Music: Adrian Johnston
The play concerns Shakespeare's daughter, Susanna and her marriage to John Hall the Stratford physician.

*Dear Mister Shakespeare*, written and performed by Allister Bain
Hackney Empire Studio: July 1996

*The Wars of the Roses*
Mouth to Mouth Theatre Company, tour of open-air sites in Suffolk: August 1996
Director: James Holloway
An adaptation of the history plays from *Henry IV* to *Richard III.*

*The Shakespeare Murders*
The Victorian Studios, Nottingham: October 1996
A one-day event, played as part of the Violence Trilogy. The production used contemporary surveillance systems to explore various scenes from Shakespeare.

*Shakespeare as I knew her*
Created and acted by Jane Lapotaire at Bristol Old Vic: November 1996
The piece purports to present incontrovertible proof that the Bard of Avon was Wilhemina Shakespeare.

*Shakespeare for my Father*
The Haymarket Theatre, London: November 1996
A one-woman show created and acted by Lynn Redgrave, concerning her relationship with her father Sir Michael Redgrave. The production made extensive use of allusions to Shakespeare, particularly the Lear–Cordelia relationship.

# THE YEAR'S CONTRIBUTIONS TO SHAKESPEARE STUDIES

## 1. CRITICAL STUDIES

*reviewed by* JANETTE DILLON

Structuring a critical review of this kind satisfactorily is an almost impossible task. Whatever system the reviewer adopts will necessarily fail to bring together work that may be usefully juxtaposed on one ground or another; and constraints of length, together with the sheer bulk of material to be covered, are such that the space for cross-reference is limited. This year I have decided to drop generic headings in order to be able to look at work that seems to group usefully around particular issues or critical approaches. This doesn't mean, however, that none of the discussion is grouped by dramatic genre. Much of it still is. I have simply tried to overcome the potential rigidity of any set of categories by allowing them to overlap.

The first category that seems to emerge out of the work I read this year turns out, with appropriate irony for the demands of a review of this kind, to be what might broadly be termed 'universality', and several important studies address this issue. Michael Bristol's *Big-time Shakespeare* has two related concerns: the commodification of 'Shakespeare' within the culture industry and the posthumous life of the artwork in 'great time'. The book falls into two parts, roughly divided between these two ways of approaching Shakespeare's work. As in his earlier work on carnival, Bristol again develops concepts explored by Bakhtin, though this is a work that draws on an eclectic and enriching range of approaches. Necessarily, Bristol confronts the problem of historical specificity versus universality, and he does so in a level tone, attempting to take criticism from both left and right with equal seriousness. His personal dilemma emerges frankly and clearly: while his interest in cultural and ideological appropriation signals a left-wing critical strategy, he feels compelled to admit to sharing a 'gut intuition that Shakespeare's plays really do represent a significant reserve of literary value'. Bristol addresses the difficulty of making such an admission within the contemporary academy by representing it ironically as a form of 'coming out'. His attempt to negotiate the problem of aesthetic value by way of Harold Bloom, David Hume and Alasdair MacIntyre is intellectually honest and usefully develops an understanding of reception in relation to the concepts of memory and gift exchange. What Bristol calls the 'pathos' of tradition is that 'gifts are not always benefits'; and part II aims to demonstrate that Shakespeare's plays display this pathos exceptionally clearly. Three plays are selected for discussion: *The Winter's Tale*, *Othello* and *Hamlet*. I find the chapter on *The Winter's Tale* problematic, since I fail to see how the discussion of what Bristol calls 'social time' in the play develops his general argument, but the chapters on *Othello* and *Hamlet* open up some of the difficulties of thinking through the question of the artwork's changing location in time.

Hugh Grady's book, *Shakespeare's Universal Wolf*, taking its title image from *Troilus and Cressida*, sets out to explore the coming together of 'autonomous rationality, power politics, the market [and] appetitive desire' in early modern writing. Like Bristol, Grady declares his approach as in reaction against New Historicism, and argues that the only way out of the critical impasse he identifies between 'aesthetic' readings on the one hand and 'political' readings on the other is what he calls 'presentism': direct confrontation of the text's meaning in the present, without losing sight of its historical situation. As his subtitle indicates, the broad concept he appropriates from twentieth-century theory in order to approach this phenomenon is 'reification', a term coined by Lukács to describe the imprisoning effect on individual subjects of the systems developed by a capitalist society; but Grady's application of the concept proceeds through avowed eclecticism, selecting from a range of theoretical writers, but especially Foucault, Althusser, Habermas and the Frankfurt School. One of his aims, he says, is 'to produce a work of Postmodernist criticism that acknowledges the "Modernism" contained within Postmodernism'. Applying twentieth-century theory to works of the early modern period, he argues, 'is not "anachronistic" if the social forms which recent theories have described in our time already existed, or were coming into existence, in a period before theoretical discourse provided clear concepts to describe them'; and Grady's analysis of the plays offers a persuasive demonstration that they were. *Troilus* is one of four plays selected for study. The sequence of chapters, Grady explains, is from negativity to optimism: chapters on *Troilus*, *Othello* and *King Lear* are followed by a chapter on the presentation of utopian alternatives to a reified social reality in *As You Like It*.

Like Bristol and Grady, Susan Bennett, in *Performing Nostalgia*, is concerned with what her subtitle calls 'Shifting Shakespeare and the Contemporary Past'. The book addresses important questions, and the introductory chapter situates the concept of nostalgia within a well-defined matrix of desire, lack, conservatism and 'authenticity'. Unfortunately, subsequent chapters do not maintain this clarity of definition. Chapter 2, for example, surveys seventeen Lears in the 1980s, including twelve productions of Shakespeare's *King Lear* and five reinventions of it; yet it seems to me that the need to restage Shakespeare's play demonstrates a quite different desire from the need to reinvent it thoroughly, and that to call both of these by the name of nostalgia is to collapse important distinctions. Similarly, the fascination for the 'Jacobean' explored via non-Shakespearian plays in chapter 3, which Bennett variously identifies as 'radical chic' or 'the return of repressed', is different again from either of the phenomena examined in chapter 2. Though Bennett's category of the 'not-Shakespeare' is a potentially useful one, the difference between other dramatists contemporary with Shakespeare and modern dramatists responding to Shakespeare is a crucial one that demands to be more explicitly theorized. Chapter 4, 'The Post-Colonial Body? Thinking through *The Tempest*', works its way irritatingly through 'the spectacular body', 'the colonial body', 'the Jacobean body', 'the sexual body', the anti-, post-, pre- and neo-colonial bodies, in a way that claims to think through the body in performance but actually reworks that all-too-familiar theoretical seam in which the use of 'the' is nearly always a give-away for a reified, academicized and entirely cerebral 'body'.

Universality is a central preoccupation of Jonathan Baldo's *The Unmasking of Drama*, which examines the act and meaning of representation in Shakespeare's tragedies. Baldo is interested in exposing an irony: that Shakespeare's plays, so long made to speak of 'universal' truths, are themselves engaged in a critique of generalizing, seen by Baldo as underpinning dominant ideas about representation in the early modern period. His focus is on representation as a political as well as an aesthetic practice, not just in the sense that all aesthetic representation is by definition political, but in the sense whereby a monarch or a member of parliament may (differently) 'represent' the people. Central to the argument is a tension between two kinds of generality, one levelling and the other confounding, the first tending to concentrate representative power in a way that reinforces hierarchy, the second tending to efface it. Baldo argues too for a chronological progression between the two, whereby an older 'particularist' culture (and I'm not sure I understand how this word functions as part of the argument) gives way to the 'universalist' culture of the nation-state. The arguments are complex and difficult to summarize, but the book is full of suggestive and provocative ways of thinking about representation, the theatre and Shakespeare's tragedies. Where I find Baldo's thesis least persuasive is in his attempts to tie in his exploration of ideas about representation and generalization to the particularity of the Renaissance theatre. I'm not convinced that the conflicts between different conceptions of political representation that Baldo investigates are neatly mirrored by conflicts within the sphere of theatrical representation, nor that all the aspects of theatrical representation that Baldo calls upon are specific to the Renaissance theatre alone. Much that Baldo argues is causally related looks to me like mere analogy. In the end, however, agreement or disagreement with the arguments of the book may be less important than being made to think about the issues it raises. Whatever conclusion the reader may come to, Baldo's book is worth reading because it raises important questions about different ways of understanding and practising representation in the Renaissance.

Allusions to 'universality' and 'bardolatry' are irritatingly scattered about Peter Hyland's *An Introduction to Shakespeare* without any discussion of the issues involved. Hyland makes reference to a number of critical issues without offering any account of or intervention in the arguments, and his references to theoretical perspectives sound flat and tired. The book is divided into three long chapters, 'Life and Times', 'Theatrical Professions' and 'The Plays'. Of these the most useful is the second, though not everything Hyland has to say there is reliable. He is reductive on the status of players and playing places, referring at different times to both as outlawed, a gross oversimplification. (A particularly wonderful misprint stands out in chapter 2, where Hyland writes of performance in the 'Great Wall' at Hampton Court.) There is a sense of obligatoriness about the whole 'Life and Times' chapter, while the chapter on plays is vitiated by the decision to cover all the plays one after the other in the last 67 pages, which results in some plays receiving just over a page of comment. Coverage at this level would seem to be self-defeating.

Bardolatry, like universality, receives fuller discussion from other critics. Robert Hume's essay, 'Before the Bard: "Shakespeare" in Early Eighteenth-Century London', offers a careful examination of when precisely bardolatry begins, arguing that the factors creating it came together rather suddenly in the 1730s. Before that, he argues, the rhetoric was in place, but 'hardly any of the practical respect'. The argument depends, however, on the view that adaptation is inherently incompatible with bardolatry, which seems to me exactly the kind of post hoc assumption Hume elsewhere exposes as unhelpful.

*Textual Practice* has been one arena where the debate between an idealist and a materialist criticism has been regularly played out, and three articles in the Spring 1997 issue take up the cudgels again. Though Edward Pechter's title, 'Making Love to our Employment; or, the Immateriality of Arguments about the Materiality of the Shakespearean Text', seems to announce an essay on text, as do his opening remarks on the revision hypothesis in regard to

*King Lear*, both his piece and the responses from de Grazia and Stallybrass and Holderness, Loughrey and Murphy are in fact about the principles underpinning different critical practices rather than about Shakespearian texts. Pechter attacks de Grazia and Stallybrass for revealing a persistent idealism beneath their promised materialism and concludes that there is no escape from responding to the text through the experience of desire; de Grazia notes the eccentricity of Pechter's 'sanguine acceptance' of the critic's entrapment; while Holderness, Loughrey and Murphy claim to find their pleasure in uncovering '*disorder* and *incoherence*' in literary texts rather than in seeking to impose orderliness. Outside the pages of *Textual Practice*, in an essay entitled 'No Spectre, No Sceptre', Stephen Buhler makes a strong case for the influence of Epicurean scepticism on the politics voiced in *Julius Caesar*, concluding that materialism is not something anachronistically brought to the study of Shakespeare by cultural materialist critics, but 'part of the age's political consciousness as well as its unconscious'.

One of the early landmark collections to contest a bardolatrous and universalizing approach to Shakespeare was *Alternative Shakespeares*, published in 1985. A successor appears this year, edited by Terence Hawkes. This second volume looks back over the decade or so since the publication of volume I to ask 'Alternative to what?' Volume I situated itself within a perceived 'crisis' in English studies and offered its contents as bringing critical pluralism to an area of study still 'largely untouched' by these developments within the academy. The dominant critical paradigm then was still the universalizing myth of a Shakespeare for all men [sic] and all time. Now, as Hawkes admits, pluralism is the order of the day. So what needs challenging? The answer is relatively unchanged, but more fully formulated. The essays still challenge that earlier, quasi-theological paradigm, which is clearly and succinctly anatomized in Hawkes's introduction, though the positions adopted by the challengers have become more nuanced and self-critical. Several of the contributors in volume II also wrote for volume I, and many of the same subjects continue to preoccupy them, notably gender, sexuality and race. Where Catherine Belsey's essay for volume I, 'Disrupting Sexual Difference', offered a then-new escape from the binarism of fixed gender categories and sexual orientations, this discourse has now become virtual orthodoxy, and several contributors, including Belsey, address and extend it in volume II. Race is also a more central topic for this volume than for the last, with essays by Ania Loomba and Dympna Callaghan moving beyond Barker and Hulme's exposure of colonialist strategies in *The Tempest* to more ad hoc analyses of racial particulars in specific contexts. Indeed John Drakakis, in his Afterword, identifies Loomba's essay, 'Shakespeare and Cultural Difference', as representative of the volume in its insistence on unravelling the multiple and different histories of colonization. The anxiety that underpins the overall enterprise, as Drakakis expresses it, is that, now that the marginal could be said to have become central, the liberal trap of accommodating all challenge within the parameters of an expressed openness to plurality opens up. This remains an unanswered and unexorcized anxiety.

James Cunningham's project in *Shakespeare's Tragedies and Modern Critical Theory* falls into precisely this liberal trap, culminating as it does in a plea for pluralism as illuminating and life-enhancing, and offering as the bland rationale for such a critique its ability to recognize 'that a reading from any one of the positions cited above will obscure some aspects of a text even while revealing others'. Yet this pluralism can turn nasty, becoming a stick to beat other critics for asserting, as literary critics will, 'that the selected evidence suggests one thing rather than another'. It's hard to see, then, what ground Cunningham stands on to make his assessments of other critics. He chastises numerous critics for seriously simplifying humanism by representing it as an undifferentiated monolith, but his own project is open to attack as similarly reductive. The attempt to define different theoretical approaches chapter by chapter, to summarize and criticize the arguments of individual landmark books and essays within the given field and to test those arguments against Shakespeare's tragedies wherever they address themselves to those plays, is unlikely to satisfy on all counts in such short space. The approach quickly becomes predictable: in every case Cunningham's account of the theoretical approach in view tends towards a 'but': x's book is thoughtful, well-informed, interesting, but. Except in the case of humanism, where the 'but' gives way to a brave new world of 'Humanism Redefined' – which seems to go by the name of pluralism.

John Hale's 'multiple approach' in *The Shakespeare of the Comedies* also exemplifies the liberal trap. While it is true that there may be value in emphasizing the difference between plays rather than attempting to impose generalizations that may falsify, the reader looks for some overall coherence of approach. As a brief survey of the chapter headings indicates, there is no comparability between the size and nature of topics treated ('Interpretation through Sources', 'Shakespeare's Art of Tonal Transition', 'The Art of Pleasing in the Mature Comedies' etc), and the book's various gestures in the direction of theorizing its own approaches are unconvincing. Hale's attempt to cover all the comedies and to condense his doctoral thesis into two chapters on the use of sources produces an unevenness of treatment verging on absurdity in places.

Not surprisingly perhaps, the recurrent concerns of *Alternative Shakespeares* are also more widespread topics of interest in work published elsewhere this year. The subject of boy-actors, regularly invoked in the Hawkes collection, is explored fully but concisely by Stephen Orgel in his *Impersonations*, the most searching and stimulating study of the boy actor and gender construction on stage to date. Orgel writes with exemplary clarity, wearing his learning lightly, asking the right questions, refusing easy answers and constantly questioning and revising his own proffered answers. His overarching question remains the one recorded in his earlier essay 'Nobody's Perfect, or Why Did the English Stage Take Boys for Women', but the examination is naturally much fuller and more satisfying here. His main point is that critics have far too easily taken the convention of boy-actors for granted without properly examining the cultural context that made it necessary in sixteenth-century England when it was not, according to his reading of the evidence, necessary either earlier in England or elsewhere in sixteenth-century Europe. Orgel, rather surprisingly, admits that the presence of women on the public stage in other European countries was a new phenomenon in the mid-sixteenth century, and at the same time attempts to argue that women did perform in the medieval English cycles (using the old chestnut of the Chester 'wives', and dismissing the argument that this record may refer to sponsorship or organization of the play rather than performance). The balance of evidence seems to me to point more clearly towards a shared European tradition of male performance up to the sixteenth century, and a postponement in England by about a century of the introduction of actresses to the stage. (One might equally reformulate the question to ask what made the advent of actresses possible at an earlier date in France, Spain and Italy.) Nevertheless, the shards of evidence that Orgel brings together for female performers in England before 1660 are important, as is the much more substantial evidence for women's participation in the guilds, which, Orgel rightly points out, has been virtually ignored by scholars. His study of boy-actors looks carefully at the context of cross-dressing off the stage as well as on, and the book brings dramatic and social contexts together creatively and productively, never losing sight of the differences between them. 'Even as the age defined its gender boundaries,' he argues, 'it also continually – one might almost say compulsively – produced figures who overstepped or violated them.' As Orgel shows, that overstepping was crucially a stimulus to desire as well as a source of anxiety. Sometimes this argument seems to become a cover for self-contradiction: Orgel, for example, wants to argue both that there may have been female performers on the public stage and that the cross-dressed boy-actor was 'indispensable' to Renaissance England. On the other hand, one of Orgel's great strengths is his willingness to allow space for contradictoriness where he finds it, and his occasionally direct confrontation of that contradictoriness (as at the opening of chapter 6) and repeated subjection of his own responses to further questioning can shed more light than many a single-track argument on the subject.

Tracey Sedinger's argument, in '"If sight and shape be true": The Epistemology of Cross-dressing on the London Stage', seems strained by comparison. She contests the assumption that the crossdresser is 'visible', arguing instead that she or he is 'not a visible object, but rather a structure enacting the failure of a dominant epistemology in which knowledge is equated with visibility'. The crossdresser stages, Sedinger argues, precisely a failure of representation, 'a moment of rupture, when knowledge and visibility are at odds'. In 'Queering the Shakespearean Family' Mario DiGangi, though he does not examine the boy actor, enters adjacent territory with an analysis of homoerotic anxiety in *As You Like It*. DiGangi lacks the subtlety and meticulousness of Valerie Traub, whose work in this area has been illuminating and influential. His argument centres on the play's use of the Ganymede myth, concluding that Rosalind plays Ganymede when she woos in order to ensure that she will not play Juno (the rejected wife) when she weds. It is a reading I find heavy-handed and overly schematic. Carolyn Brown's piece on *Measure for Measure* argues not only that the Duke's interest in Angelo is a homoerotic one, but that this supposed homoeroticism should be understood as a negative comment on King James's relations with male favourites. It seems hardly likely that the newly adopted King's Men would begin the new regime by offering such bold criticism of their patron. The writers of *Eastward Ho!* the following year were jailed for less.

The emphasis on boy-actors and crossdressing is part of a continuous interest in performance as well as gender (and of course in the performativity of gender). Many of the books reviewed elsewhere in this article share a broad emphasis on the plays in performance (Bennett, Collins and Singh, for example; even a collection of essays on *Venus and Adonis* devotes a special section to the poem in performance). Michael Cordner, however, asks a less familiar question in his 'Annotation and Performance in Shakespeare': how should this developing, performance-based scholarship be incorporated into critical editions of the plays? Cordner's conclusion, predictably, is that 'we still have some way to go' in making editions properly attentive to matters of staging; but the questions he raises are important ones that merit further discussion: what kind of attention to staging is legitimately incorporated in an edition? How can we be attentive without becoming dogmatic about matters of opinion?

In *New Theatre Quarterly*, academic presumption over matters of performance runs into furious opposition from theatre professionals. Two successive issues carry a bitter exchange on the ideology of voice training between Sarah Werner and Cicely Berry, Patsy Rodenburg and Kristin Linklater. Werner attacks the latter group for working with a naive politics that privileges the notion of 'freeing the voice' as a way of accessing a more innocent and primitive self, a focus which, Werner argues, limits the possibilities for feminist performance. Werner's essay demonstrates its own kind of naiveté, however, by using the written work of these voice teachers as if it could stand in for the practice itself. Predictably, this enrages Berry and her colleagues, who feel driven to defend themselves by citing their feminist credentials and by pointing out that their books do not primarily address an academic audience. Werner's conclusion lays her wide open to attack, and Linklater seizes the opportunity: 'I am bemused by the implications of the final statement in Werner's article: "But until actors can escape the need to be organic and true, voice training will continue to place stumbling blocks in the way of feminist performances." Does this mean that, to be politically correct, feminist performances have to be inorganic and untrue?' Much hangs here on notions of the 'organic' and 'true'.

The most searching and intelligent confrontation of questions related to performance is Harry Berger's. *Making Trifles of Terrors*, a collection of his essays from 1979 to the present, shows him repeatedly returning to the tension between text and performance and between text-centred and stage-centred readings of the plays. Though I am predisposed to resist Berger's emphasis on the writtenness of Shakespeare's plays, if any critic could break down my resistance it would be Berger, with his wit, flair and meticulous attention to detail. The title of his brilliant essay on *2 Henry IV*, 'Sneak's Noise', holds together in an inspired choice of quotation the essence of Berger's case. The name of a band of alehouse musicians in the play, Sneak's noise represents, for Berger, 'the diversionary din of carnival', the various tricks performance plays to distract attention from what is going on in the deeper structure of relations within the 'play's community' (a recurrent term in his criticism). Berger's thesis here, as in other essays, is that the play builds into itself a critique of its own theatricality and of theatricality in general. Performance privileges 'the surface play', as Berger writes in another essay; but it is the deep play of what performance represses that gives that performance its edge. Berger disarmingly admits that the text/performance opposition continues to give him 'a lot of trouble' and acknowledges the appositeness of criticism directed against his failure to show much 'appreciation or understanding of theatrical practice'; but his discussions confront the really hard questions about relations between text and performance that so many other critics duck. His acknowledgement of 'trouble' is also characteristic. As he says himself, all the essays in the book are about 'acknowledgement – the difficulty of acknowledging, the failure to acknowledge, the fear of that failure, the desire to overcome it'. The title of his book is taken from another inspired quotation, from *All's Well*, one that signals a unifying concern shared by all the essays: 'They say miracles are past; and we have our philosophical persons to make modern and familiar, things supernatural and causeless. Hence it is that we make trifles of terrors, ensconcing ourselves into seeming knowledge when we should submit ourselves to an unknown fear.' Berger is not one who flies for the refuge of seeming knowledge; his work continually returns to the unknown fear.

John Joughin's *Shakespeare and National Culture* is concerned, like *Alternative Shakespeares 2*, with plurality, and seeks to explore multiple national cultures. The collection is divided into four sections, a division which, as the editor wryly notes, is doubtless complicit with categorizations that the volume as a whole seeks to challenge. The three essays in the first section all go back, in varying degrees, to the conference on Shakespeare and the Teaching of English held at the University of Central Lancashire in April 1993 at a time of debate over the National Curriculum, the Tory government's Back to Basics campaign and a letter eventually signed by over 500 academics condemning government policy with regard to the teaching of English. These essays usefully bring together elements of that debate within the wider context. The second section, 'Contesting the Colonial' has the virtue of breaking down at least one potentially inhibiting category by bringing Willy Maley's excellent piece on the marginalization of non-English Britain into the same grouping as Martin Orkin's examination of readings of *The Tempest* in South Africa and Ania Loomba's interesting discussion of what the post-colonial concept of 'hybridity' really means in relation to the complex example of Indian theatre under British rule. The categorization of part three is more traditional: Europe. Here Robert Weimann and Thomas Healy, like Michael Bristol and others, both look at the problem of 'past significance and present meaning', or how to negotiate the text in a way that simultaneously recognizes its historical difference and allows it to make an intervention in present culture. Francis Barker's essay in this section is the only one in the collection to focus on a text at any length: he uses *Coriolanus* to examine the political dangers of an exclusionary nationalism arising out of a Heideggerian sense of rootedness and belonging. The essays in the last section, entitled 'Shakespeare and Transnational Culture', seem unconcerned with defining the meaning of this apparently idealist category. John Joughin's essay is primarily a reflection on the 'culture wars' of the 1980s and nineties and a speculation on where Shakespeare studies might go from here, while Curtis Breight's is mainly an analysis of Gus Van Sant's *My Own Private Idaho.* This leaves the volume feeling curiously incomplete. Shot through, as all the essays are, with anxieties and longings around nationalism and the possibility of escaping or transcending it, their organization in a sequence leading towards this final category seems to hint at a space for optimism that the book does not deliver. It is perhaps not surprising that this space does not emerge; what is surprising is that a volume otherwise so self-aware about its own positioning within critical discourse should signal that it might.

Jyotsna Singh's *Colonial Narratives/Cultural Dialogues* explores the interconnections between colonial encounters in India from the early seventeenth century to the present day. Within this wide remit, her fourth chapter analyses the formation of India's cultural identity via the reception of Shakespeare's plays. She shows how Shakespeare was enlisted in the 'civilizing mission' and promoted through the education system as a repository of transcendental Christian values applicable across time and place, and rightly argues that the Indian 'love' of the Shakespearian text is tied to the colonizing enterprise which makes that text into 'a form of "cultural capital" with an exchange value in terms of job opportunities'. Productions of the plays, however, tell a different story, and one which displays a much freer relationship with Shakespearian texts. Though some theatres, like the Calcutta Playhouse, modelled both their architecture and their production style on the contemporary London stage, other kinds of performance, even on the Calcutta stage, showed much greater willingness to adapt both texts and performance style to native dramatic traditions. The chapter (and the book as a whole) brings together valuable information, but has some curious blindspots and mannerisms in its mode of argument. Shakespeare is regularly referred to as 'the Bard', which is irritating, even if it is intended ironically, and key concepts such as 'transculturation' are routinely italicized. Even more curiously in a book with this project, Alyque Padamsee's productions of Shakespeare in English are described as 'culturally neutral'. Can such a category really retain credibility in any discourse, far less one than takes cultural capital as its subject?

Joyce Green Macdonald's collection, *Race, Ethnicity and Power in the Renaissance*, offers a lively and stimulating set of essays. Five out of eight are on Shakespeare, but the most interesting range much more widely than that. Rebecca Ann Bach argues that the critical silence on bearbaiting is significant and revealing in ways that are analogous to the long-dominant critical silence regarding race. Both topics, she argues, are subject to a 'colonizing logic' that naturalizes white people's dominion over animals as over black people. For modern readers who distance themselves from these early modern attitudes, it is easier to look away than to look at such troubling practices. Daryl

Palmer's analysis of 'merchants and miscegenation' in *The Three Ladies of London*, *The Jew of Malta* and *The Merchant of Venice*, brings together merchant writings and dramatic texts to make compelling parallels between the two kinds of joint-stock company (merchants and actors) and the bringing together of commerce, exhibition and entertainment in the activities of both. Kim Hall looks at the emergence of connections between apes and Africans and between both these images and discourses of mimesis through *Mr Moore's Revels*, a masque staged privately in 1636. Some of the essays focusing more narrowly on Shakespeare are also very rewarding. In a careful analysis of *The Tempest*'s investment in Claribel's husband, Marjorie Raley demonstrates that Caliban's structural position, as a commodity for exchange, offers him as the explicit site of negotiation for all that is repressed around the threat of a Tunisian son-in-law; John Michael Archer offers a learned summary of the discourses of Egypt available before and after *Antony and Cleopatra* that usefully complicates tired Roman/Egyptian binaries; and Virginia Mason Vaughan looks at relations between Romans and Goths, alongside the increasing demonization of Aaron, in *Titus Andronicus*, within the context of a colonizing nation's anxiety about the 'barbarians' it seeks to conquer. Barbara Fuchs, writing in *Shakespeare Quarterly*, also considers colonialism in *The Tempest*, with a plea for complicating the colonial nuances to extend beyond the Americas to include Ireland and the Islamic powers in the Mediterranean. Richard Wilson, in *ELH*, challenges the dominance of the American colonial context for *The Tempest* from a very different angle, reviving the question of the play's possible commission for a wedding, and arguing for its keying to the political context of the proposed marriage between the Prince of Wales and the daughter of Grand Duke Ferdinand of Tuscany.

Two essays in *Shakespeare Quarterly* pay particular attention to racial issues in *Othello*. Janet Adelman's 'Iago's Alter Ego', emphasizing that racism is the 'psychic property' of the racist as well as of the victim of racism, offers a Kleinian reading of Iago that sees him projecting his sense of his own inward contamination on to Othello, while Daniel Vitkus, like Richard Wilson, queries the framework of Western imperialist discourse in New Historicist readings of Renaissance texts. He concentrates instead on English anxiety with regard to the Ottoman Turks and argues that Othello 'turns Turk', thus coming to embody the stereotype he seemed at first to escape.

Feminist critics have made notable contributions to the year's publications. *Shakespeare Quarterly* devoted a special issue to 'Teaching Judith Shakespeare', to which writers contributed descriptions and suggestions for teaching Shakespearian texts alongside those of his female contemporaries or near-contemporaries. Texts include the obvious dramatic choices (*Mariam*, *The Concealed Fancies*, *The Convent of Pleasure*) and the lyrics of Aemilia Lanier, Mary Wroth and Elizabeth I. Though a number of useful approaches are outlined, some authors register awareness of the potential problems underpinning such a strategy. '"Teaching Judith Shakespeare"', as Nancy Gutierrez notes, 'is a pedagogical activity that inevitably puts Judith into competition with William'; and a comparative approach, as well as having 'a certain fabricated neatness', has the effect of privileging gender- and author-based criticism in a way that can encourage a reductive binarism likely to erase other complexities.

In the introduction to their anthology, *Women Reading Shakespeare 1660–1900*, Ann Thompson and Sasha Roberts cite 'a poignant moment' in their preparation for the collection when they discovered all five volumes of the first edition of Mary Cowden Clarke's *The Girlhood of Shakespeare's Heroines* 'uncut and unread in the open stacks at the Folger Shakespeare Library'. The publication of this collection speaks directly to that moment, in that it represents a body of work that most Shakespeare scholars think they 'know' – without necessarily having read. Thompson and Roberts are to be congratulated for finally putting this volume on our shelves and for doing so in such a helpful and stimulating form. The selections are arranged chronologically by author; biographical details are provided as far as possible; the contributions are indexed in a variety of useful ways; and a short introduction clarifies practice and whets the appetite. The selection also includes twelve illustrations by women, which, as the editors indicate, signal another potentially rich field for investigation. Some selections are very brief, and the nature of entries varies from uninterrupted quotation to occasional quotations interspersed with paraphrase. This creates an uneven effect, but is presumably largely based on the nature and availability of material; and one beneficial effect of such selectivity, of course, is that it may encourage readers to return to the full texts. Though character-based criticism dominates in this period, for women as for men, women writers often address wider issues concerning real women's lives in their writing on Shakespeare, and in doing so represent a wide range of opinion. M. Leigh-Noel, for example, generalizes from her reading of Lady Macbeth: 'Women there are who suffer in silence and alone. They have a dual existence: one of mental and spiritual unrest, and another of apparent calm, which is the only one palpable to their nearest and dearest'; while Anna Jameson adopts a more assertive line in offering an answer both rational and impassioned to the male view that 'political women' are 'mischievous'. In a curiously modern-sounding conclusion she points out that the personal is always political; which is also the implicit statement of this collection.

Thompson and Roberts might be pleased to note that Irene Dash begins her discussion of *All's Well That Ends Well* by quoting Charlotte Perkins Gilman, writing in 1898 on the illogicality of a society that educates girls 'to realize in all ways [their] sex-limitations and [their] sex-advantages' with a view to marrying well, but at the same time hypocritically condemns husband-hunters who are too open about their purpose. Dash's discussion is part of her book, *Women's Worlds in Shakespeare's Plays*, which concentrates on the history of production of five plays (including *A Midsummer Night's Dream*, *Hamlet*, *Macbeth* and *Twelfth Night* in addition to *All's Well*). Using the evidence of promptbooks for stage productions, and including film versions in her survey, Dash shows how cuts, transposition of scenes and other interventions reshape female roles in accordance with changing cultural expectations, frequently allowing gender stereotyping to reduce the subtlety and complexity of these characters. The study is cogently argued and well illustrated, benefiting, as does Thompson and Roberts' collection, from the inclusion of pictorial as well as textual evidence.

The first two books in a new series of Feminist Readings of Shakespeare augur well for the remaining three. Coppélia Kahn's *Roman Shakespeare* continues, as she herself suggests, the project of 'identifying a gender-specific dimension – a preoccupation with the masculine subject – in Shakespeare', but from a less psychoanalytic perspective than her earlier *Man's Estate*. Rome is especially important, she argues, for our understanding of Renaissance England, which conceived of itself in such direct relation to Rome, whether via its education system or via its myths of origin; and Kahn is careful to distinguish between the different Romes (of e.g. the Tarquins or the republic) Shakespeare represents. Women, she shows, are crucial to the formation of the ideology of *virtus*, structured as it is on an opposition between politics (from which women are formally excluded) and the household. Shakespeare's Roman works (including *The Rape of Lucrece* and *Cymbeline* as well as the more familiar group), Kahn argues, present a critique of this ideology; and she offers the wound as an explicit site of this contestation. Wounds register both the hero's *virtus*, or masculinity, and his vulnerability and permeability, qualities that potentially feminize his body. And women's wounds are equally contradictory: Portia's voluntary wounding of her own thigh in *Julius Caesar*, for example, unsettles the gendered quality of *virtus* by its appropriation of a masculine constancy, so that 'in a discursive operation akin to that of the fetish, constancy is haunted by its feminine opposites, making Portia's wound ambiguously, undecideably feminine *and* masculine'. As Kahn concludes her book, 'the wound that signifies *virtus* remains an open wound'.

*Engendering a Nation*, by Jean Howard and Phyllis Rackin, exposes the history play as itself a gendered form, and in this respect bound in a paradoxical opposition to theatre, seen by its opponents as effeminizing and destabilizing. As opposed to tragedy, for example, which inspires, according to Stephen Gosson, 'womanish weeping and mourning' in its audience, the history play offers male spectators the opportunity to reclaim their threatened masculinity. Shakespeare's history plays, like their sources, are dominated by men; women remain alien to them both literally and symbolically. While the first tetralogy is especially preoccupied with foreign women whose gender and nationality together seem to express the threat they offer both to the male protagonists and to the masculine, heroic values of history, the second tetralogy operates by excluding and domesticating its female figures. No longer do women appear on the battlefield or claim political agency; here, Howard and Rackin claim, the world we recognize, in which gender roles are naturalized according to biological difference, comes into being. Yet there is something odd about this argument, which seems to imply a historical progression for women from the political to the domestic arena, as if they had somehow been once possessed, in the not-too-distant past, of powerful agency. In fact, as the specific chapter analyses of the *Henry VI* plays make clear, these powerful women are demonized by the plays in which they figure, and seem rather to represent a male fantasy that seeks to contain the disorderly potential of woman than an image of a differently gendered social hierarchy. Neither Kahn nor Howard and Rackin, however, restrict their analyses to the role of women in the plays. As this book makes clear, conflict in the histories is gendered by definition, whether the poles of masculinity and femininity are represented via England and France, Talbot and Joan of Arc, or Bolingbroke and Richard II. Howard and Rackin's underlying thesis concerning theatre's own 'femininity' is rewarding too. It not only opens the way for some illuminating analyses of those male characters, like Richard II and Richard III, who call attention to their action as performance, but also for a broader argument about the sequence of the history plays as moving from a conception of authority as the product of patrilineal inheritance to one that replaces genealogical succession with personal performance.

Ian Moulton, writing in *Shakespeare Quarterly*, also contributes to the discussion of masculinity in the history plays with a piece entitled '"A Monster Great Deformed": The Unruly Masculinity of Richard III'. He examines the way Richard's masculinity is constructed within the cultural context of Elizabeth's sovereignty and the absence of a strong masculine figure of royal authority. By reading the disorders of patriarchy through the different kinds and degrees of masculinity encoded in its representation, the essay exposes how closely implicated political and gendered thinking are.

Several book-length publications are of a much broader and less classifiable nature. André Brink's *Destabilising Shakespeare* expands a brief lecture course, originally aimed at a non-specialist audience. Perhaps because of this context, it is highly accessible and jargon-free, and includes a particularly lucid introductory chapter outlining the basis of a deconstructive approach. The essays include separate studies of *Hamlet*, *Macbeth* and *The Tempest* and a more wide-ranging discussion, drawing on a number of plays, of the threat of gender to kingship. Together they aim to show how 'some of the apparent "constants" of the Elizabethan/Jacobean world are challenged or subverted: kingship, power, identity, gender'. Brink is generous to other critics and succinct and illuminating on the plays in question. He usefully probes the instabilities of each play without descending into either relativism or banality.

Peter Egri's *Modern Games with Renaissance Forms* is a curious and eccentric book. Totalling 114 pages, including notes, it begins with an 'introduction' which consists solely of a picture (appallingly badly reproduced) and ends with a two-page endnote. The blurb suggests an impenetrable theoretical perspective possibly resembling the Emperor's new clothes ('Value can only be vindicated by fixity in flux and flux in fixity'), but the book itself is primarily descriptive of the picture and texts it studies and offers little by way of any theory or analysis. The only argument underpinning it is the unexceptional one that the appropriations of Renaissance works of art by Warhol, Stoppard and others reverse or ironize them, and there is no real refinement or development of that broad formulation. Egri's assumption that Elizabethan 'you' always represents a move away from the intimacy of 'thou' (as opposed to a straightforward plural) does not inspire confidence in his capacity as a critic.

Incredibly, William Bache and Vernon Loggins justify the need for their book, *Shakespeare's Deliberate Art*, with the assertion that 'Shakespeare's plays have not been sufficiently recognized as works of art.' This is, according to them, because 'most critical and scholarly discourse has ignored, neglected, or misunderstood the nature of Shakespeare's art'. With this resounding self-confidence they embark on the project of telling us what Shakespeare is really about. Their approach ranges from vacuously sentimental bardolatry ('We receive but what we give' is the sugary refrain of their Introduction) to schematic reductiveness (the conclusion sums up the mechanics of any Shakespeare play with unembarrassed banality: 'the first act ... presents the plot problem and introduces the main characters; ... the next two acts comprise an extended episode; and ... the final two acts resolve the impasse reached at the end of the extended episode by a concentration on the accentuated plight of, first, the heroine and, then, the hero'). The fact that act-divisions were imposed on most of Shakespeare's plays after he wrote them is not allowed to get in the way of this grand narrative, which proceeds by rubbishing the work of most other scholars. Bache and Loggins' most characteristic stylistic device is to move from the dismissal of what other critics have thought to their own account, which recognizably begins with some variation on the phrase, 'The truth is ...' The book grates, and its lack of humility constructs an unforgiving reader.

The collection of essays brought together by Joseph Alulis and Vickie Sullivan under the title *Shakespeare's Political Pageant* has several themes running through a number of essays, but this is nowhere brought out by the editors, since the anthology is not provided with an introduction and the essays are grouped according to dramatic genre rather than thematic concerns. Two essays in separate groupings, for example (Barbara Tovey's on *Measure for Measure* and Paul Cantor's on *King Lear*), examine the relevance of the concept of the philosopher-king to their respective plays and argue for the separateness of wisdom from the capacity to rule; two more (Pamela Jensen's on *Othello* and Dennis Bathory's on *Julius Caesar* and *Coriolanus*) focus on the implications of republicanism; while at least four out of the total twelve centre on the determining influence of fathers. Only one play, *Macbeth*, elicits more than one essay, and neither of these essays is in fact very closely concerned with the politics of the play. The most interesting pieces are Vickie Sullivan's development of Dr Johnson's observation regarding Henry V that 'Shakespeare now gives the king nearly such a character as he made him formerly ridicule in Percy' and Pamela Jensen's very full exposition of the view that 'the juxtaposition of public and private events in [*Othello*] acquires its special character because of the kind of regime Venice is'.

*'Divers toyes mengled'* is indeed a very mixed collection of essays in honour of André Lascombes. The first section includes essays on non-dramatic literature and medieval theatre, while the second is devoted to English Renaissance drama. The majority of these are on Shakespeare, including three on *Romeo and Juliet*. Hanna Scolnicov is convinced that the street scenes in *Romeo and Juliet* show the influence of Italian comic scenography, but offers no external evidence for her view beyond the fact that Serlio's writings were widely published and translated across Europe. Ronnie Mulryne, focusing on Sam Mendes's 1993–4 production of *The Tempest*, displays this year's recurrent concern with the presentness of the past as he explores the 'uneasy interaction' between the categories of the political and the aesthetic in modern productions of classic plays. François Laroque, extending his work on festival, examines power and festival as two sides of the same coin. Where in earlier work, he argues, festival is primarily linked with disorder, the last plays offer 'une réhabilitation de la fête', a 'recreation' in a double sense.

Michael Neill's *Issues of Death* is one of the best books to appear this year. It is a wonderfully wide-ranging and illuminating study of death in early modern England which offers carefully nuanced readings of Shakespeare's tragedies within the wider context of English Renaissance tragedy. Four in particular are discussed in detail: *Othello, Hamlet, Titus Andronicus* and *Antony and Cleopatra*. The book is in three parts, which focus respectively on death as a moment of revelation or unveiling; the tension between end-driven narrative and the dread of ending; and the refashioning of death as triumph. Neill examines a wealth of non-literary material, from the dance of death to anatomy lectures (parallels with Jonathan Sawday's *The Body Emblazoned* here) and funeral rites, in enough detail to be satisfying without overwhelming the plays as the primary object of analysis. The writing is also a pleasure to read, and many of the book's insights are especially rewarding for being so clearly and concisely expressed. Neill has a knack for selecting the right quotation and articulating comment in a form which produces an equal sense of aptness. His familiarity with non-Shakespearian material is wider and deeper than chapter titles suggest: he selects only three non-Shakespearian plays for extended study (*The Changeling, The Duchess of Malfi* and *The Broken Heart*), but his learning almost casually enriches his analyses of *Othello* and *Hamlet* by situating those plays within a broad framework of reference to lesser-known plays. Though the book draws extensively on earlier published material, it is clear that Neill has been working on aspects of death and tragedy over a period of years and that this book finally brings the fruits of that full and wide-ranging research together into a single and coherent study.

Other work on the tragedies falls short of the standard set by Neill. Jan H. Blits explains that his project in *The Insufficiency of Virtue: Macbeth and the Natural Order* is to treat the play 'as a work of coherent, rigorous, fundamental thought, intended to arouse and sustain serious philosophical inquiry and reflection'. More specifically, he aims to provide an exposition of the play as underpinned by two tensions, which he identifies as the tension between manly virtue and Christian virtue and the tension between virtue and life. This scarcely constitutes a strikingly new approach to *Macbeth*, and it is hard to find justification for a book-length commentary that proceeds line by line through the play in order to make such a case. Indeed, one is scarcely conscious of an argument as the book proceeds. The chapters are entitled simply 'Act One', 'Act Two', and so on, and the approach is broadly New Critical, but often sinks into mere paraphrase. The book has all the appearance of a publishing venture left in the vaults since the 1960s.

John O'Meara's brief essays on Shakespeare

and the Romantic tradition, brought together under the title of *Othello's Sacrifice*, is a somewhat manic plea on behalf of Rudolf Steiner's philosophical system of Anthroposophy. In the course of the book, 'tragedy' gradually ceases to function as a generic term describing a particular dramatic form and comes to figure apocalyptically as what lies ahead for the reader who fails to respond to the call to conversion. Anything less than a commitment to embrace the truth of Anthroposophy, O'Meara warns, opens the way for a tragic existence. Much more thought-provoking on *Othello* and some of the larger questions underpinning critical activity is Edward Pechter, writing on 'Sex and Sexual Stories in *Othello*'. Pechter queries the usefulness of the current emphasis on the cultural at the expense of the aesthetic, suggesting that the large claims for social usefulness made by critics defending this approach is constructed by the current 'production-driven research culture', which insists on accountability to 'the taxpayer'. Returning to Bradley, Pechter argues that some kind of imaginative alignment with character is necessary in order to respond to the play's tragedy.

Two essays on *Lear* and *Hamlet* respectively raise again the question of how the past is to be understood through its interaction with the present. In 'Shakespeare and Hanekon, *King Lear* and Land', Nicholas Visser looks at the play from the perspective of the South African Land Reform Act of 1996 (Hanekon is South African Minister of Agriculture and Land) and sees it as capturing 'the emergence of a development that would be a salient feature of the transition to modernity, the transformation of land into private property'. Linda Charnes, in 'Dismember Me: Shakespeare, Paranoia, and the Logic of Mass Culture', examines *Hamlet* through Slavoj Žižek's use of Lacan and finds it to be the first fully *noir* text in Western literature. More empirically oriented towards history than either Visser or Charnes is Christopher Worthen's examination, in 'Shakespeare, James I and the Matter of Britain', of three of the tragedies (*Lear*, *Macbeth* and *Antony and Cleopatra*) to see whether the king's patronage has any influence on Shakespeare's writing after 1603. He argues that collectively they demonstrate three central concerns: the unification of Britain; James's vision of himself as a philosopher-king, bringing peace and harmony; and his wish to be seen as a new Augustus.

Two essays make important arguments with regard to *Coriolanus*. John Plotz, in '*Coriolanus* and the Failure of Performatives', sets out to transfer the traditional emphasis of critical approaches to *Coriolanus* from the individual to the public world. Arguing against Stanley Fish's view that 'reality is a matter of public specification' via Coriolanus' own stated commitment to exposing something more real that lies deeper, Plotz develops a critique of Fish's theory that meaning can only be created and validated by interpretative communities. The play, he argues, passes on to the audience a fundamental anxiety about the trustworthiness of language. Ann Christensen's piece, 'The Return of the Domestic in *Coriolanus*', considers issues closely related to those of Kahn's study, around the interrelation of politics and the household. For Christensen the 'home', though barely represented as a setting, is a powerful shaping force in the play, insistently representing the deep connection between private and public. Volumnia persuades Coriolanus to relent not simply by invoking the family, but by explicitly tying together familial and civic duty. By attempting to repress his bond with the home, Coriolanus invites the return of the domestic 'in the form of an angry crowd avenging families, hearths, and homes'.

Michael Collins's collection, *Shakespeare's Sweet Thunder*, brings together eleven newly commissioned essays on the early comedies. Surprisingly, critics focus most repeatedly on *The Comedy of Errors* and *Love's Labour's Lost*, while there is only one essay on *A Midsummer Night's Dream* (Jay Halio's analysis of Robert Lepage's 1993 production). The emphasis of the collection is on what Collins refers to as 'the afterlife' of the plays, and there is therefore a strong focus on performance. Two, Alan Dessen's on *The Taming of the Shrew* and Homer Swander's on *Love's Labour's Lost*, analyse the difference between variant texts, while several critics, notably Ann Thompson and Carol Rutter, focus on gender issues. I found Bruce Smith's essay particularly rewarding, bringing together, as it does, questions of masculinity with very specific historical conditions of performance in a study of the Gray's Inn performance of *Errors* in 1594.

The late plays receive special attention in Robert Henke's *Pastoral Transformations*, but the relationship between its two objects of study, Italian tragicomedy and Shakespeare's late plays, emerges less clearly than it might. Henke assembles useful material but does not shape it strongly. Genre theory, the texts of Italian tragicomedy and the dramatic practice of *commedia dell'arte* are all discussed, but their possible interaction with Shakespeare's dramaturgy is thinly sketched. Some of the perspectives on the late plays offered by Italian models seem singularly unhelpful. Henke suggests, for example, that the 'gentleman-like tears' wept by the shepherds in *The Winter's Tale* represent 'the pathos-filled tonalities of Guarinian tragicomedy', which seems to me to miss the joke. The book leaves a sense that much yet remains to be uncovered regarding relations between English and Italian drama and dramatic theory.

R. S. White's New Casebook of essays on *Twelfth Night* is a well-chosen selection organized and introduced with admirable brevity and clarity. The selection shows how dominant issues of class and gender have become in recent approaches to the play, and the extent to which attention has turned from the gulling of Malvolio to the cross-dressed Viola (though Cristina Malcolmson demonstrates how productively these two areas may be brought together by a consideration of transvestism as a crossing of class as well as gender boundaries). The least successful contributions are those by Bristol and Tennenhouse, which are extracted from longer books, though one can see why they were chosen, since they stake out particular critical areas not elsewhere represented. White carefully frames the main body of work with essays by Geoffrey Hartman and Barbara Everett which consciously stand apart from those lines of approach; but this choice is clearly not intended to ironize or belittle the very substantial contributions of critics like Greenblatt, Callaghan and Malcolmson. Everett's essay leaves the reader meditating, as the editor intends it should, on what the inevitable partiality of any critical approach leaves out. The effect here is not to banalize, but to stimulate.

Like Collins's collection on the early comedies, the terms of *Shakespeare Survey 49*'s focus on *Romeo and Juliet* emphasize its 'afterlife'. Stanley Wells's opening essay offers a well-informed and wide-ranging overview of the challenges the play presents, concluding that its greatest challenge is to 'our notions of genre'; the fullest implications of the script are made available 'only if we abandon the idea that because it is called a tragedy it must centre on the fate of individuals, and accept its emphasis on the multifarious society in which these individuals have their being'. Susan Snyder develops this perception in her piece on the feud as a model for the working of ideology in the play, which sees the lovers as torn between 'feud-assigned' subjectivities and the (hopeless) struggle to escape them. Andrew Gurr's essay on the significance of the play's tough staging requirements in the context of its dating parameters is characteristically brimming with a richness of detail that spills over into numerous aspects of the performance practices of Elizabethan theatre from the early to the later 1590s; and richness of detail is also a virtue of Ronald Knowles's analysis of the workings of carnival in the play via three Bakhtinian categories identified as body, bawdy and banquet. Other contributions look at the play on film, in pictures and in the school classroom.

Other essays on the comedies this year are disappointing. Maurice Hunt, writing on '*The*

*Countess of Pembroke's Arcadia*, Shakespeare's *A Midsummer Night's Dream*, and the School of Night: An Intertextual Nexus', argues that the long night in *Arcadia* during which Pyrocles and Musidorus try to elope with Philoclea and Pamela is related to the night of Shakespeare's play through 'a complex of values involving moonshine, disordered imagination, and discord among lovers'. The supposed connection with the School of Night is that both texts share its understanding of 'the epistemological properties of night'. Lynn Enterline's '"You speak a language that I understand not": The Rhetoric of Animation in *The Winter's Tale*' focuses on the female voice in *Winter's Tale* via Pygmalion and Petrarch, but ends up top-heavy with sources that seem to erase the positive force of the statue scene. The insistence with which the performance logic of the scene has to be repressed in order to make the logic of the sources function seems to me to imply the degree to which the argument is a lost cause.

The title of Eric Sterling's book, *The Movement Towards Subversion: The English History Play from Skelton to Shakespeare*, summarizes its general argument. Sterling works, however, with a simplistic evolutionary model of development, and fails to develop the argument beyond some fairly bland and reductive assertions. 'Skelton's *Magnificence*', we are told, for example, 'contains political and historical implications'; or, 'the Reformation plays regarding King John become more subversive and less supportive of Tudor ideology'. The only refinement of the direct assertion is the comparative assertion: plays, within this analysis, can be either just subversive, or more or less subversive than each other; but nowhere is the nature of that stated subversiveness investigated in any detail or backed up by a weight of evidence. Sterling's usual approach is to substitute quotation from literary critics for any extended first-hand exploration of the relation between the text and the political world, and his writing often degenerates into embarrassingly uncritical pastiche constructed around sentences beginning 'x says'. This is not a book that encourages the reader to think more deeply about the plays that are its subject.

If work on the histories is thin, however, there is more useful work than last year on the poems. Philip Kolin's anthology on *Venus and Adonis* performs a service similar to that of the Casebook series, though at much greater length, by bringing together a combination of early and later criticism of the poem, chronologically arranged, and seven specially commissioned essays. The volume also contains a chronological bibliography of critical work on the poem which is a useful reference tool, if made to look slightly eccentric by an entry for 1997 (presumably written in 1996) which can only include the seven new articles appearing in this anthology. Generally the new work has the effect of underlining the highlights of earlier published criticism, and female critics (Kahn, Fienberg and Belsey, for example) emerge as particularly important contributors to recent criticism of the poem. The final essay, by Georgianna Ziegler, adds a new dimension by considering the illustrative tradition of *Venus and Adonis*, and ends the volume, appropriately for this poem, by moving away from cerebral analysis into a sensual appreciation of dark ink, flowing script, the smoothness of vellum and the grain of hand-made paper.

Heather Dubrow's article on the sonnets, '"Incertainties now crown themselves assur'd": The Politics of Plotting Shakespeare's Sonnets', notes how rarely positivist assumptions about the addressees and 'narrative' of the sonnets have been questioned since Malone established sonnet 126 as a point of division in the sequence. Arguing against both Thorpe's sequence and any intended division, she proposes that the reason the sequence has been so readily accepted is because it makes criticism and discussion easier, responding as it does to the critical impulse to impose order. (There is a parallel here with the discussion of the desire for order in the *Textual Practice* debate.) Katherine Duncan-Jones, who has elsewhere made the case in favour of the coherence of the 1609 quarto, writes this year on the meaning of '*Syren* teares' in Sonnet 119 and on the question 'What Are Shakespeare's Sonnets Called?' The second piece is the more important. Noting that both the title-page of the 1609 quarto and the entry in the Stationers' Register appear to specify Shakespeare's name as part of the title, she first emphasizes the testimony of three witnesses suggesting that the text was in fact authorized by Shakespeare and then compares the title with other contemporary titles including genitives. If 'Shakespeares' is established as part of the sequence's title, she argues, the genitive gathers denotative as well as possessive force, which should affect our reception of the content.

## WORKS REVIEWED


Adelman, Janet. 'Iago's Alter Ego: Race as Projection in *Othello*', *Shakespeare Quarterly*, 48, 1997, 125–44.

Alulis, Joseph, and Vickie Sullivan, ed. *Shakespeare's Political Pageant: Essays in Literature and Politics*. Lanham, Maryland and London: Rowman and Littlefield, 1996.

Bache, William B., and Vernon P. Loggins. *Shakespeare's Deliberate Art*. Lanham, New York and London: University Press of America, 1996.

Baldo, Jonathan. *The Unmasking of Drama: Contested Representation in Shakespeare's Tragedies*. Detroit: Wayne State University Press, 1996.

Bennett, Susan. *Performing Nostalgia: Shifting Shakespeare and the Contemporary Past*. London and New York: Routledge, 1996.

Berger, Harry, Jr. *Making Trifles of Terrors: Redistributing Complicities in Shakespeare*, ed. Peter Erickson. Stanford, California: Stanford University Press, 1997.

Berry, Cicely, Patsy Rodenburg and Kristin Linklater. 'Shakespeare, Feminism, and Voice: Responses to Sarah Werner'. *New Theatre Quarterly*, 49, 1997, 48–52.

Bitot, Michel, Roberta Mullini and Peter Happé. *'Divers toyes mengled': Essays on Medieval and Renaissance Culture in honour of André Lascombes*. Tours: l'Université François Rabelais, 1996.

Blits, Jan H. *The Insufficiency of Virtue: Macbeth and the Natural Order*. Lanham, Maryland and London: Rowman and Littlefield, 1996.

Brink, André. *Destabilising Shakespeare*. Rhodes University, Grahamstown: Shakespeare Society of Southern Africa, 1996.

Bristol, Michael D. *Big-time Shakespeare*. London and New York: Routledge, 1996.

Brown, Carolyn E. 'The Homoeroticism of Duke Vincentio: "Some Feeling of the Sport"'. *Studies in Philology*, 94, 1997, 187–220.

Buhler, Stephen M. 'No Spectre, No Sceptre: The Agon of Materialist Thought in Shakespeare's *Julius Caesar*'. *English Literary Renaissance*, 26, 1996, 313–32.

Charnes, Linda. 'Dismember Me: Shakespeare, Paranoia, and the Logic of Mass Culture'. *Shakespeare Quarterly*, 48, 1997, 1–16.

Christensen, Ann. 'The Return of the Domestic in *Coriolanus*'. *Studies in English Literature 1500–1900*, 37, 1997, 295–316.

Collins, Michael J., ed. *Shakespeare's Sweet Thunder: Essays on the Early Comedies*. Newark: University of Delaware Press; London: Associated University Presses, 1997.

Cordner, Michael. 'Annotation and Performance in Shakespeare'. *Essays in Criticism*, 46, 1996, 298–301.

Cunningham, James. *Shakespeare's Tragedies and Modern Critical Theory*. Madison, Teaneck: Fairleigh Dickinson University Press; London: Associated University Presses, 1997.

Dash, Irene G. *Women's Worlds in Shakespeare's Plays*. Newark: University of Delaware Press; London: Associated University Presses, 1997.

de Grazia, Margreta, and Peter Stallybrass. 'Love Among the Ruins: a Response to Pechter'. *Textual Practice*, 11, 1997, 69–79.

DiGangi, Mario. 'Queering the Shakespearean Family'. *Shakespeare Quarterly*, 47, 1996, 269–90.

Dubrow, Heather, '"Incertainties now crown themselves assur'd": The Politics of Plotting Shakespeare's Sonnets'. *Shakespeare Quarterly*, 47, 1996, 291–305.

Duncan-Jones, Katherine. '*Syren* Teares: Enchantment or Infection in Shakespeare's Sonnet 119'. *Review of English Studies*, 48, 1997, 56–60.

Duncan-Jones, Katherine. 'What Are Shakespeare's Sonnets Called?' *Essays in Criticism*, 47, 1997, 1–12.

Egri, Peter. *Modern Games with Renaissance Forms: From Leonardo and Shakespeare to Warhol and Stoppard. Studies in Modern Philology*, 12, Budapest: Akadémiai Kiadó, 1996.

Enterline, Lynn. '"You speak a language that I understand not": The Rhetoric of Animation in *The Winter's Tale*'. *Shakespeare Quarterly*, 48, 1997, 17–44.

Fuchs, Barbara. 'Conquering Islands: Contextualizing *The Tempest*'. *Shakespeare Quarterly*, 48, 1997, 45–62.

Grady, Hugh. *Shakespeare's Universal Wolf: Studies in Early Modern Reification*. Oxford: Clarendon Press, 1996.

Gurr, Andrew. 'The Date and the Expected Venue of *Romeo and Juliet*'. *Shakespeare Survey 49*, 1996, 15–25.

Gutierrez, Nancy. 'Why William and Judith Both Need Their Own Rooms'. *Shakespeare Quarterly*, 47, 1996, 424–32.

Hale, John K. *The Shakespeare of the Comedies: A Multiple Approach*. Bern etc: Peter Lang, 1996.

Hawkes, Terence, ed. *Alternative Shakespeares, Volume 2*. London and New York: Routledge, 1996.

Henke, Robert. *Pastoral Transformations: Italian Tragicomedy and Shakespeare's Late Plays*. Newark: University of Delaware Press; London: Associated University Presses, 1997.

Holderness, Graham, Bryan Loughrey and Andrew Murphy. 'Busy Doing Nothing: a Response to Edward Pechter'. *Textual Practice*, 11, 1997, 81–7.

Howard, Jean E. and Phyllis Rackin. *Engendering a Nation: A Feminist Account of Shakespeare's English Histories*. London and New York: Routledge, 1997.

Hume, Robert D. 'Before the Bard: "Shakespeare" in Early Eighteenth-Century London'. *ELH*, 64, 1997, 41–75.

Hunt, Maurice. '*The Countess of Pembroke's Arcadia*, Shakespeare's *A Midsummer Night's Dream*, and the School of Night: An Intertextual Nexus'. *Essays in Literature*, 23, 1996, 3–20.

Hyland, Peter. *An Introduction to Shakespeare: The Dramatist in his Context*. Basingstoke and London: Macmillan, 1996.

Joughin, John J., ed. *Shakespeare and National Culture*. Manchester and New York: Manchester University Press, 1997.

Kahn, Coppélia. *Roman Shakespeare: Warriors, Wounds, and Women*. London and New York: Routledge, 1997.

Knowles, Ronald. 'Carnival and Death in *Romeo and Juliet*'. *Shakespeare Survey 49*, 1996, 69–85.

Kolin, Philip C., ed. *Venus and Adonis: Critical Essays*. New York and London: Garland, 1997.

MacDonald, Joyce Green. *Race, Ethnicity, and Power in the Renaissance*. Madison, Teaneck: Fairleigh Dickinson University Press; London: Associated University Presses, 1997.

Moulton, Ian Frederick. '"A Monster Great Deformed": The Unruly Masculinity of Richard III'. *Shakespeare Quarterly* 47, 1996, 251–68.

Neill, Michael. *Issues of Death: Mortality and Identity in English Renaissance Tragedy*. Oxford: Clarendon Press, 1997.

O'Meara, John. *Othello's Sacrifice: Essays on Shakespeare and Romantic Tradition*. Toronto, New York and Lancaster: Guernica, 1996.

Orgel, Stephen. *Impersonations: The Performance of Gender in Shakespeare's England*. Cambridge: Cambridge University Press, 1996.

Pechter, Edward. 'Making Love to our Employment; or, the Immateriality of Arguments about the Materiality of the Shakespearean Text'. *Textual Practice*, 11, 1997, 51–67.

Pechter, Edward. '"Have You Not Read of Some Such Thing?": Sex and Sexual Stories in *Othello*'. *Shakespeare Survey 49*, 1996, 201–16.

Plotz, John. '*Coriolanus* and the Failure of Performatives'. *ELH*, 63, 1996, 809–32.

Sedinger, Tracey. '"If sight and shape be true": The Epistemology of Crossdressing on the London Stage'. *Shakespeare Quarterly* 48, 1997, 63–79.

Singh, Jyotsna G. *Colonial Narratives/Cultural Dialogues: 'Discoveries' of India in the Language of Colonialism*. London and New York: Routledge, 1996.

Snyder, Susan. 'Ideology and the Feud in *Romeo and Juliet*'. *Shakespeare Survey 49*, 1996, 87–96.

Sterling, Eric. *The Movement Towards Subversion: The English History Play from Skelton to Shakespeare*. Lanham, New York and London: University Press of America, 1996.

Thompson, Ann, and Sasha Roberts, ed. *Women Reading Shakespeare, 1600–1900: An Anthology of Criticism*. Manchester and New York: Manchester University Press, 1997.

Visser, Nicholas. 'Shakespeare and Hanekon, *King Lear* and Land'. *Textual Practice*, 11, 1997, 25–37.

Vitkus, Daniel J. 'Turning Turk in *Othello*: The Conversation and Damnation of the Moor'. *Shakespeare Quarterly* 48, 1997, 145–76.

Wells, Stanley. 'The Challenges of *Romeo and Juliet*'. *Shakespeare Survey* 49, 1996, 1–14.

Werner, Sarah. 'Performing Shakespeare: Voice Training and the Feminist Actor'. *New Theatre Quarterly*, 47, 1996, 249–58.

White, R. S., ed. *Twelfth Night*. New Casebooks, Basingstoke and London: Macmillan, 1996.

Wilson, Richard. 'Voyage to Tunis: New History and the Old World of *The Tempest*'. *ELH*, 64, 1997, 333–57.

Wortham, Christopher. 'Shakespeare, James I and the Matter of Britain'. *English*, 45, 1996, 97–122.

## 2. SHAKESPEARE'S LIFE, TIMES, AND STAGE

*reviewed by* Alison Findlay

### EARLY (MODERN?)

Reactions against the term 'early modern' to describe the times in which Shakespeare wrote are gathering momentum. In spite of its title, *The Project of Prose in Early Modern Europe and the New World* aims to prioritize continuities between Renaissance and medieval culture rather than 'early modern intellectual history and modern humanism' (p. 12). In *Subject and Object in Renaissance Culture*, Margreta de Grazia offers an '*anti*-Early Modern' (p. 21) reading of *King Lear*, remarking that it is dangerous to focus exclusively on the Renaissance as the nascence of the modern and to make Shakespeare, if not our contemporary, then an early version of ourselves. De Grazia's fine analysis shows that such an approach does not mean abandoning the theoretical sophistication which has characterized so much recent work on the 'early modern'.

Richard Hillman takes an equally theoretically inspired 'backwards' look in *Self-Speaking in Medieval and Early Modern English Drama*, an exciting study of subjectivity on stage, using key aspects of Lacan. Proposing a 'middle ground' between the extremes of historicist and humanist ideas of selfhood, Hillman traces a dramatic history of inwardness which stretches back to the medieval tradition. The mirror and the book serve as key representations of Lacanian models of selfhood, and theoretical positions are usefully signposted throughout. God, conscience and the slippery medium of language are all fundamental to the constitution of the fragile speaking subject, Hillman argues, but at the very moment of self-speaking on stage, subjectivity is threatened by aphanisis, a tendency to face away. The following chapters build on this idea from contrasting perspectives. A persuasive analysis locates *Wit and Science* as a precedent for Richard II's 'fall into soliloquized self-absence following confrontation with his mirror image' (p. 72). Personal revenge is read as a tragic antidote to the threat of aphanisis in *The Spanish Tragedy* and *Richard II*, while a chapter on 'unspeakably tragic subjects' (p. 164) considers male and female characters in plays by Jonson, Chapman, Webster and Ford. Hillman's writing is energetic and critically sharp throughout these discussions.

The book also considers ways in which comic structures work to counteract aphanitic subjectivity. Tragicomic patterns in Beaumont and Fletcher and in Shakespeare's last plays demonstrate how 'self-evanescence' (p. 234) can lead to the restoration of a transcendent identity linked to supernatural powers, a model which looks back to medieval drama. The final chapter on the female subject includes an unusual, though increasingly convincing, discussion of *Love's Labour's Lost*, where Hillman sees a pattern of solitary self-speaking and masturbatory activity by both men and women. This is fascinating, but neither the chapter nor the book addresses the issue of women's different positioning in relation to Lacanian theory in any sustained discussion. Indeed, my one criticism of Hillman's study is that the problem of aphanisis which it treats so lucidly could be said to characterize certain elements of the book. Some subjects, whether texts or ideas, seem to slip in and out of focus, only to be caught in passing glimpses. This is the case with *Hamlet*, which is frequently alluded to but is not pinned down for uninterrupted analysis.

Hillman's endeavour to draw connections between medieval and Renaissance drama is shared by *A New History of Early English Drama*, an impressive collection of twenty-six essays which succeed in giving a comprehensive picture of dramatic production while never losing sight of its infinite variety. Essays are grouped under broad classifications of physical space, social space, and conditions of performance and publication, thus presenting a multi-dimensional picture of dramatic production. Traditional areas of research such as theatre and religion, public theatre buildings, audiences, acting styles, publication of playbooks, and revision of texts, are covered by writers whose obvious expertise allows them to summarize the current evidence clearly and authoritatively. Areas of more recent or renewed critical interest are also well represented, as in Michael Bristol's chapter on theatre and popular culture, Richard Dutton's on censorship, Kathleen McLuskie and Felicity Dunsworth's piece on patronage, and Jeffrey Masten's discussion of collaborative authorship. Most importantly, the volume opens up definitions of theatre to include non-professional venues, and space is given to consider the relationship of drama to other cultural activities. This is a very welcome development; many of the essays on apparently marginal topics bring fresh insights. I particularly enjoyed Heidi Hackel's analysis of printed scripts in early libraries and Barbara Mowat's use of *Pericles* as a starting point to consider relationships between the theatre and literary culture.

By endeavouring to 'erase the sharp distinction between *Medieval* and *Renaissance*' (p. 3), the volume inevitably challenges its contributors to pay attention to material from across these periods. They respond to the daunting task with varying degrees of success. Attempts to cover the whole period tend to become overburdened with information, leaving little room for interpretation, as in Suzanne Westfall's discussion of household theatre, although since this is a lesser-known area of performance, the exposure of evidence perhaps justly takes precedence. Less easy to excuse is Jean MacIntyre and Garrett Epp's tedious treatment of costumes and properties which lacks any central argument to transform its potentially interesting wealth of detail. On the other hand, Paul Werstine's discussion of many scripts in relation to Greg's repressive principles of classification is disappointingly narrow.

Between these two extremes, the majority of essays adopt a compromise position with occasional cross-period references which set up channels of communication. A good example is Diane Henderson's intricate analysis of theatre and domestic culture. Henderson identifies a precedent for patterns of shrewishness, cuckoldry and female wit in Shakespearian drama in the *Secunda Pastorum*, not the most typical of mystery plays but certainly a striking example. Essays like this make the volume live up to its name as *A New History of Early English Drama*, setting up important models for future scholarship.

The principle and practice of eliding medieval and Renaissance dramatic activity owes much to the Records of Early English Drama project and the publication of another volume, *Records of Early English Drama: Somerset*, edited by James Stokes, including Bath, edited by Robert Alexander, is to be celebrated. This volume is prepared and presented with the same meticulous care for which the series is renowned. As in other parts of the country, relationships between theatrical entertainments and the ecclesiastical authorities follow the pattern of religious politics between the Reformation and the Civil War. There are interesting examples of improvised alehouse performances parodying ecclesiastical figures, while the records for Yeovil show the persistence of Robin Hood games and Whitsun ales. Perhaps the most exciting discovery is that Bridgwater enjoyed visits from thirty-one professional troupes of players, including the Queen Elizabeth's Men, Queen Anne's Men and Worcester's Men. Professional players, notably Queen Elizabeth's and Lord Admiral's visited Bath as well. Like other REED volumes, this one uncovers details of all kinds of unusual performance, such as the case of Henry Pillchorne who was inspired to remove his trousers, 'show his privie members' to an audience of both men and women, and declare he 'did daunce Piddecocke bolt upright, and readie to fight' (p. 60)!

## RENAISSANCE DRAMATISTS

Ironically, the ninth volume of *Medieval and Renaissance Drama in England*, edited by John Pitcher, does not discuss any medieval drama, though it is good to see that the selection includes material on the Caroline theatre as well as on Elizabethan and Jacobean plays. N.W. Bawcutt introduces and presents the full range of documents on the Salisbury Court Theatre, including a previously unpublished licence for Andrew Cane. Ira Clark's discussion of dramatic treatments of the marital double standard uses examples from Brome and Shirley as well as lesser-known Jacobean texts. Such investigations contribute to a richer and more complex picture of the relationship between prevailing conventions and stage representations. Nicholas Radel's tightly argued essay on tragicomedy brings Fletcher's play *The Humorous Lieutenant* (1619) into the limelight and persuasively demonstrates that homoerotic desire, although marginalized and proscribed, helps to constitute political stability by promoting an 'appropriate, de-eroticized love of a subject for his king' (p. 171).

The instability of the masculine subject is addressed in lively discussions of Marlowe's *Tamburlaine* by Carolyn Williams, and Marston's use of boy actors by David Pascoe. Lisa Hopkins looks at a different kind of challenge to male authority in *The Changeling*, where she argues that Middleton's play takes a form of revenge on Frances Howard by rewriting her story in the fate of the heroine. The court and the city are also considered. Leeds Barroll reconstructs a detail of theatre history involving a petition to construct a playhouse at the Red Bull and the patronage of Queen Anne's brother, in order to show the complex interaction of court politics and commercial playing in London. The importance of a theatre's geographical positioning in Blackfriars is considered by Janette Dillon in her thoughtful essay on *The Knight of the Burning Pestle*, where details of crossing and recrossing boundaries play out the tensions between the city and the barbaric spaces outside. Gossip from within the city may be untrustworthy, as Susan Cerasano points out in a critical re-examination of John Chamberlain's letters as a source of theatre history. Although Chamberlain lived near St Paul's, the hub of business, his reports of events like the burning of the Globe are troubled by the presence of Rumour, 'a pipe / Blown by surmises' (*2 Henry IV* Induction.15), and so must be treated with caution.

In the case of the printed word, the process of publication introduces its own filter, as James Riddell's striking new theory about Ben Jonson's *Every Man in His Humour* reminds us. On the much-debated question of how and when the play was revised, Riddell argues that Jonson may have been forced to make cuts at relatively short notice since the printer Stansby had only allowed six quires for the play at the beginning of the *Works*.

Jonson has also been the subject of a collection of essays: *New Perspectives on Ben Jonson*, edited by James Hirsch. The book is true to its title and presents a refreshing variety of material on familiar texts such as *Volpone* and *Epicoene* and more marginalized elements of the Jonsonian corpus. Ian Donaldson's essay on the comparative reputations of Shakespeare and Jonson covers some familiar ground but Francis Teague poses a challenge to the view that Jonson was a victim of his contemporaries' failure to appreciate his art. She argues that, with the exception of *The New Inn*, there is surprisingly little evidence to support the assumption that Jonson's later plays were failures. Jonson's acute awareness of the pressures of literary reputation are explored by Jennifer Brady, who reads the *Discoveries* as an acknowledgement of his literary forebears and a legacy to his disciples. Robert C. Evans and Anne Lake Prescott both consider Jonson's use of literary sources, classical and Rabelaisian, as revealed by marginal notes in his own copies. Prescott's essay is especially engaging. As well as identifying Jonson's ownership of a copy of Rabelais' *Oeuvres* (1599), she suggests that his borrowings are not simply to create comic effects. The allusions contain elements of religious satire, intimately connected to Jonson's own conversion from Catholicism, while the festive nature of drink, which has been related to Jonson's own fondness for the bottle, disguises a much more touching quest for the truth. In Rabelais, 'The Bottle of the Oracle' is a mixture of poetry and wine which promises self-knowledge. Examining Jonson's references to it, Prescott opens up a sympathetic glimpse of a man vainly searching for answers.

The figure of the poet is also very much to the fore in Bruce Thomas Boehrer's sensible discussion of 'On The Famous Voyage'. Firmly rejecting the view of Jonson as an anal neurotic, Boehrer analyses the scatological satire in the context of other early modern attitudes to waste to show that the poem balances tendencies to retention and expulsion which were typical of Jacobean England. A bleak picture of Jonson emerges in essays on dramatic texts by George Parfitt, Alexander Leggatt and James Hirsch. Hirsch identifies an especially cynical strand in *Volpone*, a play which empties language of any moral meaning since words like 'honour' signify even less than in *Julius Caesar*. Rather than examining Jonson's subject matter, Kate Levin makes a sharp critique of his stagecraft in *Epicoene*, arguing that his dramaturgical shortcomings could be more easily accommodated in court masques. While Levin's experience of directing *Epicoene* illuminates her points helpfully, one feels that her dismissal of the tight stage-management in *The Alchemist*, *Volpone* and *Bartholomew Fair* is, to say the least, unfair. Carol Lockett's reading of the masque *Pleasure Reconciled To Virtue* identifies a tension within Jonson's work which has been explored, in many different forms, throughout the volume.

The work of a lesser-known playwright is introduced in *The Plays of John Lyly: Eros and Eliza*, written by Michael Pincombe (not 'edited', as the cover misinforms us). This enjoyable book traces a conflict in Lyly's work between the traditions of love comedy, with which he was most at ease, and royal panegyric, the form with which his plays have usually been associated. Pincombe argues that, far from being a court playwright, Lyly distanced himself from the cult of 'Eliza' and that even plays presented at court are sceptical about the monarch's mythical status. The central thesis gives a strong through-line to the following chapters, each devoted to one of the plays. Since many have received little critical attention, this balance is a real asset. Departing from critical tradition, Pincombe reads *Campaspe* as an entertainment which the queen happened to attend, rather than a courtly panegyric. Far from praising Alexander the Great, the play is weighed down with dark reminders of the historical figure who, as Fluellen reminds us, 'in his rages and his furies and his wraths and his cholers . . . did in his ales and his angers, kill his best friend Cleitus' (*Henry V* 4.6.33–7). Gower hastily points out the differences between Alexander and Henry V (4.6.38–9), and Pincombe's argument that Elizabeth I would have been no more flattered by the comparison is convincing.

The difficulties of negotiating a path between panegyric and romantic comedy are explored more fully in chapters on *Sappho and Phao* and

*Endymion*. Pincombe argues that in the latter, Lyly parodically undermines the myth of 'Eliza' by projecting the triple identity of Diana (as Luna, goddess of chastity and Hecate) in the figures of Cynthia, Tellus and Dipsas. The eponymous heroine of *Mother Bombie* is read as another 'demonic or grotesque opposite: an "anti-Eliza"' (p. 158). Lyly was also concerned about censorship at Elizabeth's court, the book argues, and later plays offer a critique of the cult of chastity over which Elizabeth sternly presided. The chapter on *Galatea* is sadly brief but offers the striking suggestion that the play dramatizes Elizabeth's attempts to dictate a standard of chastity to her ladies in waiting, exposing the cult of virginity as a 'tyrannical erotic regime' (p. 136). This is one instance where a stronger theoretical framework would have strengthened the analysis of gender and erotic love, especially in relation to performance and performativity. Nevertheless, *The Plays of John Lyly* is illuminating and entertaining. Pincombe makes the plays accessible for a student reader to whom the plots or classical allusions may be unfamiliar. His style is conversational and the lively informality of the writing gives a lightness of touch in which Pincombe is faithful to the comic mode of Lyly's work.

The mythic power of Elizabeth is anatomized in the Autumn 1996 number of *English Literary Renaissance* which concentrates on the monarchical transition from Tudor to Stuart, female to male. Jonathan Baldo reads *Macbeth* in relation to James's politics of aloofness, but it is perhaps no surprise that Elizabeth's self-imaging dominates five of the seven essays, even those which deal with her corpse and her tombs. Perhaps the most interesting is Jennifer Summit's account of the dialogue of poetry and needlework between Elizabeth and Mary Stuart, where each is shown to have created a poetics of queenship through the needle and the pen.

Relationships between women and writing are illustrated in a new anthology *Lay by Your Needles Ladies, Take the Pen*, edited by Suzanne Trill, Kate Chegdzoy and Melanie Osborne. The book prints a selection of fifty prose extracts, mostly by women, from the mid-sixteenth to the end of the seventeenth century. The omission of poetry and drama makes this a less attractive general anthology than Betty Travitsky's *Paradise of Women* which gives representative examples of women's activity in these other genres. It is a useful student text in this growth area, though, and will be welcomed by those teaching courses on Renaissance women's writing.

Helen Wilcox's edition of critical essays, *Women and Literature in Britain 1500–1700*, gives a broader sense of women as readers and writers. The structure of the book cleverly sets up a tension between women as passive and active agents in their own self-fashioning. Essays from the first section on 'constructing women' and the second on 'writing women' work in conjunction to demonstrate how women responded to their cultural definitions. Ann Thompson's discussions of patrons, spectators and occasional participants in performances is neatly paired by Ros Ballaster's survey of female dramatists, for example. Margaret Ferguson's analysis of the anxiety and practical difficulties of authorship and Jacqueline Pearson's on women as readers give strong keynotes to each section. All the essays succeed in giving detailed up-to-date introductions to the topics they address, making this a valuable sourcebook of information and debate.

## TEXTS AND CONTEXTS

The continued dominance of new historicist and cultural materialist approaches is evidenced in publications that discuss history in equal or even greater measure than literary texts. In the Winter 1996 number of *English Literary History*, for example, Ian McAdam and Huston Diehl offer readings of *The Jew of Malta* and Stuart love tragedies on the 'literary' side, but the bias of the other pieces is to interpretations of historical moments, such as Roslyn Knutson's uncovering of evidence on refugees from Ottoman tyranny, as a factor governing the market for foreign history plays. The careful research undertaken is immensely valuable but our relationship to history now needs examining more rigorously. Albert Tricomi takes up the challenge in *Reading Tudor-Stuart Texts Through New Cultural Historicism*, a really fine book which presents stimulating, practical ways of breaking out of the deadlocks and indeterminacies in which new historicism finds itself. After an astute assessment of the problems, Tricomi proposes a modified critical methodology, 'cultural historicism'. It should, he argues, shift away from totalizing readings of culture through the court, accommodate itself to the interactive use of synchronic and diachronic readings of history, and, most significantly, seek to recover the affectivity of texts.

Having made an important intervention in the theoretical debate, Tricomi puts these ideas into practice in the following chapters. Taking two broad themes of surveillance and the female sexual body, he addresses each of the theoretical issues he outlines with flair. His intelligent discussion of utopias shows that Foucault's model of surveillance characterized sixteenth-century thought and writing so that More's Utopia 'turns out to be but a version of Bentham's panopticon' (p. 29). Given the ubiquity of power, Tricomi argues that cultural historicists should examine which manifestations 'are to be preferred over other, less productive ones' (p. 41). A deliberately conversational tone allows him to debate ideas with the reader and avoid prescriptive solutions. The next chapters consider the relationship between different types of historical 'knowledge'.

Analysis of Jonson and Shakespeare's verse demonstrates how processes of surveillance were internalized and reproduced as a 'tortuous undercurrent in the tropological discourse' of literary texts (p. 61). The dangers inherent in anecdotal histories are shown by comparing the partial evidence offered by the Rainbow Portrait of Elizabeth I, documents relating to the use of informers, and the representation of those figures in popular literature. Here again, Tricomi presents specific strategies for developing our reading.

The second part of the book, on the female sexual body, is not as full or as consistently trenchant as the first, though there are suggestive ideas. In the problem play, Tricomi notes that the behaviour of women is under particularly strict surveillance because the female sexual body is always 'symbolically laden' and 'the well being of the entire culture' is read into it (p. 93). This is obvious enough in plays like *Hamlet*, *All's Well*, *Troilus* and *Measure for Measure*, but the different ways in which female characters negotiate their role as objects of scrutiny is not addressed. Tricomi's consideration of Jacobean texts produces a novel interpretation of Chapman's *Bussy D'Ambois* as a problem play about male dependence on the female sexual body, rather than a flawed political tragedy. The book ends with a powerful reading of affectivity in *The Duchess of Malfi* and *The Duchess of Suffolk*. Since the latter has been unduly neglected, especially by feminist scholars, it is pleasing to see it discussed here. Tricomi's approach is not overtly psychoanalytic but his view of Webster's Duchess as a maternal figure whose death taps into 'deep human concerns' about the loss of such unconditional love (p. 142) usefully extends work like Janet Adelman's to non-Shakespearian drama. Tricomi makes a strong case for paying attention to the emotional power of texts since this is how they achieve their cultural effects.

Paul Innes adopts a completely different historicist approach in *Shakespeare and the English Renaissance Sonnet*, a subtle reading of the Sonnets as 'verses of feigning love' (*A Midsummer Night's Dream* 1.1.31). Rejecting the view that Shakespeare's Sonnets are revealing records of an intense personal passion, Innes provocatively chooses to analyse them as constructs of a society whose aristocratic ideology and underlying homosocial bonds are deeply threatened. There is no attempt to identify the young man or the dark lady, whose existence may be 'purely fictional' (p. 103). Instead, Innes begins with an assured survey of the sonnet tradition as an aristocratic transformation of military prowess into courtly love discourse, via a woman. The power of sonnets to contest rather than uphold this discourse is seen in Shakespeare's first seventeen poems, playing out a crisis of the aristocracy through the young man who defies the ideology of his class. This is an attractive argument, although the idea that the Sonnets fail to persuade the young man to marry does imply some kind of on-going narrative, in contrast to Innes's view that they may just be literary games.

Innes explores the relationship between the young man and the sonneteer in terms of homosocial bonds involving class differences, drawing on the work of Eve Sedgwick and Lorna Hutson. With many incisive close readings, he argues that the Sonnets do not present passion between equals but a poetics of patronage (though such bonding does not preclude homosexual attraction). Shakespeare's redefinition of the young man as a sonnet lady not only unsettles identities and gender norms, but enacts a 'radical disruption of mimesis' (p. 166) where the very act of representation is brought into question. The dark lady exacerbates the problem since fixed gendered subject positions which underpin patriarchal order are 'undone by one another' in the vexed triangular relationship (p. 187). This theoretically rigorous reading returns again and again to the poems, producing a highly sensitive account of the Sonnets as socially charged artefacts.

*Subject and Object in Renaissance Culture*, edited by Margreta de Grazia, Maureen Quilligan and Peter Stallybrass, is also designed to promote a different perspective by reintroducing the object, in a critical counter-move to discussions of early modern subjectivity. The power of the desiring subject is still evident, especially in Jonathan Dollimore's reading of Shakespeare's Sonnets as a prime example of the Renaissance death-wish, an insatiable desire whose final object is the annihilation of the self. The majority of the volume is weighted towards the restoration of the object, and occasionally one feels that the pendulum has swung too far, as in Patricia Parker's consideration of joinery in *A Midsummer Night's Dream*, where the profusion of material details eclipses the play completely. For most of the very prestigious contributors though, the tension between subject and object has lent a sparky internal dynamic to the arguments, so the book recaptures the energy of debate from the conference at which papers were first presented. Particularly effective is Peter Stallybrass's analysis of how the clothes are fetishized in their recycling as theatre costumes, and thereby take on a life of their own. Objects provide the starting point for discussions of gender, colonialist appropriations, non-canonical as well as canonical texts. The diversity of material is testament to the editors' view that a return to the object opens up new dimensions of the past which complicate our understanding of subjects and texts.

The complexity of local differences in any picture of the past is set out with tremendous care in David Cressy's *Birth, Marriage and Death: Ritual, Religion and the Life Cycle in Tudor and Stuart England*. This is not a general social history but a study of specific rites of passage and conflicting attitudes towards the rituals which surrounded them. Religious differences were at the centre of disputes over what kinds of public or private ceremonies should surround the delivery of children, their incorporation into the church, the marriage or deaths of members of the community. Cressy describes the significant variations between forms of ritual in amazing detail to demonstrate that, while witnessing rites of passage supposedly united a community, in fact the heightened occasion of such ceremonies often exposed fractures in society. As well as covering the main church ceremonies, with all the points of doctrinal difference, the book considers secular or non-official festive customs. Cressy begins even before birth with an examination of the expectant parents' hopes and fears, giving ample space for the voices of the past to be glimpsed through letters and diaries. There is extensive information on such items as christening feasts, courtship tokens, bridal bouquets and 'bedding' rituals, mourning clothes and wakes. Literary editors and scholars will find the book useful. The detail is almost overwhelming at times; the clamour of different opinions and forms of behaviour means that it can be difficult to find a clear answer on any given topic, but of course this is precisely Cressy's point.

A similar picture of complexity is presented by *Religion and Culture in Renaissance England*, edited by Clare McEachern and Debora Shuger. The first section 'Form and Community' examines religion as the constructor of various communal identities, doctrinal, parochial, and national. The importance of textuality and the difficulties of incorporating disparate elements in a world where words 'do set the faith itself / Against the faith' (*Richard II* 5.3.13) are explored in essays by Patrick Collinson, Lowell Gallagher, Jesse Lander, Debora Shuger and David Scott Kastan. In each case, the authors succeed in setting out general arguments appropriate to the broad framework of this section and illustrating these with details in which the complexity of the picture is revealed.

The overlap between various forms of Catholicism and Protestantism in England becomes clear in the second part of the book on literary texts. Janel Mueller convincingly argues that the Protestant martyrs celebrated in Foxe's *Acts and Monuments* were able to appropriate and transform the Catholic ontology of presence in the Eucharist. Martyrdom paradoxically displaces the 'crucial site of human access to divinity' from the Mass to the 'physical body and agency of the believer' (p. 171), and this foundation of selfhood underlies the religious poetry of Donne and Herbert. Essays by Michael Schoenfeldt and Richard Strier on the work of Donne, Aemelia Lanyer and Milton give some breadth to this section, within traditional definitions of the 'literary' text.

The place of Shakespeare's work in the turbulent religious culture is addressed in two separate pieces. Richard McCoy reads the later sonnets as 'sacrificial' poems whose eucharistic imagery display a pattern of 'annihilation and redemptive sacrifice' (p. 201) and argues that the religious allusions in 'The Phoenix and the Turtle' deserve as much attention as the political topicality of the poem. His discussion does not lead to any new proposals about Shakespeare's religious allegiances or take account of Ernst Honigmann's pertinent theory about the poem's composition and all this implies.[1] In contrast, Robert Watson's essay on *Othello* as Protestant propaganda is brilliantly provocative. He proposes that Othello's 'crisis of faith' (p. 242) relates not just to his marriage but to his belief in himself as deserving redemption through grace. With reference to religious texts, Watson argues that Desdemona may have been seen by contemporary audiences as a Christ-like figure, and Iago as a dangerously persuasive Jesuit who tempts Othello into viewing Desdemona's love as 'the contingent reward of merit' (p. 244). *Religion and Culture in Renaissance England* is thus a very worthwhile collection, combining new insights and carefully researched analyses of the spiritual environment with which early modern subjects interacted.

Religion is a key starting point for the renaissance of the written word in Frederick Kiefer's discussion of *Writing on the Renaissance Stage*, a useful study of prevailing ideas about physical documents and metaphoric books in the sixteenth and seventeenth centuries. The opening chapter draws a richly detailed picture of the European context for the drama. Kiefer argues that Erasmus and Luther were responsible for enhancing the status of the written word and simultaneously ensuring the death

[1] E. A. J. Honigmann, *Shakespeare: the 'Lost Years'* (Manchester: Manchester University Press, 1985)

and the immortality of the author, whether it be God, Ben Jonson or Shakespeare. The essential ambiguities of writing are examined further in chapters on metaphorical books, where Kiefer does well to remind us that Derridean suspicions about language were counterbalanced by ancient beliefs about the naturalness of writing as part of a divine patterning of creation.

Each discussion is divided into an introductory context chapter followed by a paired chapter on the drama. This technique works better in the section on metaphorical books than in the opening, where analyses of Heywood's *If You Know Not Me*, Marlowe's *Doctor Faustus* and the Jack Cade rebellion in *2 Henry VI* seem too brief and curiously detached from the complex picture of the European Reformation. The three chapters on the book of conscience, the book of nature and the book of fate are very well-researched, and Kiefer shows how these books form an intrinsic part of the play texts he analyses. While discussing the book of conscience, he draws an interesting contrast between *A Woman Killed With Kindness* where Frankford's letter writing to himself symbolizes 'how circumscribed his world is becoming' (p. 136), and *Bussy D'Ambois*, where the letter is a vital source of dramatic tension. The subsequent analyses of plays (including *As You Like It* and *Pericles*) are clear and straightforward. Kiefer's opening up of metaphorical books to our modern eyes represents a significant contribution to scholarship.

A genre of writing whose ubiquity has rendered it almost invisible is accorded timely attention in *The Project of Prose in Early Modern Europe and the New World*, edited by Elizabeth Fowler and Roland Greene. Rather than examining canonized English literary texts, the book gives a selection of 'strategically identified moments' (p. 1) representative of a much wider cultural and geographical spread. There are chapters on Spanish, Portuguese and Italian works as well as on English writings. In addition to crossing national boundaries to suggest a broader context for all of these texts, the collection's interdisciplinary nature effectively dissolves traditional generic categorizations, showing how history, romance, fantasy, scientific, legal discourses circulated and intermingled in often surprising ways. Essays by Ronald Sousa and Rolena Adorno on writings from the East and the New World illustrate this point admirably. The book provides fresh angles on more familiar material too, as in Roland Greene's ingenious analysis of Puttenham's *Arte of English Poesie* and Sidney's *Apologie for Poetry*, or Amy Boesky's discussion of how the fragmentary status of Bacon's writing in the *New Atlantis* betrays acknowledgement of the inadequacy of human endeavour. The approaches taken by the contributors indicate how rich a field of study this volume begins to uncover.

Prose and verse rather than drama is the main focus of *The Custom of the Castle from Malory to Macbeth*, in which Charles Ross reconsiders the custom of the castle as a confrontation between one set of social norms and another. In five well-argued chapters on French and English romances, he shows that the castle provides a motif for the politics of integration, colonization, and relationships between individual and community. For example, the alien confronting a new castle (or institution) is in danger of being trapped in its 'foul' custom, for having succeeded in the test to enter the castle, he or she then has to uphold the custom or negotiate a way around it.

Ross sets up interesting ideas here but, sadly, does not pursue them with anything like the fullness they deserve in relation to Shakespeare's texts. Brief appendices on *Othello* and *King Lear* indicate little more than starting points, and the chapter on *Hamlet* is vague. Ross sees Hamlet as a 'knight errant who suddenly finds himself forced to defend the foul ways of a castle' (p. 106), but never develops the potential for reading Claudius as a usurping or incoming knight and Hamlet's ambiguous position as an incomer who is 'to the manner born' (1.1.17). On *Macbeth*, Ross is stronger, arguing that the hero eventually performs a type of self-exorcism at Dunsinane 'that allows an oppressive castle to be reinscribed as a sign of justice' (p. 118). As this chapter proves, the custom of the castle offers alternative ways of reading Shakespeare's plays; it is unfortunate that the book doesn't explore these adequately.

## PERFORMANCES AND REINTERPRETATIONS

Since the official opening of the new Globe, opinions about the first formal season have been shared in energetic debates across the internet. *Shakespeare's Globe Rebuilt* commemorates the opening with a celebration of the Herculean task, what Andrew Gurr calls 'the enormous labours of the past years, joining so many different kinds of expertise together' (p. 159). Specialist essays on aspects of the building process have little to say directly about Shakespeare's plays, but the book is a compact source of information and current scholarly opinion about public theatre buildings. Jon Greenfield's engaging discussion of principles of design and construction conveys a real sense of the frustrations and triumphs along the rebuilding route, while his chapter on 'Timber Framing' draws interesting conclusions about the methods of Peter Streete, Master Carpenter at the first Globe.

The book's focus on the physical aspects of the theatre is its major strength. It raises the possibility that 'the architecture of Shakespeare's Globe has an intimate connection with the themes of his plays' (p. 172), opening up material contexts for interpreting them. Especially effective are essays on the theatre's interior design by John Ronayne, Siobhan Keenan and Peter Davidson, which outline the cryptic messages encoded into decorations. Knowing that craftsmen and their customers recognized a hierarchy of stone in their decorative schemes, and that this was probably used for the *frons scenae* of the first Globe, adds a physical dimension to moments such as Ulysses' speech on degree, for example. It is to be hoped that, as the authors suggest, explanatory notes on programmes will give modern spectators access to the complex layers of visual symbolism in the theatre (p. 154).

The book's final section, 'The Globe in Performance', is not the climax which it ought to be. Andrew Gurr's essay 'Staging at the Globe' neatly summarizes much familiar material on Shakespeare's use of non-verbal languages in the texts, perhaps a little 'old hat' for those used to considering the plays as three-dimensional entities. Gurr also makes wise suggestions on how the physical dimensions of the theatre might offer us readings of specific Shakespearian lines, but we do not hear from the range of actors who have actually used the space. Instead, Mark Rylance gives a statement of artistic policy and practice. His personal philosophy is encouraging since he aims to promote collaborative interaction within the company and to incorporate both Brechtian style 'presentation' and Stanislavskian forms of 'playing'. How did the actors feel about playing the Globe during the workshop and prologue seasons, though? Unlike the builders, they are only just beginning their work, so it is perhaps too early to expect definitive statements about how the space conditions performance, but it is sad that none of their initial, and no doubt varied, impressions of working there are included.

Since one of Sam Wanamaker's goals for the Globe was to promote co-operation between theatre practitioners and academics, it is appropriate that this year should also see the publication of a collection of essays by Marvin Rosenberg, whose pioneering work has made performance such an essential dimension in the critical tradition. *The Adventures of A Shakespeare Scholar: To discover Shakespeare's Art* is presented as an ongoing quest. The volume includes thirty different pieces of work drawn from Rosenberg's experiences with the plays across the last forty years. His initial challenge to the academic world in 'Elizabethan Actors: Men or Marionettes?' and classic essays such as '*Lear*'s Theater Poetry' takes their place alongside much more recent conference papers and current, unpublished research on 'Visualising Complex Character'. One of his own contributions to theatre history, in suggesting a new interpretation of the ending to *Measure for Measure* in 1968, is also included. All the items are introduced personally as part of Rosenberg's enthusiastic travels through a land of Shakespeare scholars and performers. He invites readers to participate in the experiments he conducted with conference audiences by reading lines or passages aloud to test out ideas. He provokes active engagement with character by giving deliberately simplified definitions of Hamlet as either 'sweet' or 'powerful', and often ends the pieces with questions. These methods are indicative of the openness which is needed for genuine collaboration between theatre and academy.

While Rosenberg's insistence on character as a mainspring of the plays flies in the face of post-modern theories of the subject, their pedagogical value is obvious. The activities he has pioneered demand extra time, effort and considerable energy which makes them expensive in financial terms, and therefore increasingly vulnerable in the current economic climate. Cynical responses from highly theorized or historicist critical perspectives must be balanced with an appreciation of the invaluable contribution of work like Rosenberg's if productive links between the academy and theatre are to survive.

Film as well as theatre is considered in James Loehlin's 'Shakespeare in Performance' volume on *Henry V*. Loehlin sees productions working between the official patriotic play and the 'secret' one which threatens to deconstruct the celebration of heroism and military triumph from within. To pursue this idea, he devotes the majority of his book to post-war English interpretations. While one applauds the depth of analysis that this allows, I was sorry that some of the productions mentioned in the introduction were not given fuller treatment, even at the expense of material in the following chapters. Since Loehlin points out that the BBC film is ruined by its 'bland smoothness' (p. 83), for example, one wonders why it merits a chapter of its own. The fact that such filmed interpretations are easily accessible should not sway performance studies to a more modern focus, however commercially attractive that might appear to publishers. Creating access to Charles Calvert's anti-war *Henry V* of 1872 and Aaron Hill's interesting 1723 adaptation, as Loehlin does but briefly, is important.

Within his parameters, Loehlin gives a strongly politicized reading of the major films and theatre productions. His care in outlining the local and national contexts which influenced the interpretative choices made by directors is a real strength of the book. He rightly appreciates Olivier's subtle transformation of the idealistic patriotism of the nineteenth century, while an extensive analysis of Noble's 1984 *Henry V*, with a good range of press reviews, illustrates that even this anti-war production could be approved from a patriotic viewpoint. For Loehlin, the difficulty of breaking away from a traditional reading of Henry is evidenced by Branagh's 1989 film, 'the official version of the play disguised as the secret one' (p. 145), where a grim emphasis on suffering paradoxically promotes a celebration of heroic individualism characteristic of 1980s Tory policy. Such intelligent analysis is characteristic of the book and Loehlin is always sensitive to particular moments and good performances. He evaluates the political dynamism and vulgarity of Bogdanov's decidedly unsympathetic *Henry V* with equal skill, commenting on the dangers of subsuming the play within the tetralogy. The final chapter draws attention to some non-English interpretations, ranging from Kevin Kline's heroic Henry in Central Park to Michael Kahn's controversial production in Stratford Connecticut. With great success, this tightly focused study demonstrates how *Henry V* is itself an ideological battleground.

Gerda Taranow takes up the work of reconstructing an earlier theatre production in *The Bernhardt Hamlet: Text and Context*, working from the premiere in Paris in 1899 to its reception on tour in London and America. The reader is able to appreciate fully the radical nature of Bernhardt's decision to play the Prince as a vigorous revenger, without the traditional black plumed hat that signified the romantic dreamer, since Taranow takes great trouble to convey the pervasive power of *fin de siècle* 'Hamletism', with reference to paintings, engravings and the salon culture of Paris. Less revolutionary than it first appears is Bernhardt's appropriation of a leading male role. Taranow traces a female *travesti* tradition in opera, ballet and Parisian theatre, and female Hamlets in Britain and America. It is also striking to learn that Bernhardt's production was innovative in restoring the majority of the text to the stage in a new prose translation. A useful comparison of passages pays close attention to the sound of the performance text, Bernhardt's French pronunciation and outstanding vocal ability. A lengthy penultimate chapter painstakingly reconstructs the production from Acts 1 to 5, drawing on theatre reviews, recordings, photographs and a film recording of the duel scene. My main criticism is of the book's repetition of material: we are reminded of Bernhardt's emphasis on revenge with annoying frequency and the discussion of female *travesti* roles is fragmented across several chapters. Concentrated into a single discussion, it could have been further theorized with reference to Elaine Showalter's ideas about gender instability and performance typical of the *fin de siècle*. That said, Taranow does give an evocative analysis of Bernhardt's important contribution to the performance history of *Hamlet*.

An earlier *fin de siècle* reinterpretation of Shakespeare is explored in *The Boydell Shakespeare Gallery*, a collection of essays on the significance of Boydell's promotion of Shakespeare paintings in the late eighteenth and early nineteenth centuries. Engravings of the pictures, which were published in folio form as a 'printed' gallery, are reproduced, many of them in good-sized plates. They provide ample illustration of the shift from Augustan to Romantic modes of thought and style: from the classically ordered 'Cassandra Raving' by Romney to much wilder, expressive and even surreal pictures, such as Fuseli's pre-Kott version of Titania's bower in *A Midsummer Night's Dream*. There are many interesting engravings, such as the tragic end of *King Lear*, which the audience would not have known from performances of course, and James Northcote's interpretations of *Richard III*, combining a comically villainous Richard (based on Kemble) with a sentimental view of the princes and a chilling picture of their dead bodies being bundled away into the dungeons of the Tower. The Catalogue of Engravings is a valuable resource for those interested in visual interpretations of the plays.

The essays in the volume are of variable quality and there are some annoying errors, especially misreferencing of the engravings. In spite of this, useful guidelines are set up for reading the Boydell Gallery in relation to its artistic, literary and cultural contexts. Elinor Shaffer's discussion of the gallery facade considers its contribution to bardolatry and to the illustration of Shakespeare. Gerd Unverfehrt demonstrates how negative reactions to the venture were wittily summarized in James Gillray's caricature, *Shakespeare Sacrificed*, and extends Jonathan Bate's earlier analysis by arguing that Gillray modelled it on an etching of Garrick at the Stratford Jubilee celebrations. In a section devoted to artists and themes, Marcia Pointon and Grant Scott take contrasting perspectives to read images of *The Tempest* with reference to a time of national crisis. It is to be regretted that other engravings in the collection do not receive the same detailed, trenchant analysis. Georgianna Ziegler's essay on female characters is particularly disappointing since it deliberately omits the comedies in its attempt to fit the heroines into categories of 'suppliant women' and 'monumental maidens', then fails to notice Lady Eleanor in one image and misreads the suppliant figure of Cressida in Angelica Kauffmann's picture. The radical nature of Kauffmann's sympathetic interpretation, plus the detail that she cross-dressed in order to attend lessons at the Royal Academy, are noted in Burwick's fine discussion of the Romantic response to the Boydell Gallery. Here the tensions between past traditions and innovations which characterized the turn of the century come under close scrutiny. As the millennium approaches for us, our relationships with the past, in terms of theatre and criticism, are similarly being interrogated. Our insatiable appetite for recovering, or rebuilding, fragments of the Globe in which Shakespeare's texts were produced is being refined in a critical environment that is simultaneously drawing us back before the early 'modern' and forwards beyond 'new' historicism. The reconstructed Globe, which opens doors to both the past and the future, is the most striking material manifestation of this brave new(er) world.

## WORKS REVIEWED

Cox, John D. and David Scott Kastan, eds. *A New History of Early English Drama*. New York: Columbia University Press, 1997.

Cressy, David. *Birth, Marriage, and Death: Ritual, Religion, and the Life-Cycle in Tudor and Stuart England*. Oxford: Oxford University Press, 1997.

De Grazia, Margreta, Maureen Quilligan and Peter Stallybrass, eds. *Subject and Object in Renaissance Culture*. Cambridge: Cambridge University Press, 1996.

Hillman, Richard. *Self-Speaking in Medieval and Early English Drama: Subjectivity, Discourse and the Stage*. Basingstoke: Macmillan Press, 1997.

Innes, Paul. *Shakespeare and the English Renaissance Sonnet: Verses of Feigning Love*. Basingstoke: Macmillan Press, 1997.

Kiefer, Frederick. *Writing on the Renaissance Stage: Written Words, Printed Pages, Metaphoric Books*. Newark and London: University of Delaware Press, 1996.

Kinney, Arthur F. *English Literary Renaissance*. Vol. xxvi, no. 1. Amherst: University of Massachusetts Press, 1996.

Loehlin, James N. *Shakespeare in Performance: Henry V*. Manchester and New York: Manchester University Press, 1996.

McEachern, Clare and Deborah Shuger, eds. *Religion and Culture in Renaissance England*. Cambridge: Cambridge University Press, 1997.

Mulryne, J. R. and Margaret Shewring, eds. *Shakespeare's Globe Rebuilt*. Cambridge: Cambridge University Press, 1997.

Pape, Walter and Frederick Burwick, eds. *The Boydell Shakespeare Gallery*. Bottrop: Peter Pomp, 1996.

Pincombe, Michael. *The Plays of John Lyly: Eros and Eliza*. Manchester and New York: Manchester University Press, 1996.

Pitcher, John, ed. *Medieval and Renaissance Drama in England*. Vol. ix. Madison and Teaneck: Fairleigh Dickinson University Press/London: Associated University Presses, 1997.

Rosenberg, Marvin. *The Adventures of a Shakespeare Scholar*. Newark and London: University of Delaware Press, 1997.

Ross, Charles. *The Custom of the Castle: From Malory to Macbeth*. Berkeley, Los Angeles and London: University of California Press, 1997.

Stokes, James and Robert J. Alexander, eds. *Records of Early English Drama: Somerset, edited by James Stokes, Including Bath, edited by Robert J. Alexander*. Toronto, Buffalo and London: Toronto University Press, 1996.

Swain, Kathleen M. *English Literary Renaissance*. Vol. xxvi, no. 3. Amherst: University of Massachusetts Press, 1996.

Taranow, Gerda. *The Bernhardt Hamlet: Culture and Context*. New York: Peter Lang, 1996.

Trill, Suzanne, Kate Chegdzoy and Melanie Osborne, eds. *Lay by Your Needles Ladies, Take the Pen*. London and New York: Arnold, 1997.

Tricomi, Albert H. *Reading Tudor-Stuart Texts Through Cultural Historicism*. Gainesville: University Press of Florida, 1996.

Wilcox, Helen, ed. *Woman and Literature in Britain: 1500–1700*. Cambridge: Cambridge University Press, 1996.

# 3. EDITIONS AND TEXTUAL STUDIES

*reviewed by* JOHN JOWETT

## EDITIONS

As one of the editors of the Oxford Shakespeare *Complete Works*, I should declare an ambivalent and unmercenary interest in the Norton Shakespeare, based on the Oxford text. For the Norton editors, the value of the Oxford lies in its authoritative challenge to previous editorial practice as it is still represented in its rivals. Norton have reprinted the Oxford *Textual Companion* (1987) in a paperback edition (available in North America only). It is a reminder that the massive documentation in the Oxford Shakespeare *Companion* lies behind the Norton edition, though it remains at one remove, for the Norton edition purports to be free-standing. The Norton edition on the whole preserves the integrity of the Oxford text, and builds around it generously extensive annotations, introductions, appendices, bibliographies, and illustrations, including skeleton textual documentation for each work and a valuable essay on the Shakespearian stage by Andrew Gurr. To many, the combination of Oxford textualism, the sophisticated critical acumen of the editorial team led by Stephen Greenblatt, and the well-calculated generosity afforded by the Norton format will make this the best complete works available. The Norton edition can be considered as a major new edition in its own right, and presents a direct challenge to the Riverside and Bevington Complete Works that dominate the American market.

The Oxford text is not printed intact. The limited changes have the deliberate effect of moderating some of that edition's more controversial features. In doing so Norton generates a split focus in the overall editorial vision. Take for example the reconsidered treatment of stage directions. Not even the Oxford editors would argue that their system was definitively correct, but it does have a logic and consistency that resist mechanical readjustment. Oxford reserves broken brackets for contentious stage directions. In Norton all editorial stage-direction wording (apart from a few exceptions or inconsistencies) is placed within square brackets, irrespective of whether it is contentious. The brackets are applied to rephrasing as well as additions. When such rewording takes place, the reading of the control text is not recorded in the textual notes, and so it disappears from sight entirely. Consequently, the reader can only guess whether a bracketed reading has no equivalent in the control text or substitutes for some other unrecorded wording. As for the stage directions that are not marked off in brackets, for a number of reasons they cannot be assumed to follow the control text. Directions that have been moved escape bracketing, as does transposed wording within a stage direction and correction of '*Exit*' to '*Exeunt*'. Directions that have been supplied from a secondary early text are generally not bracketed. This procedure is followed even where the secondary text might represent an independent theatrical version of the play. In the heavily altered Q1 version of *Hamlet* Ophelia enters '*playing on a lute, and her haire downe singing*'. The Oxford text rewords the direction to read '*her hair down, with a lute*' and places it in brackets. The rewording responds to the difference in staging whereby in F but not Q1 there is dialogue before Ophelia sings 'How should I your true love know', and the brackets acknowledge that even details from Q1 that are compatible with F do not necessarily belong in the Folio version. It is questionable not only whether Ophelia is playing and singing as she enters in the Folio version, for also the use of a lute would depend on the skills of a particular boy actor and could be specific to a version or a production. In Norton the stage direction reverts to Q1 and is incorporated in that form without either bracketing or textual note. What is alarming here, because it is widespread and a matter of policy, is that the emendation of the control text is made without recourse to either brackets or documentation in the textual notes. The doubly silenced emendation affects both the theatrical substance and the wording of scores of stage directions. To gain any understanding of the stage directions of the original printed texts, the Norton reader must necessarily fall back on the Oxford *Textual Companion* itself.

Another alteration of the Oxford procedures concerns the passages that the Oxford Shakespeare prints as additional passages on the grounds that they are extraneous to the version of the play that is being presented. Norton reinserts most of them into the text. They are presented in italic type with an offset layout (just as the stage directions). As with the extended bracketing of stage directions, this change alters the intellectual basis of the editing as well as affecting the aesthetics of textual presentation. It involves at least a partial return to the composite, inclusive text presenting simultaneously lines that editors think existed at different stages in the play's textual history. This is particularly striking in the case of *Hamlet*, where the passages unique to Q2 are relatively extensive and now find themselves amidst what is otherwise a consciously Folio-oriented version of the play. Specific difficulties can arise; for instance the reintroduction of Pandarus' epilogic speech at the end of *Troilus and Cressida* means that Troilus utters his 'Hence, broker-lackey' speech dismissing Pandarus in two separate scenes (see my review of the problem in *Shakespeare Survey 50*).

With *King Lear* the Norton editors adopt a similar spirit of compromise but find a different solution. The Oxford texts of *The History* and *The Tragedy* are printed in parallel on facing pages, and a third, freshly prepared conflated text is added. Though the commentary is lavishly triplicated, the conflation appears without any textual documentation, the most heavily fabricated text therefore appearing to be the least so. Careful readers will note that the Norton editors agree entirely with the Oxford position that the quarto and Folio texts should be regarded as separate entities. In the introduction Greenblatt quietly favours the Folio over both the Quarto and the conflated text by using *The Tragedy* as the standard for line references. The conflation is included so as to enable readers to 'encounter the tragedy in the form that it assumed in most editions from the eighteenth century until very recently'. Textually naive readers may, nonetheless, find themselves resisting the parallel texts and turning to the inclusive, self-contained, and free-standing conflation. This would be unfortunate, as from the Oxford–Norton perspective its interest is merely historical.

One further major change to the Oxford text is that Oldcastle dies a martyr. Oldcastle, Russell, and Harvey, the names that Shakespeare evidently first gave to characters in *1 Henry IV* and that are re-established in the Oxford Shakespeare, now go back to the traditional Falstaff, Baldolph, and Peto. This reversion chimes with the concession of a conflated *Lear*, but with the important difference that in the case of Oldcastle the Oxford break with editorial tradition, rather than being preserved and prioritized, has now completely disappeared. The diplomatic justifications on p. 75 are not entirely convincing, but still, both 'Oldcastle' and 'Falstaff' are defensible readings. Whereas Oxford took the unfamiliar option, Norton finds the reasons for printing 'Falstaff' either convincing or convenient.

Undoubtedly the textual line of fracture between Oxford and Norton leaves traces of instability in the editions as a whole. The new textual notes can be inadequate; I noted some important unrecorded emendations, mistranscriptions from Folio and quarto readings as recorded in the *Textual Companion*, inconsistent record of modernizations, and persistent confusion over representing early modern 'u' and 'v', 'i' and 'j'. In other respects, ancillary material that is particular to the Norton edition is compendious and engaging. Annotations tend to be tactful and precise, as I found by looking at the early scenes in *Richard III*. The editor is alert to a difficulty often passed over in the expression 'wayward sickness', perceptively glossing 'wayward' as '*not easily treated*'. For 'jacks' the communicable gloss '*nobodies*' is preferred over the more literal but antiquated *OED*-ese '*knaves*', and when Anne '*offers*' at Richard's breast with his sword it is justifiably explained that she '*thrusts*' at him rather than more passively 'aiming'. There is, however, a conspicuous double slip in the explanation that Anne's 'father' is 'Edward; actually father-in-law to Henry VI': the Edward in question is Anne's betrothed husband and Henry's son. The mistake no doubt testifies to the vaguely riddling and overdetermined nature of Anne's relationship with the dead Henry, and certainly adds to the confusion.

It is the general and particular introductions that define most clearly the critical complexion. The Norton Shakespeare represents an occasionally uneasy absorption of New Historicism and feminism into the larger field of critical endeavour. The editors endorse and indeed take delight in editorial mediation; they reinforce a canonical and self-contained Shakespeare; they write of people within a broad tapestry of social life rather than creating New Historicist contiguity between isolated texts. Greenblatt's General Introduction describes Shakespeare's times, his life, and his art, the expected and fundamental duties of such a document. At times Greenblatt can stand at a slightly ironic distance from these activities, as when he notes (in an oddly mixed metaphor) that the few documents recording details of Shakespeare's life 'have come to seem like precious relics and manage to achieve a considerable resonance' (p. 42). The Introduction leans heavily towards socio-cultural matters. 'Shakespeare's World' comprises 'Haves and Have-Nots', 'Riot and Disorder', 'The Legal Status of Women', to cite three adjacent sections, but there is little attention to literary, intellectual, and artistic contexts. The theatre is excellently documented as a social and material institution, but there is no account of the drama that played in it.

Greenblatt and his colleagues are engaging writers who introduce the individual works stylishly. The scope can be considered in Katharine Eisaman Maus's introduction to *Timon*. The essay is organized around the theme 'What has love got to do with money?'. This question is related to Jacobean conspicuous consumption and economic transition, and Maus suggests that if the play was left incomplete (an unsafe assumption) this may have been because it was 'too incendiary to be safely performed'. A paragraph draws attention to the idea of the female in this highly male play. Timon himself is presented as an egocentric satirist simultaneously disengaged from but overengaged with the society that disgusts him. Maus carelessly renames Flavius as 'Fulvius'. She describes him as a figure whose own virtues suggest that Timon's misanthropy is too extreme. Alcibiades is a figure who broadens the depiction of Athens to incorporate political and military factors. Finally, 'How Alcibiades will reform Athens is hard to imagine.'

Though one might quibble that love hasn't got much to do with *Timon* either, this is a good essay on the play's qualities as satire, and will probably encourage students to read it. What is missing is a sufficient sense of dramatic technique, structure, and poetic temper. This tends to be true of the edition as a whole, and it is surely a serious limitation to a Shakespeare edition for it not to do enough to stimulate the reader to think of the plays as major achievements of theatre art. What is contentious in the account of *Timon* is its sustained attempt to efface the Oxford emphasis on Middleton as probable collaborator, and to silence the text of *Timon* as a field of communication and contestation between two distinctive dramaturgies and literary ideolects. Despite its emphasis on history, the Norton Shakespeare sometimes finds ways of preserving the *cordon sanitaire* around the authorial mind.

In his introduction to *King Lear* Greenblatt writes not only with finely controlled poise but, more to the point, with a rather traditional kind of authority. 'Shakespeare's tragedy', he concludes, 'asks us not to turn away from evil, folly, and unbearable human pain but, seeing them face-to-face, to strengthen our capacity to endure and to love'. Authorially mandated meaning, genre demarcation, and moral lesson are all firmly in place. There is a sense here of a trans-historical human condition, something perceived by Shakespeare, something that enables reference to the generality of readers. The message, sharply unsentimental, resilient, even tough as it may be, comes from a pedagogic stance that is conservative and soothingly familiar. This tendency to abate the rough edge of post-1968 radicalism is reflected in both the Norton Shakespeare's moderation of its own editors' feminist and New Historicist critical roots and its modification of the Oxford editors' sometimes disturbingly innovative text.

This is nevertheless an edition of great distinctiveness, and, apart from its inadequate sense of the plays as scripts for theatrical performance, the best representative of current thinking both textual and critical. Despite its plenitude it is physically compact, and it is highly efficient as an instrument of editorial mediation. In general appearance the text conforms to Norton's house-style. The plays and poems are printed in a single column with line-numbers to the left; the departure from the Oxford measure means that Norton generates its own line-numbering system in prose passages, a point to be kept in mind when cross-referring to the unmodified Oxford *Textual Companion*. Glosses on the right are flagged with 'bubbles', and fuller notes at the foot of the page are flagged with superscript numerals; for those accustomed to a plainer text the experience of reading will be unavoidably splintered. The Norton Shakespeare must be the fullest edition of Shakespeare ever to have been put within a single book-cover; indeed it probably contains more words than an eighteenth or nineteenth-century edition that would take up half a book-shelf. The edition runs to 3420 pages, longer than either of the two volumes of the Norton Anthology of English Literature. In both hard and paper covers, it is a miracle of book construction. The glue and bindings do a remarkable job, but the paper is noticeably thinner than the already svelte sheets of the Anthology. There is a distinct show-through of print and the pages soon start to crumple.

The new features of the updated but still relatively compact fourth edition of David Bevington's *Complete Works* can be summarized more briefly. In conformity with the Norton and new Riverside editions, Bevington now includes *A Funeral Elegy for Master William Peter* (discussed below) and *The Two Noble Kinsmen*. As with Norton but in contrast with Riverside, *Edward III* remains beyond the pale. Whereas the Norton edition confines the *Elegy* to an appendix, Bevington adds it to the canon of Shakespeare's poems, though his introduction ends with the cautionary comment that 'The attribution remains uncertain'. *Two Noble Kinsmen* is edited with the exacting care one expects of Bevington, and one play, *Troilus and Cressida*, has been partly re-edited. Whereas previously Bevington posited that the Quarto 'may represent Shakespeare's revision', he now agrees with Gary Taylor and others that it is F that 'often gives what may perhaps be Shakespeare's later decisions in a manuscript that may also have been put to use in the theater'. On this cautious basis he has extended the number of Folio readings he admits into the text, so we now read 'loud', not 'broad' (1.3.27; misnumbered 29 in the textual note), 'just', not 'right' (1.3.164), 'Jove's', not 'great Jove's' (1.3.238), and so on. Q remains nominally at least the copy text. Herein perhaps lies a silent rationale for ignoring F's more substantial and troublesome introduction of a new version of the 'Hence, broker-lackey' passage into 5.3, even though this alteration cannot be one of the 'sophistications or compositorial errors' said to render F unsuitable as copy. Bevington's willingness to reconsider *Troilus and Cressida* is nevertheless commendable. However, it cannot help but highlight the cases where he has not responded to newer textual developments. Words such as 'revision' and 'later decisions' still do not appear in the textual headnotes to *Hamlet*, *Othello*, and *King Lear*.

Amongst the series of individual plays, Arden 3 has affirmed its presence and character by adding three attractive yet distinctively individual editions to its list. The success of R. A. Foakes's *King Lear* lies in a multifaceted coverage of an astonishingly wide range of material. His edition has many points of excellence, perhaps the most striking of which is Foakes's encyclopedic knowledge of the history of criticism, performance, and artistic response that has affirmed the play's remarkable position in the twentieth-century imagination. Foakes carefully negotiates these diverse responses, keeping his own critical voice at a discreetly low key. As a record of *Lear*'s reception, not least in the theatre, his account is without rival in editions of the play. A useful section reviews reworkings from Nahum Tate's adaptation to Jane Smiley's novel *A Thousand Acres*, though the full extent of the shock-waves that spread back from Smiley's novel to Shakespeare's play lies beyond the scope of even this edition.

Foakes's treatment of the text is brave, innovative, and, above all, unignorable. An illustration will make the point:

LEAR
And my poor fool is hanged. No, no, ^F^no^F^ life!
Why should a dog, a horse, a rat have life
And thou no breath at all? ^Q^O^Q^ thou'lt come no
more,
Never, never, never, ^F^never, never.^F^
[*to Edgar*?] Pray you undo this button. Thank
you, sir.
^Q^O, o, o, o.^Q^
^F^Do you see this? Look on her: look, her lips,
Look there, look there! *He dies.*^F^

Textual variation between Q and F is critical, here as elsewhere, to the play's effect and meaning. The strength of Foakes's presentation is that it makes that variation impossible to ignore. Yet this experience of textual alterity, which has no equivalent in either original version as it was performed and published, frustrates linear concentration on the words and their meaning. The superscripts puncture what is signified by the play, or either version of it. They also demand an exacting precondition for reading, which is that the reader constructs his or her own text out of the text Foakes offers, and then reads that imaginary and variable construction rather than the words printed on the page. The choice of variants can be made at will, yet unrestrained eclecticism would very quickly begin to assemble sequences that from an editorial point of view would be indefensible. A more careful use of Foakes's edition would have to keep in view the following points:

(1) Foakes's edition does not offer a synoptic presentation of variants. The superscripts mark off words or passages that are unique to one text or the other, but they take no account of words or passages that appear in alternative forms in the two texts. These have been edited critically, with a strong preference for the Folio text.

(2) The superscripts cannot simply be ignored. Foakes, like the Norton editors, is persuaded that after rectifying error there remain two distinct versions of the play, and the conflated text presumably has no legitimacy except as an editorial construct. The text compresses together a distinct Folio track and a distinct Quarto track, and the F-only and Q-only passages are in general mutually exclusive rather than coexisting.

(3) The Quarto track lies at a considerable remove from the Quarto text, or even from an edited version of it such as is presented in the Oxford *Complete Works* or the Cambridge *Early Quartos* series. A good example of the possible pitfall for the reader alert to the sigla but not to the limitations of the sigla would be the well-known 'handy-dandy' passage, where Foakes prints 'Hark in thine ear: $^{F}$change places and$^{F}$ handy-dandy, which is the justice, which is the thief?' The text here follows F; Q reads 'harke in thy eare handy, dandy, which is the theefe, which is the Iustice'. If one mentally deletes from Foakes's edition the phrase that appears in F only, the remaining text is without equivalent in either text, varying upon Q as it does by having thief and justice in transposed positions.

(4) Even the Folio track is not the Folio text. Where Foakes chooses between simultaneous variants the principle of best reading sometimes prevails over the principle of fidelity to the preferred version. For example, at 4.7.32 Foakes has Cordelia describe Lear's face as '*opposed* against the *warring* winds'; in F his face is *opposed* against the *jarring* winds, and in Q *exposed* against the *warring* winds. The technical and aesthetic considerations here are alike delicate and indecisive. From one standpoint Foakes unjustifiably departs from F where it has an effective reading; from another standpoint he reviews the evidence of each text against the other and concludes that in this line F at least has a misreading.

(5) If there is a distinction between (a) the two-track treatment of words and passages exclusive to Q or F as marked with sigla and (b) the single-track treatment of simultaneous variants as recorded only in the collation, this distinction can be arbitrary. Single and potentially superfluous words unique to one text are sometimes given sigla, sometimes not, and the decision seems to be based on the desirability of drawing attention to the alternative reading rather than a consistent treatment of a particular kind of textual variation. In one passage, 3.1.17–29, the two-track method is abandoned more drastically. Foakes's appendix note puts forward an elegant and plausible explanation for a passage whose two versions have perplexed many critics, summarizing a fuller exposition of the problem in his article published in *Shakespeare Survey 49* last year (compare my comments on Richard Knowles's discussion of the same passage in the same volume). He suggests that F's new lines were designed to replace just four lines in Q, but that the deletion was over-extended. The text relegates the four Quarto lines to the collation line at the foot of the page, and so reserves the Quarto sigla for the lines in Q that Foakes argues should have been but were not printed in F. In this case the sigla do not, as elsewhere, identify a *difference* between the editorially corrected versions; instead they conceal the difference that Foakes envisages between the versions, so as to record the *emendation* of an error in F. Any edition aiming to display passages unique to the Quarto and Folio versions should have included Q's four lines.

The Quarto track as a whole is so remote from Q itself that it is questionable whether there is much to be gained by following it. I wonder whether it would have been more meaningful as well as less intrusive to have followed through the logic of offering a Folio-inclined text by omitting the Folio superscript markers entirely. But, given the complexity of variation between the two texts, there is not any easy position of compromise between a single-version presentation and a full display of the two versions.

Though the text runs the risk of misinterpretation by its readers, there is intellectual cohesion to Foakes's edition as a whole. He takes risks in order to highlight the contingency of editing, reading, and performance alike. The 'colossus at the centre of Shakespeare's achievement' (p. 1) is not left in stone, but comes alive through the activities of those from Shakespeare himself to Smiley who have reinterpreted it. In this ever-dividing kingdom there are many Lears.

The critical temper of E. A. J. Honigmann's

edition of *Othello* is altogether more singular, concentrated as it is on what Honigmann sees as the intrinsic nature of the play. At times his forensic style as a textual analyst can be felt in his discussion of interpretative matters. Yet the point of his criticism is not to display itself, but to display *Othello*. The patient and delicate attention to detail gradually weaves together into a convincing statement of the play's worth, and Honigmann is comfortable with insisting on its greatness. His own writing maintains an undemonstrative and quiet respect. On the 'humanity' of Othello and Iago, 'limited but convincing, as only Shakespeare could imagine it', he comments self-reflectively, 'We feel it, even if criticism cannot translate it into words', then quotes the epigrammatic line at the end of *Love's Labour's Lost*: 'The words of Mercury are harsh after the songs of Apollo.' Perhaps we should reflect that in this respect other critics are less self-aware.

As this passage in the introduction suggests, Honigmann locates the play's main claim to validity in its theatrical representation of human nature and human relationships. Here 'representation' is the key term, for Honigmann is constantly aware that Othello's character is an impression rather than a fact, that the words are written rather than spoken by the man. The words on the page 'require' us to ponder on, for example, Othello's past. If they do not deliver all that we 'need to know' and leave us puzzled about the figures who speak them, that is true to the life we know of others.

Othello's otherness is part of the play's verisimilitude in just this way. Honigmann, alert to the racial issue, reproduces on p. 2 the anonymous English portrait of the Moorish ambassador to Queen Elizabeth as an iconic figuration of the noble Moor, arguing later that 'Shakespeare knew more about racism than modern critics have cared to admit' and showed 'wonderful insight into otherness' (p. 31). Thus problems that have engaged recent critics are squeezed under the obliging arch of Shakespeare's greatness. Honigmann's own concise, carefully deliberated exploration of the play's own 'feminism' similarly takes the contestatory edge off feminist criticism. Theatre-oriented critics too may feel that Honigmann is reluctant to perform. There are, to be sure, telling comments on the play's theatricality. Honigmann envisages the effects of implicitly scripted silence and gentle touch in the Willow Song scene; he notes that the text seems to recognize and play on the Othello actor's own exhaustion in Act 5, and records how the contest between Othello and Iago is often metatheatricalized as a contest between two famous actors. Despite these excellent perceptions, the edition's emphasis on the play's life in the theatre is not especially prominent, and Honigmann's strong view that the common theatre practices of cutting, adding, and substitution of words and lines are 'inexcusable' (p. 102) expresses a reservation about theatre as it is almost invariably practised.

The concomitant respect for the finest detail of Shakespeare's text influences the textual editing, which is based on the theories developed at length in his *The Texts of 'Othello'* (reviewed in *Shakespeare Survey 50*). Honigmann exercises more freedom of choice between Q and F readings than is usual, whilst inclining to F as the script that transmits the later of two authorial versions. In some editors' hands this would prove to be a recipe for paying lip-service to revision whilst in practice choosing eclectically between texts, but Honigmann's choices are carefully anticipated in and governed by his earlier mapping-out of the textual terrain. He tends to avoid conducting explicit textual discussion in the commentary – the Arden 3 asterisks to signal such notes are few and far between – and he relegates his summary textual discussion to an appendix. A further appendix debates the date of composition, arguing for a relatively early date of 1602. Another discusses and presents source material, and here Honigmann considerately italicizes passages close to Shakespeare in wording and footnotes the Shakespeare equivalent.

A full, attentive, and precise commentary includes thorough documentation from *OED*, and is supplemented with an appendix of longer notes. Honigmann is sharply alert to connotation. Iago's 'what you will' (4.1.34) is 'A poisonous phrase: it implies "anything you like to think (or do with her)."' On 'We say lie on her when they belie her! Lie with her, zounds, that's fulsome!' (4.1.35–7) he notes that Othello 'worries about the meaning' of the phrases; '*Lie on* could = tell lies about ... But he cannot reason away lie *with* her.' On 'Nature would not invest herself in such shadowing passion without some instruction' (4.1.39–40): 'He tries to rationalize his trembling before he falls.' 'Nose' and 'lips' (4.1.42) are 'surrogate genital images'. These examples from a ten-line passage are all effectively targeted comments; they address what is puzzling and bring the text to life.

In some ways this is a traditional edition. It is attentive to dramatic character but wary towards the theatre; it is attentive to text in the spirit of W. W. Greg's 'Rationale of Copy-Text' but wary of recent textual relativism. Honigmann's Shakespeare is, as far as the materials allow, stabilized and centred. Honigmann shows a sense of unyielding care and responsibility towards the play, and his edition is impressively dependable.

The canonical position of *Two Noble Kinsmen* is fully confirmed in Lois Potter's edition for Arden 3. In her introduction Potter tends to avoid sustained critical analysis, but she nevertheless manages to insinuate into the reader's consciousness her sense of the play as a complex and coherent theatrical work. Her attention to peripheral and contextual matters always leads back to the play, and in this way she obliquely develops a rich critical account of it. A finely nuanced discussion of authorship relates the play to the themes and techniques of Fletcher and Shakespeare. Potter evolves from the attribution studies a balanced statement of what we know and don't know about the process of composition. Though she confronts the text's inconsistencies and unconformities, she explicitly avoids creating a schema of authorial stints that would work as a tool for breaking the play into fragments. Her introduction considers the 'public' contexts of the death of Prince Henry and marriage of Princess Elizabeth, and an appendix provides a full text of the masque that was performed at the wedding celebrations, Francis Beaumont's *Masque of the Inner Temple and Gray's Inn*. As Potter points out, there are possible allusions to another marriage of 1613, that between Frances Howard and the Earl of Somerset on 26 December, though it is not quite clear whether she favours dating the play's original performance to early 1613, to accord with the royal wedding, or late 1613, to accord with the court scandal. Potter argues for a vein of militant Protestantism in the play, especially in the opening scene, where she reads the three queens allegorically as embodiments of endangered Protestant states. As she notes, in the context of a revival in 1619–20 the call to arms would have resonated more strongly still.

Potter's review of source material goes back to the Greek Theban plays and thence moves on to Boccaccio and Chaucer. The following sections on the Jailer's Daughter and courtly love and friendship literature skilfully weave between text and contexts. There is a good discussion of the play's original staging at the Blackfriars, after which Potter considers the play's casting requirements and its relation to other plays staged around 1613. She then broadens the perspective again, now through time, reviewing the history of publication, theatrical revival, and interpretation. The play's record of performance, with its huge gaps between Davenant and the 1970s, allows the account to be pleasingly detailed in its handling of individual productions.

The text, though thoughtfully considered, is edited with occasional casualness. There are slips in the dialogue: 'Whilst' for 'While' (2.2.61); 'You' for 'Ye' (2.2.111), 'o'' for 'of' (2.2.128), 'Cousin' for 'Kinsman', no less (3.1.69), 'on' for 'o'er' (3.1.122), 'An' for 'A'

(5.2.109). A number of words are added to stage directions without square brackets or textual note, or are silently omitted, or silently reworded. Conversely, some words actually in the 1634 Quarto's stage directions are printed in brackets, as if they had been added editorially. A few puzzling changes are made to the original wording: *toward* for *towards* at 1.1.218.1, the omission of *Wind* before *Horns* at 3.1.96 and 108, unelaborated '*five* Countrymen' for '4. *Countrymen: and Baum*' (that is, one dressed as a bavin or baboon) at 3.5.0.1.

In Emilia's speech in 1.3 Potter retains 'fury-innocent' at l. 79 but emends 'indiuiduall' at l. 81 to 'dividual'. She follows N. Blincoe (reviewed in *Shakespeare Survey 50*) in explaining *fury-innocent* as 'innocent of fury', but her introduction refers instead, and helpfully, to Montaigne's description of pre-adolescent same-sex love as 'the first fury, inspired by the son of Venus in the lover's heart upon the object of tender youth's flower ... in his infancy and before the age of budding' (p. 56). I find this parallel from a text that clearly influenced Shakespeare particularly valuable because it enables us to correlate the allusive density of the expression with a restriction and difference in the possibilities of speaking in the period. Potter recognizes that Emilia is in effect rewriting Montaigne by transposing his account of male friendship to the opposite sex (a point addressed more fully in Laurie J. Shannon's 'Emilia's Argument', in *ELH* 64, 657–82), and that sort of cross-threaded borrowing is surely typical of how Shakespeare used Montaigne.

Like Honigmann and Potter, A. R. Braunmuller in his Cambridge edition of *Macbeth* offers what is in many directions an improvement on previously available editions. His commentary is scholarly, generous and wide-ranging, with ample notes on matters of staging and a willingness both to record and to evaluate competing interpretations of cruxes. For a modern edition it is unusually full of parallels for distinctive idioms, and analogues or sources for particular images and phrases. It attends too to matters of social custom; when Lady Macbeth urges her husband to put on his night-gown (2.2.73) there is a fourteen-line note on the garment. There are dangers of pedantry, though if one understands the objective as to describe as accurately as possible the cultural nuance of the language Braunmuller's documentation has considerable merit.

Just occasionally Braunmuller is under-demonstrative about linguistic ambiguities. Responding to Lady Macbeth's extraordinary lines 'That no compunctious visitings of nature / Shake my fell purpose nor keep peace between / Th'effect and [h]it' (1.5.43–5), Braunmuller notes a reference to menstruation, whilst adding the qualification that 'the specific meaning ... is attested from 1640'. This is a breakthrough from the usual editorial reticence, but he does not investigate the images lurking in the various early modern connotations of *visit* (nature as a punisher, or a judge, or a plague causing fever, or a blast of wind that shakes a tree, or an ecclesiastical investigation aiming to 'keep peace' in a local trouble-spot). Braunmuller follows most editors in modernizing F's 'hit' to 'it'. But *effect* can be synonymous with *purpose*; *hit* can mean simply a blow that strikes its target (for the idea, compare 'The very firstlings of my heart shall be / The firstlings of my hand' at 4.1.146–7). If this seems oblique, *hit* is helped out, almost subliminally perhaps, by an alternative sense of *fell*. Cause and effect can run both ways, and the intention to fell is implicated in the adjective describing the purpose. Are there virtues in an editor leaving this kind of explication alone? I suggest not, because the acts of recording the relevant obsolete senses of words, elucidating half-obscured imagery, and teasing out contradiction and overdetermination, are all intertwined with establishing the text itself. Despite the amplitude of Braunmuller's commentary, often indeed on matters of imagery and language, there remains space for a commentary on *Macbeth* that explicates them even more fully.

The textual editing of *Macbeth* presents few

difficulties. In reading Braunmuller's edition I was reminded that the name Lady Macbeth is an unShakespearian invention by editors. Like Queen Elizabeth in *Richard III*, Lady Capulet in *Romeo and Juliet*, and Prince Hal in *1 Henry IV*, the now familiar form of the name makes no appearance in the early printed texts. On the character's first entry and elsewhere, Braunmuller places 'LADY MACBETH' in brackets to signal the alteration from F's '*Macbeths Wife*', and the regularization is recorded in a collation note. However, the expansion of the speech-prefix, which is usually '*Lady.*' in F, is silent and without record.

This aspect of editing *Macbeth* joins it with general issues as to how the original documents come to be under-represented in the edited text. A more particular and serious challenge is how to respond to the presence of material by Thomas Middleton. Traditionally, editors have stuck with the Folio. Where they have identified non-Shakespearian lines that were evidently added to the play for an adaptation, they have let them stand. Before the Oxford Shakespeare, they did not, however, expand on the song cues to provide the full adapted text. In this respect Braunmuller is traditional; the Hecate scenes themselves remain, but the non-Folio material is dispersed. The song 'Come away, come away' and Hecate's spectacular exit in flight are reprinted from Middleton's *The Witch* only in the Textual Analysis on p. 256; a transcript of the episode as it survived in the Quarto of 1673 appears elsewhere again, in an Appendix of 'Additional Text and Music', as does a photographic reproduction of John H. Long's edited text of the musical setting ascribed to Robert Johnson. Braunmuller justifies preserving the Folio uncontaminated by quoting (p. 257) G. K. Hunter's opinion, couched in problematizing rather than problem-solving terms, that what is referred to as 'Shakespeare's *Macbeth*' needs no more than the first two lines of (Middleton's) song followed by (Middleton's) flying exit – though not even this minimum appears in the edited text. He goes on to point out that the supposed need for song to cover over the noise of the flight machine has not led to musical episodes for the Witches' departures in Act 1; but Braunmuller himself cites an article by Glynne Wickham arguing that the unmodified Shakespearian Witches of Act 1 do not fly in either version of the play.

The printed text of *Macbeth*, more clearly than any other play in the Folio, incorporates at least two performance versions, presenting most immediately the post-Shakespearian one. Braunmuller gives extensive and detailed treatment of the topicality of the original text of 1606, but the play he prints belongs more immediately to the following decade, and the revisions specific to that text probably extend, in some points of detail at least, beyond the Hecate passages. The textual situation accords strangely with the play's concerns. Braunmuller's discussion of the play's structure is entitled 'Master of his time: "double redoubled strokes"', and an awareness that the structure has been rejigged through time might have been productive. It is all the more worth making this point because Braunmuller is on the whole excellent in making connections between structure, theme, context, imagery, and so on. He notes on p. 17 that 'The crisis of succession in *Macbeth* is expressed as a crisis of metaphor', an observation that brings to mind again some of the comments already made on Lady Macbeth's language.

Braunmuller is economical in reviewing the play's main source in Holinshed, which is not reprinted. He quotes William Harrison's description of the Scots from the *Chronicles* as part of a wider consideration of the original significance of the Scottish setting. Here the account is uncharacteristically loose in its use of the overlapping terms 'Celt', 'Scot' as applying historically to the Celtic migrants from Ireland to Scotland, 'Scot' as applying transhistorically to the Scottish people as a whole, and 'Highlander'. He suggests that the English regarded Scots as like Frenchmen who spoke a form of

English (p. 9), which poses a question as to who is caricaturing whom, and he wrongly implies that the Roman armies drove the Celts out of England into Scotland (p. 11).

Having dealt with 'Macbeth in legend, *Macbeth* in history', Braunmuller divides nearly all that remains of his introduction into '*Macbeth* in the mind' and '*Macbeth* in performance'. The first of these corresponds to what used sometimes to be called 'The Play', though it makes scholarly and illuminating historicist excursions. There is strong focus on the role of the female, and Braunmuller argues persuasively from contemporary documents that Lady Macbeth wills herself to the type of an amenorrheal woman, and in doing so links herself with the witches. He goes on to suggest that the play's grounding in oracular pronouncement denies the possibility of its being straightforwardly tragic. His assumption that tragedy depends on free will is, however, questionable in the light of the classical example, as too is the assumption that tragedy offers solutions. Perhaps compatible with tragedy after all, this characteristic of 'undecidability' is certainly crucial to the play. Braunmuller discusses it early on in relation to the equivocal structure of the plot, and later (pp. 43–56) he explores that same idea as expressed in the play's referentially troubled languages. The sense of the play's linguistic range and of the recurrence of similar problems of meaning in dissimilar verbal environments is valuable here, though Nicholas Brooke's account of the play's 'baroque' illusionism in his Oxford edition (1990) remains essential reading.

The account of the stage history is the fullest and most detailed of any available edition. Braunmuller focuses the narrative onto a short list of crucial and recurrent staging problems such as the appearance of the Witches and the possible absence of Banquo's ghost. The sheer bulk of information can be overwhelming nonetheless. There is a danger too, not entirely avoided, that there may be visitings of nature between the effect and [h]it, that the imaginative object constructed in the 'mind' (whose and when?) will prove disconcertingly distinct from the staged object invoked in accounts from theatre history (there and then). Braunmuller addresses this difficulty in some measure by preserving a distinctive balance in both sections whereby Macbeth is given less attention and emphasis than usual as a tragic figure in his own right; the account constantly draws the witches and Lady Macbeth to the fore. It ends with an enigmatic coda called '*Macbeth* in the mind and in performance: Act 4 Scene 3'. But here the history of performance is not in view. The English scene is taken as a metatheatrical commentary on what is otherwise a Scottish play. Malcolm's good-guy/bad-guy routine recapitulates the 'juggling fiends' themselves and summarizes the play's own deeply equivocal nature.

Peter Davison's edition of the First Quarto of *Richard III* is the second in the Cambridge Shakespeare Early Quartos series, which supplements its main run of Shakespeare editions. Davison offers a modernized and sometimes emended text based on Q, with an introduction, a collation of Q/F variants at the foot of the page, and forty pages of textual notes at the end of the volume. The aim is to present the performance text thought to lie immediately behind Q, and to explain its origin. The edition is not, then, a reproduction of Q1 as a particular textualization. Stage directions are brought into line with theatrical need, and information unique to F such as '*She looks scornfully at him*' is imported in square brackets. Some of the textual emendations are plausible rather than necessary, and a few are distinctly unnecessary. Where, for instance, Q has 'Tell him and spare not, looke what I haue said, / I will auouch in presence of the King', Davison emends to 'Tell him and spare not. Look, what I have said / I will avouch't in presence of the King'. 'Avouch't' is a Folio reading. The textual note suggests that the first line, which is not in F, comes from an authorial addition to Q. But the two variants are related, for Q's 'look what', meaning 'whatever', provides the otherwise missing object of 'avouch'. Davison's punctuation obscures the idiom, and in a case such as this readers would be justified in expecting that the Quarto reading would be preserved. Similarly too, I would argue, with Richard's description of his plots as 'inductious' rather than 'inductions' in his opening soliloquy; here the more familiar and commonplace reading comes into F from the derivative Q3. In contrast, an edition of this kind is justified in retaining, as Davison does, 'scab', glossed 'moral or spiritual disease', in 'This sudden scab of rancour I misdoubt' (3.2.85) where F reads 'stab', and even in having grim-visaged war caper to the lascivious pleasing of a 'love' rather than a 'lute'. Though in the last case I have no confidence in Q's reading, I can understand the basis for giving it the benefit of the doubt in this particular context, and the principle might have been applied more extensively in an edition that sets itself no mandate to provide a fully Shakespearian text.

Nevertheless, and though not well printed, Q does offer the basis for a highy intelligible text that is for the most part highly Shakespearian. Davison does not leave the matter there, for he is keen to investigate the stage history and the textual history that underlies Q. Part of his hypothesis was developed in an article reviewed in *Shakespeare Survey 49*. Davison endorses David Patrick's theory that the copy for Q is a memorial reconstruction, and attempts to consolidate the particular argument that the Lord Chamberlain's Men put it together on provincial tour. In developing this highly specific account of the text's history, Davison indulges in some flamboyant risk-taking.

There is in fact no credible evidence that sustains his belief that Q was put together during a provincial tour in 1597. Davison notes to this end that *Richard III* was the first Shakespeare play whose ecclesiastical authorization is recorded in the Stationers' Register, the inference being that this particular manuscript was without licence for stage performance. But according to Peter W. M. Blayney ('The Publication of Playbooks', in *A New History of Early English Drama*, ed. by John D. Cox and David Scott Kastan (New York: Columbia University Press, 1997), 383–422, p. 397) a licence from the Master of the Revels would evidently not at this time have been acceptable as an alternative to ecclesiastical allowance for the press. As Cyndia Susan Clegg points out in her study reviewed below, by 1596, the year before Q1 was published, only 40 per cent of all books entered in the Register were officially authorized, but entries for books treating political and religious matters nearly always testified to authorization. The ecclesiastical allowance can be assumed to reflect only the political and potentially seditious subject matter; it says little about the origin of the manuscript. Indeed, what it does say points in the opposite direction, for it reminds us that the posited reconstructed and unlicensed manuscript would fail to testify to local officials that the company had authority to perform the play. Davison argues that patterns of actors' doubling indicate adaptation for touring, but he makes some highly arbitrary assumptions in order to squeeze the number of boy actors down to two; in any case it is as yet unproved that plays were adapted for provincial tour. If the allowance by the authorities cannot indicate an unlicensed manuscript, if a reconstructed manuscript would fail to legitimate provincial performance, and if Q's economization on actors' parts is limited and unexceptional, the argument for the manuscript having been produced on tour collapses. Memorial transmission in some shape or form may after all influence the text, but collaborative reconstruction in the provinces remains very speculative and in some respects demands credulity.

In his textual notes Davison is sometimes pleasingly willing to accept the intractability of the evidence, as when he notes on Q's 'dead' where F has 'deare' (4.1.64) that it 'makes good sense; it could be authorial, an actor's substitution, or even a compositor's error'. Uncertainty of this kind is indeed often the problem with this text. Elsewhere Davison astutely defends Quarto readings; where Q has 'Eagle' for F's 'Eagles' (1.1.132), he notes that 'Clarence is more properly described as a royal bird than Hastings, and only Clarence is now in prison.' At one point the defence is spurious: Davison's idea that F's 'most deadly Bore' (4.5.2) was altered authorially because it 'sounded more tedious than threatening' is witty at the cost of anachronism, as this sense of *bore* is first recorded in the nineteenth century. But perhaps more typical and certainly more troublesome are the pronouncements of memorial error. Davison supposes that the same actor played Clarence and Queen Elizabeth in order to uphold his assertion that 'perpetual rest' at 2.2.45 is a memorial echo of 'perpetual night'. At such moments the memorial vessel seems to be creaking badly. Many of Davison's diagnostically optimistic remarks could readily be interpreted differently, either within the same overall hypothesis or in support of another. A note on 'adversaries' in the line 'To watch the waning of mine adversaries' (4.4.4) describes Q's reading as a substitution for F's 'enemies'; with characteristic zeal Davison adds a list of no less than 136 other cases in this one scene of substitution, by which it seems we are to understand one kind of memorial error. Yet, to take the leading example, 'adversaries' is much the rarer word both in Shakespeare and more generally; the image of Margaret watching the decline of those 'adverse' in the literal sense of turned towards or against her sustains the metatheatrical aspect of her speech; and, in combination with waning, Q's word offers some hint of an astrological image. The inference that an actor introduced this reading by mistake is highly insecure. There are in Davison's comments some echoes of the trenchant and detailed notes that flesh out the memorial hypothesis in W. W. Greg's editions of *Merry Wives* and *Doctor Faustus* – and Greg's analyses of these texts have proved more vulnerable to the test of time than almost anything he wrote. Nevertheless, Davison is always an engaged and engaging textual critic whose remarks are often sharply observed and informed with a strong sense of theatrical reality.

The appearance of *1 Henry IV* in the Bedford Shakespeare Texts and Contexts Series can be taken as an opportunity to describe the character of the series. The text of the play, edited by David Bevington, presented with commentary footnotes and a page of textual documentation, takes up rather less than a quarter of the volume. The remainder, edited by Barbara Hodgdon, comprises documents chosen to place the play in its cultural setting. The texts are mostly modernized for the sake of intelligibility to the modern reader, which is in line with the treatment of the play itself, but a few are preserved in original spelling to give the reader a closer impression of the early modern documents. Editing is light – ampersands and some 'emphasis' capitals survive modernization – though occasionally interventionist. Hence on p. 132 'complices' is rendered '[ac]complices' and 'made belieue' becomes 'made [to] believe'; in both cases the emendation is a form of commentary rather than a needful correction of the text. Annotation is light too; on the same page the reader is told that *cautell* is trickery, but left unhelped with *fautors*.

The strength and value of the edition lies in Hodgdon's skilful selection and presentation of materials. These she distributes into six sections, each with an introduction, entitled: 'Historiography and the Uses of History', 'Civic Order and Rebellion', 'Cultural Territories', 'The "Education" of a Prince', 'Honor and Arms', and 'The Oldcastle Controversy'. The project achieves on a modest scale some of the objectives of larger electronic hypertext editions. Exclusions are inevitable, but the 400-page book format imposes a rigour that is not without its advantages. Along with selection comes presentation, contextualization of contexts. The book is designed, in the words of one of its pre-publication reviewers, as a 'pedagogical tool'. It can be distinctly helpful, from the point of view of teaching and learning, to have introduced and annotated selections rather than whole texts, and the collection of materials might realistically be read in its totality. The view of history that Hodgdon generates resonates strongly with areas of recent critical enquiry whilst remaining responsively concordant with the play's concerns. If historical contextualization is only one possible way of teaching the play, it is an important way, especially when the text itself treats history. Hodgdon's book will enable serious and effective study of this kind.

Another functional and yet pleasing educational tool, this time provided for school readers, is Rex Gibson's edition of the *Sonnets* in the Cambridge School Shakespeare series. Each sonnet is appended with a discursive summary and commentary, and with glossary notes. There are reassurances such as 'Don't worry if you have difficulty with lines 7–8 – many people do' (Sonnet 112), and each commentary ends with a task aimed at exploring the technique, tone, or meaning of the sonnet in question. The edition is usefully illustrated, and includes a short introduction and a number of appendices introducing topics such as structure, themes, language, and more general study tasks. Gibson is tirelessly innovative in suggesting ways in which the Sonnets can profitably be taught and learnt, and it is striking how effectively his approach transfers from the plays to Shakespeare's non-dramatic writing.

The Malone Society's publication for 1995, a photofacsimile of Q1 *A Midsummer Night's Dream* (1600), fills one of the gaps in the old Oxford Shakespeare Quarto series of facsimiles. The edition reproduces the exceptionally clean and clear Huntington Library copy, which happens to bring together every known press-corrected reading except a turned ornamental 'N' on sig. A2. The inner margins surrounding the photographs have through line-numbers for the Quarto text ('Q/TLN'); the outer margins cross-refer to the through line-numbers of the Folio as established in Charlton Hinman's Norton Facsimile (1968). An appendix correlates the Quarto signatures and line-numbers with the act-scene-line numbers of the Riverside edition. In his introduction, Thomas L. Berger records press variants and provides a summary of scholarship on the stationers, the copy for Q, the printing process, and the relation between Q and F. Two minor criticisms are that I would have preferred the Quarto line-numbering to be printed larger instead of smaller than the Folio numbering (this applies also to earlier Shakespeare quartos in the series), and that in the tabular list of press variants some of the line references look puzzling at first sight because there is too much space between 'Q/TLN' and the line-number itself. More important than such details, the photographic reproduction is crisper and more legible than that of the same copy in Michael J. B. Allen and Kenneth Muir's facsimile edition of *Shakespeare Plays in Quarto* (1981). The Malone Society edition will be a valuable resource for textual critics, especially those who do not have access to the Allen–Muir collection. For reasons connected variously with the printer's manuscript, the printing process, the condition of the Huntington copy, and the quality of the edition itself, the Malone Society facsimile provides an unusually good opportunity actually to read for pleasure a Shakespeare play in a form as close as is practicable to that in which it was originally printed.

In Eric Sams's edition of *Shakespeare's 'Edward III'* a clear perspective on the authorship question is reflected in the title. It is announced even more clearly in a subtitle that appears on the dust jacket and nowhere else: '*An early play restored to the canon*'. In contrast with Fred Lapides's more rounded presentation of the play (1980), Sams's edition finds its entire focus in the question of authorship. Though the text is modernized it retains some characteristics of an early document, but the polemic of authorship is present even here. The generally uncapitalized verse-lines and extremely light punctuation are designed to reflect the conventions, not of the 1596 Quarto, but of the manuscript of another play Sams attributes to Shakespeare, *Edmund Ironside*.

The notes are primarily aimed at pointing out parallels with Shakespeare's works. A forty-two page section on 'The Case for Shakespeare' is the core of the edition. Most people who have looked at the issue agree that there are indeed solid grounds for considering that Shakespeare wrote at least part of the play, and major studies by Karl Wentersdorf and Eliot Slater conclude that Shakespeare wrote it unaided. It should nevertheless be kept in mind that the extensive investigations of Elliot and Valenza, discussed further below, have produced findings that suggest that the play as a whole lies outside Shakespeare's range of writing, though this would not necessarily preclude part-authorship. There is clearly a task to be done in mediating the extensive, sometimes technical, qualitatively variable, and sometimes contradictory evidence, and there is every possibility of adding to it.

Unfortunately, Sams weakens his plausibility as a fair advocate by his apparent inability to digest, present, and make constructive use of other studies and his adversarial disrespect towards those with whom he disagrees. Unfortunately too, Sams makes little attempt to assess and evaluate his own evidence, and is sometimes seriously misleading. Much of the discussion is virtually without value in establishing Shakespeare's hand except in a most vaguely permissive way. The potentially more significant data needs identifying as such and then subjecting to a certain amount of sceptical caution. Take, as one instance, Sams's section of 'Shakespearisms' as established by C. T. Onions but, for Sams, inconveniently disestablished by the 1986 reviser of Onions's *Shakespeare Glossary*, Robert Eagleson (Sams calls him 'Eagleton', as though he were a lexicographical Marxist). Though Eagleson is crudely accused of 'emasculation' in deleting Onions's identification of certain words and phrases as peculiar to Shakespeare, he cut the balls with reason. *OED* is an inaccurate guide to earliest usages and, moreover, favours Shakespeare because its quotations are more inclusive of Shakespeare than other writers (as was demonstrated by Jürgen Schäfer, in *Documentation in the 'OED'*, 1980). Onions's 'Shakespearisms' are not without serious qualification 'an unrivalled instrument of identification' (p. 190). Even if they were, Sams's list would need thinning out. The very first item, *abstract* in the sense 'inventory', is highly dubious, as the pre-Shakespearian gloss 'epitome (of something greater)' or 'summary' fits the context in *Edward III* better than the 'Shakespearian' sense. This improvisation of evidence can be seen elsewhere, as when Sams puts forward a previously unsuspected sense of *council-house* ('private chamber') in order to establish *Edward III* and *Richard III* as the first usages of it (p. 94). Occasionally there is a more clear-cut mistake. The collation 'succeeded ... successfully' at lines 9–10 is compared with 'succeeding ... successfully' in Q *Richard III* 3.1.71–3 (p. 79). Although Sams castigates editors for ignoring the cited Quarto reading 'sucessfully', they could not have done otherwise, for Q actually shares with F in reading 'Successiuely'.

Sams realizes that there is a strong body of opinion in support of Shakespeare's authorship of the scenes involving the Countess. The very idea that Shakespeare might have collaborated in his early career is dismissed out of hand with unhelpful aggression as a 'canard' that 'needs to be shot down and silenced' (p. 161). Sams simply calls on the authority of the Folio to vindicate Shakespeare's sole authorship of *1 Henry VI* (p. 160); however the same authority testifies with equal weight to Shakespeare's non-authorship of *Edward III*. Certainly Sams should have followed the example of earlier studies in constantly comparing the evidence within the Countess scenes with the evidence in the rest of the play in order to discriminate between competing hypotheses; but he does not. His study, flawed in its methodology in several respects, is here most vulnerable of all. Ultimately, however, the point Sams makes about the stubborn marginalization of the play by 'Academia' is not entirely contingent on the debate as to whether the play is a collaboration or solely Shakespeare's. On the evidence available, and Sams does add something to that evidence, there is a case for presenting the play in the context of a Shakespeare edition or series even if it is a collaboration. The 1997 edition of the Riverside Shakespeare and the Cambridge series have done exactly that, and Arden 3 plans to do likewise.

## TEXTUAL STUDIES: MONOGRAPHS

Jeffrey Masten's *Textual Intercourse* reprints in expanded form articles that first appeared in *English Literary History* and Jonathan Goldberg's collection *Queering the Renaissance* (1993), adding an epilogue on Margaret Cavendish. His arguments are both critical and textualist. Masten traces an early modern and, he argues, homosocial practice of collaborative dramatic writing that gives way to a practice of modern authorship in the seventeenth century. He tentatively relates this shift to the beginnings of a political movement away from absolutism: 'textual production seems to move from collective making to individual authorship, while modes of government begin, however slowly, to move from singular authority to more collective action' (p. 151). The statement is not qualified by consideration as to why authorship in the specific field of drama should correlate with political developments when no such pattern is demonstrated in the fields of, say, poetry or essay-writing, nor why the modern model of authorship should begin to function for drama most noticeably during the reign of the high-absolutist James I. If serious questions such as these were answered, Masten's speculative remarks on the relation between authorship as an ideology and state would helpfully clarify why the retrospective, nostalgic, and politically absolutist 1647 Beaumont and Fletcher Folio should celebrate the authors' collaboration.

Masten is dismissive of the attempts of Cyrus Hoy, MacD. P. Jackson, and others to determine who wrote what. He rightly suggests that their work can encourage critics to view collaborations from a single-author perspective as dismembered fragments of authorial canons. But as Masten is developing an argument in part about collaboration as a practice, he must inevitably have a direct or indirect debt to such studies himself. For example, he depends heavily on attribution studies when discussing collaboration in *Pericles*, a play that was published as by Shakespeare alone. Nevertheless, G. E. Bentley's work in defining the role of the dramatist in the making of plays is acknowledged ungrudgingly. It is on this ground that Masten builds his book's foundation: the belief, repeated many times, that 'collaboration was the Renaissance English theatre's dominant mode of textual production' (p. 14). This is an entirely unwarranted interpretation of Bentley, whose needfully very provisional guess was that '*as many as* half of the plays by professional dramatists in the period incorporated the writing *at some date* of more than one man' (*The Profession of Dramatist in Shakespeare's Time, 1590–1642* (1971), p. 199; my emphases). 'As many as' is an elastic term, but even at full stretch it does not mean 'more than'. Bentley indicates that at least half the plays were written by a single dramatist, and considerably more if one sets aside the activities of revision and adaptation by a second dramatist. Masten can be right on this point only if his principal authority is wrong.

One might conclude that, after all, single authorship prevailed, but perhaps the fairest inference from Bentley is that there simply was no 'dominant mode of textual production' one way or the other, a view uncongenial to the post-Marxist strand in Masten's writing. Of course the actual practice of playmaking is one thing and the period's conceptual apparatus for describing it, what Masten calls the 'model', is another. But examination of evidence such as title-pages or allusions to dramatists might suggest the 'model' is more firmly tipped towards single authorship than the 'mode'. Relative to its practice, collaboration had consistently weak discursive recognition. Even if it were the dominant mode, collaboration would not be the dominant model.

These points do not have to emerge because *Textual Intercourse* does not attempt anything like a full study of the development of authorship in early modern drama, and instead functions as a series of exploratory excursions. However tentatively expressed, its general conclusions are undermined by the absence of a comprehensive overview of the subject. Though even the detail he scrutinizes can be conspicuously thin on context, the particles on which Masten focuses are nevertheless often handled with skill and care, and his book is both fascinating to read and a constant provocation to new thought. Masten is an observant if sometimes over-ingenious reader of textual detail. His account of disjunction between author-centred and collaboration-centred discourses in the Beaumont and Fletcher Folio preliminaries makes particularly instructive reading. But when Masten posits a model for the overall emergence of dramatic authorship it would be unsafe to suppose that the weight of evidence he puts forward sustains the larger conclusions towards which he is reaching.

In *Unediting the Renaissance* Leah S. Marcus, like Masten, explores early modern text from a distinctly postmodern perspective. She sees editors' rejection of 'bad' quarto texts as an anthropological ritual, adding that the acceptance of particular readings from such texts is consistent with this procedure: 'an ordinarily abominable object is suddenly "singled out and put into a very special kind of ritual frame that marks it off from other experience"' (p. 79, quoting Mary Douglas). The comparison is not especially exact, for editors merge the 'bad' quarto readings they adopt with the rest of the edited text rather than putting them in a ritual frame, and it is hard to see how such readings become, like the abominable object, 'a source of tremendous power'. More constructive than this critique of editing, and perhaps ultimately more valuable, are her close, perceptive, and well informed readings of two-text plays. Marcus considers *Doctor Faustus* and three Shakespeare examples: *Merry Wives*, *The Taming of the Shrew*, and *Hamlet*. A final chapter moves away from drama to explore the material specificity of John Milton's 1645 *Poems*.

In her examination of each play, Marcus adduces arguments that relate to social class and gender. She points out that in *Doctor Faustus* the impression that Helen's kiss definitively damned Faustus was – until the recent spate of A-text and two-text editions – artificially reinforced by editors' conflation of A and B. When considering *Taming of the Shrew* she argues that *A Shrew* is more sympathetic to the female position than *The Shrew*, a contentious but arguable perspective that belies the notion that in the latter Shakespeare can be commended for his at least relative liberalism. Marcus offers a detailed and largely convincing description of Q1 *Merry Wives* as a more urban, 'popular', and finally sentimental version of the play that significantly lacks nearly all the references to the court and most of the details that root the action of the Folio text in the soil of Windsor. It might be kept in mind, though, that most of the Quarto's reframing is achieved through omissions, and that Marcus's account does little to determine one way or the other whether the shorter texts are memorially transmitted. With perceptive honesty Marcus herself spells out a limitation to the consequences of her argument, when she points out that not much about the envisaged audience can be inferred from the social figuration within the text: 'In many instances, audiences may have preferred to see what they were not' (p. 98), whether they were themselves aristocratic or middling. Even the Queen can be imagined, hypothetically but in line with the blurb on the title-page, enjoying the humbler merriment of the Quarto text.

Marcus's critical, historical, and philological

forays are all very well, but they support the project described one way as to unedit Shakespeare, another way as to 'heap scorn upon past editors, their unthinking misogyny, and their seemingly desperate devices for containing and solidifying the Shakespeare canon' (p. 131). To this end she can sometimes depart from verbal or textual-critical cogency. On p. 11 the zeal to criticize editorial *annotation* for its intrusiveness leads her to describe it as 'emendation', as though it altered the words of the text. Eagerness for the declamation leads to the false 'seemingly' just quoted and obliterates the sense in sentences such as 'To the extent that they adopt readings from Q1 or confirmed by Q1, editors tend to avoid mentioning that text in their notes' (p. 134). More seriously, Marcus often invokes a model of editorial practice that most current editors would themselves see as bad editing, whereby the textual introduction and the collation line serve only to intimidate the reader and editorial choices are determined by arbitrary but conservative cultural imperatives. Noting that 'the Sly ending that is "missing" from *The Shrew* has yet to appear as part of the play in any standard edition' (p. 107; the comment is true only if one marginalizes Alexander Pope), Marcus suggests that 'editors and critics have been particularly reluctant to associate *The Taming of A Shrew* with Shakespeare' because 'it has been perceived as an affront to the editors' own manhood' (pp. 107–8). If implausibility can redeem unpleasantness, perhaps it should be allowed to do so. In fact the New Penguin editor G. R. Hibbard and the Oxford *Complete Works* editor Stanley Wells both print episodes from *A Shrew* as additional passages to *The Shrew*. It's hard to see how and indeed whether Marcus considers editors might go further in drawing *A Shrew* into the edited text, especially in view of the evasive quotation marks round 'missing' and the vague verb 'associate'.

Marcus herself enjoys playing fast and loose with the texts' history. She rehearses some old narratives about Q1 *Hamlet* being Shakespeare's first version of the play, the objections to which are unignorable, cogent, and well established. Adding insult to injury, she also toys with ideas that Q1 might be Shakespeare's own revision, or that all the short texts might be Shakespeare's own memorial reconstructions of his own works. Yet she adds too a variant of the standard theory that they represent the underlying play as the actors remembered it. Yet again, she reverts to assuming that Q1 is the earliest version when she later refers to the 'gradually increasing "literacy"' in the handling of written material from Q1 to Q2 to F (p. 172). The function of these various and variously implausible essays into conflicting hypotheses is simply to obfuscate the textual situation. We are nudged into assuming that the usual accounts of editors are no more secure, as though all uncertainties were equal. So Marcus claims that Q2 *Hamlet* 'brings us closer [than Q1] to Shakespeare as we have traditionally *liked* to imagine him' (p. 176; my emphasis), saying through the corner of the mouth that we have been ignorantly flattering our preconceptions. If Q2 doesn't bring us closer than Q1 to the historical Shakespeare, then what does it bring us closer to?

In her Introduction Marcus takes as a leitmotif the editorial construction of meaning in Prospero's account of Sycorax, 'This blew ey'd hag, was hither brought with child.' Here most conspicuously of all, a large issue is hung on a superficially clever analysis of a textual fragment. As blueness of the eyelid was considered a sign of pregnancy, editors have been able to establish a persuasive and illuminating connection between the otherwise puzzingly irrelevant 'blew ey'd' and 'with child'. Marcus indicates that they are complicit with racist attitudes in refusing to accept that the Algerian Sycorax might have blue irises, a trait more usually associated with Nordic beauty (pp. 8–11). But, as Marcus is aware, 'blue-eyed' was in Shakespeare's period a term conspicuously avoided in praising the beauty of blue eyes; the phrase then was 'grey-eyed'. The exception Marcus notes is

Sidney's mock-Petrarchan description of Mopsa, 'fair as Saturn' and with 'lips of Saphir blew'; this only confirms the rule, because the epithet is pointedly inappropriate and doesn't apply to eyes. If editors were racist they would surely have no difficulty with the idea that Sycorax's unexpected blue (but not grey) eyes made her a grotesque parody of the European ideal of beauty, or that the hag just might be a product of miscegenation. Marcus is marginally more persuasive in noting that Chapman's Homer describes Athena as 'blue-eyed', but 'This Athena-like hag was hither brought with child' is probably incommunicable from the text and certainly almost as puzzlingly incongruous as the mock-blazon. Both readings depend on the audience's precise and microscopic knowledge of other very specific literary usages. Compared with the editorial gloss, which is both undeniably relevant to the line and well attested as communicable to early audiences, these interpretations are strained. Dubious inches of moral advantage cost yards in credibility. The case is not solid as an objection to commentary because Marcus recognizes the cultural and linguistic shifts that have certainly altered the sense of 'blue-eyed', in which case commentary is rendered necessary; her own explanations are philological, arcane, and beyond most readers' knowledge. Marcus advances a serious but unsustainable charge against the political morality of editors at large. She attempts to make a virtue out of what she would have as the modern play-reader's anachronistic and uninformed misreading. The basis on which she argues for unannotating 'blue-eyed' is offensively censorial, and it is no excuse that her readers, as distinct from readers of *The Tempest*, can be let in on the doubtfully helpful insight she has to offer. It is ironic that Marcus should elsewhere accuse editors of suppression.

Marcus's attack on the New Bibliography whereby wicked male editors are scapegoated for the suppression of textual free-play is no less ritualistic than anything she finds in editors. She backhandedly admits that Q1 *Hamlet* is not necessarily to be preferred over Q2 because 'in the absence of the icon, the power of iconoclasm is lost' (p. 146), words that intimate a paradoxical impulse to break 'Shakespeare' yet to leave him still unbroken so he can be broken again. Here, strangely ritualistic urges seem to lurk in iconoclasm itself. For well over a decade, many editors have been distancing themselves from the New Bibliography, reimagining the problems presented by the extant printed texts, rewriting the language and reprioritizing the concerns of textual exposition. There is a legitimate call to extend these developments further. Marcus's book sometimes brilliantly and always interestingly continues the recent project of examining the 'bad' quartos as alternatives to the texts given (rightful) priority in Shakespeare editions. Her care about historical conditions and her frequent critical perspicacity often carry the argument. These qualities are most liable to collapse when she heaps scorn on editors, present as well as past.

Marcus Walsh's sane and often admirable *Shakespeare, Milton, and Eighteenth-Century Literary Editing* traces the foundations of practices Leah Marcus seeks to undo. Where some recent studies of the subject have found early editors hemmed in by contingency or riddled with contradiction flowing from the epistemology of the period itself, Walsh insists on the sophistication and coherence of the period's editorial thought. Walsh's longest chapter is on Shakespeare editing, but his introduction and his other chapters on biblical scholarship and Milton editing have a particular relevance to the Shakespeare scholar because they supply a vital context necessary to understand what editors were doing with Shakespeare's text. Indeed, more about the editing of classical texts might have been useful. His chapter on the Bible finds textual scholarship deriving its principles from a Protestant concept of the divine Word. Against the textual scepticism of the Catholics, Protestants sought to find determinate meaning of the very highest authority in the Bible. This attitude to text, derived from Anglican biblical scholarship with its emphasis on a discoverable underlying truth, is an enabling condition for secular editing. As for Milton, the need to define just why Richard Bentley's notorious edition of *Paradise Lost* (1732) was unacceptable despite its having been produced by the leading textual scholar of the day 'concentrated minds wonderfully' (p. 77), a process that would be repeated in the reaction against another aesthetically oriented edition, William Warburton's Shakespeare (1747). In 1748 John Upton was able to respond to both negative examples in a new Preface to his *Critical Observations on Shakespeare*.

Walsh's book, and his Shakespeare section in particular, draw on Peter Shillingsburg's distinction between the aesthetic, sociological, historical, and authorial orientations of editing in *Scholarly Editing in the Computer Age* (1986). Shillingsburg's computer-age taxonomy is not always satisfactory for the Enlightenment period, and it commits Walsh to a narrative of emergence into rationality; for instance it is hard to take account of the tenacious hold of the *textus receptus* except as an aberration, and Walsh avoids placing too much emphasis on it. Nevertheless, Shillingsburg's categories can prove helpful. Walsh shows that when the authority of the Folio was challenged by denouncing Folio readings as corruptions introduced by the players, editors were rejecting a sociological position in favour of one that was aesthetic or authorial. Pope's imposition of eighteenth-century literary taste involved an aesthetic preference. It was Lewis Theobald and Edward Capell who were the most effective proponents of author-based editing, and Walsh reminds us that Capell's innovative development of a theory of copy-text was directed at discovering 'the Poet's real habitation' (quoted p. 179) rather than preserving the historical document itself.

Walsh praises Theobald's commitment to a rational and informed approach to emendation. His practice was based on respect for the readings of what he called 'the old Copies' or 'the genuine Copies' where they could be defended, on attention to textual transmission, on openly reasoned choice, and on consideration of the language and historical context of Shakespeare's day as well as Shakespeare's own usages. That apparently oxymoronic expression 'the genuine Copies', echoing but meaning something different from the Folio title-page's similarly oxymoronic reference to 'the True Originall Copies', refers to what the more precise vocabulary of twentieth-century scholarship would call the early substantive editions. It offers clarification of his confusingly articulated suggestion in *Shakespeare Restored* (1726) that an editor might emend 'the Writings of *SHAKESPEARE*' (quoted p. 119), by which Theobald must mean the 'genuine Copies' or perhaps even the *textus receptus*. Upton was clearer still: the 'genuine text' was something that needed to be 'discovered and retrieved' from the 'various copies of authority' (quoted p. 158). Here, well before Edmond Malone, is a notion of the authentic text as something recoverable from, but not always residing in, the early editions.

Arguing against the more dismissive critiques by Jerome McGann and Margreta de Grazia, Walsh maintains that, at least after the editions of Pope and Warburton, eighteenth-century editors were engaged in a collective 'extension of scholarly humanism to the world of vernacular literature' (p. 198). Here the historical perspective broadens backwards to the Renaissance and forwards to today. Walsh declares his own predilection in quoting Meyer Abrams's description of the 'salient and persistent features of the traditional, or humanist paradigm' of literary communication (quoted p. 200).

Cyndia Susan Clegg's *Press Censorship in Elizabethan England* is a cogent and thorough study advancing a case that has already been made by other writers for the Jacobean period: that censorship was much less than a systematic instrument of oppression. Clegg's book falls in two sections. The first examines 'The Practice of Censorship' through royal privilege and proclamation, ecclesiastical authorization, and the Stationers' Company licensing system. She consistently urges that 'When the encounters between Elizabethan government and the press are taken in their economic, legal, political, and religious contexts, press censorship appears less as a product of prescriptive (and proscriptive) Tudor policy than a pragmatic situational response to an extraordinary variety of particular events' (p. 5). As compared with the picture in received Whiggish and New Historicist accounts, individual stationers enjoyed relative independence. The 1586 Star Chamber decrees put control in the hands of the stationers themselves, whose motives were independent of the crown. Elizabeth's proclamations against particular books typify the *ad hoc* nature of press censorship as a whole.

Clegg's second section advances the same point of view by turning from the mechanisms of control to specific examples of censored texts. She notes that even the oppression of Catholic writing was selective, being most urgently concerned with controlling sedition: 'The authorities discriminated between objectionable texts – those sought in and of themselves – and devotional works that were seized as evidence of illegal Catholic practices' (p. 80). George Gascoigne's *Hundred Sundry Flowers* (1573) is notable for the extent to which it was not reformed in the 1575 *Posies*. Building on Adrian Weiss's brilliant bibliographical demonstration that the prefatory material in the *Flowers* is entirely an elaborate fiction (in *Studies in Bibliography*, 45 (1992), 71–104), Clegg suggests that the prefatory materials to the *Posies* are equally unreliable as biographical information, and that the *Posies* 'reveals a rhetorical strategy that sought to deflect reception away from political and personal slander' (p. 103). Her larger argument here is that what Annabel Patterson in *Reading Holinshed's Chronicles* (1994) calls 'the codes governing sociopolitical communication' are not in themselves, as Patterson urges, stable. In 1576 the reformed *Posies* was itself called in; hence 'what was censurable in 1573 was revised and became acceptable in 1575, and what was acceptable in 1575 became censorable in 1576'. There are further chapters giving subtle, scholarly, and enlightening treatment to the notorious but unique case of John Stubbs's judicial loss of his hand for his 'seditious libel' in *The Discovery of a Gaping Gulph*, the revision of Holinshed's *Chronicles*, Martin Marprelate and the Puritan press, and the 1599 proscription of satire and censorship of Sir John Hayward's *Henry IV*. She notes that the 'litany of Tudor abuses' evident in the events of 1599, though certainly abuses indeed, reflects the 'specific political contexts of the troubled years of 1599–1601' and should not be generalized into an account of Elizabethan or early modern practices as a whole.

A brief distillation of Clegg's already distilled account of famous examples such as this may make her book sound like special pleading. Of course, part of the difficulty here is whether post-enlightenment values should be used at all as a measure of the polity of a period that definitively had different values. But no matter how one responds to this question, Clegg is right to urge that we should not build our overall picture by weaving together a number of individual notorious instances, and she makes an important and convincing case in arguing that Elizabethan press censorship was uneven and situational.

On p. 2 of *'The Contention' and 'The True Tragedy'* Yashdip S. Bains states that Shakespeare revised the plays, and the revisions are represented in the 1623 Folio texts of *2* and *3 Henry VI*. This is presented as a self-evident fact: 'One would have thought that there would be no disagreement.' Bains's technique throughout is assertion, and his strategy is to describe every attempt to challenge the self-evident fact as a failure: he himself is anchored to the sea-bed, everyone else is adrift. This is an easy game to play, because the 'correct' explanation stands in no need of assessment and justification. Bains repeatedly complains that other textual critics present arguments that lack bibliographical certainty. If this is true enough, and indeed inevitable, the inference that he himself is in confident possession of such certainty is off the mark. As far as I can see, Bains's position is based on the absurd proposition that the order in which the versions were originated must perforce correspond to the order of printing.

Laurie Osborne's *The Trick of Singularity*, a book not averse to buzz-words, examines performance editions of *Twelfth Night*, seeking to 'acknowledge a multiplicity of texts and allow free play of copies in order to explore the issues raised by performance editing' (p. 21). At this level this game too is straightforward, because any example could not fail to add to the multiplicity, but Osborne's account does something different and more useful when it traces the patterns that precipitate out of the free play. A chapter called 'Double Dating' observes how the perceived date of *Twelfth Night*, an 'external' consideration, comes to influence the perception of its meaning. She goes on to review the characteristics of nineteenth-century performance editing, showing, for example, that the editors and publishers 'self-consciously advertised their editions in connection to the theatre' (p. 36) but nonetheless 'allied their editions with other kinds of texts' (p. 42). The third chapter, the core of the book's more pragmatic scholarship, explores the ways in which different performance editions construct different theatrical meanings, noting some cuts made to consolidate a nineteenth-century perception of character, other cuts designed to highlight a contrast between Viola and Olivia. Here and elsewhere the emphasis on multiplicity becomes moderated by a picture of continuities and overlaps. So Osborne can show how the performance editions frequently betray anxiety about homoeroticism; Olivia's passion is repeatedly played down and Viola's femininity is made to show through her disguise. Comparable developments are seen when the book takes a sharp turn to the more recent phenomenon of videos, which Osborne describes as video editions, noting a similarity with performance editions insofar as both are reproducible records of a prior performance. Osborne finds the video editions reproducing some features of the earlier performance editions; she muses that 'Although there is no sign that film directors research and reinscribe nineteenth-century performance choices, their rewriting of the playtext quite possibly grows from ongoing assumptions about how theatre and film work and how *Twelfth Night* "should" work' (p. 115). Here too patterns of stability emerge.

Towards the end of the book, Osborne's historical view is given a Lacanian twist in 'Displacing and Renaming Love', a sustained examination of Malvolio and Sebastian as the play's internal interpreters of the action. If at one level this book is an empirical and straightforward study of performance texts, at another level it is a heavily and variably theorized study of text and meaning, now arguing that Lacanian slippage is intrinsic to the text from the First Folio onwards and that there is a kind of inevitability, or at least a high appropriateness, in the fractionalism of the performance tradition: 'I see in that revealing sliding of character and text [in performance editions] the historical realization of the impulse to ... stop the slippery text from sliding again' (p. 163). It is perhaps not pedantic to ask where the 'impulse' resides before its historical realizations.

But for present purposes it would be more useful to engage with Osborne in her use of textual theory. Here she sometimes becomes heavily committed to theoretical models that potentially collapse her sense of historical particulars and discussible entities, and in her concluding chapter she startlingly performs what reads as an accidental deconstruction of the model she follows, McGann's distinction between the text, the poem, and the work. These distinctions are immediately dislocated when she silently substitutes the performance term 'play' for the literary term 'poem'. She then silently redefines the 'text' as being a material object rather than, as per McGann, a 'purely lexical event' (*The Textual Condition* (1991), pp. 31–2); she says the text can be used as a doorstop, but you can't, in any simple sense, stop a door with a lexical event. She then silently shifts McGann's definition of 'poem' as 'the locus of a specific process of production (or reproduction) and consumption', offering her equivalent 'play' as 'a location where both the individual text and the collective work occur' and so 'the center of an irregular shape, an outline traced by texts and other reproductions'. This slippery and unproclaimed redefinition removes any sense of contingency other than textual; it defines the 'play' without reference to specific performance or publication, but transhistorically and in terms of what it is not. And when she urges the plasticity of that outline, suggesting that the inclusive term 'work' is unconfinable except by pragmatic and perhaps arbitrary decisions, she throws into further doubt the notion that any such thing as a 'play' might be discovered at its 'center'. This theory may reach towards its own elusive coherence, but it substitutes vague abstractions for McGann's more concrete account of the textual condition. Osborne can sometimes rescue herself with belated and basic common sense: 'Why then are we not including *Twelfth Night* in the work called *The Two Gentlemen of Verona* or the work called *The Comedy of Errors*? [new paragraph] Perhaps the answer lies in those features which distinguish *Twelfth Night* from the earlier plays' (pp. 166–7). Perhaps indeed. Perhaps inevitably, there are tensions within the Mclanian theory, and tensions between theory and practice, in this uneven but ambitious book.

G. Harold Metz's *Shakespeare's Earliest Tragedy* is a more sober study of the text, origins, and receptions of *Titus Andronicus*. It gives thorough and well documented coverage to most of the topics that would be expected in the introduction and appendices to an edition of the play, though Metz does not attempt to present his own critical perspective. The first section on authorship is a review of opinions from Edward Ravenscroft to Gary Taylor; Metz was writing too early to respond to the recent studies by MacD. P. Jackson and Brian Boyd reviewed in *Shakespeare Survey 50*, and for that matter the editions of Jonathan Bate and Alan Hughes reviewed in *Shakespeare Survey 49*. This opening chapter is followed by a survey of twentieth-century criticism, and then in turn studies of the question of revision and of the text. Metz upholds the views that the play was revised both within Q1 and between Q1 and F, and that Q1 was set from an authorial draft; he lists press variants in Q2 and Folio variants on the Q3 copy, and discusses annotations in the early texts. In reviewing 'Sources, Origins, Influences' he reiterates a case he has made previously that an ancestor of the eighteenth-century prose chapbook was 'almost certainly the primary source of Shakespeare's play'. Here he argues against Marco Mincoff and G. K. Hunter, and finds an ally in Eugene Waith in his Oxford edition; Jackson's article on the matter is not mentioned. An appendix to the chapter presents passages from the chapbook and the play in parallel.

Metz comes down in favour of an early date of 1589 for the play's composition. A later chapter upholds this dating by arguing that parallels between *Titus* and Thomas Nashe's *The Unfortunate Traveller* result from Nashe seeing the play on stage. The book presents a usefully inclusive survey of the play's more recent stage history between 1970 and 1994; for earlier productions the reader is referred to articles Metz published previously in *Shakespeare Quarterly* and *Shakespeare Survey*, and there is a long footnote on pp. 288–9 supplementing the first of these. The final chapters discuss the Longleat manuscript drawing of a scene from the play and the stage directions for music.

The book's subtitle, *Studies in 'Titus Andronicus'* is suitably distanced from any claim to thematic unity, for, as my summary will suggest, there is none. Indeed, the order of proceedings seems arbitrary, the chapters on twentieth-century criticism and recent stage history look ill at ease amidst the studies of text and origins, and the stage history chapter calls out for repackaging with Metz's earlier articles on the subject. The individual studies are usually dependable and impartial; the passions momentarily begin to rise over the chapbook, where Metz's case is most contentious. This book is a considerable repository of carefully digested information and scholarship. A more extensive index would have enhanced its value further.

Gordon Williams's *A Glossary of Shakespeare's Sexual Language* should become the standard first point of reference on its subject for editors and others. Where Eric Partridge in his groundbreaking *Shakespeare's Bawdy* (1947) sometimes relied on enthusiasm for the subject, Williams adopts a more scholarly approach, and he is keen to avoid the vice of 'kite-flying' he finds in more recent commentators such as Frankie Rubinstein (p. 7). In his introduction he examines the evasive locutions of Shakespeare's eighteenth and nineteenth-century commentators, whom he describes as knowing but élitist: 'That there has ever been a time of innocence in the reading of Shakespeare ... is a myth' (p. 9). The more pressing difficulty today is that commentators have tended to interpret Shakespeare's sexual references by the light of modern sexual perspectives and linguistic usages. He doubts whether Mistress Quickly's 'I'll drink no proofs, nor no bullets' is, as Partridge thought, a glance at oral sex, pointing out that *drink* can allude to genital sex. He points out that whereas Elizabethans would tend to giggle at *occupy* they were much less sensitized than we are to *come*.

Williams highlights the care that is needed in establishing the extent to which words such as *come* can be attributed with a sexual meaning. He cites just one instance in the whole of Shakespeare – though I would add, at least, *Measure* 2.1.114–16. Williams is well aware that the quibble occurs much more frequently in other writers such as Middleton, for his book draws on his massively detailed 3-volume *Dictionary of Sexual Language in Shakespearean and Stuart Literature* (1994). Whereas that study 'endeavours to map out broad areas of use', the present one 'must take account of more personal and idiosyncratic aspects'. A glossary such as this can scarcely do full justice to defining the pressure of the sexual in relation to the non-sexual in a particular image or a particular writer's ideolect, but in his introduction Williams warns against 'lumpish correspondences' (p. 11) and suggests the delicacy with which Shakespeare's allusions can be deployed.

This being so, the sexual referent can be hard to determine. In *Much Ado* at 5.2.9–10, Margaret's 'To have no man come over me – why, shall I always keep below stairs' has a coital implication in 'come over' (though as recent an editor as Sheldon P. Zitner in his 1993 Oxford Shakespeare edition explains the phrase as meaning no more than to assume social superiority through marriage); but what of 'keep below stairs'? Williams has an interesting discussion, even if he does not mention the possibility that the sexual meaning is simply 'keep my lower body securely locked away'. He is sympathetic to editors who have emended to sustain a contrast between male up-and-in and down-and-out, and it is useful to have attention drawn to these earlier editorial deliberations. George Steevens's emendation 'keep *men* below stairs' is supported with reference to a 1683 text in which a busy harlot's architectural/anatomical 'Stairs will be wet and the Passage slippery'. Nice emphasis capitals.

Reference to that quotation demonstrates scholarship rather than prurience, even if it shows Williams pressing rather insistently for stability and coherence in what is, after all, not the primary sense. If anything, he can sometimes say too little. Where Williams is silent it is sometimes difficult to know whether he has overlooked a sexual reference or prudently kept his kite grounded. There is no discussion of *Timon* 2.2.53–6, where Isidore's Servant says

'There's the fool hangs on your back already' and Apemantus' riposte is 'No, thou stand'st single: thou'rt not on him yet.' If this is not homosexual banter, it sounds rather like it, and comment would be helpful. Williams does not refer to Lucio's 'putting the hand in the pocket' at *Measure* 3.1.314; there is a note on other allusive uses of *hand* but no reference to *pocket* used like the more distinctively female *placket*. Must the reader conclude that *pocket* cannot be vaginal?

Part of the difficulty here, and hence the whole need for guidance, lies in the exacerbated instability of meaning when it lies at a secondary or even tertiary level. Lucio's full question is 'What, is there none of Pygmalion's images newly made woman to be had now, for putting the hand in the pocket and extracting clutched?' Passing over complexities in the reference to artificial creation or the artificial appearance of virginity, and so on to the pocket image, one might ask as to how far, if at all, *had* here means 'possessed sexually' as well as 'obtained for prostitution'. Does the image begin as a reference to coitus to resolve itself as a reference to pandarism, or does it completely overlap the roles of customer and indirect beneficiary? Is the coital image somehow sustained in 'extracting clutched', or is it abandoned? Yet finally Lucio's question eludes referentiality. As Jonathan Dollimore has famously pointed out (in *Political Shakespeare*, ed. by Dollimore and Alan Sinfield (1985), pp. 85–6), in *Measure for Measure* prostitutes remain symptomatically absent from the stage. Lucio seeks to embarrass Pompey by hinting at entirely supposititious realities. Sexual language is always like that, ranging through alarming excesses of overstatement (*yard*, *ell*) to playful and tricky hints at what may or may not be (*My mistress' eyes are nothing* ...). It cuts across the process of public and more secure reference by speaking of things often unknown, and more imagined than seen and done. Signification runs wild; lexicography is ill-equipped for such language. Paradoxically, that strengthens the need for such mapping as is possible of this shifting verbal terrain.

## ARTICLES, ESSAYS, NOTES

As has already been seen, the term 'authorship' overlies a complex negotiation between the activities of defining the authorial canon and of interrogating authorship as concept and as early modern practice. The most obvious manifestation to the general Shakespeare reader is the sudden and slightly anxious inclusion of *A Funeral Elegy* in three major editions of the works. The case in favour of identifying the *Elegy* as a poem penned by Shakespeare is made in articles by Donald W. Foster and Richard Abrams; the case against is put in a joint article by Ward E. Y. Elliott and Robert J. Valenza summarizing work conducted by the Claremont Colleges Shakespeare Clinic.

Abrams examines critical implications of placing the *Elegy* in the context of Shakespeare's works. Seizing on the known date of composition of 1612, he relates the *Elegy*'s drab style to Shakespeare's supposed rejection of the stage and its flamboyant poetics at the end of his career. The elegist blames the theatrical vices of 'fond conceit', 'disguise', and 'affect[ation]' for Peter's death (p. 439), implying that he rejects the choice of writing a play on Peter 'because to do so would belie Peter's avoidance of pretension'. This is a suspect argument surely, as it depends on a conjectural account of Shakespeare's intellectual and emotional life in order to draw him towards a position that is at once commonplace and yet still not securely his. Abrams goes on to argue that a passage about recounting a tale of woe in winter in such a way as to send the listeners weeping to their beds is an echo of *Richard II*. Does this prove more than that the elegist probably knew the play, which had been reprinted in 1608? He finds that the Sonnet theme of the immortalizing power of art is developed in the *Elegy*, as too is the dramatic theme of the 'compulsive context of masculine vanities' (p. 449); he does not take into proper consideration that both have long antecedents and numerous analogues. He finds resemblance between the *Elegy* and a passage in *Two Noble Kinsmen* 1.2 in the use of sea imagery in relation to paired characters; here it would have been helpful to address the possibility that the elegist was following conventions of his genre that were to be reflected later in Milton's *Lycidas*. Abrams provides little that positively advances the campaign for Shakespeare, but provides ingenious, sometimes over-ingenious, solutions to a number of objections.

Foster's article, adding to his *Elegy by W.S.: A Study in Attribution* (1989), summarizes the links with canonical Shakespeare that he has been able to establish through his more recent work using electronic text archives. He confirms that the 'rare words' test supports Shakespeare's authorship. Paradoxically, words *not* found elsewhere in Shakespeare cumulatively point to his authorship, for the reason that Shakespeare consistently and tirelessly expanded his vocabulary base. Hence a word associated with no writer at all is especially likely to be Shakespearian. The *Elegy* does prove to have a high incidence of such words. It also has three examples of a characteristically Shakespearian impersonal use of 'who', though I note that in each case there are other elements of personification in the passage that call in question whether the 'who' is entirely impersonal. Foster also claims that the frequency of hendiadys is uniquely Shakespearian. The *Elegy*, moreover, 'finds its highest lexical correlation with Shakespeare's plays and poems, principally with plays written or acted in the last years, 1609–13' (p. 1085). Some of the supporting arguments invite scepticism. W. S.'s alleged knowledge of *The Tragedy of Mariam* suggests that he is Shakespeare because it can be shown that the play was also known, not to Shakespeare, but to Middleton at the time the *Elegy* was written; Middleton, like Shakespeare, wrote for the King's men. John Ford's borrowings from the *Elegy* support its ascription to Shakespeare because Ford borrowed from Shakespeare. A somewhat more convincing point is that the *Elegy* has closer links in its diction with the Shakespeare canon than does *All Is True/Henry VIII*, though, as Foster notes, the play is probably a collaboration.

Elliott and Valenza respond to Foster with a devastating critique of his methods. His work has not, they point out, 'been shown to be immune to "false positives"'. They do not accept that the *Elegy*'s 'sharing of rare words and quirks with Shakespeare, even a lot of rare words and quirks, proves Shakespeare's authorship' (p. 180), pointedly urging an analogy between this 'sum of quirks' approach and some of the fallacious arguments used by the anti-Stratfordians. The fallacies can be seen by considering *Woodstock*, a play that cannot plausibly have been written by Thomas Middleton that is nevertheless, they say, full of Middleton 'rare-quirk marker words'. As for hendiadys and redundant comparatives and superlatives, Elliott and Valenza comment that identification depends on literary judgement and so can be discovered only by manually checking all occurrences of 'and' and 'more'; the use of electronic text archive does not make the procedure any more objective or reliable or checkable. They endorse MacD. P. Jackson's stricture that Foster, having identified nine common words that occur in Shakespeare's works at reasonably constant rates, discards four because the rates for them are not matched in the *Elegy*; and they confirm Jackson's observation that the *Elegy*'s frequency of 'in the' excludes it as a Shakespeare work.

The limitation is, then, that Foster records 'green light' findings but does not look for and even avoids 'red light' results. The conclusion 'must prove Shakespeare' is much harder to achieve than the conclusion 'must exclude Shakespeare'. Elliott and Valenza's exclusion tests successfully fail to show, as one might put it, that the core Shakespeare canon was not by Shakespeare. In contrast they positively show that the works of the Shakespeare Apocrypha were none of them by Shakespeare, and that none of the anti-Stratfordian claimants could have written Shakespeare's words. With 'green light' tests we have no agreement as to what really would constitute a distinctive profile made up of individually inconclusive features, and the method therefore remains of deeply uncertain validity. Meanwhile, the weight of Elliott and Valenza's argument falls where they establish a number of tests that show clearly that the *Elegy* does not fit with Shakespeare's authorship. The conclusion is that 'Despite some striking Shakespeare resemblances' the *Elegy* fails 'too many tests to look much like Shakespeare'.

The trouble is that the same is true of *A Lover's Complaint*. Quite simply, neither the *Elegy* nor the *Complaint* can be accepted as Shakespeare's unless the Claremont work is shown to be lacking. It is the finding against the *Complaint* that is the real shock, for it runs against the strong endorsement of the work as Shakespearian, not only in its presence alongside the Sonnets in the 1609 volume issued by Thomas Thorpe, but also in the modern studies by Kenneth Muir, MacD. P. Jackson, John Kerrigan, and others. Elliott and Valenza are able to rule out the main rival claimant to authorship of the *Complaint*, George Chapman. They are refreshingly willing to accept that 'Computer-aided authorship analysis is in its infancy', that 'Time will tell' (p. 201). In the meantime, the balance tips strongly against the erstwhile anonymous *Elegy* and the erstwhile Shakespearian *Complaint* alike. The very insecurity of the authorial boundary-line presents an interesting challenge to our conceptualizations of 'Shakespeare'.

The traditional distinction between 'good' and 'bad' quartos is another authorial borderline that often looks insecure. For David Farley-Hills in 'The "Bad" Quarto of *Romeo and Juliet*', as for Jay L. Halio (reviewed in *Shakespeare Survey 50*), Q1 *Romeo and Juliet* is not a memorial reconstruction. Farley-Hills proposes that Q1, 'atypical of "bad" quartos' (p. 36), is based on a redaction of the 'foul papers' (as represented in Q2) prepared by an adapter with knowledge of the play as it had been performed on stage. The redaction was probably performed by Shakespeare's company on provincial tour. The strength of the account is that Farley-Hills moves beyond the more structural differences that can readily be explained as features of adaptation to consider the finer details of the texts. Many of the features customarily attributed to faulty memory can be accommodated to his alternative theory. Farley-Hills is often persuasive, though there are moments of special pleading. A transposition of lines (to or from 3.4 in Q2, from or to a weaker position in 1.5 in Q1) is explained as 'a post-Q1 stage of revision' in Q2, the text that Farley-Hills agrees was set from 'foul papers', or alternatively as an authorial duplication that somehow escaped from Q2. The strain in the account here shows when he admits as a third possibility, the very kind of error he is trying to banish, failure of the actor-redactor's memory (p. 39). Farley-Hills later strengthens the suggestion that Shakespeare marked some revisions in his authorial draft after the Q1 redaction had been taken from it. He suggests that the Prologue may have been written by the redactor as in Q1, anticipating the 'two houres traffique of our Stage' of a short version. It would have been later revised by Shakespeare as in Q2. This intriguing idea must be treated with at least some scepticism. If the main playbook had already been prepared (as is strongly supposed, especially when Farley-Hills dates the redaction to 1596), why would the redactor and Shakespeare *both* base their further alterations on the defunct and theatrically impractical 'foul papers'?

Anyone seeking to gain familiarity with the general issues of postmodern editorial theory with respect to Shakespeare could do much worse than read the engaging essays on 'Editing Early Modern Texts' in *Shakespeare Studies 24*. This forum developed by Susan Zimmerman began with invitations to the contributors to write, in Zimmerman's words, on 'how bibliographical and textual studies, interpreted very broadly, have been affected by the poststructural critical climate; how such studies might enhance other kinds of research in the early modern period; and what major problems and projects are likely to shape the future of the field'.

Stephen Orgel, having once famously asked 'What Is a Text?' (*Research Opportunities in Renaissance Drama*, 24 (1981), 3–6), now enquires 'What is an Editor?' He recognizes that those who have both attempted to theorize 'post-Bowers bibliography' and edit texts as well, such as Jerome McGann and Orgel himself, have tended to produce texts very much like everyone else's. He goes on to suggest, as a form of editing that both preserves the 'archeology' of the text and presents 'a Shakespeare accessible to the modern reader', what he describes as 'an unedited text with an infinite commentary, the editor acting only as referee' (p. 25). As with Foakes's *King Lear* but to a far more radical extent, it would be up to the reader to construct a reading text from the materials presented. What would approximate to the 'infinite' is not, as Orgel suggests, the amount of material stored in a large but finite data-base, but the number of predicated readings, as the possibilities for interpretation are multiplied by the possibilities for each reader to select variants from any source whatsoever in order to assemble a personal lexical sequence representing 'a Shakespeare'. In this vision *accessible* might mean 'capable of being electronically accessed' rather than 'capable of being understood', and indeed one suspects that manipulation of text could become an end in itself as the characteristic act of reading.

Orgel's McLeodian objection to his own proposal is that the 'unedited text' is itself illusory, as any form of reproduction unignorably involves editorial choice. But he notes too that whereas in such models of editing 'the author has little or nothing to do with the case', in fact the author function is 'not something invented in the eighteenth century' (p. 28). Foucault's argument has too conveniently let postmodern editors and critics of the early modern period off the hook, for after all its texts could be, in an ideational as well as literal way, authored.

David Scott Kastan, like Orgel, avoids striking a single pose. In a discriminating and flexible discussion he is characteristically aware of contradiction: between the polarities of print and authorship, and, in a phrase that reaches straight to the heart of the matter, between 'the impossibility of editing and yet the inescapability of it' (p. 37). This latter, he says, 'creates and explains the excitement of textual studies today'. Kastan is cheerfully stoical in recognizing that the text's 'making and remaking are not evidence of its contamination but the enabling conditions of its being' (p. 37). His sense of symmetry enables some valuable perceptions, as when he writes 'If edited versions, then, usually idealize the activity of authorship, facsimile versions work to idealize the printed text.' But it can also exclude the sort of triangular co-ordination that is probably most fitting for dramatic texts. To the author and document must be added the event of performance, which might be more or less authorially determined, more or less in accord with the printed text. His claim that the 'social conception of textuality' (p. 35) will be inimical to editing is not necessarily true. The sociality of the play text depends very much on its writing for, treatment in, and sometimes derivation from the theatre, and these considerations are very much assimilated into current editorial practice.

W. Speed Hill's rather pessimistic contribution to the collection begins with a mapping-out of editorial choices as they stand now in contrast with the situation some thirty years ago. He identifies five new approaches, the last and certainly the least of which is 'no editing at all'. What they have in common is 'a decentering of the author' (p. 40). Hill argues with reference to editions of *Hamlet* that this reassessment of authority has happened alongside a decline in analytic bibliography. The idealist authorial project was happily underpinned by the supposedly rigorous materialism of the bibliographers. Perhaps the more recent questions as to the extent to which bibliography really enabled editors to achieve their objectives were only possible once the desire to attain the authorial mystery had itself weakened. The problem Hill addresses is that the editor is now deprived of the ideological and technical resources that previously validated, or seemed to validate, editing. Most of the new approaches to editing are more costly in terms of labour as well as money. Hill notes a migration away from both scholarly editing as a career choice and the canonical authors as the objects of their endeavours, lamenting that 'I disagree with those who stigmatize editions as authoritarian rather than authoritative, but I feel powerless to persuade them otherwise' (p. 46).

After Hill comes Paul Werstine, whose article has some grace of self-awareness. A paragraph of phrases such as 'there has been hell to pay', 'tarred another with the brush', 'flatly disowned any truck', 'open hostility', 'hammered', 'set out to trash' is an ironic prelude to the 'story' Werstine then sets out to tell, and when he goes on to describe Shakespeare textual criticism under the New Bibliography as resembling 'the splendid art of storytelling' he has already defused at least some protest. Werstine develops some familiar narrative functions, such as the hero discovering the Groundless Grounds of New Bibliography, and the hero slaying the Definitive Edition. Here Werstine unwittingly aligns himself with none other than Greg, who, contrary to what we are often told, pointedly described the notion of a definitive edition as 'silly'.

The older idea of the definitive edition has demised, and I strongly suspect that the idea of a future hypertext Shakespeare, scholarly and all-answering (but definitively undefinitive), has quietly moved in to occupy the vacuum. Hence it is that essentially the same rhetoric of disdain towards the fumbling pragmatics of editing as it is practised has been voiced from time to time almost throughout the century. Anticipating that the new Holy Grail of hypertext will eventually be reached and then enable us to cast print editions aside, Werstine asks what in the meantime can be done to ameliorate the bad books we continue to use. He advocates 'a respect for textual multiplicity and difference'. This excellent principle is not, however, easily put into practice. Werstine praises the third text of *King Lear* in the Norton Shakespeare, which in itself is conflated and anti-differential, on the grounds that it increases choice. This rather recalls Angelo's extenuation of compelled sins as standing more for number than for account. Though Werstine commends the New Folger series of his own co-editing for a presentation whereby 'The reader can take his [sic] pick of Quarto, Folio, or Quarto/Folio' (p. 53), this is actually true only of selected passages in selected texts. Despite its recourse to brackets and other intrusive sigla, such editing still sacrifices the representation of alternatives to the coherence of the continuous text, and does not bear anything like adequate witness to textual multiplicity. A solution Werstine does not endorse is the widely criticized collation line, which can, after all, be an efficient way of presenting textual multiplicity and difference on the same page as the edited text.

John Pitcher's 'Why Editors Should Write More Notes' takes us along and beyond some of the lines I explored with reference to Braunmuller's commentary on *Macbeth*. His opening pages offer a brilliant exposition of lines from *Cymbeline* in a way intended to be 'extensive enough to allow modern and postmodern critical discussion to begin in earnest' (p. 58). This, he argues, is the nature of commentary as it is now needed, even if it requires a challenge to the economics of publishing Shakespeare editions and a more energetic and challenging practice on the part of editors. Pitcher concludes by suggesting that 'passivity' (p. 61) as much as theoretical rectitude might discourage editors from the eclectic use of early editions.

Though his energized perspective differs from Hill's, they seem to agree that postmodern approaches to text can encourage a glib indifference to serious textual scholarship.

The final essay in the forum, Josephine A. Roberts's 'Editing the Women Writers of Early Modern England', helps put Shakespeare's texts into perspective by drawing attention to our imperfect understanding of the relationship between Shakespeare and a manuscript culture in which women actively participated. She draws a distinction between the primary editorial scholarship in works such as Sr Jean Klene's forthcoming edition of the Southwell–Sibthorpe commonplace book that is making the material available for the first time and Barry Weller and Margaret W. Ferguson's 1994 edition of *The Tragedy of Mariam* that builds from the Malone Society Reprints edition to provide a modernized edition for the more general reader.

*Shakespeare's Speech-Headings* is a long overdue collection emanating from a seminar at the 1986 conference of the Shakespeare Association of America in Montreal. It is worth remembering that the papers were first given four years before Paul Werstine's influential article 'Narratives About Printed Shakespeare Texts' (*Shakespeare Quarterly*, 41 (1990), 65–86). The editor, George Walton Williams, establishes the significance of the topic by reprinting R. B. McKerrow's seminal paper of 1935, 'A Suggestion Regarding Shakespeare's Manuscripts', which used highly variable speech-prefixes as key evidence for identifying foul paper copy for printed plays. The organization of the volume might imply that behind the humdrum title lies an important challenge to the orthodoxies of the New Bibliography, and this is true of at least some of the individual essays.

The interest of other papers is, however, confined to a particular reading or group of readings. Sidney Thomas conjectures that the first prefix identifying Capulet's wife as '*Old La.*' in Q2 *Romeo and Juliet* might have been modified by a printing-house editor. A. R. Braunmuller explores the unexpected identification of a Citizen at Angers as Hubert in *King John* at the speech-prefix at TLN 636 and thereafter in the scene. Where F's entry at TLN 505 reads '*Enter a Citizen vpon the walles.*' Braunmuller suggests the edited direction '*Enter Citizens on Angers, including Hubert, upon the walls*', which anticipates the arrangement in his Oxford Shakespeare edition of the play. He does not address the difficulties of casting in this, the most heavily populated scene. Such considerations might have discouraged any expansion of what evidently at least began as a single Citizen, and they offer the prospect that, for example, the first mention of Hubert's name could have appeared in the manuscript to note a possible doubling arrangement. It is difficult to say whether Hubert's appearance at Angers is some such theatrical expedient or an initial and incomplete attempt to merge the roles themselves, but I remain sceptical that the character later identified as Hubert can plausibly be understood to be the same represented figure as a citizen on the walls at Angers. Thomas Clayton's supposedly 'Preliminary' enquiry into speech-prefixes in *Coriolanus* is as attentive, detailed, and heavily documented an attempt to legislate between alternative editorial treatments as one could expect to find. Richard Proudfoot's examination of the Shakespeare Apocrypha indicates the 'range of bibliographical interest to be found in speech prefixes' (p. 132), for these texts are diverse in every respect. Proudfoot presents his case for two good conjectural emendations of *Two Noble Kinsmen*, both of which are already on record, one of them actually adopted, in the Oxford Shakespeare (*Textual Companion*, notes to 3.3.34–5 and 4.1.45). They are attractive enough to have been at least recorded by the Arden 3 editor.

Other contributions to the volume are more concerned to argue away from textual detail and towards the wider issues of editing. Preeminent here (along with Paul Werstine's short contribution, which is already available in expanded form in his 'McKerrow's "Suggestion" and Twentieth-Century Shakespeare Textual Criticism') is William B. Long's 'Perspective on Provenance'. Long posits that the inconsistencies that were allowed to stand in surviving theatrical playbooks are such that a clean 'good' quarto printed text such as Q1 *Midsummer Night's Dream* could have been set up from a playbook rather than a pre-theatrical manuscript. The standards of correctness expected of a playbook are, Long observes, those of modern editors rather than early modern theatrical personnel. He argues that even the variable speech-prefixes in Q2 *Romeo and Juliet* might remain unaltered in a playbook. It would seem true that playbook annotators tended to make limited and non-systematic changes to prefixes and that some inconsistency was tolerated, but the possibility remains that one of the purposes in going to the trouble of preparing an authorial or scribal fair copy would be to introduce a greater degree of regularity in the speech-prefixes. An example of an extant licensed manuscript that preserves as much variation as is found in Q2 *Romeo* would therefore have been crucially helpful in consolidating Long's argument. Noting that extant manuscripts of non-dramatic works have survived unmutilated after serving as printers' copy, Long argues that the same might apply to a playbook. But there are differences. The fact that particular manuscripts were not significantly damaged does not mean that a theatre company could be assured of a playbook's survival intact, and the potential loss of future revenue following from loss of a licensed playbook would have no equivalent for a non-dramatic work. Long nevertheless opens up theoretical possibilities that remind us that our understanding of the copy manuscripts for printed plays is provisional and insecure. If one reads his paper as a critique of the concept of foul papers on the basis that two manuscripts might be one too many, one might counterbalance this view with conclusions emerging from students of non-dramatic manuscripts such as Henry Woudhuysen that, for plays as well, two manuscripts might be too few. Such perspectives do not, however, cancel each other out. Previously the extant play manuscripts were regarded as local variations on general types, and a generalizable model of textual production seemed possible. We can now no longer assume that a single model based on two manuscripts, one foul and one fair, will necessarily apply. That is not to say that nothing can be surmised, and to exaggerate scepticism would be no more responsible than to exaggerate probability.

Steven Urkowitz develops his earlier articles arguing for the separate integrity of the Quarto and Folio texts of two plays, *The Contention/2 Henry VI* and *Richard III*, examining some parallel contrasts in the treatment of the murderers in each play as it develops from one text to the other. The direction in which the texts do develop is a moot point. Although Urkowitz claims that his discussion doesn't depend on a particular sequence of versions, he favours seeing the Quartos as the earlier versions. Thus he suggests an alteration from more equally balanced and less differentiated Quarto murderers to more strongly differentiated Folio murderers. He is placidly non-committal as to who might have made the changes: 'We cannot tell', but to an age less fixated on establishing a singular, genuine and isolatable Shakespeare 'This is not a big problem' (pp. 116–17).

George Walton Williams in his introduction to the book declares with cautious optimism that 'To edit is human'. Random Cloud [Randall McLeod] offers an exploration of human and editorial folly in a diverting, witty, and typographically virtuoso anti-essentialist study that addresses naming in speech-prefixes. He triangulates Williams's maxim by implying that to edit is artificially to create human-like entities; in this to edit is, he posits, to err. An opening section has already appeared in print (as 'The very names of the Persons', in *Staging the Renaissance*, ed. David Scott Kastan and Peter Stallybrass (1991)). After it, Cloud explores some examples of paradoxical speech-prefixes in modern drama and Jonson's *Epicene* before turning to the Bastards themselves: firstly, and briefly, Edmund, and then, at more length, Philip Faulconbridge – or is it Sir Robert Plantagenet? – in *King John*. The conclusion is that it 'all bumbles along very well, thank you, with unstable nomencl' (sic, 'p. 189', sic, p. 190). Cloud's business might seem finished, but his 'Pyramus and Thysbe' is a dialogue between 'Deborah', 'Ed' and 'Prof' on the instabilities in naming Starveling and Moonshine in *A Midsummer Night's Dream*. Ed's position is 'But it's OK; I can fix it. I have a system' (p. 193).

The debate between cultural materialist opponents of fixing it and their opponents continues in the February 1997 issue of *New Theatre Quarterly*, where Gabriel Egan takes issue with Andrew Spong's 'Bad Habits' (*NTQ*, No. 45 (1996), 65–70). Egan demonstrates that the materialist position has depended on blunt assertions that lack scholarly credibility, and he efficiently dismantles Spong's rejection of the value of primary materials. Spong's position was in any case surprising, as it is the early printed books that validate the Shakespearean Originals series with which he associates himself. Indeed, answering Spong's Marxist position in Marxist terms, Egan accuses the series's general editors of fetishizing print. In doing so, they reject 'the recoverable active labour of the working dramatist' (p. 46).

It is the recoverable active labour of the working printer that concerns Joseph Dane. His article is about the integrity of the pile of sheets, as it is established in the first place by the order in which they were printed on one side. The order of sheets in the pile might subsequently be affected by 'perfecting' and 'gathering'; in other words by printing the second forme of the sheet, and collating a copy of each sheet to make up a single book. Dane draws his evidence from published collations of press variants; many of these studies are of play quartos, a few of which present Shakespeare works. He confirms that in general integrity was maintained. In gathering, the 'tendency toward binding integrity' can be strong enough to suggest the probable sequence of states that are in themselves indeterminable. Dane describes perfecting integrity as 'a much stronger principle' (p. 300), but notes circumstances in which exceptions arise in a limited and mechanical way. His concluding comment is that studies of press variation need to enlarge their horizons from the unit of the forme to 'the pattern of variation within the book as a whole' (p. 301).

In an article on censorship that summarizes an increasing dissatisfaction with studies stronger on theoretical than empirical rigour, Janet Clare notes that 'The historicisms of the 1980s . . . have been cavalier about the traditional strength and skills of historical investigation . . . As with any social practice, to understand censorship in the Renaissance, we need to map its terrain, note its serial changes, explore the languages through which it was articulated by the officials who served it and the writers who chafed against its strictures' (p. 176). She finds these cavalier shortcomings alike in Greenblatt, Patterson, Steven Mullaney, and Richard Burt. Clare comments, for example, that if Greenblatt had properly identified the potential for sedition in *2 Henry IV* as lying in its presentation of a rebellion led by an archbishop, rather than in the 'contained' masterless army recruits, and if he had examined the differences between Quarto and Folio texts, he would have found his claim that the state 'was not prodded to intervene' to be inaccurate. Contrary to the 'totalizing view of "top–down" containment' (p. 160), the text evidently was regarded as seditious, and evidently was censored.

The March 1997 issue of *Notes and Queries* contains a batch of notes on the text of Shakespeare. Prompted partly by the Q1 reading 'Madame', partly by some unnecessary doubts as to whether it is appropriate for Romeo to describe Juliet as a young falcon, Horst Breuer proposes emending 'My Neece' to the banal 'Mistress' instead of the usual editorial 'My nyas' (*Romeo and Juliet*, 2.2.167). After suggesting that Shakespeare knew Cicero's *De Officiis*, Steve Sohmer finds an analogue in Cicero's work for the phrase that Jonson noted as 'ridiculous' in *Julius Caesar*, 'Caesar did never wrong but with just cause' (3.1.47). Sohmer thus finds further justification for adopting the words 'but with just cause' into the text of Shakespeare (as was done in the Oxford *Complete Works*). Paul Hammond notes that F's omission of a passage including the line 'He's mad, that trusts in ... a boyes loue' might, in the context of James I's homosexuality, have been due to censorship. The passage leads straight into the mock trial scene. Though Hammond recognizes that one would probably need a separate explanation for the omission of that episode as a whole, he seeks to question any presupposition that revision alone accounts for the variation between Q and F. Daniel Senes finds that 'internal logic' suggests reattributing 'Seest thou this object, Kent' (5.3.237) from Albany to Edmund; this entails a shared error in Q and F but is dramatically plausible. Thomas Merriam notes that the hints of pro-Catholic sympathies in the original text of *Sir Thomas More* and the play's influence on Shakespeare's works support the stylometric case for Shakespeare's authorship. His discussion of Catholic leanings depends on a contest between 'Protestant' Munday and 'Catholic' Shakespeare that would not be sustainable if, as is likely enough, Henry Chettle wrote scenes critical to the argument such as Sc. 12. The argument relating to Shakespeare's borrowing makes the decidedly vulnerable assumption that Shakespeare would only borrow from the play (even after he revised it) if it were of his original authorship. In a more plausible authorship study, MacD. P. Jackson uses phrase lengths to support James Spedding's 1850 division of *All is True/Henry VIII* between Shakespeare and Fletcher, as against Cyrus Hoy's revised estimate. Finally, in a note with implications for the substance and wording of editorial stage directions, G. K. Hunter assembles the evidence in the drama of the period for the stage device of the aside.

## ELECTRONIC RESOURCES

The prodigious *World Shakespeare Bibliography on CD-ROM* extends its coverage by swelling both backwards and forwards in time from one release to the next. The second release captures about 25,000 works published between 1987 and 1994. It includes annotated listings of books, articles, and reviews on Shakespeare; it also covers Shakespeare theatre productions, which makes it almost two archives in one. The entries are arranged in sections with up to three levels of subsections. In the table of contents the reader can expand and collapse the subsections at will, and so move straight into the bibliographical records at any point. There are indexes of subjects and persons, and a user guide. Indexes and cross-references are hypertext-linked to the main entry. It is extraordinarily easy to navigate around the bibliography using the table of contents and the basic Find facility, which is permanently displayed at the foot of the screen. Efficient use of the indexes may need searches to locate an entry, as shifting place within such large indexes is too hit-and-miss and scrolling is too slow. A string of references under an entry can be looked up without losing the index by opening a new window.

I egocentrically checked the *Bibliography* for my own publications. An article on *The Tempest* published in *The Glasgow Review* in 1993 was untraceable. The failure to register this item undermined my confidence in the apparent inclusivity of the data, though there are obvious practical difficulties in monitoring journals not specifically concerned with Shakespeare studies. Requests from the editor James L. Harner for information from authors obviously need heeding. The other works were successfully located with standard Find searches, but when searching for titles some difficulties emerged. 'The Three Texts of *2 Henry IV*' was effectively unsearchable because the word 'texts' is on a stop list (as too is the word 'short', which gives short shrift to authors of that name). An article whose title begins 'Johannes Factotum' was located by searching for 'factotum', but, whereas 'Johannes' located items authored by people with that forename, it did not locate the article. Use of the search-form 'entry title' did not help: the search engine seemed to have a blind spot.

There are, then, localized difficulties and limitations. But there is no denying the magisterial scale and elegance of the *Bibliography* as a whole. The software allows printing of selections, export to another drive, annotation, and creation of personal hypertext links. Such operations are more complex than standard searches, but they can be performed with only limited patience and experience in using the CD. The project is planned to cover 1980–96 by 1999, and so is still in its early days, but *The World Shakespeare Bibliography* is already an essential research tool for all those working in the field of Shakespeare studies.

The *Arden Shakespeare CD-ROM* gives some indication of the possible shape of future electronic editions. The publishers have developed the CD-ROM quickly by utilizing text and resources that are on the whole readily available. The standard display shows the Arden 2 text, commentary, and collation in panelled windows. Colour is used to distinguish stage directions (green), speech-prefixes (red), and line numbers (blue). Word searches can be limited to single plays or groups of plays; within the text, stage directions, songs, or specific dramatic roles can be selected for searching. A number of other documents are hypertext linked to the edited text and are searchable in their own right. These include Bevington's 1978 bibliography *Shakespeare*, Geoffrey Bullough's *Narrative and Dramatic Sources of Shakespeare*, Eagleson's revised edition of Onions's *Shakespeare Glossary*, Partridge's *Shakespeare's Bawdy*, and photofacsimiles of the Quartos and Folio. The emphasis is therefore entirely on the printed word; beyond the photofacsimiles there are no visual illustrations, let alone moving images or sound. The hypertext links are usually one-way: from edited text to facsimile or source, from glossary or grammar to edited text.

Arden's expedition has enabled them to bring out a product without any serious rival. The disadvantage is that much of the material is outdated, not least the earlier editions of the Arden 2 series itself. Though many of these remain impressive editions, time has taken its toll. The plays that have already been re-edited for Arden 3 look particularly the worse for wear. As the disc relies on existing printed books that present limited difficulties over copyright, the publishers have made little investment in the text *per se*, and the materials on the Arden CD-ROM could be bought more cheaply, albeit less conveniently, in print. Much of the publishers' costs lie in developing the electronic structure, and the cost to the user must justify itself quite largely in terms of its efficiency as a tool for searching, collocation, and simultaneous display. All in all then, the Arden disc is an expensive piece of relatively new electronic technology applied to relatively old materials. But another limitation that seems at first sight to reflect a conservative definition of the field of Shakespeare study may to some extent at least derive from the nature of hypertext itself, for the printed materials worth consideration for hypertext linkage are in fact rather limited. Analogues and allusions to the play, for instance, would offer relatively few points of linkage. A disc such as the Arden could include more of the same ilk, a dictionary of proverbs for example, but the major omissions that spring to mind are of editions, adaptations, and performance texts. To reproduce editions in general would have meant expanding the project very considerably, but by including the most influential adaptations the editors could have shown a stronger commitment to theatre than is associated with Arden 2.

Parts of the CD-ROM will nevertheless be of tremendous value to some readers, not least those with textual interests who wish to read or simply keep track of the Quarto and Folio texts. The facsimile reproductions, sometimes a little roughly linked to the Arden text, can be enlarged to reveal fine detail until the image begins to break up into pixels; resolution is more than adequate for reading purposes, but less fine than can be expected of a printed facsimile. 'Bad' quarto texts are usually included; exceptions are *The Taming of A Shrew*, which is instead reproduced from Bullough as a source text, and, regrettably, the First Quartos of *Hamlet* and *Romeo and Juliet*, where the slot for the 'Main Quarto' is occupied by Q2.

Beyond the Arden CD-ROM, the challenges in preparing textual, visual, and audio input on the scale made possible and implicitly demanded by electronic publication are very considerable indeed. At the present moment it occasions little surprise that pre-existing and even old or inadequately edited texts should be deemed suitable for a prestigious electronic Shakespeare edition. As we grow used to the capacities of hypertext the question of quality in the primary textual editing must necessarily return. The potentials of electronic editing are truly tingling, but anyone would be sobered and daunted at the task of generating huge quantities of material that has high state-of-the-art editorial value in its textual content as well as in its electronic structure. The Norton Shakespeare with its appropriated and manipulated Oxford text suggests that merely editing Shakespeare's works afresh for print can be an insurmountable challenge. Electronic text might keep editors busy.

## WORKS REVIEWED


Abrams, Richard. 'W[illiam] S[hakespeare]'s "Funeral Elegy" and the Turn from the Theatrical'. In *Studies in English Literature 1500–1900*, 36 (1996), 435–60.

*Arden Shakespeare CD-ROM: Texts and Sources for Shakespeare Studies*. Walton-on-Thames: Thomas Nelson and Sons, 1997.

Bains, Yashdip S. *'The Contention' and 'The True Tragedy': William Shakespeare's First Versions of '2 and 3 Henry VI'*. Rashtrapati Nivas: Indian Institute of Advanced Study, 1996.

Breuer, Horst. 'Romeo's Niece: A Note on *Romeo and Juliet*, II.ii.167'. In *Notes and Queries*, 242 (1997), 54–6.

Clare, Janet. 'Historicism and the Question of Censorship in the Renaissance'. In *ELR*, 27 (1997), 155–76.

Clegg, Cyndia Susan. *Press Censorship in Elizabethan England*. Cambridge: Cambridge University Press, 1997.

Dane, Joseph. 'Perfect Order and Perfected Order: The Evidence from Press-Variants of Early Seventeenth-Century Quartos'. In *PBSA*, 90 (1996), 272–320.

Egan, Gabriel. 'Myths and Enabling Fictions of "Origin" in the Editing of Shakespeare'. In *New Theatre Quarterly*, 49 (February 1997), 41–7.

Elliott, Ward E. Y., and Robert J. Valenza. 'Glass Slippers and Seven-League Boots: C-Prompted Doubts About Ascribing *A Funeral Elegy* and *A Lover's Complaint* to Shakespeare'. In *Shakespeare Quarterly*, 48 (1997), 177–207.

Farley-Hills, David. 'The "Bad" Quarto of *Romeo and Juliet*'. In *Shakespeare Survey 49* (1996), 27–44.

Fletcher, John, and William Shakespeare. *The Two Noble Kinsmen*. Ed. by Lois Potter, Arden 3. Walton-on-Thames: Thomas Nelson and Sons, 1997.

Foakes, R. A. 'French Leave, or Lear and the King of France'. In *Shakespeare Survey 49* (1996), 217–23.

Foster, Donald W. 'A Funeral Elegy: W[illiam] S[hakespeare]'s "Best-Speaking Witness"'. In *PMLA*, 111 (1996), 1080–105.

Hammond, Paul. 'James I's Homosexuality and the Revision of the Folio Text of *King Lear*'. In *Notes and Queries*, 242 (1997), 62–4.

Hunter, G. K. 'Notes on "Asides" in Elizabethan Drama'. In *Notes and Queries*, 242 (1997), 83–5.

Jackson, MacD. P. 'Phrase Lengths in *Henry VIII*: Shakespeare and Fletcher'. In *Notes and Queries*, 242 (1997), 75–80.

Marcus, Leah S. *Unediting the Renaissance: Shakespeare, Marlowe, Milton*. London and New York: Routledge, 1996.

Masten, Jeffrey. *Textual Intercourse: Collaboration, Authorship, and Sexualities in Renaissance Drama*. Cambridge Studies in Renaissance Literature and Culture, vol. 14. Cambridge: Cambridge University Press, 1997.

Merriam, Thomas. '*Sir Thomas More* Without Stylometry'. In *Notes and Queries*, 242, 67–72.

Metz, G. Harold *Shakespeare's Earliest Tragedy: Studies in 'Titus Andronicus'*. Madison, Teaneck and London: Fairleigh Dickinson University Press and Associated University Presses, 1996.

Osborne, Laurie E. *The Trick of Singularity: 'Twelfth Night' and the Performance Editions*. Iowa: University of Iowa Press, 1996.

Senes, Daniel. 'A Proposed Emendation for *King Lear*, v.iii.237'. In *Notes and Queries*, 242 (1997), 64–7.

Shakespeare, William. *The Complete Works*. Ed. by David Bevington, updated 4th edn. New York: Longman, 1997.

Shakespeare, William. *'The First Part of King Henry the Fourth': Texts and Contexts*. Ed. by Barbara Hodgdon, Bedford Shakespeare. Boston and New York: Bedford Books, 1997.

Shakespeare, William. *The First Quarto of 'King Richard III'*. Ed. by Peter Davison, New Cambridge, The Early Quartos. Cambridge: Cambridge University Press, 1996.

Shakespeare, William. *Macbeth*. Ed. by A. R. Braunmuller, New Cambridge. Cambridge: Cambridge University Press, 1997.

Shakespeare, William. *A Midsummer Night's Dream, 1600*. Ed. by Thomas L. Berger, Malone Society Reprints, vol. 157. Oxford: Oxford University Press, for the Malone Society, 1996, for 1995.

Shakespeare, William. *The Norton Shakespeare: Based on the Oxford Edition*. Gen. ed. Stephen Greenblatt, ed. by Walter Cohen, Jean E. Howard and Katharine Eisaman Maus. New York and London: W. W. Norton, 1997.

Shakespeare, William. *Othello*. Ed. by E. A. J. Honigmann, Arden 3. Walton-on-Thames: Thomas Nelson and Sons, 1996.

Shakespeare, William. *King Lear*. Ed. by R. A. Foakes, Arden 3. Walton-on-Thames: Thomas Nelson and Sons, 1997.

Shakespeare, William. *The Sonnets*. Ed. by Rex Gibson, Cambridge School Shakespeare. Cambridge: Cambridge University Press, 1997.

*Shakespeare Studies 24*. Ed. by Leeds Barroll. Book-review ed. Susan Zimmerman. Madison, Teaneck and London: Fairleigh Dickinson University Press and Associated University Presses, 1996.

*Shakespeare's 'Edward III'*. Ed. by Eric Sams. New Haven and London: Yale University Press, 1996.

Sohmer, Steve. 'What Cicero Said'. In *Notes and Queries*, 242 (1997), 56–8.

Walsh, Marcus. *Shakespeare, Milton, and Eighteenth-Century Literary Editing: The Beginnings of Interpretative Scholarship*, Cambridge Studies in Eighteenth-Century English Literature and Thought, vol. 35. Cambridge: Cambridge University Press, 1997.

Williams, George Walton, ed. *Shakespeare's Speech-Headings: Speaking the Speech in Shakespeare's Plays*, Papers of the Seminar in Textual Studies, Shakespeare Association of America, March 29, 1986, Montreal. Newark and London: University of Delaware Press and Associated University Presses, 1997.

Williams, Gordon. *A Glossary of Shakespeare's Sexual Language*. London and Atlantic Highlands: Athlone, 1997.

*World Shakespeare Bibliography on CD-ROM 1987–1994*. Ed. by James L. Harner. Cambridge: Cambridge University Press, 1997.

# BOOKS RECEIVED

This list includes all books received between September 1996 and September 1997 which are not reviewed in this volume of *Shakespeare Survey*. The appearance of a book in this list does not preclude its review in a subsequent volume.


Ford, John. *'Tis Pity She's a Whore*. Ed. by Derek Roper, Revels Student Editions. Manchester: Manchester University Press, 1997.

Gurr, Andrew. *Playgoing in Shakespeare's London*, 2nd edn. Cambridge: Cambridge University Press, 1996.

Holmer, Joan Ozark. *'The Merchant of Venice': Choice, Hazard and Consequence*. London: Macmillan, 1995.

Keyishian, Harry. *The Shapes of Revenge: Victimization, Vengeance, and Vindictiveness in Shakespeare*. New Jersey: Humanities Press, 1995.

Krane, Edna. *Shylock and the King of England*. New York: Vantage, 1996.

Lezra, Jacques. *Unspeakable Subjects: The Genealogy of the Event in Early Modern Europe*. Stanford: Stanford University Press, 1997.

Purkayastha, Jagodish. *The Supernatural and the Real in 'Macbeth'*. Laitumkhrah, Shillong: Meghalaya Modern Press, 1994.

Stapleton, M. L. *Harmful Eloquence: Ovid's Amores from Antiquity to Shakespeare*. Ann Arbor: University of Michigan Press, 1996.

Webster, John. *The Duchess of Malfi*. Ed. by John Russell Brown, Revels Student Editions. Manchester: Manchester University Press, 1997.

# INDEX TO VOLUME 51

The index does not include titles of books referred to in the review articles. These books are listed alphabetically by author at the end of the articles. Book titles in the chapters by Catherine Alexander and Marcus Walsh are not included in this index.

# INDEX TO VOLUME 51

# INDEX TO VOLUME 51

# INDEX TO VOLUME 51

# INDEX TO VOLUME 51

# INDEX TO VOLUME 51

INDEX TO VOLUME 51

# GENERAL INDEX TO VOLUMES 41–50

# GENERAL INDEX TO VOLUMES 41–50

# GENERAL INDEX TO VOLUMES 41–50